THE INTERFACE OF LANGUAGE, VISION, AND ACTION

THE INTERFACE OF LANGUAGE, VISION, AND ACTION

EYE MOVEMENTS AND THE VISUAL WORLD

EDITED BY
JOHN M. HENDERSON AND
FERNANDA FERREIRA

PSYCHOLOGY PRESS
NEW YORK • HOVE

Front cover image: Pierre Bonnard, *Before Dinner*, 1924. The Metropolitan Museum of Art, Robert Lehman Collection, 1975. (1975.1.156). Photograph © 1984 The Metropolitan Museum of Art.

Back cover image: Poster for May 2002 workshop at Michigan State University in East Lansing. Design by Brendon Hsieh.

Published in 2004 by
Psychology Press
29 West 35th Street
New York, NY 10001
www.psypress.com

Published in Great Britain by
Psychology Press
27 Church Road
Hove, East Sussex
BN3 2FA
www.psypress.co.uk

Psychology Press is an imprint of the Taylor & Francis Group.
Printed in the United States of America on acid-free paper.

10 9 8 7 6 5 4 3 2 1

Library of Congress Cataloging-in-Publication Data

The interface of language, vision, and action : eye movements and the visual world / edited by John M. Henderson and Fernanda Ferreira.
        p. cm.
    Includes bibliographical references and index.
    ISBN 1-84169-089-9 (hardcover : alk. paper)
    1. Psycholinguistics—Congresses. 2. Eye—Movements—Congresses. 3. Perceptual-motor processes—Congresses. 4. Visual perception—Congresses. I. Henderson, John M. (John Michael), 1958– II. Ferreira, Fernanda.

BF455.I48 2004
153.7'5—dc22   2003026653

Contents

Introduction to the Integration of Language,
Vision and Action   ix

Fernanda Ferreira and John M. Henderson

1 Scene Perception for Psycholinguists   1

John M. Henderson and Fernanda Ferreira

2 Visual and Linguistic Processing during Eye Fixations in 59
Reading

Keith Rayner and Simon P. Liversedge

3 Fixation Location and Fixation Duration as Indices of   105
Cognitive Processing

David E. Irwin

4 Eye Scanning and Visual Search   135

John M. Findlay

5 Thinking outside the Brain: Spatial Indices to   161
Visual and Linguistic Information

Michael J. Spivey, Daniel C. Richardson, and Stanka A. Fitneva

6 The Use of Eye Tracking in Studies of   191
Sentence Generation

Antje S. Meyer

7   Why Look? Reasons for Eye Movements   213
     Related to Language Production

     Zenzi M. Griffin

8   Putting First Things First   249

     Kathryn Bock, David E. Irwin, and Douglas J. Davidson

9   Referential Domains in Spoken Language   279
     Comprehension: Using Eye Movements to
     Bridge the Product and Action Traditions

     Michael K. Tanenhaus, Craig G. Chambers, and Joy E. Hanna

10   Children's Eye Movements during Listening: 319
     Developmental Evidence for a Constraint-Based
     Theory of Sentence Processing

     John Trueswell and Lila Gleitman

11   Now You See It, Now You Don't: 347
     Mediating the Mapping between
     Language and the Visual World

     Gerry T.M. Altmann and Yuki Kamide

     Index   387

Contributors

Gerry T. M. Altmann
University of York
United Kingdom

Kathryn Bock
University of Illinois at
    Urbana-Champaign
U.S.A.

Craig G. Chambers
University of Calgary
Canada

Douglas J. Davidson
F. C. Donders Centre for Cognitive
    Neuroimaging
The Netherlands

Fernanda Ferreira
Michigan State University
U.S.A.

John M. Findlay
University of Durham
United Kingdom

Stanka A. Fitneva
Queens University
Canada

Lila Gleitman
University of Pennsylvania
U.S.A.

Zenzi M. Griffin
Georgia Institute of Technology
U.S.A.

Joy E. Hanna
State University of New York at
    Stony Brook
U.S.A.

John M. Henderson
Michigan State University
U.S.A.

David E. Irwin
University of Illinois at
    Urbana-Champaign
U.S.A.

Yuki Kamide
University of Manchester
United Kingdom

Simon P. Liversedge
University of Durham
United Kingdom

Antje S. Meyer
University of Birmingham
United Kingdom

Keith Rayner
University of Massachusetts,
    Amherst
U.S.A.

Daniel C. Richardson
Stanford University
U.S.A.

Michael J. Spivey
Cornell University
U.S.A.

Michael K. Tanenhaus
University of Rochester
U.S.A.

John Trueswell
University of Pennsylvania
U.S.A.

Workshop Participants. Front Row, Left to Right: Michael Spivey, Antje Meyer, Michael Tanenhaus, Kay Bock, Fernanda Ferreira, Gerry Altmann. Back Row, Left to Right: David Irwin, John Trueswell, Keith Rayner, John Henderson, John Findlay, Zenzi Griffin.

Introduction

The study of language processing was dramatically enriched when psycholinguists became aware of research on eye movements. In 1978 Keith Rayner published a highly influential article describing the details of eye-movement behavior during reading. He summarized a large amount of work demonstrating that reading could be decomposed into two basic elements—fixations and saccades—which varied in their characteristics depending on the perceptual and linguistic features of the text. Around the same time, Just and Carpenter (1980) described how measures like fixation duration changed systematically, depending on the linguistic characteristics of the text being read. For example, they demonstrated that longer and rarer words receive longer fixations than shorter and more frequent words. Soon afterwards, Frazier and Rayner (1982) pioneered the use of eye movements to study syntactic processing. Their investigations spawned two decades of research focused on using eye movements as a tool to reveal the way written language is understood. This research program continues to yield important insights.

Today we may view this period as the first era of research involving eye movements and language processing. It appears that we have now entered a second era, which centers around a different type of eye-movement monitoring system: the free-viewing eyetracker. These systems allow eye movements to be monitored while people look at real or virtual visual displays, and because they tolerate movements of the head and body, they permit the viewer to interact with the available objects. The first article heralding this new technique was published in 1995 by Michael Tanenhaus and his colleagues in the journal *Science* (Tanenhaus, Spivey-Knowlton, Eberhard, & Sedivy, 1995). Tanenhaus et al. announced to the rest of the psycholinguistic world that it was now possible to investigate how people understand spoken language by measuring the eye movements they made as they listened to commands and manipulated the corresponding objects. It is an understatement to say that this technique has caught on. In the last five years, psycholinguists have used eye movements to study how speech and language are understood (Dahah, Swingley, & Tanenhaus, 2000; Fernald, Swingley, & Pinto, 2001; Spivey,

Tanenhaus, & Eberhard, 2002), to learn about the processes involved in language production (Bock, Irwin, & Davidson, 2003; Griffin, 2001; Griffin & Bock, 2000), and even to shed light on how conversations are managed (Barr & Keysar, 2002; Hannah, Tanenhaus, & Trueswell, 2003).

This second era of research combining psycholinguistics and the study of eye movements promises to be at least as productive as the first. One significant feature of this line of work is that it ties together the evolutionarily significant domains of language, vision, and action. Although it is clear that we often passively listen or read, much of the time we use language to perform specific tasks, and often those involve objects in the world around us. With free-viewing eyetrackers we can learn how language is used for action. Related to this point, in this new eyetracking era, researchers will be able to investigate spoken language processing because the focus is not on the pattern of fixations and saccades on text but rather on the real-world referents of the expressions in the linguistic stimuli. Finally, the versatility of the technique has yielded an exciting tool for language production researchers. Because the free-viewing eyetracker can tolerate head movements, it is possible to measure fixations and saccades made while people describe visual displays. The field of language production has thus been provided with a new and sensitive measure for investigating formulation processes, which is an extremely happy event given how much more challenging the experimental investigation of production is compared to comprehension (Bock, 1982, 1996).

These developments led us to set up a workshop at Michigan State University to exchange results and ideas and to discuss the issues surrounding the use of free-viewing eyetrackers for studying the cognitive systems of humans. We were particularly interested in getting investigators who worked primarily in visual cognition together with those studying language comprehension and production. It struck us that people from these two fairly distinct areas of inquiry might have results that would be of mutual interest and relevance. Moreover, we also suspected that ideas from one field were being imported into the other without a careful enough examination of whether the extensions were appropriate. For example, researchers in psycholinguistics who use eye movements and the visual world to examine comprehension and production make many assumptions about the way visual displays are processed, but those assumptions have not been the target of serious scrutiny. It seemed important, then, to set up this workshop in order to initiate a long-term conversation between researchers in visual cognition and psycholinguists. In addition, it is also clear that, as we learn more about how language is processed through the availability of this technique, it will be more and more useful to set up workshops and other similar events to allow investigators from all areas of the language sciences to talk to each other and exchange findings.

This book is the physical product of our May 2002 workshop. The first chapter is by us, the organizers of the workshop and is titled "Scene Perception for Psycholinguists." The purpose of this chapter is to provide psycholinguists and other cognitive scientists with an overview of what is known about scene and object recognition that might be relevant particularly to the use of the visual world paradigm to examine language. For example, we review what is known about the speed with which scenes can be apprehended and objects within them identified, and then we try to relate those conclusions to assumptions that psycholinguists make about the same processes. This exercise led us to a number of important discoveries: For example, it appears that what vision researchers and psycholinguists call "scenes" are very different sorts of visual displays, and it is not entirely clear that principles generalize across types. The chapter also highlights the large number of research questions that need to be studied in order for the field to make real progress trying to integrate vision, language, and action.

The next three chapters were written by the workshop participants most closely associated with eye movements and visual cognition. Keith Rayner, as mentioned above, is a pioneer in this field, and his chapter with Simon P. Liversedge provides a detailed review and analysis of what the eyes do when people read text. It focuses particularly on integrating what is known about low-level visual processes and the influence of linguistic variables. Much of the research that Rayner and Liversedge review was done with the stationary type of eye-movement monitoring system, in part because the most precise and detailed measurements of eye behavior can only be obtained with these systems. Nevertheless, the results have important implications for the use of free-viewing eyetrackers in language research. Dave Irwin, in his chapter "Fixation Location and Fixation Duration as Indices of Cognitive Processing," points out that the straightforward mapping between "fixation time on X" and "cognitive processing of X" is much too simple-minded. Fixation times are influenced by noncognitive variables; cognitive processing takes place during saccades as well as during fixations; and, occasionally, what we are looking at is not what we are currently processing. These issues do not undermine the use of eye movements to study visual and linguistic processing, but they do make clear that researchers must be cautious and sophisticated in how they interpret the data they get from eyetracking. The chapter by John Findlay is a review of eye movement behavior during one important type of visual task, visual search. A great deal of what we know about eye movements and vision has come from visual search experiments. Moreover, many psycholinguistic paradigms using the free-viewing eyetracker have visual search as an essential component; for instance, participants might be asked to pick up an object from an array, and their eye movements during execution of the command are analyzed as the utterance unfolds. Of course, to comply with the request, the observer must search the array for the relevant object. Findlay's chapter provides an extremely careful analysis of how visual acuity and attention influence the execution of saccades during visual search. We expect this summary to be invaluable to all psycholinguists who use the visual world paradigm.

Michael Spivey's chapter is a creative and fascinating discussion of what eye-movement behavior in naturalistic situations tells us about the nature of visual representations, and even cognition itself. Spivey argues that "spatial indices" mediate between the internal world of mind and the external world of objects and events. The chapter is an excellent example of the way that basic research from visual cognition can inform a psycholinguist's thinking. In turn, the insights that have emerged from that exercise might have major implications for our ideas about what vision is for and even for our conceptions of mental representation.

The next three chapters are by well-known researchers in language production. Antje Meyer's contribution, "The Use of Eyetracking in Studies of Sentence Generation," describes how people investigating syntactic formulation processes, in particular, have benefited from the availability of free-viewing eyetrackers. In addition, she addresses an important and difficult question: Why do people look at objects before they articulate their phonological forms? Zenzi Griffin discusses a related set of topics in her chapter, but as her title "Why Look? Reasons for Speech-Related Eye Movements" suggests, she focuses more closely on the functional significance of eye movements during language production. In addition, she describes her and her colleagues' intriguing research on the way eye movements are used to coordinate production processes. A thought-provoking phenomenon that Griffin describes, and that is discussed by Spivey as well, is that when people talk about objects, they often look to the locations those objects *used* to occupy, even when the objects are no longer there. Kay Bock, Dave Irwin, and Doug Davidson's chapter asks what it is about concepts, objects, or words that makes us put them into early positions in sentences. This topic is closely related to the issue of incrementality in production. Their research with eye-movement monitoring has led them to make a critical distinction between linear and hierarchical incrementality and to suggest that the latter seems to characterize the production system.

This volume also includes a lovely set of chapters on comprehension and the use of the visual world paradigm. Michael Tanenhaus's chapter with Craig Chambers and Joy Hanna looks at what eye movements can tell us about the way that referential domains are established during conversation. The authors address the important question of what context means, especially for a comprehension system that must be used for interactive dialogue. They also discuss the differences between what they term the "language as product" and "language as action" traditions, and their work provides important evidence that the best psycholinguistics will emerge from attempts to bridge these approaches. John Trueswell and Lila Gleitman focus on what the free-viewing eyetracking paradigm has revealed about children's processing of sentences. Their contribution is particularly valuable, given the themes of our volume, because it discusses a groundbreaking line of research that could not have been done without the combination of the mobile eyetracker and an emphasis on how language is used to interpret the visual world. Before the research program Trueswell and Gleitman describe began, almost nothing was known about young children's online processing of spoken, complex utterances; but now we know a great deal about children's uses of linguistic and nonlinguistic constraints to arrive at sensible and useful interpretations of language.

Last, but certainly not least, we have an outstanding contribution from Gerry Altmann and Yuki Kamide. This chapter provides a superb end to our volume because, while it describes some important results concerning the incrementality of language comprehension processes, it also highlights important areas where little is known and where we should therefore be cautious about drawing strong inferences from our results. The authors even included an extremely useful appendix that discusses issues in analyzing eyetracking data. We expect that this section alone will make their chapter indispensable to researchers working on language, vision, and action.

We are happy to take this opportunity to thank a variety of people and organizations who made this workshop and this volume possible. First, of course, we thank the participants for their thought-provoking presentations and first-rate contributions to this volume. Second, we thank our students who helped us put the event and the book together: Karl Bailey, Monica Castelhano, Dan Gajewski, Ben Hsieh, Michelle Larrabee, Aaron Pearson, and Ben Swets. Special thanks go to Ben Hsieh who put together and maintained the workshop Web site. We also thank our stimulating colleagues in the Cognitive Science Program at Michigan State University, whose influences are apparent in almost all aspects of the way we think about cognition. We are grateful to Michigan State University for providing financial support and facilities for the workshop and for other cognitive science events. We also thank the Army Research Office for their generous financial support both of this workshop and of related research in our lab (the opinions expressed in this workshop are those of the organizers and attendees and do not necessarily represent the views of the Department of the Army or any other governmental organization. Reference to or citations of trade or corporate names does not constitute explicit or implied endorsement of those entities or their products by the author or the Department of the Army). Finally, Fourward Technologies and Applied Sciences Laboratories also generously provided financial support for the workshop.

REFERENCES

Barr, D. J., & Keysar, B. (2002). Anchoring comprehension in linguistic precedents. *Journal of Memory & Language*, 46, 391-418.

Bock, J. K. (1982). Toward a cognitive psychology of syntax: Information processing contributions to sentence formulation. *Psychological Review*, 89, 1-47.

Bock, J. K. (1996). Language production: Methods and methodologies. *Psychonomic Bulletin & Review*, 3, 395-421.

Bock, K., Irwin, D. E., & Davidson, D. J. (2003). Minding the clock. *Journal of Memory & Language, 48*, 653-685.

Dahan, D., Swingley, D., & Tanenhaus, M. K. (2000). Linguistic gender and spoken-word recognition in French. *Journal of Memory & Language, 42*, 465-480.

Fernald, A., Swingley, D., & Pinto, J. P. (2001). When half a word is enough: Infants can recognize spoken words using partial phonetic information. *Child Development, 72*, 1003-1015.

Frazier, L., & Rayner, K. (1982). Making and correcting errors during sentence comprehension: Eye movements in the analysis of structurally ambiguous sentences. *Cognitive Psychology, 14*, 178-210.

Griffin, Z. M. (2000). What the eyes say about speaking. *Psychological Science, 11*, 274-279.

Griffin, Z. M. (2001). Gaze durations during speech reflect word selection and phonological encoding. *Cognition, 82*, B1-B14.

Hanna, J. E., Tanenhaus, M. K., & Trueswell, J. C. (2003). The effects of common ground and perspective on domains of referential interpretation. *Journal of Memory & Language, 49,* 43-61.

Just, M. A., & Carpenter, P. A. (1980). A theory of reading: From eye fixations to comprehension. *Psychological Review, 87*, 329-354

Rayner, K. (1978). Eye movements in reading and information processing. *Psychological Bulletin, 85*, 618-660.

Spivey, M. J., Tanenhaus, M. K., & Eberhard, K. M. (2002). Eye movements and spoken language comprehension: Effects of visual context on syntactic ambiguity resolution. *Cognitive Psychology, 45*, 447-481.

Tanenhaus, M. K., Spivey-Knowlton, M. J. Eberhard, K. M., Sedivy, J. C. (1995). Integration of visual and linguistic information in spoken language comprehension. *Science*, 268, 1632-1634.

1

Scene Perception for Psycholinguists

JOHN M. HENDERSON
FERNANDA FERREIRA

Our goal in this chapter is to provide a resource for researchers using free-viewing eyetracking and the visual world paradigm to study language comprehension and production. This enterprise has been growing rapidly over the last several years and has yielded a large body of important work. It has also become increasingly clear that the research is based on many un-examined assumptions about what scenes are, how they are processed, and how eye movements are directed through them. It seemed to us that these assumptions needed to be made explicit and that it was time to bring the ex-tant knowledge on eye movements in scene perception to bear on the use of the visual world paradigm to study psycholinguistics. We will begin by sur-veying the literature on the visual cognition of natural scenes, concentrating on what scenes are and how they are recognized. We then move on to the core of the chapter, which is a review of the literature on eye movements in scene perception. Our take-home message is that a great deal is already under-stood about scenes and how they are processed and that these findings are highly relevant to the assumptions and conclusions associated with the use of the visual world paradigm by language researchers.

GENERAL ISSUES IN SCENE PERCEPTION

*I*n the field of scene perception, investigators often preface the term *scene* with modifiers like *real-world* or *natural* to indicate that they are interested in the perceptual processing of visual input that is in some important sense like that typically encountered by the visual system during the natural course of everyday activity. Natural scenes have properties that differ from the sorts of visual stimuli that are often used in psychological experiments. For example, natural scenes fill the entire visual field (i.e., the light projected onto the retina from a natural scene covers the entire retina), and they produce specific sorts of wavelength, intensity, and spatial frequency regularities and variations that are constrained by properties of the world itself. In addition, natural scenes comprise surfaces and objects with specific semantic and syntactic constraints that in turn give rise to the semantics of the scene as a whole (Biederman, Mezzanotte, & Rabinowitz, 1982). In short, entities in the world and the image properties they produce are structured in particular ways that the visual system has evolved to handle. Natural scenes include what you are looking at right now. If you turn around and look behind you, what you see is a real-world scene too.

In practice, investigations of natural scene perception have been based on the simplifying assumption that depictions are a reasonable substitute for real-world scenes. Depictions that have been used as stand-ins for real scenes have included small collections of line drawings of a few objects arrayed in a way suggesting a meaningful scene (Mandler & Johnson, 1977; Parker, 1978), more complex line drawings (Friedman, 1979; Loftus & Mackworth, 1978), line drawings derived directly from photographs (De Graef, Christiaens, & d'Ydewalle, 1990; Henderson, Weeks, & Hollingworth, 1999), color renderings of scenes constructed from 3D models (Henderson & Hollingworth, 1999a), full-color photographs (Henderson & Hollingworth, 1998), and virtual-reality displays (Loschky & McConkie, 2003). Figure 1.1 shows examples of several of the most popular depiction formats that have been used in scene perception studies. The purpose of using scene depictions has been to capture some of the important properties of real-world object and scene perception by including in the depictions what are thought to be the important properties of scenes such as visual complexity, structural and semantic constraint, and meaning, while allowing for control over factors that would be difficult, if not impossible, to hold constant in the real world. Scene depictions such as drawings or photographs necessarily reduce the amount of information normally available to the visual system, such as nonpictorial depth cues (e.g., those involving stereopsis and motion parallax),[1] and motion.

We highlight the difference between depictions versus the real environment because many of the questions that psycholinguists would like to have answered about eye movements in scenes, such as how far into the periphery one can determine the identities of objects, or what information controls

FIGURE 1.1. Examples of the types of scene depictions that have been used in scene perception research: line drawings, computer-rendered images, and photographs. Note how different the line drawing is from the other two depiction types.

fixation placement, may depend on the specific kind of image the visual system is faced with. As one example, it is likely that information about object identity can be detected from a greater distance in the periphery when sparse images are presented (Henderson, Williams, Castelhano, & Falk, 2003). We will come back to this specific issue of the *functional field of view* in scene viewing later.

There are a few notable exceptions to the use of depictions as stand-ins for the environment, including studies of eye movements as participants engage in active tasks such as tea making or, for those with more refined tastes, preparation of peanut butter and jelly sandwiches (Hayhoe, Shrivastava, Mruczek, & Pelz, 2003; Land, Mennie, & Rusted, 1999; Land & Hayhoe, 2002). Other natural tasks that have been investigated are hand-washing (Pelz & Canosa, 2001) and, more commonly, driving (Chapman & Underwood, 1998; Land & Horwood, 1995; Land & Lee, 1994; Liu, 1999; Recarte & Nunes, 2000; Shinoda, Hayhoe, & Shrivastava, 2001). These natural-task studies suggest that some of the results from scene depiction experiments may not generalize to the real environment, though a systematic study of this question has yet to be undertaken. An example of a potential difference in eye movements from depictions to the real world is the average amplitude of a saccade. In scene depiction studies, modal saccade amplitudes are often under a degree, and few saccades exceed 10 degrees (Henderson & Hollingworth, 1998). In contrast, it has been reported that modal saccade amplitudes in viewing the real environment are closer to 5 degrees, and saccades of 20 degrees are not uncommon (Land & Hayhoe, 2002). This difference may be accounted for by factors such as the size of objects in the natural environment versus in depictions, differences in the size of the scene images themselves in the two cases (essentially the entire visual field in the natural world versus 20 to 30 degs maximum, and typically less, in depictions), differences in the kinds of tasks participants are engaged in when viewing the real environment versus a depiction, or some combination of these and other factors. Another possibility, though, is that the spatial resolution of current portable head-mounted eye-trackers is not sufficient to detect the many smaller saccades typically observed during picture viewing. Many of these smaller amplitude saccades are within-object, and these may be below the spatial resolution of head-mounted trackers. When only interobject saccades are considered in depiction studies, saccade amplitude distributions look much more similar to those observed in studies of the real environment (e.g., Henderson & Hollingworth, 1998; Hollingworth & Henderson, 2002; see also discussion below).

In short, much of what we know about eye movements during scene perception (and for that matter about scene perception in general) has come from studies using depicted scenes, where the nature of the depiction varies from study to study (see also Henderson & Hollingworth, 1998, for a summary of how stimuli have varied across studies of scene perception). It is unclear that one can generalize about basic issues like how far from fixation an object can be identified or the average saccade amplitude from one type of depiction to another, or from visual depictions of the environment to the visual environment itself. Artifacts may also arise in the use of depictions, such as the bias toward fixating near the center of a depicted scene (Mannan, Ruddock, & Wooding, 1996; Parkhurst, Law, & Neibur, 2002). This problem of generalizing from representations of the world to the world itself does not arise in reading because readers typically arrange themselves at a natural distance to text so that about 3-4 letters subtend one degree of visual angle, as discussed in this volume by Rayner & Liversedge (2004; see also Rayner, 1998). Because of the influence of reading studies, the issue of how to map from depictions to the natural case is not one that the psycholinguistic community is accustomed to grappling with.

What Is a Scene?

Henderson and Hollingworth (1999b) defined *scene* as a semantically coherent (and often nameable) human-scaled view of a real-world environment comprising background elements and multiple discrete objects arranged in a spatially licensed manner. Background elements are taken to be larger-scale, immovable surfaces and structures, such as ground, walls, floors, and mountains, whereas objects are taken to be smaller-scale, discrete entities that move (e.g., animals), or can be moved (e.g., furniture) within the scene. These definitions of background and object are not entirely adequate because they would seem to depend at least in part on spatial scale. An office viewed from the vantage point of the doorway would likely include floor, ceiling, and walls as background elements, and a desk, desk chair, bookshelves, filing cabinets, and so on as component objects, spatially arranged according to the laws of physics and the constraints associated with office tasks. But, from your vantage point sitting in a chair in front of the desk, the desktop might be considered a scene, with its surface forming most of the background and a stapler, phone, and pen serving as individuated objects. Natural scenes have this hierarchical structure, and it is difficult to determine precisely when the spatial scale becomes too small or too large to call the resulting view a scene. We introduce the idea of human scale to constrain the definition to include the kinds of images humans are likely to encounter in interactions with the environment and to exclude those they are not. A related way to place a principled boundary around the concept of scene is to limit the scale to the one that affords human locomotion and motor interaction. So, an encompassing view of a kitchen or a playground would be considered a good scene, whereas earth viewed from *Discovery* in *2001: A Space Odyssey* or a paramecium viewed through a microscope would not. This constraint captures the intuition that, unlike objects, scenes are specific views of the environment within which we are embedded. In contrast, when we look at an object, we are looking at an entity from a vantage point outside of that entity.

Spatial licensing includes adhering to the physical constraints of the universe, including gravity and space, and to the semantic constraints imposed by object identity and function (referred to by Biederman, 1981, and Biederman et al., 1982, as syntactic and semantic constraints, respectively). Examples of the former include the fact that objects generally cannot float unsupported in the air, that two objects cannot occupy the same space at the same time, and that one object cannot be seen through another opaque object (Biederman et al., 1982). Examples of the latter include the fact that a fire hydrant does not belong on top of a mailbox (Biederman et al., 1982), or that a couch is not typically found on a front lawn (college frat house lawns notwithstanding). It is often difficult to determine whether a physical constraint has been violated by an object without understanding the semantics of that object; for example, some objects can float unsupported, and some objects do allow light to pass through them so that an occluded object can be seen behind, so determining whether a physical constraint has been violated often requires knowledge of the identity and semantic attributes of an object (Henderson, 1992a). Nevertheless, the general point stands that a well-formed scene must ultimately conform to a set of basic physical and semantic constraints that impose structure on the environment.

Are visual scenes a natural kind, distinct from other types of meaningful visual entities such as letters, objects, or faces? The notion that scenes are treated differently is supported by the observation that the fovea and non-foveal regions of the retina are magnified by different factors in human visual cortex (Engel, Glover, & Wandell, 1997; Sereno et al., 1995) and that these differential degrees of magnification have implications for how brain regions devoted to visual recognition might operate. Specifically, it has been suggested that objects requiring analysis of fine detail to be recognized will be supported by central-biased representations, whereas objects requiring integration over a larger spatial scale will be more peripherally biased. So, to the extent that individual objects fall into the former category and scenes fall into the latter, the expectation is that objects and scenes will be supported by different cortical recognition areas and presumably, therefore, different computational systems (Levy, Hasson, Avidan, Hendler, & Malach, 2001; Malach, Levy, & Hasson, 2002).

Another source of evidence supporting the idea that distinguishing between objects and scenes carves nature at its joints derives from recent neuroimaging studies. For example, Epstein and Kanwisher have provided fMRI evidence that a distinct area of the inferior temporal cortex becomes activated when participants view pictures of indoor environments, outdoor environments, and even landmarks (Epstein, Harris, Stanley, & Kanwisher, 1999; Epstein & Kanwisher, 1998). This area of cortex, dubbed the parahippocampal place area (PPA), shows preferential activation to natural scenes including rooms, landscapes, and city streets, but not to objects, faces, houses, or other visual patterns unassociated with large-scale space (Epstein & Kanwisher, 1998). Furthermore, PPA is sensitive to backgrounds that preserve coherent spatial structure and geometry, but not to the individual objects that would fill those backgrounds when presented without the structure that creates the spatial interpretation (Epstein & Kanwisher, 1998). Additional evidence suggests that PPA is not affected by familiarity with the real-world environment depicted by a scene picture, or by motion, and is greater for novel than for repeated scene images (Epstein et al., 1999). Visual imagery for scenes versus faces differentially activates PPA (O'Craven & Kanwisher, 2000). Finally, PPA has been shown to be sensitive to changes in scene viewpoint but not to changes to constituent objects in a scene (Epstein, Graham, & Downing, 2003). Overall, PPA does not appear to be a memory area, is not involved in route planning, and is not dedicated to processing locomotion, but instead seems to play a role in processing novel perceptual information about scene appearance and layout (Epstein et al., 1999), perhaps specifically representing the relationship between the viewer and the surfaces defining local space (Epstein et al., 2003).

An additional study suggestive of the specific role of PPA in scene perception was presented by Steeves, Humphrey, Culham, Menon, & Goodale (2002). These investigators examined the behavioral performance of a patient (DF) with visual form agnosia (profound inability to recognize objects) in a behavioral scene recognition study and in an fMRI study in which they looked for PPA activation. Consistent with the view that the visual system treats scenes differently than it treats objects, DF was able to classify scenes, particularly when they were presented in color rather than in black and white. Furthermore, like normal control subjects, DF showed PPA activation to scenes.

Together, the results of these studies suggest that PPA is specifically dedicated to analyzing scenes. Of course, this interpretation may change as additional evidence accumulates about the function of the PPA, but the findings are intriguing in that they suggest that scene processing may require at least some dedicated neural hardware that is distinct from that used for discrete visual entities like objects or faces.

Our discussion of the literature on scene processing up to this point makes clear that we can make two critical and orthogonal distinctions. First, the input to the visual system in "scene" experiments can be either the real environment or a depiction of it. Second, a "scene" (either real environment or depiction) can be complete or can be a construction that is missing some of the critical characteristics typical of a normal real-world environment. We refer to the former type of stimulus as a *true scene*, and the latter as an *ersatz scene*. True scenes involve entities that naturally occur in the setting and that are arranged appropriately with respect to each other as well as with respect to forces such as gravity. The components of the scene also have a property we will term *proportionality*: The objects are sized appropriately (e.g., animals in a scene are about the size they should be given the scene's scale). In addition, true scenes include accurately detailed backgrounds. Examples of ersatz scenes range from visual stimuli that include no background to those with abnormally large actors and participants, to simple arrays of objects with no natural structure. These two dimensions can be conceptualized as a 2x2 matrix as shown in Table 1.1. The cells in the table provide a brief description of the type of stimulus that results from combining these two dimensions. We will continue to expand this table as we proceed through the chapter.

Are the Displays Used in Psycholinguistic Studies Scenes?

As mentioned above, most investigators in scene perception reserve the term *scene* for natural environments or depictions thereof—in other words, for the first row of Table 1.1. Interestingly, it appears that researchers in psycholinguistics who use variations of the visual world paradigm employ the term *scene* to refer to all four cells. Investigators in psycholinguistics often use the term *scene* to refer to displays that depict objects, whether or not those objects form a semantically coherent and interpretable whole. In many cases these displays consist of groups of objects arrayed in some arbitrary pattern such as a square or a random arrangement (e.g., Altmann & Kamide, 2004; Bailey & Ferreira, 2003; Tanenhaus, Spivey-Knowlton, Eberhard, & Sedivy, 1995; Barr & Keysar, 2002). Vision researchers sometimes use displays of this sort, as well, to investigate questions about the allocation of attention and eye movements in object recognition (e.g., Henderson, Pollatsek, & Rayner, 1987; 1989; Irwin & Zelinsky, 2002; Zelinsky & Murphy, 2000), but they do not call these scenes.

Of course, many images used in both psycholinguistic and visual cognition research fall somewhere between an arbitrarily arranged array of unrelated objects and a true scene—in other words, the dimensions that comprise Table 1.1 are continual. Consider an image that depicts a small set of objects interacting in a semantically coherent and interpretable manner but that falls short of containing the entire surrounding visual context that would be present

TABLE 1.1. Examples of Types of Visual Displays
and Their Relationships to Scenes

	Real environment	Depiction
True scene	The world you see in front of you at the moment	A color photograph of the world you see in front of you at the moment
Ersatz scene	A set of random objects arranged on a table in front of you	A line drawing of a set of random objects arranged on a table in front of you

in a true scene. Examples of this type of display, which we can refer to as a *scene sketch*, would be a picture of lightning hitting a church (Bock, 1986), a person giving another person a book (Bock, 1989), or a fish eating another fish (Tomlin, 1986). A second intermediate type of image would be an arbitrarily arranged set of objects that creates a semantically coherent interpretation. We can call these *interpretable arrays*. Examples used in the visual cognition literature would be arrays of objects taken from a particular semantic class such as animals (Henderson et al., 1987, 1989), or taken from a particular scene such as objects that would be found on a street, in a refrigerator, or on a tool-bench (e.g., Biederman, Blickle, Teitelbaum, & Klatsky, 1988; Rao, Zelinsky, Hayhoe, & Ballard, 2002; Zelinsky, Rao, Hayhoe, & Ballard, 1997). Interpretable arrays are often used to investigate the processing of objects (and interactions among them) rather than the meaning of the array itself, though they have been used as a substitute for a scene sketch. An example from psycholinguistics would include the images described in this volume by Altmann and Kamide (2004) in which semantically interpretable events are suggested by individual objects arranged in an array. Table 1.2 expands on Table 1.1 to include this distinction.

There are likely to be important differences in how scenes versus object arrays (interpretable or not) are processed visually and cognitively; we mention a few of the more important ones here. First, scenes are likely identified as coherent meaningful entities using global image properties that transcend the specific objects in the scene (see section below on fast scene recognition). Arrays, in contrast, have no route to semantic interpretation beyond inferences from the identities of the objects they contain and so cannot benefit from this additional level of visual analysis and interpretation. Second, the functional field of view for constituent objects in an array is likely to be larger than for scenes, partly because scenes are semantically more dense and also because objects in scenes tend to obscure each other via lateral masking.

TABLE 1.2. Expanded Examples of Types of Visual Displays and Their Relationships to Scenes

		Real environment	Depiction
True scene		The world you see in front of you at the moment	A color photograph of the world you see in front of you
Ersatz scene	Scene sketch	Undefined?	A drawing of lightning hitting a church
	Interpretable array	Four objects from a refrigerator on a psycholinguistics lab table-top	A drawing of four objects from a refrigerator
	Uninterpretable array	A set of random objects arranged on a table in front of you	A drawing of a random set of objects

Another interesting difference between the study of eye movements over scenes in visual cognition versus psycholinguistics is that the scenes used in visual cognition typically exclude people or even animate objects, because it is assumed that such objects will attract a disproportionate number of fixations (Buswell, 1935; Friedman, 1979; Yarbus, 1967). In reality, though, the belief that the presence of a human in a scene will attract fixations is based more on anecdote than strong experimental support. To our knowledge, no systematic study of this hypothesis has yet been undertaken, though we are currently pursuing it in our lab. An illustration of the type of experiment we are conducting is shown in Figure 1.2 from Weith, Castelhano, & Henderson (2003), a visual cognition study that is unusual in its purposeful inclusion of a person in many of the scenes. In this study, participants viewed a sequence of photographs of true scenes depicting a janitor cleaning and stealing from an office. When the janitor was present in a scene, a large proportion of fixations fell on the janitor's face. Unknown at this point is exactly what aspect of the human form attracts fixations; is it the fact that it is a human? Or do all biological forms attract gaze? Note also that the direction of the janitor's gaze is important in

FIGURE 1.2. Scan pattern of one subject viewing this image as a slide in a sequence of slides that told a story. Faces (and especially eyes) attract fixations, and the orientation of an observed person's gaze directs the observer's own gaze.

determining the location of an observer's fixations in the scene, especially after the eyes have been fixated.

In contrast to common practice in scene perception research, the displays used in psycholinguistic studies often include people or other actors because the scenes are meant to depict events in which an agent is actively engaged in some action. Table 1.3 expands Table 1.1 to include this additional dimension. Table 1.3 makes clear that we can distinguish among eight types of displays that differ on three dimensions: whether the scene is real or depicted, whether it is actually a scene or is degraded in some way, and whether the display includes animate entities or not. It is not at all clear that conclusions about the interface of language and vision that emerge using one type of display necessarily generalize to the others. Addressing this issue constitutes a major research program that has not yet even begun.

What we can do at this stage in our knowledge is to be explicit about the cells in Table 1.3 that have been explored in psycholinguistic research using visual paradigms. To the best of our knowledge, no true, real world scenes have ever been used, either with or without agents. A few studies have employed scene depictions, typically with people and other sorts of agents (e.g., Bock has used stimuli such as the pictures from the Thematic Apperception Test in production experiments). These depictions are not photographs or 3-D renderings; instead, they are drawings, and most include minimal background. Often the constituent objects (especially those of interest) are inappropriately large given the scene's scale. In other words, they are more like scene sketches than true scenes. Even more common is the use of arrays, both real and depicted, and (because of practicality issues) without any animate entities. Clearly, arrays are not true scenes, which means that a great deal of what is known about scene processing from visual cognition does not directly translate to the most commonly used paradigm in language-vision research.

TABLE 1.3. Examples of Types of Visual Displays (Three Dimensions)

	Real environment		Depiction	
	With agents	Without agents	With agents	Without agents
True scene	A customer passing money to a salesclerk	A store with no one in it	A photo of a customer passing money to a salesclerk	A photo of a store with no one in it
Ersatz scene	A set of random objects arranged on a table in front of you, somehow including a caged gerbil	A set of random objects arranged on a table in front of you, none of which is a caged gerbil	A photo of a set of random objects on a table, including a caged gerbil	A photo of various inanimate objects on a table

How Fast Is Scene Recognition?

In this section, we begin by narrowing our discussion to true scenes—that is, we consider only the first row of Tables 1.1-1.3. The evidence is overwhelming that *gist* can be apprehended very rapidly and can in turn influence various other visual and cognitive processes (e.g., biases about the presence of particular objects) and behaviors (e.g., eye movement control). *Gist* is another ill-defined term in the visual cognition literature, but investigators typically have in mind something like a general semantic interpretation. Gist probably includes establishing the identity of a scene (i.e., the equivalent of its basic-level category; Tversky & Hemenway, 1983), some semantic features of that class of scenes, and some aspects of the scene's global spatial layout. A number of paradigms converge on the conclusion that the information needed to determine scene gist (rather than the amount of time needed to report or respond) is acquired well within a single eye fixation, and in fact in just a fraction of that time. Here we briefly review some of the sources of that evidence.

One source of evidence suggesting that scene gist can be rapidly apprehended arises from the object detection paradigm introduced by Biederman and colleagues (Biederman, 1972; Biederman, Glass, & Stacey, 1973; Biederman, Rabinowitz, Glass, & Stacey, 1974; Biederman et al., 1982; see also Boyce, Pollatsek, & Rayner, 1989; Hollingworth & Henderson, 1998; Murphy & Wisniewski, 1989). In the most often used version of this paradigm, a scene is presented briefly and followed by a pattern mask. A label specifying a target object is presented prior to scene onset, and a spatial location marker is presented at scene offset. The participant is asked to determine whether the target object was present at the cued location. The target object might or might not be present and might or might not be consistent with the scene (consistency can be defined according to scene semantics or scene structure). The general finding is that participants are influenced by the consistency of the target object with the scene. This finding was at first taken to indicate that scene gist affects object identification. However, more recent work suggests that the consistency effect is more likely due to a response bias (Hollingworth & Henderson, 1998; 1999; see also Henderson, 1992a; Henderson & Hollingworth, 1999b). In any event, the more important conclusion for our purposes here is that sufficient information about the scene was acquired from these brief views to differentially affect participants' responses to semantically and structurally consistent and inconsistent objects. Therefore, enough information had to have been acquired from the scene to establish those relationships. This effect remains whether the target object is specified before or after the scene, and whether or not the spatial cue is presented (Hollingworth & Henderson, 1998). Recent work with Monica Castelhano in our lab has used the response bias generated for a target object by a scene as a tool to investigate rapid gist apprehension. The results suggests that sufficient information to produce this bias can be derived from a scene photograph in as little as 30 to 50 ms. These data suggest that gist begins to be available within 30-50 ms of scene onset.

A second early source of evidence for the rapid processing of scene gist came from a classic set of experiments reported by Potter using the rapid serial visual presentation (RSVP) technique (Potter & Levy, 1969; Potter, 1975, 1976; see also Potter, 1999), and subsequent related studies (Intraub 1979, 1980, 1981). In this paradigm, viewers were presented with a sequence of scene depictions (typically photographs taken from magazines). The streams were presented at rates up to 113 ms per picture, and participants were asked either to detect whether a particular preidentified target scene was present in the stream (detection condition) or to report whether a given scene was present in the stream after all scenes were presented (memory condition). The important finding for our purposes comes from the detection condition: Viewers were quite accurate at detecting scenes even at the fastest presentation rates. Potter (1976) showed that these results could be obtained when the target scene was identified with a verbal label rather than a picture, suggesting that detection did not require having the specific visual features of the target in mind. Intraub (1981) extended these results by showing that even knowledge of the general target category (again, given verbally) was sufficient for good detection. Interestingly, at these rates, the scenes could be detected but not remembered, suggesting that scenes may be rapidly identified but then lost to memory unless sufficient uninterrupted time is available for memory consolidation (Potter, 1976).

A third type of experiment that has been taken as evidence for the rapid comprehension of scene gist derives from studies showing that eye fixations are often directed toward informative scene regions after only a single initial fixation (Antes, 1974; Loftus and Mackworth, 1978; Mackworth and Morandi, 1967). Some of these early studies confounded visual saliency and semantic scene properties and so may actually have shown that the visual saliency of local scene regions rather than global scene interpretation initially directs eye movements. However, more recent studies have demonstrated that the first saccade in a scene is directed appropriately during visual search for a particular target, suggesting that enough of the scene has been interpreted in the first fixation to orient the eyes, given the nature of the target and scene (Castelhano & Henderson, 2003; Oliva, Torralba, Castelhano, & Henderson, 2003). This issue is discussed in more depth under the eye movement section below.

A further source of evidence for the rapid apprehension of scene gist comes from a series of studies showing that photographs can be very accurately categorized following presentation durations as brief as 20 ms (Thorpe, Fize, & Marlot, 1996; VanRullen & Thorpe, 2001). In these experiments, participants were asked to respond as quickly as possible whether the content of each briefly presented photograph was a member of a superordinate conceptual category such as "animal." Responses were found to be highly accurate (greater than 90% correct) and fast (averaging under 400 ms). This *ultrarapid categorization* generalized from natural categories to artifacts such as "means of transport" (VanRullen & Thorpe, 2001). The rapid categorization effect does not seem to require color, suggesting that the categories are not distinguished based on simple color cues (Delorme, Richard, & Fabre-Thorpe, 2000). The fast response times are also not made faster by familiarity with the images even after three weeks of exposure, suggesting that categorization for novel images operates at the limits of processing speed (Fabre-Thorpe, Delorme, Marlot, and Thorpe, 2001). An event-related potential (ERP) signature that distinguished the targets from nontargets in this task was generated about 150 ms after presentation of an image. Because 150 ms is insufficient time for neural activity through multiple synapses, these results have been taken to suggest that scene categorization takes place in a feed-forward manner (Thorpe et al., 1996). Performance with or without a simultaneous attention-demanding task has been shown to be similar, suggesting that, unlike other forms of visual analysis, rapid categorization of these natural images requires little, if any, attention (Li, VanRullen, Koch, & Perona, 2002).

While the ultrarapid categorization results are intriguing, it is not yet clear whether these studies truly reflect scene categorization, or whether they instead might reflect rapid object-level categorization. This question arises because the responses participants use to categorize the images have been associated with object categories (e.g., animal, food, means of transport) rather than scene categories, and because the photographs used as stimuli have depicted a single object against a relatively uniform (though natural) background. These displays, then, although depicting true scenes in the sense that they are photographs of animals against a background, are in reality closer to ersatz scenes because they are the kinds of pictures that photographers create when highlighting a single object. Thus, they are, in fact, simpler images than even object arrays (because only one object is really shown). (This issue of whether rapid categorization reflects object or scene recognition has arisen in prior rapid scene-categorization tasks as well; see discussion in Henderson, 1992, of the Potter, 1976, studies described above). Another concern with the ultrarapid categorization results is the amount of time actually available for image analysis in these studies. In most studies of scene perception, a pattern mask follows scene offset and so terminates processing in the visual system. Because the pictures in the aforementioned studies were not backward-masked after exposure, they almost certainly continued to be processed after stimulus offset. Thus, although 20 ms of unmasked image exposure may be sufficient for categorizing natural images of objects, it remains to be determined whether the ultrarapid categorization results would be obtained if masked exposure were used to constrain visual processing to that amount of time, if the images were true complex scenes, and if the response classes were true scene categories.

In summary, the term *gist* when applied to true scenes typically refers to knowledge of the scene category (e.g., kitchen) and the semantic information that may be retrieved based on that category. The weight of the evidence strongly converges on the conclusion that the gist of true scenes is apprehended very rapidly, certainly within the duration of a single fixation. Gist is also sometimes taken to include gross overall spatial layout of (possibly unidentified) scene elements. Far less research has been conducted to look at the fast apprehension of this layout information, though there is some evidence that layout can also be apprehended rapidly (Sanocki & Epstein, 1997; but see Germeys & d'Ydewalle, 2001, for an alternative interpretation).

In the case of the visual stimuli typically used in psycholinguistic research, it is far less clear that similar rapid gist comprehension is possible. For example, in the case of an array of arbitrary objects, there is no higher-level category or meaning to apprehend, so array comprehension must necessarily be based on the identification of the individual objects. Arrays of related objects do in some sense have meaning, but that meaning is likely understood via recognition of the individual objects (Biederman et al., 1988; Henderson et al., 1997, 1999). A scene sketch occupies an interesting middle ground between true scenes and object arrays. It may be that the meaning of a pair or a small group of interacting objects (e.g., a cowboy sitting on a horse, lightning striking a church) can be rapidly apprehended on the basis of some emergent (e.g., statistical) properties of the collection, as seems to be the case with true scenes (see the next section). On the other hand, it may be that scene sketches lack the regularities that are apparently available in true scenes to support rapid comprehension. If the latter hypothesis is true, then the understanding of a scene sketch is likely to rely more on processes associated with object identification than those associated with scene-level processing. This issue awaits further investigation.

How Are Scenes Recognized So Quickly?

Given that the gist of a scene can be determined very rapidly, in fact far more rapidly than would be needed to serially identify all of the constituent objects and their spatial relationships, the obvious question is exactly how it is that rapid scene comprehension happens. Several hypotheses have been advanced.

First, it could be that a *diagnostic object* is rapidly identified (or several are rapidly identified in parallel), and that the scene gist is inferred from this object (Friedman, 1979) or a few objects and their spatial relationships (De Graef et al., 1990). For example, the presence of a stove, or of a stove and a refrigerator, strongly suggests a kitchen; the presence of both nearly requires it (though not quite— the scene could be the interior of an appliance store). One could imagine a system similar to the spreading activation model of letter-and-word processing that would activate a scene representation from object representations (Henderson, 1992). One potential problem for this kind of model is that scene gist can be determined from a degraded image in which none of the component objects can easily be directly identified (e.g., Mannan, Ruddock, & Wooding, 1995; Schyns & Oliva, 1994), though perhaps, even in this case, mutual support of the degraded diagnostic objects for each other and for the scene boosts their collective activation enough to overcome the degradation, as in the TRACE model of auditory word processing (McClelland & Elman, 1986).

A second possibility for explaining rapid scene identification is that there are some scene-level features that directly suggest identity and gist without requiring identification of any of the specific objects or any specific spatial relationships among them. Past suggestions for these features include large volumetric shapes (e.g., geons, Biederman, 1995) or other similar large-scale image features.

Yet another hypothesis is that low-frequency spatial information of the sort available in the visual periphery might be used to determine scene gist. In a series of studies, Schyns and Oliva (1994) applied high- and low-pass spatial frequency filters to a set of photographs of scenes. The resulting filtered images from pairs of scenes were then combined to create images in which the low spatial frequency components of one scene were joined with the high spatial frequency components of another. These *hybrid* images can be perceived as either of the scenes, depending on which spatial frequencies the viewer attends to. The question Schyns and Oliva asked was whether viewers would be biased to use one or the other spatial frequency range to interpret a scene in the initial stages of viewing. That is, which spatial frequency components does the visual system typically use initially to determine gist? In the first experiment, viewers were biased to use the low spatial frequency component during the very early stages of scene identification (Schyns & Oliva, 1994). Furthermore, participants were quite accurate in identifying scenes using the low spatial frequency information with as little as 50 ms of exposure time. The response task was open ended so viewers were able to generate the identity of the scenes from a potentially infinite set of responses. In a second set of experiments, Oliva and Schyns (1997) showed that the use of low spatial frequencies in rapid scene identification was not mandatory: When participants were primed to use the high spatial frequency components of a hybrid image, they tended to identify the scene represented by those components. Thus, it appears that viewers are naturally biased to use low spatial frequency information during the initial stages of scene identification, but that they need not do so (Oliva & Schyns, 1997).

There is also evidence that color plays a role in rapid scene identification, at least when color is diagnostic of the scene category (Oliva & Schyns, 2000). Viewers were asked to name or verify the category of each scene. In the naming and verification tasks, scenes were presented for 120 ms each either in their normal color, in an abnormal color, or in grayscale only, and participants named the scenes. For displays in which color was diagnostic of category, the presence of normal color facilitated and the presence of abnormal color interfered with recognition compared to the grayscale baseline. For scenes in which color was not diagnostic of the category, no effect of color was found. Normal color was also found to enhance categorization for low-pass filtered scenes when color was diagnostic of the category. This latter result suggests that a coarse organization of diagnostically colored blobs can be sufficient for scene categorization (Oliva & Schyns, 2000).

A recent suggestion to explain rapid scene identification is that viewers make use of a holistic, low-dimensional representation of the scene termed a *spatial envelope* (Oliva & Torralba, 2001, 2003). The spatial envelope comprises a set of scene-level dimensions such as naturalness, openness, roughness, ruggedness, and expansion. Importantly, generating these dimensions does not require hierarchical analysis in which objects or other shape primitives must be computed to determine the scene category. Instead, the dimensions can be computed directly from coarsely coded spectral information in a scene image (Oliva & Torralba, 2001, 2003). This approach has been shown to be capable of categorizing a large set of scenes into semantically appropriate clusters that accord well with those produced by human observers (Oliva & Torralba, 2001, 2003). An intriguing question for further research is whether these clusters correspond to coherent and simple verbal labels.

In summary, the evidence suggests that the gist or general semantic category of a scene can be determined from as little as 30 to 50 ms of masked presentation. During this time, general information about a scene, including its semantic category (assuming it has one), the global structural layout (positions and orientations of large surfaces and objects), and identities of some objects (e.g., large objects near fixation), are also likely determined (Castelhano & Henderson, 2003). Identification of extrafoveal objects and processing of the precise spatial relationships among those objects, however, appears to require focused attention, typically accompanied by fixation. We turn to this topic next (see also the discussion in this volume by Findlay, 2004).

EYE MOVEMENTS IN SCENE PERCEPTION

In this section, we consider the role of eye movements in scene perception. There are at least three reasons why this topic is important, independent of the theme of this book. First, human vision is a dynamic process in which the perceiver actively seeks out visual input as it is needed. In fact, virtually all animals with developed visual systems actively control their gaze using eye, head, and/or body movements (Land, 1999). *Active vision* ensures that high-quality visual information is available when it is needed to support ongoing cognitive and behavioral activity, and also can simplify a large variety of otherwise very difficult computational problems (Ballard, 1996; Ballard, Hayhoe, Pook, & Rao, 1997; Churchland, Ramachandran, & Sejnowski, 1994). So, a complete theory of visual cognition will require understanding how ongoing visual and cognitive processes control the direction of the eyes, and in turn how vision and cognition are affected by where the eyes are pointed over time. Second, because attention plays a central role in visual processing, and because eye movements are an overt behavioral manifestation of the allocation of attention in a scene, eye movements serve as a window into the operation of the attentional system (see also discussion in this volume by Findlay, 2004, and Irwin, 2004). It has even been argued that it is misguided to study covert attention in the absence of eye movements (Findlay, 2004). Third, and of particular interest in the context of this volume, eye movements provide an unobtrusive, sensitive, real-time behavioral index of ongoing visual and cognitive processing. This fact has been exploited to a significant degree in the study of perceptual and linguistic processes in reading (Rayner, 1998; Rayner & Liversedge, 2004), and is coming to play a similarly important role in studies of language production and spoken language comprehension, a major impetus for the current volume (see Altmann & Kamide, 2004; Bock et al., 2004; Griffin, 2004; Meyer, 2004; Spivey, 2004; Tanenhaus et al., 2004; Trueswell & Gleitman, 2004).

Psycholinguists (and indeed, any cognitive scientist hoping to capitalize on the use of the eye-movement record as a window into the underlying cognitive processes associated with scene viewing) will ultimately want to base their theories on an up-to-date understanding of how visual and cognitive processing are revealed by eye movement behavior during scene viewing.

Most of what we currently know about eye movements during scene perception derives from investigations of static scene viewing, in which both the viewer and the scene remain still. Therefore, our review necessarily must focus on this work. Much of this research on eye movements over scenes was directly inspired by the successful study of eye movements in reading (for reviews, see Rayner, 1998, Rayner & Liversedge, 2004), and the questions and measures were fairly straightforwardly imported from that literature. As a result, the first questions about eye movements in scenes included the following: How long do fixations last during scene processing? What variables affect fixation durations, crucially separating "early" measures such as first-fixation durations and integrative measures such as total fixation time? Where do people tend to land within a scene, and what controls the patterns of fixations and saccades? How much information do people obtain from a single fixation during scene viewing? Are they able to see only the object on which the eye has landed, or do they see adjacent objects? Does the quality of visual information that is obtained over the functional field of view vary depending on proximity to the point of fixation? These questions all had fairly direct analogues in the reading literature (for instance, the duration of a fixation during reading tends to be about a quarter of a second; the functional field of view is about 3-4 char-acters to the left and 15 to the right of fixation for readers of languages such as English), and so it was certainly reasonable to begin investigations of scene processing with these same issues in mind. As we will see, though, the mea-sures used to study scene processing soon expanded to include several that have less meaning for reading. For instance, researchers now ask about scan patterns over scenes—that is, when people look at a scene, where do they fix-ate and in what order? This question makes less sense in reading, because the sequential nature of words in sentences highly constraints the scan pattern.

An additional complication is that researchers who use the "visual world" paradigm to study language processing rely on different types of measures than are used in the scene perception literature. In particular, the *probability of fixating* an object over some relevant period of time is a very popular depen-dent variable for describing the link between linguistic input and the visual display. For example, if a person hears "pick up the car" while looking at an array of eight toy objects, which object or objects the person will fixate prior to the onset of speech is determined by a variety of typically uncontrolled factors, including visual saliency, position in the array, and so on. Indeed, all that is known is that there is no *linguistic* motivation for looking at any one object over the others. But the probability of fixating on the named object *car* in-creases as more and more of the acoustic form of that word unfolds over time, so that by the end of the word the probability is close to 100% that the person is looking at the car. And if the array includes, say, a carp (again, a toy version), then it is possible to compare the rise and fall of the probability distribution as-sociated with fixating the car compared to the carp. It is important to bear in mind, however, that this measure is not widely used in scene perception re-search. It is certainly possible to focus on visual processing alone and to ask what the probability of fixating, say, a refrigerator in a kitchen scene is over time, but in practice this kind of dependent variable is associated mainly with studies using visual displays as tools to examine language comprehension or production (see the chapter in this volume by Altmann & Kamide, 2004, for insightful discussion and analysis of measures).

EYE MOVEMENTS: BASIC FACTS

Before moving on to a review of eye movements in scene viewing, we will pro-vide a very brief overview of the basics of eye movements. We will be particu-larly interested in saccadic eye movements, in which a distinction is drawn be-tween two temporal phases, *fixations*, when gaze position is held relatively still, and *saccades*, when the eyes are moving from one fixation location to another.[2] Saccadic eye movements are very fast (700 deg/sec or better can be observed, e.g., Carpenter, 1988), and due to a combination of visual masking and central suppression, visual uptake of pattern information is essentially shut down during the saccade, a phenomenon generically known as saccadic suppression (Thiele, Henning, Buishik, & Hoffman, 2002; Matin, 1974; Volkman, Schick, & Riggs, 1968; Volkman, 1986; see also Irwin, 2004, in the present volume, for a review of the evidence that some cognitive processes, particularly those associated with spatial cognition, are also suppressed during saccades). Saccadic suppression implies that useful pattern information is acquired from complex scenes only during fixations.

The quality of the visual information available to scene processing systems during a fixation falls off rapidly and continuously from the center of gaze (the fixation point) due to the optical properties of the cornea and lens and the neuroanatomical structure of the retina and visual cortex. The highest quality visual information is acquired from the foveal region of a viewed scene, a spatial area subtending roughly 2 degrees of visual angle at and immediately surrounding the fixation point. The fovea is centered at the optical axis of the eye, and has a high density of cones with minimal spatial summation. Although the cones require a relatively high level of luminance to operate, they are sensitive to the differences in wavelength that give rise to the perception of color, and they are able to preserve the high spatial frequency changes in reflected light over space that support the perception of fine detail. Furthermore, a disproportionately large amount of primary visual cortex is devoted to the fovea (a property known as *cortical magnification*), providing the neural machinery needed for initial visual computation that can take advantage of this high-resolution input.

The foveae must be oriented rapidly and accurately to ensure that important stimuli in the environment receive the highest quality visual analysis as information is required to perform complex visuocognitive and visuomotor tasks. On average the eyes move to a new fixation position during scene viewing about three times each second, though there is a good deal of variability in the durations of fixations in a given image within individuals as well as across individuals (see Henderson, 2003; Henderson & Hollingworth, 1998; Rayner, 1998), and there is some evidence that these distributions may also differ depending on whether the viewer is examining a scene depiction or a real environment (Land & Hayhoe, 2002). Two important issues for understanding eye movements during scene perception are *where* a fixation tends to be directed and *how long* it typically remains there. We will consider these issues of fixation position and fixation duration next. As we mentioned above, a third characteristic of eye movements that has received some attention in the scene perception literature (but that has not been as relevant in reading research) is the pattern of eye movements in a scene over time. We will come back to this issue of scan pattern after introducing some fixation position and fixation duration measures. For other reviews of eye movements during scene perception, we point the interested reader to Henderson and Hollingworth (1998, 1999b), Henderson (2003), and Rayner (1998).

Where Do Viewers Look in a Scene?

It has been known at least since the classic study by Buswell (1935) that fixations are not randomly distributed in a scene. Buswell asked a group of viewers to examine 55 pictures of different types of artwork. In an ingenious set-up, Buswell reflected light from the viewer's cornea onto photographic film, and quantized the light into time slices by interposing the blades of a fan rotating at 30 Hz into the reflection. In this way, Buswell was able to determine both the viewer's direction of gaze and the duration of each fixation. Despite the rudimentary nature of this eye-tracking system, Buswell learned that viewers tend to cluster fixations on informative image regions, and he was also able to estimate accurately the mean fixation durations and saccade amplitudes as well as the degree of variability within and across viewers, and within and across images, for these measures. Based on his observations, Buswell concluded that there was an important relationship between eye movements and visual attention, and suggested that "[e]ye movements are unconscious adjustments to the demands of attention during a visual experience" (Buswell, 1935, p. 9).

Yarbus (1967) also asked viewers to examine pictures of scenes and objects under a variety of viewing instructions. Like Buswell (1935), Yarbus (1967) concluded that eye movement patterns are influenced by characteristics of the stimulus as well as by the viewer's task and goals. Indeed, many of the classic illustrations of eye movement patterns on scenes found in textbooks are taken from the study reported by Yarbus (1967).

Both Buswell (1935) and Yarbus (1967) concluded that informative scene regions are more likely to receive fixations than less informative regions. This conclusion was based on a "natural history" approach, in the sense that naturalistic observations rather than controlled experiments were used to support it. Perhaps the first experimental study designed to investigate fixation placement in scene perception analytically was reported by Mackworth and Morandi (1967). In this study, each of two color photographs was divided into 64 square regions. An independent group of viewers rated the "informativeness" of each of these regions based on how easy that portion would be to recognize on its own. An independent group of viewers examined the complete pictures while judging which picture they preferred. The number of discrete fixations in a given region was greater the higher its informativeness rating. Regions that were considered relatively uninformative (i.e., that received low ratings) were often not fixated at all, suggesting that the uninformative regions could be rejected as potential fixation sites based on analysis in the visual periphery. Mackworth and Morandi (1967) also reported that fixations made during the first 2 seconds of scene viewing were as likely to be placed on informative regions as fixations made during later 2-second intervals. Mackworth and Morandi argued that these data provided evidence for an early analysis of the information content of peripheral scene regions.

It is important to note that Mackworth and Morandi (1967) used visually simple and somewhat unusual pictures as stimuli (e.g., a pair of eyes within a hooded mask, a coastal map), and it might have been easy for viewers to find visually informative regions in the periphery with these images. Using a more complex set of pictures of scenes taken predominantly from the Thematic Apperception Test, Antes (1974) reported additional evidence that informative scene regions draw eye fixations. One group of participants rated each scene region according to the degree to which it contributed to the total amount of information conveyed by the whole picture. The eye movements of a second group of participants were recorded while they judged the scenes to decide which one they preferred. Antes (1974) found that regions rated more informative received more fixations, replicating Mackworth and Morandi (1967). In addition, the first viewer-determined fixation position in a picture (the first fixation after a saccade away from the experimenter-determined initial fixation position) was more likely to be within an informative than an uninformative scene region, demonstrating that even initial fixation placement is controlled by the information content of local regions.

Uniform and empty regions of a scene are typically not fixated, as can be seen in Figure 1.3, showing all fixations from six subjects trying to commit the scene to memory. As can be seen in the figure, fixations tended to land on objects and clusters of objects such as the boat and the statue. The eyes never landed on the empty scene regions such as the water in the foreground. A safe conclusion, then, is that nothing is of no interest to the eye-movement system. A caveat must be added, however: New research (some of which is being reported for the first time in this volume) shows that viewers do sometimes look to an empty region when it previously contained an interesting object of some sort (see Altmann & Kamide, 2004; Bock et al., 2004; Griffin, 2004; Spivey, Richardson, & Fitneva, 2004).

In summary, it has been known since early studies of scene perception that viewers concentrate their fixations on interesting and informative scene regions. But what makes something "interesting and informative?"

What Image Properties Influence Where Viewers Look in a Scene?

In recent scene perception studies, investigators have begun to explore the nature of the image properties that influence where a viewer will fixate. Three general approaches have been taken to studying this issue. First, investigators have manipulated the nature of the scene images presented to viewers so that only some potentially useful visual information is available and then examined whether fixation placement is similar in these images to fixation placement for the original. For example, Mannan et al.

FIGURE 1.3. All fixations (white squares) from six subjects viewing this scene in preparation for a later memory test (the scene was originally presented in color). Fixations tend to cluster on objects; uniform, uninformative scene regions tend to receive few, if any, fixations.

(1995, 1996) low-pass filtered scenes to remove all of the mid- and high spatial frequency information, producing what is essentially a blurry version of the original picture. Over the first 1.5 sec of viewing, participants' fixations on the low-pass filtered scenes were found to be in similar positions to those of participants who saw the original images. Because the objects in many of the low-pass filtered scenes were not identifiable (though the gist of the scene may have been clear in some of the images), these data suggest that eye-movement control does not rely on object identification in the scene, a result that is consistent with the finding that the meaning of peripheral objects does not influence fixation position selection until after an object has already been fixated (Henderson et al., 1999; see discussion in Henderson & Hollingworth, 1998, and below[3]).

A second method for determining the stimulus properties that control fixation placement is to allow subjects to freely view scenes and then to attempt to determine after the fact which image properties correlate with fixation placement. In this type of analysis, viewers are asked to examine a set of images (scenes, objects, or meaningless patterns such as fractal images) for a variety of purposes. Patches of the scene centered at each fixation are then examined to determine whether they possess more (or less) of some property than do nonselected or randomly selected patches. Using this method, investigators have found evidence that high spatial frequency content and edge density are weakly related to fixation sites (Mannan et al., 1997b), and local contrast (the standard deviation of intensity in a patch) and two-point decorrelation (the difference between the intensity of the fixated point and nearby points) are higher for fixation sites than randomly chosen sites in the same images (Parkhurst & Neibur, 2003; Reinagel & Zador, 1999).

In a third method, investigators have begun to build computational models of visual saliency based on the known properties of V1 (the region of the visual cortex associated with initial visual analysis), a general framework known as the *saliency map* approach (Itti & Koch, 2000, 2001; Itti, Gold, & Koch, 2001; Itti, Koch, & Niebur, 1998; Kock & Ullman, 1985; see also Torralba, 2003). In this approach, visual properties present in a scene give rise in a bottom-up manner to a representation (the saliency map) that makes explicit the locations of the most visually prominent regions in the image. In essence, saliency maps explicitly mark regions of a scene that are different from their surround on one or more dimensions such as color, intensity, contrast, orientation, and so forth. Computation of these differences of each region from its surround typically takes place over multiple spatial scales. The maps generated for each dimension are then combined to create a single saliency map. The intuition behind this approach is that uniform regions are uninformative, whereas areas that are different from neighboring regions are potentially informative. These models are then used to derive predictions about the spatial distribution of eye fixations in a scene, which can then be correlated with observed human fixations (Oliver et al., 2003; Parkhurst et al., 2002).

A critical issue in this framework is how the salient points should be prioritized. For example, one method has been to compute a single saliency map across the entire image and to assign an ordered set of fixation sites based on the ordered saliency derived from that single map, with inhibition of return assuring that the same sites are not re-selected (Itti & Koch, 2000). This view assumes that a single map is retained over multiple fixations. Another approach is to compute a new saliency map in each successive fixation. Parkhurst and colleagues have taken the latter approach and have demonstrated that by generating a new map in which saliency is weighted by the distance of each point to the current fixation position, better correlations with observed human fixation sites are obtained (Parkhurst et al., 2002). A second important question in this approach involves determining what image properties should be included in computing the saliency map. One current model assumes that the saliency map can be derived from a weighted linear combination of orientation, intensity, and color (Itti & Koch, 2000; Itti et al., 2001; Itti, Koch, & Niebur, 1998), though other properties could be considered. A final issue concerns biological implementation: Where in the brain is the saliency map computed and represented (Findlay & Walker, 1999; Gottlieb, Kusunoki, & Goldberg, 1998; Li, 2002)? Is there a single saliency map, perhaps computed directly over image properties in V1 (Li, 2002)? Or might there be multiple maps computed over multiple brain areas combining input from a variety of bottom-up and top-down sources, as has been suggested in the spatial attention literature (Corbetta & Shulman, 2002).

A potentially important factor in determining the degree to which fixation positions are determined by image-based saliency is the time epoch in scene viewing. For example, stimulus factors may play a stronger role in determining fixation sites early in scene viewing than later, because over the course of viewing, visual and semantic information acquired from fixations on individual objects and other scene elements will have more of an opportunity to control subsequent fixation placement (Henderson et al., 1999). This issue has been explored to some extent by examining separately the role of scene statistics on early versus later fixations (Mannan et. al., 1995, 1996, 1997b; Parkhurst et al., 2002).

The saliency map framework is a very promising approach to fixation site selection, but there are a few qualifications. First, while it is clear that visual properties of a scene do influence fixation positions, it has been difficult for investigators to determine exactly what stimulus properties are critical, and how they are combined to influence fixation locations. Stimulus properties that have been investigated in eye-movement experiments include color, contrast, intensity, symmetry, and contour density. One saliency map model is based on a specific set of features (orientation, intensity, and color, Itti et al.,2001; Itti & Koch, 2000), but there is as yet no strong evidence that these specific features have a unique or even central role in determining fixation placement in scenes. At best, predictions of fixation positions based on these specific features correlate somewhat weakly with actual fixation locations in scenes, though the correlations increase when the visual patterns are meaningless (Parkhurst et al., 2002). Furthermore, although there is some relationship between these postulated features and fixations (e.g., Mannan et al., 1996; Parkhurst et al., 2002), results using direct manipulation and measurement of scene statistics at fixation points provide evidence only for contour density and local contrast as predictors of fixation positions (Kreieger, Rentschler, Hauske, Schill, & Zetsche, 2000; Mannan et al., 1996, 1997b; Reinagel & Zador, 1999).

Second, these approaches focus on stimulus-driven control of fixation placement at the expense of top-down factors, even though saliency does not seem strongly related to actual fixation placement, particularly for meaningful stimuli and active tasks (Henderson et al., 1999; Oliva et al., in press; also Land & Hayhoe, 2002; Pelz & Canosa, 2001). Most investigators working within the saliency map paradigm are aware of the shortcoming of focusing only on stimulus influences and explicitly note that top-down factors will need to be incorporated into a complete model. The approach, though, is predicated on the assumption that top-down factors will modulate the fixation sites determined from bottom-up information. This is a reasonable first step, but we wonder whether substantial progress can be made without including top-down information in these types of models; for example, even initial saccades tend to take the eyes in the direction of a search target in a scene, presumably because information about the global scene gist and spatial layout generated from the first fixation provides important information about where a particular object is likely to be found (Castelhano & Henderson, 2003; Henderson et al., 1999; Oliva et al., 2003). Later fixation placement, after objects have initially been fixated and identified, is even more likely to be based on knowledge about the identities and meanings of specific objects and their relationships to each other and to the scene (Henderson et al., 1999; Land & Hayhoe, 2002; Pelz & Canosa, 2001).

Perhaps an important contribution of the bottom-up approach will be the demonstration that it does not do a very good job alone of predicting individual fixation positions or sequences of fixations (scan patterns). This conclusion is actually a happy one for researchers in psycholinguistics who want to use the visual world paradigm because it means that more than just the visual, stimulus properties of a display influence eye-movement behavior. Next we discuss several of the sources of top-down information likely to affect fixation location, and we speculate about the possible top-down role of language.

What Cognitive Factors Influence Where Viewers Look in a Scene? We can divide sources of information available to the eye-movement system into a variety of types (see Table 1.4). Information about a specific scene can be learned over the short term in the current perceptual encounter (*short-term episodic scene knowledge*) and over the long term across multiple encounters (*long-term episodic scene knowledge*). For example, knowing that you have recently placed your keys on your desk to the right of your keyboard (short-term episodic knowledge), you would be in a position to direct your eyes more effectively when you realize you need to rush off to a meeting. Short-term knowledge also allows for the tendency of viewers to refixate previously visited scene areas that are semantically interesting or informative, as we will discuss below, and ensures that objects are fixated when needed during motor interaction with the environment over the course of a complex visuomotor task (Hayhoe et al., 2003; Land et al., 1999). Short-term priming (e.g., Castelhano & Henderson, 2003) can also be considered a form of (very) short-term learning.

Long-term episodic knowledge provides a second source of top-down information about specific scene instances that can influence eye movements. An example might be the knowledge that your coffeemaker always sits to the left of the kitchen sink, a fact you can use to direct your blurry eyes when you stumble into the kitchen in the morning.

TABLE 1.4.

Knowledge Sources Influencing Eye Movements in Scenes	Description	Example
Short-term episodic scene knowledge	Specific knowledge about a particular scene at a particular time	My keys are currently next to my keyboard
Long-term episodic scene knowledge	Specific knowledge about a particular scene that is stable over time	My coffeemaker always sits to the left of the sink
Scene schema knowledge	Generic knowledge about a particular category of scene	Mailboxes are typically found on sidewalks
Task knowledge	Generic knowledge about a particular category of task	Changing lanes while driving requires checking the side-view mirror

A third important source of knowledge is generic semantic regularities in the environment (e.g., the locations of mailboxes in the outdoors) of the sort that have traditionally been considered aspects of scene schemas (Biederman et al., 1982; Friedman, 1979; Mandler & Johnson, 1977). We will call this *scene schema knowledge*. Scene schema knowledge is assumed to arise from semantic regularities across multiple episodes with token-level scenes. Generic semantic regularities may include semantic-semantic knowledge (e.g., mailboxes are found on sidewalks), and semantic-visual knowledge (e.g., mailboxes are found on flat surfaces). Semantic regularities can also involve knowledge about relationships within and across spatial scale. An example of the former is the assumption that where there is a fork, there is likely to be a knife as well (Henderson et al., 1997); an instance of the latter is a viewer's assumption that in a kitchen a toaster will typically be found on a counter (Henderson et al., 1999). Schema knowledge also appears to include information about specific image regularities that are predictive of the scene's semantic category and gist (Oliva & Torralba, 2003) and of spatial information such as the positions of particular objects (Oliva, et al., 2003). This short- and long-term knowledge may be used to direct attention without the viewer's awareness. For example, Chun has shown using non-scene stimuli in a visual search task that abstract relationships among visual elements can be learned implicitly and used to direct attention (Chun, 2000). Although this phenomenon has not been directly investigated with eye movements, we see no reason to believe that the results would not generalize.

A fourth type of knowledge we can consider is *task knowledge*, that is, knowledge about how to move one's eyes in the service of a particular goal or set of goals. In a classic example of task effects on gaze control, Yarbus (1967) noted that viewers change their scan patterns in a static scene depending on the specific viewing task they are engaged in, though this observation was qualitative. Under more controlled conditions, it has been shown that the distribution of fixations in a scene differs depending on whether a viewer is searching for an object or trying to memorize that scene (Henderson et al., 1999). Oliva, et al.(2003) described an additional example of task influence on fixation placement. Participants were asked to count the number of people who appeared in a variety of photographs of true scenes. Each scene contained anywhere from six people to none. The eye-movement results showed that the eyes were directed toward regions of the scenes likely to contain people (see also Henderson et al., 1999). The regions chosen for fixation were not well predicted by a purely stimulus-driven saliency map model.

There is also a good deal of data suggesting that specific tasks generate specific kinds of eye-movement behavior. Land et al. (1999) and Hayhoe et al. (2000) have shown this in their tea-making and sandwich-making studies: People had a strong tendency to fixate a task-relevant object (e.g., a knife just before picking it up) rather than the most visually salient object. Pelz and Canosa (2001) reported that viewers in a hand-washing task sometimes produced what they called *look-ahead fixations* that were related to future actions associated with the high-level goals of the task rather than to the salience of the visual properties of the immediate environment. Eye movements also have particular patterns during other complex and well-learned activities such as driving (Land & Lee, 1994; Liu, 1999 and cricket batting (Land & McLeod, 2000). Yet another example of gaze behavior that requires more than saliency for an explanation is the finding that people often fixate the location of an absent object if they remember that an object had been in that location previously (Altmann & Kamide, 2004; Bock et al., 2004; Griffin, 2004; Ryan, Althoff, Whitlow, & Cohen,.2000; Spivey et al., 2004). Finally, as documented by many of the chapters in this volume, human gaze is strongly influenced by language processing (Bock et al., 2004; Griffin, 2004; Meyer & Lethaus, 2004; Tanenhaus et al., 2004; Trueswell & Gleitman, 2004).

In summary, the positions of fixations during scene viewing are not random; fixations cluster on both visually and semantically informative scene regions. In memorization tasks, visual characteristics of local scene regions appear to exert an early effect on fixation site selection, with semantic characteristics of local scene regions playing a greater role once those regions have initially been fixated. Once a local region has been fixated (or the eyes have at least landed nearby), then the semantics of that region appear to play a much larger role in its subsequent selection as a fixation site. In more goal-directed visual tasks, such as visual search, other types of contextual influences, such as those based on a global interpretation of the scene (rather than interpretation of local regions) may come into play even earlier in scene viewing (Henderson et al., 1999; Oliva, et al., 2003). The influence of linguistic input as another possible source of top-down contextual information is an important issue that has not been systematically studied yet.

More speculatively, if viewers are required to process a scene while listening to a sentence or attempting to formulate an utterance to describe that scene, the linguistic task may be viewed as a source of top-down control. For instance, if someone is asked to point to the toaster in a kitchen scene, decisions about where to fixate will be influenced by the linguistic input. Viewers will concentrate their fixations on the horizontal surfaces that look like plausible sites for toasters and other small appliances, and they will probably stop looking around the scene once the target has been located (Henderson et al., 1999). The process can be broken down even further, although assumptions must be made about when the scene is first presented to the viewer relative to the onset of the linguistic material (and this point is true for all of the studies that have used visual displays to reveal how people understand language). Let us imagine that the scene and the utterance onset at the same time and that the viewer's initial point of fixation is in the center of the display. Within the duration of the first fixation on the scene, the participant would know that the scene is a kitchen, possibly even before the end of the word *point* in an instruction such as "Point to the toaster." During the two short syllables that make up the function words *to the*, the eye might move to some salient or interesting object (which could, of course, be the toaster, but we will ignore that possibility in order to keep matters simple). When the participant hears even a fragment of *toaster*, he or she will probably direct the eyes to the proper object, because the visual system knows what the scene is, knows enough about the layout to be able to find the horizontal surfaces at the right height, and knows linguistically that the sounds *toa-* make up the beginning of *toaster*. It must be acknowledged, however, that a great deal depends on whether the toaster is itself salient in some way, on the presence of other objects (e.g., is there a blender and a coffeemaker on the countertop as well), and on the availability of linguistic competitors (e.g., a plate of toast on a kitchen table; in principle the word *toad* could be a competitor as well, of course, but kitchens rarely contain amphibians unless their legs are being prepared as part of a meal). Notice that in this hypothetical example it is possible to imagine that the viewer never fixates on the refrigerator, for instance, because the task of locating the toaster is a source of top-down information for directing the eyes to various objects. The refrigerator is likely not relevant to locating the toaster, and therefore it would not be surprising to find that it was entirely ignored (particularly since the eye-movement system will probably stop searching once the target is located).

Few studies of language comprehension using the visual world paradigm conform to this description of how linguistic input might exert top-down control over eye movements because most use visual arrays rather than true scenes. Recall that two of the critical differences between arrays and scenes are that arrays have no gist, and they also cannot take advantage of scene-based constraints on object locations. Thus, an array of, say, eight objects that includes a toaster does not have any type of high-level description (unless all the items are small appliances, for instance, but this is never done in visual world studies), and therefore the toaster could be anywhere. As a result, the visual system has *only* the linguistic input to guide eye movements. Indeed, with arrays, the participant is really engaged in something more like arbitrary visual search rather than true scene viewing. The implications of these points for research integrating vision and language are completely unknown at this stage.

In summary, humans have a great deal of experiential knowledge that can be used to guide eye movements intelligently in scenes. All of these sources of information likely interact with each other (and with the current bottom-up stimulus information) to determine the path of the eyes through a scene. A final shortcoming of current approaches to fixation site selection, based on stimulus properties alone, is that they have not yet attempted in any serious way to account for the durations of individual fixations, an important aspect of human eye movements and an issue we will return to later in the chapter.

Does Object Meaning Influence Where Viewers Initially Look?

We have just reviewed the evidence that general cognitive sources of information influence where people look in scenes. Now we turn to a more specific type of cognitive effect and one that is particularly relevant to the use of the visual world paradigm: object meaning. We begin by considering whether the semantic properties of objects that have not been attended and fixated can affect the selection of a fixation site. In other words, are the identities and meanings of objects in a scene outside of the currently fixated area typically processed to a level that they can affect fixation placement? Another way to cast this question is to ask whether the semantic properties of a scene region can modulate its image-generated visual saliency. This issue is important for a number of reasons. First, if the identities and meanings of a substantial number of objects that are located in the visual periphery can be determined before fixation, then it becomes less clear why fixations on those objects would be needed. Second, this issue has been a source of a good deal of controversy in the visual cognition literature. Third, this issue has important implications for the use of scenes in psycholinguistics, because some investigators seem to assume erroneously that all objects in a complex display are identified within a brief fixation. This confusion possibly arises because investigators tend to equate getting the gist of a scene in a single fixation with knowing the identities of all its constituent objects based on that same, single fixation. But as we discussed in the section on rapid scene identification, extracting gist does not entail identifying all or even any of the objects the scene contains.

In perhaps the first study to investigate this issue, Loftus and Mackworth (1978) manipulated predetermined target objects in line drawings of scenes. The scenes varied considerably in complexity, but approximated true scenes. Each target object was either consistent or inconsistent with the overall semantics. For example, a tractor appeared in a farm scene and an underwater scene. The assumption was that a semantically anomalous object is more informative than a semantically consistent object, and so should draw fixations if object identities and meaning can influence eye-movement control. In the experiment, participants were asked to view each scene for four seconds to prepare for a recognition memory test. The results regarding fixation location were straightforward. First, the target objects tended to be fixated earlier when they were inconsistent with the rest of the scene than when they were consistent. These data suggested that semantically informative scene regions attracted fixations. Second, and extending the findings of Antes (1974) to semantically defined informativeness, the inconsistent target objects were much more likely to be fixated immediately following the first saccade within the scene. Furthermore, the average amplitude of the saccade to the target objects was 6.5 deg to 8 deg of visual angle, suggesting that viewers could determine the semantic consistency of an object with its scene, based on peripheral information obtained in a single fixation, and that this semantic information could then exert an immediate effect on gaze control.

The finding that early fixations in a scene can be immediately directed to semantically informative peripheral regions would have been significant had it held up to further empirical scrutiny because it would have supported the following assumptions about eye movements in scenes. First, this result is indeed consistent with other studies showing that information about the gist of a scene is available within the first fixation (as we discussed earlier in this chapter). Second, the finding that the eyes were immediately directed to semantically anomalous objects in the visual periphery seems to imply that the semantic relationship between the scene and specific objects in the visual periphery can be rapidly (i.e., within a single fixation) understood. Such rapid understanding would require that objects be processed to a semantic level over a wide scene area in a short amount of time. Third, the results seem to suggest that information about the semantics of both the scene and peripheral objects can be used by the gaze control system to orient the eyes quickly to a semantically informative peripheral scene region.

As we have seen, there is good converging evidence that the gist or overall meaning of a scene can be determined within a single fixation. However, the second and third points are more controversial because they require that the identities and/or semantics of a large number of objects be processed in the visual periphery in parallel (or with very rapid serial processing) without an eye fixation. This assumption is inconsistent with the results from other lines of research on scene perception. For example, in studies of object detection in briefly presented scenes, detection performance is relatively poor, even when the identity of the target object is known before the scene appears (Biederman et al., 1982; Boyce & Pollatsek, 1989; Hollingworth & Henderson, 1999)[4]. Similarly, studies of both change detection and object memory suggest that a fixation near or on an object is necessary to encode the visual properties and identities of objects in scenes (Henderson & Hollingworth, 1999; Henderson, Williams, Castelhano, & Falk, 2003; Hollingworth, Williams, & Henderson, 2001; Nelson & Loftus, 1980; Nodine, Carmody, & Herman, 1979; Parker, 1978).

More recent studies using the semantic anomaly manipulation in scenes have not replicated the semantic attraction effect (De Graef et al., 1990; Henderson et al., 1999; see Henderson & Hollingworth, 1998, for a more complete discussion). For example, De Graef et al. (1990) asked participants to search line drawings of scenes for non-objects—object-like figures that were not identifiable and so did not carry any semantic content. Following Loftus and Mackworth (1978), semantically consistent and inconsistent target objects were placed in the scenes. But in contrast to them, De Graef et al. (1990) found no evidence that the target objects were fixated earlier when they were semantically inconsistent with the scene than when they were consistent. In fact, a plot of the cumulative probability of fixating a target as a function of semantic status showed that viewers were no more likely to examine the inconsistent than the consistent objects for the first eight fixations in the scene, and after that, they actually were more likely to fixate the *consistent* objects. Similarly, no effects of other types of anomalies, such as spatial inconsistencies, were found on early fixation site selection.

Henderson et al. (1999) reported an experiment that attempted to closely replicate the Loftus and Mackworth (1978) study. Semantically consistent target objects were created independently for each of 24 complex line drawings generated from photographs of natural environments. For example, a farm and a kitchen scene contained a chicken and a mixer, respectively, as target objects. Pairs of scenes and target objects were then yoked, and target objects were swapped across the scenes to control the visual characteristics of the objects themselves at the same time that their semantic relationships to the scenes were changed. The two target objects in a pair were chosen to be about the same real-world size and were always placed in the same location in the paired scenes so that the distance from the initial fixation point and lateral masking from surrounding contours would be controlled. In the first experiment, participants were instructed to view the scenes in preparation for a later memory test (which was, in fact, never given); these were the same instructions used by Loftus and Mackworth (1978). Viewers were no more likely to move their eyes directly to the target object when it was semantically anomalous than when it was consistent with the scene, either for the first or second saccade in the image. Overall, viewers landed on a target object for the first time after an average of about 11 fixations in a scene, and this value did not change as a function of the semantic relationship between the object and the scene. In addition, the average amplitude of the initial saccade to the target object was about 3°, and there was no evidence that saccades were longer to the targets when they were semantically inconsistent with the scene than when they were consistent. Together, these data suggest that gaze was not initially attracted by individual objects analyzed semantically in the periphery. Therefore, it does not appear that people can identify peripheral objects based on initial, centrally located fixations.

In a second experiment designed to extend these results, Henderson et al. (1999) asked participants to search for a target object in each scene. The search targets, identified by a visually presented word presented prior to each trial, were the same as the target objects in the first experiment and so were either consistent or inconsistent with their context scene. The scene was then presented, and participants searched for the target as quickly as possible. If semantically anomalous objects are highly salient in the visual periphery, then they should "pop out" and be found more quickly than consistent objects. Instead, participants were no more likely to fixate a target after the first saccade in the scene when that target was anomalous, compared with when it was semantically consistent.[5] In fact, consistent search targets were fixated about half a fixation sooner on average than anomalous targets, probably because the scene could be used to constrain the search to areas likely to contain the consistent target. For example, a blender in a kitchen is likely to appear on a countertop rather than on the floor or elsewhere, but the location of a blender in a farmyard is harder to predict. This is a point we will return to below.

Why have the recent studies failed to replicate the Loftus and Mackworth (1978) result? First, as suggested by several authors, semantic anomaly and visual distinctiveness may have been confounded (Antes & Penland, 1981; De Graef et al.,1990; De Graef, De Troy, & d'Ydewalle, 1992; Rayner & Pollatsek, 1992). An examination of a large set of the scenes used by Loftus and Mackworth suggest that this likely was the case.[6] In contrast, all of the scenes used in Henderson et al. (1999) were created in the same way and in the same style, and target objects were drawn independently of the scene backgrounds and then inserted into both the consistent and inconsistent scenes.

Second, the scenes used in the De Graef et al. (1990) and Henderson et al. (1999) studies were generated from photographs of natural scenes and so were visually more complex and cluttered than those used by Loftus and Mackworth (1978). It is likely that less cluttered scenes produce less lateral masking and so increase the functional field of view for object identities and hence the distance at which object semantics can influence eye movements. In reading, letter identification declines more steeply as a function of eccentricity when contours that produce lateral masking are present in the display compared to conditions when they are not (Bouma, 1978). Line drawings of objects subtending only two degrees of visual angle can be identified with good accuracy at up to 20 deg of visual angle when presented alone in the visual field (Pollatsek, Rayner, & Collins, 1984). Because the line drawings of scenes used by De Graef et al. (1990) and Henderson et al. (1999) were more visually complex and so included more contours than those used by Loftus and Mackworth (1978), it is likely that peripheral identification of objects was much more difficult in the former experiments than in the latter. The question, of course, is which of these two conditions best reflects the situation found in natural visual environments. Recent experiments in our lab with photographs of true scenes suggest that the more complex line drawings produce results that are consistent with more accurate depictions of the world (see Note 5).

In summary, the weight of the evidence suggests that initial fixation placement in a complex true scene is influenced by the visual properties of local scene regions (e.g., objects), but not by the semantic properties of those local regions. What might this conclusion mean for psycholinguists wishing to use the visual world paradigm to study language processing? One implication is that regardless of whether a participant is asked to look for an expected or an unexpected object in a display, the earliest fixations will be determined by the visual properties of the objects. Therefore, it is important to ensure that the visual saliency of the objects of interest is controlled across conditions. Second, it is also important to be clear in any study of vision and language about whether viewers are able to preview the displays before the linguistic input begins, or whether information from the two modalities becomes available simultaneously. If the former is true, then it will be no surprise to find that naïve participants are able to go immediately to a target object; they will already know where the objects are located and so can go to the right one when the linguistic input begins (see section below on later effects of object identity and meaning on fixation site selection). If no preview is given, however, then it could be much more newsworthy to find that participants can move quickly to a target object. Of course, even this conclusion would have to be qualified because a great deal depends on the complexity of the display. In simple arrays of a small number of discrete objects, it is more likely that participants would be able to acquire information from objects beyond fixation and to use that information to direct their gaze efficiently, compared to a true scene with many irrelevant objects and background features (imagine a Victorian living room with busy wallpaper, books on tables with pictures on the covers, artwork on the walls and on furniture, and so on). Also, thus far, we have been implicitly focusing mainly on studies of language interpretation, but similar issues arise for research in language production as well. For instance, the degree to which eye fixations and speech are time-locked may be influenced by whether a participant has preknowledge of the display as well as by the complexity of the display used to elicit a particular kind of utterance.

Does Object Meaning Affect Where Viewers Look Later? Although a semantic analysis of local scene regions may not be able to attract the eyes, meaning does affect the probability of refixating the region once it has initially been fixated. A standard measure of fixation density is the number of discrete fixations within a given region in some given amount of display time. As reviewed above, viewers tend to cluster their fixations on informative regions of a scene (Antes, 1974; Buswell, 1935; Mackworth & Morandi, 1967; Yarbus, 1967; see Figure 1.3). An examination of the figures presented by Buswell (1935) and Yarbus (1967) suggests that in their studies, these fixation clusters were not entirely determined by visual factors. Instead, viewers tended to concentrate their fixations on regions that were semantically interesting. In a widely cited example, Yarbus (1967) found that viewers tended to concentrate their fixations on the faces in, for example, Repin's *An Unexpected Visitor* when instructed to determine the ages of the people. In contrast, when asked to estimate the material circumstances of the family in the same picture, viewers distributed their fixations more widely over the scene, fixating the furniture and other artifacts (in addition to the faces).

Fixation densities in a scene region are a function of the likelihood that the region is fixated at all (*probability of region entry*), the number of times the eyes move to the region from elsewhere in the scene (*number of entries*), the number of fixations in the region each time it is entered (*gaze fixation count*), and the number of total fixations made within that region summed over entries (*total fixation count*). These measures are often correlated, but not perfectly, and discrepancies among them can often be important sources of information about scene processing. For example, viewers may be unlikely to look at a particular region (low probability of entry), but given that they do look, they may fixate multiple times in that region before exiting (high first-gaze fixation count), may return to the region multiple times (high number of entries), and may fixate multiple times on each entry (high total-fixation count). This type of pattern can be found, for example, when a previously present object is deleted from a scene (Ryan et al., 2000). This manipulation often creates a uniform empty region that has a lower probability of entry. However, when the eyes do happen to land in the region that had previously contained an object no longer present, that region tends then to receive many more fixations, presumably because once the region has been fixated, the absence of the object is noted and the discrepancy leads to additional fixations (e.g., Henderson et al., 2003; Hollingworth & Henderson, 2002).

The figures presented by Buswell (1935) and Yarbus (1967) certainly suggest that the number of entries, the number of gaze fixations, and the total number of fixations in a given scene region are affected by amount of semantic information. There is also quantitative evidence supporting this observation. First, the number of fixations viewers make in a region when it is first entered is affected by scene semantics (Henderson et al., 1999). In addition, viewers tend to return their gaze to semantically informative regions over the course of scene viewing, leading to increases in the number of entries to such regions (Loftus & Mackworth, 1978; Henderson et al., 1999). In Henderson et al. (1999), viewers looked to (entered) informative object regions about 3.3 times and uninformative object regions about 2.6 times on average over the course of 15 seconds of scene viewing.

There is one study in the literature suggesting that the semantic content of an object region does not influence the number of region entries (Friedman and Liebelt, 1981; Friedman, 1979). Participants viewed line drawings of real-world scenes in preparation for a memory test involving discrimination of the details of objects in the scenes. Each scene contained objects that had been rated for their likelihood within the scene by a separate group of participants and ranged continuously from very likely to somewhat likely. No differences in fixation density as a function of semantic ratings were observed. Because none of the objects were truly unlikely (or anomalous) in the scenes, a possible explanation for the lack of effect of semantic content is that the overall manipulation of semantics was relatively weak. In contrast, in Henderson et al. (1999) as well as Loftus and Mackworth (1978), the semantically inconsistent objects were highly anomalous in their scenes, so the semantic manipulation was probably stronger, making the effect easier to detect (Henderson & Hollingworth, 1998).

The studies showing semantic influences on fixation density indicate that a purely stimulus-driven saliency map approach to explaining fixation site selection is not sufficient to explain the relevant findings. For example, these models cannot account for increased fixation densities on semantically informative scene regions. Henderson et al. (1999; see also Parkhurst et al., 2002; Mannan et al., 1995) suggested that visual saliency may play a larger role in decisions about fixation placement early during scene viewing as the viewer attempts to identify specific objects and the spatial relationships among them, but even these initial fixations are likely to be affected by an interaction of scene information apprehended in the first fixation (see above section on gist), information in memory relevant to the current viewing task, and the task itself.

How Long Do Viewers Look at a Given Scene Region?

Early studies of eye movements during scene viewing did not report fixation-time measures (Antes, 1974; Buswell, 1935; Mackworth & Morandi, 1967; Yarbus, 1967), and recent approaches to fixation placement based on the saliency map approach have similarly neglected fixation time. There is, however, extensive evidence that fixation time is affected by the information carried by the fixated region. For example, the *total fixation time* (the sum of the durations of all fixations) is longer for visually and semantically informative regions (DeGraef et al., 1990; Friedman, 1979; Henderson et al., 1999). This result is to be expected because total fixation time in a region is correlated with the number of fixations in that region, and as noted above, fixation density is affected by visual and semantic factors.

At a more fine-grained level of analysis, we can ask whether the durations of individual fixations and temporally contiguous clusters of fixations in a region (rather than the sum of all fixations) are also affected by the properties of the fixated region. Several commonly used measures of fixation time include *first-fixation duration* (the duration of the initial fixation in a region) and *first-pass gaze duration* (the sum of all fixations from first entry to first exit in a region); other similar measures such as *second-pass (or n^{th} pass) gaze duration* (the sum of all fixations from second (or n^{th}) entry to second (or n^{th}) exit in a region), and total fixation duration (the sum of all fixations from all entries) can also be used (Henderson et al.,1999). In this section we briefly review the types of factors that influence fixation durations in scenes.

Do Visual Factors Influence Fixation Time?

This issue has not been explored to a great degree. There is evidence that individual fixation durations are affected by the luminance (Loftus, 1985) and contrast (Loftus, Kaufman, Nishimoto, & Ruthruff, 1992) of a scene image. Henderson and Hollingworth (1998) compared distributions of fixation durations for full-color photographs, full-color renderings of scenes, and black-and-white line drawings and found that the distributions of fixation durations were very similar, with small differences in means across conditions. In an unpublished study, we have also compared full-color scenes with their grayscale counterparts. The data again suggested that fixation duration distributions were very similar in the two conditions. A difficulty with this sort of global image manipulation, however, is that it is not possible to disentangle the influence of image properties at fixation from image properties in the parafovea and periphery. To tease apart these influences, it is necessary to manipulate the image at fixation and beyond fixation independently.

Van Diepen and colleagues used a moving mask paradigm to manipulate the quality of the visual information available at fixation independently of the information available extrafoveally (van Diepen, De Graef, & d'Ydewalle, 1995; van Diepen, Wampers, & d'Ydewalle, 1998). Viewers searched for nonobjects in line drawings of real-world scenes, and the image at fixation was either normal or was degraded by reducing the contrast or overlaying a noise mask on the fixated region. The mask moved with the eyes so that it was always centered at the fixation point and included the region of the scene covered by the fovea. When the image was degraded at the onset of each fixation, first-fixation durations were longer than in a control condition, suggesting that the duration of the initial fixation was influenced by the acquisition of visual information from the fixated region. We have recently replicated this effect in our lab using full-color photographs of natural scenes.

Another source of evidence about the influence of visual properties on fixation time derives from work using change detection in scenes. In this paradigm, participants view pictures of real-world scenes while attempting to detect changes to them. In the transsaccadic version of this paradigm, changes are contingent on the execution of a saccade (Bridgeman, Hendry, & Stark, 1975; Bridgeman & Stark, 1979; Currie, McConkie, Carslon-Radvansky, & Irwin, 2000; Grimes, 1996; Henderson & Hollingworth, 1999a; McConkie, 1990; McConkie & Currie, 1996). In one version of this *transsaccadic change detection paradigm*, only a single region of the scene changes contingent on a saccade to that region (Henderson & Hollingworth, 1999a, 2003, in press; Hollingworth & Henderson, 2002; Hollingworth, Williams, et al. 2001). This paradigm allows investigation of the influence of changes to the visual properties of a region on fixation duration. The results show that even when the viewer does not explicitly notice a change, an increase in fixation time is often observed (Henderson & Hollingworth, 2003; Hollingworth & Henderson, 2002; Hollingworth et al., 2001; see also Hayhoe, Bensinger, & Ballard, 1998). These increases are found when the object changes from one basic-level concept to another, changes from one visual token of a given basic-level concept to another, and rotates 90 deg around its vertical axis. The latter two manipulations affect visual details but preserve the identity, concept, and semantics of the object with respect to the scene, so the increased fixation times suggest that visual properties (or at least changes between pre- and post-saccade visual properties) are able to influence gaze durations in a relatively immediate manner.

In summary, there is evidence from several paradigms that fixation time in scenes is affected by the visual properties of the fixated image, but considerably more work is needed to determine exactly what image properties affect precisely which measures. The Van Diepen et al. (1998) study and our replication are the only direct explorations of the influence of visual factors from the fixated area alone (that is, separating foveal and extrafoveal stimulus properties) on fixation duration during scene viewing that we are aware of, and there is currently no direct data concerning whether first-fixation durations or gaze durations in a scene are affected by other visual properties such as brightness, contrast, contour density, and color. Until this research is conducted, psycholinguists would be wise to exercise caution and hold constant the object from which performance is measured in any visual world study (as well as its position in the display). If indeed some objects are fixated longer due to their visual properties, then changing objects haphazardly across conditions could introduce serious confounds into the experimental designs.

Do Semantic Factors Influence Fixation Time?

The influence of semantic factors on fine-grained measures of fixation time during scene viewing has been studied more extensively than have visual factors. One common manipulation used to investigate this issue is the semantic consistency of a specific object with its scene context. For example, in the study described above, Loftus and Mackworth (1978) found that first-pass gaze durations were longer for semantically informative (i.e., semantically anomalous) than for uninformative (i.e., semantically consistent) objects in scenes. Friedman (1979) similarly showed that first-pass gaze duration on an object was correlated with that object's rated likelihood in its scene, with longer gaze durations on less likely objects (see also Antes & Penland, 1981).[7] Using the nonobject counting task described above, De Graef et al. (1990) also found that first-pass gaze durations were longer for semantically inconsistent objects in scenes, though this difference appeared only in the later stages of viewing. Hollingworth et al. (2003) replicated this gaze duration effect but observed it for all periods of scene viewing. Finally, Henderson et al. (1999) found that first-pass, second-pass, and total-fixation duration were longer for anomalous than for semantically consistent objects in scenes. All of these studies used line-drawing depictions as stimuli.

The influence of semantic factors on the duration of the very first fixation on an object (i.e., *first-fixation duration*) is less clear. De Graef et al. (1990) found that overall, first-fixation durations on an object did not differ as a function of semantic consistency (see also De Graef et al., 1992). However, when first-fixation duration was examined as a function of fixation moment (whether an object was fixated during the first or second half of all fixations on its scene), first-fixation durations on objects that were first encountered relatively late during scene exploration (following the median number of total fixations) were shorter on semantically consistent than anomalous objects (De Graef et al., 1990). On the other hand, Henderson and Hollingworth (1998) reported an analysis of the first-fixation duration data from Henderson et al. (1999) and found no overall effect of semantic consistency on first-fixation duration, nor an effect when the data were divided by a median split into fixations that occurred during the first versus second half of scene exploration. We have similarly failed to find first-fixation duration effects in our studies manipulating semantic consistency (e.g., an unreported analysis from Hollingworth et al., 2001). It appears that if these effects of region semantics on first-fixation durations during scene viewing exist, they are fragile. We note that we have also typically found effects of object changes in scenes on gaze durations but not first-fixation durations. This tendency of effects to be observed only in gaze durations during scene viewing differs from reading, where effects often appear in both measures, or even primarily in first-fixation duration (Rayner, 1998). It is not clear why effects do not typically show up in first-fixation durations in scenes, but the issue is worthy of further investigation.

As we argued in the previous section, it would seem to be prudent for psycholinguists to design their visual world experiments so that the same object is a target in different experimental conditions. Here we urge this approach because of the virtual certainty that the semantic characteristics of objects have important effects on eye movement behavior. Even if the effects are not detectable in the earliest measures of fixation time, they still seem to emerge fairly early, and they are quite robust.

Does Scene Viewing Produce Systematic Scan Patterns?

In addition to measuring where viewers look in a scene and for how long, we can also examine the sequence in which specific regions are fixated. The study of eye-movement (scan) patterns has received less attention than perhaps it should in the scene perception literature. There are probably two reasons for this relative lack of interest. First, there was an initial theory suggesting that the *scan path* produced during complex image viewing was an integral part of the memory for that image (Noton & Stark, 1971a, 1971b; Stark & Ellis, 1981). According to this scan path theory, learning a new image involved coding both the visual features of the image as well as the eye-movement motor sequence used to encode them. Recognition of the image at a later time would then involve recapitulating the eye-movement sequence encoded during learning. This scan path theory was subsequently shown to be incorrect. For example, recognition experiments demonstrate that it is not necessary to make eye movements to recognize scenes, as highlighted by the studies of rapid scene identification and gist comprehension reviewed above. Another finding inconsistent with scan path theory is that there is very little similarity in the temporal sequences of fixations from one viewing to another of a given image by the same viewer (Groner, Walder, & Groner, 1984; Mannan et al., 1997a; Walker-Smith, Gale, & Findlay, 1977). We have recently demonstrated that the eye-movement pattern generated during face recognition is essentially the same whether the face was learned with or without the viewer making eye movements (Henderson, Williams, & Falk, submitted). The fact that scan path theory was not empirically supported led to a general reduction in interest in the issue of scan patterns in vision, a case, perhaps, of throwing the baby out with the bathwater, in the sense that although scan path theory is incorrect, there may still be regularities in the scan patterns produced by viewers due to control of those patterns by the stimulus and/or the task.

A second factor that has tended to undermine the study of scan patterns in scene perception (we use the term *scan pattern* to dissociate the temporal sequence of fixations from the particular assumptions of scan path theory) has been the difficulty of quantitatively capturing patterns or sequences of fixations. One issue is that determining whether fixations are in the same area or not is difficult because objects in scenes are not discretely arrayed in a nonoverlapping, spatially segregated manner. Instead, because true real-world scenes occur in three dimensions, objects visually overlap and occlude each other. When a fixation lands near a pair of objects in such an arrangement, it can be difficult to determine whether the fixation is on the occluding or occluded object.

Furthermore, issues of spatial scale come into play; for example if a fixation is found on the handle of a cup that is sitting on a plate on a table, what was actually fixated from the perspective of ongoing visual analysis: the handle, the cup, the plate, or the table? This issue of course arises in computing fixation durations and fixation locations as well, but it is compounded in the case of patterns because multiple regions must be defined for sequences of fixations to be described. Several approaches have been taken to solving this problem: statistical cluster analysis, in which the fixations themselves are used to define the regions in a data-driven manner; arbitrary predefinition, in which regions are defined by imposing a grid over the scene (e.g., Groner et al., 1984); and intuitive predefinition, in which judgments are used to parse the scene into regions based on the image or on the fixation positions (e.g., Stark & Ellis, 1981). None of these approaches is optimal. This general problem does not arise in the study of reading, because of the two-dimensional nature of text and because words are clearly separated from each other visually with spaces (at least in English).

Ignoring for the moment the issue of the difficulty of parsing scenes into multiple regions to be able to apply a scan pattern analysis, there is also the problem of quantifying the pattern itself. Essentially, the challenge is to devise a method for capturing sequences of the spatial distributions of points in two dimensions for scene depictions or three dimensions for the actual environment. Although there are quite a few methods for capturing clusters and densities of such points, there are far fewer methods for capturing their temporal sequential ordering, and very few of these methods (some developed for analyzing migrations of animals over terrain, and some for other issues in geography) have been ported over for use in analyzing eye movements. Two exceptions are the use of Markov analyses to look for dependencies in pairs or triplets of fixation positions (e.g., Henderson, Falk, Minut, Dyer, & Mahadevan, 2001; Liu, 1998), and string analyses used to compare the similarities of fixation sequences across conditions (Brandt & Stark, 1997). We anticipate that more of these kinds of analyses will be adopted in the study of eye movements in scene perception in the near future.

A final factor that has tended to reduce interest in scan patterns has been the observation that there is a relatively low level of consistency of scan patterns either within or across individuals when viewing a given scene image (e.g., Mannan et al., 1997a; see also Groner et al., 1984). The general conclusion seems to be that although viewers tend to fixate the same regions of a scene (so fixation clusters occur on informative regions), the sequence in which they view those regions is much more variable. However, we again caution that this issue has been much less studied than other aspects of eye movements in scenes, and it may be that with more careful examination, more consistency in scan patterns will be found, especially as analysis tools become more sophisticated.

It is also worth noting here that even the degree of consistency in basic eye-movement measures such as fixation durations and saccade amplitudes varies significantly across studies of scene perception. Individual viewers are somewhat idiosyncratic in that their fixation durations, and saccadic amplitudes tend to differ from each other. Interestingly, Andrews and Coppola (1999) observed that fixation durations and saccade amplitudes covaried within individuals across reading and visual search tasks, but not from those tasks to scene perception. Also, differences in basic measures like average fixation durations and average saccade amplitudes are observed across scene perception studies, though these differences lessen as the studies become more similar (Henderson & Hollingworth, 1998). It is often difficult to determine the precise cause of these cross-study differences because a number of potentially important factors typically vary from study to study. We've already discussed the difference between the actual environment and depictions of the environment, as well as the difference between scenes and arrays. Other important factors that cut across these dimensions include viewing task (Yarbus, 1967), viewing time per image, and image content. Furthermore, within depictions, we can add differences in the size of the viewed image, the resolution of the image, whether color is present, and the nature of the depiction (e.g., line drawing, rendered scene, photograph). Henderson and Hollingworth (1998) summarized the values of several of these factors for a large number of studies that had been published up to that point in time, and they observed very little consistency from one study to the next. These factors could interact with each other in complex ways to influence dependent measures of eye movement behavior such as saccadic amplitudes, fixation positions, and fixation durations, as well as estimates of the functional field of view for perceptual and semantic information. The issues are obviously similar for the use of visual world paradigms to study language, but caution is probably more important there because even less is known about these questions when a new source of information as complex as language is added to the paradigm. We see two options that the field can adopt for dealing with this problem: (1) settle on one set (or at least a small set) of values for these dimensions (e.g., use only color photographs of the natural environment), or (2) undertake a systematic study of the ways in which these factors do (or don't) influence eye-movement parameters of interest. The former approach might make some sense within psycholinguistics. The latter approach would require a Herculean effort and is unlikely to be completed in the near future.

What Is the Functional Field of View in Scene Perception?

Given that human vision is structured with a high resolution central region and a lower resolution visual surround, and given also that eye movements are used to orient the fovea to important and informative scene regions, an important question in scene perception is the specific size and nature of the region from which useful information can be acquired during a given eye fixation, a region that we will refer to as the *functional field of view*.[8]

Psycholinguists using the visual world paradigm are interested in a number of basic questions about the functional field of view in scene perception. The most important of these, perhaps, is how far from fixation an object can be identified. Unlike reading, where there is a relatively narrow range of natural letter sizes given typical reading distances (Rayner & Pollatsek, 1992), it is difficult to provide a straightforward answer to the functional field-of-view question in the visual world paradigm because, as discussed above, displays vary tremendously across labs and experiments. It is, in principle, possible to define the functional field of view for vision operating over the natural world (though for technical reasons this has not yet been done), but the field of view for the natural world would not generalize to the visual world paradigm because a natural visual stimulus and the stimuli presented in the lab differ. For example, a number of factors affect the distance at which an object can be identified, including the size of the object, the amount of additional visual information in the image, the quality of the image, whether attention is directed to the object, whether eye movements are allowed, whether foveal information is being processed, whether the images are from a small and repeated set or from a potentially infinite set of objects, and whether the objects in the set are visually similar. To take one extreme, Pollatsek et al. (1984) showed that participants could identify about 85% of line drawings of simple objects subtending 2 deg of visual angle at an eccentricity of up to 10 deg. A number of factors undoubtedly contributed to this high degree of peripheral identification, including the limited and repeated set of target objects, presentation of the objects alone on the monitor (no lateral masking), lack of presentation of any stimuli at the fovea (no foveal processing load), low visual similarity across objects in the set, and presentation of the objects at a spatially predictable position in the periphery (allowing prior allocation of attention to the object position).

A variety of approaches have been adopted to investigating the nature of the functional field of view in scene perception, including the moving-window technique and tasks such as semantic anomaly detection and object change detection. In the moving-window technique, fixation-contingent display changes are used to manipulate the image presented to the viewer contingent on where the viewer is currently fixated (Saida & Ikeda, 1979; van Diepen et al., 1998; see Rayner, 1998, for a description of the origin of this technique). A window region is defined at fixation, within which the scene is visible. Outside of this window region, the scene is degraded in some way (e.g., filtered, masked, eliminated). An estimate of the functional field of view can be obtained by manipulating the size of the window. The minimum window size at which performance is the same as a no-window control provides an estimate of the maximum functional field of view for all types of information that might be acquired during a fixation (Rayner, 1998). Studies using the moving-window technique during scene viewing have suggested that the functional field of view is quite large, encompassing about half of the total scene regardless of its absolute size, at least for scene depictions up to 14.4 x 18.8 deg (Saida & Ikeda, 1979).

Detection of semantic anomalies has been used to provide an estimate of the degree to which semantic information is processed from objects that appear beyond the fovea (Loftus & Mackworth, 1978; Henderson et al., 1999), or what we might call the functional field of view for object semantics. As discussed above, an initial investigation using this method led to the conclusion that semantic information about objects in scenes is acquired relatively far into the periphery, with semantically anomalous objects drawing the eyes from eccentricities of 8 deg on average (Loftus & Mackworth, 1978). These results suggested that the functional field of view for object semantics has a radius of 8 deg or more. Subsequent studies using more complex scenes, however, were unable to replicate this large field of view effect, and instead found that semantically anomalous objects in scenes were more likely processed out to the parafoveal region of about 3-4 deg from fixation (De Graef et al., 1990; Henderson et al., 1999), a finding that we have recently replicated with photographs of scenes (Hsieh & Henderson, in preparation). Notice, though, that given the sparse kinds of displays that people tend to use in psycholinguistic studies, it is likely that the field of view for object semantics is fairly large.

A third method for investigating the functional field of view in scene perception was introduced by Parker (1978) and involved analyzing the fixation patterns of viewers who were trying to find differences between previously learned and currently visible images. The logic of this method is that the distance at which various kinds of differences can be detected (and thus can either be responded to directly or can draw the eyes) is an indication of how far from fixation the information needed to detect such differences is acquired. In Parker's study, participants were shown line drawings containing six objects arranged in a scene-like manner. Each picture was presented in one form during an initial viewer-timed learning phase, and then was shown 12 more times in a test phase (6 "same" and 6 "different" trials). This sequence was repeated until the viewer had taken part in a session of 65 presentations of a given picture (5 learning and 60 test presentations). Viewers participated in seven such sessions, one for each picture. In the test presentations, the pictures were changed through manipulations to the objects, which were deleted, increased, or decreased in size by 67%, replaced with an object from a different conceptual category, and replaced with an object from the same conceptual category.

In this study, viewers were able to detect object deletions very quickly, and 85% of the detections were accomplished without fixation on the region of the picture that had contained the deleted object. Furthermore, viewers tended to jump ahead to a changed object in a picture. Because the average center-to-center distance between objects was 10 deg and because no background elements were present upon which viewers might fixate, it appeared that viewers could detect changes and either move to them sooner or, in the case of deletions, respond directly to them, given information acquired from at least 10 deg away from fixation. As Parker concluded, "The results indicated that during recognition, information is encoded from a wide area and utilized both to direct additional eye fixations and to reach response decisions" (p. 284).

The results from Parker (1978) suggested that the functional field of view for the presence and categories of the specific objects in a picture is quite large (with a radius of at least 10 deg around fixation, for a functional field of view of up to 20 deg). However, these results seem to be at odds with other evidence suggesting that the functional field of view for these sorts of object properties is a relatively small area around the current fixation point. For example, Nelson and Loftus (1980) recorded viewers' eye movements while they examined a set of line drawings of scenes in preparation for a difficult memory test. Performance in the memory test was found to be a function of the nearest fixation to the tested object during learning, with good performance if the tested object had been fixated and a rapid drop off to near-chance levels if the nearest fixation during learning was greater than about 2.6 deg from the object subsequently tested (see also Nodine et al., 1979). Thus, Nelson and Loftus (1980) concluded that the functional field of view for memory encoding during scene viewing appeared to be restricted to a small area around fixation.

Parker's (1978) results also appear to be at odds with recent evidence about the functional field of view obtained from online change-detection tasks. For example, Henderson and Hollingworth (1999a) employed a saccade-contingent, display-change technique in which, during ongoing scene viewing, a critical object was changed during a saccade toward that object, during a saccade away from that object after it was initially fixated, or during a saccade toward another control region of the scene. Change detection was found to be a function of the distance of the fixation prior to the saccade to the changing object when the eyes were moving toward it, and the distance of the first fixation after the saccade from the changing object when the eyes were moving away from it. The exception to this finding was a deletion to the target of the saccade when the eyes were moving toward it; in this condition, change detection was not contingent on the distance of the fixation prior to the saccade toward the target (Henderson & Hollingworth, 1999a, 2003). In the other conditions, performance started falling off when the before- or after-change fixation was beyond 4 deg from the changing object. Furthermore, in the case of the control condition in which the change was contingent on a saccade to a different region of the scene (and so the critical object was fixated neither before nor after the change), detection was at chance. Finally, in those cases where the change was not immediately detected, later detections took place only when the eyes happened to refixate the changed object.

Together, these results suggest that the functional field of view is relatively large for the presence of the target of a saccade, but is far more restricted for other object information and other locations, with an asymptote in these scene depictions at a maximum of about 4 deg, and a minimum of the currently fixated object. The 4 deg maximum value for detecting object changes also converges with the 4 deg estimate of the functional field of view for object processing found with semantic anomaly attraction reviewed above (Henderson et al., 1999).

Evidence for a relatively restricted functional field of view has also been obtained in the "flicker paradigm" in which participants are asked to detect and report scene changes across brief blank periods that alternate with two versions of the scene (Rensink, O'Regan, & Clark, 1997). The fact that viewers typically take a considerable amount of time to find changes in this paradigm suggests that there is a severe restriction in the amount of information that can be acquired during each fixation. Hollingworth, Schrock, and Henderson (2001) examined the role of fixation in change detection in this flicker paradigm by monitoring eye position and found that participants typically needed to fixate either directly on or very close to (within 2 deg) a changing object before they detected the change.

Why were Parker's (1978) results so different from those of other scene-viewing studies? Several design features of the experiment may have led to an overestimate of the functional field of view. First, the images used in Parker (1978) were schematic, consisting of an array of six discrete line-drawing objects against a blank background. These images would fall somewhere between interpretable arrays and scene sketches in our typology. The objects were large (judging from other measurements reported in the paper, they subtended about 7 deg of visual angle on average) and were relatively distant from each other (10 deg center to center, and 6.5 deg center to nearest edge on average). As mentioned above, line drawings of objects presented in an uncluttered field can be identified quite far from fixation (Pollatsek et al., 1984). The sparseness of the arrays and the large distances between objects may also have led to saccade lengths that were inflated compared to those typically observed in more natural scene images (Henderson & Hollingworth, 1999b). In studies examining the ability of semantic information to attract the eyes, what at first appeared to be a relatively large functional field of view (Loftus & Mackworth,

1978) was found to be much smaller when more complex scenes were used as stimuli (De Graef et al., 1990; Henderson et al., 1999). Second, the experiment included only seven base pictures, and variants of each of these pictures were presented 65 times to each viewer. Given the simplicity of the pictures and the large number of repetitions, viewers may have been able to learn specific visual cues that would be sufficient to detect object differences in the periphery. Again, this might be misleading about the nature of the functional field of view and peripheral image processing in natural scene perception.

In a study that attempted to replicate the Parker results with color computer renderings of complex true scenes, Henderson, Williams, Castelhano, & Falk (2003) reported several results that contrasted with those reported by Parker (1978). First, objects that were deleted between scene learning and test were relatively difficult to notice, and recognition time for correctly noticing deletions was numerically slower than for noticing that a different object had been substituted for the original object. Contrary to Parker (1978), then, deleted objects were easily missed rather than easily noticed. Second, although there was some tendency for changed objects to be fixated sooner than unchanged objects, the average distance of the saccade to the changed object was about 4°, considerably smaller than the average distances between objects in Parker (1978). Again, this 4° value is consistent with other studies exploring eye movements in pictures of scenes, as documented by Henderson et al. (1999; see also Henderson & Hollingworth, 1998, Henderson & Hollingworth, 1999b).

We are not suggesting that the functional field of view is equally limited for all types of scene information. For example, as discussed in the section on rapid scene recognition, it is likely that scene gist and global layout are processed over a significantly larger area of a scene than are the identities of specific objects. An analogous situation exists in reading, where the total functional field of view (including word length cued by the spaces between words) is considerably larger (about 3 to 4 characters to the left of fixation and 15 to the right) than it is for word identities (the *word span*), which is, at best, two words and probably closer to one (Rayner, 1998). Similarly, in scene perception, it is likely that different types of information can be acquired at different distances from fixation. For example, the gross large-scale visual characteristics of a given object (such as its presence) may be acquired at a greater distance from the fovea than conceptual or identity information for that object. Again, this is an issue that awaits further direct investigation.

In summary, the functional field of view for global scene properties is likely quite large. At the same time, the contrast between the functional field of view for object properties given a display of a single object (e.g., Pollatsek et al., 1984), an array of objects (e.g., Parker, 1978), and a full scene (e.g., Henderson et al., in press) suggests that the functional field of view for object information differs markedly depending on the complexity of the presented image, and that for complex true scenes, it is quite small.

Why is the functional field of view important in the visual world paradigm? If the objects in the experiment have already been identified before linguistic input is provided, then those objects provide a lexical and semantic context for interpreting that utterance. This context could lead to a situation in which the linguistic input is compared directly to the limited set of possibilities, rather than the natural case in which the input must generate the possibilities as well as selecting among them. The presence of this context might result in the use of features to make the decisions that differ from those that would be used in normal language processing. If these features could be processed faster than those that are typically used, estimates of the time-course of typical processing would also be biased toward greater speed. As a simple example, imagine a case in which participants are shown two objects on either side of fixation with names that can be distinguished by the first phoneme (*dog* versus *sock*). Imagine too that these objects are relatively large and are presented on an uncluttered field close to fixation, so that they can be quickly identified. Now imagine that at the onset of the display, an auditory stimulus is presented naming one of the objects, e.g., "dog." It might be found that participants can begin moving their eyes to the dog before the acoustic signal has ended. The interpretation might then be that the acoustic signal can be linguistically analyzed very rapidly. But does this result really require the conclusion that a word is normally identified this rapidly, or using the initial phoneme? It could be instead that the signal required to discriminate between these two possibilities is simple and that the system in essence bypasses normal acoustic lexical linguistic analysis and instead taps into cues that are chosen specifically to optimize performance in this task. This is possible because in a simple display of this sort, the objects can be identified quickly enough that the determination of such cues is possible.

CONCLUSION

In this chapter we have tried to pull together a review of the basic facts about eye movements and the visual cognition of scene viewing that psycholinguists should take into account when using the visual world paradigm. We have seen that the two literatures do not mesh seamlessly. One major and critical difference is in the nature of the visual displays that are used: Scenes in visual cognition studies are typically quite different from the stimuli used in the visual world paradigm. This difference has major implications for the kinds of eye movements that will be observed; for instance, the functional field of view for object identity can vary widely depending on the complexity of the visual display. We have seen too that although the meaning of a scene is extracted within the first fixation on it, this process is based on the extraction of scene features and does not depend on the identification of any individual objects. Also, because image properties can have major influences on eye-movement behavior, particularly in the absence of any kind of scene meaning, researchers should more carefully control the visual properties of the objects used in visual world studies. For example, the same objects should be used in different linguistic conditions; otherwise, condition and visual saliency are confounded.

We have of necessity left out of our review several important areas of research in the visual cognition of scene viewing. These include visual memory for scene information, effects of scene context on object recognition, and transsaccadic integration during scene perception. All of these topics have relatively large literatures associated with them. For reviews of the first two topics, we point the interested reader to Henderson and Hollingworth (2003b) and Henderson and Hollingworth (1999b), respectively. For review of the latter topic, see Pollatsek & Rayner (1992), Irwin (1992), and Irwin's chapter in this volume (2004).

The visual world paradigm has revolutionized the study of how language is processed. With greater communication between those who study psycholinguistics and those who study visual cognition, both fields will advance even further in understanding the interface between language, vision, and action.

ACKNOWLEDGMENTS

Preparation of this chapter was supported by grants from the National Science Foundation (BCS-0094433) and the Army Research Office (DAAD19-00-1-0519; the opinions expressed in this article are those of the authors and do not necessarily represent the views of the Department of the Army or any other governmental organization. Reference to or citations of trade or corporate names does not constitute explicit or implied endorsement of those entities or their products by the author or the Department of the Army). We thank the members of the Psycholinguistics and Visual Cognition Labs at Michigan State University for their spirited feedback on this work, and Keith Rayner for comments on an earlier draft of the chapter. Correspondence can be addressed to either author at Psychology Research Building, Michigan State University, East Lansing, MI 48824-1117 (e-mail: john@eyelab.msu.edu or fernanda@eyelab.msu.edu).

NOTES

1. Recently, three-dimensional scene images such as those produced by virtual reality displays have become available for use in eye-movement experiments. This development could be significant because three-dimensional VR displays preserve these ad-

ditional depth cues, and little is currently known about how depth interacts with other image properties in their influence on eye movements in complex scenes.

2. Other types of eye movements include microsaccades, which help keep the image from fading on the retina due to fatigue, optokinetic nystagmus, which keeps fixation stable within a moving pattern, vergence movements, which direct the two eyes to a common point in depth, and smooth pursuit, which support visual tracking over object or viewer motion. All of these types of eye movements are relevant during dynamic real-world scene perception, though they are thought be less directly reflective of ongoing cognitive processing than are saccadic eye movements and fixations.

3. The role of high versus low spatial frequency information in determining early initial fixation placement in a scene is not yet clear. On the one hand, the Mannan et al., data suggest that initial fixation placement may be controlled in part by low-spatial frequency information initially acquired from a scene. On the other hand, van Diepen, Wampers, & d'Ydewalle (1998) demonstrated with a moving-window technique that high-spatial frequency information (i.e., edges) is more important in determining future fixation sites than is low-spatial frequency information. It is possible that although low-spatial frequency information can be used to select fixation sites, high-spatial frequency information is preferred, with the system flexibly switching across spatial frequency channels as required (Oliva & Schyns, 1997). This topic should be investigated further.

4. The main issue at stake in these studies has been whether scene context actually affects perceptual identification of objects in scenes (Biederman et al., 1982) or only affects decision bias (Hollingworth & Henderson, 1998, 1999). The point here, though, is that in all of these studies, overall detection rates for both contextually-consistent and inconsistent objects viewed briefly in the visual periphery are often quite low.

5. This issue continues to produce controversy. A recent study reported by Becker, Pashler, & Lubin (2001) appeared to show that initial fixations were attracted to semantically anomalous target objects in the periphery of photographs of scenes. However, in this experiment, only two scenes were used, the scenes were not controlled in the same way that they typically have been (e.g., the same target objects were not used across conditions), and one of the two scenes did not produce the effect. Henderson and Hsieh (in preparation) have recently redone the Henderson et al. (1999) study with a large set of photographs of true scenes, and they failed to find that semantic anomaly attracted initial fixations.

6. We thank Geoff Loftus for his generosity in making the original pictures available to us.

7. Loftus and Mackworth as well as Friedman called their measures *duration of the first fixation*, though the measures are equivalent to what is now referred to as gaze duration. Their eye-tracking equipment did not have the spatial resolution to allow these investigators to examine the true first fixation duration.

8. This region has also been called the effective field of view, the span of effective vision (Rayner & Pollatsek, 1992), the span of the effective stimulus (Bertera & Rayner, 2000; McConkie & Rayner, 1975), the functional visual field (Nelson & Loftus, 1980), the visual span (Reingold, Charness, Pomplun, & Stampe, 2001), the perceptual span (Rayner, 1975), and the attentional span (Henderson, 1992b).

REFERENCES

Altmann, G. T. M., & Kamide, Y. (2004). Now you see it, now you don't: Mediating the mapping between language and the visual world. In J. M. Henderson & F. Ferreira (Eds.), *The interface of language, vision, and action: Eye movements and the visual world*. New York: Psychology Press.

Andrews, T. J., & Coppola, D. M. (1999). Idiosyncratic characteristics of saccadic eye movements when viewing different visual environments. *Vision Research, 39,* 2947-2953.

Anstis S. M. 1974. A chart demonstrating variations in acuity with retinal position. *Vision Research, 14,* 589-92.

Antes, J. R. 1974. The time course of picture viewing. *Journal of Experimental Psychology, 103,* 62-70.

Antes, J. R., & Penland J. G. (1981). Picture context effect on eye movement patterns. In D. F. Fisher, R. A. Monty, & J. W. Senders (Eds.), *Eye movements: Cognition and visual perception*. Hillsdale, NJ: Erlbaum.

Bailey, K. G. B., & Ferreira, F. (2003, March). Eye movements and the comprehension of disfluent speech. Poster presented at the annual CUNY Conference on Human Sentence Processing, Boston, MA.

Ballard, D. H. (1991). Animate vision. *Artificial Intelligence, 48,* 57-86.

Ballard, D. H. (1996). On the function of visual representation. In K. Akins (Ed.), *Perception: Vancouver studies in cognitive science*. Oxford: Oxford University Press.

Ballard, D. H., Hayhoe, M. M., Pook, P. K., & Rao, R. P. (1997). Deictic codes for the embodiment of cognition. *Behavioral & Brain Sciences, 20,* 723-767.

Barr, D.J., & Keysar, B. (2002). Anchoring comprehension in linguistic precedents. *Journal of Memory and Language, 46,* 391-418.

Becker, M., Pashler, H., & Lubin, J. (2001, November). Semantic oddities draw early saccades. Presented at the 42nd annual meeting of the Psychonomic Society, Orlando, Florida.

Biederman, I. (1972). Perceiving real world scenes. *Science 177,* 77-80.

Biederman, I.(1981). On the semantics of a glance at a scene. In M. Kubovy & J. R. Pomerantz (Eds.), *Perceptual Organization* (pp. 213-253). Hillsdale, NJ: Erlbaum.

Biederman, I. (1995). Visual object recognition. In S. M. Kosslyn & D. N. Osherson (Eds.), *An invitation to cognitive science: Visual cognition*. Cambridge, MA: MIT Press.

Biederman, I., Blickle, T. W., Teitelbaum, R. C., & Klatsky, G. J. (1988). Object search in non-scene arrays. *Journal of Experimental Psychology: Learning, Memory, and Cognition, 14,* 456-467.

Biederman, I., Glass, A. L., & Stacy, E. W. Jr. (1973). Searching for objects in real-world scenes. *Journal of Experimental Psychology, 97,* 22-27.

Biederman, I., Mezzanotte, R. J., & Rabinowitz, J. C. (1982). Scene Perception: detecting and judging objects undergoing relational violations. *Cognitive Psychology, 14,* 143-177.

Biederman I., Rabinowitz, J. C., Glass, A. L., & Stacy, E. W., Jr. (1974). On the information extracted from a glance at a scene. *Journal of Experimental Psychology, 103,* 597-600.

Bock, J.K. (1986). Meaning, sound, and syntax: Lexical priming in sentence production. *Journal of Experimental Psychology: Learning, Memory, and Cognition, 12,* 575-86.

Bock, J.K. (1989). Closed-class immanence in sentence production. *Cognition, 31,* 163-186.

Bock, K., Irwin, D. E., & Davidson, D. J. (2004). Putting first things first. In J. M. Henderson & F. Ferreira (Eds.), *The interface of language, vision, and action: Eye movements and the visual world*. New York: Psychology Press.

Bouma, H. (1978). Visual search and reading: Eye movements and functional visual field. A tutorial review. In J. Requin (Ed.), *Attention and performance VII* (pp. 115-147). Hillsdale, NJ: Erlbaum.

Boyce, S. J., & Pollatsek, A. (1992b). The identification of objects in scenes: The role of scene backgrounds in object naming. *Journal of Experimental Psychology: Learning, Memory, & Cognition, 18,* 531-543.

Brandt, S. A., & Stark, L. W. (1997). Spontaneous eye movements during visual imagery reflect the content of the visual scene. *Journal of Cognitive Neuroscience, 9,* 27-38.

Bridgeman, B., Hendry, D., & Stark, L. (1975). Failure to detect displacements of the visual world during saccadic eye movements. *Vision Research, 15,* 719-722.

Bridgeman, B., & Stark, L. (1979). Omnidirectional increase in threshold for image shifts during saccadic eye movements. *Perception & Psychophysics, 25,* 241-243.

Buswell, G. T. (1935). *How people look at pictures.* Chicago: University of Chicago Press.

Carpenter, R. H. S. (1988). *Movements of the eyes.* London: Pion.

Castelhano, M. S., & Henderson, J. M. (2003, May). *Flashing scenes and moving windows: An effect of initial scene gist on eye movements.* Presented at the Annual Meeting of the Vision Sciences Society, Sarasota, Florida.

Chapman, P. R., & Underwood, G. (1998). Visual search of dynamic scenes: event types and the role of experience in viewing driving situations. In G. Underwood (Ed.), *Eye guidance in reading and scene perception.* Amsterdam: Elsevier.

Churchland, P. S., Ramachandran, V. S., Sejnowski, T. J. (1994). A critique of pure vision. In C. Koch & S. Davis (Eds.), *Large scale neuronal theories of the brain.* (pp. 23-60). Cambridge MA: MIT Press.

Chun, M. M. (2000). Contextual cueing of visual attention. *Trends in Cognitive Sciences, 4,* 170-178.

Corbetta, M., & Shulman, G. L. (2002). Control of goal-directed and stimulus-driven attention in the brain. *Nature Reviews Neuroscience, 3,* 201-215.

Currie, C., McConkie, G., Carlson-Radvansky, L. A., & Irwin, D. E. (2000). The role of the saccade target object in the perception of a visually stable world. *Perception & Psychophysics, 62,* 673-683.

De Graef P, Christiaens D, d'Ydewalle G. 1990. Perceptual effects of scene context on object identification. *Psychological Research, 52,* 317-329.

De Graef, P., De Troy, A., & d'Ydewalle, G. (1992). Local and global contextual constraints on the identification of objects in scenes. *Canadian Journal of Psychology, 46,* 489-508.

Delorme, A., Richard, G., & Fabre-Thorpe, M. (2000). Ultra-rapid categorization of natural scenes does not reply on color cues: A study in monkeys and humans. *Vision Research, 40,* 2187-2200.

Engel, S. A., Glover, G. H., & Wandell, B. A. (1997). Retinotopic organization in human visual cortex and the spatial precision of functional MRI. *Cerebral Cortex, 7,* 181-192.

Epstein, R., Graham, K. S., & Downing, P. E. (2003). Viewpoint-specific scene representations in human parahippocampal cortex. *Neuron, 37,* 865-876.

Epstein, R., Harris, A., Stanley, D., & Kanwisher, N. (1999). The parahippocampal place area: Recognition, navigation, or encoding. *Neuron, 23,* 115-125.

Epstein, R., & Kanwisher, N. (1998). A cortical representation of the local visual environment. *Nature, 392,* 598-601.

Fabre-Thorpe, M., Delorme, A., Marlot, C., Thorpe, S. (2001). A limit to the speed of processing in ultra-rapid visual categorization of novel natural scenes. *Journal of Cognitive Neuroscience, 13,* 171-180.

Findlay, J. M. (2004). Eye scanning and visual search. In J. M. Henderson & F. Ferreira (Eds.), *The interface of language, vision, and action: Eye movements and the visual world.* New York: Psychology Press.

Findlay, J. M., & Walker, R. (1999). A model of saccade generation based on parallel processing and competitive inhibition. *Behavioral and Brain Sciences, 22,* 661-721.

Friedman, A. (1979). Framing pictures: The role of knowledge in automatized encoding and memory for gist. *Journal of Experimental Psychology: General, 108,* 316-355.

Friedman, A., & Liebelt, L. S. (1981). On the time course of viewing pictures with a view towards remembering. In D. F. Fisher, R.

A. Monty, & J. W. Senders (Eds.), *Eye movements: Cognition and visual perception* (pp. 137-155). Hillsdale, NJ: Erlbaum

Germeys, F., & d'Ydewalle, G. (2001). Revisiting scene primes for object locations. *The Quarterly Journal of Experimental Psychology, 54A,* 683-693.

Gottlieb, J. P., Kusunoki, M., & Goldberg, M. E. (1998). The representation of salience in monkey parietal cortex. *Nature, 391,* 481-484.

Griffin, Z. (2004). Why look? Reasons for speech-related eye movements. In J. M. Henderson & F. Ferreira (Eds.), *The interface of language, vision, and action: Eye movements and the visual world.* New York: Psychology Press.

Grimes, J. (1996). On the failure to detect changes in scenes across saccades. In K. Akins (Ed.), *Perception: Vancouver studies in cognitive science* (pp. 89-110). Oxford: Oxford University Press.

Groner, R., Walder, F., & Groner, M. (1984). Looking at faces: Local and global aspects of scanpaths. In A. G. Gale & F. Johnson (Eds.), *Theoretical and applied aspects of eye movement research* (pp. 523-533). Amsterdam: Elsevier.

Hayhoe, M. M., Bensinger, D. G., & Ballard, D. H. (1998). Task constraints in visual working memory. *Vision Research, 38,* 125-137.

Hayhoe, M. M., Shrivastava, A., Mruczek, R., & Pelz, J. B. (2003). Visual memory and motor planning in a natural task. *Journal of Vision, 3,* 49-63.

Henderson J. M. (1992a). Object identification in context: The visual processing of natural scenes. *Canadian Journal of Psychology, 46,* 319-341.

Henderson, J. M. (1992b). Visual attention and eye movement control during reading and picture viewing. In K. Rayner (Ed.), *Eye movements and visual cognition: scene perception and reading* (pp. 260-283). New York: Springer-Verlag.

Henderson, J. M. (1992c). Identifying objects across eye fixations: Effects of extrafoveal preview and flanker object context. *Journal of Experimental Psychology: Learning, Memory, and Cognition, 18,* 521-530.

Henderson, J. M. (1993). Visual attention and saccadic eye movements. In G. d'Ydewalle

& J. Van Rensbergen (Eds.), *Perception and cognition: Advances in eye movement research* (pp. 37-50). Amsterdam: North Holland.

Henderson, J. M. (1994). Two representational systems in dynamic visual identification. *Journal of Experimental Psychology: General, 123,* 410-426.

Henderson, J. M. (1996). Visual attention and the attention-action interface. In K. Aikens (Ed.), *Perception: Vancouver studies in cognitive science* (pp. 290-316). Oxford: Oxford University Press.

Henderson, J. M. (1997). Transsaccadic memory and integration during real-world object perception. *Psychological Science, 8,* 51-55.

Henderson, J. M. (2003). Human gaze control in real-world scene perception. *Trends in Cognitive Sciences, 7,* 498-504.

Henderson, J. M., & Anes, M. D. (1994). Effects of object-file review and type priming on visual identification within and across eye fixations. *Journal of Experimental Psychology: Human Perception and Performance, 20,* 826-839.

Henderson, J. M., & Hollingworth, A. (1998). Eye movements during scene viewing: An overview. In G. Underwood (Ed.), *Eye Guidance in Reading and Scene Perception* (pp. 269-283). Oxford: Elsevier.

Henderson, J. M., & Hollingworth, A. (1999a). The role of fixation position in detecting scene changes across saccades. *Psychological Science, 10,* 438-443.

Henderson, J. M., & Hollingworth, A. (1999b). High-level scene perception. *Annual Review of Psychology, 50,* 243-271.

Henderson, J. M., & Hollingworth, A. (2003a). Eye movements and visual memory: Detecting changes to saccade targets in scenes. *Perception & Psychophysics, 65,* 58-71.

Henderson, J. M., & Hollingworth, A. (2003b). Eye movements, visual memory, and scene representation. In M. Peterson & G. Rhodes (Eds.), *Perception of faces, objects, and scenes: Analytic and holistic processes.* Oxford University Press.

Henderson, J. M., & Hollingworth, A. (2003c). Global transsaccadic change blindness during scene perception. *Psychological Science, 14,* 493-497.

Henderson, J. M., & Hsieh, B. (in preparation). Semantic oddities do not pop out in scenes.

Henderson, J. M., McClure, K. K., Pierce, S., Schrock, G. (1997). Object identification without foveal vision: evidence from an artificial scotoma paradigm. *Perception & Psychophysics, 59*, 323-346.

Henderson, J. M., Pollatsek, A., & Rayner, K. (1987). The effects of foveal priming and extrafoveal preview on object identification. *Journal of Experimental Psychology: Human Perception and Performance, 13,* 449-463.

Henderson, J. M., Pollatsek, A., & Rayner, K. (1989). Covert visual attention and extrafoveal information use during object identification. *Perception & Psychophysics, 45*, 196-208.

Henderson, J. M., Weeks, P. A. Jr., & Hollingworth, A. (1999). Effects of semantic consistency on eye movements during scene viewing. *Journal of Experimental Psychology: Human Perception and Performance, 25*, 210-228.

Henderson, J. M., Williams, C. C., & Castelhano, M. S., & Falk, R. J. (2003). Eye movements and picture processing during recognition. *Perception & Psychophysics, 65,* 725-734.

Hollingworth, A., & Henderson, J. M. (1998). Does consistent scene context facilitate object perception? *Journal of Experimental Psychology: General, 127*, 398-415.

Hollingworth, A., & Henderson, J. M. (1999). Object identification is isolated from scene semantic constraint: Evidence from object type and token discrimination. *Acta Psychologica, 102 (Special Issue on Object Perception and Memory)*, 319-343.

Hollingworth, A., & Henderson, J. M. (2000a). Semantic informativeness mediates the detection of changes in natural scenes. *Visual Cognition, 7*, 213-235.

Hollingworth, A., & Henderson, J. M. (2002). Accurate visual memory for previously attended objects in natural scenes. *Journal of Experimental Psychology: Human Perception and Performance, 28*, 113-136.

Hollingworth, A., Schrock, G., & Henderson, J. M. (2001). Change detection in the flicker paradigm: The role of fixation position within the scene. *Memory & Cognition, 29*, 296-304.

Hollingworth, A., Williams, C. C., & Henderson, J. M. (2001). To see and remember: Visually specific information is retained in memory from previously attended objects in natural scenes. *Psychonomic Bulletin & Review, 8*, 761-768.

Intraub, H. (1979). Presentation rate and the representation of briefly glimpsed pictures in memory. *Journal of Experimental Psychology: Human Learning and Memory, 5*, 78-87.

Intraub, H. (1980). The role of implicit naming in pictorial encoding. *Journal of Experimental Psychology: Human Learning and Memory, 6*, 1-12.

Intraub, H. (1981). Rapid conceptual identification of sequentially presented pictures. *Journal of Experimental Psychology: Human Perception and Performance, 7*, 604-610.

Irwin, D. E. (1992). Visual memory within and across fixations. In K. Rayner (Ed.), *Eye movements and visual cognition: Scene perception and reading* (pp. 146-165). New York: Springer-Verlag.

Irwin, D. E. (2004). Fixation location and fixation duration as indices of cognitive processing. In J. M. Henderson & F. Ferreira (Eds.), *The interface of language, vision, and action: Eye movements and the visual world*. New York: Psychology Press.

Irwin, D. E., & Zelinsky, G. J. (2002). Eye movements and scene perception: Memory for things observed. *Perception & Psychophysics, 64*, 882-895.

Itti, L., Gold, C., & Koch, C. (2001). Visual attention and target detection in cluttered natural scenes. *Optical Engineering, 40*, 1784-1793.

Itti., L., & Koch, C. (2000). A saliency-based search mechanism for overt and covert shifts of visual attention. *Vision Research, 40*, 1489-1506.

Itti, L., & Koch, C. (2001). Computational modeling of visual attention. *Nature Reviews: Neuroscience, 2*, 194-203.

Itti, L., Koch, C., & Niebur, E. (1998). A model of saliency-based visual attention for rapid scene analysis. *IEEE Transactions on pattern Analysis and Machine Intelligence, 20*, 1254-1259.

Krieger, G., Rentschler, I., Hauske, G., Schill, K., & Zetsche, C. (2000). Object and scene analysis by saccadic eye-movements: an investigation with higher-order statistics. *Spatial Vision, 13*, 201-214.

Land, M. F. (1999). Motion and vision: Why animals move their eyes. *Journal of Comparative Physiology A, 185*, 341-352.

Land, M. F., & Hayhoe, M. (2001). In what ways do eye movements contribute to everyday activities? *Vision Research, 41*, 3559-3565.

Land, M. F., & Horwood, J. (1995). Which part of the road guides steering? *Nature, 377*, 339-340.

Land, M. F., & Lee, D. N. (1994). Where we look when we steer. *Nature, 369*, 742-744.

Land, M. F., & McLeod, P. (2000). From eye movements to actions: How cricket batsmen hit the ball. *Nature Neuroscience, 3*, 1340-1345.

Land, M. F., Mennie, N., & Rusted, J. (1999). Eye movements and the roles of vision in activities of daily living: Making a cup of tea. *Perception, 28*, 1311-1328.

Levy, I., Hasson, U., Avidan, G., Hendler, T., & Malach, R. (2001). Center-periphery organization of human object areas. *Nature Neuroscience, 4*, 533-539.

Li, F. F., VanRullen, R., Koch, C., & Perona, P. (2002). Rapid natural scene categorization in the near absence of attention. *Proceedings of the National Academy of Sciences, 99*, 9596-9601.

Li, Z. (2002). A saliency map in primary visual cortex. *Trends in Cognitive Sciences, 6*, 9-16.

Liu, A. (1998). What the driver's eye tells the car's brain. In G. Underwood (Ed.), *Eye Guidance in reading and scene perception* (pp. 431-452). Oxford: Elsevier.

Loftus, G. R. (1985). Picture perception: Effects of luminance on available information and information-extraction rate. *Journal of Experimental Psychology: General, 114*, 342-356.

Loftus, G. R., Kaufman, L., Nishimoto, T., & Ruthruff, E. (1992). Effects of visual degradation on eye-fixation durations, perceptual

processing, and long-term visual memory. In K. Rayner (Ed). *Eye movements and visual cognition: Scene perception and reading* (pp. 203-226). New York: Springer.

Loftus, G. R., & Mackworth, N. H. (1978). Cognitive determinants of fixation location during picture viewing. *Journal of Experimental Psychology: Human Perception and Performance, 4*, 565-572.

Loftus, G. R., & Nelson, W. W., & Kallman, H. J. (1983). Differential acquisition rates for different types of information from pictures. *Quarterly Journal of Experimental Psychology, 35A*, 187-198.

Loschky, L. C., & McConkie, G. W. (2002). Investigating spatial vision and dynamic attentional selection using a gaze-contingent multiresolution display. *Journal of Experimental Psychology: Applied, 8*, 99-117.

Mackworth, N. H., & Morandi, A. J. (1967). The gaze selects informative details within pictures. *Perception & Psychophysics, 2*, 547-552.

Malach, R., Levy, I., & Hasson, U. (2002). The topography of high-order human object areas. *Trends in Cognitive Sciences, 6*, 176-184.

Mandler, J. M., & Johnson, N. S. (1977). Some of the thousand words a picture is worth. *Journal of Experimental Psychology: Human Learning and Memory, 2*, 529-540.

Mannan, S., Ruddock, K. H., & Wooding, D. S. (1995). Automatic control of saccadic eye movements made in visual inspection of briefly presented 2-D images. *Spatial Vision, 9*, 363-386.

Mannan, S. K., Ruddock, K. H., & Wooding, D. S. (1996). The relationship between the locations of spatial features and those of fixations made during visual examination of briefly presented images. *Spatial Vision, 10*, 165-188.

Mannan, S. K., Ruddock, K. H., & Wooding, D. S. (1997a). Fixation sequences made during visual examination of briefly presented 2D images. *Spatial Vision, 11*, 157-178.

Mannan, S. K., Ruddock, K. H., & Wooding, D. S. (1997b). Fixation patterns made during brief examination of two-dimensional images. *Perception, 26*, 1059-1072.

Matin, E. (1974). Saccadic suppression: A review and an analysis. *Psychological Bulletin, 81*, 899-917.

McConkie, G. W. (1990). *Where vision and cognition meet.* Paper presented at the Human Frontier Science Program Workshop on Object and Scene Perception, Leuven, Belgium.

McConkie, G. W. (1991). Perceiving a stable visual world. In J. Van Resnbergen, M. Devijver, & G. d'Ydewalle (Eds.), *Proceedings of the sixth European conference on eye movements* (pp. 5-7). Leuven, Belgium: Laboratory of Experimental Psychology.

McConkie, G. W., & Currie, C. B. (1996). Visual stability while viewing complex pictures. *Journal of Experimental Psychology: Human Perception and Performance, 22,* 563-581.

McConkie, G. W., & Rayner, K. (1975). The span of the effective stimulus during a fixation in reading. *Perception & Psychophysics, 17,* 578-586.

McClelland, J. L., & Elman, J. L. (1986). The TRACE model of speech perception. *Cognitive Psychology, 18,* 1-86.

Meyer, A. S., & Lethaus, F. (2004). The use of eye tracking in studies of sentence generation. In J. M. Henderson & F. Ferreira (Eds.), *The interface of language, vision, and action: Eye movements and the visual world.* New York: Psychology Press.

Murphy, G. L., & Wisniewski, E. J. (1989). Categorizing objects in isolation and in scenes: What a superordinate is good for. *Journal of Experimental Psychology: Learning, Memory, and Cognition, 4,* 572-586.

Nelson, W. W., & Loftus, G. R. (1980). The functional visual field during picture viewing. *Journal of Experimental Psychology: Human Learning and Memory, 6,* 391-399.

Nodine, C. F., Carmody, D. P., & Herman, E. (1979). Eye movements during visual search for artistically embedded targets. *Bulletin of the Psychonomic Society, 13,* 371-374.

Noton, D., & Stark, L. (1971a). Scan paths in eye movements during pattern perception. *Science, 171,* 308-311.

Noton, D., & Stark, L. (1971b). Scan paths in saccadic eye movements while viewing and recognizing patterns. *Vision Research, 11,* 929-944.

O'Craven, K. M., & Kanwisher, N. (2000). Mental imagery of faces and places activates corresponding stimulus-specific brain regions. *Journal of Cognitive Neuroscience, 12,* 1013-1023.

Oliva, A., & Schyns, P. G. (1997). Coarse blobs or fine edges? Evidence that information diagnosticity changes the perception of complex visual stimuli. *Cognitive Psychology, 34,* 72-107.

Oliva, A., & Schyns, P. G. (2000). Colored diagnostic blobs mediate scene recognition. *Cognitive Psychology, 41,*176-210.

Oliva, A., & Torralba, A. (2001). Modeling the shape of the scene: A holistic representation of the spatial envelope. *International Journal in Computer Vision, 42,* 145-175.

Oliva, A., & Torralba, A. (2003). Scene-centered description from spatial envelope properties. In H. H. Bulthoff et al. (Eds.), *Lecture notes in computer science: Biologically motivated computer vision.* New York: Springer-Verlag.

Oliva, A., & Torralba, A., Castelhano, M. S., & Henderson, J. M. (2003). Top-down control of visual attention in object detection. *IEEE Proceedings of the International Conference on Image Processing, 1,* 253-256.

Parker, R. E. (1978). Picture processing during recognition. *Journal of Experimental Psychology: Human Perception and Performance, 4,* 284-293.

Parkhurst, D., Law, K., & Niebur, E. (2002). Modeling the role of salience in the allocation of overt visual attention. *Vision Research, 42,* 107-123.

Parkhurst, D. J., & Niebur, E. (2003). Scene content selected by active vision. *Spatial Vision, 6,* 125-154.

Pelz, J. B., & Canosa, R. (2001). Oculomotor behavior and perceptual strategies in complex tasks. *Vision Research, 41,* 3587-3596.

Pollatsek, A., & Rayner, K. (1992). What is integrated across fixations? In K. Rayner (Ed.), *Eye movements and visual cognition: Scene perception and reading* (pp. 166-191). New York: Springer-Verlag.

Pollatsek, A., Rayner, K., & Collins, W. E. (1984). Integrating pictorial information across eye movements. *Journal of Experimental Psychology: General, 113*, 426-442.

Pollatsek, A., Rayner, K., & Henderson, J. M. (1990). Role of spatial location in integration of pictorial information across saccades. *Journal of Experimental Psychology: Human Perception & Performance, 16*, 199-210.

Potter, M. C. (1975). Meaning in visual search. *Science, 187*, 965-966.

Potter, M. C. (1976). Short-term conceptual memory for pictures. *Journal of Experimental Psychology: Human Learning and Memory, 2*, 509-522.

Potter, M. C. (1999). Understanding sentences and scenes: The role of conceptual short-term memory. In V. Coltheart (Ed.), *Fleeting memories* (pp. 13-46). Cambridge, MA: MIT Press.

Potter, M. C., & Levy, E. I. (1969). Recognition memory for a rapid sequence of pictures. *Journal of Experimental Psychology, 81*, 10-15.

Rao, R. P. N., Zelinsky, G. J., Hayhoe, M. M., & Ballard, D. H. (2002). Eye movements in iconic visual search. *Vision Research, 42*, 1447-1463.

Rayner, K. (1975). The perceptual span and peripheral cues in reading. *Cognitive Psychology, 7*, 65-81.

Rayner, K. (1998). Eye movements in reading and information processing: 20 years of research. *Psychological Bulletin, 124*, 372-422.

Rayner, K., & Liversedge, S. P. (2004). Visual and linguistic processing during eye fixations in reading. In J. M. Henderson & F. Ferreira (Eds.), *The interface of language, vision, and action: Eye movements and the visual world*. New York: Psychology Press.

Rayner, K., & Pollatsek, A. (1992). Eye movements and scene perception. *Canadian Journal of Psychology, 46*, 342-376.

Recarte, M. A., & Nunes, L. M. (2000). Effects of verbal and spatial imagery tasks on eye fixations while driving. *Journal of Experimental Psychology: Applied, 6*, 31-43.

Reinagel, P., & Zador, A. M. (1999). Natural scene statistics at the centre of gaze. *Network: Computer and neural systems, 10*, 1-10.

Reingold, E. M., Charness, N., Pomplun, M., & Stampe, D. M. (2001). Visual span in expert chess players: Evidence from eye movements. *Psychological Science, 12*, 48-55.

Rensink, R. A., O'Regan, J. K., & Clark, J. J. (1997). To see or not to see: The need for attention to perceive changes in scenes. *Psychological Science, 8*, 368-373.

Riggs, L. A. (1965). Visual acuity. In C. H. Graham (Ed.), *Vision and visual perception* (pp. 321-349). New York: Wiley.

Ryan, J. D., Althoff, R. R., Whitlow, S., & Cohen, N. J. (2000). Amensia is a deficit in relational memory. *Psychological Science, 11*, 454-461.

Saida, S., & Ikeda, M. (1979). Useful visual field size for pattern perception. *Perception & Psychophysics, 25*, 119-125.

Sanocki, T., & Epstein, W. (1997). Priming spatial layout of scenes. *Psychological Science, 8*, 374-378.

Schyns, P., & Oliva, A. (1994). From blobs to boundary edges: Evidence for time- and spatial-scale-dependent scene recognition. *Psychological Science, 5*, 195-200.

Sereno, M. I., Dale, A. M., Reppas, J. B., Kwong, K. K., Belliveau, J. W., Brady, T. J., Rosen, B. R..Tootell, R. B. H. (1995). Borders of multiple visual areas in humans revealed by functional magnetic-resonance-imaging. *Science, 268*, 889-893.

Shinoda, H., Hayhoe, M. M., & Shrivastava, A. (2001). What controls attention in natural environments? *Vision Research, 41*, 3535-3545.

Simons, D. J. (1996). In sight, out of mind: When object representations fail. *Psychological Science, 7*, 301-305.

Spivey, M. J., Richardson, D. C., & Fitneva, S. A. (2004). Thinking outside the brain: Spatial indices to visual and linguistic information. In J. M. Henderson, and F. Ferreira (Eds.), *The interface of language, vision, and action: Eye movements and the visual world*. New York: Psychology Press.

Stark, L., & Ellis, S. R. (1981). Scanpaths revisited: Cognitive models direct active looking. In D. F. Fisher, R. A., Monty, & J. W. Senders (Eds.), *Eye movements: Cognition and visual perception* (pp. 193-226). Hillsdale, NJ: Erlbaum.

Steeves, J. K. E., Humphrey, G. K., Culham, J. C., Menon, R. S., & Goodale, M. A. (in press). Behavioral and neuroimaging evidence for a contribution of color information to scene recognition in a patient with impaired form recognition. *Journal of Cognitive Neuroscience.*

Tanenhaus, M. K., Chambers, C. G., & Hanna, J. E. (2004). Referential domains in spoken language comprehension: Using eye movements to bridge the product and action traditions. In J. M. Henderson & F. Ferreira (Eds.), *The interface of language, vision, and action: Eye movements and the visual world.* New York: Psychology Press.

Tanenhaus, M. K., Spivey-Knowlton, M. J., Eberhard, K. M., & Sedivy, J. E. (1995). Integration of visual and linguistic information in spoken language comprehension. *Science, 268,* 632-634.

Thiele, A., Henning, M., Buischik, K., Hoffman, P. (2002). Neural mechanisms of saccadic suppression. *Science, 295,* 2460-2462.

Thorpe, S. J, Fize, D., & Marlot, C. (1996). Speed of processing in the human visual system. *Nature, 381,* 520-522.

Tomlin, R. S. (1986). The Identification of Foreground-Background Information in On-Line Oral Descriptive Discourse. *Papers in Linguistics, 19,* 465-494.

Torralba, A. (2003). Modeling global scene factors in attention. *Journal of the Optical Society of America, 20,* 1407-1418.

Trueswell, J., & Gleitman, L. (2004). Children's eye movements during listening: Developmental evidence for a constraint-based theory of sentence processing. In J. M. Henderson & F. Ferreira (Eds.), *The interface of language, vision, and action: Eye movements and the visual world.* New York: Psychology Press.

Tversky, B., & Hemenway, K. (1983). Categories of environmental scenes. *Cognitive Psychology, 15,* 121-149.

van Diepen, P. M. J., De Graef, P., & d'Ydewalle, G. (1995). Chronometry of foveal information extraction during scene perception. In J. M. Findlay, R. Walker, & R. W. Kentridge (Eds.), *Eye movement research: Mechanisms, processes and applications* (pp. 349-362). Amsterdam: Elsevier

van Diepen, P. M. J., Wampers, M., & d'Ydewalle, G. (1998). Functional division of the visual field: moving masks and moving windows. In G. Underwood (Ed.), *Eye guidance in reading and scene perception* (pp. 337-355). Oxford: Elsevier.

VanRullen, R., & Thorpe, S. J. (2001). Is it a bird? Is it a plane? Ultra-rapid visual categorisation of natural and artifactual objects. *Perception, 30,* 655-668.

Volkmann, F. (1986). Human visual suppression. *Vision Research, 26,* 1401-1416.

Volkman, F., Schick, A., & Riggs, L. (1968). Time course of visual inhibition during voluntary saccades. *Journal of the Optical Society of America, 58,* 1310-1414.

Walker-Smith, G. J., Gale, A. G., & Findlay J. M. (1977). Eye movements strategies involved in face perception. *Perception, 6,* 313-326.

Weith, M., Castelhano, M. S., & Henderson, J. M. (2003, May). *I see what you see: Gaze perception during scene viewing.* Presented at the annual meeting of the Vision Sciences Society, Sarasota, Florida.

Yarbus, A. L. (1967). *Eye movements and vision.* New York: Plenum Press.

Zelinsky, G., & Murphy, G. (2000). Synchronizing visual and language processing: An effect of object name length on eye movements. *Psychological Science, 11,* 125-131.

Zelinsky, G., Rao, R. P. N., Hayhoe, M. M., & Ballard, D. H. (1997). Eye movements reveal the spatiotemporal dynamics of visual search. *Psychological Science, 8,* 448-453.

2

Visual and Linguistic Processing during Eye Fixations in Reading

KEITH RAYNER AND SIMON P. LIVERSEDGE

In this chapter we provide a discussion of eye movement research investigating aspects of processing during reading. We first provide a general introduction, drawing attention to two different fields of research within the area of eye movements and reading: visual processing during reading and linguistic processing during reading. We then discuss some of the main areas of research within the field of visual processing during reading, followed by a section discussing some of the main areas of linguistic processing during reading. In both sections, we discuss studies that have had a substantial impact within the field along with more recent research examining questions that are currently under investigation. Throughout the chapter we emphasize methodological issues stressing the importance of fully understanding different aspects of the eye movement record in order to provide the most fully specified account of eye movement behavior. We conclude by arguing that researchers working in the area of linguistic processing during reading should be aware of the work conducted in the area of visual processing during reading and vice versa. Finally, we claim that a full understanding of research in each of these areas is necessary if we are ever to develop a formal and comprehensive model of reading.

Not only is the skill of reading essential in modern society, it is also the topic of a considerable amount of research. What is particularly interesting is the fact that reading has been used as the context to study numerous questions about visual processing and also about linguistic processing.

That is, some research questions about basic vision issues have been addressed in the context of reading research, while other basic questions about language processing have also been addressed in the context of reading research. In this chapter, we will discuss examples of each of these two types of research and also provide a brief review of the research findings. We will also focus on research that has used eye movement data to study each type of issue.

We (see Rayner, 1995, 1998; Liversedge & Findlay, 2000) have previously pointed out that within the context of eye movement research on reading, two distinct types of research groups have developed that use eye movement data to slightly different ends. The first group is primarily concerned with understanding the programming of eye movements in their own right; they are particularly interested in how relatively low-level visual factors influence eye movements. Researchers in this group often appear to be much more interested in eye movements per se than in reading; reading simply provides a convenient way to study oculomotor control (i.e., the visual stimuli are very structured and constrained, and eye movement behavior is relatively easy to characterize). The second group is primarily interested in higher-order language processes (such as discourse processing, syntactic parsing, ambiguity resolution, and the like). Those in this group often appear to have little interest in eye movements per se; eye movements simply represent a convenient online measure of processing. Those in the oculomotor group are most likely to publish their research findings in journals such as *Vision Research, Perception & Psychophysics*, and the *Journal of Experimental Psychology: Human Perception and Performance*. Those in the language group are most likely to publish their research findings in journals such as *Cognition, Journal of Memory and Language*, and the *Journal of Experimental Psychology: Learning, Memory, and Cognition*. Obviously, these are not the only journals in which researchers in either group would publish their papers. We simply point these out as examples to indicate that researchers working in different areas can place the same kind of data (eye movement data) in markedly different journals that, in the main, report work addressing qualitatively different research issues. Unfortunately, it is often the case that many researchers in the oculomotor group have little interaction with those in the language group and vice versa. Thus, members of both groups are often largely unaware of important developments and findings emerging from the other group.

There are obviously exceptions to this broad generalization, and indeed, in our own work we have engaged in both types of research since our goal is, very generally, to understand the relationship between eye movements and the psychological processes that occur when we read. This approach, necessarily, ensures that we maintain an interest in eye movements and reading at the oculomotor level and the linguistic processing level (as well as levels in between the two extremes). In this chapter, we will discuss a broad range of work, starting with studies investigating issues of lower level oculomotor control and then moving on to work investigating higher-order psycholinguistic processing. Part of our message in this chapter is that researchers in each of the two groups cannot continue to ignore one another's work. Researchers measuring eye movements in the language processing group must pay attention to the work produced by the oculomotor group since eye movements themselves are the behavioral response that mediates, and from which they infer, the psychological processes in which they are interested. Similarly, it is our belief that researchers in the oculomotor group should take note of the research produced by the language-processing group since, to a very great degree, cognitive processes are what drive eye movements during reading.

It is at this point that we should make clear a strong bias that we share. Namely, we believe that eye movements during reading are largely driven by linguistic processing. To be sure, there are occasions when visual/oculomotor processes have effects. To qualify this, consider the important distinction between the decision of when to move the eyes and the decision of where to move the eyes. We would like to argue that the *when* decision is primarily driven by linguistic processing (though there are cases where low-level visual/oculomotor processes also have an effect), while the decision of *where* to move the eyes is largely influenced by low-level visual/oculomotor processes (though there are some obvious cases where linguistic processing has some impact). Some of this distinction is captured in the E-Z Reader model of eye movement control (Reichle, Pollatsek, Fisher, & Rayner, 1998; Reichle, Rayner, & Pollatsek, 1999, 2003; Rayner, Reichle, & Pollatsek, 1998). Very much consistent with the distinction we have made is the finding that variables such as word frequency and word predictability have major influences on when readers move their eyes, while word length information has a major influence on where readers move their eyes (see Rayner, 1998, for a review).

The other issue that we need to discuss at the outset is the measures of processing times that can be gleaned from the eye movement record. We (Liversedge & Findlay, 2000; Liversedge, Paterson, & Pickering, 1998; Rayner, 1998; Rayner, Sereno, Morris, Schmauder, & Clifton, 1989) have discussed these measures in greater detail elsewhere. Here, we simply provide a quick overview of different measures and some of their more important defining features (see also Henderson & Ferreira, this volume, for a similar discussion of eye movement measures in scene perception). When the unit of analysis is a single target word, the following measures are typically reported: first fixation duration (the duration of the first fixation on a word independent of the number of fixations that are made on that word), single fixation duration (the duration of the only fixation on the target word), gaze duration (the sum of all fixations on the word prior to moving to another word), and total fixation time (the sum of all fixations on a word, including regressions to the word). If readers made only a single fixation on a word, then the issue of the most appropriate measure to use would be obvious. However, the reality is that readers often skip words and some words are refixated (receive more than one fixation before the reader moves to another word). Thus, a large number of measures must be used since single fixation duration would exclude consideration of too much data. Other measures such as spillover (the duration of the fixation after leaving the target word), average saccade length (to and from the target word), and the number of regressions (to and from the target word) are also typically reported. Note that this is not intended to be an exhaustive list of all measures of processing time for single words, but instead represents the main measures that are typically discussed in eye movement studies investigating reading.

When the unit of analysis is larger than a single word (so that it is a phrase or a group of words), then the following measures are typically reported: first-pass reading time (the sum of fixations from the first fixation in the region until moving out of it either forward or regressively), second-pass reading time (the amount of time devoted to rereading a target region), the go-past or regression path duration (the time from first entering a region until moving past that region forward in the text; unlike the first-pass reading time, this measure includes reading time following regressions out of the region), and total reading time (which includes all fixations in a given region). In addition, measures such as the frequency of regressions to and from a region are typically reported.

One way of characterizing different reading time measures is to consider whether they sum spatially, temporally, or both spatially and temporally contiguous fixations (see Liversedge et al., 1998, for a more in-depth discussion). When we record a reader's eye movements as a sentence is read, we obtain a stream of fixations, each of a particular duration and occurring one after the other until the reader indicates that they have understood the sentence (usually by pressing a button that terminates the display). The fixations are localized at different points within the sentence (see Figure 2.1) and, as we have already indicated, we obtain reading time measures by summing collections of fixations in different ways. Importantly, in most eye movement experiments, researchers are primarily interested in localizing exactly where within the eye movement record differences in reading time lie. To do this they often consider the full range of reading time measures for different portions of their sentences. However, it is important to note that some reading time measures, such as total reading time, involve summing fixations made within the same region of the sentence (e.g., on the same word). For example, the total reading time for Region 5 in Figure 2.1 is 1902 ms obtained by summing all the fixations (246, 384, 268, 244, 286, 164, and 310 ms) that are localized in that region. These fixations can be termed *spatially contiguous* fixations since they all fall within the same spatial location within the sentence. In contrast, other reading time measures, such as second-pass reading time or regression path duration, involve summing fixations that occur adjacently within the stream of fixations that form the eye movement record; that is to say, the fixations are *temporally contiguous*. For example, the regression path duration for Region 5 in Fig-

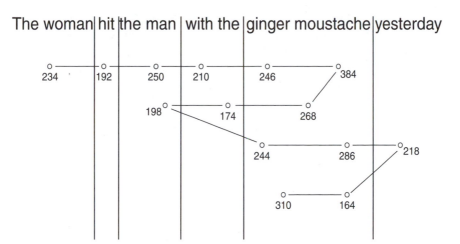

FIGURE 2.1. A hypothetical eye movement record showing a typical sequence of fixations with durations (in ms) made while reading a sentence. The sentence has been split into regions (indicated by the vertical bars) for which different reading time measures may be computed.

ure 2.1 is 1800 ms obtained by summing 246, 384, 268, 174, 198, 244, and 286 ms. These fixations occur contiguously over time. The distinction between these qualitatively different kinds of measures may not initially appear important. However, when analyzing eye movement records, both types of measure should be used to determine reading time differences since it is not necessarily the case that differences in fixation durations will be exclusively localized to a specific region of the sentence, or exclusively localized to a particular sequence of fixations within the record.

An important follow-up point to this discussion is to make it quite clear that we are not suggesting that experimenters adopt the blanket use of all types of reading time measures in all experiments in the hope that at least one of them will show an effect. Instead, we favor the use of reading time measures that sum fixations spatially, temporally, or both to dissect the eye movement record in a scientific manner in order to localize where within the stream of fixations differences in patterns and durations of fixations lie.

VISUAL PROCESSES IN READING

In this section, we will discuss a number of visual and oculomotor issues that have been addressed within the context of reading. Many of these issues are rather general and need not be limited to reading (and we will typically note instances of how a specific issue has also been addressed outside of the context of reading). Furthermore, some of the research we discuss represents attempts to determine if a certain effect, obtained using simple oculomotor tasks, generalizes to the more complex task of reading. As we shall see, some findings obtained in simpler situations do generalize to reading whereas others don't. We will discuss in order (1) the perceptual span, (2) preview effects, (3) integration of information across saccades, (4) saccade programming, (5) the center of gravity effect and landing position effects, (6) range effects, (7) binocular coordination of the eyes, (8) inhibition of saccade return, (9) the gap effect, and (10) express saccades.

The Perceptual Span

The perceptual span is typically defined as the region around a fixation point from which useful information can be obtained. The idea of the perceptual span, or span of effective vision, has been around since the earliest days of experimental psychology. Psychologists have long sought to know how much information can be processed in a single glance, and the issue has been addressed both in and out of the context of reading. Within the context of reading, Huey (1908) had an entire chapter devoted to the perceptual span in his classic early book on reading. Indeed, the tachistoscope was developed in part as a way to investigate how much information could be obtained in a single glance. Over the years, there have been many attempts to estimate the size of the perceptual span in reading. Unfortunately, these attempts have involved the use of techniques such as tachistoscopic presentations, or presentation of text at different rates from right to left during reading aloud. Such techniques have severe limitations associated with them, the most fundamental of which are that they may lead readers to adopt different strategies than they would adopt in normal reading, and that they are, at best, based on questionable assumptions (see Rayner, 1975, 1978a, for a more detailed overview). Here, we will focus on studies using eye-contingent display change techniques: the moving-window, moving-mask, and boundary paradigms. These techniques were developed to overcome the difficulties associated with less satisfactory methodologies. Furthermore, they have been employed very widely within many laboratories and have been extremely valuable and successful in investigating many different aspects of non-foveal processing during reading.

In the moving-window paradigm (McConkie & Rayner, 1975; Rayner & Bertera, 1979), the text around the point of fixation is altered in some way (see Figure 2.2) except for an experimenter-defined window region (where the text is normal). Wherever the reader looks, the normal text is available, while outside of this window area, the text is altered. Readers are free to move their eyes wherever and whenever they wish, but the amount of useful information that is available on each fixation is controlled. Each time the eyes move, a new window region is exposed. In some cases (see Figure 2.2), the window is defined in terms of letter spaces, while in others the window is defined in terms of word boundaries. Sometimes, the spaces between words outside of the window are preserved, and other times they are filled in. Sometimes the text outside of the window is perturbed only on selected fixations. Finally, the size of the window is set by the experimenter (so that it remains constant throughout a trial in some cases and changes from fixation to fixation on other trials) and the characteristics of the altered text varies; sometimes the text outside of the window is replaced with a homogenous string of letters, for example, and in other cases the original letters are replaced by other letters. The basic assumption with the moving-window paradigm is that when the window is as large as the region from which a reader can obtain useful information, there will be no difference between reading in that situation and when text is presented normally (that is, there is no window).

The moving-mask paradigm (Rayner & Bertera, 1979) is the opposite of the moving-window paradigm in that wherever the reader looks, a visual mask obscures the text (see Figure 2.3). As with the moving window paradigm, the size of the mask can be varied. In moving-mask experiments, the goal is to examine decrements in reading as a function of the size of the mask. Interestingly, a mask of one letter, so that the letter the eyes fall on is masked, cuts reading rate in half. And, when the mask obscures foveal vision (the 6-8 letters in the center of vision), reading is next to impossible (Rayner & Bertera,1979; Fine & Rubin, 1999).

In the boundary paradigm (Rayner, 1975), a single critical target word is initially replaced by another word or by a nonword, and when the reader's eye movement crosses an invisible boundary location in the text, the initially

reading has been used as the context to study interesting

xxxxxxx xas been used xx xxx xxxxxxx xx xxxxx xxxxxxxxxxx
        *

xxxxxxx xxx xxxx xxed as the conxxxx xx xxxxx xxxxxxxxxxx
               *

ncobrmp bas been used sr fbc ocmfcvf fc rfvhp rmfcnczfrmp
        *

ncobrmp bcz dccm vzed as the confcvf fc rfvhp rmfcnczfrmp
               *

FIGURE 2.2. Examples of the moving window paradigm. The first line shows a normal line of text. The second and third lines show a moving window of 13 letter spaces (six letters to the left and six letters to the right of the fixation point) and x's outside of the window. The fourth and fifth lines show a moving window of 13 letter spaces and incorrect letters outside of the window. The asterisk indicates the fixation location.

reading has been used as the context to study interesting

reading hasxxxxxxxxxxd as the context to study interesting
                    *

reading has beenxxxxxxxxxxxthe context to study interesting
                       *

FIGURE 2.3. An example of a moving mask paradigm with a nine letter mask in the center of vision. The asterisk indicates the fixation location.

displayed stimulus is replaced by the target word (see Figure 2.4). The assumption with this paradigm is that if the reader obtains information from the initially presented stimulus, any inconsistency between what is available on the fixation after crossing the boundary location and with what was processed on the prior fixation (when information about the initially displayed stimulus was processed) should be registered in the fixation time on the target word. A number of variations of the boundary technique have also been employed (see Rayner, 1998, for a review).

While these three eye-contingent display change techniques have been widely used to study reading (Rayner, 1998), they have also recently been used to study a number of other visual cognition tasks such as scene perception (Henderson & Hollingworth, 1999; McConkie & Currie, 1996; van Diepen, Ruelens, & d'Ydewalle, 1999), visual search (Bertera & Rayner, 2000; Greene & Rayner, 2001; Pomplun, Reingold, & Shen, 2001; Rayner & Fisher, 1987), music reading (Truitt, Clifton, Pollatsek, & Rayner, 1997; Gilman & Underwood, 2002), and chess (Reingold, Charness, Pomplun, & Stampe, 2001).

Here, we will not review all of the experiments using the eye-contingent display change techniques that have been done to examine the size of the perceptual span in reading. Rather, we will simply summarize the general findings that have emerged (see Rayner, 1998, for descriptions of individual studies). First, the span extends to 14-15 letter spaces to the right of fixation for readers

reading has been used as the control to study
                        *
reading has been used as the context to study
                        *
reading has been used as the rcmfnct to study
                        *
reading has been used as the context to study
                                          *

FIGURE 2.4. An example of the boundary paradigm. The first and second lines show an initially displayed word (control) which changes to the target word (context) when the reader's eye movement crosses an invisible boundary (the letter e in the). The third and fourth lines show a random letter string in the preview location prior to the boundary change. The asterisk represents the fixation location.

of alphabetic orthographies like English which are printed from left-to-right (Den Buurman, Boersma, & Gerrissen, 1981; McConkie & Rayner, 1975; Rayner, 1986; Rayner & Bertera, 1979; Rayner, Inhoff, Morrison, Slowiaczek, & Bertera, 1981; Rayner, Well, Pollatsek, & Bertera, 1982). Second, the span is asymmetrically extended to the beginning of the currently fixated word, or no more than 3-4 letters to the left of fixation (Binder, Pollatsek, & Rayner, 1999; McConkie & Rayner, 1976; Rayner, Well, & Pollatsek, 1980; Underwood & McConkie, 1985). Third, the span does not extend below the currently fixated line in reading (Pollatsek, Raney, LaGasse, & Rayner, 1993), though when the task was to find a target word in the passage, it was occasionally possible to obtain information below the fixated line (see also Prinz, 1984). Fourth, the word identification span (or area from which words can be identified on a given fixation) is smaller than the total perceptual span (Rayner et al., 1982; McConkie & Zola, 1987; Underwood & McConkie, 1985) and generally does not exceed 7-8 letter spaces to the right of fixation. Fifth, the size of the span is not constant, but varies as a function of text difficulty (Henderson & Ferreira, 1990; Inhoff, Pollatsek, Posner, & Rayner, 1989; Rayner, 1986). Sixth, and finally, the size and characteristics of the perceptual span are very much influenced by the orthography: the span is much smaller for languages like Japanese (Ikeda & Saida, 1978; Osaka, 1987, 1992) and Chinese (Inhoff & Liu, 1998) than for English; it is also smaller for Hebrew than English and is asymmetric to the left of fixation for Hebrew (Pollatsek, Bolozky, Well, & Rayner, 1981).

Preview Effects

Dodge (1907) first demonstrated that if subjects have a preview of a stimulus before their eyes get to it, they can respond to it faster than if they have no preview. Preview effects in reading have now likewise been widely demonstrated. Most of this research has relied on the use of the boundary paradigm (or a variation of it) described above and has demonstrated a preview benefit effect which is obtained by comparing how long readers look at a target word when they had a valid preview (or an orthographically similar preview) of the target on fixation n-1 compared to an invalid or unrelated preview. Generally, the preview benefit effect is on the order of 50 ms.

A study by Rayner (1975) was the first to demonstrate preview effects in the context of reading. In that study, the boundary paradigm was used and it was found that a valid preview of the target word to the right of fixation yielded shorter fixations on that word when it was subsequently fixated on the next fixation. The study also demonstrated preview benefit effects for conditions that shared orthographic similarity in the beginning few letters of the preview and target. A subsequent study by Rayner et al. (1982) demonstrated that individual letters to the right of fixation were more critical than word integrity and that the acquisition of letters is not dependent on words being intact. This suggests that readers acquire partial word information from the word to the right of fixation. Further evidence for this conclusion comes from the fact that Rayner et al. (1982) found that when the first three letters of the word to the right of fixation were available and the remainder of the letters were replaced by visually similar letters, readers read at about the same rate as when the entire word to the right of fixation was available. Lima and Inhoff (1985) and Lima (1987) also found that the time readers looked at a word decreased when the first three letters of the word were available on the prior fixation (compared to when these were not available). Inhoff (1989a) subsequently demonstrated that the beginning letters effect was not due to the fact that they are closer to fixation than end letters of words: he had readers read sentences in which words were printed from right-to-left but letters within the word were left-to-right. Thus, in his experiment, the first three letters were further from fixation than the end letters. He found facilitation in reading when the first three letters were available. Numerous other studies have found significant effects of partial word information (Balota, Pollatsek, & Rayner, 1985; Henderson & Ferreira, 1990; Inhoff, 1989b).

In addition to partial word information being obtained to the right of fixation, word length information is also acquired and used in computing where to fixate next (O'Regan, 1979, 1980; Morris, Rayner, & Pollatsek, 1990; Pollatsek & Rayner, 1982; Rayner, 1979; Rayner & Morris, 1992). The fact that readers skip words to the right of fixation about a third of the time (Rayner, 1998) suggests that those words can be fully identified. We shall discuss word skipping more fully in the section on Word Predictability.

Integration of Information across Saccades

The preview benefit effect is highly robust and has been demonstrated many times, not only in reading, but in scene perception and visual search (see Rayner, 1998, for a review). The fact that the effect exists has led many researchers to try to determine the basis for the effect. Many of these experiments have been conducted under the rubric of integration of information across saccades. When we read, we do not have the experience of seeing text for about 250 ms followed by a gap or blank period (resulting from the saccade[1]). Rather, the visual signal is processed in the brain such that the discrete inputs are smoothed out so that we maintain a stable coherent view of the text we are reading. Note also that such integration across fixations also occurs during scanning of nonlinguistic visual scenes. Three observations are relevant to the current discussion of integration of information across saccades. First, many of the experiments that have investigated this phenomenon have utilized a variation of the boundary paradigm (Rayner, 1978b) in which a word or letter string is initially presented parafoveally, and when the subject makes an eye movement toward the parafoveal stimulus, it is replaced by a target word, which must be named as rapidly as possible. While the results of the naming task variation of the boundary paradigm have been quite influential, all the important results with respect to reading have also been replicated in a normal reading context. Second, this type of paradigm (in which a parafoveal stimulus is initially presented and then replaced by a target stimulus during the saccade) has subsequently been used by many investigators to study the issue of integration of information across saccades outside of the context of reading (e.g., see Saida & Ikeda, 1979; Van Diepen, Wampers, & d'Ydewalle, 1998). Third, these experiments (including both the original boundary paradigm and the naming variation) are, although not widely recognized as such, the antecedents of "change blindness" studies (Rensink, O'Regan, & Clark, 1997).

In the context of reading, the question about the basis of the preview benefit and integration of saccades has generally been formulated as follows: when readers are fixated on word n, what kind of information do they obtain from word n+1 that enables them to identify it faster on the next fixation? If readers obtain information from word n+1 that helps them identify that word faster, what kind of information is it? We will not review all of the experiments that have been carried out to address this issue. Rather, we will focus on studies showing the different types of information that are extracted from non-foveal locations.

When the experiments first appeared, it was a somewhat surprising finding that preview benefit is not due to the integration of purely visual codes across saccades. While it is the case that a visually similar preview will produce less disruption than a visually dissimilar preview, it has also been demonstrated that the (upper or lower) case of each letter in the word can change from preview to target and this has little effect on performance (McConkie & Zola, 1979; Rayner, McConkie, & Zola, 1980). If purely visual information were being combined across fixations or in a visual integrative buffer, then the case change should be highly disruptive. McConkie and Zola (1979) had readers read text in alternating case, and each time they moved their eyes, the text shifted from one version of alternated case to another (e.g., *ChAnGe* shifted to *cHaNgE*). Readers did not notice that the change was taking place, and their reading behavior was not different from a control condition in which they read alternated case in which the letters did not change case from fixation to fixation. If visual codes were important to the preview benefit effect and in integrating information across saccades, then the change of features between upper and lower case letters should have disrupted reading. Other evidence (see Rayner, 1998) is likewise consistent with the conclusion that visual codes are not integrated across saccades.

A further surprising finding was that semantic codes do not mediate the preview benefit and are apparently not integrated across saccades. Rayner, Balota, and Pollatsek (1986) tested the idea that semantic codes influence subsequent fixation time using the boundary paradigm. Prior to fixating on a target word (such as *tune*), the preview for that word was either orthographically similar (*turc*), semantically similar (*song*), or unrelated (*door*). Rayner et al. found that the semantically related pair yielded a priming effect in a standard priming paradigm (where the prime word *song* was presented for 200 ms followed by a 50 ms blank period and then the target word *tune* until a response was made). However, in the reading situation, although fixation time on the target word was shorter when the preview was orthographically similar to the target word, there was no difference between the semantically related and unrelated conditions. More recently, Altarriba, Kambe, Pollatsek, and Rayner (2001) obtained similar results. The twist in the Altarriba et al. experiments is that fluent Spanish-English bilingual readers were subjects, and they read sentences where the previews were either identical to the target, cognates that look very much alike across the two languages (*crema* was a preview for *cream* and vice versa), translations (that look nothing alike across the two languages), or pseudocognates (like *grasa* as a preview for *grass*, but the two words do not mean the same thing). There was no facilitation from the translation, and the cognate and the pseudocognate conditions yielded the same amount of facilitation, thus again demonstrating that orthographic similarity yields facilitation.

Given that visual codes and semantic codes are not the primary basis of the preview and integration effects, what is? Basically, the preview effect seems to be due to some combination of (1) visual orthographic codes, particularly beginning letters of words[2] as we discussed in the prior section, (2) abstract letter codes, and (3) phonological codes. Thus, the argument is that visual orthographic codes (in the form of the beginning letters of a word) are quickly transformed into abstract letter codes that serve as the basis for the facilitation that emerges as a preview benefit. Furthermore, there is clear evidence that some type of phonological code also aids in conveying information across saccades in reading (Pollatsek, Lesch, Morris, & Rayner, 1992; Henderson, Dixon, Petersen, Twilley, & Ferreira, 1995). For example, Pollatsek et al. found greater facilitation from a homophone preview (*beech* as a preview for *beach*) than an orthographically related preview (*bench* as a preview for *beach*).

Saccade Programming

Nowhere has research on basic oculomotor issues had such a major influence on reading research as has research on basic saccade programming. In simple oculomotor tasks in which subjects must move their eyes from a central fixation location to a (generally) sudden onset of a new fixation target, there is a latency period associated with making a saccade since they are motor movements that require time to plan and execute. Even if uncertainty about when or where to move the eyes is eliminated, saccade latency is at least 150-175 ms (Abrams & Jonides, 1988; Rayner, Slowiaczek, Clifton, & Bertera, 1983; Salthouse & Ellis, 1980; Salthouse, Ellis, Diener, & Somberg, 1981, though see Wenban-Smith & Findlay, 1991). Given that the average fixation during reading is approximately 230-250ms, and yet saccade planning up to the point of execution takes 150-175ms, it seems very likely that saccade programming is done in parallel. More directly, double-step experiments (where subjects must move their eyes from a central fixation to a new location, but at some point relative to the new location onset, the target location jumps to another location) indicate that the decision where to move the eyes can be modified as late as 80 ms before the actual movement of the eyes. Furthermore, these experiments provide clear evidence for parallel programming of saccades (Aslin & Shea, 1987; Becker & Jürgens, 1979) and separate decision processes involved in computing when and where to move the eyes.

The notion of parallel programming of saccades has become a central component in influential models of eye movement control in reading (Morrison, 1984; Reichle et al., 1998). While the double-step experiments are quite compelling in indicating separate decision processes involved in deciding where to move and when to move the eyes, it is instructive to note that Rayner and McConkie (1976) reached the same conclusion based on reading research prior to the most compelling double-step evidence (Becker & Jürgens, 1979), and Rayner and Pollatsek (1981) provided empirical support for the notion around the same time.

Center of Gravity and Landing Position Effects

In basic oculomotor experiments, when saccades are made to targets consisting of two elements, in reasonably close proximity, the first saccade goes to some intermediate location between the two. This is referred to as the *global effect* or the *center of gravity effect* (Deubel, Wolf, & Hauske, 1984; Findlay, 1982). If one element is larger, more intense or brighter, then the saccade tends to land closer to that target in comparison to a condition in which the two elements are identical. The more visually salient stimulus has a larger influence over the location to where the saccade is made. Findlay and Walker's (1999) inclusion of a *salience map* within their framework of saccadic eye movement control accounts for exactly these types of effects. These global and center of gravity effects are often assumed to be very much related to landing position effects that have been observed in reading.

Although there is variability in where the eyes land on a word, readers tend to make their first fixation on a word about halfway between the beginning and middle of the word (Deutsch & Rayner, 1999; Dunn-Rankin, 1978; McConkie, Kerr, Reddix, & Zola, 1988; McConkie, Kerr, Reddix, Zola, & Jacobs, 1989; Rayner, 1979; Rayner, Sereno, & Raney, 1996). Rayner (1979) originally labeled this prototypical location as the *preferred viewing location*. Subsequently, O'Regan and Lévy-Schoen (1987) distinguished between the preferred viewing location and the *optimal viewing position*. The optimal viewing position is a bit to the right of the preferred viewing location, closer to the center of the word. Extensive research efforts have examined the consequence of making fixations at locations other than this optimal viewing position (see O'Regan, 1992, for a review). For words presented in isolation, two general effects have emerged. First, there is a *refixation* effect: The further the eyes are from the optimal viewing position, the more likely it is that a refixation will be made on the word. Second, there is a *processing-cost* effect: For every letter that the eyes deviate from the optimal viewing position, the associated cost amounts to about 20 ms (O'Regan, Lévy-Schoen, Pynte, & Brugaillère, 1984). When words are read in text rather than in isolation, however, although the refixation effect remains, the processing-cost effect is greatly attenuated or absent (Rayner et al., 1996; Vitu, O'Regan, & Mittau, 1990). This indicates that contextual information overrides low-level visual processing or the information acquired about a word before it is directly fixated influences its later fixation location and duration.

Range Effects

A given fixation location in a word can be viewed not only as a landing position but also as the takeoff point or *launch* site to the next word. Furthermore, the distance between a launch site and a landing position is dictated by the extent of the saccade. It is important to realize that in terms of oculomotor behavior, any particular landing position on a word is entirely dependent upon two variables: launch site and saccade extent.

Although the mean landing position in a word lies between the beginning and the middle of a word, the distribution of landing positions varies as a function of the distance from the prior launch site (McConkie et al., 1988; Radach & Kempe, 1993; Rayner et al., 1996). Thus, if the distance to a target word is large, landing positions are shifted to the left or beginning of the word, whereas if the distance is small, they are shifted to the right.

To explain the launch site effect, McConkie et al. (1988) suggested that something like a *range* effect might explain the results. The range effect (Kapoula, 1985; Kapoula & Robinson, 1986) occurs when the eyes saccade toward isolated targets at various eccentricities: they tend to land around the mean of the range of possible eccentricities instead of directly saccading onto the actual position of the target. Thus, targets presented at a small or large eccentricity are overshot and undershot, respectively. Vitu (1991) presented words at different distances from fixation and showed that the eye's landing position did not differ as a function of eccentricity. She argued that a center of gravity effect (in which subjects target the middle of a word for the next saccade) better explained the results than a range effect. However, more recently, Radach and McConkie (1998) provided analyses that are more consistent with a range effect explanation than a center of gravity effect. Given that most findings favor a range effect account over a center of gravity account, the range effect notion has been incorporated into the E-Z Reader model to help explain landing position effects (Reichle et al., 1999; Rayner et al., 2000).

In addition to these basic findings regarding where we fixate when we read, there is a growing body of evidence to indicate that the orthographic characteristics of a word influence where the eyes land on that word. In Finnish, Hyönä, (1993; 1995) has shown that readers fixate closer to the beginning of a word with an infrequent word initial letter sequence than they do for a similar word with a frequent word initial letter sequence. Furthermore, White and Liversedge (2004a, 2004b) have shown similar effects in English for both misspelled and correctly spelled words. These small, but reliable, effects suggest a sensitivity on the part of the mechanism responsible for the *where* aspect of oculomotor control to non-foveal orthographic information.

Binocular Coordination of the Eyes

Most research on eye movements during reading (and indeed eye movement research in general) has typically involved recording the movements of only one of the eyes (though vision is typically binocular). But, of course, readers have two eyes. Do the two eyes move together when we read? Or is their timing different (does one eye move before the other)? Also, do the landing positions differ? Obviously, these questions need not be limited to reading, but are of rather general interest to vision researchers. Surprisingly, while there has been some research investigating binocular eye movements in vision, there has been very little investigating binocular eye movements during reading. The standard explanation has been that the two eyes move together, or conjugately, during reading (see Rayner, 1978a, for a review). Smith, Schremser, and Putz (1971) claimed that, typically, the left eye moved about 6-7 ms prior to the right eye in reading. However, Williams and Fender (1977) argued that this was an artifact of the way they measured saccades and showed that the two eyes do move at the same time. While it appears that saccadic eye movements of both eyes are initiated at the same time, in a recent paper, Heller and Radach (1999) provided data suggesting that there is substantial variability in the fixation location of the two eyes when we read.

Heller and Radach (1999) showed that on average the eyes fixate 1.5-2 characters apart. Although the mean distance between fixated points is two characters, the actual distance between fixation points is related to the amplitude of the preceding saccade (5% of saccade length for a 10-12 letter saccade, 15% of a 2-3 letter saccade). After a saccade, at the start of a fixation when the two fixation points are disparate, there was a relatively slow vergence movement that persisted throughout the fixation (although the two eyes were still apart at the end of the fixation). Note that such vergence movements are unlikely to be a consequence of depth cues within the visual stimulus since text was presented normally on a computer screen. Thus, there was very little visual disparity in the signal received by the two eyes that could provide cues to depth. An alternative possibility is that this vergence movement serves to bring the points of fixation onto the same position within a word. However, this did not appear to be the case. Vergence movements persisted in an identical manner to those that occurred when a word was fixated binocularly even when text was viewed monocularly. Therefore, vergence movements during reading do not appear to be caused by binocular fixation of the text. Heller and Radach also showed that vergence movements are not constant. In the case of saccadic undershoot or overshoot, the eye whose point of fixation is farthest from the target location makes the biggest movement to the target. It is not a case of the eyes simply centralizing on a mid-point location.

Heller and Radach (1999) also found that when the text being processed was in MiXeD case (difficult to process), then vergence movements were slower than when the text was presented normally (easy to process). This fascinating finding is suggestive of the possibility that such low-level oculomotor control may be sensitive to the influence of processing difficulty. In addition, Heller and Radach showed that readers made longer saccades for normal text than for mixed-case text. Since fixation disparity varies as a function of preceding saccade amplitude, then average fixation disparity was greater for normal text than for mixed-case text. It appears that when normal text is read, the visual system is able to tolerate a larger fixation disparity than when mixed case text is read.

Recently, we have started testing subjects in the first of a series of experiments to explore a number of aspects of binocular coordination of the eyes during reading. As yet, we only have preliminary data from three subjects in a simple reading experiment. Consequently, we are still cautious in forming our conclusions. However, we believe that the data strongly suggest a number of very interesting possibilities.

In our study, subjects were presented with single sentences on a computer screen. Participants viewed the sentences on the screen normally through a pair of Cambridge Research Systems shutter goggles. The shutter goggles were used to permit dichoptic presentation of one target word embedded within the sentence. We will not further discuss the dichoptic target word manipulation in this chapter. However, it is important to note that the whole of the sentence other than the target word was viewed under normal binocular conditions. Consequently, data from this study are informative concerning binocular control during normal reading and allow us to verify some of the claims made by Heller and Radach (1999).

In our experiment, the screen was positioned 80 cm from the reader's eye and one character covered 0.29 degrees of visual angle. Subjects were required to read the sentences normally and answer comprehension questions where necessary. Eye movements of both eyes were measured using left and right Dual Purkinje Image eyetrackers. The left and the right eye were calibrated monocularly (visual stimulation to the left eye was blocked using the shutter goggles while the right eye was calibrated and vice versa). Subjects were recalibrated after every five sentences or more often if required to ensure accurate recordings from both eyes.

For the analyses, we computed the mean proportion of fixations on which the line of gaze from each eye was aligned (fixation positions of both eyes were disparate by one character or less), crossed (the fixation position of the right eye was greater than a character to the right of the position of the left eye), or uncrossed (the fixation position of the left eye was greater than a character to the left of the position of the right eye). We also computed the mean magnitude of disparity in fixations categorized as aligned, crossed, or uncrossed. These data are shown in Figures 2.5 and 2.6. It should be noted that for both these measures there were differences between the data from each of the subjects, and therefore, we only discuss here those aspects of the data that were consistent across all three subjects.

In line with the data from Heller and Radach (1999), it can be seen from Figure 2.5 that readers' points of fixation were not aligned on a substantial proportion of fixations. Indeed, readers' points of fixation were aligned on 40% of fixations, but were not aligned on 60% of fixations. That is to say, on the majority of fixations, readers' point of fixation from each eye fell upon different letters of the word they were fixating. Furthermore, while the lines of gaze were uncrossed on 5% of fixations, they were crossed on 55% of fixations. Thus, for the three subjects tested so far, the pattern of data consistently shows that fixation disparity is primarily a consequence of overconvergence rather than overdivergence.

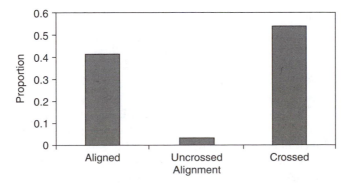

FIGURE 2.5. The mean proportion of aligned, uncrossed, and crossed fixations for the three subjects tested in the binocular eye-tracking experiment.

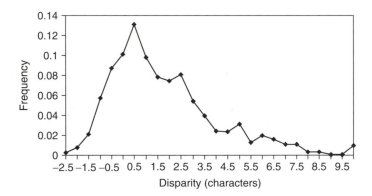

FIGURE 2.6. Frequency distribution of the magnitude of the disparity in aligned, uncrossed and crossed fixations for the three subjects in the binocular eye-tracking experiment (positive numbers represent crossed disparity, negative numbers uncrossed).

In Figure 2.6 the magnitude of fixation disparity is plotted along the horizontal axis with frequency on the vertical. Crossed lines of gaze are represented by a negative disparity and uncrossed by a positive disparity and the unit of disparity is a character. The distribution clearly shows that the most frequent disparity occurs when the lines of gaze are crossed by one character. Also, the data are skewed to the left with the distribution showing a longer tail for crossed disparate fixations than for uncrossed disparate fixations. The results clearly indicate that when lines of gaze were crossed, fixation disparity was greater than when lines of gaze were uncrossed. The range of disparity for uncrossed fixations is from 0.5 characters to as much as 8 characters, though the vast majority of disparate fixations fall within the range of 0.5 to 4.5 characters disparate. By contrast, for uncrossed fixations, the range of disparate fixations is 0.5 to 2.5 characters. Perhaps the most striking conclusion that may be drawn from the current data (and those of Heller and Radach, 1999) is that the default assumption that both eyes fixate the same position within a word is not correct for the majority of fixations made when reading a sentence.

A final aspect of the data that we examined was whether fixation disparity changed as a function of fixation position within the sentence. To do this, we segmented the sentences into word-long regions. The sentences we used in the current experiment were up to 12 words in length. Thus, we measured the magnitude of the disparity for each of the three disparity categories across each region of the sentence from the leftmost word to the rightmost. Once more, we stress that the data are provisional and must be treated cautiously. However, the results of the current analyses show a consistent pattern such that the frequency of crossed fixation disparity was greatest when readers fixated the leftmost regions of the sentence. Furthermore, the frequency of crossed fixation disparity decreased systematically as the reader fixated regions further to the right. By contrast, the frequency with which readers made aligned fixations was lowest when the leftmost regions of the sentence were fixated, but increased systematically as the reader fixated more rightward regions. We anticipate that future experiments investigating these and other aspects of binocular eye movement control during reading will provide very interesting data that will pose a challenge for existing models of eye movement control and possibly undermine models of lexical identification that assume a cyclopean point of fixation in order that lexical identification may take place (e.g., Shillcock, Ellison, & Monaghan, 2000).

Inhibition of Saccade Return

Posner and Cohen (1984) first observed that when attention is moved from one location to another in a visual array, processing of stimuli at a previously attended location is somewhat inhibited in comparison to a location that has not recently been attended. This inhibition effect is often measured by an increase in response latency to material in a previously attended region. It has been termed *inhibition of return* (Posner, Rafal, Choate, & Vaughan, 1985) and presumably reflects the difficulty of returning attention to a previously attended location (for a review, see Klein, 2000).

While many inhibition of return studies have utilized reaction time measures, some have investigated the phenomenon by measuring eye movements in a visual array. For example, Abrams and Dobkin (1994) found that subjects were slower to initiate an eye movement to a previously attended location than to a previously unattended location (see also Maylor, 1985; Rafal, Egly, & Rhodes, 1994; Ro, Pratt, & Rafal, 2000; Vaughan, 1984). Likewise, Hooge and Frens (2000) found that latencies for eye fixations preceding *return saccades* (saccades returning to previously fixated positions) were 40% longer than latencies of fixations preceding saccades to previously unfixated positions. Klein and MacInnes (1999) suggested that inhibition of return acts to facilitate visual search when multiple saccades are involved because it reduces the likelihood that the eyes will return to items that have been previously inspected.

Recently, we (Rayner, Juhasz, Ashby, & Clifton, 2003) asked the question: Does the inhibition of return effect generalize to the more complex task of reading? Are fixation durations increased before readers move their eyes to a word that they previously fixated? We thought that it would be remarkable if the effect generalized to reading because it is well known that eye fixations in reading are quite sensitive to linguistic variables like word frequency and word predictability, which may dominate low-level effects like inhibition of return (see Liversedge & Findlay, 2000; Rayner, 1998; Starr & Rayner, 2001, for reviews).

Of course, it is impossible to control where readers fixate as they read and the extent to which they do or do not move their eyes back to a word that they have immediately just fixated. Therefore, the analyses we carried out were based on culling instances of return saccades from a large corpus of eye movement data from readers reading text or sentences under instructions to comprehend the reading material. Logically, in reading, there are two types of return saccades: (a) those in which a saccade returns the eyes to a previously fixated word via a regression (termed *regressive return saccades*), and (b) those in which a saccade takes the eyes forward in the text to a region from which they had originally regressed (termed *forward return saccades*). Fixations preceding these two types of return saccades were compared to fixations in which the ensuing saccade did not return to the word fixated on the immediately preceding fixation. We found that fixations preceding regressive return saccades were 36 ms longer than nonreturn saccades and those preceding forward return saccades were 44 ms longer than nonreturns. The fact that forward return saccades showed the same effect as regressive return saccades suggests that the effect is not simply due to readers only partially processing the word to which they regressed. Furthermore, Rayner et al. (2003) found that the effect combined additively with the usual effect of word frequency so that fixations preceding both return and nonreturn saccades were longer when the eyes were on a low frequency word than a high frequency word. This finding suggests that the systems responsible for producing frequency and inhibition of return effects are independent.

The Gap Effect

Saslow (1967) first showed that when subjects are fixating a stimulus and are about to make a saccade to a target elsewhere in the visual field, the time to make the saccade is reduced if the stimulus that is currently fixated disappears compared with when it does not. Thus, the saccade latency is shorter when the fixation stimulus disappears than when the fixation stimulus remains visible. This phenomenon, the *gap effect*, has been the subject of much subsequent study. The gap effect is unchanged if instructions are given to attend elsewhere than fixation (Kingstone & Klein, 1993; Walker, Kentridge, & Findlay, 1995) and thus appears to be intrinsic to the fixational part of the oculomotor system rather than being attentional (Dorris & Munoz, 1995; Findlay & Walker, 1999).

Would such a low-level visuomotor effect occur in reading if the text disappeared prior to the initiation of a saccade? It has been demonstrated that if readers are allowed to see text for 50-60 ms before a masking pattern obliterates the text that reading proceeds quite normally (Rayner et al., 1981;

Slowiaczek & Rayner, 1987; Ishida & Ikeda, 1989). This does not mean that all of the processing needed for reading can be completed in 60 ms. Rather, the finding suggests that readers are able to get the visual information needed for reading into the processing system in 60 ms. So, given that a 60 ms presentation of text is sufficient for reading to proceed quite normally, if we extinguish the text, will the time to make a saccade be reduced, resulting in an increase in the reading rate?

We (Liversedge, Rayner, White, Vergilino-Perez, Findlay, & Kentridge, 2004; Rayner, Liversedge, White, & Vergilino-Perez, 2003) tested this possibility in experiments in which readers either read normal text or *disappearing text* (see Figure 2.7). In the latter condition, whenever the reader fixated a word within a sentence, 60 ms after the word was fixated, it disappeared. The rest of the sentence remained on the monitor after the word disappeared and when the reader moved his/her eyes to look at the next (or any other) word in the sentence, it too disappeared after 60 ms (with the word that had previously been fixated reappearing immediately following the saccade out of the word). In this way, readers could fixate the sentence as they would when reading it normally, but each word of the text disappeared before their eyes as they read.[3] This methodology may sound somewhat bizarre and might lead one to suspect that it would be impossible to read and understand a sentence under such circumstances. However, we found that reading text under such conditions is surprisingly easy and language processing appears to proceed unimpaired. We were thus able to ask the critical question: Does a gap effect occur during reading resulting in an increased reading rate?

Basically, our research revealed that there is no gap effect in reading. When the fixated text disappeared, readers did not read faster than when the text was normal. Indeed, individual fixations increased by about 20 ms. This may well be due to some type of saccade inhibition (Reingold & Stampe, 2002) due to the sudden offset. But, interestingly, readers compensated for the slightly longer fixations by making fewer overall fixations (and especially fewer refixations on a word prior to moving to another word) in the disappearing text

reading has been used as the context to study interesting
*

reading has been used as the   to study interesting
*

reading has been used as the context to study interesting
*

reading has been used as the context to   interesting
*

FIGURE 2.7. An example of disappearing text. When the reader fixates on a word (context in the example), it is removed from the monitor 60 ms after the beginning of the fixation and it does not reappear until the reader moves to another word. That word (study in the example) likewise disappears after 60 ms.

condition. This led to virtually equivalent reading times between the disappearing and normal text conditions. What emerged most strikingly from the experiments was that cognitive processes associated with understanding the text is what drives the eyes through the text. That is, we found as strong an effect of word frequency when the text disappeared as when it was normal; readers looked longer at low-frequency words than high-frequency words independent of whether the text was normal or disappeared (Liversedge et al., 2004; Rayner et al., 2003).

Express Saccades

Another basic oculomotor effect that has a clear relationship to the gap effect is the phenomenon of express saccades. Research using the gap effect paradigm has suggested that when the fixation point is extinguished, there is a separate category of saccades, express saccades, with very short latencies under 120 ms (see Fischer & Weber, 1993, for a review). The defining feature of express saccades is that they represent a separate distribution of saccade latencies. There has been some debate about (a) whether or not there is a bimodal distribution of saccade latencies (with express saccades representing one peak of the distribution and normal saccades representing the other) and (b) the phenomenon in general (Findlay, 1992; Kingstone & Klein, 1993). Even if there were no controversy surrounding express saccades, there are questions about the functional utility of such short latency saccades for normal information processing tasks (Fischer & Rayner, 1993). In a specific test of the extent to which express saccades might occur in reading, Inhoff, Topolski, Vitu, and O'Regan (1993) found no evidence of a bimodal distribution of fixation durations or express saccades.[4]

Linguistic Processing in Reading

Reading is very much a linguistic processing activity. We read to understand some aspect of the printed message, and so reading is inherently a form of language processing. Accordingly, reading is often used as the context in which to study how various properties of words influence fluency, how we parse sentences, and how we understand discourse. In this section, we will discuss a number of language processing issues. Once again, many of the issues are rather general and need not be limited to reading (so that studies in the context of speech perception could just as easily speak to some of these issues). This said, it is clear that studies using eye movements in the context of reading have made significant contributions to our understanding of language processing.

Considerable data have demonstrated that eye movements are intimately related to the moment-to-moment cognitive processing activities of readers. Our discussion will deal with studies at the word level, the sentence level, and the discourse level. There are a number of other issues, only some of which, due to space limitations, can we very briefly mention. Thus, issues such as priming effects due to semantic relationships between words (Carroll & Slowiaczek, 1986; Morris, 1994; Sereno & Rayner, 1992) and morphological effects (Hyönä & Pollatsek, 1998; Inhoff, Radach, & Heller, 2000; Pollatsek, Hyönä, & Bertram, 2000) will not be discussed. We do note that a number of recent studies have started to examine the processing of long, complex words (Andrews, Miller, & Rayner, 2004; Juhasz, Starr, Inhoff, & Placke, 2003; Niswander, Pollatsek, & Rayner, 2000) rather than simple monomorphemic words. In our view, this is a positive step, given that complex words are ubiquitous in text. In this section of the chapter, we will discuss in order (1) word frequency, (2) word predictability, (3) lexical and phonological ambiguity, (4) sentence parsing, (5) wrap-up effects, (6) pronoun resolution, and (7) on-line inferences.

Word Frequency

One of the most robust effects in the reading literature is the *word frequency* effect, wherein it takes longer to process a low frequency word than a high frequency word. Likewise, in terms of eye movements, readers look longer at low frequency words than high frequency words. The size of the frequency effect typically ranges from a 20ms effect up to a 60 ms effect for gaze duration. This effect was first noted informally by Rayner (1977) and then validated by Just and Carpenter (1980) via regression analyses. However, in natural language, word length and word frequency are confounded: high frequency words tend to be shorter than low frequency words, and this was true in Just and Carpenter's analysis. Since word length exerts a strong effect on fixation times (as word length increases, gaze duration increases, Just & Carpenter, 1980; Rayner et al., 1996), it was necessary to control word length while varying word frequency. Inhoff and Rayner (1986) and Rayner and Duffy (1986) were the first to do so, and both found strong frequency effects. Since then, it has been demonstrated many times (see Rayner, 1998, for a review) that readers look longer (in terms of first fixation duration, gaze duration, and single fixation duration) at low frequency words than at high frequency words.

In addition to differences in fixation times on the target word, three other findings have been observed. First, there is often a *spillover* effect from fixating low frequency words as fixation time on the next word is also inflated (Rayner & Duffy, 1986). Second, although the duration of fixation *n* is influenced by word frequency, the duration of fixation *n-1* (when the target word is to the right of fixation) is not (Carpenter & Just, 1983; Henderson & Ferreira, 1993; Rayner, Fischer, & Pollatsek, 1998). Third, for words that are six letters or fewer, high frequency words tend to be skipped more than low frequency words (Gautier, O'Regan, & LaGargasson, 2000; O'Regan, 1979; Rayner et al., 1996).

Word Predictability

A second variable that affects fixation time on a word is word predictability. Ehrlich and Rayner (1981) found that words that are constrained by preceding context are fixated for less time and skipped more often than unconstrained words. This *predictability* effect has now been demonstrated a number of times, and the size of the effect in fixation times is on the order of 20-30 ms for gaze duration (so the size of the effect typically isn't as large as for word frequency). More recently, Rayner and Well (1996) found that readers fixated low constraint target words longer than they fixated medium or high constraint target words. They also found that readers skipped high constraint target words more than they did either medium or low constraint target words. In experiments examining contextual constraint (or predictability), constraint is usually determined via a modified cloze task in which subjects who do not participate in the actual experiment are given a sentence frame up to the target word and asked to write down what the next word is; high constraint words are produced a high proportion of the time whereas low constraint words are generally not filled in by subjects.

The predictability effect is quite interesting since not only does contextual constraint influence fixation time, as we noted above, it also affects word skipping. The strongest influence on skipping is word length (Brysbaert & Vitu, 1998; Rayner & McConkie, 1976), but predictability also influences skipping. Although there is currently some controversy about this point, there is some evidence suggesting that when words are skipped, the fixation duration prior to the skip and after the skip is inflated (Pollatsek, Rayner, & Balota, 1986; Reichle et al., 1998). So, in this sense the fact that a word is skipped is still registered in the eye movement record. Part of the issue surrounding the controversy (Engbert, Longtin, & Kliegl, 2002) is that the size of the effect when a word is skipped is on the order of 30-40 ms (combining the fixation before the skip and the fixation after the skip). One might expect the size of the effect to be larger since fixation times on a word are typically over 200 ms. This is an interesting issue that has yet to be fully worked out.

Lexical and Phonological Ambiguity

There have been many studies (see Gorfein, 2001) of lexical ambiguity using naming time, lexical decision time, and the cross-modal priming paradigm to examine the issue of whether both (or all) meanings of an ambiguous word are immediately activated when the word is processed, or if only the contextually appropriate meaning is activated. However, the problem with such studies is that they usually require some form of response regarding a target word that is presented in isolation, usually centrally, on a computer screen that the participant is centrally fixating. Such tasks may therefore be regarded as artificial in the sense that the participant may not necessarily process words presented in this manner in the same way that he or she would when reading. Note that during normal reading, participants obtain a parafoveal preview and therefore partially process a word prior to direct fixation of the word. Furthermore, since the eyes saccade (most of the time) from left to right during reading, information regarding a word's identity becomes available incrementally from left to right (this is particularly true of long words where two or three fixations on the word will be necessary prior to a saccade from the word onto the next word in the sentence). Note that we are not suggesting a left-to-right letter scan of words. Instead, we are arguing that (at least partial) information becomes available for processing first from non-foveal locations, and then later much more detailed information becomes available from the fovea when the word is directly fixated. Thus, to examine lexical processing as it occurs during normal reading, in our view, it is preferable to utilize eye-tracking methodology since this permits the most appropriate examination of the time course of the availability of information and its influence on processing during normal reading. Indeed, a number of eye movement experiments have examined the issue of lexical processing during reading and, in particular, the resolution of lexically ambiguous words.

The pattern of results in these eye movement experiments is quite interesting as fixation time on the lexically ambiguous word is modulated by the characteristics of the word and the prior context (Kambe, Duffy, & Rayner, 2000; Rayner & Duffy, 1986; Sereno, 1995). The basic finding is that when preceding context is neutral (so that it does not bias either meaning of the word), readers look no longer at a biased, ambiguous word (one with a highly dominant meaning, such as *bank*) than an unambiguous control word (matched on length and frequency); however, they do look longer at a balanced ambiguous word (with two equally likely meanings) than at a control word. On the other hand, when the context biases one meaning, readers look no longer at a balanced ambiguous word than the control; however, if the context biases the subordinate meaning of the word, they look longer at a biased word than a control word (Duffy, Morris, & Rayner, 1988).

Studies have also been reported dealing with phonological ambiguity (the homophones *bear* and *bare* are phonologically ambiguous since, although they are spelled differently, they sound the same). These studies are interesting in that they try to determine how early during processing of a fixated word a phonological representation of that word is activated. Studies (Pollatsek et al., 1992; Rayner, Sereno, Lesch, & Pollatsek, 1995) using the eye-contingent display change paradigms mentioned earlier in this chapter have suggested that phonological codes are activated very early in processing.

In other studies, a homophone target word is included (so that if the context calls for the word *bear*, the word *bare* actually appears) and fixation time on the word is examined. Readers typically look longer at such homophone target words (Daneman & Reingold, 1993) unless the context is highly constraining of the correct word (Rayner, Pollatsek, & Binder, 1998). These studies also reveal differences due to the visual similarity of the homophone pairs, the frequency difference between the two members of the homophone pairs, and reading skill (Jared, Levy, & Rayner, 1999).

Sentence Parsing

Of all the areas of language processing that have been examined, there are more studies of eye movements of readers reading syntactically ambiguous (or *garden path* sentences such as *The woman hit the man with the handlebar moustache*) than any other type of study (Rayner, 1998). Although many studies of parsing have been done using the self-paced reading method in which readers advance (either word-by-word or phrase-by-phrase) through the sentence by pushing a button, it is clear that eye movement methodology represents the gold standard for research on parsing because it allows for precise moment-to-moment examination of readers' attempts to deal with the ambiguity. The problems with self-paced reading are twofold: (1) reading rate is about half that of normal reading, and readers may therefore perform processes that they would not carry out when reading normally; and (2) readers can't look back when they encounter problems, since the text has disappeared, and we know that regressions are important for reanalysis and are very much an index of comprehension difficulty (Altmann, 1994; Rayner & Sereno, 1994b).

The impetus for eye movement research investigating parsing was work by Frazier and Rayner (1982), who argued that if a syntactically ambiguous phrase is initially misanalyzed, fixation times on the disambiguating word increase and readers quickly make a regression to facilitate reanalysis. Both predictions were confirmed. Additionally, Frazier and Rayner (1982) presented data suggesting that readers were very good at regressing back to the part of the sentence where they had first starting going wrong in terms of their parse of the sentence. This finding has recently been further supported by Meseguer, Carreiras, and Clifton (2002). The important point to note about the arguments of Frazier and Rayner is that the syntactic processor assigns a single syntactic analysis to an ambiguous sentence fragment in an informationally encapsulated manner. Furthermore, upon encountering information that syntactically disambiguates the sentence in favor of an initially unpreferred analysis, the processor is forced to abandon its initial analysis and compute an alternative analysis. It is the detection of an initial misanalysis and the reanalysis of the misparsed sentence that causes the increased fixation times and regressive eye movements.

Recently, however, the Garden Path theory advocated by Frazier, Clifton, Rayner, and their colleagues has been challenged by researchers favoring a constraint-based model of processing (MacDonald, 1994; MacDonald, Pearlmutter, & Seidenberg, 1994a, 1994b; Pearlmutter & MacDonald, 1992; Spivey-Knowlton, & Sedivy, 1994; Tabossi, Spivey-Knowlton, McRae, & Tanenhaus, 1994; Trueswell, Tanenhaus, & Kello, 1993; Trueswell, Tanenhaus, & Garnsey, 1994). These researchers claim that alternative syntactic analyses of an ambiguous fragment compete against each other, and multiple sources of information (e.g., frequency information, semantic information, contextual information, etc.) activate each of the alternatives. According to this view, then, the longer fixation times and regressive eye movements that are typically observed when a garden path sentence is read are very often due to the process of competition between alternatives rather than misanalysis detection and syntactic reanalysis.

The debate concerning which of these alternative theories that existing and new experimental data favor is still very much alive, and it is beyond the scope of this chapter to evaluate the evidence for or against each position. For a while, the pendulum seemed to be swinging mostly in the direction of the constraint satisfaction view. However, a number of recent studies (Binder, Duffy, & Rayner, 2001; Clifton, Traxler, Mohamed, Morris, Williams, & Rayner, 2003; Traxler, Pickering, & Clifton, 1998) suggest that the pendulum may be beginning to swing in the other direction. Suffice it to say, for our purposes in this chapter, that the consequence of syntactic processing difficulties in terms of the eye movement record is disruption in the form of increased reading times and increased regressive eye movements.

It would perhaps be misleading to leave the discussion of syntactic processing at this point without further discussion of the time course of effects. From the preceding paragraphs, it may seem that whenever a reader experiences disruption to processing due to syntactic factors, the disruption will occur immediately at the point of syntactic disambiguation. However, this is not always the case. Very often in experiments investigating aspects of syntactic processing where disruption is predicted at a particular word within the sentence, no such effect appears until downstream of that word (Van Gompel, Pickering, & Traxler, 2001). That is to say, fixations on and regressions from the critical word will not be increased compared with fixations on the same word in an unambiguous control sentence. Instead, increased fixations or regressions occur on the next word or two following the critical word. At the present time it is unclear why disruption to processing due to different syntactic manipulations occurs at different points in the eye movement record after a critical word has first been encountered. However, through careful examination of different measures of processing difficulty (such as first fixation duration, first pass, regression path, and total reading time) for the critical and postcritical region, it is usually possible to determine exactly when disruption to processing first occurred.

Sentence and Clause Wrap-Up

Just and Carpenter (1980) first demonstrated sentence wrap-up effects. They found that readers fixated longer at the end of a sentence than within the sentence. Subsequently, Rayner et al. (1989) demonstrated that when a target word ended a clause, readers fixate on it longer than when the same word does not end a clause. Once again, the longer fixation times reflect some type of clause wrap-up effect. More recently, Rayner, Kambe, and Duffy (2000) found that readers fixated longer on a target noun when it was clause final than when it was not. However, they also found that readers made longer saccades when their eyes left the target noun when it was clause final than when it was not. This last result suggests that sometimes higher-order processes that are related to making a decision about when to move the eyes impinge on lower-level decisions that are typically associated with deciding where to send the eyes.

Pronoun Resolution

In order to form a coherent representation of what a text means, it is necessary to form referential links between pronouns and their antecedents within the text. For example, in order to understand the meaning of the second clause in the sentence *As the man walked down the street, he tripped and fell over* the reader must form a referential link between the anaphoric pronoun *he* and its antecedent noun phrase *the man*. That is to say, the reader must work out that the individual who fell over is the same individual who was walking down the street. This process, *pronoun resolution*, may appear from the example to be a quite simple process, but it is in fact extremely complex. Furthermore, pronoun resolution is absolutely necessary in order for the reader to form a rich and meaningful representation of the text.

There have been a large number of studies conducted to investigate pronoun resolution and most of these studies have used methodologies other than eye tracking. Probe recognition methodology (e.g., Chang, 1980; Corbett & Chang, 1983; Gernsbacher, 1989; McDonald & MacWhinney, 1995) and probe naming (e.g., Rigalleau & Caplan, 2000) involve participants reading a sentence and then responding as quickly as possible to a probe word that is presented to them. Participants are required either to make a *Yes/No* recognition decision, a lexical decision, or to name the word. The time to make a response is taken to indicate the degree to which a potential antecedent of the referring expression (i.e., a pronoun) was activated when the response was made. While such studies have contributed to our understanding of the process of pronoun resolution, the methodology has recently been criticized on the grounds that it may not reflect only those processes associated with normal pronoun resolution (Gordon, Hendrick, & Foster, 2000; Foster, 2000; Stewart, Pickering, & Sanford, 2000). In particular, the work of Gordon et al. demonstrates that response times in probe studies can be influenced by a memory list of key words that the participant believes are likely to be probed. Gordon et al. also showed that similar probe recognition effects can be obtained for sentences presented normally or with a scrambled word order, suggesting that this methodology may tap into something other than natural language processing.

An alternative methodology that has been used to investigate pronoun resolution (as well as the process of syntactic processing) is self-paced reading (Cacciari, Carreiras, & Cionini, 1997; Crawley, Stevenson, & Kleinman, 1990; Garnham, Oakhill, Ehrlich, & Carreiras, 1995; Stevenson & Vitkovitch, 1986). However, the problems identified with this methodology for investigating questions concerning the process of parsing also hold for research investigating pronoun resolution. Indeed, Clifton and Ferreira (1989) argued that self-paced reading is not sufficiently sensitive to very early effects in reading, particularly when the sentences are presented clause by clause.

Once again, it is our belief that eye tracking is probably the best methodology to use to investigate pronoun resolution during normal reading. Despite the strengths of this technique, there have been relatively few eye movement studies investigating this process. Two early studies investigated the influence of gender information on pronoun resolution (Ehrlich & Rayner, 1983; Vonk, 1984). Gender information can provide a strong cue to the reader concerning which of a number of potential antecedents a pronoun is co-referent with. Vonk showed that when a sentence contained a gender cue, readers spent longer fixating the pronoun and less time reading the remainder of the sentence than when it did not.

Although Vonk (1984) observed effects of gender at the pronoun, two other eye-tracking studies in which there was no secondary task did not show such early effects. Ehrlich and Rayner (1983) observed their earliest effects of gender on fixations made shortly after readers had first encountered the pronoun. They argued that at least some pronoun resolution processes are delayed until after the pronoun has been fixated. Similarly, Garrod, Freudenthal, and Boyle (1994) showed effects of gender on the verb following a gender-marked pronoun, but not on the pronoun itself. Note that pronouns are very short and are fixated quite infrequently during reading. Hence, it is possible that reading time differences do not often occur on the pronouns themselves since on the majority of trials they are skipped, resulting in a zero first-pass reading time for that portion of the sentence.

Finally, a very recent study by Van Gompel and Liversedge (2002) also investigated the influence of gender and number information on pronoun resolution. However, in their study they used cataphoric rather than anaphoric pronouns. Cataphoric pronouns refer forward rather than backward in the text. Thus, in the sentence *When he was waiting, the man noticed the woman*, the cataphoric pronoun *he* refers forward in the text to the subsequent noun phrase *the man*. Van Gompel and Liversedge showed that readers attempted to form a co-reference relation between the cataphoric pronoun and the first noun phrase in the main clause regardless of whether the pronoun and noun phrase matched in gender or number. Interestingly, their results showed increased fixations on the region following the first noun phrase in the main clause rather than on the noun phrase itself; again, this is another demonstration of effects appearing downstream from the critical region.

On-line Inferences

In many ways, it is quite surprising that there isn't more research on discourse processing using eye movements as the dependent variable. In the past, the level of question that has been asked about comprehension processes and discourse processing have been such that experimenters have been quite happy to use gross reading times (sentence or discourse reading time) or self-paced reading time as their primary measure. On-line experiments dealing with discourse processing have typically relied on probe experiments in which a probe word appears at some point during self-paced reading. While such experiments are needed to determine the nature of the discourse representation that readers build as they move through a passage, we also suspect that the time is ripe for the use of eye movement techniques to study higher order comprehension issues. Indeed, Kambe, Duffy, Clifton, and Rayner (2003) have recently developed an eye-contingent probe paradigm in which a probe word appears at a certain time with respect to the readers' fixation on a given target word.

Even so, the few studies that have been done using eye movements to examine on-line inferences have yielded interesting results (see Garrod & Terras, 2000; Garrod, O'Brien, Morris, & Rayner, 1990; O'Brien, Raney, Albrecht, & Rayner, 1997; O'Brien, Shank, Myers, & Rayner, 1988). For example, O'Brien et al. (1988) found that when the phrase *stabbed her with his weapon* was read early in a passage, readers subsequently fixated no longer on the target word *knife* than when the earlier phrase read *stabbed her with his knife*; in the *weapon* case, the reader presumably inferred that the weapon was a knife. In contrast, when the original phrase read *assaulted her with his weapon*, readers fixated longer on the subsequent mention of *knife*.

A slightly different, but equally important, type of inference that readers make during on-line processing is the computation of contrasting sets of entities within their discourse representation. In the English language there are a small number of focus particles, such as words like *only*, *just*, *even*, *also* and *too*, that indicate contrastive focus to the reader. That is to say, when they appear in a sentence they serve to inform the reader to instantiate two contrasting sets of distinct elements within their semantic representation of what the sentence means (Rooth, 1992). For example, consider the sentence *Only horses raced in the Derby were sold at auction the following month.* For this sentence the focus operator *only* indicates that one of the two contrasting sets will be in focus (the focus set), and the other will be out of focus (the contrast set). Importantly, the reader is frequently required to infer the exact nature of the contrast sets. For example, given the sentence fragment *Only horses raced in the Derby...,* the reader must make a decision about whether the focus set is comprised of horses and that the contrast set is comprised of other animals, or alternatively, whether the focus set is the set of horses that were raced in the Derby and the contrast set those horses that were not. The point is that when a focus operator is encountered, the reader must make such a decision and frequently make an inference about the nature of the sets they must represent in their discourse model.

Several recent studies have examined whether using focus particles to indicate contrastive focus influences how syntactically ambiguous sentences are initially processed (Ni, Crain, & Shankweiler, 1996; Clifton, Bock, & Rado, 2000; Paterson, Liversedge, & Underwood, 1998; Liversedge, Paterson, & Clayes, 2002; Sedivy, 2002). Ni et al.'s original work suggested that upon reading a sentence fragment such as *only horses...,* readers initially instantiated a discourse representation containing two contrasting sets of horses rather than one contrasting a set of horses with another set of all other animals. In line with Referential Theory (Crain & Steedman, 1985), readers were then predisposed to process the remainder of the sentence as modifying the head noun and thereby specifying the nature of the distinction between the two contrasting sets of horses. However, more recently, Paterson et al. and Liversedge et al. criticized the Ni et al. eye movement experiment on methodological grounds. They also conducted two eye-tracking experiments. In the first of these, Paterson et al. showed that for relative clause sentences with a noun, verb, noun structure, readers did not instantiate contrasting sets of the type stipulated by referential theory. By contrast, Liversedge et al. used relative clause sentences with a noun, verb, prepositional phrase structure, and for such sentences readers did appear to construct a discourse representation in line with Referential theory. Paterson et al. and Liversedge et al. argued that the particular types of contrasting sets that readers infer when they read sentences containing focus operators depends critically upon the particular syntactic structure of the sentence within which the focus operator appears.

Implications of Visual Processing Research for Language Processing Research, and Vice Versa

In this chapter, we have reviewed two basic types of research. First, we reviewed research using eye movement data to examine some basic questions about visual processing during reading. Second, we reviewed research using eye movement data to examine some basic questions about linguistic processing during reading. Hopefully, it is clear that both research traditions have been highly successful in dealing with a number of important and interesting questions. In this concluding section, we argue that it is extremely important for researchers in each tradition to be aware of the research in the other area. We also argue that the formalization of the relationship between eye movement behavior and the psychological processes associated with written language comprehension is critical in the development of a comprehensive model of reading.

Given the current availability of "off-the-shelf" eye-tracking hardware and software, it is now relatively easy for researchers to buy an eye-tracker, plug it in, and start collecting data. However, this ease of availability can cause researchers to fail to fully consider how they are going to deal sensibly with the great volume of data that eye-tracking research generates. Of particular importance is the consideration of the eye movement measures that are most appropriate for the task in hand, and how the data stream is sampled in order that the indices of processing difficulty (i.e., the measures) do indeed locate those differences in fixations and eye movement patterns that a linguistic manipulation within an experiment has caused.

Why is it important for researchers interested in language processing to be aware of findings in the area of visual processing? Very often, in our experience, researchers in the former area simply think of eye movement measurement as a convenient way to study on-line language processing, and they remain uninterested in the specifics of the patterns of eye movements that the linguistic stimuli that are being processed evoke. Furthermore, they often do not make themselves knowledgeable concerning the theoretical claims that low-level researchers make about when and where readers move their eyes as they read and, importantly, which visual, as well as linguistic, characteristics of text influence eye movements. Such information is important if researchers are not to ignore low-level influences that might impinge on their results.

Consider the fact that psycholinguistic researchers most often focus (often exclusively) upon detecting differences in reading times during the first or second pass through the sentence and differences in the number of regressive saccades readers make from some critical region of the sentence. While such effects are often obtained and are clearly highlighted as important within psycholinguistic research, their implications for oculomotor control decisions frequently appear not to have been fully understood and are usually not reported.

For example, when a difference in first-pass reading time has been obtained for a critical word (or region) of the sentence, this necessarily indicates that the linguistic manipulation within the experiment has somehow affected the *when* decision component of the oculomotor control system. In particular, the increased processing time can come from two possible sources that may be regarded to reflect two qualitatively different types of decision concerning when to move the eyes. The first of these two possibilities is that the decision is delayed concerning when to terminate the current fixation, or fixations, on a word (or region) within the sentence. That is, disruption to processing causes longer fixations on a word (or region), necessarily indicating that the decision regarding when to terminate the current fixation on a word has been delayed. The second possible source for increased processing time comes, not from readers making fixations of longer duration but, instead, from them making a greater number of fixations on a word (or region). For example, if a word in one experimental condition produced little difficulty, then the reader may make a single fixation of 220 ms before making a saccade to inspect the next word in the sentence. However, if the same word under a different experimental condition did produce processing difficulty, then the reader may make two fixations on it, one of 220 ms as before plus one other fixation of, say, 200 ms before fixating the next word. In such a situation, the decision of when to terminate the fixation of 220 ms was not delayed since this fixation duration was not inflated. Instead, the decision about when to leave the currently fixated word was delayed.

Delaying both these types of decision concerning when to move the eye will produce increased first-pass and total reading times for the word (or region) under consideration. However, it is very important to realize that accounting for the increased reading time in terms of increased fixation durations on a word, or alternatively, in terms of an increase in the number of fixations (with no corresponding increase in fixation duration), involves explaining disruption in terms of very different decisions and operations within the system responsible for eye movement control. Note also, that it is quite possible that both these types of eye movement behavior could occur together or independent of each other when disruption to processing is experienced. However, very few psycholinguistic researchers ordinarily check to see whether one, or the other, or both of these possibilities did contribute to their effects.

The point this discussion serves to make is that, in our view, it is not sufficient simply to obtain a difference in reading time for a region of a sentence. Instead, it is important to conduct detailed analyses of the eye movement record in order to determine exactly the source (in terms of patterns of eye movement behavior) of those reading time differences. Only then is it possible to form a fully specified account of where and for how long readers fixated as they read the sentence. This, in turn, is important for developing a comprehensive account of the process of reading.

In a similar way, psycholinguistic researchers tend not to be particularly concerned with where within a region a reader fixates. However, exactly where the eyes fixate can have rather profound effects on processing time measures for a region. Thus, if one reader makes one fixation in a region while another makes two fixations in the region, it is highly likely that the latter reader will have longer first-pass reading times for that region. Of course, it is likely that the longer times for the second reader are reflecting processing difficulties. However, if the first reader's initial fixation was much further into the region than the second reader's initial fixation, at least some of the time associated with the additional fixation is undoubtedly due to where the reader initially fixated rather than being due to the linguistic characteristics of the text in that region being difficult to process. Differing landing positions and their consequences for reading time measures are particularly important to consider when a region of a sentence that is being compared across different conditions contains different words. Such content differences can produce different inspection strategies, which, in turn, can influence reading time differences.

Similarly, disruption to processing is often identified through increased regressive saccades in order that readers might reinspect text they have already read. In such a situation the experimental manipulation has usually disrupted some aspect of psycholinguistic processing. However, in terms of eye movement behavior, the experimental manipulation has impacted upon the *where* decision component of the oculomotor control system. The mechanism responsible for controlling the eye is directing the point of fixation to a particular location earlier in the sentence in order to facilitate the comprehension process. That is to say, the regressive saccade indicates that, at a very basic level, the default left-to-right programming of eye movements has somehow been interrupted (or overridden) in order that a qualitatively different psychological operation may take place, given that disruption has occurred. Note also that very often a regressive saccade from a region will terminate the reading time for that region. Thus, decisions concerning where the eye is directed also have important implications for whether differences in processing time are obtained at critical points in the sentence.

The discussion above should indicate that very rarely do psycholinguists characterize precisely reading time differences and differences in the frequency of regressions in terms of patterns of eye movement behavior. And yet, this is actually extremely important if we are ever to develop a fully specified model of reading. Let us be clear. It is our belief that any fully specified model of reading necessarily must account for not only the psycholinguistic operations associated with the comprehension process, but also the oculomotor processes by which the visual linguistic information is delivered to the psychological system concerned with processing that information. From this perspective, it is imperative that researchers characterize disruption to the reading process, not only in terms of the additional time required to attain comprehension, but also in terms of the precise patterns of eye movement behavior that occur when such disruption is experienced as that behavior is a central aspect of the reading process itself.

We'll end our discussion of why language researchers need to be concerned about low-level oculomotor effects with three specific examples. First, it is the case that psycholinguistic researchers sometimes report first fixation duration for a target region that is three to five words long. However, first fixation duration is generally taken to be a measure of processing difficulty associated with the word on which the fixation occurs. Consequently, it simply does not make sense to report first fixation duration as a viable measure when the target region is longer than a couple of short words. This is particularly the case if the critical word within the target region that drives the experimental manipulation does not occur until the end of the region. Why? Because the first fixation on an extended target region will very probably land on the first or second word of that region, and we know that it is extremely unlikely that readers are preprocessing text to the right of that word such that they are able to identify those words prior to direct fixation. Given that this is the case, the first fixation measure will simply be insensitive to any effect the experimental manipulation might have (or any reliable effects that are obtained are almost certainly spurious). In such a situation, a measure such as first-pass reading time or go-past reading time would provide a much more informative indication of processing difficulty.

Another reason why language researchers need to be aware of results from the visual processing domain is that intuitions about processing may not always be correct. For example, in a well-known paper by Trueswell, Tanenhaus, and Garnsey (1994) arguments were made to the effect that readers are able to disambiguate the correct reading of ambiguous phrases like *the defendant examined* or *the evidence examined* (which can continue as either a subject plus main verb interpretation or as a reduced relative) when the next word was the beginning of a prepositional phrase (*by the lawyer*). So, when fixated on *examined*, the reader should be able to process *by the* parafoveally and hence arrive at the correct interpretation. While this assumption seems intuitively quite plausible, when Clifton et al. (2003) experimentally controlled for this by masking the *by*-phrase prior to readers fixating on it, they found little evidence consistent with the assumption.

The final reason that researchers working within the psycholinguistic tradition must not ignore research examining lower-level aspects of oculomotor behavior is because researchers working within that tradition have made real attempts to formalize the relationship between psychological processes and eye movement behavior using modeling techniques (Reichle et al., 1998; Engbert et al., 2002). At present, there has been no attempt within the psycholinguistic community to formalize the relationship between eye movement behavior and higher order cognitive processes that occur during reading. In our view, such a formalization is vital if psycholinguistic research is to proceed in a less ad hoc manner. Clearly, to fully develop our understanding of psycholinguistic processing during reading, it is absolutely necessary to have a clear and comprehensive mapping of the relationship between oculomotor behavior and cognitive processes. To this extent, researchers working within the visual processing tradition have provided a good example of valuable future directions for research that psycholinguistic researchers interested in reading may pursue.

Why is it important for researchers interested in visual processing to be aware of research on language processing? Here, the answer is quite simple: numerous psycholinguistic studies have clearly documented that how long readers look at words in reading is strongly influenced by the ease or difficulty associated with understanding that word (Rayner, 1998). It is typically the case that researchers interested in visual processing have a bias to explain things in the simplest possible fashion. Many of the initial models of eye movement control (see Bouma & deVoogd, 1974), for example, tried to explain eye movements without recourse to any aspect of language processing. And, indeed, some current models (O'Regan, 1992; Yang & McConkie, 2001) attempt to account for eye movements with limited input from linguistic influences. For example, Yang and McConkie (2001) argue that "...much, and probably most, of the variation on saccade onset times is the result of physiological processes (time to resolve competition, random waiting times) that have little relation to the current cognitive activity" (p. 3584). Such a notion is frequently greeted with a sense of incredulity by psycholinguistic eye movement researchers, and it often comes as something of a surprise to them that there is any debate at all within the eye movement community as to whether linguistic variables influence how long readers fixate a word. To be clear—most psycholinguists generally believe that linguistic characteristics of the text being processed have a very significant influence on eye movement behavior (or else why on earth would eye movement recording be such a prevalent methodology within the area?). Indeed, as we have documented, one of the most robust effects in the field is the frequency effect in which readers look longer at low frequency words than high frequency words. Even in the data of those who wish to explain eye movements almost exclusively on the basis of low-level visual and oculomotor processes, there is clear evidence of frequency effects (see Vitu, McConkie, Kerr, & O'Regan, 2001). Thus, in our view, it is imperative that researchers working in the visual processing tradition must not ignore the massive body of experimental data that exists to demonstrate that eye movement behavior is significantly influenced by the linguistic characteristics of the text being processed.

To summarize, we have attempted to provide a brief summary of a number of research topics that have been investigated in two distinct areas of eye movement research that exist within the field of reading: low-level visual processing and higher-level psycholinguistic processing. We have argued that researchers working in each of these two traditions often fail to pay attention to relevant work that has been published by researchers working in the other tradition. We have also argued that great care must be taken when analyzing eye movement records to ensure that appropriate measures of eye movement behavior are employed to determine where within an eye movement record differences in behavior lie. Perhaps the most important point that we have tried to make in this chapter is that it is essential to develop a more complete understanding of the relationship between eye movements and higher-order psycholinguistic processing. Furthermore, we believe that the formalization of that relationship, in the form of explicit testable models, is essential and that the attainment of such models necessarily has to be the ultimate goal of all researchers who use eye movement methodology to investigate the process of reading. Without a full understanding of research findings within both the low-level visual processing tradition and the higher-order psycholinguistic processing tradition, such a formalization will not be possible.

ACKNOWLEDGMENTS

This chapter was written when the first author held a Leverhulme Visiting Professorship at the University of Durham (supported by the Leverhulme Trust). Grants HD17246 and HD26765 from the National Institute of Health to KR and 12/S19168 from the BBSRC to SPL provided further support. We are grateful to John Findlay, John Henderson, and Sarah White for their helpful comments on an earlier draft of the chapter.

NOTES

1. Vision is suppressed during saccades, which explains why readers typically do not see display changes in the boundary paradigm.
2. There is some facilitation from ends of words as well, but not as much as from beginning (Inhoff, 1989).
3. To ensure that readers were not reading off of an after-image when the fixated word disappeared, we performed a shutter test in which when a fixated word disappeared, a shutter closed simultaneously with the fixation. The shutter then opened simultaneously with the offset of the word. Readers could not read anything under these circumstances.
4. Indeed, there are occasionally very short fixations (around 50 ms) in the eye movement record during reading. However, the incidence of these short fixations is not affected by manipulations expected to influence higher level attentional processes.

REFERENCES

Abrams R. A., & Dobkin, R. S. (1994). The gap effect and inhibition of return: Interaction effects on eye movement latencies. *Experimental Brain Research, 98,* 483-487.

Abrams, R. A., & Jonides, J. (1988). Programming saccadic eye movements. *Journal of Experimental Psychology: Human Perception and Performance, 14,* 428-443.

Altarriba, J., Kambe, G., Pollatsek, A., & Rayner, K. (2001). Semantic codes are not used in integrating information across eye fixations in reading: Evidence from fluent Spanish-English bilinguals. *Perception & Psychophysics, 63,* 875-890.

Altmann, G. T. M. (1994). Regression-contingent analyses of eye movements during sentence processing: A reply to Rayner and Sereno. *Memory & Cognition, 22,* 286-290.

Andrews, S., Miller, B., & Rayner, K. (2004). Eye movements and morphological segmentation of compound words: There is a mouse in mousetrap. *European Journal of Cognitive Psychology, 16,* 285-311.

Aslin, R. N., & Shea, S. L. (1987). The amplitude and angle of saccades to double-step target displacements. *Vision Research, 27,* 1925 -1942.

Balota, D. A., Pollatsek, A., & Rayner, K. (1985). The interaction of contextual constraints and parafoveal visual information in reading. *Cognitive Psychology, 17,* 364-390.

Becker, W., & Jürgens, R. (1979). Analysis of the saccadic system by means of double step stimuli. *Vision Research, 19,* 967-983.

Bertera, J. H. & Rayner, K. (2000). Eye movements and the span of the effective stimulus in visual search. *Perception & Psychophysics, 62,* 576-585.

Binder, K. S., Duffy, S. A., & Rayner, K. (2001). The effects of thematic fit and discourse context on syntactic ambiguity resolution. *Journal of Memory and Language, 44,* 297-324.

Binder, K S., Pollatsek, A., & Rayner, K. (1999). Extraction of information to the left of the fixated word in reading. *Journal of Experimental Psychology: Human Perception and Performance, 25,* 1162-1172.

Bouma, H., & deVoogd, A. H. (1974). On the control of eye saccades in reading. *Vision Research, 14,* 273-284.

Brysbaert, M. and Vitu, F. (1998). Word skipping: implications for theories of eye movement control. In G. Underwood (Ed.) *Eye guidance in reading and scene perception* pp. 125-147. Amsterdam: Elsevier

Cacciari, C., Carreiras, M., & Cionini, C. B., (1997). When words have two genders: Anaphor resolution for Italian functionally ambiguous words. *Journal of Memory and Language, 37,* 517-532.

Carpenter, P.A., & Just, M.A. (1983). What your eyes do while your mind is reading. In K. Rayner (ed.), *Eye movements in reading: Perceptual and language processes* (pp 275-307). New York: Academic Press.

Carroll, P. J., & Slowiaczek, M. L. (1986). Constraints on semantic priming in reading: A fixation time analysis. *Memory & Cognition, 14,* 509-522.

Chang, F.R. (1980). Active memory processes in visual sentence comprehension: Clause effects and pronominal reference. *Memory and Cognition, 8,* 58-64.

Clifton, C., Jr., Bock, J., & Rado, J. (2000). Effects of the focus particle only and intrinsic contrast on comprehension of reduced relative clauses. In A. Kennedy & R. Radach & D. Heller & J. Pynte (Eds.), *Reading as a perceptual process,* (pp 591-619). Amsterdam: Elsevier Press.

Clifton, C., Jr. & Ferreira, F., (1989). Parsing in context. *Language and Cognitive Processes, 4,* 77-104.

Clifton, C. Jr., Traxler, M. J., Mohamed, M. T., Williams, R. S., Morris, R. K., & Rayner, K. (2003). The use of thematic role information in parsing: Syntactic parsing autonomy revisited. *Journal of Memory and Language, 49,* 317-334.

Corbett, A. T., & Chang, F. R. (1983). Pronoun disambiguation: Accessing potential antecedents. *Memory & Cognition, 11,* 283-294.

Crawley, R. A., Stevenson, R. J., & Kleinman, D. (1990). The use of heuristic strategies in the interpretation of pronouns. *Journal of Psycholinguistic Research, 19*, 245-264.

Daneman, M., & Reingold, E. (1993). What eye fixations tell us about phonological recoding during reading. *Canadian Journal of Experimental Psychology, 47*, 153-178.

Den Buurman, R., Boersma, T., & Gerrissen, J.F. (1981). Eye movements and the perceptual span in reading. *Reading Research Quarterly, 16*, 227-235.

Deubel, H., Wolf, W., & Hauske, G. (1984). The evaluation of the oculomotor error signal. In A. G. Gale & F. Johnson (eds.), *Theoretical and applied aspects of eye movement research* (pp 55-62). Amsterdam: North Holland.

Deutsch, A., & Rayner, K. (1999). Initial fixation location effects in reading Hebrew words. *Language and Cognitive Processes, 14*, 393-421.

Dodge, R. (1907). An experimental study of visual fixation. *Psychological Review Monograph Supplements, 8*(4).

Dorris, M. C., & Munoz, D. P. (1995). A neural correlate for the gap effect on saccadic reaction times in monkey. *Journal of Neurophysiology, 73*, 2558-2562.

Duffy, S. A., Morris, R. K., & Rayner, K. (1988). Lexical ambiguity and fixation times in reading. *Journal of Memory and Language, 27*, 429-446.

Dunn-Rankin, P. (1978). The visual characteristics of words. *Scientific American, 238*, 122-130.

Ehrlich, K., & Rayner, K. (1983). Pronoun assignment and semantic integration during reading: Eye movements and immediacy of processing. *Journal of Verbal Learning and Verbal Behavior, 22*, 75-87.

Engbert, R., Longtin, A., & Kliegl, R. (2002). A dynamical model of saccade generation in reading based on spatially distributed lexical processing. *Vision Research, 42*, 621-636.

Findlay, J. M. (1982). Global processing for saccadic eye movements. *Vision Research, 22*, 1033-1045.

Findlay, J. M. (1992). Programming of stimulus-elicited saccadic eye movements. In K. Rayner (ed.), *Eye movements and visual cognition: Scene perception and reading.* New York: Springer-Verlag.

Findlay, J. M., & Walker, R. (1999). A model of saccadic eye movement generation based on parallel processing and competitive inhibition. *Behavioral and Brain Sciences, 22*, 661-721.

Fine, E. M. & Rubin, G. S. (1999). Reading with a central field loss: number of letters masked is more important than the size of the mask in degrees. *Vision Research, 39*, 747-756.

Fischer, B., & Weber, H. (1993). Express saccades and visual attention. *Behavioral and Brain Sciences, 16*, 553-567.

Fischer, M. H., & Rayner, K. (1993). On the functional significance of express saccades. *Behavioral and Brain Sciences, 16*, 577.

Frazier, L., & Rayner, K. (1982). Making and correcting errors during sentence comprehension: Eye movements in the analysis of structurally ambiguous sentences. *Cognitive Psychology, 14*, 178-210.

Garnham, A., Oakhill, J. V., & Cruttenden, H. (1992).The role of implicit causality and gender cue in the interpretation of pronouns. *Language and Cognitive Processes, 7*, 231-255.

Garnham, A., Oakhill, J. V., Ehrlich, M-F., & Carreiras M. (1995). Representations and processes in the interpretation of pronouns: New evidence from Spanish and French. *Journal of Memory and Language, 34*, 41-62.

Garrod, S.C., Freudenthal, S., & Boyle, E. (1994). The role of different types of anaphor in the on-line resolution of sentences in a discourse. *Journal of Memory and Language, 33*, 39-68.

Garrod, S. C. , O'Brien, E. J., Morris, R. K., & Rayner, K. (1990). Elaborative inferencing as an active or passive process. *Journal of Experimental Psychology: Learning, Memory, and Cognition, 16*, 250-257.

Garrod, S. C. & Terras, M. (2000). The contribution of lexical and situational knowledge to resolving discourse roles: Bonding and resolution. Journal of Memory and Language, *42*, 526-544.

Gautier V, O'Regan J K and Le Gargasson J. F. (2000). 'The-skipping' revisited in

French: programming saccades to skip the article 'les'. *Vision Research, 40*, 2517-2531.

Gernsbacher, M. A.(1989). Mechanisms that improve referential access. *Cognition, 32*, 99-156.

Gilman, E., & Underwood, G. (2003). Restricting the field of view to investigate the perceptual spans of pianists. *Visual Cognition, 10*, 201-232.

Gordon, P. C., Hendrick, R., & Foster, K.L. (2000). Language comprehension and probe-list memory. *Journal of Experimental Psychology: Learning, Memory, and Cognition, 26*, 719-750.

Gorfein, D. S. (2001). *On the consequences of meaning selection*. Washington: APA Books.

Greene, H. H., & Rayner, K. (2001). Eye movements and familiarity effects in visual search. *Vision Research, 41*, 3763-3773.

Henderson, J. M., Dixon, P., Petersen, A., Twilley, L. C., & Ferreira, F. (1995). Evidence for the use of phonological representations during transsaccadic word recognition. *Journal of Experimental Psychology: Human Perception and Performance, 21*, 82-97.

Henderson, J. M., & Ferreira, F. (1990). Effects of foveal processing difficulty on the perceptual span in reading: Implications for attention and eye movement control. *Journal of Experimental Psychology: Learning, Memory, and Cognition, 16*, 417-429.

Henderson, J. M., & Ferreira, F. (1993). Eye movement control during reading: Fixation measures reflect foveal but not parafoveal processing difficulty. *Canadian Journal of Experimental Psychology, 47*, 201-221.

Henderson, J. M., & Hollingworth, A. (1998). Eye movements during scene viewing: An overview. In G. Underwood (Ed), *Eye guidance in reading, driving, and scene perception*. Amsterdam: Elsevier.

Heller, D. & Radach, R. (1999). Eye movements in reading: Are two eyes better than one? In W. Becker, W., H. Deubel, & T. Mergner, (Eds.). *Current oculomotor research: Physiological and psychological aspects*, (pp. 341-348). New York: Kluwer Academic, Plenum.

Hooge, I. T. C., & Frens, M. A. (2000). Inhibition of saccade return (ISR): spatial-temporal properties of saccade programming. *Vision Research, 40*, 3415-3426.

Huey, E. B. (1908). *The psychology and pedagogy of reading*. New York: Macmillan.

Hyönä, J. (1993). *Eye movements during reading and discourse processing*. [Psychological Research Rep. No. 65]. Turku, Finland: University of Turku.

Hyönä, J. (1995). Do irregular letter combinations attract readers' attention? Evidence from fixation locations in words. *Journal of Experimental Psychology: Human Perception and Performance, 21*, 68-81.

Hyönä, J., & Pollatsek, A. (1998). Reading Finnish compound words: Eye fixations are affected by component morphemes. *Journal of Experimental Psychology: Human Perception and Performance, 24*, 1612-1627.

Ikeda, M., & Saida, S. (1978). Span of recognition in reading. *Vision Research, 18*, 83-88.

Inhoff, A.W. (1989a). Parafoveal processing of words and saccade computation during eye fixations in reading. *Journal of Experimental Psychology: Human Perception and Performance, 15*, 544-555.

Inhoff, A. W. (1989b). Lexical access during eye fixations in reading: Are word access codes used to integrate lexical information across interword fixations? *Journal of Memory and Language, 28*, 444-461.

Inhoff, A. W., & Liu, W. (1998). The perceptual span and oculomotor activity during the reading of Chinese sentences. *Journal of Experimental Psychology: Human Perception and Performance, 24*, 20-34.

Inhoff, A. W., Pollatsek, A., Posner, M. I., & Rayner, K. (1989). Covert attention and eye movements during reading. *Quarterly Journal of Experimental Psychology,41A*, 63-89.

Inhoff, A.W., Radach, R., & Heller, D. (2000). Complex compounds in German: Interword spaces facilitate segmentation but hinder assignment of meaning. *Journal of Memory and Language, 42*, 23-50.

Inhoff, A. W., & Rayner, K. (1986). Parafoveal word processing during eye fixations in reading: Effects of word frequency. *Perception & Psychophysics, 40*, 431-439.

Inhoff, A. W., Topolski, R., Vitu, F., & O'Regan, J. K. (1993). Attention demands during reading and the occurrence of brief (express) fixations. *Perception & Psychophysics*, 54, 814-823.

Ishida, T. & Ikeda, M. (1989). Temporal properties of information extraction in reading studied by a text-mask replacement technique. *Journal of the Optical Society A: Optics and Image Science*, 6, 1624-1632.

Jared, D., Levy, B. A., & Rayner, K. (1999). The role of phonology in the activation of word meanings during reading: Evidence from proofreading and eye movements. *Journal of Experimental Psychology: General*, 128, 219-264.

Juhasz, B. J., Starr, M. S., Inhoff, A. W., & Placke, L. (2003). The effects of morphology on the processing of compound words: Evidence from naming, lexical decisions and eye fixations. *British Journal of Psychology*, 94, 223-244

Just, M. A., & Carpenter, P.A. (1980). A theory of reading: From eye fixations to comprehension. *Psychological Review*, 87, 329-354.

Kambe, G., Duffy, S. A., Clifton, C., & Rayner, K. (2003). An eye movement contingent probe paradigm. *Psychonomic Bulletin & Review*, 10, 661-666.

Kambe, G., Rayner, K., & Duffy, S. A. (2001). Global context effects on processing lexically ambiguous words. *Memory & Cognition*, 29, 363-372.

Kapoula, Z. A. (1985). Evidence for a range effect in the visual system. *Vision Research*, 25, 1155-1157.

Kapoula, Z. A., & Robinson, D. A. (1986). Saccadic undershoot is not inevitable: Saccades can be accurate. *Vision Research*, 26, 735-743.

Kingstone, A., & Klein, R. M. (1993). What are human express saccades? *Perception & Psychophysics*, 54, 260-273.

Klein, R. (2000). Inhibition of return. *Trends in Cognitive Sciences*, 4, 138-147.

Klein R. M., & MacInnes, W. J. (1999). Inhibition of return is a foraging facilitator in visual search. *Psychological Science*, 10, 346-352

Lima, S. D. (1987). Morphological analysis in sentence reading. *Journal of Memory and Language*, 26, 84-99.

Lima, S. D., & Inhoff, A. W. (1985). Lexical access during eye fixations in reading: Effects of word-initial letter sequences. *Journal of Experimental Psychology: Human Perception and Performance*, 11, 272-285.

Liversedge, S. P., & Findlay, J. M. (2000). Eye movements reflect cognitive processes. *Trends in Cognitive Sciences*, 4, 6-14.

Liversedge, S. P., Paterson, K. B. & Pickering M. J. (1998). Eye movements and measures of reading time. Underwood, G. (Ed.) *Eye guidance in reading and scene perception*, pp 55-75, Elsevier, Oxford.

Liversedge, S. P., Paterson, K. B., & Clayes, E. L. (2002). The influence of *only* on syntactic processing of "long" relative clause sentences. *Quarterly Journal of Experimental Psychology*, 55A, 225-240.

Liversedge, S. P., Rayner, K., White, S. J., Vergilino-Perez, D., Findlay, J. M., & Kentridge, R. W., (2004). Eye movements when reading disappearing text: Is there a gap effect in reading? *Vision Research*, in press.

Maylor E. (1985). Facilitatory and inhibitory components of orienting in visual space. In M. I. Posner and O. S. M. Marin (Eds.), *Attention and performance XI*, pp 189-202. Hillsdale, NJ: Lawrence Erlbaum..

MacDonald, M. C. (1994). Probabilistic constraints and syntactic ambiguity resolution. *Language and Cognitive Processes*, 9, 157-201.

MacDonald, M. C., Pearlmutter, N. J., & Seidenberg, M. S. (1994a). The lexical nature of syntactic ambiguity resolution. *Psychological Review*, 101, 676-703.

MacDonald, M. C., Pearlmutter, N. J., & Seidenberg, M. S. (1994b). Syntactic ambiguity resolution as lexical ambiguity resolution. In C. Clifton, Jr., L. Frazier, and K. Rayner(Eds.), *Perspectives on sentence processing*. Hillsdale, NJ: Erlbaum.

McConkie, G. W., & Currie, C. B. (1996). Visual stability across saccades while viewing complex pictures. *Journal of Experimental Psychology: Human Perception and Performance*, 22, 563-581.

McConkie, G. W., Kerr, P. W., Reddix, M. D., & Zola, D. (1988). Eye movement control during reading: I. The location of initial eye fixations in words. *Vision Research, 28,* 1107-1118.

McConkie, G. W., Kerr, P. W., Reddix, M. D., Zola, D., & Jacobs, A. M. (1989). Eye movement control during reading: II. Frequency of refixating a word. *Perception & Psychophysics, 46,* 245-253.

McConkie, G. W., & Rayner, K. (1975). The span of the effective stimulus during a fixation in reading. *Perception & Psychophysics, 17,* 578-586.

McConkie, G. W., & Rayner, K. (1976). Asymmetry of the perceptual span in reading. *Bulletin of the Psychonomic Society, 8,* 365-368.

McConkie, G. W., & Zola, D. (1979). Is visual information integrated across successive fixations in reading? *Perception & Psychophysics, 25,* 221-224.

McDonald, J. L., & MacWhinney, B. (1995). The time course of anaphor resolution: Effects if implicit verb causality and gender. *Journal of Memory and Language, 34,* 543-566.

Meseguer, E., Carreiras, M., & Clifton, C. (2002).Overt reanalysis strategies and eye movements during the reading of garden path sentences. *Memory & Cognition, 30,* 551-561.

Morris, R. K. (1994). Lexical and message-level sentence context effects on fixation times in reading. *Journal of Experimental Psychology: Learning, Memory, and Cognition, 20,* 92-103.

Morris, R.K., Rayner, K., & Pollatsek, A. (1990). Eye movement guidance in reading: The role of parafoveal letter and space information. *Journal of Experimental Psychology: Human Perception and Performance, 16,* 268-281.

Morrison, R. E. (1984). Manipulation of stimulus onset delay in reading: Evidence for parallel programming of saccades. *Journal of Experimental Psychology: Human Perception and Performance, 10,* 667-682.

Ni, W., Crain, S., & Shankweiler, D. (1996). Sidestepping garden paths: The contribution of syntax, semantics and plausibility in resolving ambiguities. *Language and Cognitive Processes, 11,* 283-334.

Niswander, E., Pollatsek, A., & Rayner, K. (2000). The processing of derived and inflected suffixed words during reading. *Language and Cognitive Processes, 15,* 389-420.

O'Brien, E. J., Raney, G. E., Albrecht, J. E., & Rayner, K. (1997). Processes involved in the resolution of explicit anaphors. *Discourse Processes, 23,* 1-24.

O'Brien, E. J., Shank, D. M., Myers, J. L., & Rayner, K. (1988). Elaborative inferences during reading: Do they occur on-line? *Journal of Experimental Psychology: Learning, Memory, and Cognition, 14,* 410-420.

O'Regan, J. K. (1979). Eye guidance in reading: Evidence for linguistic control hypothesis. *Perception & Psychophysics, 25,* 501-509.

O'Regan, J. K. (1980). The control of saccade size and fixation duration in reading: The limits of linguistic control. *Perception & Psychophysics, 28,* 112-117.

O'Regan, J. K. (1992). Optimal viewing position in words and the strategy-tactics theory of eye movements in reading. In K. Rayner (ed.), *Eye movements and visual cognition: Scene perception and reading* (pp. 333-354). Springer-Verlag.

O'Regan, J. K., & Lévy-Schoen, A. (1987). Eye movement strategy and tactics in word recognition and reading. In M. Coltheart (ed), *Attention and performance XII: The psychology of reading* (pp 363-383). Erlbaum.

O'Regan, J. K., Lévy-Schoen, A., Pynte, J., & Brugaillère, B. (1984). Convenient fixation location within isolated words of different length and structure. *Journal of Experimental Psychology: Human Perception and Performance,10,* 250-257.

Osaka, N. (1987). Effect of peripheral visual field size upon eye movements during Japanese text processing. In J. K. O'Regan & A. Lévy-Schoen (eds.), *Eye movements: From physiology to cognition* (pp. 421-429). North Holland.

Osaka, N. (1992). Size of saccade and fixation duration of eye movements during reading: Psychophysics of Japanese text processing. *Journal of the Optical Society of America, 9,* 5-13.

Paterson, K.B., Liversedge, S.P., & Underwood, G., (1998). Quantificational constraints on parsing "short" relative clause sentences. *Quarterly Journal of Experimental Psychology*, 52A, 717-737.

Pearlmutter, N. J., & MacDonald, M. C. (1992). Plausibility and syntactic ambiguity resolution. In *Proceedings of the 14th Annual Conference of the Cognitive Society* (pp. 498-503). Hillsdale, NJ: Erlbaum.

Pollatsek, A., Bolozky, S., Well, A. D., & Rayner K. (1981). Asymmetries in the perceptual span for Israeli readers. *Brain and Language*, 14, 174-180.

Pollatsek, A., Hyönä J., & Bertram, R. (2000). The role of morphological constituents in reading Finnish compound words. *Journal of Experimental Psychology: Human Perception and Performance*. 26, 820-833.

Pollatsek, A., Lesch, M., Morris, R. K., & Rayner, K. (1992). Phonological codes are used in integrating information across saccades in word identification and reading. *Journal of Experimental Psychology: Human Perception and Performance, 18*, 148-162.

Pollatsek, A., & Rayner, K. (1982). Eye movement control in reading: The role of word boundaries. *Journal of Experimental Psychology: Human Perception and Performance, 8*, 817-833.

Pollatsek, A., Rayner, K., & Balota, D.A. (1986). Inferences about eye movement control from the perceptual span in reading. *Perception & Psychophysics, 40*, 123-130.

Pollatsek, A., Raney, G. E., LaGasse, L., & Rayner, K. (1993). The use of information below fixation in reading and in visual search. *Canadian Journal of Experimental Psychology, 47*, 179-200.

Pomplun, M., Reingold, E. M., & Shen, J. (2001). Peripheral and parafoveal cueing and masking effects on saccadic selectivity in a gaze-contingent window paradigm. *Vision Research, 41*, 2757-2769.

Posner, M. I., & Cohen, A. (1984). Components of visual orienting. In H. Bouma & D. Bouwhuis (Eds.), *Attention and performance 10* (pp. 531-556). London: Erlbaum.

Posner, M. I., Rafal, R. D., Choate, L., & Vaughan, J. (1985). Inhibition of return: Neural basis and function. *Cognitive Neuropsychology, 2*, 211-228.

Prinz, W. (1984). Attention and sensitivity in visual search. *Psychological Research, 45*, 355-366.

Radach, R., & Kempe, V. (1993). An individual analysis of initial fixation positions in reading. In G. d'Ydewalle, & J. Van Rensbergen (Eds.), *Perception and cognition: Advances in eye movement research* (pp. 213-226). Amsterdam: Elsevier.

Radach, R., & McConkie, G. W. (1998). Determinants of fixation positions in words during reading. In G. Underwood (ed.), *Eye guidance in reading, driving, and scene perception*. Oxford: Elsevier.

Rafal, R. D., Egly, R., & Rhodes, D. (1994). Effects of inhibition of return on voluntary and visually guided saccades. *Canadian Journal of Experimental Psychology, 48*, 284-300.

Rayner, K. (1975). The perceptual span and peripheral cues in reading. *Cognitive Psychology, 7*, 65-81.

Rayner, K. (1977). Visual attention in reading: Eye movements reflect cognitive processes. *Memory & Cognition, 4*, 443-448.

Rayner, K. (1978a). Eye movements in reading and information processing. *Psychological Bulletin, 85*, 618-660.

Rayner, K. (1978b). Eye movement latencies for parafoveally presented words. *Bulletin of the Psychonomic Society, 11*, 13-16.

Rayner, K. (1979). Eye guidance in reading: Fixation locations within words. *Perception, 8*, 21-30.

Rayner, K. (1986). Eye movements and the perceptual span in beginning and skilled readers. *Journal of Experimental Child Psychology, 41*, 211-236.

Rayner, K. (1995). Eye movements and cognitive processes in reading, visual search, and scene perception. In J.M. Findlay, R. Walker, and R.W. Kentridge (Eds.), *Eye movement research: Mechanisms, processes and applications* (pp 3-22). Amsterdam: North Holland.

Rayner, K. (1998). Eye movements in reading and information processing: 20 years of research. *Psychological Bulletin, 124*, 372-422.

Rayner, K., Balota, D. A., & Pollatsek, A. (1986). Against parafoveal semantic preprocessing during eye fixations in reading. *Canadian Journal of Psychology, 40,* 473-483.

Rayner, K., & Bertera, J. H. (1979). Reading without a fovea. *Science, 206,* 468-469.

Rayner, K., & Duffy, S. A. (1986). Lexical complexity and fixation times in reading: Effects of word frequency, verb complexity, and lexical ambiguity. *Memory & Cognition, 14,* 191-201.

Rayner, K., & Fisher, D. L. (1987). Letter processing during eye fixations in visual search. *Perception & Psychophysics, 42,* 87-100.

Rayner, K., Fischer, M.H., & Pollatsek, A. (1998). Unspaced text interferes with both word identification and eye movement control. *Vision Research,* 38, 1129-1144.

Rayner, K., Inhoff, A. W., Morrison, R., Slowiaczek, M. L., & Bertera, J. H. (1981). Masking of foveal and parafoveal vision during eye fixations in reading. *Journal of Experimental Psychology: Human Perception and Performance, 7,* 167-179.

Rayner, R., Juhasz, B., Ashby, J., & Clifton, C. (2003). Inhibition of saccade return in reading. *Vision Research, 43,* 1027-1034.

Rayner, K., Kambe, G., & Duffy, S. A. (2000). The effect of clause wrap-up on eye movements during reading. *Quarterly Journal of Experimental Psychology, 53A,* 1061-1080.

Rayner, K., Liversedge, S. P., White, S. J. & Vergilino-Perez, D., (2003). Reading disappearing text: Cognitive control of eye movements. *Psychological Science,* 14, 385-388.

Rayner, K., McConkie, G. W., & Zola, D. (1980). Integrating information across eye movements. *Cognitive Psychology, 12,* 206-226.

Rayner, K., & Morris, R. K. (1992). Eye movement control in reading: Evidence against semantic preprocessing. *Journal of Experimental Psychology: Human Perception and Performance, 18,* 163-172.

Rayner, K., & Pollatsek, A. (1981). Eye movement control during reading: Evidence for direct control. *Quarterly Journal of Experimental Psychology, 33A,* 351-373.

Rayner, K., Pollatsek, A., & Binder, K. S. (1998). Phonological codes and eye movements in reading. *Journal of Experimental Psychology: Learning, Memory, and Cognition, 24,* 476-497.

Rayner, K., Reichle, A. D., & Pollatsek, A. (1998). Eye movement control in reading: An overview and model. In G. Underwood (ed), *Eye guidance in reading, driving, and scene perception.* Oxford: Elsevier.

Rayner, K., & Sereno, S. C. (1994a). Eye movements in reading: Psycholinguistic studies. In M. Gernsbacher (Ed.), *Handbook of psycholinguistics.* New York: Academic Press.

Rayner, K., & Sereno, S. C. (1994b). Regressive eye movements and sentence parsing: On the use of regression-contingent analyses. *Memory & Cognition, 22,* 281-285

Rayner, K., Sereno, S. C., Lesch, M. F., & Pollatsek, A. (1995). Phonological codes are automatically activated during reading: Evidence from an eye movement priming paradigm. *Psychological Science, 6,* 26-32.

Rayner, K., Sereno, S. C., & Raney, G. E. (1996). Eye movement control in reading: A comparison of two types of models. *Journal of Experimental Psychology: Human Perception and Performance, 22,* 1188-1200.

Rayner, K., Sereno, S.C., Morris, R.K., Schmauder, A.R., & Clifton, C. (1989). Eye movements and on-line language comprehension processes. *Language and Cognition Processes, 4*(Special issue), 21-49.

Rayner, K., Slowiaczek, M. L., Clifton, C., & Bertera, J. H. (1983). Latency of sequential eye movements: Implications for reading. *Journal of Experimental Psychology: Human Perception and Performance, 9,* 912-922.

Rayner, K., & Well, A. D. (1996). Effects of contextual constraint on eye movements in reading: A further examination. *Psychonomic Bulletin & Review, 3,* 504-509.

Rayner, K., Well, A. D., & Pollatsek, A. (1980). Asymmetry of the effective visual field in reading. *Perception & Psychophysics, 27,* 537-544.

Rayner, K., Well, A. D., Pollatsek, A., & Bertera, J. H. (1982). The availability of useful information to the right of fixation in reading. *Perception & Psychophysics, 31,* 537-550.

Reichle, E. D., Pollatsek, A., Fisher, D. L., & Rayner, K. (1998). Toward a model of eye movement control in reading. *Psychological Review, 105*, 125-157.

Reichle, E. D., Rayner, K., & Pollatsek, A. (1999). Eye movement control in reading: accounting for initial fixation locations and refixations within the E-Z reader model. *Vision Research, 39*, 4403-4411.

Reichle, E. D., Rayner, K., & Pollatsek, A. (2003). The E-Z Reader model of eye movement control in reading: Comparisons to other models. *Behavioral and Brain Sciences, 26*, 445-526.

Reingold, E. M., Charness, N., Pomplun, M., & Stampe, D. M. (2001). Visual span in expert chess players: Evidence from eye movements. *Psychological Science, 12*, 48-55.

Reingold, E .M., & Stampe, D. M. (2002). Saccadic inhibition in voluntary and reflexive saccades. *Journal of Cognitive Neuroscience, 14*, 371-388.

Rensink R.A., O'Regan J.K., and Clark J.J. (1997). To see or not to see: The need for attention to perceive changes in scenes. *Psychological Science, 8*, 368-373.

Rigalleau, F., & Caplan, D., (2000). Effects of gender marking in pronoun coindexation. *Quarterly Journal of Experimental Psychology: Human Experimental Psychology, 53A*, 23-52.

Ro, T., Pratt, J., & Rafal, R. D. (2000). Inhibition of return in saccadic eye movements. *Experimental Brain Research, 130*, 264-268.

Rooth, M. (1992). A theory of focus interpretation. *Natural Language Semantics, 1*, 75-116.

Saida, S., & Ikeda, M. (1979). Useful field size for pattern perception. *Perception & Psychophysics, 25*, 119-125.

Salthouse, T. A., & Ellis, C.L. (1980). Determinants of eye-fixation duration. *American Journal of Psychology, 93*, 207-234.

Salthouse, T. A., Ellis, C. L., Diener, D. C., & Somberg, B. L. (1981). Stimulus processing during eye fixations. *Journal of Experimental Psychology: Human Perception and Performance, 7*, 611-623.

Saslow, M. G. (1967a) Effects of components of displacement-step stimuli upon latency for saccadic eye movement. *Journal of the Optical Society of America, 57*, 1024-29.

Sedivy, J. C. (2002) Invoking discourse-based contrast sets and resolving syntactic ambiguities. *Journal of Memory and Language, 46*, 341-370.

Sereno, S.C. (1995). Resolution of lexical ambiguity: Evidence from an eye movement priming paradigm. *Journal of Experimental Psychology: Learning, Memory, and Cognition, 21*, 582-595.

Sereno, S. C., & Rayner, K. (1992). Fast priming during eye fixations in reading. *Journal of Experimental Psychology: Human Perception and Performance, 18*, 173-184.

Shillcock, R., Ellison, T. M. & Monaghan, P. (2000). Eye-fixation behaviour, lexical storage and visual word recognition in a split processing model. *Psychological Review, 107*, 824-851.

Slowiaczek, M. L., & Rayner, K. (1987). Sequential masking during eye fixations in reading. *Bulletin of the Psychonomic Society, 25*, 175-178.

Smith, K. U., Schremser, R., & Putz, V. (1971). Binocular coordination in reading. *Journal of Applied Psychology, 55*, 251-258.

Spivey-Knowlton, M. J., & Sedivy, J. (1994). Resolving attachment ambiguities with multiple constraints. *Cognition, 55*, 227-267.

Starr, M. S., & Rayner, K. (2001). Eye movements during reading: Some current controversies. *Trends in Cognitive Sciences, 5*, 156-163.

Stevenson, R. J., & Vitkovitch, M. (1986). The comprehension of anaphoric relations. *Language and Speech, 29*, 335-360.

Stewart, A.J., Pickering, M.J. & Sanford, A.J. (2000) The time course of the influence of implicit causality information: Focusing versus integration accounts. *Journal of Memory & Language, 42*, 423-443.

Tabossi, P., Spivey-Knowlton, M. J., McRae, K., & Tanenhaus, M. K. (1994). Semantic effects on syntactic ambiguity resolution: Evidence for a constraint-based resolution process. In C. Umilta & M. Moscovitch (Eds.), *Attention and Performance XV* (pp. 589-616). Cambridge, MA: MIT Press.

Traxler, M. J., Pickering, M. J., & Clifton, C., Jr. (1998). Adjunct attachment is not a form of lexical ambiguity resolution. *Journal of Memory and Language, 39,* 558-592.

Trueswell, J. C., Tanenhaus, M. K., & Garnsey, S. M. (1994). Semantic influences on parsing: Use of thematic role information in syntactic ambiguity resolution. *Journal of Memory and Language, 33,* 285-318.

Trueswell, J. C., Tanenhaus, M. K., & Kello, C. (1993). Verb-specific constraints in sentence processing: Separating effects of lexical preference from garden-paths. *Journal of Experimental Psychology: Learning, Memory, and Cognition, 19,* 528-553.

Truitt, F. E., Clifton, C., Pollatsek, A., & Rayner, K. (1997). The perceptual span and the eye hand span in sight reading music. *Visual Cognition, 4,* 143-162.

Underwood, N. R., & McConkie, G. W. (1985). Perceptual span for letter distinctions during reading. *Reading Research Quarterly, 20,* 153-162.

van Diepen, P. M. J., Ruelens, L., & d'Ydewalle, G. (1999). Brief foveal masking during scene perception. *Acta Psychologica, 101,* 91-103.

van Diepen, P. M. J. & Wampers, M. (1998). Scene exploration with Fourier-filtered peripheral information. *Perception, 27,* 1141-1151.

van Gompel, R. P. G., Pickering, M. J., & Traxler, M. J. (2000). Unrestricted race: A new model of syntactic ambiguity resolution. In: A. Kennedy, R. Radach, D. Heller, & J. Pynte (Eds.), *Reading as a perceptual process.* Oxford: Elsevier, 621-648.

van Gompel, R. P. G., & Liversedge, S.P. (2002). The influence of morphological information on cataphoric pronoun assignment. *Journal of Experimental Psychology: Learning, Memory and Cognition, 29,* 128-139.

Vaughan, J. (1984). Saccades directed at previously attended locations in space. In A. G. Gale & F. Johnson (Eds.), *Theoretical and applied aspects of eye movement research* (pp 143-150). Amsterdam: North Holland.

Vitu, F. (1991). Against the existence of a range effect during reading. *Vision Research, 31,* 2009-2015.

Vitu, F., McConkie, G. W., Kerr, P., & O'Regan, J. K. (2001). Fixation location effects on fixation durations during reading: an inverted optimal viewing position effect. *Vision Research, 41,* 3513-3533.

Vitu, F., O'Regan, J.K., & Mittau, M. (1990). Optimal landing position in reading isolated words and continuous text. *Perception & Psychophysics, 47,* 583-600.

Vonk, W. (1984). Eye movements during comprehension of pronouns. In A. G. Gale & F. Johnson (eds.), *Theoretical and applied aspects of eye movement research* (pp. 203-212). Amsterdam: North Holland.

Walker R., Kentridge R. W., & Findlay J. M., (1995). Independent contributions of the orienting of attention, fixation offset and bilateral stimulation on human saccadic latencies. *Experimental Brain Research, 103,* 294-310.

Wenban-Smith M. G., & Findlay, J. M. (1991). Express saccades : Is there a separate population in humans? *Experimental Brain Research, 87,* 218-222.

White, S. J., & Liversedge, S.P. (2004a). Orthographic familiarity influences initial eye fixation positions in reading. *European Journal of Cognitive Psychology, 16,* 52-78.

White, S. J., & Liversedge, S.P. (2004b). Orthographic regularity influences the eyes' landing positions in reading, submitted.

Williams, R. A., & Fender, D. H. (1977). The synchrony of binocular saccadic eye movements. *Vision Research, 17,* 303-306.

Yang, S.-N., & McConkie, G. W. (2001). Eye movements during reading: a theory of saccade initiation times. *Vision Research, 41,* 3567-3585.

3

Fixation Location and Fixation Duration as Indices of Cognitive Processing

DAVID E. IRWIN

INTRODUCTION

*T*he use of eye movements to study cognitive processing is increasing rapidly. Although eye movements have long been used to study reading (Huey, 1908) and more recently to study various issues in perception and memory (see Rayner, 1978, 1998, for comprehensive reviews), the development of less-expensive and easier-to-use eyetrackers, coupled with the ready availability of powerful computers and display devices, has allowed innovative researchers to conduct sophisticated and groundbreaking research into increasingly complex areas of cognitive functioning, ranging from the perception and representation of pictures of real-world scenes (e.g., Henderson & Hollingworth, 1999; Hollingworth & Henderson, 2002; Ryan, Althoff, Whitlow, & Cohen, 2000) to the processes involved in online auditory sentence comprehension (e.g., Tanenhaus, Spivey-Knowlton, Eberhard, & Sedivy, 1995; see also the chapters by Tanenhaus and Altmann in this volume) and sentence production (e.g. Griffin & Bock, 2000; Meyer, Sleiderink, & Levelt, 1998; see also the chapters by Bock, Irwin, & Davidson, by Griffin, and by Meyer, in this volume).

Eye position may seem to be an ideal dependent variable because eye movements are a natural and frequently occurring human behavior; people typically look at something when they want to acquire information from it. It may thus seem reasonable to assume that fixation location corresponds to the spatial locus of cognitive processing and that fixation or gaze duration corresponds to the duration of cognitive processing of the material located at fixation. This idea was expressed most forcefully in *the eye-mind assumption* in the theory of reading proposed by Just and Carpenter (1980): "the eye remains fixated on a word as long as the word is being processed. So the time it takes to process a newly fixated word is directly indicated by the gaze duration" (p. 330).

There are several problems that complicate the interpretation of eye-movement data, however. In this chapter I focus on four specific issues: 1) the locus of cognitive processing may include not only the fixation location, but areas of space much wider than that; 2) the locus of cognitive processing can be, and frequently is, dissociated from fixation location; 3) the control of eye position is not always under cognitive control; and 4) cognitive processing can occur during eye movements as well as during eye fixations. The existence of these problems means that although fixation location and fixation duration are valuable dependent measures, they do not necessarily provide completely precise and accurate information about the locus and duration of cognitive processing under all circumstances. As I discuss below, these problems are particularly troublesome for studies involving picture perception, visual search, and everyday vision, but less so for studies of reading.

FIXATION LOCATION
AND THE FUNCTIONAL FIELD OF VIEW

A single eye fixation provides a view of the world that is roughly elliptical, approximately 200 deg of visual angle wide and 130 deg high (Harrington, 1981). Thus, the binocular visual field encompasses an area of about 20,000 deg square. In principle, therefore, a large amount of information is available in a single glance. Various limitations of the visual system and of the cognitive processing system restrict considerably our ability to perceive and process information from this vast area, however. The distribution and characteristics of rods and cones, for example, limit our perception of color in the periphery and of dim light in the fovea. Our best visual acuity is provided by foveal vision, corresponding to the center of our gaze, but the fovea is very small, subtending only approximately 3 deg square. Visual acuity drops rapidly as distance increases from the fovea, being reduced by 50% at 5 deg from the fovea and by 90% at 40 deg from the fovea (Hochberg, 1978). The limited-capacity nature of the cognitive system restricts us even further, often making it impossible for us to process all information from the environment even when visual acuity is not an issue. Because of these limitations, we must direct visual-spatial attention from one region of space to another to select specific stimulus information for further processing from the vast array of information that is available. Visual-spatial attention can be directed either overtly, by moving the eyes and/or body to foveate a visual target, or covertly, by allocating cognitive resources to process information arising from an object or region of space without orienting the eyes or body to it (see chapter by Findlay in this volume).

Eyetrackers equate fixation location with the center of gaze, the fovea, and thus fixation duration corresponds to the amount of time that the fovea is directed at some location. Although vision is most acute at the fovea, cognitive processing is not restricted to this location. Rather, there is a *functional*, or *useful, field of view* surrounding the fixation location from which information is processed during the execution of any visual task (e.g., Mackworth, 1976). This region has also been called the *perceptual span* or *span of the effective stimulus* (McConkie & Rayner, 1975). The size of the functional field of view depends upon the nature of the task, the number of items in the visual field, and whether other cognitive demands are placed on the subject.

For example, several studies have investigated the detection and identification of isolated objects in peripheral vision. Geissler (1926) reported that simple geometric forms presented monocularly could be identified accurately even when they were presented 25 deg of visual angle from the fovea, while Munn and Geil (1931) found that binocular discrimination of these forms could be performed accurately up to 45 deg from the center of gaze. More recently, Menzer and Thurmond (1970) found in a forced-choice task that solid-surface polygons could be identified above chance even when they appeared 80 degrees away from the fixation point. All of these studies demonstrate that the locus of cognitive processing is not necessarily restricted to the center of fixation, but, rather, can extend far into the visual periphery.

Edwards and Goolkasian (1974) compared performance on four different tasks at four different distances from the fovea. The four tasks were detection of light onset, recognition of the position of a U-shaped figure, letter identification, and categorization of three-letter words. They found that all four tasks could be performed accurately at 10 deg from central fixation, but only detection, recognition, and identification could be performed accurately at 15 and 25 deg from the fovea. At 58 deg from the center of fixation, only detection of light onset was possible. Thus, this study shows that the size of the functional field of view depends on the task that the subject has to perform.

While the studies reviewed above show that information can be extracted from single objects far into the visual periphery, others have shown that the functional field of view is much smaller when multiple items are present in a display. For example, Viviani and Swenson (1982) found that subjects could accurately locate a star-shaped target among 15 disk-shaped distractors when the target appeared 4.1 deg from the fixation point but not when it appeared

12.7 deg away. Using a moving-window technique (in which a window moves in synchrony with the eyes, so that only part of the visual field is exposed), Bertera and Rayner (2000) found that the effective span for visual search (for a target letter among distractor letters) was 5 deg around the fixation point. Target-distractor similarity has a large effect on the size of the functional visual field in visual search studies such as these, however; for example, Engel (1971) found that detecting a single short line in a field of slightly longer lines was nearly impossible unless the short line was fixated exactly, while more discriminable objects such as a U-shaped figure or a square could be detected up to 4 deg and 10 deg away from fixation, respectively (see also Findlay, 1997; Rayner & Fisher, 1987).

The size of the functional visual field has also been studied in reading and in picture viewing. In reading, Rayner and colleagues (e.g., McConkie & Rayner, 1975; Rayner, 1975; Rayner, Well, & Pollatsek, 1980; Rayner, 1986; see also the chapter by Rayner & Liversedge in this volume) have found that gross visual characteristics such as word shape and initial and final letter identities can be extracted about 1 deg to the left of fixation and about 5 deg to the right of fixation (for readers of left-to-right languages such as English), but semantic information is available only at the fovea. In recognition tests following picture viewing, Nelson and Loftus (1980) found that detection of a critical visual detail depended upon its distance from the nearest fixation; they estimated that the functional visual field was 2.6 deg from the point of fixation (see also, Saida & Ikeda, 1979; Shioiri & Ikeda, 1989). Henderson, Williams, Castelhano, and Falk (2003) estimated that useful information about object presence and object identity in pictures of full-color scenes is limited to a region less than 4.5 deg around the fovea. Using less detailed pictorial stimuli (line drawings that contained only six objects), Parker (1978) estimated that useful information about a picture was available from a region subtending 6.5 to 10 deg around the fovea.

The results of the preceding studies indicate that the size of the useful field of view depends on several factors, such as scene composition and the nature of the task being performed. Some of this variability is most likely due to low-level perceptual factors such as acuity limitations and lateral inhibition in the visual pathway (Bouma, 1978). The cognitive load or attentional processing demands required by a task (or by tasks performed concurrently) also influences the size of the functional field of view, however. Several studies have shown that a "foveal load" (i.e., requiring a judgment to a stimulus presented at the fovea) reduces the size of the functional visual field. For example, Ikeda and Takeuchi (1975) presented subjects a load stimulus at the fovea and a peripheral target stimulus (a star) in a field of distractors (distorted triangles). Subjects were required to report the foveal load (which varied across four levels of difficulty), then the location of the target stimulus. Ikeda and Takeuchi found that the size of the functional field of view decreased as foveal load difficulty increased, such that the functional field under the heaviest load condition was roughly two-thirds the size of the functional field when there was no foveal load (for similar findings, see Leibowitz & Appelle, 1969; Pomplun, Reingold, & Shen, 2001; Webster & Haslerud, 1964). In reading, Henderson and Ferreira (1990) found that the size of the perceptual span in reading became smaller (i.e., less information was acquired from the parafovea) when word processing at the fovea was difficult.

The preceding studies demonstrate that dividing attention reduces the size of the useful field of view; perhaps not surprisingly, then, there is also evidence that directing or focusing attention appropriately can increase the size of the useful field of view. For example, Grindley and Townsend (1968) found that a directional attention cue (i.e., an arrow pointing toward the target location) increased the retinal eccentricity at which a target stimulus could be detected, as long as other items were also in the visual field (see also Engel, 1971; Henderson, 1996; Ikeda & Takeuchi, 1975). In reading, Rayner et al. (1980) argued that the asymmetric (biased to the right) effective visual field is due to attentional factors tied to the direction of eye movements. This argument was supported by the finding that bilingual Israeli readers have effective visual fields that are asymmetric to the left while reading Hebrew and asymmetric to the right while reading English (Pollatsek, Bolozky, Well, & Rayner, 1981). Henderson, Pollatsek, and Rayner (1989) also found that eye-movement direction produced a perceptual span asymmetry in the processing of pictures of objects.

Finally, there are also substantial individual differences in the size of the functional field of view. It is well known that the size of the functional field of view declines with age (e.g., Ball, Beard, Roenker, Miller, & Griggs, 1988; Scialfa, Thomas, & Joffe, 1994; Sekuler & Ball, 1986), for example, but Pringle, Irwin, Kramer, and Atchley (2001) found that even within a group of 25 young subjects (mean age = 23 years) that the size of the functional field of view varied from 12 to 28 degs of visual angle in a simple visual search task in which subjects had to localize an oblique line appearing among 11 vertical distractors. They also found that the size of the functional visual field correlated strongly with the time it took subjects to detect a change between two alternating versions of a picture (i.e., in a change-detection task), presumably because more attentional "samples" were required to detect the change when one had a smaller useful field of view. Reingold, Charness, Pomplun, and Stampe (2001) also found large individual differences in perceptual span between novice and expert chess players viewing a chess board; the experts had dramatically larger perceptual spans when viewing meaningful, but not random, chess positions.

Summary and Implications

The research summarized above indicates that eye position (i.e., the position of the fovea) is not necessarily an accurate index of the spatial locus of cognitive processing. Rather, it is possible that information is being extracted and interpreted from a large area around the fixation location, with the size of this region dependent upon the number of items in the display, their similarity to each other, the task to be performed upon them, the presence of concurrent processing demands, cues for the guidance of visual attention, and subject characteristics such as age and knowledge of the stimulus domain. Thus, merely knowing where the fovea is pointing is not sufficient to specify precisely what information a subject is processing from a visual display and how effectively it is represented and interpreted by the cognitive system. Although it seems reasonable to assume that information at the fovea is being processed during a fixation, it seems likely that information outside the fovea is being processed as well, muddying the interpretation of temporal variables such as fixation duration. In the next section I review evidence that indicates that the interpretation of fixation location and fixation duration data is even more vexed because the locus of cognitive processing can be, and frequently is, completely separate from fixation location.

EYE POSITION, EYE MOVEMENTS, AND THE LOCUS OF VISUAL ATTENTION

As noted above, our vision is most acute at the fovea, the center of gaze. In order to make out the fine details of objects in the world around us, we must reposition the fovea so that it is directed at these objects. We typically do this three or four times each second by making rapid eye movements called *saccades*. In recent years several studies have demonstrated that covert visual attention actually precedes the eyes' overt movement to a location in space. That is, the detection and the identification of stimulus items presented at the saccade target location are facilitated relative to items presented at other spatial locations (e.g., Currie, McConkie, Carlson-Radvansky, & Irwin, 2000; Deubel & Schneider, 1996; Henderson, 1993; Henderson & Hollingworth, 2003; Henderson et al., 1989; Hoffman & Subramaniam, 1995; Klein, 1980; Klein & Pontefract, 1994; Kowler, Anderson, Dosher, & Blaser, 1995; Rayner, McConkie, & Ehrlich, 1978; Shepherd, Findlay, & Hockey, 1986). This occurs even if the stimulus is presented and removed before the saccade actually occurs and even if subjects are instructed to attend to a location other than the saccade target (e.g., Deubel & Schneider, 1996; Hoffman & Subramaniam, 1995; Kowler et al., 1995).

Consider the study by Deubel and Schneider (1996), for example. In one experiment, each trial began with the presentation of a small fixation cross in the center of the screen. Then, two strings of characters appeared left and right of the fixation cross; each string consisted of five figure-8 characters. Each character was approximately 0.5 deg wide and the distance between characters was approximately 1 deg; the central character in each string was centered 5 deg away from the fixation cross. The three central characters in each string were set on ellipses that were colored red, green, and blue. After a delay of 700 ms, the central fixation cross turned into an arrow colored red, green, or blue that pointed to the right or to the left. The pointing direction of the arrow signified saccade direction, while the color of the arrow signified to which location (colored ellipse) the eyes should be sent. After a further delay of 500 - 1000 ms (during which time the subject was instructed to program a saccade to the designated location) the arrow disappeared. This cued the subject to execute the saccade. Sixty ms later the figure-8 characters changed into nine distractor characters (randomly selected among "2" and "5") and one target character, either an "E" or a reversed "E." The target character always appeared on the side indicated by the arrow cue, but appeared with equal probability in one of the three colored ellipses (i.e., not always at the saccade target location). The target and distractor characters remained visible for 120 ms and were then removed from the screen, leaving only the colored ellipses behind. The subject attempted to report which target character had been presented ("E" vs. reversed "E") after moving their eyes to the cued ellipse. Mean saccade latency was 225 ms, which meant the characters disappeared well before the eyes actually moved away from central fixation. Of major interest was the finding that discrimination accuracy for the target character ("E" vs. reversed "E") was much higher when the target character appeared at the saccade target location (approximately 83% correct) than when it appeared in another, nearby location (approximately 56% correct). These results indicate that even before the eyes left the central fixation cross, the subject's attentional processing resources had been allocated to the saccade target location, thereby facilitating target discrimination. In other words, the locus of cognitive processing was separate from the locus of fixation. Deubel and Schneider (1996) found that the actual landing position of the saccade had very little effect on discrimination accuracy, suggesting that attention was allocated to the intended saccade target location rather than being bound to the actual landing position of the eyes.

In a second experiment, Deubel and Schneider (1996) showed that attention was allocated to the saccade target location even if subjects were instructed to attend to a different location in the display. The procedure for this experiment was identical to that described above, except that subjects knew that the target character would always appear at the center position of the character string. Despite this, discrimination accuracy was high only when the target location corresponded to the saccade target location. Even though subjects knew where the target would appear (and hence where they should allocate their attention), discrimination accuracy was approximately 60%, when the eyes moved to a location different from the target location, and approximately 80%, when the eyes moved to the location that corresponded to where the discrimination target was presented. These results indicate that when a saccade is made to some location, covert visual attention precedes the eyes to that location in an obligatory and involuntary fashion (see Hoffman & Subramaniam, 1995, and Kowler et al., 1995, for similar results). People apparently cannot direct their covert visual attention to one position in space while moving their eyes to a different position.

The fact that covert visual attention precedes overt movements of the eyes to positions in space indicates that the spatial locus of cognitive processing is not always tied to eye (fovea) position, but rather, with every saccade, is directed elsewhere (specifically, to the target of the next saccade). Furthermore, there is evidence that these saccade-induced shifts of visual attention not only facilitate stimulus processing at the saccade target location, but also influence the contents of mental representations as well. For example, consider a study by Irwin (1992). In this study, subjects were presented with an array of letters while they fixated a central point. A peripheral saccade target was then presented that indicated the direction that the eyes should move. The array of letters disappeared as soon as the eyes began to move. Following the eye movement, a partial-report cue (i.e., a bar marker) appeared near one of the previously occupied array positions. Subjects were required to report the letter that had been presented in the spatial location indicated by the report cue. Thus, in order to respond correctly, subjects had to remember the position and the identity of the cued letter across the eye movement. Irwin found that subjects could remember only three to four letters (i.e., position + identity units) across an eye movement, regardless of the number of letters presented in the letter array. Report of the letters spatially near the saccade target was much more accurate than report of other letters in the array, however. This suggests that information near the saccade target was more likely to be attended and encoded into memory than the other information in the display. Indeed, report of the letters that had appeared near the initial fixation point (at the fovea) was quite poor by comparison, indicating that even though the subject's eyes were foveating these letters, they were not receiving much cognitive processing. Rather, it was the information in the periphery, at the saccade target location, that was the locus of cognitive processing. In other words, eye position and the locus of cognitive processing were dissociated (see Irwin & Andrews, 1996, and Irwin & Zelinsky, 2002, for similar results).

Irwin and Gordon (1998) investigated directly the relationship between attention movements and eye movements in the encoding of information into memory. Their procedure was similar to that of Irwin (1992), but subjects were instructed to attend to one region of a display while they moved their eyes either to the region they were attending or to a different spatial region. On each trial in their first experiment an array of 10 letters was presented while subjects viewed a central fixation point. Saccade direction was signalled by one of two tones and varied from trial to trial. The array disappeared when a saccade was initiated to the appropriate saccade target. After the saccade, a partial-report probe appeared near one of the previously occupied letter positions and subjects attempted to report the identity of the letter that had been presented there. But, in addition, subjects were instructed to pay more attention to one side of the letter array than the other. To encourage subjects to follow this instruction, the side of the array that they were instructed to attend to was probed much more often than the other side of the array. On half of the trials the subjects moved their eyes toward the side of the array to which they were instructed to attend, and on half of the trials they moved their eyes away from the side to which they were instructed to attend. Of interest was how voluntary attentional allocation (manipulated by instruction) and saccade-induced attention shifts would influence the contents of memory.

Irwin and Gordon (1998) found that accuracy was much higher when high-probability (i.e., instructed-to-attend) positions were probed than when low-probability positions were probed when the eyes moved away from these positions. These results indicate that the attention instructions did influence which array positions were remembered. In addition, report of the letters near the saccade target was facilitated when a saccade was made to the low-probability side of the array. This result indicates that information near the saccade target location was encoded into memory even when subjects were trying to attend elsewhere. The effect of making a saccade to some location yielded approximately as much benefit as biasing a subject to attend to that location through instruction and probe probability; little additional benefit was gained by having voluntary attention and saccade-induced attention directed to the same side of the letter array. The amount of information that could be remembered across these different conditions was roughly constant. In all cases about four items were retained in memory across a saccade; what attention did was influence which items were remembered. As in Irwin (1992), memory for the center items in the array was quite poor, even though these items were at the fovea when the array was presented. Thus, what people remember across eye movements is not necessarily what they are foveating, but rather what they are attending.

To obtain additional information about the effects of attention on memory across saccades, Irwin and Gordon (1998) conducted a second experiment using letters that appeared in different colors. Subjects viewed an array of colored letters in one fixation, then executed a saccade to a target. The letters disappeared when the saccade was initiated; after the saccade ended, a partial report probe appeared near one of the previously occupied letter positions. Subjects attempted to report the identity and the color of the letter that had been presented there. Subjects were again instructed to pay attention to one side of the letter array, which was probed much more often than the other side; saccades (whose direction was cued by a tone) were made equally often to each side of the letter array. It is generally believed that one function of attention is to combine separate features (e.g., color, shape) that appear at the same spatial location into an integrated whole or object (e.g., Treisman & Gelade, 1980); in the absence of attention, illusory conjunctions, or incorrect combinations of features, may occur. Thus, Irwin and Gordon (1998) reasoned that letter report and color report for the high-probability locations should be very accurate and few illusory conjunctions should occur if subjects followed the attention instructions because the features present at those locations should be accurately conjoined via attention into integral objects. Similarly, letter report and color report for the items near the saccade target should be very accurate and few illusory conjunctions should occur if attention automatically precedes the eyes to the saccade target location.

Irwin and Gordon (1998) found that report of letter and color for the high-probability (i.e., instructed-to-attend) locations was very accurate and few illusory conjunctions occurred when these positions were probed, especially if a saccade was made in their direction. These results indicate that subjects followed the instruction to attend to the high-probability side of the letter array. Nonetheless, correct report of letter and color for the array items that appeared near the saccade target was facilitated when a saccade was made to the low-probability side of the array, and few illusory conjunctions occurred. These results support the conclusion that attention shifts obligatorily to the location of the saccade target before the eyes move, thereby increasing the likelihood that features near that location will be conjoined and encoded as integrated objects into memory. The effect of making a saccade to some location yielded approximately as much benefit as biasing a subject to attend to that location through instruction and probe probability; in this experiment, having voluntary attention and saccade-induced attention directed to the same side of the letter array led to additional improvements in memory. Memory for the center items in the array was again quite poor, and many illusory conjunctions occurred there, even though these items were at the fovea when the array was presented. This illustrates again that what people remember across eye movements is not necessarily what they are foveating, but rather what they are attending.

The results of the studies summarized above indicate that the locus of cognitive processing is not necessarily the same as the locus of fixation; in fact, they suggest that the locus of cognitive processing is dissociated from the locus of fixation every time one makes a saccadic eye movement. This raises an interesting question: Do people know where they are looking, or might they confuse their locus of attention with the locus of fixation? It seems obvious that we would know where we are looking, because foveated objects appear clearly and in the center of our visual space. Nonetheless, Deubel and Schneider (1996) reported that subjects in their experiments (summarized above) sometimes said that they had moved their eyes to the saccade target location when in fact their eyes remained fixated on the central fixation cross. Deubel and

Schneider suggested that these reports might arise from subjects confusing shifts of visual attention for shifts of the eyes.

This question was investigated directly by Deubel, Irwin, and Schneider (1999). In their first experiment, subjects began each trial by fixating a central cross. Potential saccade targets (peripheral crosses) were located 6 deg on either side of fixation. After a random time period the central fixation cross turned into an arrow signalling saccade direction. A test stimulus consisting of an open circle appeared for 20 ms somewhere in the visual field with a temporal asynchrony that varied randomly between -50 ms and 600 ms. Depending on the timing of test appearance, the eyes would have moved or not before the circle was presented. The subject's task was to indicate whether his or her gaze had been on the central fixation point or on the saccade target when the test stimulus occurred. Deubel et al. found that visual stimuli presented at the saccade target location as early as 250 ms before saccade onset were reported as occurring *after* the saccade. In other words, the perceived direction of gaze shifted well before the eyes moved. This result shows that people don't always know what they are looking at, or at least, *when* they are looking *where*. This presumably occurs because shifts of visual attention are mistaken for shifts of the eyes — when that happens, the subjective direction of gaze does not correspond to objective eye position. Visual attention moves to the saccade target location before the eyes move, making that location the new center of visual space.

Summary and Implications

The studies described above demonstrate that the locus of cognitive processing can be, and frequently is, dissociated from fixation location; in fact, this occurs every time we make a saccadic eye movement to some location in space. The locus of cognitive processing shifts to the intended saccade target location sometime before the eyes actually move there and our perceived direction of gaze shifts with it. Just before saccadic eye movements, then, the position of the fovea does not correspond to the location where cognitive processing is taking place; accordingly, fixation duration will not correspond to the duration of cognitive processing at the fovea's position, either. Rather, processing is taking place at the intended landing position of an upcoming saccade.

EYE POSITION AND COGNITIVE CONTROL

As reviewed above, when people intend to move their eyes to some location in space, their visual-spatial attention arrives at that location some time before the eyes arrive. This implies that the locus of cognitive processing is not always tied to fixation location. The converse of this also seems to be true; specifically, the eyes can be captured involuntarily by suddenly appearing stimuli, indicating that the control of eye position is not always under cognitive control.

Reflexive, involuntary saccades are sometimes made to a stimulus that appears abruptly in the visual field. For example, in a study by Theeuwes, Kramer, Hahn, and Irwin (1998; see also, Irwin, Colcombe, Kramer, & Hahn, 2000; Kramer, Cassavaugh, Irwin, Peterson, & Hahn, 2001; Kramer, Hahn, Irwin, & Theeuwes, 1999, 2000; Theeuwes, Kramer, Hahn, Irwin, & Zelinsky, 1999) subjects began each trial by fixating a central point that was surrounded by four or five gray circles that contained figure-8 premasks. After some period of time all of the circles but one turned red and the figure-8 premasks turned into small letters. The subject's task was to move his or her eyes to the remaining gray circle and to identify the small letter it contained. On some trials an additional circle, or sudden onset, was also presented when the original circles changed color. This onset stimulus was completely irrelevant to the subject's task because it never contained the target. Nonetheless, it was observed that subjects frequently moved their eyes to the sudden onset circle for a very brief time before moving their eyes to the remaining gray circle. That is, the sudden onset stimulus captured the eyes even though subjects intended to look somewhere else. Interestingly, subjects reported being unaware of ever looking at the abrupt onset, or sometimes even of its existence. In other words, eye position was not under cognitive control.

A similar phenomenon occurs in the antisaccade paradigm (Fischer & Weber, 1996; Hallett, 1978; Mokler & Fischer, 1999). In this paradigm subjects are instructed to move their eyes in the opposite direction of an abruptly appearing stimulus. Despite this instruction, on some trials subjects execute an erroneous prosaccade to the abrupt onset before making a correct antisaccade in the opposite direction. The erroneous prosaccades to the abrupt onset have much shorter latencies than do correct antisaccades, and the eyes linger on the abrupt onset stimulus for only a very brief time before moving correctly in the opposite direction. Furthermore, a large number of the erroneous prosaccades go unnoticed by the subjects who are making them (Mokler & Fischer, 1999). Thus, the erroneous prosaccades appear to be reflexive or involuntary in nature, outside the subject's cognitive control.

Similar explanations have been put forward to account for the "oculomotor capture" results of Theeuwes et al. (1998) and for the occurrence of erroneous prosaccades in the antisaccade paradigm (Mokler & Fischer, 1999). Specifically, it has been proposed that the appearance of the sudden onset stimulus causes the oculomotor system to generate a reflexive or involuntary saccade to the stimulus, which races against the voluntary saccade that is being programmed to the instructed location. If the involuntary saccade program wins the race, the eyes will go to the onset before moving on to the instructed location upon completion of programming of the voluntary saccade. Dual programming of concurrent saccades, one reflexive and one voluntary, is required to explain the very brief fixations that are made on the sudden onset stimulus (too brief to allow for the programming of a second voluntary saccade) and for other aspects of performance, such as the fact that the proportion of involuntary saccades in the Theeuwes et al. paradigm is reduced when the appearance of the sudden onset is delayed in time.

Because these reflexive saccades are not under cognitive control, one might wonder whether they, like voluntary saccades, are preceded by covert movements of visual-spatial attention. Theeuwes et al. suggested that they were, but Mokler and Fischer (1999) argued that attention movements do *not* precede involuntary saccades. They based this conclusion on the fact that subjects are frequently unaware that they have made an involuntary saccade. Based on this lack of awareness, Mokler and Fischer argued that subjects' attention must not have preceded the eyes on these trials.

Although awareness is one criterion that might be used to distinguish attended processing from unattended processing (e.g., Posner, 1978), it is not the only one. In particular, one frequently used signature of attended processing is facilitation in target detection and discrimination, as in the studies described in the previous section that demonstrated that attention precedes voluntary saccadic eye movements. Thus, to address the question of whether attention precedes involuntary saccadic eye movements, Irwin, Brockmole, and Kramer (2000) combined the antisaccade task used by Mokler and Fischer (1999) with a target discrimination task.

In a standard antisaccade task (e.g., Hallett, 1978) subjects begin each trial by fixating a central point. After some delay the central point disappears and a new point suddenly appears elsewhere in the visual field. The subject is instructed to move his or her eyes an equal distance in the *opposite* direction. These antisaccades are voluntary in nature because they require the subject to move away from the visual stimulus to another (usually empty) location in space. On most trials subjects do this correctly, but on some proportion of trials (usually 5-10% under such presentation conditions) the subject makes a rapid, erroneous prosaccade toward the sudden onset before making a correct antisaccade in the opposite direction. These prosaccades are presumably reflexive or involuntary in nature because the subject did not intend to look at the sudden onset.

It is possible to increase the proportion of erroneous prosaccades in this task by introducing a temporal gap between the offset of the central fixation point and the onset of the antisaccade stimulus (e.g., Fischer & Weber, 1992) and by inserting a precue in that interval (Fischer & Weber, 1996; Mokler & Fischer, 1999). Irwin et al. (2000) wanted to maximize the number of erroneous prosaccades that subjects made, so they adopted both of these techniques. In addition, to assess the allocation of attention in the visual field, they presented briefly an array of letters sometime after the presentation of the antisaccade stimulus but (ideally) before the eyes moved. Subjects searched for one of two target letters in this array, and Irwin et al. (2000) examined whether search accuracy was affected by eye-movement behavior. In particular, they examined whether search accuracy depended on where the target letter was presented relative to where the eyes (and thus perhaps attention) moved and whether this differed for voluntary, correct antisaccades, as opposed to involuntary, erroneous prosaccades. Furthermore, on each trial, subjects also reported whether they thought they had moved their eyes correctly so that the relationship between awareness and movements of attention when erroneous prosaccades occurred could be examined.

Irwin et al. (2000) found that when subjects made correct antisaccades, target letter discrimination was higher when the target letter appeared at the location that the eyes moved toward than when the target letter appeared on the opposite side of the display. Since correct antisaccades are voluntary saccades, this result replicates the many previous studies that have shown that attention precedes voluntary saccades. More importantly, Irwin et al. found this to be true for erroneous prosaccades as well; in fact, the effect of eye-movement direction on target discrimination was statistically the same regardless of the type of eye movement that was made. Furthermore, target letter discrimination was more accurate at the location the eyes moved toward regardless of whether or not subjects were aware that they had made an erroneous prosaccade.

In sum, the results of Irwin et al. (2000) indicate that visuospatial attention *does* precede involuntary saccades in addition to voluntary saccades (see also Peterson, Kramer, & Irwin, in press). Furthermore, these movements do not depend on subjects' awareness that they have made an involuntary saccade. These results thus support the assumption of Theeuwes et al. (1998) that attention is captured whenever the eyes are captured, but they are inconsistent with the conclusion of Mokler and Fischer (1999) that involuntary saccades are not preceded by shifts of attention.

Summary and Implications

The phenomenon of oculomotor capture is interesting because it demonstrates that eye position is not always under cognitive control; rather, the eyes can be captured, without awareness, for at least a brief time, by stimuli that appear suddenly in the visual field. In this case, information is extracted from the environment even though the subject is unaware of having fixated the onset location. Interestingly enough, even though eye position is not under cognitive control in this case, cognitive processing still takes place; as with voluntary saccades, however, the spatial locus of processing is not tied to the position of the fovea, but rather to the location where the eyes will be sent on the next (in this case involuntary) saccade.

COGNITIVE PROCESSING DURING SACCADIC EYE MOVEMENTS

A final factor that complicates the use of eye position as an index of cognitive processing is that under some circumstances cognitive processing continues even while the eyes are moving from one fixation location to the next. The first empirical investigations of this issue were conducted by Sanders and colleagues (e.g., Sanders & Houtmans, 1985; Sanders & Rath, 1991; Van Duren & Sanders, 1995), who argued that perceptual processes such as stimulus encoding are confined to eye fixations while postperceptual processes such as response selection take place not only during eye fixations but during the saccades which separate successive fixations as well. More recent investigations have suggested that the critical distinction is not between perceptual and postperceptual processes, however, but rather between processes that conflict with the demands of saccade programming and execution and those that do not (Irwin, 2003). In particular, it appears that cognitive processing is confined to eye fixations only if the cognitive task requires the same processes or structures that are active during saccade programming and execution; if such conflicts do not exist, then cognitive processing takes place during saccades as well as during eye fixations. Evidence supporting this conclusion is described next.

Visuospatial Processing Is Confined to Eye Fixations

Eye movements involve visuospatial processing. A position in space must be selected as the target of the eye movement, and the spatial positions of at least some of the objects in the world are updated across eye movements (e.g., Andersen, Batista, Snyder, Buneo, & Cohen, 2000; Currie, McConkie, Carlson-Radvansky, & Irwin, 2000; Duhamel, Colby, & Goldberg, 1992). Recently, several experiments have shown that cognitive operations that also require visuospatial processing are suppressed during saccades, meaning that visuospatial processing takes place during eye fixations only.

For example, two separate studies have demonstrated that mental rotation does not take place during saccades. Mental rotation (imagining the rotation of an object or of oneself in the environment) is a visuospatial process used for activities such as reading a map, packing a box, deciding whether a book will fit in a crowded bookshelf, and parking a car. Irwin and Carlson-Radvansky (1996) found that mental rotation is suppressed during saccadic eye movements. Subjects judged whether a letter presented in some orientation (0, 90, 180, or 270 degs from upright) was a normal or mirror-image version of the letter. Information about the identity and the orientation of the letter was provided while the subject fixated a leftward fixation mark, and then the subject executed a 15 deg or a 45 deg saccade to a rightward fixation mark. The target letter was presented at the rightward point, and the subject's reaction time and accuracy to make the normal/mirror judgment were recorded. Of interest was whether the prime information presented before the saccade would be more beneficial when a 45 deg saccade (which lasts about 100 ms) rather than a 15 deg saccade (which lasts about 50 ms) was executed to the target letter. No such effect was found, even though a control condition showed that a 100 ms preview of the prime was more beneficial than a 50 ms preview of the prime when the eyes did not move. These results suggest that mental rotation does not occur during saccadic eye movements, but rather is confined to discrete eye fixations.

A limitation of the Irwin and Carlson-Radvansky (1996) study is that the conclusion that mental rotation is suppressed during saccades relies on accepting a null hypothesis (i.e., no difference in performance between the 15-deg and 45-deg eye-movement conditions). Thus, Irwin and Brockmole (2000) conducted another study in which suppression during saccades would be manifested by significant differences among conditions, rather than by a null effect. On each trial in this study the subject first fixated a fixation box that appeared on the left side of the display. Then a single character (presented either 0, 90, 180, or 270 deg rotated from the upright, either in its normal or mirror-reversed configuration) was presented within it. Three hundred ms later, a saccade target box was presented on the right side of the display, or the fixation box remained on the left side of the display (for no-saccade control trials). Distributed randomly across trials, the fixation box remained on the left, or the saccade target box appeared either 7.5 deg or 40 deg away from the leftward fixation box. On no-saccade trials subjects made their normal/mirror-reversed decision by pressing one of two response buttons as soon as they could while maintaining fixation on the fixation box; on saccade trials the subject was instructed to make his or her decision *while making a saccade to the target box*. Reaction time (measured from character onset) and accuracy were recorded. Irwin and Brockmole reasoned that if mental rotation is suppressed during saccades, then RT should be longer when subjects have to execute a 40 deg saccade (which takes about 93 ms) as opposed to a 7.5 deg saccade (which takes about 28 ms). In fact, if suppression is complete, RT should be 65 ms longer in the 40 deg condition than in the 7.5 deg condition, because this is the difference in saccade duration (93 - 28).

Reaction time (measured from stimulus onset) as a function of saccade distance and stimulus orientation was the main dependent measure. The results showed that responses were significantly longer in the 40-deg saccade condition (M = 946 ms) than in the 7.5-deg saccade condition (M = 873 ms). The main effect of orientation was also significant, but the interaction between saccade distance and orientation was not. All subjects showed the same pattern of results. The error rate was higher in the 40-deg saccade condition than in the 7.5-deg saccade condition, as well (13.2% vs. 10.8%). These results show clearly that processing is suppressed during the saccade; the difference between the 40-deg and 7.5-deg saccade conditions was 73 ms, suggesting that mental rotation was suppressed completely while the eyes were moving.

To verify that it was mental rotation and not some other aspect of stimulus processing that was suppressed, subjects also completed a no-rotation control condition in which the procedure was the same as described above but the stimuli were always upright and thus never required rotation. In this version of the experiment RT and errors were identical in the 40-deg and 7.5-deg saccade conditions. Thus, suppression during the saccade was found only when mental rotation was required.

The results of Irwin and Carlson-Radvansky (1996) and Irwin and Brockmole (2000) indicate that mental rotation is suppressed during saccadic eye movements. Two additional studies have examined whether other kinds of visuospatial processing are also suppressed during saccades. Irwin and Brockmole (in press) conducted an experiment similar to that of Irwin and Brockmole (2000), but the stimuli were pictures of individual objects, always in an upright orientation. The subject had to respond whether the object (e.g., a bird, a chair, a bicycle, etc.) faced to the left or faced to the right while executing either a short or a long saccade. Making this judgment requires subjects to identify the stimulus and to impose a spatial frame of reference upon it in order to identify the front of the stimulus and which direction it is facing. This is a visuospatial operation, and it was found that saccades interfered with this process: RT to make the left/right judgment was 45 ms longer in the long-saccade condition than in the short-saccade condition, as would be expected if visuospatial processing is suppressed during saccades. Brockmole, Carlson, and Irwin (2002) found that people cannot execute changes of spatial scale during saccades. On each trial, subjects saw a pair of objects made up of smaller objects (e.g., a large square made out of smaller squares, a large rectangle made out of smaller squares, a large square made out of smaller rectangles, or a large rectangle made out of smaller rectangles). During one fixation, they made a judgment about one of the objects at one level of spatial scale (e.g., the local or small-object level) and then they executed a saccade to the other object in the pair and made a judgment about it at the other level of spatial scale (e.g., the global or large-object level in this case). Of interest was whether people could change from a local to global level of analysis (and vice versa) while their eyes were moving. The results indicated that they could not; RT was prolonged by the duration of the saccade, indicating that people can not execute changes of spatial scale while their eyes are moving. These two studies provide additional support for the hypothesis that visuospatial processes (i.e., processes that compete with saccade programming and execution) are suppressed during saccades.

In sum, several studies have shown that cognitive processing is confined to eye fixations if the cognitive task requires the same processes or structures that are active during saccade programming and execution; the next section summarizes several studies that have shown that if such conflicts do not exist, then cognitive processing takes place during saccades as well as during eye fixations.

Stimulus Recognition and Stimulus Identification Take Place During Saccades

The generation of saccadic eye movements relies on a complex network of brain structures, but the key cortical areas appear to be the frontal and supplementary eye fields and the posterior parietal cortex (Schall, 1995). The posterior parietal cortex is also heavily involved in visuospatial processing, so the results of the studies summarized above are consistent with the hypothesis that cognitive tasks that require the same brain structures that are active during saccade generation and execution are suppressed during saccades. Stimulus recognition and stimulus identification do not rely on the parietal cortex, however, but rather on more ventral areas of the brain such as inferotemporal cortex (Mishkin, Ungerleider, & Macko, 1983). Several recent studies have shown that saccades do not interfere with stimulus recognition and stimulus identification tasks, but, rather, that processing continues while the eyes are in motion. These are described next.

Irwin, Carlson-Radvansky, and Andrews (1995) found that identity priming takes place during saccades. Their procedure was based on the Posner and Snyder (1975) primed letter-matching task in which subjects had to judge whether two *target* letters were identical or different. Subjects' reaction time (RT) and accuracy to make this judgment were recorded. Presentation of the two target letters was preceded by a *prime* stimulus. On some trials the prime was a neutral warning signal (a + sign), but on other trials it was a letter that either matched or mismatched the target letters. When the prime was a letter, it was much more likely to match the target letters than to mismatch them (by a 4:1 ratio). Posner and Snyder (1975) found that RT on *same* trials (i.e., trials in which the target letters were identical to each other) was faster when the prime matched the target letters than when the prime mismatched the target letters, even though the prime was irrelevant to the subjects' task (i.e., only the congruence of the target letters was relevant to the response). Furthermore, the difference in RT between match and mismatch prime conditions increased as the stimulus onset asynchrony (SOA) between the prime and the targets increased from 10 to 300 ms. Posner and Snyder (1975) argued that the difference in RT between match and mismatch prime conditions consisted of two components: *facilitation* (assessed by subtracting RT on prime-match trials from RT on neutral prime trials) and *inhibition* (assessed by subtracting RT on neutral prime trials from RT on prime-mismatch trials). They found that the amount of facilitation rose quickly as SOA increased, whereas inhibition did not occur until the SOA exceeded 150 ms, at which point it increased rapidly. Posner and Snyder (1975) attributed these effects to two processes: a rapid, automatic activation of the processing pathway and identity code shared by the prime and the targets, and a slower, attentional expectancy based on the highly-predictive nature of the prime.

To determine whether either (or both) of these processes operate during saccades, Irwin et al. (1995) modified the Posner and Snyder (1975) procedure by presenting the prime while subjects fixated a leftward fixation mark, then presenting the target letters at a rightward fixation mark after subjects initiated either a 7.5 degree saccade or a 40 degree saccade to that location. Of interest was whether the prime would have more effect during a long as opposed to a short saccade, as would be the case if the processes set into motion by the prime continue to operate while the eyes are moving.

On each trial a fixation box appeared on the left side of the display. The subject fixated the point centered within this box, and then a saccade target box was presented on the right side of the display. In separate blocks of trials, the saccade target box appeared either 7.5 deg or 40 deg away from the left-ward fixation point. The subject was instructed to initiate a saccade to the point centered within the saccade target box as soon as it appeared. Of course, the eyes do not move instantaneously; typically, saccade latencies are between 250-300 ms. The prime was presented within the leftward fixation box before the eyes moved. Irwin et al. wanted subjects to view the prime for only 100 ms before they moved their eyes, however, because Posner and Snyder (1975) found that most of the growth in facilitation and inhibition in their task occurred at SOAs between 100 and 300 ms. To achieve a prime duration of 100 ms, the fixation box and the saccade target box were presented alone for some period of time and then the prime was presented in the center of the fixation box until the eyes began to move toward the saccade target box. For example, suppose that a subject's saccade latency was always 250 ms; to achieve a prime duration of 100 ms, the empty fixation box and the saccade target box would be presented for 150 ms before presenting the prime. Of course, saccade latency varies across subjects and across trials within a subject, so a fixed headstart value like 150 ms could not be used. Instead, each subject's saccade latency was monitored continuously during the experiment, and the headstart value on each trial was adjusted to track a 100 ms mean exposure time for the prime. This tracking procedure not only ensured that the prime would be viewed for approximately 100 ms, but it also served to equate the mean prime exposure duration across experimental conditions.

On one-third of the trials (neutral trials) the prime consisted of a plus sign. On the remaining trials the prime consisted of an uppercase letter drawn randomly from the set of consonants, excluding Q, W, and Y. The target letters (also uppercase consonants excluding Q, W, and Y) were presented in the saccade target box during the subject's saccade, and they remained there until the subject made the *same/different* response. On half of the trials the two target letters were (physically) identical to each other, and on half they were different. On 54% of the *same* trials the prime letter was identical to the two target letters, whereas on 13% of the *same* trials the prime letter was different from the two target letters (recall that on 33% of the *same* trials the prime consisted of a neutral + sign). Thus, the prime was highly predictive of target identity. On 54% of the *different* trials the prime letter was identical to one of the two target letters, whereas on 13% of the *different* trials all three letters (prime and targets) were different from each other.

The results on *same* trials are of most importance in this experiment, so only those findings will be discussed. There was significant facilitation and inhibition at both saccade distances, but significantly more facilitation when the eyes moved 40 deg (48 ms) than when the eyes moved 7.5 deg (23 ms). Inhibition increased slightly with saccade distance (40 ms vs. 44 ms), but this increase was not significant. The increase in total prime effect (facilitation + inhibition) as saccade distance increased (63 ms vs. 92 ms) was significant, however. These results indicate that the prime continued to be processed during the saccade. Analysis of the error rates was consistent with the reaction time analysis.

In sum, this experiment showed that a prime had a larger effect following a long, as opposed to a short, saccade. There was a significant increase in the amount of facilitation generated by the prime, but no evidence for increased inhibition. Viewed within the context of the Posner and Snyder (1975) two-process theory of attention, this pattern of results suggests that only the automatic process of identity node or pathway priming was in operation during the saccade; if subjects had been generating an attention-requiring expectation based on the highly predictive nature of the prime, then inhibition also should have increased with saccade duration. Henderson and colleagues also found that facilitation, but not inhibition, increased with increasing saccade distance in a transsaccadic semantic priming paradigm (Henderson, 1992; Henderson, Pollatsek, & Rayner, 1987), providing additional support for the conclusion that priming operations continue during saccadic eye movements.

Irwin (1998) investigated whether processes directly involved in word recognition are suppressed during saccades. The procedure was very similar to that of Irwin and Brockmole (2000) described earlier. The subject fixated a box on the left side of the display, and then a letter-string was presented within it. The string was always four letters long; on half the trials it formed a word (e.g., *land*), and on half the trials it formed a pronounceable nonword (e.g., *mafe*). A saccade target box was presented on the right side of the display at the same time as the letter string was presented on the left side of the display. The saccade target box appeared either 7.5 deg or 40 deg away from the letter string. The subject was instructed to press one of two response buttons to indicate whether the letter string was a word or a nonword while making a saccade to the target box. A no-saccade control condition, during which letter-strings were presented at central fixation, was also conducted. Reaction time (measured from letter-string onset) and accuracy were measured. If processing (word recognition in this case) is suppressed during saccades, then RT should have been longer when subjects had to execute a 40 deg saccade vs. a 7.5 deg saccade because of the difference in saccade duration.

Stimulus type (word vs. nonword) did not interact with any other factor, so the results reported next are averaged over all stimuli. Reaction time was 522 ms in the no-saccade condition, 571 ms in the 7.5-deg saccade condition and 573 ms in the 40-deg saccade condition. The error data were consistent with the RT data. Thus, saccades interfered with stimulus processing, but short saccades were just as interfering as long saccades. Most importantly, RT was identical in the two saccade conditions, indicating that lexical processing was not suppressed *during* the saccade itself. Rather, subjects continued to process the stimulus while the eyes were moving.

These results were confirmed in a second experiment using the "head-start" procedure described above (Irwin et al., 1995). In this version of the experiment, the saccade target box was presented for some period of time before the letter-string was presented, so that saccade programming could begin and the letter-string could be presented for a brief time before the eyes moved. This experiment also showed that word recognition processes continue to operate during saccades.

To obtain additional information about lexical processing during saccades, Irwin (1998) also investigated whether word identification (rather than recognition) is suppressed during saccades. Subjects fixated a fixation box on the left side of the display. Then the empty saccade target box was presented on the right side of the display, either 7.5 or 30 deg away. The subject was instructed to initiate a saccade to the saccade target box as soon as it appeared. Shortly before the eyes moved, the word to be identified (5-8 letters long) was presented within the leftward fixation box. When saccade onset was detected, the word was erased from the fixation box and a visual pattern mask was presented in the saccade target box. The subject's task was to identify the word.

Except at extreme exposure durations, identification accuracy was higher when the eyes moved 30 deg before landing on the pattern mask than when the eyes moved 7.5 deg. These results show that word identification is not suppressed during saccades; rather, subjects continue to process the word while their eyes are in motion.

Irwin and Brockmole (in press) investigated the effect of saccades on object recognition. The object recognition task that was employed was based on one used by Kroll and Potter (1984) that required subjects to distinguish pictures of objects from pictures of nonobjects. The experimental procedure was very similar to that of Irwin and Brockmole (2000) described above. The subject fixated a box on the left side of the display, and then a stimulus picture was presented within it. At the same time, a saccade target box was presented on the right side of the display, either 10 deg or 40 deg away. Subjects were instructed to saccade to the saccade target box and, while moving their eyes, to decide whether the stimulus was an object or a nonobject. They pressed one of two response buttons to indicate their response, and their response time and accuracy were measured. Irwin and Brockmole (in press) found that saccade distance had no effect on reaction time or accuracy. Subjects performed the object-decision task just as quickly and just as accurately during long saccades as during short saccades. Thus, object processing must not have been suspended while the eyes were in motion.

Summary and Implications

The results described above demonstrate that in some cases cognitive processing takes place during the saccades that separate successive eye fixations, while in other cases it does not. The results are consistent with the notion that cognitive suppression arises from interference from mechanisms that control or are active during saccade programming and execution. The existence of cognitive processing during saccades complicates the interpretation of eye movement data in several ways. One complication is that the position of the eyes does not correspond to the locus of cognitive processing; that is, processing is being done on material located at the eyes' previous fixation location even though the eyes are no longer there. Another complication concerns the proper definition of gaze duration, a commonly used dependent variable in eye-movement research. Gaze duration is usually defined as the sum of all fixation durations on a word or region of text; saccade durations are not included. When cognitive processing occurs during saccades, then saccade durations should be included in the calculation of gaze duration, however, because fixation durations alone will underestimate the duration of cognitive processing.

CONCLUSIONS

Because of recent advances in technology, eye position can be measured very accurately in a relatively unobtrusive fashion in a variety of natural situations, and on the surface, it might seem to afford both time-locked and spatially specific information about the locus of cognitive processing. In this chapter I have described four problems that complicate the interpretation of eye-movement data. The first problem is that cognitive processing is not necessarily restricted to the fixation location (i.e., the position of the fovea), but may include regions of space much larger than that (the useful field of view). The second problem is that the locus of cognitive processing shifts away from the current fixation location to the location of the next fixation (i.e., to the saccade target location) some time before the eyes actually move. The third problem is that the eyes are sometimes captured in an involuntary fashion by stimuli that appear suddenly in the field of view, which means that the control of eye position is not always under cognitive control. Finally, cognitive processing is not always restricted to eye fixations, but sometimes takes place during eye movements as well. The existence of these problems means that fixation location and fixation duration do not provide time-locked and spatially specific information about the locus and duration of cognitive processing under all circumstances.

The severity of these various problems will depend upon the stimulus domain and upon the nature of the cognitive task being performed. For example, the size of the useful field of view is relatively small in the case of reading because of visual acuity limitations; in this case, then, fixation location provides a reasonably accurate estimate of the location of cognitive processing. In studies that use pictures as stimuli, however, the size of the useful field of view may be quite large, especially if the pictures are undetailed and contain only a small number of objects; in this situation, fixation location will not necessarily correspond to the locus of cognitive processing. Because the size of the useful field of view depends upon the number of items in the display, their similarity to each other, the task to be performed upon them, the presence of concurrent processing demands, cues for the guidance of visual attention, and subject characteristics such as age and knowledge of the stimulus domain, one should use displays with a large number of items that are hard to discriminate from each other, use elderly subjects who have no knowledge of the stimulus domain, and have them perform another task concurrently with the task of interest, if one wants to ensure that the locus of fixation corresponds to the locus of cognitive processing!

In contrast, the second problem, the fact that the locus of cognitive processing is dissociated from fixation location before every saccadic eye movement, is always a problem, even when the eyes are captured in an involuntary, reflexive fashion. Whenever eye movements are being made, the position of the fovea will not always correspond to the location where cognitive processing is taking place. The existence of this problem also means that fixation duration on stimulus n will not be a precise measure of the duration of cognitive processing of stimulus n, but, rather, will be affected by peripheral processing of stimulus n during fixation $n-1$, as well as peripheral processing of stimulus $n+1$ during fixation n. It seems likely that the severity of this problem will depend upon the size of the useful field of view, however; if little information can be extracted from the visual periphery, the effects of that information on fixation duration should be small. Again, this implies that there may be a closer link between eye position and the locus of cognitive processing in reading than in picture perception, scene perception, and visual search; consistent with this hypothesis, Rayner and colleagues have found that the characteristics of the currently fixated word (e.g., its frequency and predictability) primarily determine fixation duration on that word, despite the existence of peripheral preview and spillover effects (e.g., Reichle, Pollatsek, Fisher, & Rayner, 1998; see also the chapter by Rayner & Liversedge in this volume).

The third problem, the fact that the eyes can be captured involuntarily by suddenly appearing stimuli, is only a problem if dynamic scenes are being viewed; during reading and during static-scene viewing, the control of eye position is largely under cognitive control, although other salient stimulus characteristics, such as color, luminance, and stimulus complexity, may also draw the eyes in a bottom-up fashion (e.g., Parkhurst, Law, & Niebur, 2002).

Finally, the fact that cognitive processing sometimes take place during saccades as well as during eye fixations implies again that under some circumstances fixation location does not precisely specify the locus of cognitive processing and that fixation duration alone is not always an accurate measure of the duration of cognitive processing; rather, saccade duration should be taken into consideration when the task being performed (e.g., word and object recognition) is one that is not suppressed during eye movements. The severity of this problem will depend on the size of the region over which gaze duration is defined. It is likely to be small when individual words are the unit of analysis (e.g., Rayner, 1998, compared the difference in gaze duration on high- vs. low-frequency words during reading when saccade durations were and were not included and found that the difference was only 3- 8 ms). The difference may be considerably larger, however, if the region includes several words (e.g., Ferreira & Clifton, 1986; Trueswell, Tanenhaus, & Garnsey, 1994) or a large area of space (e.g., Germeys, De Graef, & Verfaillie, 2002).

Although this chapter has emphasized problems associated with the use of fixation location and fixation duration as indices of cognitive processing, this is not to say that these measures are worthless. Rather they are very valuable, and it is clear from many studies of reading and of object and scene perception that fixation duration at least partly reflects relatively localized processing. Nonetheless, these measures must be used and interpreted cautiously. For example, ordinal comparisons of fixation (or gaze) durations among conditions are likely to be more justifiable than comparisons or calculations based on the "actual" values themselves. Perhaps the main conclusion to be drawn from this chapter is that eyetrackers provide only an imperfect estimate of the locus of cognitive processing; because attentional processing resources can be dissociated from the position of the eyes, what researchers really need are "attention trackers" that will specify the location of these resources. This awaits further advances in technology.

ACKNOWLEDGMENT

Preparation of this chapter was supported by NSF Grant BCS 01-32292 to the author. I thank Keith Rayner and John Henderson for their helpful comments.

Address all correspondence to the author at Department of Psychology, University of Illinois, 603 E. Daniel St., Champaign, IL 61820 or via email to dirwin@s.psych.uiuc.edu.

REFERENCES

Andersen, R. A., Batista, A. P., Snyder, L. H., Buneo, C. A., & Cohen, Y. E. (2000). Programming to look and reach in the posterior parietal cortex. In M. S. Gazzaniga (Ed.), *The new cognitive neurosciences, 2nd edition*, (pp. 515-524). Cambridge, MA: MIT Press.

Ball, K., Beard, B., Roenker, D., Miller, R., & Griggs, D. (1988). Age and visual search: Expanding the useful field of view. *Journal of the Optical Society of America A, 5*, 2210-2219.

Bertera, J. H., & Rayner, K. (2000). Eye movements and the span of the effective stimulus in visual search. *Perception & Psychophysics, 62*, 576-585.

Bouma, H. (1978). Visual search and reading: Eye movements and functional visual field: A tutorial review. In J. Requin (Ed.), *Attention and performance VII*, (pp. 115-147). Hillsdale, NJ: Erlbaum.

Brockmole, J. R., Carlson, L. A., & Irwin, D. E. (2002). Inhibition of attended processing during saccadic eye movements, *Perception & Psychophysics, 64*, 867-881.

Currie, C., McConkie, G. W., Carlson-Radvansky, L. A., & Irwin, D. E. (2000). The role of the saccade target object in the perception of a visually stable world. *Perception & Psychophysics, 62*, 673-683.

Deubel, H., Irwin, D. E., & Schneider, W.X. (1999). The subjective direction of gaze shifts long before the saccade. In W. Becker, H. Deubel, & T. Mergner (Eds.), *Current oculomotor research: Physiological and psychological aspects* (pp. 65-70). New York: Plenum.

Deubel, H., & Schneider, W.X. (1996). Saccade target selection and object recognition: Evidence for a common attentional mechanism. *Vision Research, 36*, 1993-1997.

Duhamel, J.-R., Colby, C., & Goldberg, M. (1992). The updating of the representation of visual space in parietal cortex by intended eye movements. *Science, 255*, 90-92.

Edwards, D. C., & Goolkasian, P. A. (1974). Peripheral vision location and kinds of complex processing. *Journal of Experimental Psychology, 102*, 244-249.

Engel, F. L. (1971). Visual conspicuity, directed attention, and retinal locus. *Vision Research, 11*, 563-576.

Ferreira, F., & Clifton, C. (1986). The independence of syntactic processing. *Journal of Memory and Language, 25*, 348-368.

Findlay, J. M. (1997). Saccade target selection during visual search. *Vision Research, 37*, 617-631.

Fischer, B., & Weber, H. (1992). Characteristics of 'anti' saccades in man. *Experimental Brain Research, 89*, 415-424.

Fischer, B.,& Weber, H. (1996). Effects of procues on error rate and reaction times of antisaccades in human subjects. *Experimental Brain Research, 109*, 507-512.

Geissler, L. R. (1926). Form perception in indirect vision. *Psychological Bulletin, 23*, 135-136.

Germeys, F., De Graef, P., & Verfaillie, K. (2002). Transsaccadic perception of saccade target and flanker objects. *Journal of Experimental Psychology: Human Perception and Performance, 28*, 868-883.

Griffin, Z. M., & Bock, K. What the eyes say about speaking. *Psychological Science, 11*, 274-279.

Grindley, G., & Townsend, V. (1968). Voluntary attention in peripheral vision and its effects on acuity and differential thresholds. *Quarterly Journal of Experimental Psychology, 20*, 11-19.

Hallett, P. E. (1978). Primary and secondary saccades to goals defined by instructions. *Vision Research, 18*, 1279-1296.

Harrington, D. (1981). *The visual fields: A textbook and atlas of clinical perimetry*. St. Louis: Mosby.

Henderson, J. M. (1992). Identifying objects across saccades: Effects of extrafoveal preview and flanker object context. *Journal of Experimental Psychology: Learning, Memory, and Cognition, 18*, 521-530.

Henderson, J. M. (1993). Visual attention and saccadic eye movements. In G. d'Ydewalle and J. Van Rensbergen (Eds.), *Perception and cognition: Advances in eye-movement research* (pp. 37-50). Amsterdam: North-Holland.

Henderson, J. M. (1996). Spatial precues affect target discrimination in the absence of visual noise. *Journal of Experimental Psychology: Human Perception and Performance, 22*, 780-787.

Henderson, J. M., & Ferreira, F. (1990). Effects of foveal processing difficulty on the perceptual span in reading: Implications for attention and eye movement control. *Journal of Experimental Psychology: Learning, Memory, and Cognition, 16*, 417-429.

Henderson, J. M., & Hollingworth, A. (1999). The role of fixation position in detecting scene changes across saccades. *Psychological Science, 10*, 438-443.

Henderson, J. M., & Hollingworth, A. (2003). Eye movements and visual memory: Detecting changes to saccade targets in scenes. *Perception & Psychophysics, 65*, 58-71.

Henderson, J. M., Pollatsek, A., & Rayner, K. (1987). Effects of foveal priming and extrafoveal preview on object identification. *Journal of Experimental Psychology: Human Perception and Performance, 13*, 449-463.

Henderson, J. M., Pollatsek, A., & Rayner, K. (1989). Covert visual attention and extrafoveal information use during object identification. *Perception & Psychophysics, 45*, 196-208.

Henderson, J. M., Williams, C. C., Castelhano, M. S., & Falk, R. J. (2003). Eye movements and picture processing during recognition. *Perception & Psychophysics, 65*, 725-734.

Hochberg, J. (1978). *Perception*. Englewood Cliffs, NJ: Prentice-Hall.

Hoffman, J. E., & Subramaniam, B. (1995). The role of visual attention in saccadic eye movements. *Perception and Psychophysics, 57*, 787-795.

Hollingworth, A., & Henderson, J. M. (2002). Accurate visual memory for previously attended objects in natural scenes. *Journal of Experimental Psychology: Human Perception and Performance, 28*, 113-136.

Huey, E. B. (1908). *The psychology and pedagogy of reading*. New York: Macmillan.

Ikeda, M. & Takeuchi, T. (1975). Influence of foveal load on the functional visual field. *Perception & Psychophysics, 18*, 255-260.

Irwin, D. E. (1998). Lexical processing during saccadic eye movements. *Cognitive Psychology, 36*, 1-27.

Irwin, D. E. (2003). Eye movements and visual cognitive suppression. In D. Irwin & B. Ross (Eds.), *The psychology of learning and motivation volume 42: Cognitive vision,* (pp. 265-293). San Diego: Academic Press.

Irwin, D. E., & Andrews, R. (1996). Integration and accumulation of information across saccadic eye movements. In T. Inui and J. L. McClelland (Eds.), *Attention and performance XVI: Information integration in perception and communication* (pp. 125-155). Cambridge, MA: MIT Press.

Irwin, D. E., & Brockmole, J. R. (2000). Mental rotation is suppressed during saccadic eye movements. *Psychonomic Bulletin and Review, 7*, 654-661.

Irwin, D. E., & Brockmole, J. R. (in press). Suppressing where but not what: The effect of saccades on dorsal- and ventral-stream visual processing. *Psychological Science*.

Irwin, D. E., Brockmole, J. S., & Kramer, A. F. (2000). *Does attention precede involuntary saccades?* Paper presented at Attraction, Distraction, and Action: An Interdisciplinary Conference and Workshop, Villanova, PA.

Irwin, D. E., & Carlson-Radvansky, L. A. (1996). Suppression of cognitive activity during saccadic eye movements. *Psychological Science, 7*, 83-88.

Irwin, D. E., Carlson-Radvansky, L. A., & Andrews, R. V. (1995). Information processing during saccadic eye movements. *Acta Psychologica, 90,* 261-273.

Irwin, D. E., Colcombe, A. M., Kramer, A. F., & Hahn, S. (2000). Attentional and oculomotor capture by onset, luminance, and color singletons. *Vision Research, 40,* 1443-1458.

Irwin, D. E., & Gordon, R. D. (1998). Eye movements, attention, and transsaccadic memory. *Visual Cognition, 5,* 127-155.

Irwin, D. E., & Zelinsky, G. J. (2002). Eye movements and scene perception: Memory for things observed. *Perception & Psychophysics, 64,* 882-895.

Just, M. A., & Carpenter, P. A. (1980). A theory of reading: From eye fixations to comprehension. *Psychological Review, 87,* 329-354.

Klein, R. (1980). Does oculomotor readiness mediate cognitive control of visual attention? In R. S. Nickerson (Ed.), *Attention and performance VIII* (pp. 259-276). Hillsdale, NJ: Erlbaum.

Klein, R., & Pontefract, A. (1994). Does oculomotor readiness mediate cognitive control of visual attention? Revisited! In C. Umilta & M. Moskovitch (Eds.), *Attention and performance XV* (pp. 333-350). Cambridge, MA: MIT Press.

Kowler, E., Anderson, E., Dosher, B., & Blaser, E. (1995). The role of attention in the programming of saccades. *Vision Research, 35,* 1897-1916.

Kramer, A. F., Cassavaugh, N. D., Irwin, D. E., Peterson, M. S., & Hahn, S. (2001). Influence of single and multiple onset distractors on visual search for singleton targets. *Perception & Psychophysics, 63,* 952-968.

Kramer, A. F., Hahn, S., Irwin, D. E., & Theeuwes, J. (1999). Attentional capture and aging: Implications for visual search performance and oculomotor control. *Psychology and Aging, 14,* 135-154.

Kramer, A. F., Hahn, S., Irwin, D. E., & Theeuwes, J. (2000). Age differences in the control of looking behavior: Do you know where your eyes have been? *Psychological Science, 11,* 210-217.

Kroll, J. F., & Potter, M. C. (1984). Recognizing words, pictures, and concepts: A comparison of lexical, object, and reality decisions. *Journal of Verbal Learning & Verbal Behavior, 23,* 39-66.

Leibowitz, H., & Appelle, S. (1969). The effect of a central task on luminance thresholds for peripherally presented stimuli. *Human Factors, 11,* 387-392.

Mackworth, N. H. (1976). Stimulus density limits the useful field of view. In R. A. Monty and J. W. Senders (Eds.) *Eye movements and psychological processes* (pp. 307-321). Hillsdale, NJ: Erlbaum.

McConkie, G. W., & Rayner, K. (1975). The span of the effective stimulus during a fixation in reading. *Perception & Psychophysics, 17,* 578-586.

Menzer, G. W., & Thurmond, J. B. (1970). Form identification in peripheral vision. *Perception & Psychophysics, 8,* 205-209.

Meyer, A. S., Sleiderink, A. M., & Levelt, W. J. M. (1998). Viewing and naming objects: Eye movements during noun phrase production. *Cognition, 66,* B25-B33.

Mishkin, M., Ungerleider, L. G., & Macko, K. A. (1983). Object vision and spatial vision: Two cortical pathways. *Trends in Neuroscience, 6,* 414-417.

Mokler, A., & Fischer, B. (1999). The recognition and correction of involuntary prosaccades in an antisaccade task. *Experimental Brain Research, 125,* 511-516.

Munn, N. L., & Geil, G. A. (1931). A note on peripheral form discrimination. *Journal of General Psychology, 5,* 78-88.

Nelson, W., & Loftus, G. (1980). The functional visual field during picture viewing. *Journal of Experimental Psychology: Human Learning and Memory, 6,* 391-399.

Parker, R. (1978). Picture processing during recognition. *Journal of Experimental Psychology: Human Perception and Performance, 4,* 284-293.

Parkhurst, D., Law, K., & Niebur, E. (2002). Modeling the role of salience in the allocation of overt visual attention. *Vision Research, 42,* 107-123.

Peterson, M. S., Kramer, A. F., & Irwin, D. E. (in press). Covert shifts of attention precede involuntary eye movements. *Perception & Psychophysics.*

Pollatsek, A., Bolozky, S., Well, A., & Rayner, K. (1981). Asymmetries in the perceptual span for Israeli readers. *Brain and Language, 14,* 174-180.

Pomplun, M., Reingold, E., & Shen, J. (2001). Investigating the visual span in comparative search: The effects of task difficulty and divided attention. *Cognition, 81,* B57-B67.

Posner, M. I. (1978). *Chronometric explorations of mind.* Hillsdale, NJ: Erlbaum.

Posner, M., & Snyder, C. (1975). Facilitation and inhibition in the processing of signals. In P. M. A. Rabbitt and S. Dornic (Eds.), *Attention and performance V* (pp. 669-682). New York: Academic Press.

Pringle, H., Irwin, D., Kramer, A., & Atchley, P. (2001). The role of attentional breadth in perceptual change detection. *Psychonomic Bulletin & Review, 8,* 89-95.

Rayner, K. (1975). The perceptual span and peripheral cues in reading. *Cognitive Psychology, 7,* 65-81.

Rayner, K. (1978). Eye movements in reading and information processing. *Psychological Bulletin, 85,* 618-660.

Rayner, K. (1986). Eye movements and the perceptual span in beginning and skilled readers. *Journal of Experimental Child Psychology, 41,* 211-236.

Rayner, K. (1998). Eye movements in reading and information processing: Twenty years of research. *Psychological Bulletin, 124,* 372-422.

Rayner, K., & Fisher, D. L. (1987). Eye movements and the perceptual span during visual search. In J. K. O'Regan & A. Levy-Schoen (Eds.), *Eye movements: From physiology to cognition* (pp. 293-302). Amsterdam: North Holland.

Rayner, K., McConkie, G., & Ehrlich, S. (1978). Eye movements and integrating information across fixations. *Journal of Experimental Psychology: Human Perception and Performance, 4,* 529-544.

Rayner, K., Well, A., & Pollatsek, A. (1980). Asymmetry of the effective visual field in reading. *Perception & Psychophysics, 27,* 537-544.

Reichle, E. D., Pollatsek, A., Fisher, D. L., & Rayner, K. (1998). Toward a model of eye movement control in reading. *Psychological Review, 105,* 125-157.

Reingold, E., Charness, N., Pomplun, M., & Stampe, D. (2001). Visual span in expert chess players: Evidence from eye movements. *Psychological Science, 12,* 48-55.

Ryan, J., Althoff, R., Whitlow, S., & Cohen, N. (2000). Amnesia is a deficit in relational memory. *Psychological Science, 11,* 454-461.

Saida, S., & Ikeda, M. (1979). Useful visual field size for pattern perception. *Perception & Psychophysics, 25,* 119-125.

Sanders, A. F., & Houtmans, M. J. M. (1985). There is no central stimulus encoding during saccadic eye shifts: A case against general parallel processing notions. *Acta Psychologica, 60,* 323-338.

Sanders, A. F., & Rath, A. M. (1991). Perceptual processing and speed-accuracy trade-off. *Acta Psychologica, 77,* 275-291.

Schall, J. D. (1995). Neural basis of saccade target selection. *Reviews in the Neurosciences, 6,* 63-85.

Scialfa, C., Thomas, D., & Joffe, K. (1994). Age differences in the useful field of view: An eye movement analysis. *Optometry & Vision Science, 71,* 736-742.

Sekuler, R., & Ball, K. (1986). Visual localization: Age and practice. *Journal of the Optical Society of America A, 3,* 864-867.

Shepherd, M., Findlay, J., & Hockey, R. (1986). The relationship between eye movements and spatial attention. *Quarterly Journal of Experimental Psychology, 38A,* 475-491.

Shioiri, S., & Ikeda, M. (1989). Useful resolution for picture perception as a function of eccentricity. *Perception, 18,* 347-361.

Tanenhaus, M. K., Spivey-Knowlton, M. J., Eberhard, K. M., Sedivy, J. C. (1995). Integration of visual and linguistic information in spoken language comprehension. *Science, 268,* 1632-1634.

Theeuwes, J., Kramer, A. F., Hahn, S., & Irwin, D. E. (1998). Our eyes do not always go where we want them to go: Capture of the eyes by new objects. *Psychological Science, 9,* 379-385.

Theeuwes, J., Kramer, A. F., Hahn, S., Irwin, D. E., & Zelinsky, G. J. (1999). Influence of attentional capture on eye movement control. *Journal of Experimental Psychology: Human Perception and Performance, 25,* 1595-1608.

Treisman, A., & Gelade, G. (1980). A feature integration theory of attention. *Cognitive Psychology, 12,* 97-136.

Trueswell, J., Tanenhaus, M., & Garnsey, S. (1994). Semantic influences on parsing: Use of thematic role information in syntactic ambiguity resolution. *Journal of Memory and Language, 33,* 285-318.

van Duren, L., & Sanders, A. F. (1995). Signal processing during and across saccades. *Acta Psychologica, 89,* 121-147.

Viviani, P., & Swennson, R. G. (1982). Saccadic eye movements to peripherally discriminated visual targets. *Journal of Experimental Psychology: Human Perception and Performance, 8,* 113-126.

Webster, R., & Haslerud, G. (1964). Influence on extreme peripheral vision of attention to a visual or auditory task. *Journal of Experimental Psychology, 68,* 269-272.

4

Eye Scanning and Visual Search

JOHN M. FINDLAY

During visual search, a number of processes operate to direct the eyes efficiently to the search target. Our understanding of these processes has advanced considerably in the last 10 years, and this chapter gives a perspective about how the eyes are controlled during search activity. During each fixation, visual information is analyzed in a way that emphasizes the central part of the visual field. This analysis proceeds in parallel on the basis of an internal salience map, which develops over time. The point of highest salience is selected as the saccade destination. There is no convincing evidence supporting serial scanning by covert attentional processes within a normal fixation during free viewing. However, the analysis may be assisted by information gained during the preceding fixation through the process of non-foveal preview. If the analysis is adequate to locate the search target, the eyes are moved to it; otherwise, a new fixation location is selected. Particularly with large search displays, more strategic processes are also important that distribute fixations over the area to be searched.

INTRODUCTION

*L*ooking for something is a common everyday visual activity. Visual search forms a fruitful terrain to investigate the way in which perceptual and cognitive factors interact. This chapter will review research in the area, paying particular attention to the eye-scanning process that redirects the fovea to different locations of a search display. One tradition of research in the area emphasizes *covert attention*, the ability to attend to a location in the

135

visual field other than the point of regard. It will be argued that emphasis on covert attention is misguided. Rather, visual search shows how the active interplay of visual processes and *overt attention*, i.e., eye scanning, typifies the way visual attention is normally deployed.

Fovea and Periphery

A fundamental aspect of the organization of vision is the inhomogeneity of the visual pathways (see chapter in this volume by D. Irwin). The fovea of the retina provides maximum visual resolution and provides the natural center of visual attention. Away from the fovea, visual resolution declines. This resolution decline has been measured for a variety of visual tasks; in many (such as vernier acuity), the differential magnification in the projection from retina to cortex is critical; for some (such as grating acuity), the decline can be related to receptor spacing (Wilson, Levi, Maffei, Rovamo, & DeValois, 1990). A further loss of discrimination occurs if the resolution target is not present in isolation but is accompanied by flanking visual material (Bouma, 1970). This loss is termed *lateral masking*, and the separations at which lateral masking becomes important are surprisingly large (Toet & Levi, 1992). A fully adequate explanation of lateral masking is still lacking (Huckauf, Heller, & Nazir, 1999). One relevant factor may be that the tasks used to measure it require endogenous covert attention to be directed to the periphery. The ability to localize a target with endogenous covert attention proves also to be remarkably poor (Intriligator & Cavanagh, 2001).

The low ability of the visual periphery to resolve detail has substantial consequences for visual search. Before discussing these, it is worth giving some consideration to the question of why we are so little aware of the visual limitations imposed. Indeed, both naïve individuals and many visual scientists consistently overestimate their abilities to use peripheral vision and are surprised by the "change-blindness" demonstrations that our vision is not like a photographic recording (Levin, Momen, Drivdahl, & Simons, 2000). Two reasons can be adduced for our lack of awareness. First, we constantly move our eyes around a visual scene. High visual resolution occurs where we are looking and, to an extent as discussed later, where we contemplate looking next. Second, many significant visual properties in the environment have low visual detail, and while we obtain substantial "gist" information from one glimpse at a scene (Delorme, Richard, & Fabre-Thorpe, 2000; Henderson & Hollingworth, 1999), this information relates to scene layout (Sanocki & Epstein, 1997) and statistical properties rather than any detailed representation at the object level.

In the case of visual search, peripheral vision is clearly involved since the issue generally concerns detection of a possible target in peripheral vision. Most work on visual search has, to date, been concerned with search displays containing multiple isolated items. The target item forming the object of the search is displayed with a number of other items, termed *distractors*. Two tasks, in particular, have been very extensively studied. In the first the observer is required to make a speeded present/absent response to indicate whether a target is present or not. In the second, the observer must locate a target (if present), usually by directing the eyes to it. An early instance of the second task was reported by Williams (1966). Williams required individuals to locate a target in a display consisting of cluttered, but nonoverlapping, geometric shapes of different shape, size, and color. The task was to identify a target specified by a small indicator number, only legible if the item was fixated. He found that prespecification of the target color led to faster searches, whereas prespecification of target shape or size was almost ineffective. A further result from his study related this finding to the subject's eye scanning. Properties that promoted faster searches, in particular color, were found also to allow observers to restrict their eye fixations to distractors having the appropriate property. Conversely prespecification of other properties, such as target shape, resulted neither in faster search nor in effective selection by the eye-movement control system.

This study predated and in some ways anticipated the much more well-known work of Anne Treisman (citation counts show about 60 citations for Williams compared with many thousand for Treisman). Her great contribution was to differentiate between cases where search was easy and the target seemed to pop out of the display with cases where search was more difficult. She proposed that the easy searches could be carried out "pre-attentively," whereas the second type required attentional resources. Her classic first paper in the area (Treisman & Gelade, 1980) introduced the "search function," in which the time taken to make a present-absent response is plotted against the number of elements in the display. Pop-out tasks are characterized by a "flat" search function, in which the time taken to make the response is independent of the number of display elements. More difficult tasks are generally slower, and the search function increases in a linear manner with the number of elements in the display. The terms *parallel* and *serial search* describing these two cases have rightly become highly familiar.

Treisman and Gelade (1980) also suggested an explanatory framework. Targets that offer pop-out are generally targets that can be differentiated from the distractor items in the display by means of a simple visual feature. In cases where two features must be conjoined in order to differentiate the target from the distractors, serial search is normally found. Subsequent work has in general supported this distinction with apparent counterexamples often proving equivocal on closer examination. Thus, search for conjunctions involving stereo-depth (Nakayama & Silverman, 1986) is often described as an exception. But the flat search functions in these conjunction searches have a high baseline (> 1 sec), and other evidence suggests that the general rule is not broken (McSorley & Findlay, 2001). Treisman and Gelade proposed that the two cases differed in their attentional requirements. Pop-out search represented discriminations that could be made in parallel across the whole visual field and thus do not require attention. Serial search involves attentional scanning. In the original version of feature integration theory, this scanning was assumed to be *covert* mental scanning without actual eye movements and to occur on an item-by-item basis (it should be acknowledged that Treisman has made modifications to her theory subsequently, e.g., Treisman, 1993, although the emphasis on covert scanning has been retained). The rate of the presumed item-by-item, serial attentional scan may be deduced from the search function, and rates in the range 30 ms/item to 60 ms/item were typically found. These rates are, of course, too fast to represent overt scanning with the eyes, and thus it was postulated that they corresponded to scanning using the covert attentional processes that Posner (1980) was investigating at the same point in time.

In the next section of this chapter, we shall analyze search tasks in which the eyes are free to move, reiterating arguments made previously (Findlay & Gilchrist, 1998; Findlay, Brown, & Gilchrist, 2001) that, in this case, covert attention is only involved through its association with the overt scanning process and no autonomous movements of covert attention occur. The position reached is that, during the course of each eye fixation, visual material is analyzed in parallel, even for conjunction searches. This conclusion is, of course, at variance with the traditional interpretation of the search function in terms of covert attentional scanning and thus joins a growing body of work critical of the traditional account (Eckstein, 1998; Pashler, 1987).

WHAT OCCURS DURING EACH FIXATION OF AN ACTIVE VISUAL SEARCH?

The previous section introduced the possibility that covert attention might scan through a set of items in a search display. How might such covert scanning link to the overt eye movement scan? We shall consider four possibilities for the way in which such covert scanning might link with an overt eye scan, assuming for the moment that it may be postulated that covert attention can be redeployed at a fast enough rate for the possibilities discussed as 1 and 2 below.

1. Covert attention scans until the target is found and then the eye is directed to it.

    On this account, incorrectly directed saccades would never occur.

2. Covert attention scans a subset of items. If the target is located during this time, the eyes make a saccade to the target; otherwise a saccade is made following some deadline.

Two predictions can be made from this account. First, saccades which are directed to the search target should have shorter latencies than those directed to distractors. Second, saccades directed to distractors should not show any preference to be directed towards a particular type of distractor. The latter prediction might be relaxed if a further assumption is made that the covert attentional scan can intelligently select items that resemble the target in preference to dissimilar ones (e.g., Wolfe, 1994).

3. Covert attention operates independently of overt eye movements.

Under this extreme position, no predictions are made about the pattern of eye movements, and thus the position cannot be refuted through eye scan studies. However, there are numerous studies showing a linkage between the covert and overt attentional systems (Hoffman & Subramaniam, 1995; Shepherd, Findlay, & Hockey, 1986), and it is hard to envisage a covert attentional system that operated entirely independently of the overt one.

4. Covert attentional scanning plays no role in the selection of the search target.

Under this proposal, the whole idea of a covert attention scan is rejected in favor of the alternative that the whole visual field, or at least the parafoveal region, is processed in parallel. The basic idea of a covert attentional process is that certain parts of the visual field are given preferential treatment. As will be discussed subsequently, there is good evidence that in many situations, visual processing at the location of an upcoming saccade target is enhanced, and thus covert attention may still, in some sense, have a role to play. What is rejected is the idea of a separate independent covert scanning mechanism.

Turning to relevant evidence, it is immediately clear that proposal 1 is not in accord with the many demonstrations that multiple fixations occur in most search tasks before a target is found (Binello, Mannan, & Ruddock, 1995; Findlay, 1995, 1997; Hooge & Erkelens, 1996, 1999; Motter & Belky, 1998a,b; Rao, Zelinsky, Hayhoe, & Ballard, 2002; Zelinsky, 1996; Zelinsky, Rao, Hayhoe, & Ballard, 1997).

The suggestion that covert attention can scan through several locations within the duration of a fixation is plausible only if it is assumed that covert attention can be redeployed very rapidly. This assumption must be regarded as questionable. Estimates of the time necessary for covert attention to be redeployed have ranged from 10-20 ms up to several hundred milliseconds (Egeth & Yantis, 1997). However, in general, the faster redeployment rates are deduced from indirect evidence, and indeed, many of these estimates come from the interpretation of the search function that is being criticized in this section.

A study from our laboratory (Brown, Huey, & Findlay, 1997) is relevant to this issue. We investigated a task in which a pictorial face stimulus was the target. The face target was presented together with a small number of distractors, consisting of scrambled faces. Target and distractors were presented in a ring arrangement ensuring that all items were equidistant from the fixation point and thus equally visible. The observers were asked to move their eyes to the target. Naïve observers were unable to do this task. The proportion of first saccades directed to the intact face was no greater than that towards each of the scrambled faces. We showed that the difficulty was not one of peripheral discrimination since a short period of training could produce a dramatic improvement in performance. After training, subjects took longer to initiate their eye movement and achieved much better search accuracy. The improvement was particularly marked for upright faces but also occurred for inverted faces. One possible reason for the performance improvement is that the prolonged initial fixation allowed time for a slow scan through the items using covert attention. However, an alternative account, not involving such serial processing, can also be given (Findlay & Gilchrist, 1998). A conclusion from this study is that, even in a task where it might be advantageous to use a covert attentional scan, individuals do not spontaneously adopt such a strategy. The eye-movement system prefers to operate on a "move now, think later" basis.

The predictions from proposal 2 are also not upheld. This was demonstrated independently by Findlay (1997) and by Motter and Belky (1998b), following detailed analysis of eye-movment patterns in tasks of conjunction search in humans and in monkeys, respectively. Both studies compared the latency of eye movements to targets and to distractors and found no support for the prediction that target-directed eye movements should have shorter latency. In the Motter and Belky study the two measures did not differ; in the Findlay study, target-directed eye movements had slightly longer latency. Likewise, both studies found that saccades that did not go to the target were more likely to land on distractors sharing a target feature rather than the random pattern predicted by proposal 2.

Both studies arrived at the conclusion that the best account of eye-movement control in visual search was given by option 4 above, in which visual material was analyzed in parallel across the visual field. This leads to the concept of a *salience map*. The salience map, an idea introduced into work on human vision by Koch and Ullman (1985), is a two-dimensional representation of the visual world in terms of a single property, salience. It may be envisaged as a pattern of hypothesized neural activity in a neural network. The network is two-dimensional with the visual field being mapped spatially in a retinotopic way. The level of neural activity at each point encodes the salience. In the case of visual search, it is assumed that neurocomputational processes have operated so that the level of activity varies corresponding to the level of evidence that the search target is present at a location. Items sharing a feature with the target will thus generate a higher level of activation than items sharing no target feature. Proximity to fixation also increases an item's salience. It is then assumed that the saccade will be made to the location of highest activity on the salience map. The final assumption is that the system is not able to encode visual properties perfectly but is subject to random noise fluctuations (cf. Eckstein, 1998). The pattern of erroneous saccades can then be readily accounted for.

An added attraction of proposal 4 is that it accords with recent work in visual neurophysiology. Visual representations in the brain are universally found to take the form of two dimensional retinotopic maps. Two studies reported 10 years ago (Chelazzi, Miller, Duncan, & Desimone 1993; Schall & Hanes, 1993) how processes of lateral inhibition across different map locations might lead to the formation of a task directed salience map. This idea has undergone considerable development with salience maps for different purposes identified in a variety of visual areas of the brain (Bichot & Schall, 1999; Gottlieb, Kusunoki, & Goldberg, 1998; Hasegawa, Matsumoto, & Mikami, 2000; Kusunoki, Gottlieb, & Goldberg, 1998; Schall, 1995). We also have a good understanding of the way these spatiotopic representations are transformed into the appropriate saccadic orienting movement (Wurtz, 1996).

HOW ACCURATELY CAN THE EYES BE DIRECTED TO A TARGET DURING VISUAL SEARCH?

Zelinsky et al. (1997) recorded eye movements during a visual search task using pictorial displays consisting of small (up to six) numbers of realistic objects (toys in a crib; tools on a workbench, etc). They also rejected the idea that serial deployment of covert attention during fixations occurred (termed by them the *serial spotlight model*). However, their eye-movement records led them to propose an elaboration of the parallel processing account. As shown in Figure 4.1, they found that the first saccade appeared to be directed to the center of group of objects, rather than at individual objects. Their interpretation, termed a *zoom lens model,* involves multiple scene representations at different spatial scales and has been elaborated recently (Rao et al. 2002). In some of the coarse scale representations, individual items are not differentiated, and thus a salience peak may emerge from a weighted, center-of-gravity combination of information from several different objects. As they note, many studies have found such center-of-gravity averaging when studying saccades to

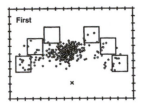
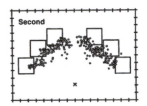
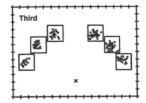

FIGURE 4.1. Search eye movements showing an incremental strategy. Observers were asked to look for a specified target in controlled but realistic displays of the type shown in the top panels. Landing positions of the first, second and third saccades are shown in the lower panels. From Zelinsky et al. (1997).

simple targets (Findlay, 1982; McGowan, Kowler, Sharma, & Chubb, 1998; Ottes, Van Gisbergen, & Eggermont, 1984).

Two recent experiments carried out in my laboratory both address the issue of saccade targeting accuracy. In both cases, it is shown that center-of-gravity effects can occur in search situations. However, such effects appear not to be obligatory, although they are a default option in some circumstances.

The first experiment, carried out with McSorley and Findlay (2003), showed evidence of center-of-gravity effects in a search situation but also produced an intriguing paradox. These effects *decreased* as the number of nontarget distractors increased. In our experiments, the eyes achieved greater accuracy in a search task when more distractors were presented with the target.

The specific task we investigated reflected our interest in the mechanisms of early vision. Our display elements were Gabor patches, and we required participants to search for a target defined by its spatial frequency in the presence of distractors of a different spatial frequency. Figure 4.2 shows an example of the task: for naïve subjects, the search task was described as searching for a target with fatter (or thinner) lines. We required subjects to locate the target by directing the eyes to it as rapidly as possible. The display elements were located at 3 deg or 6 deg eccentricity and control single item targets were presented on some of the trials.

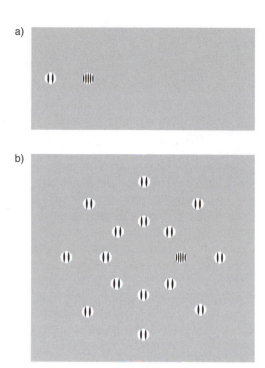

FIGURE 4.2. Search displays with a single distractor (a) and with 15 distractors (b). The task was to move the eyes to a target of specified spatial frequency. When a distractor intervened between the fixation point and the target, this tended to capture the first saccade in the single distractor display but did not prevent accurate saccades to target in the fifteen-distractor displays.

When we presented a target with just one distractor in the configuration of Figure 4.2a, subjects were not able to direct a single saccade to the target when it was more distant than the distractor. Rather their first saccade was directed close to the near display element irrespective of whether that was target or distractor. There was some indication of the "global" or "center-of-gravity" effect, whereby saccades to two stimuli in neighboring locations are directed toward a midway location (Findlay, 1982). However, there was also substantial undershoot for both the single and double targets, and less than 10% of first saccades landed within 1 deg of the target center when the target was located in the more distant (6 deg) location.

We then obtained results from a similar saccade-to-target task where we increased the number of distractors to 15, in a ring configuration as shown in Figure 4.2b. Saccadic accuracy improved dramatically. Now, when the target was located in the outer ring, about 80% of saccades landed within 1 deg of target center, even though there were intervening distractors in the inner ring.

In this case, when the target occurred in the remote location on the horizontal axis, the immediate on-axis configuration of target and distractor replicated that of the two-element displays described in the previous paragraph. Contrary to the normal finding, we found much *better* performance with the increased number of distractors.

Although it is much more normal for search studies to show increasing search difficulty with an increase in the number of distractor items, Bravo and Nakayama (1992) noted a case that was an exception to the rule. They interpreted the finding as resulting from the increased perceptual grouping that can occur when a large number of perceptually similar items are present in the visual field. To test whether such grouping might account for the improved search accuracy in the 16 item displays, we made random perturbations in various parameters of the displays (distractor item location, distractor item size, distractor item spatial frequency, distractor item contrast). None were effective in reducing search efficiency substantially in terms of our measure of the proportion of first saccades reaching the target. We concluded that an alternative explanation was needed of the paradoxical result, and this will be discussed following presentation of a second set of results demonstrating that center-of-gravity effects can occur in a search like task.

In the second experiment, carried out with Valerie Brown, we were able to demonstrate that gravity-of-gravity effects occur during the course of continuous scanning. This is significant because it has been reported that target-elicited saccades made to stimuli with sudden onsets are less accurate than saccades in the general free-scanning situation (Lemij & Collewijn, 1989). Thus while gravity-of-gravity effects are consistently found when the eyes are directed to newly appearing target, they have not been clearly demonstrated in free viewing.

Our result came as an incidental finding from analysis of the eye-scanning patterns in the task shown in Figure 4.3a. The display consists of a collection of "rings," each surrounding a small indicator letter. The rings operate to mask the letter so that it is necessary to fixate accurately in order to identify it and virtually no information about the letter identity is available in parafoveal or peripheral vision. The subjects were instructed to perform the following task. They had to look initially at the ring on the top left, colored red (each display had a red ring in the same top left location). The letter in this ring formed the search letter. Subjects then had to scan the black rings, counting the number of occasions that the search letter was present. They finally had to compare this count with the number present inside the blue ring on the bottom right (present in every display in the same location) and give a match/mismatch judgment. Each display seen contained one red ring and one blue ring, always in the same location. The remaining rings varied in both their number (which could be 3, 6, 9, or 12) and their location, chosen at random from all locations in

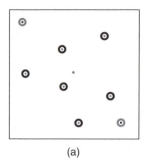 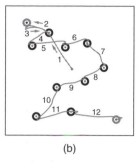 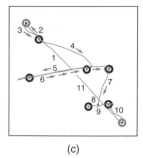

(a)   (b)   (c)

FIGURE 4.3. The "Rings" task. The top left panel shows the display as seen by the participants. Participants were asked to look first at a red ring, always located in the same location on the far top left. This ring contained a small indicator letter, and the task required checking how many of black rings contained an identical letter. Finally, this number was to be compared with the number in a blue ring located in a fixed location in the bottom right corner and a same/different response given. On different trials the red and blue rings were always in the same location but the number and location of black rings was varied in a quasi-random way (number was chosen from 3, 6, 9, or 12; black ring location was chosen randomly with the constraint that a separation of at least one ring diameter occurred between all rings). The second and third panels show example records with eye scans superimposed. The eye scan is shown by the thin, gray lines with successive saccades numbered.

the square whose corners were the red and blue rings, with the constraint that there was always at least one ring diameter separating each pair of rings.

The experiment was set up to inquire how efficiently the eye/brain system could choose a path through the randomly ordered rings and what generative process led to the search path. For the present purposes, it is sufficient to note that the scanning process was, in general, very efficient, with omissions (failure to fixate a ring) being very rare and rescanning (multiple fixations on the same ring) also relatively rare. Interestingly, this efficient scanning during a visual search task (see also Engel, 1977) contrasts with a report that during a task of scene memorization, eye scanning does not appear to operate by distributing scans around different objects (Melcher & Kowler, 2001).

Figure 4.3b shows a typical eye scan. Our in-house software used allows superposition of the eye-scan trace on a copy of the display and also selects each saccadic movement in turn for analysis. Two small circular markers at the beginning and end of the eye-movement trace show the particular saccade selected. The markers in Fig 3b show the first saccade made after the display was presented. This saccade moved from the display center to land close to a black ring. Subsequently, a saccade was made to the red (top left) ring, the black ring was refixated, and each other black ring was fixated in turn before the scanpath ends at the blue ring. Apart from the first, each scanning saccade lands accurately on the target to which it was directed (the small hooks and loops in the trace are the characteristic of traces obtained from the dual-Purkinje eye-tracking system and are presumed to occur as a results of lens overshoot as shown by Deubel and Bridgeman, 1995).

Figure 4.3c shows a further eye scan. As in Figure 4.3b, the scanpath starts in the center, moves to a black ring close to the red, then on to the red ring, and then back to the proximal black ring previously fixated. There follows a large, slightly curved, saccade (saccade 4) to another black ring. The next saccade (5) is directed left to an isolated black ring on the left of the display. The following two movements are of particular interest. The first is a large saccade (saccade 6) to the right, accurately targeting a ring on the right of the display. The first part of its trajectory superimposes almost exactly that of its predecessor but it does not stop at the intermediate ring. The following saccade (saccade 7—marked with the small circle markers) lands almost midway between the two remaining black rings. These are then fixated in turn before the saccade to the blue ring. A further final saccade back to the center of the display was made before the response button was pressed that terminated the recording.

This record thus shows two cases of a saccade to a target in the presence of a potentially interfering neighboring distractor. In one case, an accurate saccade is made; in the other the saccade is inaccurate. Saccade, 6 shows an instance of an accurate saccade to a target that involved crossing an intermediate display element. Saccade 7 shows a saccade apparently directed to the center of gravity of two targets. To establish whether the averaging saccades were part of a regular pattern, records from four subjects were analyzed in detail. A previous study on saccade targeting in the presence of sudden onset distractors had shown that such distractors influence targeting when inside a rather narrow sector centered on the target axis (Walker, Deubel, Schneider, & Findlay, 1997). Outside this sector, a distractor does not affect the accuracy of the saccade to the target, although it does result in a latency increase. The sector is illustrated in Figure 4.4. Although the study by Walker et al. involved sudden onset targets and distractors, it provided some guidance about looking for an effect in search scanning.

We analyzed all saccades directed to a black ring made subsequent to the fixation on the red ring. For each saccade, it was assumed that the saccade "target" was the ring closest to the saccade landing point. The first analysis divided the population of saccades into cases where a second distractor ring was present in the sector and cases where no distractor was present in the sector. The shape of the sector was as shown in Figure 4.4 and derived from the findings of Walker et al. (1997). The size extended from the launch site to a distance that was twice the target distance. Targeting accuracy was coded as illustrated in Figure 4.4 (right hand diagram). Each saccade was assigned an accuracy score, "4" represented a "bull's eye" landing in the central 0.5 deg diameter region of the ring (the letter area), "3" represented a saccade which landed within the remainder of the 1 deg diameter ring target, "2" represented

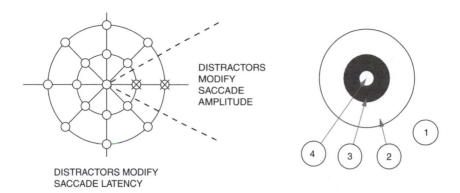

FIGURE 4.4. The left-hand plot summarizes results from a study by Walker et al. (1997). On each trial, participants were required to saccade to a target, which appeared in one of the two locations marked with a cross on the axis to the right. Simultaneously with target appearance, a visual distractor appeared at one of the locations marked with a circle (control trials with no distractor also occurred). On the basis of a number of experiments of this type, it was concluded that a distractor located centrally or in most of the remainder of the visual field, would effect an increase in latency of the elicited saccade. Only in the narrow sector on each side of the axis of the movement was no latency increase observed. When a distractor occurred within this sector, the latency of the elicited saccade was normal, but its amplitude and direction were influenced by the appearance of the distractor so that saccades tended to land at the center-of-gravity of target and distractor location. The right-hand plot shows the coding scheme for measuring saccadic accuracy in the rings task.

a saccade whose end point was in the exterior annulus a further 0.5 deg in size and "1" coded the remainder of cases, in which the saccade landed over 1.5 deg from the target center.

For rings where there was no distractor within the sector, accuracy was high with 18% landing in region 4 (bulls eye), 41% in region 3, 23% in region 2, and 18% outside. The latter figure included occasional cases of multistepping saccades where a sequence occurred with the second saccade accurately on target. Figure 4.5 demonstrates that the proportion of misdirected saccades increased dramatically when a distractor occurred within the designated sector. The proportion of saccades landing more than 0.5 deg away from the ring increased to around 40%. Further analyses showed that the majority of these inaccurate saccades landed at an intermediate position between target and distractor.

Figure 4.6 shows a more detailed analysis which broadly supports the proposal made on the basis of the findings from the study by Walker et al. (1997) concerning the sector within which distractors can influence saccade targeting. This figure considers all cases in which a distractor was located within a sector ± 45° either side of the target axis. The data from distractors on axes anticlockwise

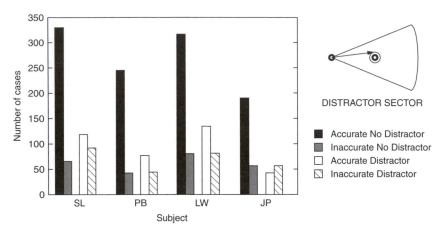

FIGURE 4.5. Comparison of on-target (codes 2, 3 and 4) saccades when a second ring was located within the critical sector as described in Figure 4.4, with cases where only the saccade target ring lay within the critical sector. Data from four participants.

to the target axis and those clockwise to it have been combined. The figure shows this sector schematically with the radial axis representing the relative distance of the distractor and the target. Thus the closest four segments to the saccade launch site shows cases where the distractor distance was less than half the target distance, the next four segments show cases where the distractor distance/target distance ratio was between 1/2 and 1, etc. The figures in each segment show the proportion of cases where an inaccurate saccade occurred when there was a distractor located in the segment and can be compared with a baseline figure of around 0.2 for cases with no distractor in the identified sector. The relatively small number of cases within each segment result in some fluctuations, but the data show that distractor influence operates within a confined region of similar shape to that identified in the Walker et al. (1997) study. Interestingly, there is a suggestion that distractors on the same axis of the target, i.e., exactly in line, may have less effect than those on an adjacent axis.

A further question of interest concerns the status of the distractor in relation to the overall eye scanpath. We again considered cases with a distractor within the sector discussed previously (Figure 4.4) and compared cases where the distractor was a ring that had already been scanned with those where both target and distractor were novel. This comparison is shown in Table 4.1. The accuracy coding shown in Figure 4.4 is used to compute a mean accuracy score, and thus high figures represent accurate saccades.

The data are clear in showing that previously scanned distractors and new distractors both result in reduced saccade targeting accuracy. This suggests

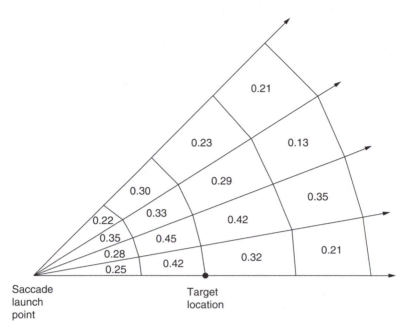

FIGURE 4.6. Plot showing the effect of a second target ring at various locations with respect to the target ring for the saccadic movement. The target for the saccade was established as the ring nearest the saccade landing point. The location of the nearest distractor ring to the target was categorized into 16 radial sectors. The angular classification was made by noting the angle between the saccade launch point to target vector and the saccade launch point to distractor vector, which was then classified as in the diagram. The relative distances of saccade launch point to distractor vector and saccade launch point to target vector were categorized in the bands 0-0.5; 0.5 -1.0; 1.0 - 1.5 and 1.5 -2.0. For each of the 16 segments, the figure in the segment shows the probability of an inaccurate saccade (classification 1 from Figure 4.4).

that the distracting effect is operating at a relatively low level and is unaffected by whatever memorial process allows the scanpath to avoid refixating items already scanned.

Each of the studies described has shown that saccadic targeting is not invariably accurate, and, in particular, is subject to center-of-gravity influences when a distractor is present in a neighboring location. This "global effect" is a well-known feature of eye scanning, but there has been considerable debate about whether it should be seen as a default option imposed by the physiology of the visuomotor transformation for eye movements or as a much more strategic effect (He & Kowler, 1989; Vitu, 1991). We argue in the next section that neither approach on its own can encompass the findings.

TABLE 4.1. Mean Accuracy Scores with Distractors within the Critical Sector as Described in Figure 4.4 (first two columns)* and with no Distractor within This Sector (final column)

Observer	Previously scanned distractor	New distractor	No distractor
SL	2.41	2.30	2.95
PB	2.48	2.63	3.01
LW	2.37	2.48	2.84
JP	2.06	2.13	2.73
Mean	2.33	2.38	2.88

*When a distractor fell within the sector, cases were separated into those where this distractor had already been scanned and those where the distractor had not yet been scanned.

SACCADE TARGETING ACCURACY: SELECTION OPERATES USING A DYNAMIC REPRESENTATION OF VISUAL INFORMATION

In the first experiment described in the previous section we reported a paradoxical finding. Eye targeting was accurate when locating a target presented with 15 other distractors, but inaccurate when only a single distractor was present. We argued that this was not due to any form of perceptual grouping among the distractors. Instead, our preferred account (McSorley & Findlay, 2003) takes account of the underlying dynamical nature of visual processes. We propose that the visual information for target selection is changing rapidly with time. The critical factor that determines the saccade end point is the exact point in time at which the saccade is triggered, with the saccadic destination being then determined by the state of the visual salience signal at that time. The dissociation of a "when" signal, concerning the point in time at which a saccade is initiated, and a "where" signal, concerning the computation of saccade destination, is well established in thinking about the saccadic system (Becker & Jürgens, 1979; Findlay & Walker, 1999). The "when" decision, the decision about when to release the movement, is largely dependent on events and processing at the point of fixation. Once this decision is made, the system is irrevocably committed to making a saccadic movement, but the destination is determined in a more or less automatic way by the visual salience. This is the basis of the finding that, when the eyes are ready to move, they can often be "captured" by the appearance of a novel stimulus (Theeuwes, Kramer, Hahn, & Irwin, 1998).

In the experiment involving searching for Gabor pattern, the latencies of the first eye movement differs considerably in the two critical conditions. In the two-item display, the latency of the first saccade is, on average, about 200 ms, while in the 15 item case, the latency increases to 250 ms. Further detailed analyses showed that a substantial part of the increased target selection accuracy could be attributed to the increased latency. A form of speed-accuracy tradeoff characterizes the search. Our conclusion is that the established global effect can be found in a visual search task, but it introduces a qualification that it is strong for saccades with short latencies but decreases dramatically for saccades with longer latencies (see also Findlay & Gilchrist, 1997).

Why should the latencies differ so dramatically between the 2-item and the 16-item tasks? We believe that the explanation is an effect that has already been alluded to in connection with Figure 4.3. Walker et al. (1997) showed that, when distracting stimuli occur simultaneously with a saccade target, their effect is to modify the saccade destination if they occur within a narrow sector centered on the saccade axis. If they occur outside this sector, then a different effect is found: the saccade destination is not modified but the latency of the saccade is increased. They introduced the term *remote distractor effect* to describe the latter finding and suggested that it results from the way saccadic programming is shaped by the neural center of the superior colliculus (see also Reingold & Stampe, 2003). In the case of the 16-item display, half the display elements are contralateral, and all but two fall in the region where the remote distractor effect has been found.

The salience map that determines the saccade destination is likely to be dominated initially by the powerful early transient visual information resulting from the display onset. This condition produces a strong center-of-gravity effect, and one extreme possibility is that the center of gravity occurs solely when short latency saccades are made to stimuli displayed with a transient onset. Lemij and Collewijn (1989) noted that saccades to stimuli with transient onsets are less accurate than those to already visible targets. Although the very earliest study to report the global effect (Coren & Hoenig, 1972) did not use abrupt onsets, almost all subsequent ones have done so. This possibility, however, can be rejected from the further analysis of the inaccurate saccades in the "rings" experiment of Figure 4.3.

Table 4.2 presents average accuracy measures, now divided according to the duration of the previous fixation. Although, in all cases, saccades with a dis-

TABLE 4.2. Saccadic Accuracy in Relation to the Duration
of the Prior Fixation*

Observer	Short (< 200 ms)	Median (200–300 ms)	Long (< 300 ms)	No distractor
SL	2.60	2.47	2.19	2.95
PB	2.66	2.42	2.33	3.01
LW	2.55	2.26	2.49	2.84
JP	2.00	2.17	1.86	2.73
Mean	2.45	2.33	2.22	2.88

*The first three columns show average accuracy in cases where a distractor was present in the critical sector. The final column repeats the third column of Table 4.1 and shows accuracy when no distractor was present.

tractor in the critical sector are less accurate than those without such a distractor, it is not the case that accuracy is worse when the previous fixation is short—the result that would be predicted if the global effect were merely a consequence of dominance by transient stimulation. The findings suggest, rather, that the inverse of a speed-accuracy trade-off is present. Saccades following short fixations show greater accuracy. This is a surprising finding, but a link may be made with other studies looking for a speed-accuracy tradeoff in visual search.

SACCADE SELECTION ACCURACY: IS THERE A SPEED-ACCURACY TRADEOFF?

In the discussion above, saccadic accuracy has been used to describe targeting accuracy, that is, whether or not a saccade lands on the target item to which it was directed. A different form of accuracy can be termed *saccade selection accuracy*. The measure here concerns the likelihood of a saccade being directed to the search target as opposed to a distractor. One expectation might be that the longer the delay before a saccade is made, the more information can be accumulated and the greater the probability that the target can be located. Indeed, we have already noted cases where evidence has been found to suggest that such a trade-off occurs (the face search task of Brown et al. 1997, and the Gabor search task of Figure 4.2). In their study of oculomotor capture by irrelevant onsets, Theeuwes et al. (1998) found that capture was more likely when saccade latency was short than when it was long.

Both these effects occurred with the first saccade made after a search display was presented, and the evidence for a trade-off in subsequent scanning is not so clear-cut. A positive trade-off was reported by Hooge and Erkelens (1999). These workers investigated a search task in which display elements were Landolt-C acuity targets (the target was a complete small ring without a gap; all distractors were similar rings with a small gap in one side). The rings were arranged in a regular hexagonal lattice. Their displays ingeniously allowed separate manipulation of the central and peripheral discriminability of the items (gap size and a "fat vs. thin" manipulation of the ring thickness of the Landolt-C). Selectivity was measured as the proportion of fixations falling on distractors having the same ring thickness as the target. Hooge and Erkelens found that a difficult foveal task resulted in increased fixation durations and better search selection accuracy.

Nevertheless, two other studies have failed to find such a result. Shen, Reingold, Pomplun, and Williams (2002) employed a task similar to that of Hooge and Erkelens (1999). Shen et al. confirmed the finding that foveal processing difficulty led to increased fixation duration. However, neither of these variables affected the search selection accuracy. Another study that failed to find an effect of fixation duration on search selection accuracy was that of Findlay, Brown, and Gilchrist (2001), who used a task requiring search for a color-shape conjunction amongst 16 display items arranged in two concentric rings. The critical measure was the probability of locating the conjunction target with the second saccade in the search sequence, given that the first saccade had not landed on the target. Findlay et al. showed that search selection accuracy, measured in this way, was independent of the duration of the prior fixation, although it did depend strongly on the distance of the target from the new fixation location.

PREPLANNING IN THE SACCADIC SYSTEM

A surprising result from the Findlay et al. (2001) study just described was the relative accuracy of saccades made following extremely brief fixations. A substantial number of cases occurred when saccades were made after fixations of considerably less than 100 ms duration. Such saccades were as likely to land on the target as those following fixations of longer duration. In some extreme cases, accurate target directed saccades occurred after fixation durations as short as 50 ms., too short to allow the analysis of new visual information. The existence of such cases suggests that the decision about saccade destination was made during the penultimate, rather than the previous, fixation.

A study by McPeek, Skavenski, and Nakayama (2000) reached a similar conclusion that a saccadic destination can be preprogrammed and stored in a way that allows an intermediate movement to intervene. McPeek et al. used displays consisting of just three elements in a triangular array with fixation at the center. Thus all elements were equidistant from the initial fixation position. The elements were colored red or green. Two elements were of one color and the third the alternative color. The observer's task was to move the eyes to the oddball element. As found previously (Findlay, 1997), this task is surprisingly difficult, with frequent erroneous saccades occurring. However, as in the Findlay et al. (2001) study, erroneous saccades were often followed with a short-latency, second movement directed to the target.

McPeek et al. used an ingenious manipulation to shed further light on these cases. On some trials, the colors of two display elements were changed during the initial saccadic movement, taking advantage of the well-known result that visual changes occurring during a saccadic movement do not result in any immediate awareness of the change since the visual transients that would normally signal an attention-grabbing event are masked. For these cases, the target was in one location during the fixation prior to the initial saccade, but was in a different location during the fixation after this saccade and before the critical second saccade. The question of interest was where the second saccade was directed. In particular, two main possibilities can be distinguished. The second saccade might go to the initial location of the target, indicating that it had been preplanned prior to the first movement. Alternatively, it might go to the new location of the target, indicating that the decision was made in the fixation immediately preceding the actual movement.

The results were clear. The great majority (almost 90%) of saccades were directed to the former target location, even when these saccades were no longer appropriate and a further movement was required to bring the eye on target. Only if there was an abnormally long fixation was the saccade target modified. When the saccade destination was plotted against the intersaccadic interval between first and second saccade, the data showed a sharp transition between the two possibilities. Cases where the intersaccadic interval was less than about 250 ms were directed to the old location, while the few relatively rare cases with longer intersaccadic intervals had the following saccade directed to the new location.

The study demonstrates in a particularly obvious way that the saccadic system is able to prepare two successive movements in parallel. This result has been long known (Becker & Jürgens, 1979), and the parallel programming of saccades has been a major feature of some recent theories of eye-movement control during reading (Reichle, Pollatsek, Fischer, & Rayner, 1998). Another set of studies addressing the issue of double, or pipelined, programming of saccades has come from the laboratory of Cécile Beauvillain (Beauvillain, 1999; Vergilino & Beauvillain, 2000, 2001). When an observer is required to move the eyes to a single long word presented in the visual parafovea, a saccade pair is planned with the second saccade having a fixed length. This was demonstrated by showing that the size of the second saccade was unaffected by a displacement of the stimulus during the first saccade. However, a different pattern emerges if, in a similar situation, the requirement is to make a saccade to two shorter words in sequence. Once again a pair of saccades is planned, shown by the continued production of a second saccade if the stimulus is removed during the execution of the first one. However, the size of the second saccade in this condition is now modified when the word pair is displaced during the initial saccade.

Future work will be required to find the generality of these results and to obtain a full understanding of both the prevalence and detailed operation of advance saccade preparation. However, the phenomenon may well account for the inconsistent finding discussed above concerning whether there is a speed-accuracy trade-off in saccadic search selection.

Peripheral Preview and the Role of Covert Attention

Some of the results discussed in the previous section provide a further demonstration that saccadic planning can depend, sometimes in quite subtle ways, on information taken in from parafoveal and peripheral vision during the previous fixation. It is well known from studies of reading (Rayner, 1998; this volume) that the processing of information from the text in advance of the current fixation location speeds the reading process. Information, principally at the orthographic level, is taken in from a word when in the parafovea and assists lexical identification when the word is later viewed foveally. The phenomenon has been termed *preview advantage.*

Preview advantage has also been demonstrated with pictorial material (Pollatsek, Rayner, & Collins, 1984; see also discussion in chapter in this volume by D. Irwin). Henderson, Pollatsek, and Rayner (1989) sought evidence that preview could operate from regions of the visual field remote from the saccade target. They found no evidence for this and concluded that the process was an attentional phenomenon associated with the saccade target. However, there is no need for precise spatial correspondence of the pre- and post-saccadic pictures. Pollatsek, Rayner, and Henderson (1990) carried out an experiment in which the preview consisted of two items in adjacent locations in the periphery. After the saccade, the subject saw one picture together with an abstract shape, and the task was to name the picture. The preview benefit when the identical picture was present in the preview was almost as large when the picture location was switched during the saccade as when it was not. The saccade target in this study was defined in a general way by the items. If a more specific saccade target is given, the spatial selectivity resulting from saccade preparation can perhaps be higher. Deubel and Schneider (1996) worked with a display containing three visual locations separated by 1 deg, centered at 5 degs eccentricity. One of the items was designated as the saccade target, and the task was to detect a visual character probe appearing for 100 ms whilst the saccade was in preparation. Discrimination was high at the designated saccade target and reduced for material positioned even as little as 1 deg distance.

These demonstrations of preview advantage are often described in terms of a close and obligatory coupling between the mechanism conferring visual processing advantage and the saccadic targeting mechanism. The former mechanism is usually regarded as attentional in nature. The findings are thus consistent with the "pre-motor" theory of visual attention (Rizzolatti, Riggio, Dascola, & Umiltà, 1987), placing the emphasis on the link between attention and the preparation of orienting movements. Since the visual processing advantage occurs prior to the actual movement of the eye, it has seemed natural to assign priority to the attentional operation. Statements are found frequently to the effect that "attention selects the target for the saccadic eye movement" and several well-known theories of eye control have developed along these lines (Henderson, 1992; Morrison, 1984; Reichle et al. 1998).

I would like to conclude by proposing that we should query whether endogenous covert visual attention should be given this primacy and whether it really has a "life of its own." The analysis of visual search earlier in this chapter rejected the idea that attention could scan freely and rapidly to different locations within each fixation. Of course, it is possible to comply with instructions to look at one location and attend to another. However, this situation seems effortful and somewhat abnormal in comparison with the ease with which the eyes can be moved. Why should covert attention be used separately? Situations can be found in which it is advantageous to attend covertly without moving the eyes. The most convincing ones involve social activities where overt eye shifts would provide information that an individual wishes to conceal. In competitive sports it may be desirable to mislead an opponent. For some social animals, it may be inadvisable to gaze at a higher- ranked conspecific. Yet these situations surely occur far less frequently than everyday active vision in which the eyes scan several times each second. It seems more plausible to suppose that covert attention coevolved with eye scanning to support active vision.

The ready demonstration that it is possible to attend to one location while looking elsewhere has led to a wealth of studies of the phenomenon. The assumption is often implicit that covert attention can substitute for eye movements and thus is in some way more basic. I suggest that this conclusion is misleading. Covert attention generally acts to supplement eye movements rather than substitute for them.

CONCLUSIONS

This review of eye movements during visual search considered first the way in which the organization of vision into fovea and periphery complemented the ready ocular mobility so that vision operates as an active process with frequent and rapid saccadic shifts. The traditional view of visual search giving primacy to movements of covert attention was analyzed and rejected in favor of an alternative in which no covert eye scanning occurred within each fixation although saccadic eye scanning became an important feature. The next topic to be considered was the accuracy of scanning eye movements in search, and two forms of accuracy were distinguished. Saccade selection accuracy refers to the ability to select the search target from distractors. Saccade targeting accuracy refers to the ability to position the eyes to land exactly on the selected target. Studies of saccade targeting accuracy showed evidence of a speed-accuracy trade-off relating to a dynamic representation of visual information. Some evidence supported a speed-accuracy trade-off in the case of saccade selection accuracy, but this was less clear cut, possibly because of the extent to which two or more saccades can be planned in parallel. Finally, a brief discussion of peripheral preview led to a position integrating a form of covert attention into the active vision cycle.

REFERENCES

Beauvillain, C. (1999). Change in motor plan with a change in selection of the to-be-recognized object. *Behavioral and Brain Sciences, 22*, 674-675.

Becker, W., & Jürgens, R. (1979). An analysis of the saccadic system by means of double step stimuli. *Vision Research, 19*, 967-983.

Bichot, N. P., & Schall, J. D. (1999). Saccade target selection in macaque during feature and conjunction search. *Visual Neuroscience, 16*, 81-89.

Binello, A., Mannan, S., & Ruddock, K. H. (1995). The characteristics of eye movements made during visual search with multi-element stimuli. *Spatial Vision, 9*, 343-362.

Bouma, H. (1970). Interaction effects in parafoveal word recognition. *Nature, 226*, 177-178.

Bravo, M.J., & Nakayama, K. (1992). The role of attention in different visual search tasks. *Perception and Psychophysics, 51*, 465-472.

Brown, V., Huey, D., & Findlay, J. M. (1997). Face detection in peripheral vision. Do faces pop out? *Perception, 27*, 1555-1570.

Chelazzi, L., Muller, E. K., Duncan, J., & Desimone, R. (1993). A neural basis for visual search in inferior temporal cortex. *Nature, 363*, 345-347.

Coren, S., & Hoenig, P. (1972). Effect of nontarget stimuli on the length of voluntary saccades. *Perceptual and Motor Skills, 34*, 499-508.

Delorme, A., Richard, G., & Fabre-Thorpe, M. (2000). Ultra-rapid categorization of natural scenes does not rely on color cues: A study in monkeys and humans. *Vision Research, 40*, 2187-2200.

Deubel, H., & Bridgeman, B. (1995). Fourth Purkinje image signals reveal eye-lens deviations and retinal image distortions during saccades. *Vision Research, 35*, 529-538.

Deubel, H. & Schneider, W. X. (1996). Saccade target selection and object recognition: Evidence for a common attentional mechanism. *Vision Research, 36*, 1827-1837.

Eckstein, M. P. (1998). The lower visual search efficiency for conjunctions is due to

noise and not serial attentional processing. *Psychological Science, 9*, 111-118.

Egeth, H. E., & Yantis, S. (1997). Visual attention: Control, representation, and time course. *Annual Review of Psychology, 48*, 269-297.

Engel, F. R. (1977). Visual conspicuity, visual search and fixation tendencies of the eye. *Vision Research, 17*, 95-108.

Findlay, J. M. (1982). Global processing for saccadic eye movements. *Vision Research, 22*, 1033-1045.

Findlay, J. M. (1995). Visual search: Eye movements and peripheral vision. *Optometry and Vision Science*, 461-466.

Findlay, J. M. (1997). Saccade target selection in visual search. *Vision Research, 37*, 617-631.

Findlay, J. M., Brown, V., & Gilchrist, I.D. (2001). Saccade target selection in visual search: The effect of information from the previous fixation. *Vision Research, 41*, 87-95.

Findlay, J. M., & Gilchrist, I. D. (1997). Spatial scale and saccade programming. *Perception, 26*, 1159-1167.

Findlay, J. M., & Gilchrist, I. D. (1998). Eye guidance during visual search. In G. Underwood (Ed.), *Eye guidance in reading and scene perception* (pp. 297-314). Amsterdam: Elsevier.

Findlay, J. M., & Walker, R. (1999). A model of saccadic eye movement generation based on parallel processing and competitive inhibition. *Behavioral and Brain Sciences, 22*, 661-721.

Gottlieb, J., Kusunoki, M., & Goldberg, M. E. (1998). The representation of visual salience in monkey parietal cortex. *Nature, 391*, 481-484.

Hasegawa, R. P., Matsumoto, M., & Mikami, A. (2000). Search target selection in monkey prefrontal cortex. *Journal of Neurophysiology, 84*, 1692-1696.

He, P., & Kowler, E. (1989). The role of location probability in the programming of saccades: Implications for "center-of-gravity" tendencies. *Vision Research, 29*, 1165-1181.

Henderson, J. M. (1992). Visual attention and eye movement control during reading and picture viewing. In K. Rayner (Ed.), *Eye movements and visual cognition* (pp. 260-283). New York: Springer-Verlag.

Henderson, J. M., & Hollingworth, A. (1999). High-level scene perception. *Annual Review of Psychology, 50,* 243-271.

Henderson, J. M., Pollatsek, A., & Rayner, K. (1989) Covert visual attention and extrafoveal information use during object identification. *Perception and Psychophysics, 45,* 196-208.

Hoffman, J. E., & Subramaniam, B. (1995). The role of attention in saccadic eye movements. *Perception and Psychophysics, 57,* 787-795.

Hooge, I. T. C., & Erkelens, C. J. (1996). Control of fixation duration in a simple search task. *Perception and Psychophysics, 58,* 969-976.

Hooge, I. T. C., & Erkelens, C. J. (1999). Peripheral vision and oculomotor control during visual search. *Vision Research, 39,* 1567-1575.

Huckauf, A., Heller, D., & Nazir, T. A. (1999). Lateral masking: Limitations of the feature interaction account. *Perception and Psychophysics, 61,* 177-189.

Intriligator, J., & Cavanagh, P. (2001). The spatial resolution of visual attention. *Cognitive Psychology, 43,* 171-216.

Koch, C., & Ullman, S. (1985). Shifts in visual attention: Towards the underlying circuitry. *Human Neurobiology, 4,* 219-222.

Kusunoki, M., Gottlieb, J., & Goldberg, M. E. (2000). The lateral intraparietal area as a salience map: The representation of abrupt onset, stimulus motion, and task relevance. *Vision Research, 40,* 1459-1468.

Lemij, H. G., & Collewijn, H. (1989). Differences in accuracy of human saccades between stationary and jumping targets. *Vision Research, 29,* 1737-1748.

Levin, D. T., Momen, N., Drivdahl, S. B., & Simons, D. J. (2000). Change blindness blindness: The metacognitive error of over-estimating change-detection ability. *Visual Cognition, 7,* 397-412.

McGowan, J. W., Kowler, E., Sharma, A., & Chubb, C. (1998). Saccadic localization of random dot targets. *Vision Research, 38,* 895-909.

McPeek, R. M., Skavenski, A. A., & Nakayama, K. (2000). Concurrent processing of saccades in visual search. *Vision Research, 40,* 2499-2516.

McSorley, E., & Findlay, J. M. (2001). Visual search in depth. *Vision Research, 41,* 3487-3496.

McSorley, E., & Findlay, J. M. (2003). Saccade target selection in visual search: Accuracy improves when more distractors are present. *Journal of Vision, 3(11),* 877-892. http://journalofvision.org.

Melcher, D., & Kowler, E. (2001). Visual scene memory and the guidance of saccadic eye movements. *Vision Research, 41,* 3597-3611.

Morrison, R. E. (1984). Manipulation of stimulus onset delay in reading: Evidence for parallel programming of saccades. *Journal of Experimental Psychology, Human Perception and Performance, 5,* 667-682.

Motter, B. C., & Belky, E. J. (1998a). The zone of focal attention during active visual search. *Vision Research, 38,* 1007-1022.

Motter, B. C., & Belky, E. J. (1998b). The guidance of eye movements during active visual search. *Vision Research, 38,* 1805-1818.

Nakayama, K., & Silverman, G. H. (1986). Serial and parallel processing of feature conjunctions. *Nature, 320,* 264-265.

Ottes, F. P., Van Gisbergen, J. A M., & Eggermont, J.J. (1984). Metrics of saccadic responses to double stimuli: Two different modes. *Vision Research, 24,* 1169-1179.

Pashler, H. (1987). Detecting conjunction of color and form: Re-assessing the serial search hypothesis. *Perception and Psychophysics, 41,* 191-201.

Pollatsek, A., Rayner, K., & Collins, W. E. (1984). Integrating pictorial information across saccadic eye movements. *Journal of Experimental Psychology, General, 113,* 426-442.

Posner, M. I. (1980). Orienting of attention. *Quarterly Journal of Experimental Psychology, 32,* 3-25.

Rao, R. P. N., Zelinsky, G. J., Hayhoe, M. M., & Ballard, D. H. (2002). Eye movements in iconic visual search. *Vision Research, 42,* 1447-1463.

Reichle, E. D., Pollatsek, A., Fisher, D. F., & Rayner, K. (1998). Toward a model of eye movement control in reading. *Psychological Review, 105,* 125-147.

Reingold, E. M., & Stampe, D. M. (2002). Saccadic inhibition in voluntary and reflex saccades. *Journal of Cognitive Neuroscience, 14,* 371-388.

Rizzolatti, G., Riggio, L., Dascola, I., & Umiltà, C. (1987). Reorienting attention across the horizontal and vertical meridians: Evidence in favor of a premotor theory of attention. *Neuropsychologia, 25,* 31-40.

Sanocki, T., & Epstein, W. (1997). Priming spatial layout of scenes. *Psychological Science, 8,* 374-378.

Schall, J. D. (1995). Neural basis of saccade target selection. *Reviews in the Neurosciences, 6,* 63-85.

Schall, J. D., & Hanes, D. P. (1993). Neural basis of target selection in frontal eye field during visual search. *Nature, 366,* 467-469.

Shen, J., Reingold, E. M., Pomplun, M., & Williams, D. E. (2003). Saccadic selectivity during visual search: The influence of central processing difficulty. In J. Hyönä, R. Radach, & H. Deubel (Eds.) *The mind's eye: Cognitive and applied aspects of eye movement research.* Amsterdam: Elsevier.

Shepherd, M., Findlay, J. M., & Hockey, G. R. J. (1986). The relationship between eye movements and spatial attention. *Quarterly Journal of Experimental Psychology, 38A,* 475-491.

Theeuwes, J., Kramer, A. F., Hahn, S., & Irwin, D. E. (1998). Our eyes do not always go where we want them to go. *Psychological Science, 9,* 379-385.

Toet, A., & Levi, D. M. (1992). Spatial interaction zones in the parafovea. *Vision Research, 32,* 1349-1357.

Treisman, A. (1993). The perception of features and objects. In A. Baddeley & L. Weiskrantz (Eds.), *Attention, selection, awareness and control.* Oxford: Clarendon Press.

Treisman, A. M., & Gelade, G. (1980). A feature integration theory of attention. *Cognitive Psychology, 12,* 97-136.

Vergilino, D., & Beauvillain, C. (2000). The planning of refixation saccades in reading. *Vision Research, 40,* 3527-3538.

Vergilino, D., & Beauvillain, C. (2001). Reference frames in reading: Evidence from visually and memory-guided saccades. *Vision Research, 41,* 3547-3557.

Vitu, F. (1991). The existence of a center of gravity effect during reading. *Vision Research, 31,* 1289-1313.

Williams, L. G. (1966). The effect of target specification on objects fixated during visual search. *Perception and Psychophysics, 1,* 315-318.

Wilson, H. R., Levi, D., Maffei, L., Rovamo, J., & DeValois, R. (1990). The perception of form: Retina to striate cortex. In L. Spillman & J.S. Werner (Eds.), *Visual perception: The neurophysiological foundations* (pp. 231-272). San Diego: Academic Press.

Wolfe, J. M. (1994). Guided search 2.0 A revised model of visual search. *Psychonomic Bulletin and Review, 1,* 202-228.

Wurtz, R. H. (1996). Vision for the control of movement. The Friedenwald Lecture. *Investigative Ophthalmology and Visual Science, 37,* 2131-2145.

Zelinsky, G. J. (1996). Using eye saccades to assess the selectivity of search movements. *Vision Research, 36,* 2177-2187.

Zelinsky, G. J., Rao, R. P. N., Hayhoe, M. M., & Ballard, D. H. (1997). Eye movements reveal the spatiotemporal dynamics of visual search. *Psychological Science, 8,* 448-453.

5

Thinking outside the Brain: Spatial Indices to Visual and Linguistic Information

MICHAEL J. SPIVEY
DANIEL C. RICHARDSON
STANKA A. FITNEVA

In vision research, accumulating evidence suggests that the coherence of our visual experience involves not only internal representations in the brain but also the external visual environment itself. In this chapter, we discuss a collection of eye-movement experiments that lend further support for this important role of the external visual environment in visual imagery, in visual memory, as well as in linguistic memory and even in naturalistic conversation and insight problem solving. We argue that eye fixations serve as the cognitive liaisons (or "spatial indices" or "pointers") between internal and external objects and events. Essentially, the visual environment can be treated as an additional memory database, with eye movements being the most typical method for accessing such data. The spatial indices to which eye movements interface appear to be used not just for organizing perceptual-motor routines but also for organizing relatively high-level cognitive processes. These findings point to an externalist philosophy of mind, in which the concept of mental activity is not solely defined over neural states, but also includes peripheral bodily states, as well as objects and events in the surrounding environment.

INTRODUCTION

*I*t just might be that your mind is bigger than your brain. Not because you have an ethereal soul that influences your brain via the pineal gland, as proposed by Descartes, but because your external physical environment contains information that you can *perceptually* access as quickly and directly as you can *cognitively* access information from internal memory. One might even say, what is in your immediate physical environment is "part of what you know." For example, do you know what time it is? If looking at your wristwatch is about as quick as (perhaps quicker than) recalling from memory what time it was 30 seconds ago when you last looked at your watch and involves functionally quite similar processes (i.e., content-addressable memory), then perhaps both processes can constitute "knowing the time."

In this chapter, we walk through a range of experimental demonstrations of ways in which people tend to rely on the external environment to store information for them rather than storing it all in their brains. On the surface, the phenomenon that we report—use of spatial indices, or deictic pointers—may appear intriguing, but not necessarily revolutionary. At a deeper level, however, this constellation of findings hints at the potential upheaval of some very old and fundamental assumptions in cognitive science: a mindset that philosophers have called *internalism* (Segal, 2001; see also Putnam, 1975).

INTERNALISM AND EXTERNALISM

Internalism holds that the contents of the mind at any point in time can be fully accounted for by a description of the state of the brain. While a full description of the state of the brain is, of course, impossible with current technology, it is noteworthy that an internalist account of mental content rules out any need for reference to the organism's environment in this description of mental content. Thus, although philosophy will certainly never be able to provide a full account of mental content (since it will not be the field that produces a full description of a brain-state), an internalist philosopher will at least tell us where not to look for one. The environment contains stimuli that influence the organism, and the environment undergoes changes due to that organism's actions, but the environment is not part of that organism's mind (cf. Newell, 1990). According to internalism, it is separate. This internalist conception of mental states seems intuitively obvious, but such intuitions can be severely troubled in the case of the "Twin Earth" thought experiments proposed by Putnam (1975) and others.[1]

Much of the debate between externalism and internalism employs such Twin Earth thought experiments to test for a relatively static inclusion of the environment in determining the truth value of belief states (e.g., Fodor, 1980;

Wilson, 1994; Segal, 2001). However, a recent version of externalism that focuses rigorously on the immediate participatory role of the environment (in addition to brain and body, of course) in constructing mind has been called *active
externalism* (Clark & Chalmers, 1998). This perspective marshals demonstrations from self-organized artificial intelligence research (Beer, 1989; Brooks,
1991), demonstrations from dynamical systems theory (Kelso, 1995; Thelen &
Smith, 1994), observations of situated action (Greeno, 1998; Suchman, 1987),
of collective action (Hutchins, 1995), and collective intelligence (Lévy, 1997), as
well as thought experiments (Wilson, 1994), to argue for the importance of
"cognitive properties of systems that are larger than an individual" (Hutchins,
1995; for a review, see Clark, 2001). Haugeland (1995) has dubbed it the "embodied and embedded" account of mind. Not only does the central nervous system's *embodiment* in a particular vehicle with particular sensors and effectors
pose as a crucial expansion of the old-fashioned concept of mind-as-just-brain,
but that brain-body dyad's *embedding* in a particular environment makes the
whole system a richly interactive brain-body-environment triad.

Although the case for an embodied and embedded mind is compelling for
some (cf. McClamrock, 1995; Ross, 1997), with its robot implementations,
computer simulations, natural observations, and thought experiments, the one
thing this literature has been short on is controlled laboratory experimentation. Importantly, as some of the most devoted (and sometimes unwitting) cus-
tomers of the mind-as-just-brain assumption, cognitive psychologists have
found it easy to ignore this new embodied and embedded perspective precisely because it has lacked controlled experimental results. Perhaps it should
not be surprising that so many people accept internalism, at first glance, as a
foregone conclusion. Lakoff (1987, 1997) provides a number of naturally occurring linguistic examples of people taking for granted the conceptual metaphor "the mind is a container." If the mind is a container, then it must have discrete boundaries delineating what is "inside" and what is "outside," and in the
case of the human mind, the human skull seems to be the best box for the job.
Indeed, the intuition that a complete description of mental activity will come
solely from properties of the organism's central nervous system is so powerful
that it has successfully resisted quite a few attempts to dispel it. Not only has
the internalist mindset survived the recent critiques of contemporary philosophers such as Putnam (1975), Haugeland (1995), Dreyfus (1996), and Clark
(2001), but decades ago it survived Dewey (1896), Le Bon (1916), Ryle (1949),
Merleau-Ponty (1962), and Gibson (1966), just to name a few.

INTERNALISM IN PSYCHOLOGY

As one example manifestation of this internalist mindset in psychology, a
popular framework for theories of visual perception, the "spatiotopic fusion hy-

pothesis" critiqued by Irwin (1992), assumes that the successive retinal images that are acquired in between saccadic eye movements are metrically combined to construct and store an internal representation of the external visual world inside the brain (cf. Marr, 1980). This assumption of an "internal screen" (O'Regan, 1992) on which is projected an image of the external visual world for the inspection of some central executive has—despite its obvious homunculus problems—driven a great deal of research in visual psychophysics, visual neuroscience, visual cognition, as well as computer vision. A number of theories have been proposed to account for the problem of how such noisy, illusion-prone, ballistic optical devices as the eyes can avail the construction of a contiguous, metrically accurate, internally represented 3-D model of the visual environment (for a review, see O'Regan, 1992). O'Regan (1992) notes that over the years a number of researchers have proposed not to *solve* this problem, but instead to *dissolve* it (e.g., Gibson, 1950; Haber, 1983; Turvey, 1977; see also Bridgeman, van der Heijden, & Velichkovsky, 1994). If we do *not* actually have a contiguous, metrically accurate, internally represented 3-D model of the visual environment in our brains, then there is no need to figure out how our eyes and visual systems build one (and perhaps computer vision should stop trying things that way too, cf. Ballard, 1989). O'Regan (1992) suggests that, rather than visual perception being a passive process of accumulating retinal images from which to build an internal 3-D model, "seeing constitutes an active process of probing the external environment as though it were a continuously available external memory...if we so much as faintly ask ourselves some question about the environment, an answer is immediately provided by the sensory information on the retina, possibly rendered available by an eye movement." (p. 484). Not unlike the externalist philosophers, O'Regan and Noë (2001) claim that "activity in internal representations does not generate the experience of seeing. The outside world serves as its own, external, representation." (p. 939).

If it is the case that rather little of the external visual environment is actually internalized, then, logically, unexpected changes in the visual environment should go unnoticed. For example, one should be able to change the color, location, and other properties as well—even the very presence—of large objects in a complex scene and have it frequently go unnoticed. This, however, clashes sharply with our intuition that we are continuously aware of the complete contents of the visual scene laid out before our eyes. This logical, but counterintuitive, prediction of O'Regan's (1992) brand of visual externalism led directly to the recent cottage industry of change blindness research (for a review, see Simons, 2000).

Abrupt changes in a display will typically attract attention immediately if they take place during an uninterrupted fixation (e.g., Yantis & Jonides, 1990). However, it turns out that a range of minor ocular and attentional disturbances are sufficient to mask this ability. If the image flickers briefly during the scene change, participants rarely notice the change (Rensink, O'Regan, & Clark,

1997). If the scene is briefly overlaid by a few blobs, or "mudsplashes," flashed on the screen during the change—without occluding the region that changes—participants rarely detect the change (O'Regan, Rensink, & Clark, 1999). If the scene change takes place during a saccade, it is likely to go unnoticed (McConkie & Currie, 1996). And if the scene change takes place during a blink, it is rarely detected (O'Regan, Deubel, Clark, and Rensink, 2000). In fact, even if the eyes were fixating within a degree of the object to be changed, right before the blink, when the eyelids open back up, and the object has changed, participants notice the change only 40% of the time (O'Regan et al. 2000).

Change blindness also works in dynamic real-world scenarios. For example, inspired by a gag from the old Candid Camera television show, Simons and Levin (1998) had a confederate accost passersby on the Cornell University campus and ask for directions on a map. During the conversation, two young men carrying a door walked between the confederate and the passerby. The confederate and one of the door carriers exchanged places, and the door carrier took up the conversation as if nothing unusual had happened. Only about 50% of the time did the passerby notice that the person he was talking to had changed!

The dramatic effects observed in change blindness experiments provide compelling support for an externalist claim that the locus of perception is as much in the environment itself as it is in the organism interacting with that environment (e.g., Noë, Pessoa, & Thompson, 2000). This is not to say that nothing about the environment is stored internally. As the reports show, many of these scene changes are detected as much as 50% of the time (e.g., Hollingworth & Henderson, 2002), and implicit measures often reveal greater change detection than that seen with explicit verbal protocol (Hayhoe, 2000; Hollingworth, Williams, & Henderson, 2001). Thus, certain attended aspects of the scene are stored in internal memory, and when those aspects are altered in the scene, the mismatch between internal and external representations is detected at least somewhere in the visual system. This point will become especially important in our later discussion of exactly how visual properties that are *not* stored internally can be accurately indexed and accessed from the external environment, via an internally stored label for the index.

THINKING OUTSIDE THE BRAIN

If the external environment is even just occasionally relied upon as a source of visual memory, one can ask whether it is possible, in those circumstances, to purposefully take advantage of and optimize that external memory? In fact, Kirsh (1995; see also Kirsh & Maglio, 1994) cites numerous real-world examples of people doing exactly that. Kirsh (1995) makes the observation that we physically "jig" our environment with physical constraints that structure and optimize our interaction with it. For example, when moving into a new house, deciding what utensils, dishes, and pans to put in which kitchen drawers and cabinets is often done with imagined plans of when and where the various accoutrements will be needed during cooking and cleaning. When arranging one's office desk, the computer, the telephone, the stapler, the tape dispenser, "in" and "out" boxes, etc. are all placed in locations that the user expects will maximize their coordinated and sequential use. Similarly, a colleague of ours, who worries that he paces too much while lecturing, deliberately places chairs, overhead projectors, etc, blocking the way of the most natural pacing routes. These are all examples of physically jigging one's environment so that accessibility and restriction of various objects and actions is optimally timed. This means that information is being built into the environment and thus that information will not always need to be cognitively represented. In a way, a properly jigged work environment can be counted on to "do some of the thinking for you."

Additionally, Kirsh (1995) notes that one way of *informationally* jigging an environment is to "seed" it with attention-getting cues. For example, to help oneself remember to bring a book to school, one might place the book next to the front door inside one's house. Also, many people have specific wall-hooks or dishes near the front door inside their house where they keep their keys. Thus, the knowledge that one's keys will be needed when leaving the house need not be an active component of the cognitive plan to go to the store because that knowledge is built into the environment to become perceptually salient at just the right time. In these kinds of circumstances, we've externalized (offloaded, if you will) information onto our environment, thereby freeing up internal processing capacity, and thus certain crucial bits of information that are necessary for complex behavior are provided not by neural-based memory representations but by the environment itself on a need-to-know basis.

A concrete example of this kind of phenomena comes from a recent study by Grant and Spivey (2003), in which participants' eye movements were recorded while they attempted to solve a diagram-based version of Duncker's (1935) classic tumor-and-lasers problem. The schematic diagram was simply a filled oval, representing the tumor, with a circumscribing oval representing the stomach lining (which must not be injured). Nothing else in Duncker's problem description was depicted in the schematic diagram. As this problem is a very difficult insight problem, only a third of the participants solved it without needing hints. Although the eye-movement patterns were very similar for successful and unsuccessful solvers, one difference stood out. Successful solvers tended to look at the stomach lining more than unsuccessful solvers. We then used this observation to try to influence participants' cognitive performance by manipulating the perceptual salience of components of the diagram.

In a second experiment, the schematic diagram was animated (with a single pixel increase in diameter pulsating at 3 Hz) to subtly increase the perceptual salience of either the stomach lining, or the tumor. A control condition had no animation. In the control and pulsating tumor conditions, one third of the participants solved the problem without hints, as expected. However, in the pulsating stomach lining condition, *two* thirds of the participants solved the problem without hints! Grant and Spivey (2003) hypothesized that the increased perceptual salience of the stomach lining helped elicit patterns of eye movements and attention that were conducive to developing a *perceptual simulation* (Barsalou, 1999) of the correct solution, which involved multiple weak lasers from different locations converging on the tumor. Essentially, Grant and Spivey (2003) "jigged" the environment, with a subtle manipulation in perceptual salience, such that a creative cognitive inference was facilitated. Thus, one might say, having an intelligent environment is just as important as having an intelligent brain.

POINTERS IN SPACE

In the next sections, we will outline several examples of the bidirectional interaction between the environment and cognition and discuss examples of salient external information triggering internal processes, as well as internally generated information being linked back to external objects and locations. In fact, we humans have quite a penchant for externalizing our internal information. Of course, we communicate to others by linguistic means (speaking and writing) as well as nonlinguistic means (hand gestures, facial expressions, prosody, etc.). But we also externalize internal information purely for our own benefit. We recite phone numbers out loud to ourselves so that the environment can deliver the information to our ears, mimicking the phonological loop. We make lists of things to do and of groceries to buy. Some of us talk to ourselves. Some of us even write on our hands. We write down appointments on calendars. We occasionally point a finger at an object when we're silently reminding ourselves to do something with it. And sometimes when we imagine things, our eyes virtually paint our imagery on the world.

In a recent headband-mounted eye-tracking experiment, Spivey and Geng (2001, Experiment 1; see also Spivey, Tyler, Richardson, & Young, 2000) recorded participants' eye movements while they listened to spoken descriptions of spatiotemporally dynamic scenes and faced a large white projection screen that took up most of their visual field. For example, "Imagine that you are standing across the street from a 40-story apartment building. At the bottom there is a doorman in blue. *On the 10th floor, a woman is hanging her laundry out the window. On the 29th floor, two kids are sitting on the fire escape smoking cigarettes. On the very top floor, two people are screaming.*"

While listening to the italicized portion of this passage, participants made reliably more upward saccades than in any other direction. Corresponding biases in spontaneous saccade directions were also observed for a downward story, as well as for leftward and rightward stories. Thus, while looking at ostensibly nothing, listeners' eyes were doing something similar to what they would have done if the scene being described were actually right there before them. Instead of relying solely on an internal "visuospatial sketchpad" (Baddeley, 1986) on which to illustrate their mental model of the scene being described, participants also recruited the external environment as an additional canvas on which to depict the spatial layout of the imagined scene.

Although eye movements may not be required for vivid imagery (Hale & Simpson, 1970; but cf. Ruggieri, 1999), it does appear that they often naturally accompany it (e.g., Antrobus, Antrobus, & Singer, 1964; Brandt & Stark, 1997; Demarais & Cohen, 1998; Neisser, 1967; see also Hebb, 1968). But what is it that the eyes are trying to do in these circumstances? Obviously, it is not the case that the eyes themselves can actually externally record this internal information. When the eyes move upward from the imagined 10th floor of the apartment building to the imagined 29th floor, no physical mark is left behind on the external location in the environment that was proxying for that 10th floor.

Rather than a physical mark, perhaps what they "leave behind" is a deictic pointer, or spatial index. According to Ballard, Hayhoe, Pook, and Rao (1997; see also Pylyshyn, 1989, 2001), deictic pointers can be used in visuomotor routines to conserve the use of working memory. Instead of storing all the detailed properties of an object internally, one can simply store an address (or pointer) for the object's location in the environment, along with some labeling information, and access those properties perceptually when they are needed.

In the case of Spivey & Geng's (2001) eye movements during imagery, a few pointers allocated on a blank projection screen will obviously not reference any external visual properties, but they can still provide perceptual-motor information about the relative spatial locations of the *internal* content associated with the pointers. If one is initially thinking about x (e.g., the 10th floor) and then transitions to thinking about y (e.g., the 29th floor), then storing in working memory the relation *above* (y,x) may not be necessary if the eye movements, and their allocation of spatial indices, have embodied that spatial relationship already (cf. Pylyshyn, 1989). In this way, a "low-level" motor process, such as eye movements, can actually do some of the work involved in the "high-level" cognitive act of visual imagery.

Although it is the address in the pointer that allows one to rely on the external environment to store information, the *label* for the pointer is also a very important ingredient in this recipe. The internally represented label could be something as simple as "target," or it could be rich information such as "the doorman in blue at the bottom of the 40-story apartment building." A pointer must have some internal content attached to it so that one can know when and why to use it. Otherwise, you wind up like Ernie, on Sesame Street, trying to explain to Bert why he has a string tied around his finger when he can't remember what it was that the string was supposed to remind him about. A pointer with no internal information attached to it is useless.

POINTERS TO OBJECTS

To illustrate the use of such spatial indices in visual attention, Pylyshyn introduced a multiple object tracking task (e.g., Pylyshyn & Storm, 1988; Scholl & Pylyshyn, 1999). In this task, participants view an initial display of indistinguishable discs or squares, of which a subset flash several times to indicate that they are the targets. Then all the objects begin to move in pseudorandom directions across the screen, and the participant's task is to "keep track" of the handful of target discs while maintaining central fixation. Participants can successfully track up to about four or five such targets, but if there are more than that, they begin to make errors (attributing targethood to nontarget objects). As participants must maintain central fixation throughout this task, these spatial indices are clearly being allocated and updated extrafoveally.

In another experimental paradigm that demonstrates the use of spatial indices in natural visuomotor processing, Ballard, Hayhoe, and Pelz (1995) recorded participants' eye movements during a block pattern copying task, with a model pattern, a resource of blocks, and a workspace in which to copy the model. In this kind of framework, eye position serves the function of allocating spatial pointers for working memory, in which a pointer stores an *address* in spatial coordinates along with little more than a *label* for when and why to use the pointer. For example, a pointer's address might be something like "the block just to the right of the top-leftmost block in the model," and its label might be "the block I am working on now." Thus, if the participant has just finished placing the previous block in the incomplete block pattern in the workspace, then this pointer can guide the eyes to this new block in the model block pattern in order to access and store its color. With the color of this block now stored internally, the eyes can then move to the resource space, containing many blocks of various colors, and search for a block of the same color. Once that new block is picked up, in order to put it in the appropriate location in the workspace, one needs to know its position relative to the other blocks in the incomplete block-pattern. As the pointer's address itself may make reference to blocks that have not yet been placed in the workspace, the eyes must once again call up this pointer allocated to "the block just to the right of the top-leftmost block in the model" and perceptually access its spatial relationships with the adjacent blocks. With this new information stored in working memory, the eyes can move down to the workspace for placement of the new block. The pointer with the label "the block I am working on now" must then delete its current address and find a new one elsewhere on the model block pattern, and begin the process all over again. This sequence of fixating the model, then the resource, then back to the model, before finally looking at the workspace for block placement was indeed the modal pattern of eye movements observed in Ballard et al.'s (1995) experiments.

But what happens if the external information referred to by these spatial indices changes? According to the framework, one should expect the person copying the block pattern not to notice when a block changes color, except under those circumstances where the process is at a stage where the visual property that's been changed is the one currently being stored in working memory. This is, indeed, exactly what happens (Hayhoe, 2000; Hayhoe, Bensinger, & Ballard, 1998). If a few deictic pointers have been allocated to particular objects or regions of space, and the current task calls upon the label of one of those pointers, the system will automatically seek the address associated with that pointer—fixate the indexed object or location—and perceptually access the external information at that address. If neither the pointer's label nor working memory contain information that conflict with this externally accessed information, then, naturally, any change that took place in that external information will go undetected. The newly accessed visual properties will be trusted as if they had been that way all along.

POINTERS TO ABSENT OBJECTS

Interestingly, this accessing of a pointer when its label is called upon is so automatic that it can even happen when the object to which it was originally allocated is no longer present at all. In Spivey and Geng's (2001) second experiment, they presented four different shapes of varying colors, tilted 15 degs leftward or rightward, in the four quadrants of the screen. Participants were instructed to look at the object in each quadrant, and then back to a central fixation cross. One of the four shapes then disappeared, and participants were asked to recall either its color or its direction of tilt. On as many as 50% of the trials, as they formulated their answer, participants spontaneously fixated the empty quadrant that used to contain the shape being queried—despite the fact that they could easily determine in peripheral vision that the object was no longer there. Participants rarely looked at the other remaining shapes. This is exactly what one should expect if observers are employing pointers to rely on the external world to store object properties in addition to what is stored in the pointers' labels themselves and in working memory. The task calls upon the shape's name (e.g., "diamond"), which activates the pointer with that label, and queries a property of that shape (e.g., "color"). If the pointer's label does not include the attribute (e.g., "green"), then the pointer's address to the external environment is the next obvious resource. A relatively automatic eye movement to that address verifies that the queried information is absent from the external environment. At this point, internal working memory is the only resort. On the trials where participants fixated the empty quadrant, as well as on the trials where they did not fixate it, the same information resource, internal working memory, is used to answer the question. Thus, one should actually *not* expect a difference in memory accuracy between trials in which the empty quadrant was fixated and those in which it was not. And that is, indeed, what Spivey and Geng (2001, Experiment 2) found.

Spivey and Geng (2001) concluded that, since there is no improvement of memory, the eye movement to the empty quadrant does not appear to be an attempt to recruit visual surroundings in order to encourage a context-dependent improvement of memory. Nor is it a deliberate, strategic, attempt to answer the question by looking at the queried object because participants can easily tell from peripheral vision, as well as from previous trials, that the object is not there. Rather, the eye movement to the empty quadrant is an automatic attempt by an embodied working memory system to access the contents of a pointer's address in the external environment. Just as in the change blindness studies, this embodied working memory system does not know that the content in that external location has been removed until it accesses the pointer with that address. Although it is possible to attend to and access these pointers without eye movements when the task instructions require it (Pylyshyn & Storm, 1988), a wide range of research indicates that eye movements naturally follow such allocations of attention (e.g., Ballard et al., 1997; Corbetta & Shulman, 1999; Henderson, 1993; Hoffman, 1998; Tanenhaus, Spivey-Knowlton, Eberhard, & Sedivy, 1995).

HOLLYWOOD SQUARES

It might not be too surprising that the embodied working memory system, relying on pointers that reference visual objects, elicits eye movements to the addresses of those pointers when the system is trying to access memory of *visual* properties. But what about when the queried content associated with that pointer is not visual, but auditory? In a series of experiments, affectionately referred to as Hollywood Squares because the task somewhat resembles the television game show, Richardson and Spivey (2000) presented four talking heads in sequence, in the four quadrants of the screen, each reciting an arbitrary fact and then disappearing (e.g., "Shakespeare's first plays were historical dramas. His last play was The Tempest."). With the display completely blank except for the lines delineating the four empty quadrants, a voice from the computer delivered a statement concerning one of the four recited facts, and participants were instructed to verify the statement as true or false (e.g., "Shakespeare's first play was The Tempest."). See Figure 5.1.

While formulating their answer, participants were twice as likely to fixate the quadrant that previously contained the talking head that had recited the relevant fact than any other quadrant. Despite the fact that the queried information was delivered auditorily, and therefore cannot possibly be visually accessed via a fixation, something about that location drew eye movements during recall. Richardson and Spivey (2000) suggested that spatial indices had been allocated to the four quadrants to aid in sorting and separating the events

A.

The Pyrenees is a mountain range separating France and Spain.

B.

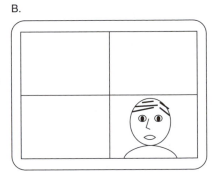

Shakespeare s first plays were historical dramas; his last was The Tempest.

C.

Jim has recently moved to London to look for a job working for the government.

D.

A spaggler is a Roman hook-like used to scrape oil off the body after bathing.

FIGURE 5.1. In the 'Hollywood Squares' experiment, participants looked at talking heads that delivered arbitrary facts (A-D). At the end of the trial, with the four quadrants empty, the computer delivered a spoken statement that the participant verified as true or false (e.g., "Shakespeare's first play was The Tempest.").

that took place in them. Thus, when the label of one of those pointers was called upon (e.g., "Shakespeare"), attempts to access the relevant information were made both from the pointer's address in the external environment and from internal working memory. As before with Spivey and Geng's (2001) findings, since the external environment no longer contained the queried information, internal working memory was the sole determinant of memory accuracy. Therefore, verification accuracy was the same on trials that did have fixations of the queried quadrant as on trials that did not.

Richardson and Spivey (2000, Experiment 2) replicated these results using four identical spinning crosses in the quadrants during delivery of the facts, instead of the talking heads. Participants seemed perfectly happy to allocate pointers to the four facts in those four locations, even when spatial location was the only visual property that distinguished the pointers. Moreover, in the "tracking" condition (Richardson & Spivey, 2000, Experiment 5), participants viewed the grid through a virtual window in the center of the screen. Behind this mask, the grid moved, bringing a quadrant to the center of the screen for fact presentation. Then, during the question phase, the mask was removed. Even in this case, when the spinning crosses had all been viewed in the center of the computer screen, and the relative locations of the quadrants implied by translation, participants continued to treat the quadrant associated with the queried fact as conspicuously worthy of overt attention. In fact, even if the crosses appear in empty squares which move around the screen following fact delivery, participants spontaneously fixate the square associated with the fact being verified (Richardson & Kirkham, in press, Experiment 1). Thus, once applied, a deictic pointer— even one that attempts to index auditorily delivered semantic information—can dynamically follow the moving object to which it was allocated (e.g., Scholl & Pylyshyn, 1999; see also Tipper & Behrmann, 1996).

It actually should not be surprising that an embodied working memory system using deictic pointers would attempt to index information from events that are over and done with. The pointer doesn't "know" that the sought-after information at its address is long gone precisely because it has offloaded that knowledge onto the environment —it wouldn't be a pointer otherwise. These findings demonstrate the robustness and automaticity with which spatial indices are relied upon in order to employ the body's environment as sort of notice board of "virtual post-it notes" that complement our internal memory.

ON CONTEXT-DEPENDENT MEMORY

Some researchers acquainted with context-dependent memory results have expressed bemusement—in some cases, even disappointment—that memory accuracy in these studies was not improved on the trials where the participant fixated the quadrant that had been associated with the fact being verified. There might, in principle, be the possibility for visual context helping a pattern completion process for internally accessing a memory in this task (e.g., Eich, 1980). However, the nondistinctive visual contexts at the participants' disposal in this display would clearly not have been conducive to such an effect.[2]

Figure 5.2 demonstrates why it should not be surprising at all that memory was not improved on trials where the participant fixated the critical quadrant, compared to trials in which he/she did not. As the visual input is extremely similar regardless of which quadrant the participant looks at, it seems unlikely that the view of any one quadrant would provide sufficiently unique contextual memory cues compared to any other quadrant.

Importantly, this makes it all the more striking that we continue to observe participants producing this effect in study after study. Participants get no memory benefit from looking at the empty quadrant; indeed they shouldn't ex-

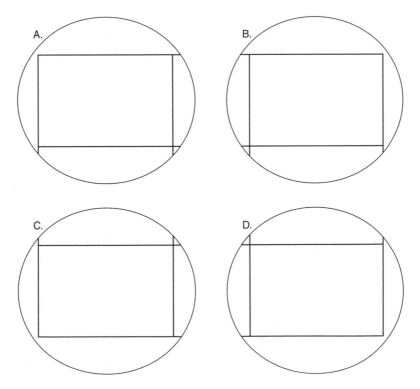

FIGURE 5.2. Panels A-D are schematic examples of the images on the central retina when viewing the empty quadrants during the verification phase of the Hollywood Squares task. Rather little distinguishing information is available for assisting a context-dependent memory effect.

pect to since there is little if any distinguishing contextual input provided from doing so. And yet the spatial indexing system is so accustomed to information in the physical environment being relatively stable from moment to moment that it erroneously treats even ephemeral information sources, such as spoken utterances, as if they are "still out there," waiting for their content to be addressed. This is externalism.

POINTERS IN INFANCY

Is externalism something we come to only late in life? In other words, is the type of spatial indexing we have discussed only a feature of the mature, literate (perhaps even computer-literate) adult brain? Or is the tendency to treat objects and spatial locations as though they were "keepers of information" evinced at early stages of development? Leslie, Scholl and colleagues have argued that theories of adult spatial indexing can be related to infants' emerging concept of "'objecthood" (e.g., Leslie, Xu, Tremoulet, & Scholl, 1998; Scholl & Leslie, 1999). Spatial indexing is believed to play an important role in infants' developing ability to individuate and enumerate items in the world. Thus, theories of spatial indexing have typically been employed in developmental research primarily as an explanation for infants' developing object knowledge. Surprisingly, though, this hypothetical mechanism has not itself been directly studied until recently.

In their Experiment 2, Richardson and Kirkham (in press) familiarized 6-month-olds with animated pictures of toys that danced inside square frames in time to their distinctive sounds. As in the Hollywood Squares experiments, the sounds always came from the same pair of stereo speakers located on the left and right sides, equidistant from the center of the display. In the test phase, one of the sounds was played while the two squares remained empty, and the infants' eye movements were recorded. The infants spent more time gazing at the empty square frame that had previously contained the toy associated with that sound. This first result with the infants is reminiscent of findings by Marshall Haith (e.g., Haith, Hazan, & Goodman, 1988; Haith, Wentworth, & Canfield, 1993), and may be essentially an expectation-based gaze.

However, Kirkham and Richardson's (submitted) Experiment 3 shows something distinctly more sophisticated. Here, the square frames traveled to new locations on the screen right before the test sound was presented. Once again, the 6-month-olds spent more time gazing at the empty square frame that had previously contained the toy associated with that sound. At this age, it has been found that infants are only just beginning to move from retinocentric to egocentric reference frames for representing locations in space (Gilmore & Johnson, 1998). However, even at this early point in development, infants already have the ability to index a sound to a location in space, and even to allow that location to be spatially updated—just like the updating of pointers' addresses in experiments with adults (Richardson & Kirkham, in press, Experiment 1; Scholl & Pylyshyn, 1999; see also Wang, 1999).

POINTERS IN READING AND CONVERSATION

This ability to use space to organize components of sensory input is relevant not just for memory, attention, and action, but also for language processing as well. Spatial organization is used in many aspects of language processing (cf., Bryant, 1997; Chaterjee, 2001; Glenberg & Robertson, 1999; Richardson, Spivey, Barsalou, & McRae, 2003), and particularly explicitly in sign language (e.g., Emmorey, 2002). For example, signers of American Sign Language will use a *signing space*, of perhaps 2 feet in diameter in front of them, and after discourse entities have been introduced and assigned to specific locations, they can be deictically referred to by pointing at the appropriate location in the signing space. In fact, transitive events with a subject and a direct object can often be communicated by simply signing the transitive verb in a fashion such that the hand's trajectory begins at the location assigned to the entity acting as subject and ends at the location assigned to the entity acting as direct object (Emmorey, 2001). No explicit reference or pointing to the entities is necessary. Thus, during sign-language production and comprehension, locations in space must be kept track of as place holders for the various objects and entities in the discourse.

Maintenance of multiple spatial indices appears to be employed in naturalistic spoken conversation as well. In fact, in an experimental design that extends the Hollywood Squares paradigm to somewhat more ecologically valid circumstances, Fitneva (in preparation) recently collected data suggesting that this kind of use of spatial place holders occurs while people talk about different documents in the room with them. Participants were given two separate passages to read at different tables in the room. One was on corporate law, the other on ancient Egyptian burial practices. After the two passages had been read, they were enclosed in folders on their individual tables, and the participant sat facing the experimenter, with the two tables to his/her left and right. The experimenter read aloud random questions about the two passages from index cards (keeping her eyes on the cards), and the participant's eye movements were recorded during his/her attempts to answer the questions. The left/right position of the two passages was counterbalanced between subjects, and the experimenter was always blind to which passage was at which table.

Somewhat similar to this experimental design, Glenberg, Schroeder, and Robertson (1998) reported that people tend to look away from a speaker when they answer difficult questions (see also Kendon, 1967). However, in the present study, participants did not simply look away anywhere, they conspicuously looked *toward* an object that was relevant to, though unmentioned in, the question. Participants tended to gaze left of center when answering a question that concerned the content of the document on the participant's left-hand side, and right of center when answering a question that concerned the content of the document on the participant's right-hand side. As with the previous studies, accuracy was no better on the trials where participants did look at the correct side versus those where they did not.

To be sure, the participants in this study were fully aware that, during the question period, they could not possibly read anything on the pages enclosed in their folders on the tables 6 feet away. These fixations of the tables were certainly not explicit attempts to acquire external information from the environment. Rather, we suggest that they were relatively automatic—absent-minded, if you will—perusals of the spatial indices that had been allocated to the bundles of information inside the respective folders. A portion of the queried information was still available in short-term memory, and among that information was a pointer to the source of the entire set of information to be tested on. Participants' fixation of that source while recalling its content might even be thought of as a concrete manifestation of the process of source monitoring in memory (e.g., Johnson, Hashtroudi, & Lindsay, 1993).

POINTERS IN CONVERSATION AND GESTURE

As noted above, the idea that spatial properties of hand gestures can be informative in language processing seems natural enough for *signed* languages. However, gestures also play an important role in *spoken* languages (e.g., Goldin-Meadow, 1997; Rauscher, Krauss, & Chen, 1996). There are many categories of hand gesture that have been catalogued in natural speech, including *deictic* gestures (e.g., Levelt, Richardson, & la Heij, 1985), *interactive* gestures (Bavelas Chovil, Lawrie, & Wade, 1992), *iconic representational* gestures (McNeill, 1992), but the category that is most relevant to this next experiment is that of *metaphoric representational* gestures (McNeill, 1992). A metaphoric representational gesture is one in which the speaker indicates spatial locations in the present environment to metaphorically refer to non-present objects, entities, or temporal phases in a story. For example, one might extend a hand outward in front of one's body while saying, "So, he's getting C's in college and flirting with a cocaine habit," then move the hand rightward 1 foot, and say, "Then he enters big business and gets rich off of investors' money," then move the hand rightward again one foot, and say, "And now he's responsible for decisions that directly affect the entire world." In this example, the indicated spatial locations stand as place holders for periods of time, which can even be gestured to again later when revisiting discussion of the appropriate time period.[3] A listener's sensitivity to these kinds of gestures was tested in a recent experiment, again extending the Hollywood Squares paradigm to somewhat more ecologically valid circumstances. Richardson (in preparation) played digital video clips for participants, in which an actor talked about two alternative types of objects, animals, people, holiday destinations, etc. Each time the monologue discussed one alternative, a particular hand would always make a subtle movement (e.g., imagine the sort of gestures someone might make when saying 'On the one hand...but on the other hand...'). Although, these small movements resemble simple prosodic *beat* gestures (McNeill, 1992), after several correlated occurrences (e.g., left-hand moves for cats, right-hand moves for dogs), it becomes clear that they are acting as metaphoric representational gestures that metaphorically "place" one referent in one location in space and the other referent in another location in space. Left and right sides were counterbalanced between subjects by using mirror-image reversals of the digital video clips.

After each monologue, a blank display was shown, and a recorded voice asked a question about one of the referents (e.g., "What animal does my aunt own?"). While giving their answers, they tended to look at the half of the blank screen that the actor's subtle gestures had associated with the question's referent. For example, if the actor's right hand had been making metaphoric representational gestures during comments about dogs, then the participant tended to look at that side of the blank screen when giving the answer "a Labrador." Thus, much like in American Sign Language, a region of space had been recruited to serve as a place holder for the referent "dogs," and a different region of space had been recruited to serve as a place holder for the referent "cats." As in a signer's *signing space*, this layout of spatial indices not only allows for a topographic arrangement of the objects, entities, and topics of discussion, but also supports later deictic reference.

THE LOOK OF A MIND

As we have shown, spatial indices appear to be employed not just in low- and mid-level perception, such as perceptual-motor routines (Hayhoe, 2000) visual working memory (Ballard et al., 1995) and visual imagery (Spivey & Geng, 2001), but also in higher-level cognition, such as memory for semantic information (Richardson & Spivey, 2000) and even naturalistic conversation (Fitneva, in preparation; Richardson, in preparation). Based on these findings, we suggest that the objects of thought, the very things upon which mental processes directly operate, are not always inside the brain (e.g., O'Regan & Noë, 2001). The cognitive processing that gives rise to mental experience may be something whose functioning cuts across the superficial physical boundaries between brain, body, and environment (cf. Jarvilehto, 1998).

But what does such a non-brain-based mind look like? The mind, to an externalist, must be a rather graded entity, like a fuzzy set (Zadeh, 1973). In fuzzy set theory, the inclusion of members in a set is graded rather than all or none. For example, in traditional set theory, the set of *apples* would include, with full membership, all objects that are genuinely apples and nothing else. In contrast, fuzzy set theory would assign degrees of membership on a scale from 0 to 1. A fuzzy set is often depicted as something like a probability distribution, with a mode and tails that gradually approach zero. Fuzzy set theory is useful to an externalist because determining the discrete boundary in the external environment where things suddenly go from being "part of the mind" to being "not part of the mind" would presumably be impossible. Instead, one can hypothesize graded membership of external objects and events to the set of *mental contents*, gradually falling off with greater distance and with more mediated causes (e.g., Clark & Chalmers, 1998).

According to this version of externalism, the fuzzy set for *your mental contents* would include your brain, your body, as well as objects in the environment, and partially overlapping—at multiple spatial scales—with other mind-like fuzzy sets. Figure 5.3 presents an idealized sketch of this fuzzy set. The small oval in the middle of the diagram represents the classical set of *your brain contents*. Things inside that Venn diagram are part of your brain. Things outside it are not. The circumscribing oval represents the classical set of *your body contents*. Things inside that Venn diagram are part of your body. Things outside it are not. The fuzzy set of *mental contents* subsumes these two sets, and extends somewhat beyond them in x- and y-space. The third dimension of height in the diagram indicates degree of membership.

Importantly, the fuzzy set of *mental contents* includes to varying degrees, not just physical material in the present (such as a brain, a body, and other objects in the immediate environment), but also causal forces in that fuzzy set's history. As one traces back the causal forces of the environment's role in determining the set of *mental contents*, one must include—with some nonzero degree of membership—social influences accrued over days, parental influences accrued over decades, cultural influences accrued over centuries, and evolutionary influences accrued over many millennia.

An individual's personal (seemingly internally generated) sense of "intention" actually self-organizes across multiple coupled time scales from a combination of evolutionary, biological, cultural, parental, and social constraints (e.g., Gibbs, 1999; Juarerro, 1999; Van Orden & Holden, 2002; Van Orden, Holden, & Turvey, 2003), not the least of which is—for evidence admissible to cognitive psychology, anyway—experimenter instructions and specific task constraints. In this view, mind becomes something not completely dependent on the body, although certainly not completely independent of it either. Rather, mind appears to be an emergent property that arises among

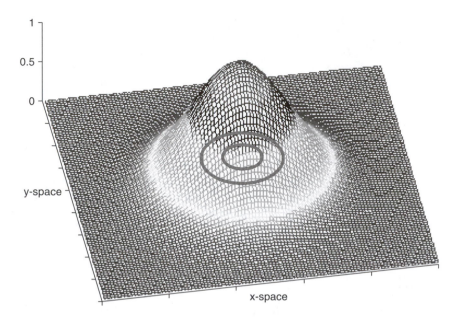

FIGURE 5.3. Along two spatial dimensions (*x* and *y*) the classical set of *body contents* (larger oval) circumscribes the classical set of *brain contents* (smaller oval). However, according to externalism, the fuzzy set of *mental contents* subsumes them both, as well as some of the properties of the surrounding environment, with a distribution function indicating degree of set membership (*z*-axis). Non-spatial dimensions that are likely to be relevant, such as semantic features and causal forces, are not depicted.

the interactions of a brain, its body, and the surrounding environment—which, interestingly, often includes other brains and bodies. Multiple brains, bodies, and environmental properties will often interact and function in a coherent manner that most decidedly resembles what we mean when we say "mind," as seen in collaborative task performance, mimicry, and other examples of social embodiment and embeddedness (Barsalou, Niedenthal, Barbey, & Ruppert, in press; Hutchins, 1995; Knoblich & Jordan, 2000; Stary & Stumptner, 1992).

Thus, the temporal dynamics of these fuzzy minds/sets become crucial for their accurate description— especially when one considers what happens as one fuzzy mind/set interacts with other fuzzy minds/sets over time. Figure 5.4A presents a schematic depiction of three bodies (and brains), like the one in Figure 5.3, moving in space as a function of time. Only one spatial dimension is shown so that the second dimension, of time, can be easily graphed. In Figure 5.4A, two bodies travel near one another for a period of time, then they diverge, and one of them begins traveling near a different body. As time is probably fractal, or self-similar, in this framework, the scale of the temporal dimension for these interactions could be just about anything. The bodies

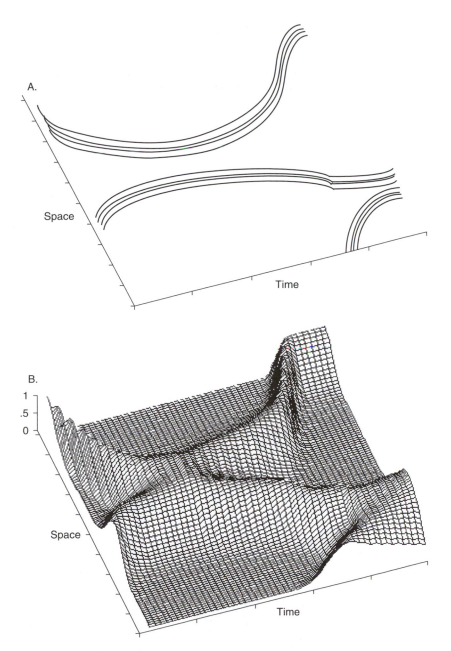

FIGURE 5.4. Using only one of the spatial dimensions from Figure 5.3, and adding a temporal dimension, panel A presents spatial trajectories of three bodies interacting over time. In panel B, the fuzzy set distributions intended to characterize the minds of those bodies do more than interact, they merge into one another at times.

could be interacting over the course of minutes (going from one hallway conversation to another), over the course of hours (going from one meeting to another), over the course of weeks or years or decades (going from one friendship/relationship to another).

For a fuzzy externalist, the depiction of these trajectories looks importantly different when they are defined over how the *minds* interact instead of how the *bodies* interact. Note, in Figure 5.4B, how the fuzzy set distributions merge as they approach one another. When two bodies are particularly close in space (and presumably close in other nondepicted semantic dimensions), the envelope of their distributions approaches having *one mode* instead of two. This demonstration offers a portrayal of how multiple different brains can cohere to such a degree that they function, at least to some extent, as though they were one mind. We suggest, in this chapter, that many of the interfacing links that maintain such phenomena are the spatial indices that connect bundles of information in one brain to bundles of information in other brains and in the rest of the environment.

A BROADER MINDSET

By looking at the use of spatial indices in a wide range of tasks and environments, we believe we have demonstrated some of the ways in which perception and cognition rely heavily on external objects and locations as the very stuff of mental activity. If we picture "mind" as the conglomeration of cooperating processes from both internal and external sources, we are logically forced—a little bit like the metaphysical functionalists (cf. Block, 1980; Fodor, 1981)[4] — to hypothesize group minds, nation minds, and even technologically expanded minds (e.g., Hewitt & Scardamalia, 1998).

Imagine sitting at your computer with the Internet browser open, and you've got an annoying mental block on a particular actor's name. You've spoken his name a hundred times before, you know his work well, but for some reason you have a habit of blanking on his name. (And by now you've probably *trained* the neural networks in your brain to do that.) You're in a "tip-of-the-tongue" state. You can recall that he was in Spike Lee's *Jungle Fever*, Quentin Tarantino's *Pulp Fiction*, as well as Francois Girard's *The Red Violin*, and many, many other movies as well. You can see his face in your mind clearly. His last name is a common two-syllable one that starts with J, and he uses his middle initial in his name. Aside from that, you can't quite dredge up his full name, but you *are* staring at your web browser. So you go to the Internet movie database, look up one of those films, skim through the cast credits, and his name pops right out.

What went on there? You knew some bits and pieces of a memory internally, but were unable to access one of the most important properties of that memory: its label. You were, however, able to internally access some potential addresses for that missing piece of memory. By going to the uniform resource locator (URL) http://www.imdb.com and finding its Web page for *Pulp Fiction*, you accessed the external content of one of the addresses that was available internally. Just like when you look at your watch to tell someone what time it is. And just like when our experimental participants, attempting to recall certain information, looked at particular regions in space that used to be home to a perceivable version of that information. When interfaced with the Internet, we have "minds" more expansive than ever before dreamt of in human history.

RAMIFICATIONS

As with the Internet, where knowledge is about navigation, not about storage, the mind, too, is best measured by its capabilities, not by its capacities—by its processing, not by its representations (cf. Jones & Smith, 1993; see also Pirolli & Card, 1999). Crucially, the mind's capabilities and processing are inextricably linked to the organism's interaction with the environment. Indeed, according to active externalism, it is that interaction between organism and environment from which "mind" emerges.

It should be noted that a wide adoption of this externalist concept of mind would have profound and far-reaching consequences for society. More than just reshaping the theories and experimental methods of psychology and cognitive science, by legitimizing the concepts of distributed cognition, transactive memory systems, and the collective mind (Jonasse, 1995; Nowak, Vallacher, & Burnstein, 1998; Yoo & Kanawattanachai, 2001), externalism promises new and different applied understandings of social behavior, group decision making, and relationships (e.g., Hutchins, 1995; Larson, Christensen, Franz, & Abbott, 1998; Pedersen & Larsen, 2001). For example, when you spend time with different groups from different demographic backgrounds, you don't just *act* like someone else, you *are* someone else. And for a couple to "be one" becomes more than a pleasing metaphor; it becomes scientific fact (cf. Hollingshead, 1998). Externalism has implications for culture as well, explaining how a tradition or fashion or sociological pattern might literally "have a mind of its own" (Cole & Engestroem, 1997). Indeed, the re-examination of the concept of individual responsibility instigated by externalism would shake the very foundations of (at least Western) legal theory, shifting much of the focus of reform from individual criminals to the criminogenic conditions that foster them (Haney, 2002). Finally, and possibly most important of all, a sincere espousing of externalism radically alters one's phenomenological sense of self. When the self is no longer conceived of as an ivory tower in the skull, it can be understood as an amalgam of interweaving influences from both internal and external sources. And so, perhaps, despite the intuitive appeal of one of Lakoff's (1987) favorite conceptual metaphors, the mind is not a container after all.

NOTES

1. Take, for example, Twin Earth, where Twin Gerry interacts with a fluid he calls "water" in just the same way that Gerry on Earth interacts with a fluid he calls "water," but the two fluids actually have very different chemical structures and thus are fundamentally different things. So what happens when our Gerry visits Twin Earth to go swimming with Twin Gerry, and they exclaim in unison, "Gosh, I like swimming in this water.?" If you think their respective mental states are not quite identical, then, like it or not, you're an externalist.
2. Although future research might benefit from providing distinctive markings in each stimulus port in order to provide unique visual contexts for memory primes, that would be more a study of context-dependent memory than of spatial indices.
3. Another example of a metaphoric representational gesture, that has a great deal in common with literal deictic gestures, is when someone points directly at an empty chair that was recently vacated by someone who has left the room (let's say, John) and says something like, "Wasn't John just making that same point?"
4. Except that externalism itself is agnostic as to whether an organic nervous system is required as part of the conglomeration in order for the system to be considered "a mind."

ACKNOWLEDGMENTS

We are grateful to Larry Barsalou, Fernanda Ferreira, Monica Gonzalez-Marquez, Antje Meyer, Melinda Tyler, Becca Webb, and the group-mind of the entire workshop for helpful discussions and comments. We are also grateful to Carmela Alcántara, James May, Janice Ng, Adam November, and Anna Waisman for assistance with data collection. The new work described herein was supported by a Neuroscience Research Fellowship from the Alfred P. Sloan Foundation and by a Research Grant from the Consciousness Studies Program at the University of Arizona.

REFERENCES

Alibali, M. W., Heath D. C., & Myers, H. J. (2001). Effects of visibility between speaker and listener on gesture production: Some gestures are meant to be seen. *Journal of Memory and Language, 44,* 169-188.

Antrobus, J. S., Antrobus, J. S., Singer, J. L. (1964). Eye movements accompanying daydreaming, visual imagery, and thought suppression. *Journal of Abnormal and Social Psychology, 69,* 244-252.

Baddeley, A. D. (1986). *Working memory*. Oxford: Oxford University Press.

Ballard, D. H. (1989). Behavioral constraints on animate vision. *Image and Vision Computing, 7,* 3-9.

Ballard, D. H., Hayhoe, M. M., & Pelz, J. B. (1995). Memory representations in natural tasks. *Journal of Cognitive Neuroscience, 7,* 66-80.

Ballard, D. H., Hayhoe, M. M., Pook, P. K., and Rao R. P. N. (1997). Deictic codes for the embodiment of cognition. *Behavioral and Brain Sciences, 20,* 723-767.

Barsalou, L. W. (1999). Perceptual symbol systems. *Behavioral and Brain Sciences, 22,* 577-660.

Barsalou, L. W., Niedenthal, P. M., Barbey, A. K., & Ruppert, J. A. (in press). Social embodiment. In B. H. Ross (Ed.), *The psychology of learning and motivation* (Vol. 43). San Diego, CA: Academic Press.

Bavelas, J. B., Chovil, N., Lawrie, D. A., & Wade, A. (1992). Interactive gestures. *Discourse Processes, 15,* 469-489.

Beer, R. (1989). *Intelligence as adaptive behavior.* New York: Academic Press.

Block, N. (1980). Introduction: what is functionalism? In N. Block (Ed.), *Readings in philosophy of psychology* (pp.171-184). Cambridge, MA: Harvard University Press.

Brandt, S. A., and Stark, L. W. (1997). Spontaneous eye movements during visual imagery reflect the content of the visual scene. *Journal of Cognitive Neuroscience, 9,* 27-38.

Bridgeman, B., Van der Hejiden, A. H. C., Velichkovsky, B. M. (1994). A theory of visual stability across saccadic eye movements. *Behavioral and Brain Sciences, 17,* 247-292.

Brooks, R. (1991). Intelligence without representation. *Artificial Intelligence, 47,* 139-159.

Bryant, D. J. (1997). Representing space in language and perception. *Mind and Language, 12,* 239-264.

Chatterjee, A. (2001). Language and space: Some interactions. *Trends in Cognitive Sciences, 5,* 55-61.

Clark A. (2001). Reasons, robots and the extended mind. *Mind and Language, 16,* 121-145.

Clark, A., & Chalmers, D. (1998). The extended mind. *Analysis, 58,* 7-19.

Cole, M., & Engestroem, Y. (1997). A cultural historical approach to distributed cognition. In S. Gavriel (Ed), *Distributed cognitions: Psychological and educational considerations* (pp. 46).

Corbetta, M., & Shulman, G. L (1999). Human cortical mechanisms of visual attention during orienting and search. In G. Humphreys & J. Duncan, John (Eds.), *Attention, space, and action: Studies in cognitive neuroscience* (pp. 183-198). London: Oxford University Press.

Demarais, A. M., & Cohen, B. H. (1998). Evidence for image scanning eye movements during transitive inference. *Biological Psychology, 49,* 229-247.

Dewey, J. (1896). The reflex arc concept in psychology. *Psychological Review, 3,* 357-370.

Dreyfus, H. L. (1996). The current relevance of Merleau-Ponty's Phenomenology of Embodiment. Electronic *Journal of Analytical Philosophy, 4* (Spring).

Duncker, K. (1945). On problem solving. *Psychological Monographs, 58,5.doc"> No. 270.*

Eich, J. E. (1980). The cue dependent nature of state dependent retrieval. *Memory and Cognition, 8,* 157-173.

Emmorey, K. (2001). Space on hand: The exploitation of signing space to illustrate abstract thought. In G. Merideth (Ed), *Spatial schemas and abstract thought* (pp. 147-174).

Emmorey, K. (2002). *Language, cognition, and the brain: Insights from sign language research.* Mahwah, NJ: Erlbaum.

Fodor, J A. (1980). Methodological solipsism considered as a research strategy in cognitive psychology. *Behavioral and Brain Sciences, 3,* 63-109.

Fodor, J. A. (1981). The mind body problem. *Scientific American, 244,* 114-123.

Frazier, L., & Rayner, K. (1982). Making and correcting errors during sentence comprehension: Eye movements in the analysis of structurally ambiguous sentences. *Cognitive Psychology, 14,* 178-210.

Gibbs, R. W. Jr. (1999). *Intentions in the experience of meaning.* NY: Cambridge University Press.

Gibson, J. J. (1950). *The perception of the visual world.* Boston: Houghton Mifflin.

Gibson, J. J. (1966). *The senses considered as perceptual systems.* Boston: Houghton Mifflin.

Gilmore, R. O., & Johnson, M. H. (1998). Learning what is where: Oculomotor contributions to the development of spatial cognition. In S. Francesca & G. Butterworth (Eds.), *The development of sensory, motor and cognitive capacities in early infancy: From perception to cognition* (pp. 25-47). Hove, UK: Psychology Press.

Glenberg, A. M., Schroeder, J. L., & Robertson, D. A. (1998). Averting the gaze disengages the environment and facilitates remembering. *Memory and Cognition, 26,* 651-658.

Glenberg, A. M., & Robertson, D. A. (1999). Indexical understanding of instructions. *Discourse Processes, 28,* 1-26.

Goldin-Meadow, S. (1997). When gestures and words speak differently. *Current Directions in Psychological Science, 6,* 138-143.

Grant, E. R., & Spivey, M. J. (2003). Eye movements and problem solving: Guiding attention guides thought. *Psychological Science, 14,* 462-466.

Greeno, J. G. (1998). The situativity of knowing, learning, and research. *American Psychologist, 53,* 5-26.

Haber, R. N. (1983). The impending demise of the icon: A critique of the concept of iconic storage in visual information processing. *Behavioral and Brain Sciences, 6,* 1-54.

Haith, M. M., Hazan, C., & Goodman, G. (1988). Expectation and anticipation of dynamic visual events by 3.5 month old babies. *Child Development, 59,* 467-479.

Haith, M. M., Wentworth, N., & Canfield, R. L (1993). The formation of expectations in early infancy. *Advances in Infancy Research, 8,* 251-297.

Hale, S M., & Simpson, H. M. (1970). Effects of eye movements on the rate of discovery and the vividness of visual images. *Perception and Psychophysics, 9,* 242-246.

Haney, C. (2002). Making law modern: Toward a contextual model of justice. *Psychology, Public Policy, and Law, 8,* 3-63.

Haugeland (1995). Mind embodied and embedded. In Y. Houng and J. Ho (Eds.), *Mind and cognition.* Taipei: Academia Sinica.

Hayhoe, M. M. (2000). Vision using routines: A functional account of vision. *Visual Cognition, 7,* 43-64.

Hayhoe, M. M., Bensinger, D. G, & Ballard, D. H. (1998). Task constraints in visual working memory. *Vision Research, 38,* 125-137.

Hebb, D. O. (1968). Concerning imagery. *Psychological Review, 75,* 466-477.

Henderson, J. M. (1993). Visual attention and saccadic eye movements. In G. d'Ydewalle & J. Van Rensbergen (Eds.), *Perception and cognition: Advances in eye movement research. Studies in visual information processing* (Vol. 4, pp. 37-50). Amsterdam, Netherlands: North Holland/Elsevier Science Publishers.

Hewitt, J., & Scardamalia, M. (1998). Design principles for distributed knowledge building processes. *Educational Psychology Review, 10,* 75-96.

Hoffman, J. E. (1998). Visual attention and eye movements. In H. Pashler (Ed.), *Attention* (pp. 119-153). Hove, UK: Psychology Press.

Hollingshead, A. B. (1998). Retrieval processes in transactive memory systems. *Journal of Personality and Social Psychology, 74,* 659-671.

Hollingworth, A., & Henderson, J. M. (2002). Accurate visual memory for previously attended objects in natural scenes. *Journal of Experimental Psychology: Human Perception and Performance, 28,* 113-136.

Hollingworth, A., Williams, C. C. & Henderson, J. M. (2001). To see and remember: Visually specific information is retained in memory from previously attended objects in natural scenes. *Psychonomic Bulletin and Review, 8,* 761-768.

Hutchins, E. (1995). *Cognition in the wild.* Cambridge, MA: MIT Press.

Irwin, D. E. (1993). Perceiving an integrated visual world. In D. Meyer & S. Kornblum (Eds.), *Attention and performance 14: Synergies in experimental psychology, artificial* intelligence, cognitive neuroscience (pp. 121-142). Cambridge, MA: The MIT Press.

Jarvilehto, T. (1998). The theory of the organism environment system: I. Description of the theory. *Integrative Physiological and Behavioral Science, 33,* 321-334.

Johnson, M. K., Hashtroudi, S., & Lindsay, D. S. (1993). Source monitoring. *Psychological Bulletin, 114,* 3-28.

Jonasse, R. (1995). Collectively seeing the wind: Distributed cognition in smoke-jumping. *Mind, Culture, and Activity, 2,* 81-101.

Jones, S. S., & Smith, L. B. (1993). The place of perception in children's concepts. *Cognitive Development, 8,* 113-139.

Juarrero, A. (1999). *Dynamics in action.* Cambridge, MA: MIT Press.

Kelso, J. A. S. (1995). *Dynamic patterns.* Cambridge, MA: MIT Press.

Kendon, A. (1967). Some functions of gaze direction in social interaction. *Acta Psychologica, 26,* 22-63.

Kirsh, D. (1995). The intelligent use of space. *Artificial Intelligence, 73,* 31-68.

Kirsh, D., & Maglio, P. (1994). On distinguishing epistemic from pragmatic action. *Cognitive Science, 18,* 513-549.

Knoblich, G., & Jordan, S. (2000). Constraints of embodiedness on action coordination. In L. R. Gleitman and A. K. Joshi, (Eds.), *Proceedings of the 22nd annual conference of the Cognitive Science Society* (pp. 764-769). Mahwah, NJ: Lawrence Erlbaum Associates.

Lakoff, G. (1987). *Women, fire, and dangerous things: What categories reveal about the mind.* Chicago: University of Chicago Press.

Lakoff, G. (1997). The internal structure of the self. In U. Neisser & D. A. Jopling, (Eds.), *The conceptual self in context: Culture, experience, self understanding. The Emory symposia in cognition* (pp. 92-113). New York: Cambridge University Press.

Larson, J. R., Jr., & Christensen, C., Franz, T. M., & Abbott, A. S. (1998). Diagnosing groups: The pooling, management, and impact of shared and unshared case information in team based medical decision making. *Journal of Personality and Social Psychology, 75,* 93-108.

Le Bon, G. (1916). *The crowd, a study of the popular mind.* London: T.F. Unwin.

Leslie, A. M., Xu, F., Tremoulet, P, & Scholl, B. J. (1998). Indexing and the object concept: Developing "what" and "where" systems. *Trends in Cognitive Sciences, 2,* 10-18.

Levelt, W. J., Richardson, G., & la Heij, W. (1985). Pointing and voicing in deictic expressions. *Journal of Memory and Language, 24,* 133-164.

Lévy, P. (1997). Collective intelligence: Mankind's emerging world in cyberspace. New York: Plenum Press.

Marr, D. (1980). *Vision: A computational investigation into the human representation and processing of visual information.* New York: W.H. Freeman.

McClamrock, R. A. (1995). *Existential cognition: computational minds in the world.* Chicago: University of Chicago Press.

McConkie, G. W., & Currie, C. B. (1996). Visual stability across saccades while viewing complex pictures. *Journal of Experimental Psychology: Human Perception and Performance, 22,* 563-581.

McNeill, D. (1992). *Hand and mind: what gestures reveal about thought.* Chicago: University of Chicago Press.

Merleau-Ponty, M. (1962). *Phenomenology of perception* (C. Smith, Trans.). New York: Humanities Press.

Neisser, U. (1967). *Cognitive psychology.* Englewood Cliffs, NJ: Prentice Hall.

Newell, A. (1990). *Unified theories of cognition.* Cambridge, MA: Harvard University Press.

Nowak, A., Vallacher, R. R., & Burnstein, E. (1998). Computational social psychology: A neural network approach to interpersonal dynamics. In W. Liebrand & A. Nowak, (Eds.), *Computer modeling of social processes* (pp. 97-125). London: Sage Publications.

O'Regan, J K. (1992). Solving the "real" mysteries of visual perception: The world as an outside memory. *Canadian Journal of Psychology, 46,* 461-488.

O'Regan, J. K., Deubel, H., Clark, J. J., & Rensink, R. A. (2000). Picture changes during blinks: Looking without seeing and seeing without looking. *Visual Cognition, 7,* 191-211.

O'Regan, J K., & Noe, A. (2001). A sensorimotor account of vision and visual consciousness. *Behavioral and Brain Sciences, 24,* 939-1031.

O'Regan, J. K., Rensink, R. A., & Clark, J. J. (1999). Change-blindness as a result of 'mudsplashes'. *Nature, 398,* 34.

Pedersen, M. K., & Larsen, M. H. (2001). Distributed knowledge management based on product state models the case of decision support in health care administration. *Decision Support Systems, 31,* 139-158.

Pirolli, P., and Card, S. (1999). Information foraging. *Psychological Review, 106,* 643-675.

Putnam, H. (1975). The meaning of 'meaning'. In K. Gunderson (Ed.), *Language, mind, and knowledge.* Minneapolis: University of Minnesota Press.

Pylyshyn, Z. W. (1989). The role of location indexes in spatial perception: A sketch of the FINST spatial index model. *Cognition, 32,* 65-97.

Pylyshyn, Z. W. (2001). Visual indexes, preconceptual objects, and situated vision. *Cognition, 80,* 127-158.

Pylyshyn, Z. W., & Storm, R. W. (1988). Tracking multiple independent targets: Evidence for a parallel tracking mechanism. *Spatial Vision, 3,* 179-197.

Rauscher, F. H., Krauss, R. M. & Chen, Y. (1996). Gesture, speech, and lexical access: The role of lexical movements in speech production. *Psychological Science, 7,* 226-231.

Rensink, R. A., O'Regan, J. K., & Clark, J. J. (1997). To see or not to see: The need for attention to perceive changes in scenes. *Psychological Science, 8,* 368-373.

Richardson, D. C., & Kirkham, N. Z. (in press). Multi modal events and moving locations: Eye movements of adults and 6 month olds reveal dynamic spatial indexing. *Journal of Experimental Psychology: General.*

Richardson, D. C. & Spivey, M. J. (2000). Representation, space and Hollywood Squares: looking at things that aren't there anymore. *Cognition, 76,* 269-295.

Richardson, D. C., Spivey, M. J., Barsalou, L., & McRae, K. (2003). Spatial representations activated during real-time comprehension of verbs. *Cognitive Science, 27,* 767-780.

Ross, D. (1997). Critical notice of Ron McClamrock's "Existential Cognition." *Canadian Journal of Philosophy, 27,* 271-284.

Ruggieri, V. (1999). The running horse stops: The hypothetical role of the eyes in imagery of movement. *Perceptual and Motor Skills, 89,* 1088-1092.

Ryle, G. (1949). *The concept of mind.* New York: Barnes & Noble.

Scholl, B. J., & Leslie, A. M. (1999). Explaining the infant's object concept: Beyond the perception/cognition dichotomy. In E. Lepore & Z. Pylyshyn (Eds.), *What is cognitive science?* (pp. 26-73). Oxford: Blackwell.

Scholl, B. J., & Pylyshyn, Z. W. (1999). Tracking multiple items through occlusion: Clues to visual objecthood. *Cognitive Psychology, 38,* 259-290.

Segal, G. (2001). *A slim book about narrow content.* Cambridge, MA: MIT Press.

Simons, D. J. (2000). Current approaches to change blindness. *Visual Cognition, 7,* 1-15.

Simons, D. J., & Levin, D. T. (1998). Failure to detect changes to people during a real world interaction. *Psychonomic Bulletin and Review, 5,* 644-649.

Spivey, M. J., & Geng, J. J. (2001). Oculomotor mechanisms activated by imagery and memory: eye movements to absent objects. *Psychological Research, 65,* 235-241.

Spivey, M. J., Tyler, M. J., Richardson, D. C., & Young, E. E. (2000). Eye movements during comprehension of spoken scene descriptions. *Proceedings of the 22nd annual conference of the Cognitive Science Society* (pp. 487-492). Mahwah, NJ: Erlbaum.

Stary, C., & Stumptner, M. (1992). Representing organizational changes in distributed problem solving environments. *IEEE Transactions on Systems, Man, and Cybernetics, 22,* 1168-1177.

Suchman, L. A. (1987). *Plans and situated actions: The problem of human-machine communication.* Cambridge: Cambridge University Press.

Tanenhaus, M., Spivey Knowlton, M., Eberhard, K., & Sedivy, J. (1995). Integration of visual and linguistic information during spoken language comprehension. *Science, 268,* 1632-1634.

Thelen, E., & Smith, L. B. (1994). *A dynamic systems approach to the development of cognition and action.* Cambridge, MA: MIT Press.

Tipper, S. P. & Behrmann, M. (1996). Object centered not scene based visual neglect. *Journal of Experimental Psychology: Human Perception and Performance, 22,* 1261-1278.

Turvey. M. T. (1977). Contrasting orientations to the theory of visual information processing. *Psychological Review, 84,* 67-88.

Van Orden, G. C., & Holden, J. C. (2002). Intentional contents and self control. *Ecological Psychology, 14,* 87-109.

Van Orden, G. C., Holden, J. C., & Turvey, M. T. (2003). Self-organization of cognitive performance. *Journal of Experimental Psychology: General, 132,* 331-350.

Wang, R. F. (1999). Representing a stable environment by egocentric updating and invariant representations. *Spatial Cognition and Computation, 1,* 431-445.

Wilson, R. (1994). Wide computationalism. *Mind, 103,* 351-372.

Yantis, S., & Jonides, J. (1990). Abrupt visual onsets and selective attention: Voluntary versus automatic allocation. *Journal of Experimental Psychology: Human Perception and Performance, 16,* 121-134.

Yoo, Y., & Kanawattanachai, P. (2001). Developments of transactive memory systems and collective mind in virtual teams. *International Journal of Organizational Analysis, 9,* 187-208.

Zadeh, L. A. (1973). Outline of a new approach to the analysis of complex systems and decision processes. *IEEE Transactions on Systems, Man, and Cybernetics, 3,* 28-44.

6

The Use of Eye Tracking in Studies of Sentence Generation

ANTJE S. MEYER

INTRODUCTION

*E*ye monitoring has been used less frequently in studies of language production than in other areas of psycholinguistics, most notably visual
word recognition, reading, and auditory language comprehension (for
discussions of the use of eye tracking in these research areas see the chapters
by Altmann & Kamide (2004), Rayner & Liversedge (2004), Tanenhaus,
Chambers, & Hanna (2004) in the present volume). One reason for this is that
many eye-tracking systems offering high spatial resolution require the participants to sit absolutely still, which is often enforced by using a bite bar or chin
rest. However, high-accuracy eye-tracking systems that allow for some head
and body movements have now been available for more than a decade. But
one may wonder why anyone would *want* to use eye tracking to study language
production. Widely used research methods in this area are analyses of spontaneously occurring and induced speech errors, disfluencies, and tip-of-the-
tongue (TOT) states and the elicitation of single words (usually nouns) using
drawings of objects or definitions. Sentence-level planning processes are often
studied using sentence-completion or recall tasks (for further discussion of
methods of language production research see Bock, 1996). It is not obvious
what could be gained by combining any of these paradigms with eye tracking.

However, in studies of phrase and sentence production, researchers often ask speakers to describe pictures of several objects or of scenes or events. In this task speakers must process the visual input, understand the scene or event, and find a way of verbalizing what they see. Their eye movements provide information about the uptake of visual information; they show which regions of the pictures they inspect and when they do so. This information can be linked to the content and form of the verbal descriptions. One can, for instance, determine which areas speakers inspect before committing themselves to a particular type of utterance, or whether entities that are fixated upon early are likely to assume particular syntactic roles or positions in the utterance. Thus, as Bock, Irwin, and Davidson (2004) explain in more detail in Chapter 8 of the present volume, eye tracking can be used to study how speakers map visual-conceptual representations onto linguistic structures.

Another application of eye tracking is to use it to assess the time required for specific components of sentence planning. The processing time can be used to estimate processing difficulty. As Rayner and Liversedge (2004) describe in Chapter 2 of the present volume, readers look longer at words that are difficult to comprehend than at easier words, and they are less likely to process difficult than easy words without fixating upon them (see also Rayner, 1998; Starr & Rayner, 2001). Therefore, one might expect speakers to look longer or more regularly at regions of a picture that are difficult to describe than at less challenging regions.

Finally, eye monitoring can be used to study the coordination of speech planning and speech output, in similar ways as the eye-voice span has been used in studies of reading aloud (e.g., Levin, 1979; Stuart Hamilton & Rabbitt, 1997). One can examine whether speakers usually look at the region they are currently describing or whether (and if so how far) their eyes, and presumably their speech planning, run ahead of their speech output. It can also be determined whether the coordination of speech planning and speech output is fairly invariant across speakers and speaking situations, or whether it is, for instance, tighter when the descriptions are difficult than when they are easier to give.

Obviously, eye tracking will only be a useful tool for language production research if a speaker's visual inspection of a picture and the cognitive processes underlying the production of an utterance about the picture are systematically and transparently related. In this chapter we review eye-tracking studies that were primarily concerned with the time course and coordination of speech-planning processes, and we will examine whether this condition is met.

EYE MOVEMENTS DURING THE PRODUCTION OF SIMPLE NOUN PHRASES

In this section we summarize experiments in which the speakers' eye movements were recorded while they were naming two or more objects in a fixed order, using noun phrase conjunctions such as "the cat and the chair" or "the cat, the chair, and the ball."[1] Meyer, Sleiderink, and Levelt (1998) set out to obtain basic descriptive data about the speakers' eye movements in this multiple-object naming task. Speakers were shown line drawings of pairs of objects. The objects were small enough and far enough apart to render object identification without fixation quite difficult. Therefore, it is not surprising that the speakers almost always (on 98% of the trials) fixated upon both objects they were shown. A slightly more interesting finding was that the speakers almost always inspected the objects in the order of mention and only once before naming: They looked at the left object, which they had to name first, for about 450 ms, initiated the shift of gaze to the right object, and shortly afterwards (about 800 ms after picture onset) said the first object's name. Thus, at speech onset, speakers were usually looking at the second object.

This regular pattern—that speakers look at each of the objects to be named in the order of mention and just once before naming them—has been replicated in all multiple-object naming experiments we know of. For instance, van der Meulen (2001, 2003) examined the gaze patterns of speakers naming sets of four objects. She found that the alignment of gaze and speech was very regular. Speakers looked at the objects in the order of mention, just once, and their eye gaze usually ran ahead of their overt speech by no more than one or two objects.

These studies showed that, contrary to what one might have thought, speakers naming several objects do not preview all objects before beginning to speak, but produce the object names in a highly incremental fashion. However, it is important to note that the shift of gaze from the first to the second object usually takes place before, rather than after the onset of the first object's name. This is not surprising: If the shift of gaze (and, presumably, the processing of the second object) were initiated only after name onset, speakers would often not be able to produce the utterances fluently (see Griffin, 2003). Given that the shift of gaze precedes the speech onset, some of the planning of the first object's name must take place while another object is being inspected. We will now review studies that examined *which* planning steps for the name of the first object speakers complete before initiating the shift of gaze to the second object and which planning steps they carry out afterwards.

Current models of object naming differ in the processing levels they postulate and in their assumptions about information transmission between levels (i.e., processing is taken to be strictly serial or cascading, with or without feedback from lower to higher processing levels). However, all models agree that object naming involves two main sets of processes: Visual-conceptual processes leading to the identification of the object and lexical retrieval processes. Each of these main stages (or phases) can be further divided into subcomponents, and the existing models differ in these divisions. Our own working model assumes that the retrieval of a single word from the mental lexicon consists of the selection of a lemma (a syntactic word representation), morphological and phonological encoding, and the retrieval of articulatory commands (for details see Levelt, Roelofs, & Meyer, 1999; for discussions of alternative models see, for instance, Humphreys, Price, & Riddoch, 1999; Johnson, Paivio, & Clark, 1996; Levelt, 1999; Rapp & Goldrick, 2000).

One way of determining how far speakers plan the name of one object before shifting gaze to a new object is to vary factors that are already known to affect specific planning steps and to examine whether these variations affect how long the first object is inspected. If they do, the shift of gaze must occur after the processing at the targeted levels has been completed. Following this general logic, Meyer, Sleiderink, and Levelt (1998) presented object pairs either as intact line drawings or in a degraded version, thereby varying the ease of object recognition. Orthogonally, they varied the frequency of the object names. Name frequency primarily affects the ease of retrieving the morphological form of object names (e.g., Dell, 1990; Jescheniak & Levelt, 1994; Jescheniak, Meyer, & Levelt, 2003; but see Caramazza, Miozzo, & Bi, 2001). As expected, speakers named the degraded drawings significantly more slowly than the intact ones, and they named the objects with low-frequency names more slowly than those with high-frequency names. Importantly, contour type and frequency also significantly affected the viewing times[2] for the objects: Speakers looked for a shorter period at the objects with intact contours than at those with degraded contours, and they looked for a shorter period at objects with high-frequency names than at objects with low-frequency names. These findings suggest that speakers orchestrate their speech planning and the uptake of new visual information in a sequential fashion: They complete the visual-conceptual analysis of one object, select a lemma, and retrieve the corresponding morphological form before shifting gaze to the next object.

The findings from a similar experiment by Griffin (2001) corroborate this conclusion. Griffin asked speakers to name sets of three objects. She varied the name frequency of the first object and the codability and name frequency of the second and third object. Codability is the ease of selecting a suitable lemma; objects with several plausible names (e.g., couch/sofa, sailboat/boat/ship) are less codable than objects with a single plausible name. Griffin found that the speech onset latencies depended only on the frequency of the first object, but not on the codability or frequency of the second or third object, suggesting that the names of these objects were accessed after speech onset. However, the viewing times (or gaze durations, in Griffin's terminology) for the first and second object depended on the frequency of their names; the viewing time for the second object also depended on the codability of that object. (The codability of the first object was not varied).

Meyer and van der Meulen (2000) examined whether the viewing times for objects to be named would be sensitive to phonological priming. This would imply that speakers complete not only the morphological, but also the phonological encoding of object's name before the shift of gaze. Again, speakers were asked to name object pairs. At trial onset, they heard an auditory distracter word that was phonologically related or unrelated to the name of the first object. As in earlier experiments (e.g., Meyer & Schriefers, 1991), the speech onset latencies were shorter after phonologically related than after unrelated distracters. Importantly, the viewing time for the first object was also shorter in the phonologically related than in the unrelated condition, which shows that the speakers fixated upon the first object at least until they had retrieved the phonological form of its name and only then started to inspect the next object.

Finally, several investigators have studied the effect of name length, which is another phonological variable, on viewing times for objects. In a pioneering study, Pynte (1974) determined how long speakers looked at triplets of numerals they were to recall later. The experiment was carried out with native speakers of French. The critical item was the middle one in the row. In Experiment 1, its name had either one syllable (French "trente," 30) or three syllables ("quatre-vingt-dix," 90); in Experiment 2, the name of the target had either two or three syllables ("vingt-huit," 28, or "quatre-vingt-deux," 82). In both experiments, Pynte found that the item with the short name was looked at for shorter (by about 110 ms) than the item with the longer name. He concluded that the time required to plan the numeral names (to achieve "readiness for pronunciation," as he called it), depended on the length of the names.

Noizet and Pynte (1976) asked participants to inspect objects with monosyllabic names and objects with names including four or five syllables. The participants knew that no overt reaction to the pictures would be required. Noizet and Pynte found that the objects with long names were inspected for longer (by about 115 ms) than those with shorter names. They concluded that the participants implicitly labeled the targets, which took longer for items with long than with short names.[2]

Zelinski and Murphy (2000) used a memory task in which speakers on each trial first studied a display of four objects. After a brief interval they saw one of the objects again and had to indicate whether it had been part of the studied set. In each display two objects had monosyllabic names and two had trisyllabic names. Monosyllabic and trisyllabic items were matched for ease of object recognition. Zelinski and Murphy found that during the study phase, participants looked longer at objects with long than with shorter names. This was true for the first inspection times for the objects (differing by 130 ms) as well as for the total inspection times (differing by 210 ms). Thus, as part of their efforts to remember the objects, the speakers apparently generated the names of the objects, which took substantially longer for trisyllabic than for monosyllabic names.[3]

In the studies carried out by Pynte (1974), Noizet and Pynte (1976), and Zelinski & Murphy (2000), eye movements were recorded while the participants carried out various inner speech tasks. By contrast, Meyer, Roelofs, and Levelt (2003) asked speakers to name pairs of objects with monosyllabic and disyllabic names overtly and recorded their eye movements before and after speech onset. As one might expect, given the results of the studies reviewed above, they observed shorter naming latencies and viewing times for the objects with short names than for the objects with longer names. However, this was only true when the items with long and short names were tested in separate blocks of trials. When they were mixed, no length effects were found for latencies or viewing times. Meyer et al. argued that in mixed and pure blocks speakers used different criteria in deciding when to begin to speak. In pure blocks they fully prepared the phonological form of the targets and retrieved the corresponding articulatory commands before speech onset. For monosyllabic targets they generated one syllable at the phonological and articulatory level; for disyllabic targets they generated two syllables at both levels. In mixed blocks, they still fully prepared the monosyllabic targets at the phonological and articulatory levels. But for the disyllabic targets, they prepared the complete phonological form, but initiated articulation as soon as they had retrieved the articulatory program for the first syllable. Thus, irrespective of the length of the target, articulation was initiated as soon as the syllable program for one syllable had been retrieved. The results of computer simulations using the WEAVER++ model (Roelofs, 1997), which implements the model proposed by Levelt et al.(1999), are consistent with this view. Here, the most important point to note is that parallel patterns of results were obtained for the latencies and viewing times: When a length effect was obtained for the latencies, there was a length effect for the viewing times as well. When no length effect was observed for the latencies, there was no such effect for the viewing times either. This suggests that the criteria governing the timing of the speech onset and of the shift of gaze to a new object were similar: Speakers began to speak and initiated the saccade to a new object when they had generated the complete phonological form of the first object's name and the articulatory commands for one syllable (in mixed blocks) or for all syllables (in pure blocks).

However, the criteria for speech onset and the initiation of the shift of gaze, though similar, were not identical. This follows from the fact that the length effect was significantly larger for the viewing times (60 ms) than for the latencies (37 ms). Therefore, the time lag between the end of the inspection of the first object and the beginning of articulation was longer before short than before long words. In other words, when the name of the first object was short, speakers spent slightly more time looking at the second object before speech onset than when the first name was long. Griffin (2003) reported a similar pattern of results. She also presented pairs of objects for naming, the first of which had a monosyllabic or disyllabic name. Objects with long and short names were mixed and, as in the corresponding condition of the experiment by Meyer et al., no word length effect was obtained for the viewing times for the first object. However, Griffin observed a *reversed* length for the latencies: Speakers initiated the utterances slightly later when the first word was short than when it was long, and they spent the extra time before speech onset looking at the second object. Griffin concluded that in deciding when to begin to speak, speakers can take into account how much planning time for later utterance fragments they will have during the articulation of the first word. If the first word is long, offering plenty of planning time during articulation, the utterance will be initiated slightly earlier than if it is short.[5]

In summary, when people generate object names in inner speech, they look at the objects at least until they have retrieved the phonological form of their names. This may actually be the most detailed representation that can be generated in inner speech (for further discussion, see Wheeldon & Levelt, 1995). When speakers generate object names for overt speech, at least part of the articulatory commands are generated before the shift of gaze as well. Thus, speakers generate noun-phrase conjunctions such as "the cat and the dog" in a highly sequential fashion, starting to look at the second object just in time to be able to generate fluent speech, but not earlier.

EYE MOVEMENTS DURING THE PRODUCTION OF COMPLEX NOUN PHRASES

In the studies described above, speakers referred to objects in simple noun phrases, such as "cat" or "the cat." When the target words appeared in utterance-initial position, very similar results were obtained for the speech onset latencies and the viewing times for the targets. The relationship between viewing times and speech onset latencies changes dramatically when speakers describe objects in longer utterances. Meyer and Forti (submitted, see also Levelt & Meyer, 2000) showed speakers pictures of objects appearing in different sizes and colors. In the first experiment Dutch speakers named the objects in simple noun phrases such as "de step en de muts" ("the scooter and the hat") or, in a different block of trials, mentioned the size and color of the objects as well, as in "de kleine zwarte step en de muts" ("the little black scooter and the hat"). The speech onset latencies for the two phrase types did not differ significantly. This is not too surprising given that earlier studies have shown that speakers often initiate complex phrases before having planned all of their constituents (e.g., Schriefers & Teruel, 1999; see also Costa & Caramazza, 2002; Ferreira & Swets, 2002). Thus, speakers saying "de kleine zwarte step" probably fully planned only part of the first phrase, e.g., the determiner and the first adjective, before speech onset. This did not take much longer than preparing the determiner and noun for "de step." By contrast, the mean

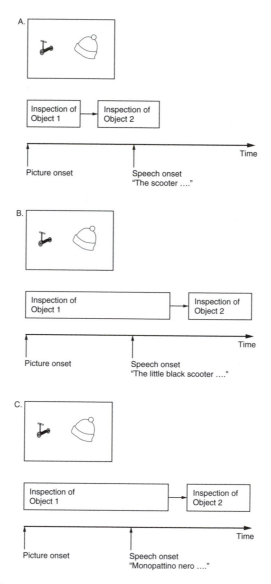

FIGURE 6.1. Schematic representation of speech-to-gaze alignment for Dutch noun phrases (Figure 6.1A) and adjective-noun phrases (Figure 6.1B) and Italian noun-adjective phrases (Figure 6.1C).

viewing time for the target objects was more than twice as long when complex than when simple noun phrases were required (see Figure 6.1). Analyses of the temporal coordination of the speakers' eye movements and the speech output showed that for both phrase types, the shift of gaze to the second object was initiated about 250 ms before the onset of the phrase-final noun.

To determine whether the shift of gaze was time-locked to the onset of the noun or the onset of the phrase-final word, Meyer and Forti carried out a second experiment in which Italian speakers described the similar pictures in utterances such as "monopattino" ("scooter") or "monopattino nero" ("scooter black"), exploiting the fact that in Italian the color adjective follows the noun. As in the Dutch experiment, the speech onset latencies did not differ significantly between the two phrase types. However, the viewing times for the target objects were again much longer for the complex than for the simple noun phrases. The Italian speakers, like the Dutch speakers, initiated the shift of gaze shortly before the onset of the last word of the phrase referring to the first object. Thus, when speakers produce complex noun phrases, their eyes remain on the referent object until they have fully planned the phrase about the object and are about to initiate the phrase-final word.

Van Tuinen (2000) monitored the eye movements of speakers describing paths through networks of objects (see Ferreira & Henderson, 1998, and Levelt, 1981, for earlier uses of this task). She found that the viewing times were longer at choice points, where the network branched and the speaker had to decide which branch to describe first, than at nonchoice points. Contrary to the author's expectation, the mean eye-voice span, measured as the time interval between the onset of the first fixation on an object and the onset of the referring expression, was the same for choice and nonchoice points. In this study, speakers often produced complex phrases to describe the objects and the trajectories between them. Given the results obtained by Meyer and Forti, we would not expect the eye-voice span, but the time interval between the onset of fixation and the onset of the *last* word about an object to be different for choice and nonchoice points.

Why do speakers look at the objects for such long periods? Theories of lexical access usually assume that the input to the mental lexicon is a conceptual, not a visual representation. Thus, one might have thought that after a target object has been identified, visual information would no longer be required for, or even supportive of, lexical access. In addition, lexical access is often assumed to be a fairly automatic process (e.g., Levelt, 1989); thus, one might expect that it could easily be carried out "in the background" while visual attention is directed at another object. As Bock, Irwin, and Davidson (2004) describe in Chapter 8 of the present volume, speakers can name objects that are presented for much shorter periods than the viewing times typically observed in the multiple-naming experiments (see also Bock, Irwin, Davidson, & Levelt, 2003). However, they clearly prefer to look at them for a longer time. There are a number of reasons why looking at the referent object may facilitate speaking, which are discussed in more detail by Griffin (2004) in Chapter 7 of the present volume. First, the sustained visual input may help to maintain a high level of activation of the associated concepts and linguistic units. Within a cascaded processing model, one might assume that as long as an object is looked at (or perhaps as long as it is attended to), activation spreads from the activated visual representation to the conceptual and linguistic units. Within a serial stage model, one might assume that as long as an object is looked at (or attended to), the corresponding conceptual and lexical processing units are periodically reactivated. Second, the sequential visual processing of objects may serve to minimize interference among processing units of the same type and insure that they are produced in the correct order. Two coactivated lemmas or phonological forms, which are selected almost simultaneously, might interfere more with each other and might be more likely to be exchanged than two units that are activated and selected in sequence. Finally, sequential visual processing may facilitate self-monitoring processes. Current theories of self-monitoring (e.g., Postma, 2000) assume that speakers compare the phonological representation for a planned utterance against the conceptual input. However, when describing pictures of objects and events, speakers may prefer to compare the planned utterance against the visual input rather than a memory representation thereof. This would be in line with findings from other research areas showing that people generally prefer to rely on external visual information to using memory representations of the environment (see, for instance, Ballard, Hayhoe, Pook, & Rao, 1997; Hayhoe, 2000; Spivey, Richardson, & Fitneva, 2004, in the present volume).

PROCESSING OF EXTRAFOVEAL OBJECTS

As discussed above, speakers naming several objects fixate upon them until shortly before they say their names. Thus, when an object is fixated at trial onset and has not been seen before, the viewing time for the object is a good indicator of the total processing time for the object. However, objects that are visible extrafoveally may begin to be processed before fixation. In an experiment by Pollatsek, Rayner, and Collins (1984), participants first fixated a point on the left side of the screen.[6] Then a line drawing of an object appeared on the right side, and the participants moved their eyes towards it. During the saccade, this interloper picture was replaced by a target picture, which the participants had to name as fast as possible. In one experimental condition, interloper and target were identical, whereas in another condition, they had homophonous names (such as "bat," "pen," or "pitcher"). Pollatsek et al. found that the targets were named faster in the homophone condition than in a control condition, in which the interloper was a square, though not as fast as in the identity condition. The homophone effect demonstrates that the participants accessed the name of the interloper, which they only saw extrafoveally.

Morgan and Meyer (submitted) are currently using a similar paradigm to investigate extrafoveal object processing in the multiple-object naming task. In these experiments, the participants see and name triplets of line drawings. On some trials, the middle object changes during the saccade from the first object towards it. As in the experiment by Pollatsek et al., the relationship between the target and the interloper picture, which is only seen extrafoveally, is varied. They can, for instance, be identical, unrelated, or conceptually related objects. The available results suggest that the visual analysis of the second object begins while the first object is being fixated upon. Whether access to the name of the second object also begins before fixation remains to be determined.

As noted, Griffin (2001) obtained effects of the codability and frequency of the name of the second of three objects on the viewing time for that object. This suggests that the name of the object may have begun to be activated before fixation, but that the lexical retrieval processes were not completed before the object was fixated upon. If these processes had been completed before fixation onset, no effects of codability and frequency on the viewing times should have been obtained.

More research is required to determine how far objects that are about to be named are processed before fixation. This may depend on properties of the visual displays (such as the size of the objects and their distance; for further discussion see Henderson & Ferreira, 2004, and Irwin, 2004, in the present volume) as well as linguistic variables (such as the ease of retrieving the name of the fixated and the extrafoveal object). The results of such studies should have important implications for the interpretation of viewing times. The serial inspection of objects, observed in many multiple-object naming experiments, can only be taken to indicate a highly incremental way of processing of objects and generating phrases about them if the extrafoveal processing of upcoming target objects is minimal.

REPEATED REFERENCE

In the experiments discussed above, the speakers saw different objects on each trial. One simple reason why they usually fixated upon the objects is that objects are easiest to recognize when fixated upon. Van der Meulen, Meyer, and Levelt (2001) studied what happened when speakers repeatedly referred to the same object, as one often does in spontaneous speech. Would speakers still look at the object before naming it, or would they, when the referent object is known and fixation is not necessary for object recognition, rely on a memory representation of the object instead? On successive trials, speakers saw pairs of displays that shared the left object. In one block of trials, the speakers were asked to use noun phrases, such as "The angel is next to the camel. *The angel* is now next to the bed." In another block of trials, the speakers were asked to use a pronoun to refer to the repeated object ("The angel is next to the camel. *It* is now next to the bed.") This experiment was carried out in Dutch, where the pronoun was "hij" ("it") on all trials, and in German, where speakers had to select one of three pronouns depending on the grammatical gender of the corresponding noun ("er," "sie," or "es"). In the German experiment, there were only three target objects in each block of trials, which differed in the grammatical gender of their names. On each trial, the speakers in the noun phrase condition selected one of three noun phrases, and the speakers in the pronoun condition selected one of three pronouns.

The German and Dutch experiments yielded very similar results: Speakers were most likely to look at the left object on the first trial of a pair (on about 82% of the trials in the German experiment), less likely to do so on the second trial when they produced a noun phrase (on 67% of the trials), and least likely when they produced a pronoun (on 50% of the trials). The same pattern of results was obtained for the viewing times on trials where the targets were fixated upon: The mean viewing time was longest on the first trial of a pair, intermediate in the second trial noun phrase condition, and shortest in the pronoun condition. Thus, speakers did not look at *every* object they referred to, but were quite likely to "skip" known objects, especially when they used pronouns.

In these experiments, a blank intertrial interval intervened between the first and the second trial of a pair. Perhaps the speakers used this interval to prepare for the next utterance, which would explain why the fixation rates on the targets were quite low. In a recent series of experiments, Morgan and Meyer (in preparation) examined how likely speakers were to fixate upon a known object that was to be named as the middle object between two new objects. The speakers named triplets of objects (as in "cat, chair, doll"). In one condition, three different objects appeared on each trial. In the other condition, the middle object remained constant across blocks of 12 trials. Speakers knew ahead of time whether they would be working on a block with constant or variable middle objects. In the variable blocks they almost always inspected all three objects in the order of mention. By contrast, in the constant blocks, the repeated object was named without prior fixation on about 20% of the trials. When it *was* inspected, the average viewing time was shorter than in the variable condition. Across experiments Morgan and Meyer varied the size of the repeated object, making it easy or almost impossible for the speakers to identify while fixating the first object. This manipulation affected how long the repeated object was inspected (when it was fixated at all), but it did not affect the likelihood of inspection. These preliminary results suggest that when speakers named objects without fixating upon them, they did not rely heavily on extrafoveal processing of the objects but more on a stored representation of the object or its name.

In sum, when speakers repeatedly refer to the same object, using either the same or a different expression, they may or may not look at the object again. What determines whether a person will fixate upon a known object again before naming it? The proposal by van der Meulen et al. was inspired by the model of eye-movement control during reading proposed by Reichle, Pollatsek, Fisher, & Rayner (1998). They assumed that speakers plan an eye movement to each object to be named. However, if the name of an object becomes available fast enough, i.e., before the planning of the eye movement to the object has reached a stage where it cannot be cancelled any more, the eye movement may be cancelled and an eye movement to another object will be planned. An object name may be readily available when the speaker has named the object before and has stored a relevant representation in working memory. Interestingly, in the experiments by van der Meulen et al., the inspection rate was lower in the pronoun than in the noun condition, although in the latter condition the speaker used the same phrase as on the preceding trial. This suggests that the speakers' working memory representation was a conceptual representation of the object rather than a representation of the linguistic expression used before. On the basis of this representation the pronoun could be generated more readily than the noun phrase, which accounts for the difference in the inspection rates. Obviously, this account is tentative. So far, we have no direct evidence that the speakers sometimes planned and then cancelled eye movements to the target objects; alternatively, they may never have planned eye movements to these objects in the first place.

In the studies just described the speakers referred twice to the object category in noun phrases or pronouns. Meyer, van der Meulen, and Brooks (in press) asked speakers to describe object pairs in utterances such as "the green ball is next to the block" or "the ball next to the block is green." In the latter type of utterance, speakers first referred to the object category and a little later to the color of the object. The main question was whether speakers would usually look at the target object again before naming its color, or whether they would rely on a memory representation of the color information, which they might have generated during the initial inspection of the object. When speakers produced adjective-noun phrases ("the green ball"), they fixated upon the left object for about 1400 ms and then turned to the right object. By contrast, when they produced adjective-final utterances ("the ball next to the block is green"), they initially looked at the left object for about 800 ms, then turned to the right object just before naming it; on approximately 80 % of the trials they looked at the left object again about 600 ms before the onset of the adjective. On the remaining trials they named the color of the object without inspecting it again. These results are quite similar to those reported by van der Meulen et al.: When speakers refer to an object they have named before either naming the object again or naming its color, they *usually* look at the object again, but they don't always do so. In the latter case, an appropriate referring expression (the name of the object or the name of its color) may be very fast to be retrieved, which leads to the cancellation of the eye movement to the object.

EYE MOVEMENTS DURING SCENE AND EVENT DESCRIPTION

In the experiments described above, speakers were asked to name sets of objects in a predefined order. One may ask how much of the orderly coordination between eye gaze and speech will be maintained when speakers produce more complex utterances and when they decide themselves, as speakers usually do in spontaneous speech, what to name and in which order to do so. Van der Meulen (2001, 2003) compared the speakers' gaze patterns when they described objects in a fixed order using a prescribed sentence structure and when they determined the order of mention and syntactic structure themselves. On each trial, she presented a set of four objects. The objects were to be described in utterances such as "the cat is above the pen and the fork is above the watch" when all four objects were different, and in utterances such as "the cat and the fork are above a pen" when the bottom two objects were identical. In one condition, the materials were blocked such that throughout a block of trials the bottom objects were always identical, or they were always different. Therefore, the same syntactic structure could be used on all trials of a block. Van der Meulen again observed the tight coordination between eye gaze and speech described above: Speakers fixated upon each object just before naming it, about 500 to 600 ms before noun onset. In another condition, the two types of displays were mixed. Here the speakers had to determine on each trial whether the two bottom objects were identical or different and had to select the appropriate sentence structure. Here, the speakers were far more likely than in the blocked condition to inspect the bottom objects during the first 500 ms of the trial. Usually, they looked at the bottom objects again just before naming them. In fact, the speakers' likelihood of inspecting one of the bottom objects during the 500 ms preceding the onset of the object's name was independent of whether they had looked at the object at trial onset. This suggests that the early inspection of the objects was functionally different from the later one: During the early inspection the speakers probably determined whether the objects were identical and perhaps began to plan the utterance structure accordingly, whereas during the later inspection, they retrieved the objects' names.

This suggestion is related to a proposal by Griffin and Bock (2000; see also Griffin, 1998), who were, to our knowledge, the first to study the speakers' eye movements during the description of pictures of actions (e.g., of a man chasing a dog). They asked speakers to carry out different tasks on the same set of pictures, among them a picture description task and a so-called patient detection task, in which the participants had to identify the event participant who was undergoing (rather than carrying out) the action. Griffin and Bock found that, as early as about 300 ms after picture onset, the likelihood of fixations on the agent and patient regions began to differ between the two tasks: In the description task, speakers were far more likely to fixate upon the agent (who was usually mentioned first) than upon the patient. The reverse held for the patient detection task. Griffin and Bock concluded that in both tasks viewers spent the first 300 ms or so in an effort to comprehend the event and to identify who was doing what to whom. Following this apprehension phase, the participants describing the displays formulated the utterance, and during this phase looked at most of the event participants before referring to them. In Chapter 8 of the present volume, Bock et al.(2004) discuss the distinction between these phases and their properties in more detail. Here it is important to note that when speakers describe actions and events or, more generally, when they have to consider more than one object in order to determine what to say (see also Belke, 2001; Belke & Meyer, 2002) there may be an apprehension phase preceding formulation that we don't see when speakers just name sets of objects in fixed order. During the formulation phase, eye gaze and speech appear to be coordinated in much the same way as discussed above for multiple object naming.

CONCLUSIONS

There is a substantial literature showing that young children follow their interlocutors' gaze and exploit this information in learning the meanings of words (e.g., Caron, Butler, & Brooks, 2002; Carpenter, Nagell, & Tomasello, 1998; Emery, 2000). This would be impossible if speakers did not regularly look at the object they are talking about. The studies reviewed above showed that the speakers' tendency to look at the intended objects is very strong, in particular where new objects or new properties of objects are concerned. They also showed that during formulation, speakers usually begin to look at an object about a second or so before naming it and that their eyes tend to remain on the object until they are about to say the last word about it. Whether this fine-grained temporal information is used by children or adults learning a language may be an interesting topic for further research.

Given the developmental evidence and the observation that people in general tend to look at the objects involved in their everyday actions (e.g., Ballard et al., 1997; Hayhoe, 2000), it is surprising that speakers sometimes do not look at the objects they are referring to. Further research is necessary to determine under which conditions speakers name objects without looking at them first. We suspect that, as in reading, there will be several variables that jointly determine the likelihood of fixating an item. Among them are, most likely, the existence of a memory representation of the object, the ease of generating an appropriate referring expression and perhaps the availability of extrafoveal information about the object. How important each of these variables is and how they interact remains to be seen. In order to produce coherent discourse, i.e., to refer appropriately to given and new entities, speakers must keep a record of their own speech. Surprisingly little is known about the properties of this record. When the determinants of the speakers' eye movements are better understood, we may be able to use the rate of fixating upon old and new objects in order to study how long speakers maintain representations of entities referred to before and to explore the properties of these representations (whether they are, for instance, conceptual or linguistic).

Finally, we have observed that the speakers' eye gaze usually remains on the object until just before utterance onset, when they name objects in single nouns or determiner noun phrases and until just before the onset of the phrase-final word, when they produce more complex descriptions. As noted, in most of this work the target was the first object to be named, but Griffin's (2001) experiments suggest that eye movements and speech are coordinated in very similar ways for objects mentioned later in an utterance. Thus, it appears that the time spent looking at an object is a good estimate of the processing time for the object and the corresponding expression.

From a methodological viewpoint this may be a disappointing outcome. If we had, for instance, found that speakers only looked at the objects until they had recognized them or until they had retrieved the lemma of the object name, we could use eye tracking to measure the time required for the selection of a concept or a lemma, respectively. However, the evidence available so far suggests that the viewing time for an object is best regarded as an indicator for the total preparation time for the utterance about the object.

For a theory of speech planning, the results reviewed here imply that speakers prefer to attend to new visual information as late as possible without jeopardizing the fluency of their utterances. We have noted above that such a strategy may be beneficial for a number of reasons: It may minimize the interference between processing units for different objects and the risk of ordering errors, and it may facilitate speech monitoring.

In most of the studies reviewed in this chapter, participants described simple arrays in short utterances as requested by an experimenter, who typically was not present while the participants carried out the task. Of course, speakers usually talk about more complex scenes, they generate longer and far more complex utterances, and, most importantly perhaps, they talk to other people. It remains to be established how the speech-planning processes and the alignment of speech and gaze in such situations differ from those examined in most laboratory studies. For instance, in conversations, speakers and listeners often look at the same object, and the listener can use information about the speaker's eye gaze to determine the intended referent object. But speakers and listeners also look frequently at each other; mutual eye contact has a number of important functions in conversations, e.g., in turn taking and securing the listeners' understanding (e.g., Clark, 1996). How speakers allocate attention to the objects they talk about and to the listener they talk to, and how this is reflected in their eye gaze might be a very interesting question for further research.

NOTES

1. We review experiments using eye tracking to study language production. The review does not cover research in which object naming was used to study object or scene perception (e.g., Boyce & Pollatsek, 1992; see also Henderson & Ferreira (2004) in the present volume) or studies of the communicative functions of eye gaze in conversation (e.g., Egbert, 1996; Kalma, 1992; Lasalle & Conture, 1991; Ruusuvuori, 2001; Sidnell, 2001).

2. We define the viewing time for a region of interest as the time period during which a person is continuously looking at that region. The viewing time is computed as the time interval between the onset of the first fixation on the region and onset of a saccade to a new region. Thus, viewing times include intraregion saccades and occasionally blinks. Griffin (2001) and Griffin and Bock (2000) use the terms gaze and gaze duration instead of viewing time.

3. The authors acknowledged that the objects with long and short names were probably not perfectly matched for ease of object recognition. Thus, differences in object recognition times may have contributed to the length effect.

4. Curiously, the length effects on viewing times observed by Pynte (1974), Noizet and Pynte (1976), and Zelinski & Murphy (2000) were quite similar in size (about 110 ms), although the length difference between long and short stimuli used in different studies varied between one and four syllables. Further research is required to understand the significance of the constant increment in viewing time.

5. An alternative account is that the speakers were reluctant to begin to speak after having planned just one syllable. When the first word was disyllabic, they began to speak as soon as its form had been planned. When it was monosyllabic, they sometimes also retrieved the phonological form of the second word before speech onset, which accounts for the reversed length effect. Thus, according to this account, speakers do not use estimates of word durations to decide when to begin to speak, but monitor how many syllables have been fully planned and sometimes postpone speech onset if it is only one syllable. The reason for this may be the same as invoked by Griffin, namely, to make sure that the utterance can be produced fluently.

6. See Henderson, 1992a, b, 1997; Henderson, Pollatsek & Rayner, 1987, 1989; McConkie & Rayner, 1975; Pollatsek, Rayner & Henderson 1990, for experiments using similar paradigms.

REFERENCES

Altmann, G., & Kamide, Y. (2004). Now you see it, now you don't: Mediating the mapping between language and the visual world. In J.M. Henderson and F. Ferreira (Eds.), *The interface of language, vision, and action: Eye movements and the visual world.* New York: Psychology Press.

Ballard, D. H., Hayhoe, M. H., Pook, P. K., & Rao, R. P. N. (1997). Deictic codes for the embodiment of cognition. *Behavioral and Brain Sciences, 20,* 723-767.

Belke, E. (2001). On the time course of naming multidimensional objects in a referential communication task. Analyses of eye movements and processing times in the production of complex object specifications. Doctoral dissertation, University of Bielefeld. Germany.

Belke, E., & Meyer, A. S. (2002). Tracking the time course of multidimensional stimulus discrimination: Analyses of viewing patterns and processing times during "same" - different decisions. *European Journal of Cognitive Psychology, 14,* 237-266.

Bock, K. (1996). Language production: Methods and methodologies. *Psychonomic Bulletin & Review, 96,* 395-421.

Bock, K., Irwin, D. E., Davidson, D. J. (2004). Putting first things first. In J. M. Henderson and F. Ferreira (Eds.), *The interface of language, vision, and action: Eye movements and the visual world.* New York: Psychology Press.

Bock, K., Irwin, D. E., Davidson, D. J., & Levelt, W. J. M. (2003). Minding the clock. *Journal of Memory and Language, 48,* 653-685.

Boyce, S. J., & Pollatsek, A. (1992). Identification of objects in scenes: The role of scene background in object naming. *Journal of Experimental Psychology: Learning, Memory, and Cognition, 18,* 531—543.

Caramazza, A., Costa, A, Miozzo, M., & Bi, Y. (2001) The specific-word frequency effect: Implications for the representation of homophones in speech production. *Journal of Experimental Psychology: Learning, Memory, and Cognition, 27,* 1430 -1450.

Caron, A. J., Butler, S., & Brooks, R. (2002). Gaze following at 12 and 14 months. Do the eyes matter? *British Journal of Developmental Psychology, 20,* 225-239.

Carpenter, M., Nagell, K., & Tomasello, M. (1998). Social cognition, joint attention, and communicative competence from 9 to 15 months of age. *Monographs of the Society for Research in Child Development, 63,* V - 143.

Clark, H. H. (1996). *Using language.* Cambridge: Cambridge University Press.

Costa, A., & Caramazza, A. (2002). The production of noun phrases in English and Spanish: Implications for the scope of phonological encoding in speech production. *Journal of Memory and Language, 46,* 178 -198.

Dell, G. S. (1990). Effects of frequency and vocabulary type on phonological speech errors. *Language and Cognitive Processes, 5,* 313-349.

Egbert, M. M. (1996). Context-sensitivity in conversation: Eye gaze and the German repair initiator bitte. *Language and Society, 25,* 587 -612.

Emery, N. J. (2000). The eyes have it: the neuroethology, function and evolution of social gaze. *Neuroscience and Biobehavioral Reviews, 24,* 581 -604.

Ferreira, F., & Henderson, J. M. (1998). Linearization strategies during language production. *Memory & Cognition, 26,* 88-96.

Ferreira, F., & Swets, B. (2002). How incremental is language production? Evidence from the production of utterances requiring the computation of arithmetic sums. *Journal of Memory and Language, 46,* 57-84.

Griffin, Z. M. (1998). *What the eye says about sentence planning.* Doctoral dissertation, University of Illinois.

Griffin, Z. M. (2001). Gaze durations during speech reflect word selection and phonological encoding. *Cognition, 52,* B1-B14.

Griffin, Z. M. (2003). A reversed word length effect in coordinating the preparation and articulation of words in speaking. *Psychonomic Bulletin & Review.*

Griffin, Z. M. (2004). Why look? Reasons for speech-related eye movements. In J. M. Henderson and F. Ferreira (Eds.), *The interface of language, vision, and action: Eye movements and the visual world.* New York: Psychology Press.

Griffin, Z. M., & Bock, K. (2000). What the eyes say about speaking. *Psychological Science, 11,* 274-279.

Hayhoe, M. (2000). Vision using routines: A functional account of vision. *Visual Cognition, 7,* 43-64.

Henderson, J. M. (1992a). Identifying objects across saccades: Effects of extrafoveal preview and flanker object context. *Journal of Experimental Psychology: Learning, Memory and Cognition, 18,* 521-530.

Henderson, J. M. (1992b). Object identification in context: The visual processing of natural scenes. *Canadian Journal of Psychology, 46,* 319-341.

Henderson, J. M. (1997). Transsaccadic memory and integration during real-world object perception. *Psychological Science, 8*, 51-55.

Henderson, J. M., & Ferreira, F. (2004). Scene perception for psycholinguists. In J. M. Henderson and F. Ferreira (Eds.), *The interface of language, vision, and action: Eye movements and the visual world*. New York: Psychology Press.

Henderson, J. M., Pollatsek, A., & Rayner, K. (1987). Effects of foveal priming and extrafoveal preview on object identification. *Journal of Experimental Psychology: Human Perception and Performance, 13*, 449-463.

Henderson, J. M., Pollatsek, A., & Rayner, K. (1989). Covert visual attention and extrafoveal information use during object identification. *Perception & Psychophysics, 45*, 196-208.

Humphreys, G. W., Price, C. J., & Riddoch, M. J. (1999). From objects to names: A cognitive neuroscience approach. *Psychological Research, 62*, 118-130.

Irwin, D. E. (2004). Fixation location and fixation duration as indices of cognitive processing. In J. M. Henderson and F. Ferreira (Eds.), *The interface of language, vision, and action: Eye movements and the visual world*. New York: Psychology Press.

Jescheniak, J. D., & Levelt, W. J. M. (1994). Word frequency effects in speech production: Retrieval of syntactic information and of phonological form. *Journal of Experimental Psychology: Learning, Memory, and Cognition, 20*, 824-843.

Jescheniak, J. D., Meyer, A. S., & Levelt, W. J. M. (2003). Specific-word frequency is not all that counts in speech production. Some comments on Caramazza et al. (2001) and new experimental data. *Journal of Experimental Psychology: Learning, Memory, and Cognition, 29*, 432-438.

Johnson, C. J., Paivio, A., & Clark, J. M. (1996). Cognitive components of picture naming. *Psychological Bulletin, 120*, 113-139.

Kalma, A. (1992). Gazing in triads - a powerful signal in floor apportionment. *British Journal of Social Psychology, 31*, 21-39.

Lasalle, L.R., & Conture, E. G. (1991). Eye contact between young stutterers and their mothers. *Journal of Fluency Disorders, 16*, 173-199.

Levelt, W. J. M. (1981). The speaker's linearization problem. *Philosophical Transactions of the Royal Society of London. Series B, 295*, 305-315.

Levelt, W. J. M. (1989). *Speaking: From intention to articulation*. Cambridge: MIT Press, 1989.

Levelt, W. J. M. (1999). Models of word production. *TRENDS in Cognitive Sciences, 3*, 223-232.

Levelt, W. J. M., & Meyer, A. S. (2000). Word for word. Sequentiality in phrase generation. *European Journal of Cognitive Psychology, 12*, 433-452.

Levelt, W. J. M., Roelofs, A., & Meyer, A. S. (1999). A theory of lexical access in language production. *Behavioral and Brain Sciences, 22*, 1-38.

Levin, H. (1979). *The eye-voice span*. Cambridge, MA: MIT Press.

McConkie, G.W., & Rayner, K. (1975). The span of effective stimulus during a fixation in reading. *Perception & Psychophysics, 17*, 578-586.

Meyer, A. S., & Forti, S. (submitted). Eye movements during the production of long and short noun phrases.

Meyer, A. S., & van der Meulen, F.F. (2000). Phonological priming of picture viewing and picture naming. *Psychonomic Bulletin & Review, 7*, 314-319.

Meyer, A. S., van der Meulen, F. F., & Brooks, A. (in press). Referring to present and remembered objects. *Visual Cognition*.

Meyer, A. S., Roelofs, A., & Levelt, W. J. M. (2003). Word length effects in language production: The effects of a response criterion. *Journal of Memory and Language, 47*, 131-147.

Meyer, A. S., & Schriefers, H. (1991). Phonological facilitation in picture-word-interference experiments: Effects of stimulus onset asynchrony and type of interfering stimuli. *Journal of Experimental Psychology: Learning, Memory, and Cognition, 17*, 1146-1160.

Meyer, A. S., Sleiderink, A. M., & Levelt, W. J. M. (1998). Viewing and naming objects: Eye movements during noun phrase production. *Cognition, 66*, B25-B33.

Morgan, J., & Meyer, A. S. (submitted). Extra-foveal processing in multiple-object naming.

Morgan, J., & Meyer, A. S. (in preparation). The use of visual information and working memory representations in picture naming.

Noizet, G., & Pynte, J. (1976). Implicit labeling and readiness for pronunciation during the perceptual process. *Perception, 5,* 217-223.

Pollatsek, A., Rayner, K., & Collins, W. E. (1984). Integrating pictorial information across eye movements. *Journal of Experimental Psychology: General, 113,* 426-442.

Pollatsek, A., Rayner, K., & Henderson, J. M. (1990). Role of spatial location in integration of pictorial information across saccades. *Journal of Experimental Psychology: Human Perception & Performance, 16,* 199-210.

Postma, A. (2000). Detection of errors during speech production: A review of speech monitoring models. *Cognition, 77,* 97-131.

Pynte, J. (1974). Readiness for pronunciation during the reading process. *Perception & Psychophysics, 16,* 110-112.

Rapp, B., & Goldrick, M. (2000). Discreteness and interactivity in spoken word production. *Psychological Review, 107,* 460-499.

Rayner, K. (1998). Eye movements in reading and information processing: 20 years of research. *Psychological Bulletin, 124,* 372—422.

Rayner, K., & Liversedge, S. P. (2004). Visual and linguistic processing during eye fixations in reading. In J. M. Henderson and F. Ferreira (Eds.), *The interface of language, vision, and action: Eye movements and the visual world.* New York: Psychology Press.

Reichle, E. D., Pollatsek, A., Fisher, D. L., & Rayner, K. (1998). Towards a model of eye movement control in reading. *Psychological Review, 105,* 125-157.

Roelofs, A. (1997). The WEAVER model of word-form encoding in speech production. *Cognition, 64,* 249-284.

Ruusuvuori, J. (2001). Looking means listening: coordinating displays of engagement in doctor-patient interaction. *Social Science & Medicine, 52,* 1093-1108.

Schriefers, H., & Teruel, E. (1999). Phonological facilitation in the production of two-word utterances. *European Journal of Cognitive Psychology, 11,* 17-50.

Sidnell, J. (2001). Conversational turn-taking in a Caribbean English Creole. *Journal of Pragmatics, 33,* 1263-1290.

Spivey, M. J., Richardson, D. C., & Fitneva, S. A. (2004). Thinking outside the brain: Spatial indices to visual and linguistic information. In J.M. Henderson and F. Ferreira (Eds.), *The interface of language, vision, and action: Eye movements and the visual world.* New York: Psychology Press.

Starr, M. S., & Rayner, K. (2001). Eye movements during reading: some current controversies. *TRENDS in Cognitive Sciences, 5,* 158-163.

Stuart Hamilton, I., & Rabbitt, P. (1997). The decline of eye-voice span in elderly readers. *Educational Gerontology, 23,* 389-400.

Tanenhaus, M. K., Chambers, C. G., & Hanna, J.E. (2004). Referential domains in spoken language comprehension: Using eye movements to bridge the product and action traditions. In J.M. Henderson and F. Ferreira (Eds.), *The interface of language, vision, and action: Eye movements and the visual world.* New York: Psychology Press.

van der Meulen, F. F. (2001). *Moving eyes and naming objects.* MPI series in Psycholinguistics. Nijmegen, The Netherlands.

van der Meulen, F. F. (2003). Coordination of eye gaze and speech in sentence production. In H. Härtl & H. Tappe (Eds.) *Mediating between concepts and grammar.* Mouton de Gruyter: Berlin/New York.

van der Meulen, F. F., Meyer, A. S., & Levelt, W. J. M. (2001). Eye movements during the production of nouns and pronouns. *Memory and Cognition, 29,* 512-521.

van Tuinen, M. (2000). *Augenblick mal! Ist die Blick-Sprech-Spanne ein Mass fuer kognitive Verarbeitungsprozesse bei der Beschreibung von raeumlichen Objektkonfigurationen? [One moment! Is the eye-voice-span a measure of cognitive processing during the description of spatial object configurations?].* M. Phil thesis, University of Bielefeld.

Wheeldon, L.R., & Levelt, W. J. M. (1995). Monitoring the time course of phonological encoding. *Journal of Memory and Language, 34,* 311-334.

Zelinsky, G. J., & Murphy, G. L. (2000). Synchronizing visual and language processing: An effect of object name length on Eye movements. *Psychological Science, 11,* 125-131.

7

Why Look? Reasons for Eye Movements Related to Language Production

ZENZI M. GRIFFIN

*C*ompared to generating an utterance, comprehending one is a piece of cake. Comprehenders have information from multiple sources to draw on as they form an interpretation that is good enough for their current purposes (e.g., Clark, 1996; Ferreira, Ferraro, & Bailey, 2002). For example, in face-to-face conversation listeners have access to background knowledge about the current situation and experience with the person speaking, in addition to the actual words said and how they are uttered. As a result, listeners are often able to recognize a word before it is completely articulated (Cooper, 1974; Marslen-Wilson, 1973). Studying a process that takes so little time and that benefits so greatly from context is a challenge. One way in which this challenge has been met is by using the eye movements of listeners as a reflection of moment-to-moment changes in how they interpret utterances (Tanenhaus, Spivey-Knowlton, Eberhard, & Sedivy, 1995; for review see Tanenhaus, Chambers, & Hanna, 2004, in this volume).

In typical experiments that use eye movements to investigate spoken language (a.k.a. the *visual world* paradigm), listeners sit in front of a display of real or pictured objects, listen to an instruction to act on one object, and then carry out the action. The listeners shift their gaze to objects as they interpret what they hear, based on knowledge of their language, its use, and of their environment. Simply put, the listeners tend to look at objects as they recognize the spoken words referring to them. One of the strengths of this method is that people naturally tend to look at objects before reaching for them (e.g., Abrams, Meyer, & Kornblum, 1990). This allows researchers to study the time course of spoken sentence comprehension with a measure that is naturally associated with carrying out the actions expressed in the sentences.

With success in comprehension research, eye tracking soon came to be used in the study of language production as well (Griffin, 1998; Griffin & Bock, 2000; Meyer, Sleiderink, & Levelt, 1998; Meyer & van der Meulen, 2000; see Meyer, 2004, in this volume). In typical experiments, speakers view scenes on a computer monitor and are asked to describe them. As in language comprehension, eye movements and speech tend to be time-locked. Speakers begin gazing at objects about 900 ms before referring to them.

A typical time course for eye movements related to speaking is illustrated in Figure 7.1. In this hypothetical example, the speaker produces the request, "Please pass the salt over here." Slightly before beginning to say "Please," the speaker programs a saccade to the saltshaker (hatched bar); she gazes at the shaker for 700 ms (solid white bar), and 200 ms after looking away from the shaker, she begins articulating the word "salt," which has a duration of 400 ms. From the onset of programming the saccade to the offset of the word, the speaker spends about 1300 ms in processes related to salt. Figure 7.1 also illustrates a hypothetical time course for a listener's eye movements while hearing the request. The listener begins programming an eye movement (hatched bar) after having heard only half of the word *salt* (Cooper, 1974; Tanenhaus et al., 1995) and begins gazing at a saltshaker (solid bar) before the speaker finishes articulating the word *salt*. The listener quickly recognizes the word *salt* and identifies the relevant object.

Eye-movement measures in comprehension and production reflect the factors that are important in each process. For instance, phonological similarity between words (Tanenhaus et al., 1995), word frequency (Dahan, Magnuson, & Tanenhaus, 2001), contextual constraint (see Altmann & Kamide, 2004, in this volume), and syntactic ambiguity (Eberhard, Spivey-Knowlton, Sedivy, & Tanenhaus, 1995) influence the speed with which listeners identify and fixate correct referents. In speaking, speakers gaze at objects for less time when object names are more common (Meyer et al., 1998), phonologically primed (Meyer & van der Meulen, 2000), the dominant name for the object (Griffin, 2001), and are uttered fluently (Griffin & Bock, 2000). Moreover, the time courses for processing stages that have been inferred from other methods tend to be transparently reflected in eye movements when the time (100-200 ms) needed to plan and execute a saccade (see Fischer, 1998, for a review) is taken into account.

Despite the many parallels between gaze and speech in the two domains, there is one glaring difference. Eye movements seem naturally linked to planning actions and thereby to understanding commands. Thus, developing a linking hypothesis to relate eye movements to comprehension has been a rela-

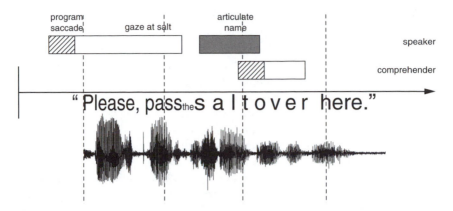

FIGURE 7.1. Illustration of the time course of speech and eye movements to a salt-shaker for a listener and a speaker.

tively straightforward affair (see Tanenhaus, Dahan, Magnuson, & Chambers, 2000). However, eye movements are less intuitively tied to planning speech, beyond speakers' need to identify the objects they talk about. Nevertheless, gazes are highly correlated with speech when people describe visual scenes. The first section of this paper presents evidence for a tight relationship between gaze and speech (see also Meyer, 2004, in this volume). In subsequent sections, hypotheses about the role of eye movements in language production are proposed and evaluated. Ultimately, the available evidence suggests that although the gaze-speech link in production is very strong, the link might not provide any functional benefit. Alternatively, speech-related eye movements may support the message representations that are expressed in speech, in a manner similar to the support provided by gestures (e.g., Iverson & Goldin-Meadow, 1998; Kita & Özyürek, 2003; Krauss, 1998; McNeill, 1985, 1992).

WHEN DO SPEAKERS GAZE?

Language production involves numerous cognitive processes that could be reflected in eye movements. Producing an utterance first involves creating a communicative intention, which is considered to be a conceptual and prelinguistic process. An utterance-sized chunk of this intention is called a *message* (Garrett, 1975). Speakers use messages to guide the sequential preparation of words (e.g., Chang, 2002). Word preparation is divided into two major processes, word selection and phonological encoding (Kempen & Huijbers, 1983). In the first process, an abstract word representation (*lemma*) is selected based on its ability to express semantic and pragmatic specifications in the message. For example, a speaker might select the lemma for *salt* rather than the lemma for *sodium* to request a saltshaker. In the second process, the phonological form of a selected lemma is assembled and coordinated with the sounds of the words that precede it. For *salt*, this would involve retrieving the knowledge that it has four phonemes that may be articulated in one stressed syllable (see Levelt, Roelofs, & Meyer, 1999, for a detailed theory). Word production processes overlap in time such that one word may be articulated while another word is selected (e.g., Kempen & Hoenkamp, 1987; Levelt, 1989). Speakers may also inspect or *monitor* the phonological forms of prepared words prior to saying them aloud (e.g., Levelt, 1983).

A priori, gazing at referents could overlap with any or all of these language production processes. However, the evidence reviewed below suggests that speakers do not consistently gaze at every included object when forming a message, nor do they look at objects while articulating the words that refer to these objects. Instead, speakers primarily gaze at objects while selecting names and assembling phonological forms. These gazes will be referred to as name-related gazes.

The term *name-related* highlights the fact that these gazes differ from those of people not directly and immediately involved in language production. People spend much more time looking at objects prior to describing them than when simply inspecting them to gain an impression of a scene (Griffin & Bock, 2000). Objects may be recognized in less than 170 ms (Potter, 1975; see Henderson & Ferreira, 2004, in this volume, for a review). In searching scenes for objects, people typically spend no more than 300 ms gazing[1] at any single one (for review, see Rayner, 1998). Yet, when called upon to label common objects, people gaze at them for over half a second (Meyer et al., 1998[2]) and often much longer (Griffin, 2001). Indeed, the time from beginning to gaze at an object to articulating its name is very similar to the time from presentation of a single pictured object to articulation of its name in speeded object naming, approximately 900 ms (Griffin & Bock, 2000). Moreover, the amount of time spent gazing at an object before referring to it reflects the difficulty speakers have in preparing its name. So, name-related gaze durations are longer for objects with the multiple appropriate names to choose among, such as *TV* and *television* (Griffin, 2001), and when speakers utter object names disfluently (Griffin & Bock, 2000). Disfluencies and the multiple-names effect primarily reflect difficulty in selecting a particular name or lemma to use (e.g., Goldman-Eisler, 1968; Lachman, 1973). Name-related gaze durations are also shorter when objects have very common names (Meyer et al., 1998) and when they are primed by the presentation of a similar-sounding word (Meyer & van der Meulen, 2000). These effects are often attributed to assembling the phonological forms of selected words (e.g., Jescheniak & Levelt, 1994; Schriefers, Meyer, & Levelt, 1990). Importantly, objects in these studies took equivalent amounts of time to categorize, suggesting that the effects are specific to tasks involving word production. Across studies, when naming objects, people usually gaze at them until they have retrieved the phonological forms of their names (Meyer et al., 1998).

The latency between starting to gaze at an object and beginning to say its name is relatively consistent in spontaneous scene descriptions. Even if they have previously fixated an object, speakers tend to return their gaze to it about a second before saying its name (Griffin & Bock, 2000). Analogous to the eye-voice span in reading aloud (Buswell, 1935) and eye-hand spans in typing and playing sheet music (e.g., Inhoff, Briihl, Boheimer, & Wang, 1992; Rayner & Pollatsek, 1997), one can calculate an *eye voice span* in speaking. An eye-voice span is calculated by first determining when a speaker began to say a word referring to an object. The speaker's eye movement record is searched backwards from the onset of the object's name to find the last gaze on the object prior to its name. The eye-voice span is the time from the onset of this last pre-name gaze and the onset of the name. In the first study of eye movements in spontaneous scene descriptions, eye-voice spans for fluently spoken subject nouns were 902 (SE = 50) ms on average and 932 (50) ms for object nouns (Griffin & Bock, 2000). Other studies in which speakers referred to multiple objects without time pressure or high fluency demands tend to show similar values.[3]

Another way of capturing the regular relationship between gaze and word onset is to plot when speakers look at an object relative to when they say its name. One such plot is shown in Figure 7.2. At each 8-ms point in time relative to the start of a word at time 0, the y-axis shows the proportion of trials when speakers gazed at the object to which they referred at time 0. The peak indicates that on 88 per cent of trials, speakers were gazing at object A about 600 ms before fluently uttering its name. The data are for naming the first (A, thin light gray line) and second (B, thick black line) of three objects named in the frame *The A and the B are above the C* in Griffin (2001).

ARTICULATING OBJECT NAMES

As shown in Figure 7.2, speakers rarely look at objects while articulating their names. Instead, they tend to shift their gazes to the next object to be named 100-300 ms prior to name onset (Meyer et al., 1998; Meyer & van der Meulen, 2000). Articulating a name does not coincide with gazing at the object to which it refers. Also, everything else being equal, speakers do not spend more time gazing at objects that have longer names (Griffin, 2003; Meyer, Roelofs, & Levelt, 2003). This indicates that gaze durations on an object do not normally reflect any length-sensitive processes in producing its name, just as object-naming latencies do not tend to vary with word length (Bachoud-Levi, Dupoux, Cohen, & Mehler, 1998).[4]

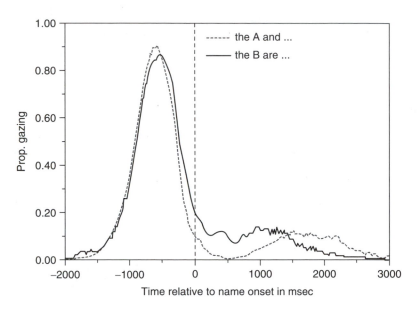

FIGURE 7.2. Relative to the onset of an object name, the grand mean proportion of speakers gazing at objects during every 8-ms sample. Data come from Griffin (2001).

Maybe the only reason that speakers do not gaze at objects while articulating their names is because they are occupied with preparing the name of the next object. Speakers' lingering gazes on the objects mentioned at the end of utterances support this idea (Griffin, 2001; van der Meulen, 2001). To see if this is the case, the preparation and articulation of sentences can be pulled apart so that they do not overlap in time. Speakers seem to plan entire utterances in advance if the scene to be described is removed before they begin speaking. Under these circumstances, speakers gaze at objects in the sequence that they later mention them (Griffin, 2002; Griffin & Bock, 2000). The duration of the gazes is equivalent to the total amount of time that spontaneous speakers (who can gaze at the scenes while speaking) spend gazing at objects before, plus during, speech. The gaze durations during advanced planning are greater for objects that have multiple names or low-frequency names (Griffin, 2002). It is as if speakers silently say the object names when they plan all of their words before speaking. The speech following this apparent advanced planning is significantly more fluent than spontaneous speech (Griffin, 2002; Griffin & Bock, 2000).

Speakers prepare scene descriptions in advance when they believe that the scenes will disappear before they begin speaking. What happens when the scene is unexpectedly present while the speaker articulates a prepared description? In this situation, the speaker no longer needs to prepare the names of any late-mentioned objects. If spontaneous speakers abstain from gazing at objects while articulating their names only in order to prepare later- object names, prepared speakers should gaze at objects while articulating their names when scenes reappear. Even under these circumstances, speakers make relatively few gazes to the objects while articulating their names (Griffin, 2002). In general, speakers have little interest in gazing at objects while articulating their names, gazing instead while selecting and phonologically encoding them.

IDENTIFYING OBJECTS

Speakers gaze at objects while selecting and phonologically encoding the words that refer to them but not while articulating the words. What about the earliest processes in naming an object? Common sense suggests that people fixate objects to identify them. So, one would expect speakers to gaze at objects while identifying them and perhaps while deciding if they are worthy of mention. Indeed, making objects difficult to identify increases the time that speakers spend gazing at them (e.g., Meyer et al., 1998). Other findings, however, suggest that participants in many production studies are able to identify objects before fixating them or without fixating them directly. In sparse scenes, objects may be correctly identified while fixating over 5 degrees of visual angle away (e.g., Mackworth & Morandi, 1967; Parker, 1978; see Henderson & Ferreira, 2004, in this voulme, for a review). In general, the more cluttered a scene is, the closer to objects people must fixate to identify them, but in most language production studies, scenes and object displays are sparse.

A final example illustrates how speakers may identify objects and plan to include them in utterances before fixating them. In an event apprehension task, observers viewed line drawings of simple events such as a horse kicking a cow (Griffin & Bock, 2000). When asked to find and fixate the patient of the action (e.g., the cow), observers directed their gaze to it within 500 ms of the picture's presentation. Although identifying a patient may presuppose identifying an agent and action, observers rarely fixated agents like the horse (see also Segalowitz, 1982). Similarly, when other people were asked to describe these events, they directed their gazes to the character that was mentioned as the subject of their sentence within the first 500 ms of viewing the scene. One might be tempted to think that speakers directed their eyes to the most perceptually salient character first and made this character the grammatical subject (e.g., Forrest, 1993; see Bock, Irwin, & Davidson, 2004, in this volume, for a review). However, the decision about which character became the grammatical subject was contingent on the roles the characters played in the event and their relative animacy. If one character were more animate or human than the other, it was encoded as grammatical subject; otherwise the agent of the action was made subject. Furthermore, speakers began to name grammatical subjects equally soon after scene onset when the grammatical subject was the first, second, or third object fixated. This suggests that speakers perceived at least gross properties about objects and their roles in the events prior to fixating them (see Henderson & Ferreira, 2004, in this volume, for conditions that reduce perceptual span).

With respect to language production, it is disappointing that the objects in most studies may be recognized prior to fixation. If this were not the case, the eye-movement records would indicate when object information became available to speakers. This would permit researchers to infer the earliest point in time when speakers accessed the information that they included in their speech. Although people usually recognize the objects they fixate, failure to fixate an object does not suggest that it has not been recognized or included in a message.

PLANNING MESSAGES

Although object recognition may not be directly inferable from eye movements, message planning may be reflected in eye movements to some degree (Holsánová, 2001). Speakers seem to outline a proposition- or clause-sized message before they begin sequentially preparing the words they will utter (see Bock & Levelt, 1994, for review). This is most clearly demonstrated in an experiment by van der Meulen and Meyer (2000; van der Meulen, 2001). Speakers viewed four pictured objects arranged in a square. When the bottom two objects were identical, speakers were supposed to use plural nouns to refer to them, as in "The spoon and the napkin are above the cups." When the bottom objects differed, a two-clause construction was called for, such as "The spoon is above the cup and the napkin is above the jar." When the two types of displays were presented in separate blocks, speakers immediately gazed at the first object to be mentioned without any scanning of the other objects. Apparently, the fixed nature of the sentence frame provided adequate message information for speakers to begin speaking comfortably once the first noun was prepared (the same was found in Griffin, 2001). However, when the two types of displays were intermixed, speakers looked at the bottom objects before starting a name-related gaze on the first object to be mentioned. This suggests that prior to preparing the first word of an utterance, speakers sought information about either the number of clauses to be produced or the number of entities in the first clause. This tendency for speakers to outline messages approximately one proposition or clause at a time is consistent with other research in language production (e.g., Ferreira & Swets, 2002; see also Bock et al., 2004). Gazes related to message planning are less identifiable than are name-related gazes, but they can be discerned.

MONITORING SPEECH

Speakers sometimes return their gazes to objects after mentioning them in a way that suggests that they are evaluating their utterances (Meyer et al., 1998). These post-name gazes occur far less often than name-related gazes do, as can be seen in Figure 7.2. Aside from intuitions, there is no current support for the idea that these gazes are related to monitoring.

Conclusion

In summary, regardless of variations in the scope of word preparation that occurs before rather than during an utterance, speakers tend to gaze at objects while selecting names for them and assembling the sounds of the names (Griffin, 2001, 2002; Meyer et al., 1998). However, object identification and message planning may often occur before speakers fixate objects in these typically sparse scenes and displays. Speakers rarely gaze at objects while articulating the objects' names although they sometimes refixate the objects later. As hypotheses about speakers' gazes are evaluated in the remainder of this chapter, additional evidence will demonstrate the strength of this speech-gaze relationship. The following sections begin by considering the social-communicative functions of gaze, then general cognitive ones, before moving onto more language-specific hypotheses about the function of speakers' gazes.

THE COMMUNICATION HYPOTHESIS: GAZES ARE FOR COMMUNICATION

Thus far, speaking has been considered a cognitive process within a speaker. However, speaking is often just one part of how people communicate with and gain information about each other (e.g., Argyle & Cook, 1976; DePaulo & Friedman, 1998; Duncan & Fiske, 1977). People have strong intuitions about the value of gaze information. Within North American culture, there is a notion that it is more difficult to lie to someone when looking him or her in the eye. Likewise, a speaker with a shifty gaze is thought more likely to be dishonest. Although these notions about the informativeness of gaze in deception turn out to be misplaced (e.g., DePaulo et al., 2003), gaze remains an important source of information during social interactions. Gaze communicates how speakers may feel about their audiences (e.g., Lesko & Schneider, 1978). A speakers' gaze may be related to turn taking in conversation and who may take the floor (e.g., Kendon, 1967; see Clark, 1996; Krauss & Chiu, 1998, for reviews). Following a speaker's gaze may help infants learn language. Babies as young as 3 months old will follow a person's gaze (Hood, Willen, & Driver, 1998), while caregivers in turn tend to monitor the gaze of their infants and label the things they attend to (Lempert & Kinsbourne, 1985). Thus, gaze can be used to point at objects and locations.

Despite the informative aspects of gaze, the extent to which communication regularly motivates name-related gazes is unclear. People spend much more time gazing at an interlocutor when listening to them than when speaking to them (Kendon, 1967). When speakers occasionally gaze at listeners, it is presumably to monitor their understanding and attention (Clark, 1996; Krauss & Chiu, 1998). Looking at a listener may reassure a speaker that the listener will perceive a name-related gaze when the topic of conversation makes such a gaze possible. Alternatively, gazes to a listener could disrupt or prevent name-related gazes. Researchers have begun tracking the eye movements of speakers while they communicate with another person in carrying out card-matching tasks. These studies suggest that speakers make name-related gazes when real listeners are present (Griffin & Garton, 2003; Horton, Metzing, & Gerrig, 2002). Furthermore, listeners can take advantage of name-related gazes to identify referents (Hanna & Brennan, 2003). However, even in non-communicative speaking tasks, speakers make name-related gazes when no human listener can naturally observe them. It is unclear whether name-related gazes show the same timing relative to words when they are intended to be perceived by listeners as when they just happen. Name-related gazes may fall in the same category as other hotly debated behaviors such as saying "um" and reducing repeated words, which speakers produce in the absence of listeners, but that listeners perceive and use (see e.g., Arnold, Fagnano, & Tanenhaus, 2003; Clark & Fox Tree, 2002; Fowler, Levy, & Brown, 1997).

THE EFFORT HYPOTHESIS: GAZES REFLECT ATTENTION AND MENTAL EFFORT

To some extent it seems unavoidable that eye movements have a similar relationship with language production as they do with other cognitive tasks. People tend to look at the things they think about and even look at things that are only somewhat related to what they think about (e.g., Just & Carpenter, 1976; Kahneman, 1973). Further, the more effort that a task requires, the more likely eye movements may be to reflect cognitive processes. If so, the most demanding aspects of speaking should be reflected in gazes.

Although word production may usually feel relatively effortless, it does recruit limited capacity resources (e.g., Ford & Holmes, 1978; Hyönä, Tommola, & Alaja, 1995). The production processes that appear to be resource demanding, based on dual-task performance, pupil dilation, and other measures of mental effort, are the same ones that are reflected in the duration of name-related gazes. Specifically, these processes are word selection and phonological encoding. For example, using a dual-task paradigm, Ferreira and Pashler

(2002) showed a central processing bottleneck for responding to a tone while selecting a name for an object and while retrieving the phonological form of the object. The longer these word production processes took, the later participants responded to a tone. This suggests a tidy correspondence between the resource-demanding processes in word preparation and the processes reflected in name-related gaze durations.[5]

Message planning is considered more resource demanding than is word preparation (e.g., Bock, 1982), so it should also be reflected in eye movements. However, name-related gazes are observed far more reliably than message-related gazes are. One reason may be the simplicity of the scenes and description tasks used thus far in eye- tracking studies of language production. Message elements in scene description are primarily concrete concepts, which are far easier to talk about than abstract ones (e.g., Taylor, 1969). Furthermore, description is an easier task than, for example, interpretation (Goldman-Eisler, 1968). We will return to this issue in considering other hypotheses.

Although eye movements and attention may be dissociated, eye movements typically follow the allocation of visual attention (see Fischer, 1998). Speakers attend to objects when preparing their names. The question then becomes what aspect of the objects are speakers attending to and why? The reason that eye movements typically follow attention appears functional, related to performing actions or just getting better sensory information (e.g., Abrams et al., 1990). Even if speakers do not identify objects before fixating them, identifying objects takes far less time than name-related gazes do. Do name-related gazes have a function in preparing utterances?

THE MEMORY-SUPPORT HYPOTHESES: GAZES FOR REMEMBERING OBJECTS

Although objects may often be identified very rapidly, the resulting representations might not suffice for word production. Indeed, in the landmark studies on the speed of object recognition, rapid identification of objects was contrasted with weak memory for them (Potter, 1975; Potter & Levy, 1969). Participants readily detected target objects that appeared in a stream of briefly presented ones, but after the stream ended, they were miserable at remembering which objects they had seen. It was as if images were only processed for the duration they were presented and a display change halted their further processing and continued availability.

Based on such observations, speakers may persist in gazing at objects after identifying them so that they do not forget what they are naming. If so, one would expect speakers to perform poorly in describing briefly presented displays of objects. However, several studies suggest that this is not the case. Mean object-naming latencies are about 900 ms (Snodgrass & Yuditsky, 1996), with faster means for item sets of uniformly highly codable objects and repeated presentations. In studies where speakers only view an object for 320 ms, they do not forget the object they are naming (e.g., LaHeij, Mak, Sander, & Wildeboordse, 1998). Speakers are even able to produce accurate time expressions after as little as a 100 ms exposure to analog or digital clocks (Bock et al., 2003). These results make it unlikely that speakers forget the objects that they want to talk about when they disappear from view.[6]

In contrast to describing a display that just disappeared, eye movements may be important in accessing information after a delay or when items are easily confused. In a mental imagery and memory experiment, participants were assigned to one of three eye-movement conditions (Laeng & Teodorescu, 2002). The stimuli were photographs of tropical fish that appeared in the corners of the computer monitors. One group could move their eyes freely while studying the fish and later, while forming mental images and answering questions about the fish. A second group fixated points in the center of the displays while studying the fish, but they could move their eyes freely later. A third group could move their eyes freely during study but fixated a central point during imaging and question answering. While imaging the fish, the first two groups gazed at the black monitor in the same manner as during study. So, those who had fixated a central point at study tended to stare at the same point during imaging, although they were free to do otherwise. Critically, the two groups who could freely reenact their eye movements during study while imaging the fish remembered details significantly better than the third group, who could not freely move their eyes to reenact their eye movements at study. The researchers argued that if eye movements during imaging simply followed the allocation of attention to different locations associated with the fish, the participants who fixated steadily during study would move their eyes to the earlier fish locations during imaging. That these participants did not do so suggested that reenacting eye movements rather than simple allocation of attention was important. In addition, the poorer performance of the participants who maintained fixation during imaging but not during study suggests that reenacting eye movements served a real function in retrieving information rather than being epiphenomenal.

Similarly, Richardson and Spivey (2002) reported that observers made eye movements to blank regions of space while they recalled auditory information that was associated with the regions. In their experiments, participants heard facts that were presented with twirling fixation points in one quadrant of a computer monitor. When later asked a question about one of the facts, participants tended to refixate the quadrant in which a fixation point had co-occurred with the relevant fact (see also Altmann & Kamide, 2004, in this volume). However, Richardson and Spivey's participants showed no benefit from fixating these locations.

Eye movements to the previous locations of stimuli suggest that eye movements are tied to the retrieval and organization of information, sometimes aiding recall. Given such a compulsion to gaze at locations associated with information undergoing mental processing, it could be considered surprising if speakers did not habitually gaze at visually presented objects while preparing their names. Furthermore, the probability of making name-related gazes may be directly related to the strength of the memory or message representation guiding word preparation. Consistent with such an influence of memory strength, speakers are less likely to gaze at referents that they have just named, particularly when the objects are referred to with a pronoun rather than a full noun phrase (van der Meulen, 2001; van der Meulen, Meyer, & Levelt, 2001). Likewise, preliminary results from a study in which speakers viewed photographs of the same objects hundreds of times in different arrays further suggests that speakers become less likely to fixate objects before naming them as the objects become more and more familiar (Griffin & Garton, 2004). However, when speakers repeat sentences they have just heard, they tend to gaze at characters within 1 s of repeating their names in over 85% of cases (Arnold & Griffin, 2004). The percentage of fixations barely declines for referring to the same character a second time in a self-generated sentence about a second, related scene. In other words, speakers tend to look at objects when they seem perfectly aware of what they are, where they are, and have no reason to suspect that they have changed. Is the glass half empty or half full? The data is still scanty, but speakers seem less likely to gaze at an object as its location, appearance, and name become more familiar, especially if identical pictures are repeated. Even so, speakers tend to look at an object remarkably often when they have already looked at it, referred to it, and its image is static.[7]

THE INTERFERENCE-AVOIDANCE HYPOTHESIS: GAZES TO AVOID INTERFERENCE FROM VIEWING OTHER OBJECTS

A complementary hypothesis is that speakers gaze at objects while retrieving their names to avoid interference from the names of other objects (Meyer et al., 1998). This hypothesis assumes that viewing objects leads to the activation of their names or, more specifically, their lemmas. Therefore, gazing at one object while preparing a name for another increases competition for selecting the intended object's lemma. If so, removing a target object from view after it was identified might have no effect as long as another did not replace it. Consistent with this idea, in studies of picture memory, such as Potter's (1975), picture processing seemed to continue after pictures were removed as long as nothing terribly novel or interesting replaced the picture (see Intraub, 1981).

   In one study testing the interference-avoidance hypothesis, speakers viewed a pair of pictured objects presented such that one replaced the other

(Meyer, personal communication). The display durations for the pictures varied, as did the instructions about which object to name and in what order. So, speakers might only name the first object, only the second one, both in the order presented, or both in reverse order. As long as the first object was displayed for at least 120 ms, its naming latency and error rate did not vary as a function of condition. It made no difference whether another object or a mask replaced the first object. Second objects did not even interfere with naming first objects when speakers had to identify them for subsequent naming. This result contrasts with the robust and common finding that presenting a written word under similar circumstances does disrupt object naming (e.g., Glaser & Düngelhoff, 1984), which was replicated for the same materials. This study suggests that perceiving a new object while naming another is not a problem, even when the new object must be identified and named. Two published studies using object naming (Damian & Bowers, 2003) and word translation (Bloem & LaHeij, 2003) demonstrate a similar lack of interference from objects and even facilitation under some circumstances. Therefore, interference-avoidance in lemma selection is not a compelling motivation for gazing at the object-to-be-named.

For more complex visual displays, however, there is evidence supporting an interference-avoidance account for memory retrieval (Glenberg, Schroeder, & Robertson, 1998) and message planning (Kendon, 1967). For instance, Kendon (1967) observed that speakers looked away from their partners prior to starting most utterances. Also, when speakers hesitated during speech, they were much more likely to look away from their partners than when they were fluent (also Duncan & Fiske, 1977). Such observations are consistent with the idea that speakers minimize the processing of irrelevant visual information when planning utterances and selecting difficult words. However, these observations are also consistent with the idea that speakers take steps to avoid interruption when they pause (Beattie, 1979). Interpretation of gaze aversion in conversation is complicated by the many other nonlinguistic influences on the amount of gaze aversion such as social norms, the intimacy of the topic, like or dislike for an interlocutor, as well as the number, proximity, status, and genders of the interlocutors (see Argyle & Cook, 1976; Exline & Fehr, 1978).

People, however, do not only avert their gaze from human interlocutors. People also avert their gaze from computer monitors that display questions (Glenberg et al., 1998). Moreover, people were more likely to avert their gaze as the questions increased in difficulty. Going beyond observation of avoidance behavior, Glenberg and colleagues tested the consequences of denying people the use of gaze aversion. Their participants were asked to recall word lists while gazing at a monitor. Their recall accuracy was much better when the monitor displayed a static scene rather than a dynamic one. Thus, participants' responses appear to suffer interference from irrelevant and visually interesting information.[8]

The results of object-naming studies and the question-answering studies provide conflicting information about the effects of visual information that is unrelated to speech content. A potential reason for the discrepancy is that question answering requires more complex message planning than simple object naming does. The same holds for recalling word lists. In naming common objects, message planning or conceptualization only requires basic level identification of an object and may therefore be too rapid and easy to suffer interference from other visual information. As message planning (or the question to be answered) becomes more difficult, gaze aversion becomes more likely (e.g., Glenberg et al., 1998). Rather than being directly related to word production processes per se, irrelevant visual information seems to interfere with earlier processes, related to figuring out and remembering what to say. Once this message content is clear, unrelated visual information becomes irrelevant. When the content of speech is simple, there is no risk of interference, and so speakers are not motivated to avert their gaze from unrelated objects.

THE PRODUCTION-SUPPORT HYPOTHESIS: GAZES TO SUPPORT OBJECT NAME PRODUCTION

In evaluating the interference-avoidance hypothesis, the evidence addressed interference from perceiving visual information that is inconsistent with the content of speech. One might also ask whether longer gazes on consistent visual information facilitates or supports speaking about it. Meyer's unpublished results suggested that continued exposure to an object after it was recognized did not facilitate producing its name. There was no advantage to seeing an object for 300 or 800 ms rather than 120 ms. Likewise, Bock and colleagues found that speakers were significantly faster in telling time when clocks were presented for only 100 ms rather than 3000. However, those studies focused on successful production. There may be better places to look for evidence. Perhaps some speech errors that speakers produce can be traced to gazing too briefly at misnamed objects. Hypothetically, speakers may continue to gaze at objects after identifying them because they use the visual forms as external semantic representations to guide word production. If so, speech errors such as calling an axe a "saw" (i.e., a semantically related word substitution) may be associated with briefer gazes on a referent than successful name productions. This prediction was tested with a small corpus of 41 self-corrected word substitution errors collected from a number of speech and eye-movement experiments (Griffin, in press). Counter to the prediction, speakers gazed at the objects they intended to refer to before producing erroneous words, just as they did when word selection was successful. This is illustrated in Figure 7.3.

This word-support hypothesis has also been put to a stronger test. If the semantic relationship between an object and its reference form is reduced,

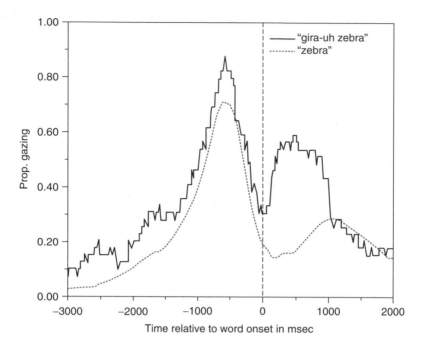

FIGURE 7.3. Grand mean proportion of trials in which speakers gazed at the correct target object at each 8-ms sample relative to the onset of an erroneous word (choppy dark line) or the onset of a correct word (smooth dotted line). $N = 41$ errors. Data from multiple experiments.

speakers should be less motivated to gaze at the object. Thus, gaze durations to such an object should be shorter. This prediction was tested in two scene description experiments (Griffin & Oppenheimer, 2003). Before each trial, speakers were instructed to provide either an accurate or an inaccurate description of the character performing the action in the following scene. For instance, if a scene showed a firefighter saving a baby from a burning building, after the *accurate* instruction, speakers would be asked to label the firefighter normally (e.g., "firefighter") and, after the *inaccurate* instruction, with the name of a similar object (e.g., "police officer"). Counter to the support hypothesis, speakers spent significantly more time gazing at objects when naming them inaccurately rather than accurately. That is, speakers gazed at firefighters for twice the normal amount of time before intentionally calling them "police officers" instead of "firefighters." Speakers even gazed longer at inaccurately named characters when only fluent references were considered. This indicates that the effect was not due to the tendency to be disfluent when uttering inaccurate names. The gaze proportions on target objects for fluent accurate and inaccurate names are shown in Figure 7.4. This study suggests that name-related gazes might not be not driven by the relationship between the name to be prepared and the nature of the fixated object.

The results of the inaccurate-naming study raise the question of why speakers would gaze at objects for more time when describing them inaccurately. There are two plausible reasons. First, speakers had fewer constraints to use in selecting an inaccurate conceptualization or message than an accurate one, because the "inaccurate name" category is bigger and more ill-defined than "accurate" is. One constraint they did have was to relate the inaccurate label to the real object, so the real object was relevant for creating a different conceptualization. This relevance may have motivated gazes during conceptualization, while the lack of constraints may have made selecting an alternative conceptualization more difficult and time consuming. However, if speakers only gazed at the objects during conceptualization processes in the inaccurate condition, one would expect the time between ending the gaze and saying the name to be longer in the inaccurate condition than the accurate one. That is, speakers might end their gaze after finally arriving at an alternative conceptualization for the object in the inaccurate condition, leaving name selection, phonological retrieval, and articulatory planning to occur before articulating

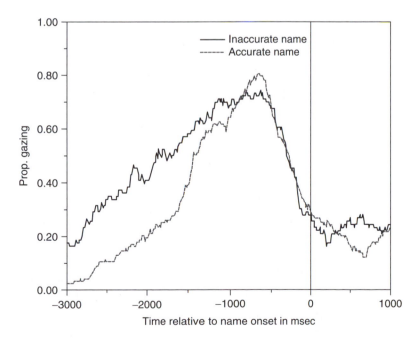

FIGURE 7.4. Grand mean proportion of trials in which speakers gazed at agents that were intentionally labeled accurately or inaccurately. Data from Griffin & Oppenheimer (2003).

the name. In contrast, speakers would end their gaze after retrieving a phonological form in the accurate condition, leaving only processes related to articulation to occur between the end of the gaze and the onset of the name. As Figure 7.4 shows, there was no sign of such a difference in when speakers ceased gazing at objects in the two conditions. Although the lack of constraint on inaccurate names probably extended the time needed to arrive at an inaccurate name, the gaze durations also reflected processes that followed name selection such as phonological encoding.

A second possible reason for gazing at objects while naming them inaccurately is that inaccurately named objects were still more related to the inaccurate names that speakers were asked to generate than other objects in the scene were. To test this, participants in a second experiment were provided with a nonword to use in inaccurately naming objects. Despite the lack of any relationship between the nonword and the objects to which it was applied, speakers gazed at each object for a similar amount of time immediately before naming it with the nonword or a real word. Name-related gazes require no preexisting link between the visual object and the sounds used to refer to it.

In summary, speakers gaze at objects immediately before inaccurately naming them, whether intentionally or unintentionally. They even gaze at objects when the labels they give them are completely unrelated to the objects. These studies indicate that name-related gazes need not be tied to the actual content of the visual area fixated. Instead, gazes appear motivated by a more abstract relationship between gaze location and words.

THE WHY-NOT HYPOTHESIS: GAZES ARE OPTIONAL

Thus far, we have looked at situations in which speakers were free to look at the objects they were talking about. Speakers were surprisingly consistent in gazing at the referents of their speech. The Bock et al. (2003) study indicated that speakers could easily tell time after viewing clocks for a scant 100 ms. Griffin (2004) tested whether speakers would be able to prevent themselves from gazing at objects in the scenes they described, and if they could, whether their utterances would be deficient in any way.

Participants viewed and described pictured events that involved two or three event participants, typically described with transitive and dative verbs, respectively (Griffin, 2004). For one group of speakers, there was a fixation point in the middle of every scene that they were asked to gaze at continuously. Their eye-movement records indicated that they fixated this point most of the time. Nevertheless, they were perfectly capable of describing events, although they occasionally complained about the difficulty of seeing the scene while fixating on a single point. Figure 7.5A shows the fixation of a speaker who described the scene as "two kids are sho:wing a piece of artwork to: a:y female

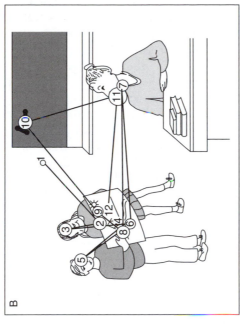

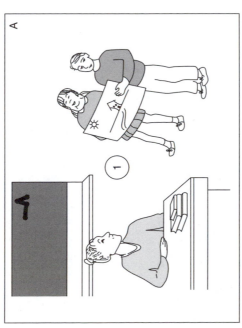

FIGURE 7.5. Circles mark locations of fixations, with greater size indicating longer durations. Fixation order is indicated with numbers and links between successive fixations. (A) The single fixation of a speaker who described the scene while fixating on the central fixation point. (B) Fixations of a speaker who described the scene while freely viewing it.

teacher" (colons indicate prolonged syllables). The utterances of this fixed-view group were compared to those from another experiment in which speakers described the same events while moving their eyes freely. Figure 7.5B shows the fixations of a speaker who described the scene as "two students are probably showing their picture to a teacher." Viewing condition had little impact on utterances. All speakers began their descriptions about two seconds after events appeared, with fixed-viewers starting a nonsignificant 161 ms later than the free viewers did. The fixed- and free-viewing speakers were equally disfluent and equally likely to refer to all of the participants in each event. Although the dependent measures showed little effect of viewing condition, all measures of speed, content, and fluency showed that transitive events involving two event roles were easier to describe than the dative events with three roles. However, the number of event roles did not interact with viewing condition on any measures.

A research assistant with no knowledge of the conditions under which speakers described the events rated the quality of the descriptions on a scale from one (unrelated to scene) to seven (perfect description). The descriptions from the fixed-viewers were rated significantly lower in quality than those of the free-viewers although their means were very similar and very high, 6.43 and 6.74, respectively. The small difference seemed primarily due to the fixed-viewers being more likely to get a detail such as character gender incorrect, probably due to the poorer quality of the parafoveal perceptual information they had available. This study suggests that name-related eye movements are unnecessary in describing simple scenes and do not facilitate descriptions beyond getting details right (which is good to do).

HYPOTHESES SO FAR

Thus far, we have established that when describing simple, visually presented scenes, speakers have a strong preference for gazing at objects while preparing words to refer to them (Griffin & Bock, 2000). The more difficulty speakers have in naming an object, the longer they spend gazing at it (e.g., Griffin, 2001; Meyer et al., 1998). This tendency to make name-related gazes is not diminished by eliminating the meaning relationship between the visual object and the word referring to it (Griffin & Oppenheimer, 2003). These gazes appear relatively unnecessary, based on the lack of interference from irrelevant objects (e.g., Damian & Bowers, 2003), from removing scenes (Bock et al., 2003), or gazing elsewhere (Griffin, 2004). Speakers gaze at referents while preparing their words, regardless of whether the words are spoken immediately after each is prepared or later after the entire utterance is ready. As speakers articulate utterances they have prepared in advance, there are few speech-related eye movements (Griffin & Bock, 2000), even when there is visual information available that is related to speech (Griffin, 2002). This pattern suggests that name-related gazes are associated with planning to speak rather than articulating words and with spatial locations rather than visual information. The place where gaze seems most important to speech is in performing some communicative and interpersonal functions in dialogue (e.g., Argyle & Cook, 1976; Duncan & Fiske, 1977) and in organizing weakly represented message content as in the gaze aversion literature (e.g., Glenberg et al., 1998). Name-related gazes appear unnecessary. If so, why do they occur so consistently?

Speakers probably create representations linking conceptual information to spatial locations as an automatic consequence of attending to objects in scenes. Representations that relate conceptual information to spatial locations have been proposed and studied under the names *object files* (e.g., Kahneman, Treisman, & Gibbs, 1992), *deictic codes* (Ballard, Hayhoe, Pook, & Rao, 1997), *positional markers* (Spivey & Geng, 2001), and *visual/spatial indices* or *fingers of instantiation* (e.g., Pylyshyn, 2001). These spatial indices underlie the gazes to locations associated with information (see Spivey, Richardson, & Fitneva, 2004, in this volume). When speakers activate a message element to linguistically encode it, the message element may activate its associated spatial index, triggering eye movements to that region of space. Indeed, it may be more effortful for speakers to prevent themselves from fixating objects and locations than simply allowing themselves to do so. A similar account could explain listeners' gazes to related images when listening to stories or sentences (see Spivey, Richardson, & Fitneva, 2004). With respect to processing aspects of language production, gaze may be epiphenomenal except when message content is weak. The next hypothesis considers why this might be the case.

THE SEQUENCING HYPOTHESIS: GAZES SUPPORT SEQUENCING WORDS

Speakers seem to prefer creating a skeletal proposition-sized message representation before starting to speak (e.g., Ferreira & Swets, 2002; Griffin & Bock, 2000; van der Meulen, 2001; see Bock & Levelt, 1994, for review). But having multiple message elements in mind means that there is more than one potential element to lexically encode at any particular moment. So, one of the difficulties of language production is that it involves mapping unordered multidimensional conceptual content onto a grammatically ordered sequence of words (e.g., Wundt, 1900/1970). Several production models posit that linguistically encoding a message may involve selectively attending to portions of it (Chang, 2002; Chang, Dell, Bock, & Griffin, 2001; Gordon & Dell, 2002). Loosely based on such models, Figure 7.6 illustrates the interrelationships between message or event roles, semantic/pragmatic specifications, spatial indices, and lexical en-

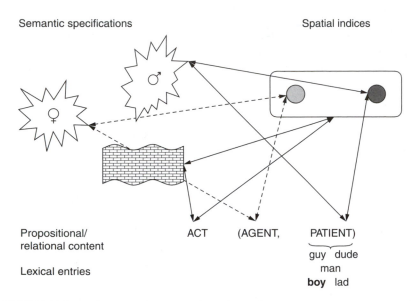

FIGURE 7.6. A diagram illustrating the relationships between semantic specifications, propositional/relational content of messages, spatial indices, and lexical entries for describing a scene of a girl hitting a boy.

tries for a speaker describing a scene of a girl hitting a boy. Linguistically encoding the patient of the event involves concurrent activation of the patient role, the semantic specifications for the boy, a spatial index for the boy in the scene, and potential words for referring to him. It is assumed that activation of the spatial index leads to fixating the associated region in space unless the speaker actively inhibits such movement or a spatial index is lacking.

While words to express the content of a message are prepared and articulated, speakers must remember the message. For unimpaired speakers under normal circumstances, maintaining a message while expressing it rarely produces any sense of difficulty. However, in speakers with impaired working memory (Martin & Freedman, 2001; Schwartz & Hodgson, 2002) or worse yet, impaired word retrieval skills too (Luria, 1972), the effort to maintain a message can be overwhelming. With heroic and prolonged effort, one of Luria's patients was able to describe his efforts to write:

> An idea for something occurred to me, an image of what I wanted to say, and I began to try to remember the right words to express this. No sooner had I got two words down when the very idea that had just taken shape in my mind suddenly disappeared. I forgot what I wanted to write. I looked at the two words I'd written but couldn't remember what I intended to say.
>
> Luria, 1972, p.121, translated from Russian by L. Solotaroff)

In addition to maintaining a message while retrieving words, speakers must also maintain information about which message elements have already been expressed and how. Without this information, expression of the remaining message elements would not be grammatically constrained by earlier words and repetition would be hard to avoid. Indeed, individuals with lexicosemantic working memory deficits seem very prone to repetition when attempting multiword utterances (Martin & Freedman, 2001; Schwartz & Hodgson, 2002). Even unimpaired speakers occasionally produce sequence errors. For example, a speaker may fail to produce words in the correct sequence, as in "Although murder is a form of suicide,..." (Garrett, 1975; see also Dell, Burger, & Svec, 1997; Ferreira & Humphreys, 2001). In this account, such sequencing errors could be due to erroneous links between semantic specifications and relational information such as roles in propositions.

Unlike the generation of mental images (e.g., Laeng & Teodorescu, 2002), sentence generation obligatorily has a sequential component. The ordering of message elements for expression has been called the speaker's linearization problem (Levelt, 1981). Eye movements to referents or their associated regions of space may help prevent sequencing errors by providing converging kinesthetic and spatial order cues for message elements. For example, in Figure 7.6, strong links from the patient role to the boy's spatial index and from the spatial index to the boy's semantic specifications could support the linguistic encoding of the correct semantic specifications for the patient even if the patient role were only weakly linked to the boy's semantic specifications. By reinforcing activation of a particular spatial cue, gaze to an object or its associated location could serve as a cue to which message element the speaker is currently lexicalizing. Similarly, the sequence for gazing at objects or locations could support the successful sequencing of words in sentence production.

Conversations about one's immediate environment probably form a small percentage of language production. A role for eye movements in sequencing may also hold for abstract topics and relationships. Cognitive Grammars (e.g., Langacker, 1987) posit abstract spatial paths for sentences such as *His mood went from bad to worse* and *I sold my soul to the devil*. Knowledge of how objects move from one position to another in space is the basis for understanding how a property like mood changes from one state to another. Chang (2002) argues that these abstract spatial paths may be the result of perceptual-spatial bootstrapping in language acquisition. He notes that such bootstrapping gibes well with the idea that even the most abstract high-level aspects of cognition may be based on perceptual experience gained through interacting with the world (e.g., Barsalou, 1999; also see Spivey et al., 2004). Having posited a relationship between spatial and message representations starting from the computational needs of language production, Chang sees the tight relationship between eye movements and speech as further support for links between grammatical sequences and space.

THE SPACE-Y HYPOTHESIS: SPEECH-RELATED GAZES ARE LIKE SPEECH-RELATED GESTURES

The literature on gestures also links together abstract message content, language production, and spatial representations (McNeill, 1985, 1992). The same hodge-podge of hotly debated functions for gestures (particularly those termed ideational, iconic, metaphorical, or lexical) arises in considering gaze and speech. Note that gestures do not simply co-occur with speech about concrete objects or spaces. Speakers gesture when discussing abstract topics as well as concrete ones. For example, McNeill (1992) describes the gestures of mathematicians discussing mathematical concepts. Likewise, if gaze aversion is considered part of the same phenomenon as name-related gazes in scene descriptions, both gaze and gesture can be meaningfully related to speech beyond the here and now.

Among the reasons for positing a strong relationship between speech and gesture is their overlapping content, temporal relationship in production, related development in children, and parallel break downs in aphasia (McNeill, 1985). In addition, speakers are more likely to gesture when they are disfluent than when fluent (e.g., Beattie & Shovelton, 2000; Christenfeld, Schachter, & Bilous, 1991), and preventing speakers from gesturing increases disfluencies (see Krauss, 1998, for review). Gestures are increasingly associated with Slobin's (1996) notion of "thinking for speaking" (e.g., Iverson & Goldin-Meadow, 1998; Kita & Özyürek, 2003; McNeill & Duncan, 2000).

Debate over the function of gestures in language production, thought, and communication overlaps with most of the hypotheses discussed here for gazes in language production. One branch of gesture research examines its use and usefulness as a mode of communication (e.g., Bavelas, 1994; Beattie & Shovelton, 2002a). Like gaze, gesture can play a role in control of turn taking (e.g., Duncan & Fiske, 1977). But speakers frequently gesture when they know that their interlocutors cannot perceive them (Iverson, 1999). Like gaze aversion in message planning, ideational gestures seem to play a role in helping speakers package information for expression (e.g., Alibali, Kita, & Young, 2000; Özyürek, McNeill, & Kita, 2000). Both gazes and ideational gestures can show a strong tie to the preparation of individual words. For example, ideational gestures anticipate related words (McNeill, 1985) by approximately one second (Morrel-Samuels & Krauss, 1992). Likewise, both may have correct referents or forms even when word retrieval fails (McNeill, 1985). The timing of gestures with respect to related words is influenced by word frequency or familiarity (Morrel-Samuels & Krauss, 1992). Finally, there are increases in ideational gestures (e.g., Beattie & Shovelton, 2000) and gaze aversion (e.g., Kendon, 1967) with disfluencies and mental effort, along with decreases in gestures (e.g., Chawla & Krauss, 1994) and gaze attraction (Meyer et al., 2000) with repetition and the lessening of mental effort.

So, ideational gestures have been argued to be often communicative (e.g., Bavelas, 1994; McNeill, 1985) or more for the speaker's own benefit (e.g., Krauss & Hadar, 1998); to support information packaging at a propositional level for the speaker (e.g., Kita & Özyürek, 2003) or rather signal syntax for the listener (Beattie & Shovelton, 2002b); and to support lemma selection (Krauss, 1998) or not (Beattie & Coughlan, 1999). Increasingly, gesture is argued to have multiple functions (e.g., Bavelas, 1994; Goldin-Meadow, 1999a; McNeill, 1985, 1992). It does not seem far-fetched to suggest that gestures *and* gaze are regularly involved in communication, information packaging, and supporting word retrieval via activating message elements to varying degrees depending on the circumstances.

Is there any evidence that gestures aid in *sequencing* words in production? Research on gesture and speech in child development is consistent with a supporting role for gesture. Children typically produce utterances with multiple elements first by combining a gesture and a word. Significant variation in children's language acquisition is accounted for by variation in their use of gesture-word combinations (e.g., Capirici, Iverson, Pizzuto, & Volterra, 1996; see Goldin-Meadow, 1999b; Iverson & Thelen, 1999, for review). Furthermore, the development of counting skills may show a transition from gesture to gaze (Alibali & DiRusso, 1999). Around the age of 4, touching and pointing at objects helps children maintain a one-to-one correspondence between spoken numbers and counted objects. Alibali and DiRusso suggested that in college students, counting is more likely to be observed in eye movements. Indeed, Holšánová (2001) has observed counting-like gazes in scene descriptions when speakers produced quantifiers and Demarais and Cohen (1998) reported that saccade rate increased with rate of subvocal counting. In addition, the form that gestures take varies with the transitivity of the clause they accompany, suggesting parallels with syntactic structure (Beattie & Shovelton, 2002b). Suggestively, many researchers argue for common evolutionary and neuroanatomical bases for manual movement and speech (e.g., Corballis, 2002; Iverson & Thelen, 1999; but see Feyereisen, 1999, for a different view).

So, both ideational gestures and speaker gazes may reflect the activation of spatial indices for message elements during message planning and word preparation. Although the appearance of irrelevant visual information does not interfere with producing simple picture descriptions, disrupting spatial indices may lead to speech disruptions when message planning is difficult and messages lend themselves to spatial coding. As semantic representations for message elements and the relationships between them become weaker, spatial indices and thereby gaze may play a larger supportive role in sentence production. Such effects should be similar to the increase in disfluencies when gestures are prevented (see Krauss, 1998). Experiments testing these predictions are under way.

SUMMARY OF HYPOTHESES

Properties of gazes are an important part of communication, whether or not speakers intend them to be so. As in other tasks, there is good reason to think that the gazes that accompany language production reflect the allocation of mental resources (e.g., Just & Carpenter, 1976). In particular, the weaker speakers' representations are of what they plan to say, the more likely they are to avert their gaze from unrelated visual information and, instead, direct their gaze to blank spaces (see Glenberg et al., 1998) or locations associated with message content (see van der Meulen et al., 2001). This seems to hold at the level of global message planning as well as successively lexicalizing elements of a message. When message content is simple and rapidly planned, speakers do not make message-related gazes and their name-related gazes appear invulnerable to interference from irrelevant information. When messages are more difficult to create, message planning seems more likely to be reflected in eye movements. One view of the gaze-production relationship predicts that name-related gazes to spatial locations associated with message elements become more important for producing utterances as messages become more complex, abstract, and weakly represented. In short, name-related gazes may support successful production and sequencing of message elements, but this idea itself awaits empirical support.

WHAT IF NAME-RELATED GAZES ARE EPIPHENOMENAL?

Finding evidence that gaze ordering is related to ordering message elements would be satisfying. Unless or until that happens, however, we are left with the possibility that word-production gazes are perfectly useless in speaking. By "perfectly useless," I mean that executing them provides no detectable processing benefit of any kind (speed, fluency, etc) over not executing them. The answer to why speakers gaze would simply be "Why not?" In such a situation, researchers might consider whether eye-movement monitoring deserved any consideration in the study of language production.

I argue that even if speech-related gazes were epiphenomenal, monitoring speakers' eye movements would still provide very useful measures (see also Just & Carpenter, 1976). Of course, one could not argue an absence of word preparation based on an absence of speech-related eye movements, but that is already the case (darn those null results!). Furthermore, we already know that speakers can describe simple scenes quite well while maintaining central fixation (see Henderson & Ferreira, 2004, in this volume, for ways to increase the need for eye movements). Name-related gazes may just indicate when speakers prepared particular words. This is not trivial, because such information supports information about the time course of language production that cannot be culled from speech measures alone.

BEYOND NAME-RELATED GAZES IN SPEAKING

Thus far, gazes in description tasks have primarily been related to preparing noun phrases (Meyer et al., 1998) and adjectives (Levelt & Meyer, 2000; van der Meulen, 2001). In one study, gazes to action-relevant regions of pictures were consistently observed only when speakers hesitated before verbs (Griffin & Bock, 2000). In an experiment with instrument-based actions, such as a camera for photographing characters, speakers fixated instruments regularly before producing verbs (Repp & Sommer, 2003). Holšánová (2001) noted that, in addition to gazing at objects before referring to them or producing a modifier, speakers also gazed at them before describing objects' locations or actions. When verbs are strongly associated with a single object such as a camera, speakers may fixate that object while preparing the verb. Such observations may be critical in establishing when verbs are typically selected in language production, and by extension, how utterances are structured (see e.g., Ferreira, 2000, for a verb-based production theory).

Another potential way of using gazes to track individual word preparation within sentence production comes from the use of written words. In a sentence construction task, participants view a scrambled set of words that they are to use in a sentence. On about 50% of trials, participants gazed at words immediately before producing them in their sentences (Lawler & Griffin, 2003). Production researchers may make use of the tendency to fixate previous locations of objects (e.g., Richardson & Spivey, 2000) or imagined locations (Altmann & Kamide, 2004, in this volume).

More complex processes in production may be discerned by going beyond fixations on individual items and instead studying potentially meaningful sequences or combinations. For example, before uttering plural nouns, speakers tend to fixate the multiple objects referred to by plurals. They also do so both when the objects are related by a common activity such as "flying objects" and when they belong to a common taxonomic category such as "three birds" (Holšánová, 2001). A more abstract gaze-production link may be reflected in a speaker's gaze to flowers and leaves before suggesting that a scene depicts "early summer" (Holšánová, 2001). The challenge however is to predict such relationships between eye movements and speech content instead of simply explaining possible relationships post-hoc. For example, if speakers decide the order of mention for message elements incrementally (e.g., Chang, 2002), they should show indecision during speech when given the opportunity of producing a prepositional dative such as *A woman is throwing a bone to a dog* or double-object dative like *A woman is throwing a dog a bone*. Consistent with this prediction, even when speakers produced sentences perfectly fluently, they gazed back and forth between the two objects mentioned after the verb (bone and dog) significantly more often when generating a sentence themselves rather than repeating it back (Griffin & Garton, 2003). Similarly, in a sentence construction task, syntactic flexibility and indecision about order of mention was reflected in speakers' eye movements between written words (Lawler & Griffin, 2003).

Although speech-related eye movements may be epiphenomenal, the tendency to make them appears remarkably strong. Furthermore, parallels between speech-related gazes and gaze aversion and speech-related gestures suggest that under more challenging speaking conditions, gazes may play a functional role in message planning and lexicalization. Epiphenomenal or not, research has only begun to tap the insights that may be gained from the study of speakers' gazes.

NOTES

1. Here the term *gaze* is used to refer to a period spent inspecting a particular object or region of space before the eye moves to another region. Gazes collapse over fixations made to the same object.
2. In the experiments of Meyer and colleagues, participants view all experimental objects and their names before the experiment begins. This pre-exposure greatly reduces gaze durations and object naming latencies, resulting in very different estimates for the time needed to name objects.
3. When speakers strive to be fluent, eye voice span begins to include time preparing later words, while gaze duration continues to be a fairly pure measure of processing time for a particular object name (Griffin, 2003). See Bock et al. (2003, 2004, in this volume) for another interpretation of eye-voice latency differences.
4. Exceptions to this rule arise when people attempt to remember object names (Noizet & Pynte, 1976; Zelinsky & Murphy, 2000) and when they are informed of the length of object names in advance (Meyer et al., 2003). Thus, gazes only seem correlated with name length when people silently rehearse object names or alter their pre-speech monitoring of words. This seems to be related to using the inner ear as opposed to word-production processes and the inner voice (see e.g., Smith, Wilson, & Reisberg, 1995).
5. There is one gap in the correspondence. Priming an object's name with a written distractor word that was phonologically related to an object's name facilitated picture naming in Ferreira and Pashler's study, as is usually the case (Schriefers et al., 1990). However, phonological primes did not alter when participants responded to tones. The authors concluded that phoneme selection, which their primes presumably affected, was not a demanding process. In contrast, gaze durations before naming objects were shortened by phonologically related distractors (Meyer & van der Meulen, 2000). In other words, in one study, phonological priming affected a resource-demanding process while in the other it did not. However, the discrepancy

may be due to differences in the utterances produced in the two studies, which in turn affected the attention allocated to phoneme selection. Specifically, Meyer et al.'s speakers named two objects whereas Ferreira and Pashler's only named one. In naming two objects fluently, speakers must take into account the duration of the first name to allow enough time to prepare the second name (Griffin, 2003). If this information about the first word's duration is related to the phoneme selection, speakers in Meyer's experiment may have needed to attend to processing the first object's name for longer than they otherwise would if no other word followed it as in the Ferreira and Pashler experiment. Additional research is required to test whether the demands of producing multiple words really underlies the observed differences between these studies.

6. It is possible that speakers engage in effortful memory encoding in such cases that would not occur if the objects remained in view. This interpretation would match that for eye movements to blocks during a copying task (Ballard et al., 1997).

7. This stubbornness is reminiscent of observers persistent scanning of repeated objects in a visual search task (Wolfe, Oliva, Butcher, & Arsenio, 2002).

8. Although speakers avert their gaze as little from a face displayed in black and white as from a gray oval, according to Erlichman (1981).

REFERENCES

Abrams, R. A., Meyer, D. E., & Kornblum, S. (1990). Eye-hand coordination: Oculomotor control in rapid aimed limb movements. *Journal of Experimental Psychology: Human Perception and Performance, 16*, 248-267.

Alibali, M. W., & DiRusso, A. A. (1999). The function of gesture in learning to count: More than keeping track. *Cognitive Development, 14*, 37-56.

Alibali, M. W., Kita, S., & Young, A. J. (2000). Gesture and the process of speech production: We think, therefore we gesture. *Language and Cognitive Processes, 15*, 593-613.

Altmann, G. T. M., & Kamide, Y. (2004). Now you see it, now you don't: Mediating the mapping between language and the visual world. In J. M. Henderson & F. Ferreira (Eds.), *The interface of language, vision, and action: Eye movements and the visual world*. New York: Psychology Press.

Argyle, M., & Cook, M. (1976). *Gaze and mutual gaze*. Cambridge: Cambridge University Press.

Arnold, J. E., Fagnano, M., & Tanenhaus, M. K. (2003). Disfluencies signal thee, um, new information. *Journal of Psycholinguistic Research, 32*, 25-36.

Arnold, J. E., & Griffin, Z. M. (2004). *The role of competition in the production of referring expressions*. Manuscript in preparation.

Bachoud-Levi, A. -C., Dupoux, E., Cohen, L., & Mehler, J. (1998). Where is the length effect? A cross-linguistic study of speech production. *Journal of Memory and Language, 39*, 331-346.

Ballard, D. H., Hayhoe, M. M., Pook, P. K., & Rao, R. P. N. (1997). Deictic codes for the embodiment of cognition. *Behavioral & Brain Sciences, 20*, 723-767.

Barsalou, L. W. (1999). Perceptual symbol systems. *Behavioral and Brain Sciences, 22*, 577-660.

Bavelas, J. B. (1994). Gestures as part of speech: Methodological implications. *Research on Language & Social Interaction, 27*, 201-221.

Beattie, G. W. (1979). Planning units in spontaneous speech: Some evidence from hesitation in speech and speaker gaze direction in conversation. *Linguistics, 17*, 61-78.

Beattie, G., & Coughlan, J. (1999). An experimental investigation of the role of iconic gestures in lexical access using the tip-of-the tongue phenomenon. *British Journal of Psychology, 90*, 35-56.

Beattie, G., & Shovelton, H. (2000). Iconic hand gestures and the predictability of words in context in spontaneous speech. *British Journal of Psychology, 91*, 473-491.

Beattie, G., & Shovelton, H. (2002a). An experimental investigation of some properties of individual iconic gestures that mediate their communicative power. *British Journal of Psychology, 93*, 179-192.

Beattie, G., & Shovelton, H. (2002b). What properties of talk are associated with the generation of spontaneous iconic hand gestures? *British Journal of Social Psychology, 41*, 403-417.

Bloem, I., & La Heij, W. (2003). Semantic facilitation and semantic interference in word translation: Implications for models of lexical access in language production. *Journal of Memory and Language, 48*, 468-488.

Bock, J. K. (1982). Toward a cognitive psychology of syntax: Information processing contributions to sentence formulation. *Psychological Review, 89*, 1-47.

Bock, K., Irwin, D. E., & Davidson, D. J. (2004). Putting First Things First. In J. M. Henderson & F. Ferreira (Eds.), *The interface of language, vision, and action: Eye movements and the visual world*. New York: Psychology Press.

Bock, K., Irwin, D. E., Davidson, D. J., & Levelt, W. J. M. (2003). Minding the clock. *Journal of Memory and Language, 48*, 653-685.

Buswell, G. T. (1935). *How people look at pictures*. Chicago: University of Chicago Press.

Capirici, O., Iverson, J. M., Pizzuto, E., & Volterra, V. (1996). Gestures and words during the transition to two-word speech. *Journal of Child Language, 23*, 645-673.

Chang, F. (2002). Symbolically speaking: A connectionist model of sentence production. *Cognitive Science, 93*, 1-43.

Chang, F., Dell, G. S., Bock, K., & Griffin, Z. M. (2000). Structural priming as implicit learning: A comparison of models of sentence production. *Journal of Psycholinguistic Research, 29*(2), 217-229.

Chawla, P., & Krauss, R. M. (1994). Gesture and speech in spontaneous and rehearsed narratives. *Journal of Experimental Social Psychology, 30*, 580-601.

Christenfeld, N., Schachter, S., & Bilous, F. (1991). Filled pauses and gestures: It's not coincidence. *Journal of Psycholinguistic Research, 20*, 1-10.

Clark, H. H. (1996). *Using Language*. Cambridge: Cambridge University Press.

Clark, H., & Fox Tree, J. (2002). Using uh and um in spontaneous speaking. *Cognition, 84*, 73-111.

Cooper, R. M. (1974). The control of eye fixation by the meaning of spoken language: A new methodology for the real-time investigation of speech perception, memory, and language processing. *Cognitive Psychology, 6*, 84-107.

Corballis, M. C. (2002). *From hand to mouth: The origins of language*. Princeton: Princeton University Press.

Dahan, D., Magnuson, J. S., & Tanenhaus, M. K. (2001). Time course of frequency effects in spoken-word recognition: Evidence from eye movements. *Cognitive Psychology, 42*(4), 317-367.

Damian, M. F., & Bowers, J. S. (2003). Locus of semantic interference in picture-word interference tasks. *Psychonomic Bulletin and Review, 10*, 111-117.

Dell, G. S., Burger, L. K., & Svec, W. R. (1997). Language production and serial order: A functional analysis and a model. *Psychological Review, 104*, 123-147.

Demarais, A. M., & Cohen, B. H. (1998). Evidence for image-scanning eye movements during transitive inference. *Biological Psychology, 49*, 229-247.

DePaulo, B. M., & Friedman, H. S. (1998). Nonverbal communication. In D. T. Glbert, S. T. Fiske & G. Lindzey (Eds.), *The handbook of social psychology* (4th ed., Vol. II, pp. 3-40). Boston: McGraw-Hill.

DePaulo, B. M., Lindsay, J. J., Malone, B. E., Muhlenbruck, L., Charlton, K., & Cooper, H. (2003). Cues to deception. *Psychological Bulletin, 129*, 74-112.

Duncan, S., & Fiske, D. W. (1977). *Face-to-face interaction: Research, methods, and theory*. Hillsdale NJ: Erlbaum.

Eberhard, K. M., Spivey-Knowlton, M. J., Sedivy, J. C., & Tanenhaus, M. K. (1995). Eye movements as a window into real-time spoken language comprehension in natural contexts. *Journal of Psycholinguistic Research, 24*, 409-436.

Ehrlichman, H. (1981). From gaze aversion to eye-movement suppression: An investigation of the cognitive interference explanation of gaze patterns during conversation. *British Journal of Social Psychology, 20,* 233-241.

Exline, R. V., & Fehr, B. J. (1978). Applications of semiosis to the study of visual interaction. In A. W. Seigman & S. Feldstein (Eds.), *Nonverbal behavior and communication* (pp. 117-157). Hillsdale NJ: Erlbaum.

Ferreira, F. (2000). Syntax in language production: An approach using tree-adjoining grammars. In L. Wheeldon (Ed.), *Aspects of language production* (pp. 291-330). London: Psychology Press.

Ferreira, F., Ferraro, V., & Bailey, K.G.D. (2002). Good-enough representations in language comprehension. *Current Directions in Psychological Science, 11,* 11-15.

Ferreira, F., & Swets, B. (2002). How incremental is language production? Evidence from the production of utterances requiring the computation of arithmetic sums. *Journal of Memory and Language, 46,* 57-84.

Ferreira, V. S., & Humphreys, K. R. (2001). Syntactic influences on lexical and morphological processing in language production. *Journal of Memory and Language, 44,* 52-80.

Ferreira, V. S., & Pashler, H. (2002). Central bottleneck influences on the processing stages of word production. *Journal of Experimental Psychology: Learning, Memory, and Cognition, 28,* 1187-1199.

Feyereisen, P. (1999). Neuropsychology of communicative movements. In L. S. Messing & R. Campbell (Eds.), *Gesture, speech, and sign* (pp. 3-26). Oxford: Oxford University Press.

Fischer, B. (1998). Attention in saccades. In R. D. Wright (Ed.), *Visual attention* (pp. 289-305). New York, NY: Oxford University Press.

Ford, M., & Holmes, V. M. (1978). Planning units and syntax in sentence production. *Cognition, 6,* 35-53.

Forrest, L. (1993). *Syntactic subject and focus of attention.* Doctoral dissertation, University of Oregon.

Fowler, C. A., Levy, E. T., & Brown, J. M. (1997). Reductions of spoken words in certain discourse contexts. *Journal of Memory and Language, 37,* 24-40.

Garrett, M. F. (1975). The analysis of sentence production. In G. H. Bower (Ed.), *The psychology of learning and motivation* (pp. 133-177). New York: Academic Press.

Glaser, W. R., & Düngelhoff, F. -J. (1984). The time course of picture-word interference. *Journal of Experimental Psychology: Human Perception and Performance, 10,* 640-654.

Glenberg, A. M., Schroeder, J. L., & Robertson, D. A. (1998). Averting the gaze disengages the environment and facilitates remembering. *Memory and Cognition, 26,* 651-658.

Goldin-Meadow, S. (1999a). The role of gesture in communication and thinking. *Trends in Cognitive Sciences, 3,* 419-429.

Goldin-Meadow, S. (1999b). The development of gesture with and without speech in hearing and deaf children. In L. S. Messing & R. Campbell (Eds.), *Gesture, speech, and sign* (pp. 117-132). Oxford: Oxford University Press.

Goldman-Eisler, F. (1968). *Psycholinguistics: Experiments in spontaneous speech.* London: Academic Press.

Gordon, J., & Dell, G. (2002). Learning to divide the labor between syntax and semantics: A connectionist account of deficits in light and heavy verb production. *Brain and Cognition, 48,* 376-381.

Griffin, Z. M. (1998). *What the eye says about sentence planning.* Doctoral dissertation, University of Illinois at Urbana-Champaign.

Griffin, Z. M. (2001). Gaze durations during speech reflect word selection and phonological encoding. *Cognition, 82,* B1-B14.

Griffin, Z. M. (2002, Sept.). *What do speakers prepare when they prepare words in advance?* Paper presented at the eighth annual meeting of Architectures and Mechanisms of Language Processing, Tenerife, Spain.

Griffin, Z. M. (2003). A reversed word length effect in coordinating the preparation and articulation of words in speaking. *Psychonomic Bulletin and Review, 10,* 603-609.

Griffin, Z. M. (2004). *Don't move your eyes.* Unpublished raw data.

Griffin, Z. M. (in press). The eyes are right when the mouth is wrong. *Psychological Science.*

Griffin, Z. M., & Bock, K. (2000). What the eyes say about speaking. *Psychological Science, 11,* 274-279.

Griffin, Z. M., & Garton, K. L. (2003, March). *Procrastination in speaking: Ordering arguments during speech.* Poster presented at the 16th Annual CUNY Conference on Human Sentence Processing, Boston, MA.

Griffin, Z. M., & Garton, K. L. (2004). *Naming photographed objects ad nauseum.* Unpublished raw data.

Griffin, Z. M., & Oppenheimer, D. (2003). *Looking and lying: Speakers' gazes reflect locus of attention rather than speech content.* Paper presented at 12th European Conference on Eye Movements, Dundee, Scotland.

Hanna, J., & Brennan, S. (2003, May). *Eye gaze has immediate effects on reference resolution in conversation.* Paper presented at the 15th Annual Convention of the American Psychological Society, Atlanta GA.

Henderson, J., & Ferreira, F. (2004). Scene perception for psycholinguists. In J. M. Henderson & F. Ferreira (Eds.), *The interface of language, vision, and action: Eye movements and the visual world.* New York: Psychology Press.

Holšánová, J. (2001): *Picture viewing and picture description: Two windows to the mind.* Doctoral dissertation. Lund, Sweden: Lund University Cognitive Studies 83.

Hood, B. M., Willen, J. D., & Driver, J. (1998). Adult's eyes trigger shifts of visual attention in human infants. *Psychological Science, 9,* 131-134.

Horton, W. S., Metzing, C. A., & Gerrig, R. J. (2002, Nov.). *Tracking Speakers' Use of Internal and External Information During Referential Communication.* Poster presented at the 43rd Anuual meeting of the Psychonomic Society, Kansas City, MO.

Hyönä, J., Tommola, J., & Alaja, A. M. (1995). Pupil-dilation as a measure of processing load in simultaneous interpretation and other language tasks. *Quarterly Journal of Experimental Psychology Section a: Human Experimental Psychology, 48,* 598-612.

Inhoff, A. W., Briihl, D., Bohemier, G., & Wang, J. (1992). Eye and span and coding of text during copytyping. *Journal of Experimental Psychology: Learning, Memory, & Cognition, 18,* 298-306.

Intraub, H. (1981). Identification and processing of briefly glimpsed visual scenes. In D. F. Fisher, R. A. Monty & J. W. Senders (Eds.), *Eye movements: Cognition and visual perception* (pp. 181-190). Hillsdale NJ: Lawrence Erlbaum.

Iverson, J. M. (1999). How to get to the cafeteria: Gesture and speech in blind and sighted children's spatial descriptions. *Developmental Psychology, 35,* 1132-1142.

Iverson, J. M., & Goldin-Meadow, S. (1998). Why people gesture when they speak. *Nature, 396,* 228.

Iverson, J. M., & Thelen, E. (1999). Hand, mouth, and brain: The dynamic emergence of speech and gesture. *Journal of Consciousness Studies, 6,* 19-40.

Jescheniak, J. -D., & Levelt, W. J. M. (1994). Word frequency effects in speech production: Retrieval of syntactic information and of phonological form. *Journal of Experimental Psychology: Learning, Memory, and Cognition, 20,* 824-843.

Just, M. A., & Carpenter, P. A. (1976). Eye fixations and cognitive processes. *Cognitive Psychology, 8,* 441-480.

Kahneman, D. (1973). *Attention and effort.* Englewood Cliffs, NJ: Prentice-Hall.

Kahneman, D., Treisman, A., & Gibbs, B. J. (1992). The reviewing of object files: Object-specific integration of information. *Cognitive Psychology, 24,* 175-219.

Kempen, G., & Hoenkamp, E. (1987). An incremental procedural grammar for sentence formulation. *Cognitive Science, 11,* 201-258.

Kempen, G., & Huijbers, P. (1983). The lexicalization process in sentence production and naming: Indirect election of words. *Cognition, 14,* 185-209.

Kendon, A. (1967). Some functions of gaze-direction in social interaction. *Acta Psychologica, 26,* 22-63.

Kita, S., & Özyürek, A. (2003). What does cross-linguistic variation in semantic coordination of speech and gesture reveal?: Evidence for an interface representation of spatial thinking and speaking. *Journal of Memory and Language, 48,* 16-32.

Krauss, R. M. (1998). Why do we gesture when we speak? *Current Directions in Psychological Science, 7,* 54-60.

Krauss, R. M., & Chiu, C. -Y. (1998). Language and social behavior. In D. T. Gilbert, S. T. Fiske, & G. Lindzey (Eds.), *The Handbook of social psychology* (4th ed., Vol. II, pp. 41-88). Boston: McGraw-Hill.

Krauss, R. M., & Hadar, U. (1999). The role of speech-related arm/hand gestures in word retrieval. In L. S. Messing & R. Campbell (Eds.), *Gesture, speech, and sign* (pp. 93-116). Oxford: Oxford University Press.

Lachman, R. (1973). Uncertainty effects on time to access the internal lexicon. *Journal of Experimental Psychology, 99,* 199-208.

Laeng, B., & Teodorescu, D. -S. (2002). Eye scanpaths during visual imagery reenact those of perception of the same visual scene. *Cognitive Science, 26,* 207-231.

La Heij, W., Mak, P., Sander, J., & Willeboordse, E. (1998). The gender-congruency effect in picture-word tasks. *Psychological Research-Psychologische Forschung, 61*(3), 209-219.

Langacker, R. W. (1987). *Foundations of cognitive grammar: Theoretical prerequisites* (Vol. 1). Stanford, CA: Stanford University Press.

Lawler, E. N., & Griffin, Z. M. (2003, May). *Gaze anticipates speech in sentence-construction task.* Poster presented at the 15th Annual Convention of the American Psychological Society, Atlanta GA.

Lempert, H., & Kinsbourne, M. (1985). Possible origin speech in selective orienting. *Psychological Bulletin, 97,* 62-73.

Lesko, W. A., & Schneider, F. W. (1978). Effects of speaking order and speaker gaze level on interpersonal gaze in a triad. *Journal of Social Psychology, 104*(2), 185-195.

Levelt, W. J. M. (1981). The speaker's linearization problem. *Philosophical Transactions of the Royal Society of London B, 295,* 305-315.

Levelt, W. J. M. (1983). Monitoring and self-repair in speech. *Cognition, 14,* 41-104.

Levelt, W. J. M. (1989). *Speaking: From intention to articulation.* Cambridge, MA: MIT Press.

Levelt, W. J. M., & Meyer, A. S. (2000). Word for word: Multiple lexical access in speech production. *European Journal of Cognitive Psychology, 12*(4), 433-452.

Levelt, W. J. M., Roelofs, A., & Meyer, A. S. (1999). A theory of lexical access in speech production. *Behavioral and Brain Science, 22,* 1-45.

Luria, A. R. (1972). *The Man with a shattered world: The history of a brain wound* (L. Solotaroff, Trans.). Cambridge MA: Harvard University Press.

Mackworth, N. H., & Morandi, A. J. (1967). The gaze selects informative details within pictures. *Perception and Psychophysics, 2,* 547-551.

Marslen-Wilson, W. (1973). Linguistic structure and speech shadowing at very short latencies. *Nature, 244,* 522-523.

Martin, R. C., & Freedman, M. L. (2001). Short-term retention of lexical-semantic representations: Implications for speech production. *Memory, 9,* 261-280.

McNeill, D. (1985). So you think gestures are nonverbal? *Psychological Review, 92,* 350-371.

McNeill, D. (1992). *Hand and mind: What gestures reveal about thought.* Chicago: University of Chicago Press.

McNeill, D., & Duncan, S. D. (2000). Growth points in thinking-for-speaking. In D. McNeill (Ed.), *Language and gesture.* Cambridge.

Meyer, A. S., & Lethaus, F. (2004). The use of eye tracking in studies of sentence generation. In J. M. Henderson & F. Ferreira (Eds.) *The interface of language, vision, and action: Eye movements and the visual world.* New York: Psychology Press.

Meyer, A. S., Roelofs, A., & Levelt, W. J. M. (2003). Word length effects in object naming: The role of a response criterion. *Journal of Memory and Language, 48,* 131-147.

Meyer, A. S., Sliderink, A., & Levelt, W. J. M. (1998). Viewing and naming objects: Eye movements during noun phrase production. *Cognition, 66*, B25-B33.

Meyer, A. S., & van der Meulen, F. F. (2000). Phonological priming effects on speech onset latencies and viewing times in object naming. *Psychonomic Bulletin and Review, 7*(2), 314-319.

Morrel-Samuels, P., & Krauss, R. M. (1992). Word familiarity predicts the temporal asynchrony of hand gestures and speech. *Journal of Experimental Psychology: Learning, Memory and Cognition, 18*, 615-623.

Noizet, G., & Pynte, J. (1976). Implicit labelling and readiness for pronunciation during the perceptual process. *Perception, 5*, 217-223.

Özyürek, A., McNeill, D., & Kita, S. (2000). What do gestures reveal about thinking-for-speaking: A cross-linguistic and developmental investigation on motion event descriptions. In R. Berman, D. Slobin, S. Stromqvist & L. Verhoeven (Eds.), *Frog story revisited*. NJ: Erlbaum.

Parker, R. E. (1978). Picture processing during recognition. *Journal of Experimental Psychology: Human Perception & Performance, 4*, 284-293.

Potter, M. C. (1975). Meaning in visual search. *Science, 187*, 965-966.

Potter, M. C., & Levy, E. L. (1969). Recognition memory for a rapid sequence of pictures. *Journal of Experimental Psychology, 81*, 10-15.

Pylyshyn, Z. (2001). Visual indexes, preconceptual objects, and situated vision. *Cognition, 80*, 127-158.

Rayner, K. (1998). Eye movements in reading and information processing: 20 years of research. *Psychological Bulletin, 124*, 372-422.

Rayner, K., & Pollatsek, A. (1997). Eye movements, the eye-hand span, and the perceptual span during sight-reading of music. *Current Directions in Psychological Science, 6*, 49-53.

Repp, S., & Sommer, K. (2003, March). *The early coding of verbs in complex sentences: Evidence from eye-movements in the production of ellipsis, full clauses and object naming*. Poster presented at the 16th Annual CUNY Conference on Human Sentence Processing, Cambridge, MA.

Richardson, D. C., & Spivey, M. J. (2000). Representation, space and Hollywood Squares: looking at things that aren't there anymore. *Cognition, 76*(3), 269-295.

Schriefers, H., Meyer, A. S., & Levelt, W. J. M. (1990). Exploring the time course of lexical access in language production: Picture-word interference studies. *Journal of Memory and Language, 29*, 86-102.

Schwartz, M. F., & Hodgson, C. (2002). A new multiword naming deficit: Evidence and interpretation. *Cognitive Neuropsychology, 19*(3), 263-288.

Segalowitz, N. S. (1982). The perception of semantic relations in pictures. *Memory & Cognition, 10*, 381-388.

Slobin, D. I. (1996). From "thought and language" to "thinking for speaking." In J. Gumperz & S. C. Levinson (Eds.), *Rethinking linguistic relativity. Studies in the social and cultural foundations of language* (pp. 70-96). New York: Cambridge University Press.

Smith, J. D., Wilson, M., & Reisberg, D. (1995). The role of subvocalization in auditory imagery. *Neuropsychologia, 33*, 1433-1454.

Snodgrass, J. G., & Yuditsky, T. (1996). Naming times for the Snodgrass and Vanderwart pictures. *Behavior Research Methods, Instruments, & Computers, 28*, 516-536.

Spivey, M. J., Richardson, D. C., & Fitneva, S. A. (2004). Thinking outside the brain: Spatial indices to visual and linguistic information. In J. Henderson & F. Ferreira (Eds.), *The interface of language, vision, and action: Eye movements and the visual world*. New York: Psychology Press.

Tanenhaus, M. K., Chambers, C. C., & Hanna, J. E. (2004). Referential domains in spoken language comprehension: Using eye movements to bridge the product and action traditions. In J. M. Henderson & F. Ferreira (Eds.), *The interface of language, vision, and action: Eye movements and the visual world*. New York: Psychology Press.

Tanenhaus, M. K., Magnuson, J. S., Dahan, D., & Chambers, C. (2000). Eve movements and lexical access in spoken-language comprehension: Evaluating a linking hypothesis between fixations and linguistic processing. *Journal of Psycholinguistic Research, 29,* 557-580.

Tanenhaus, M. K., Spivey-Knowlton, M. J., Eberhard, K. M., & Sedivy, J. C. (1995). Integration of visual and linguistic information in spoken language comprehension. *Science, 268,* 1632-1634.

Taylor, I. (1969). Content and structure in sentence production. *Journal of Verbal Learning and Verbal Behavior, 8,* 170-175.

van der Meulen, F. (2001). *Moving eyes and naming objects.* Dissertation, Katholieke Universiteit Nijmegen.

van der Meulen, F. F., & Meyer, A. S. (2000, November). *Coordination of eye gaze and speech in sentence production.* Poster presented at the 41st Annual Meeting of the Psychonomic Society, New Orleans, LA.

van der Meulen, F. F., Meyer, A. S., & Levelt, W. J. M. (2001). Eye movements during the production of nouns and pronouns. *Memory & Cognition, 29,* 512-521.

Wolfe, J. M., Oliva, A., Butcher, S. J., & Arsenio, H. C. (2002). An unbinding problem? The disintegration of visible, previously attended objects does not attract attention. *Journal of Vision, 2,* 256-271.

Wundt, W. (1900/1970). Die Sprache (A. L. Blumenthal, Trans.). In A. L. Blumenthal (Ed.), *Language and psychology: Historical aspects of psycholinguistics* (First published 1900, Vol. 1). New York: Wiley.

Zelinsky, G. J., & Murphy, G. L. (2000). Synchronizing visual and language processing: An effect of object name length on eye movements. *Psychological Science, 11,* 125-131.

8

Putting First Things First

KATHRYN BOCK
DAVID E. IRWIN
DOUGLAS J. DAVIDSON

*S*peech has to start somewhere. Utterances unfold in time, with virtually everything that adults say consisting of more than one word. Even when directed to a 9-month old child, over 93% of adult utterances consist of a connected series of words (van de Weijer, 1998, excluding vocatives and interjections). The problem this creates should be obvious. If words and phrases are separately retrieved, assembled, and articulated, there has to be a starting point. For this reason, one of the classic issues in the psychology of language is how speakers decide where to begin. Our aims in this chapter are to consider how eye-tracking methods can help answer this question and to address the perceptual and psycholinguistic considerations that are most relevant to the enterprise.

Many hypotheses about starting points hinge on the speaker's focus of attention or, more broadly, on what the speaker regards as most important or prominent at the moment of speaking. On these hypotheses, what is most prominent to the speaker at the moment of utterance becomes the starting point. This is the traditional *starting point hypothesis*. Because of the intimate relationship between prominence to the eye and prominence to the mind's eye (Rayner, 1998), eye tracking seems to offer unprecedented validity as a method for addressing this traditional hypothesis.

To evaluate the merits of such a program, we begin with an effort to de-limit a testable version of the starting point hypothesis. We then survey two general traditions in the study of language that make different predictions about starting points to illustrate that the prominence account, which is some-times seen as self-evident, has worthy competitors. Then, to evaluate existing evidence for the starting point hypothesis, we summarize the definitions of prominence available in the perceptual literature and review psycholinguistic studies of starting-point effects that have loosely relied on perceptual defini-tions of prominence. Finally, we consider the implications for the starting point hypothesis of results available from studies of eye tracking during pro-duction, including some preliminary findings of our own. Because these re-sults suggest that the traditional starting point hypothesis is at best insufficient and in most respects probably wrong, we conclude with a prospectus for how eye tracking can be used to find better answers to the question of where speak-ers start.

WHAT IS THE STARTING POINT HYPOTHESIS?

Despite its intuitive appeal, it is hard to pin down the idea that people lead off with what is most important to them. To give the hypothesis enough precision to escape circularity, we identify three problems that plague discussions of starting points and indicate how we deal with the problems in what follows.

The first problem is arriving at consistent, independent criteria for what makes something important or worthy of attention. We call this the *framework* problem. What is important in one framework or context may be unimportant in another. What is important by virtue of its relevance to an argument may be rivaled by something that is important by virtue of its novelty. And so on. In linguistics, such distinctions are acknowledged in a plethora of divisions be-tween information that is given or new, topic or comment, focus or presupposi-tion, theme or rheme, light or heavy, and so on, but these distinctions are often made with respect to the language used, rather than the status of the entities referred to. Without objective evidence for the importance or informativeness of referents within a referent model, there is no way to evaluate the validity or generality of a starting point hypothesis.

The second problem is actually a version of the framework problem that has to do with specifying the conceptual or linguistic level to which any defini-tion of importance should apply. We call this the *levels* problem. Although the default construal of importance is in terms of prominence within a referent model, other kinds of information or levels of linguistic formulation can come into play. Among the claims to be found in the literature on starting points, some are framed in terms of perceptual or quasi-perceptual properties, such as salience (Osgood & Bock, 1977) and foregrounding in a figure-ground organization (Osgood, 1980). Other ideas involve "concepts" and "elements," which could cover cases when individual words or phrases are placed early, not so much because of what they represent in particular as because of what they mean or imply in general. Males may precede females in stock expressions such as *men and women, husband and wife,* and *king and queen* because of the traditional preeminence of men in most societies (Cooper & Ross, 1975). Even more narrowly, some words might occur earlier than others because they are more accessible to lexical retrieval processes or more readily formulated linguistically, regardless of what they refer to on any one occasion (Bock, 1982, 1987; Levelt & Maassen, 1981). For instance, frequent words may tend to precede infrequent ones (Fenk-Oczlon, 1989) simply because they are easier to retrieve from memory.

The third problem is the role of grammatical restrictions in limiting the options for placing information at the beginning of an utterance. This is the *language variation* problem. Leaving aside the obvious restrictions on where closed-class words (*the, a,* and so on) are positioned with respect to open-class words, languages are notoriously different in the degree to which they permit the order of constituents to vary in the absence of changes in the form of the verb. English is a standard example of a language that is relatively rigid about its word order; Hungarian is an example of a language with fairly free order. English makes it hard to put objects of affection in the forefront, so we say "I like dogs" rather than "Dogs like I," while other languages make it easier. Correlated with freedom of order is whether a language requires the case-marking of constituents, since the functions served by location with respect to the verb in word-order languages can be taken over by case-marking. This can make it easy to place an indirect object (for example) initially in a sentence without brooking misinterpretation.

The framework problem is one to which eye tracking promises a partial solution, and much of what follows can be seen as an effort to address it. We sidestep the levels problem by confining our attention to the consequences of message preparation for the nomination of a starting point. By definition, in assembling a message, it is the intended referents of the upcoming utterance that are immediately relevant to how the utterance is formulated. This ignores any effects of the relative accessibility of alternative categorizations of the referents (i.e., conceptual accessibility or codability) or of the ease of retrieving lexical realizations for concepts (i.e., lexical accessibility). Regarding language variation, we will have little to say about how differences among languages or the constraints of the grammar within a language influence formulation options in general or starting points in particular. Instead, we take what evidence the psycholinguistic literature offers, which is often (although not exclusively) about English and about the ordering of noun phrases within sentences. Because the first noun phrase in an English sentence is often its subject, the offerings of the literature tend to be about the selection of subjects, explicitly or by default. The selection of a subject has complications and consequences that go beyond simple word order, which we will largely circumvent (see the discussion in Bock, Loebell, & Morey, 1992). This allows us to entertain generalizations about starting points that may span different grammatical roles and to extend our sights beyond English to research on starting points in other languages.

THE STARTING POINT TRADITION

The idea that what comes first is somehow more important than what follows is compelling, widespread, and long-standing. It is readily found in some of the foundational writings of modern experimental psychology and linguistics. Wundt, Jespersen, Bloomfield and others argued that speakers order words "according to the degree of emphasis on the concepts" (Wundt, 1900/1970, p. 29), "according as we shift our point of view from one to the other of the primaries contained in the sentence" (Jespersen, 1924, p. 167), if necessary, by placing "the emotionally dominant element in some way out of its usual position, preferably first or last" (Bloomfield, 1914, pp. 113-114). The same ideas, little altered, appear in contemporary linguistics and psycholinguistics.

The emphasis in this literature is on language production. Starting points matter in language comprehension, too (Gernsbacher, 1990; MacWhinney, 1977), since listeners are as much in thrall to the serial nature of language as speakers. Still, the election of starting points is the speaker's problem, making the question of *how* they are elected especially important to theories of language production. After all, speakers (and writers) are responsible for the variations in order that occur when they talk (and write).

The election of starting points can be and has been explained within competing views of how language works. Naturally, the explanations are different and differentially compatible with the basic tenets of the alternative approaches. We can divide existing sorts of explanation into two broad camps that will be familiar to most psychologists. There are those that emphasize the elements that must be ordered and those more concerned with the structures that play the ordering options out. We will call the first *elemental* (since individual elements, such as perceived objects or single words, spark the ordering) and the second *structural* (since some abstract relational scheme controls the ordering).

Among elemental views are some found in late 19th century linguistics (Paul, 1886/1970) and in the behaviorist accounts of language that dominated psychology in the middle of the twentieth century (Lounsbury, 1965; Mowrer, 1954; Osgood, 1971; Skinner, 1957). Contemporary connectionism, along with functionalist linguistics and psycholinguistics (MacWhinney & Bates, 1989), are more recent examples. Less obviously, we include modern lexicalist leanings within linguistics (Grimshaw, 1990; Pinker, 1989), psycholinguistics in general (MacDonald, Pearlmutter, & Seidenberg, 1994; Tanenhaus & Trueswell, 1995), and language production in particular (Bock, 1982; Kempen & Hoenkamp, 1987; Levelt, 1989). All of these approaches incorporate principles that emphasize the roles played by individual elements—typically words—in language use, and a common thread in psychological writings within this tradition is the idea that accessible, experientially frequent, attentionally salient elements should enjoy certain prerogatives in language use.

Complementary structuralist views can likewise be found, starting with Wundt's opposition (1900/1970) to Paul's linguistics, continuing with Bühler (see Blumenthal, 1970, pp. 48-64), and reemerging in telling objections to behaviorist theorizing from linguists and psychologists (Chomsky, 1959; Lashley, 1951). More recent counterparts are found in linguistics (Goldberg, 1995) and in psycholinguistic approaches to language comprehension (Frazier, 1989) and language production (Bock, 1990; Bock et al., 1992; Ferreira, 1993; Garrett, 1975, 1988). In this framework the explanation of ordering variations is harder, and, accordingly, tends not to be a central aim of the theoretical enterprise. Instead, ordering variations must be accommodated within the same theoretical frameworks that account for the generation of sentence structure generally. Consequently, ordering variation tends to be explained in terms of subtle differences in the relational meaning of one variant compared to another or the relative accessibility of structures as wholes, rather than in terms of the relative strength, attention, interest, and the like of individual elements.

Consider how the use of a passive or an active sentence might be (and has been) motivated within these alternative frameworks. In the event depicted in Figure 8.1, a dog is pursuing a mailman. If a speaker chooses to say *A mailman is being chased by a dog*, one might argue that the speaker's attention was first drawn to the mailman. This capturing of attention could in turn be explained in terms of the larger size of the mailman or his humanness, the latter presumably important for the same reasons that conspecifics are always important across the animal kingdom. If the speaker instead says *A dog is chasing a mailman*, the starting point might be argued to be driven by attention to the leftmost object in the picture (literate English speakers naturally tending to scan pictures from left to right) or by selective attention to cause, source, or agent of an action. Attention to causes and agents is readily explainable, in turn, by their normal association with the onset of motion (a perceptually imperative cue) and their normal significance for predictions of or reactions to events, including defensive preparation and reaction. All of these are varieties of elemental explanation.

Structural alternatives, instead, emphasize the relational properties of an utterance or event in explaining the form of the utterance. Active structures occur more frequently than passives in English and are presumably easier to produce. Simple causal schemas involve causes and effects, which are fairly

FIGURE 8.1. What's going on here?

directly reflected in the agent-patient structure of simple active sentences. A change in the normal perspective on cause and effect or a reversal of figure-ground organization may encourage passivization. That is, it is not the capturing of attention by a single element of an event, but a complementary highlighting and backgrounding of the components of a gestalt that leads to the use of passive sentences. Critically, something about the relationship between components is available to the message-creation or sentence-formulation process, but for a passive, the perspective on the relationship is different.

Both elemental and structural considerations are likely to apply to the election of starting points, to some degree, and the outlines for compromise positions have a history as long as the debate itself. Wundt (1900/1970) and Bühler (1908/1970), for instance, both argued for an initial state in which some structural, relational kernel guides the serial spell-out of an utterance. Lashley (1951) likewise argued for a determining tendency that oversees the creation of word order in sentences. The mechanisms responsible for the creation of order, for spelling out individual units, could be sensitive to the relative strength of the mental or perceptual links that establish the structural kernel.

The question, then, is whether there is in fact a relational structure that typically guides the elaboration of an utterance from the start. If there is, a further set of questions is whether and how the differential strength or prominence of related elements plays a role in elaboration and formulation. But preliminary to these further questions is the problem of identifying suitable criteria that can serve to establish what is prominent in different message contexts and whether prominence alone is sufficient to predict the starting points of utterances. This brings us back to the framework problem and to the role that the behavior of the eyes can play in identifying what is salient to a speaker at a given moment in time.

SALIENCE IN PERCEPTION, ATTENTION, AND LANGUAGE

Perceptual and Attentional Prominence

Perceptually salient items in visual scenes are items that are conspicuous, standing out from the background or from other elements in the scene. These items are usually unique or novel along some featural dimension such as color, orientation, motion, or luminance. Such items may "pop out" in a display, so that they are detected very rapidly despite the presence of multiple distractors (e.g., Treisman & Gelade, 1980). In this sense they may be described as capturing attention, which means that they are processed first, or at least preferentially to other items in a display, producing effects on reaction time or accuracy (facilitatory if the item captured is a search target, inhibitory if the item captured is a distractor).

In some cases, salient items capture attention even when they are completely irrelevant to a viewer's task (e.g., Remington, Johnston, & Yantis, 1992; Theeuwes, 1994). So, Remington et al. (1992) found that visual search for a target was slowed by the presentation of an abrupt onset stimulus even when viewers were told that onsets should be ignored because they never corresponded to the location of the target. Abrupt onsets appear to be especially effective in this regard, capturing not only covert attention (i.e., processing resources that are not necessarily tied to the locus of eye fixation) but overt attention (eye fixations) as well. For example, Theeuwes, Kramer, Hahn, and Irwin (1998) found that the eyes were captured by the appearance of a sudden onset in a display even when viewers intended to move their eyes elsewhere. Irwin, Colcombe, Kramer, and Hahn (2000) found that luminance increments also elicit such reflexive, involuntary saccades whereas transient color changes do not.

In the domain of picture perception, perceptual cues such as color (Williams, 1967) and visual complexity (Berlyne, 1958; Buswell, 1935; Hochberg & Brooks, 1978; Mackworth & Morandi, 1967) have been found to attract the eye. People rarely fixate empty regions in a picture, for example. Instead, their eyes are drawn to unpredictable contours and regions of discontinuity (e.g., Mackworth & Morandi, 1967). Krieger, Rentschler, Hauske, Schill, and Zetzsche (2000) found that most fixations fall on curved lines and edges and areas of local contrast and occlusion. These results suggest that the eyes are drawn to nonredundant regions of a picture defined by low-level perceptual contrasts. Indeed, Parkhurst, Law, and Niebur (2002) have shown that the fixations of humans who were viewing scenes freely were predicted very well by a biologically motivated computational model of stimulus salience (Itti & Koch, 2000) that was based purely on contrasts in color, luminance, and orientation.

This is not to say that covert and overt attention are driven only by stimulus factors such as perceptual salience. There is ample evidence that conceptual, expectation-driven, top-down cognitive factors influence attention and eye movements as well. Capture of attention by salient stimuli appears to be at least somewhat contingent on conceptually driven control, or <u>set</u>, so that unique or novel items in a display usually capture attention only if they are consistent with a viewer's search goals (e.g., Folk, Remington, & Johnston, 1992, 1993; Folk & Annett, 1994; Folk & Remington, 1996). Attention (e.g., Jonides, 1981) and eye movements (e.g., Yarbus, 1967) can also be directed voluntarily in response to endogenous cues. For example, Yarbus (1967) found that viewers' fixation patterns on a scene differed greatly depending on task instructions. Conceptual factors also appear to affect attentional guidance during scene viewing, in that there are longer and more frequent fixations on items that are inconsistent with the scene context (e.g., De Graef, Christiaens, & d'Ydewalle, 1990; Henderson, Weeks, & Hollingsworth, 1999; Loftus & Mackworth, 1978). The gist or global meaning of a scene can be extracted very rapidly, during the initial fixation (e.g., Biederman, Mezzanotte, & Rabinowitz, 1982; Boyce, Pollatsek, & Rayner, 1989; Hollingworth & Henderson, 1998), and there is some evidence that this can influence early fixation locations depending on the viewer's search goals (e.g., Henderson et al. 1999).

In short, both stimulus-driven perceptual factors and conceptually driven cognitive ones influence and guide attention and the eyes during scene viewing. If similar factors induce variations in word order in language, one might conclude with confidence that attention (and the eyes) exert strong control over sentence structure. Surprisingly, however, little systematic use has been made in psycholinguistic research on phrase and sentence production of the findings from the literature on visual attention and perception. Instead, investigators have relied on intuitive estimations of salience and attention getting to evaluate the control of starting points. We now turn to this work.

Salience and Linguistic Starting Points

There is a large and diverse literature on factors that influence where speakers start. To corral it, we divide demonstrations of starting-point effects into two broad groups that roughly parallel the division between stimulus-driven and goal-driven attentional capture. The first group focuses on perceptual prominence, where physical properties of objects or object locations are emphasized. The second group is concerned with conceptual prominence, where the emphasis instead is on the goals, interests, and cognitive set of speakers.

Perceptual Prominence   The most striking conclusion regarding the effects of perceptual prominence on word order is how fragile the effects are. A study by Flores d'Arcais (1975, Experiment 3) illustrates the problem. Flores d'Arcais argued that the figure in a figure-ground relationship is likely to become the subject of a sentence used in describing the relationship. More generally, Flores d'Arcais proposed that perceptual organization would affect linguistic organization, following arguments by Osgood (1957, 1971). According to this hypothesis, perceptually prominent objects should tend to precede perceptually recessive ones in language production. To test this, Flores d'Arcais manipulated factors presumed to affect salience, including the relative sizes of pictured objects or the direction of the implied action relating two objects (putting the source of the action on the left or right of the picture).

Speakers were shown the scenes and asked to describe them. For scenes in which objects varied in size and position, the results suggested that when speakers produced active sentences, they were generally faster to initiate utterances in which the larger object or the object on the left side of the scene served as the sentence's subject. For passives, the effects were sometimes in the same direction but weakly so, and in some cases were in the opposite direction. That is, when speakers produced passives, the hypothesis about perceptual effects was not supported. In a second type of scene, for which speakers were able to use verbs that allowed either the left-hand or the right-hand object to serve as the subject of an active sentence (like *lead* and *follow*), actives and passives were both initiated more rapidly when the subject of the sentences produced appeared on the left side of the picture.

What the Flores d'Arcais results hint at is that speakers do not readily give up a structural preference in order to put a perceptually salient element into subject position. On the occasions when speakers opted for a less-favored passive structure to place a salient object first, they initiated sentences more slowly unless a readily accessible verb allowed them to use the left-hand object as the sentence subject. In short, speakers tended not to launch an utterance with what first struck them in a scene unless they knew they could easily continue what they had begun. Rather than putting first things first, they did not start something that they could not finish.

Other reports suggest the same thing. Osgood (1971; Sridhar, 1988) manipulated the size and color of objects involved in actions and found little tendency to use passives to front what were presumably the perceptually more salient elements. Bates and Devescovi (1989) reported similar results in a comparison of English and Italian. Although Clark and Chase (1974) found a strong tendency for static displays to be described from top to bottom, reminiscent of the left-to-right effects reported by Flores d'Arcais (1975), no structural variations were required to accomplish this. Speakers said either *The star is above the plus* or *The plus is below the star* (see also Forrest, 1995), using the same structural frame and the same verb in both cases.

It might be objected that the perceptual manipulations in these studies were simply too weak. Without independent measures of perceptual salience within the scenes presented, this is a valid concern. Somewhat better evidence for perceptual determination of starting-point effects comes from Tomlin (1995, 1997). In Tomlin's study, speakers viewed animated cartoons of two differently colored fish swimming toward each other on collision course. When they met, one of the fish appeared to swallow the other, in a perceptually striking motion event that consumed 50 ms. Speakers were instructed on each trial to keep their eyes on just one of the fish (either the left or the right), and to describe the event as it occurred. For 10 of 12 speakers, this yielded a tendency to produce active sentences when the visually pursued fish was the swallower (e.g., "The blue fish ate the red fish"), but passive sentences when the eyed fish was the swallowee (e.g., "The red fish was eaten by the blue fish").

Objectively, the remarkable feature of these results is the brutality of the manipulations required to elicit a starting-point effect. Speakers were instructed to watch just one fish. They were instructed to describe the event immediately as it happened, implying that the perspective taken should be that of the fish they were told to watch. The only action was eating, so the verb was always a form of eat (*ate* or *was eaten by*). Even at this level of task demand, two speakers produced no passives at all. The data from only one of the speakers who did produce passives are broken down by condition, and this speaker produced passives on 81% of the trials when the eaten fish was the instructed focus of attention. Because speakers were told what to look at, these results cannot be used to evaluate the normal impact of perceptual prominence on starting-point differences, but they do suggest an upper bound on how strong the impact can be expected to be in the most conducive of circumstances. At best, 83% of speakers on 81% of possible occasions could be induced to make what was perceptually prominent at a given moment into the starting point for an utterance when there was some structural uncertainty.

At the same time, this is as impressive as psychological effects get. It suggests that when other factors are controlled, starting points might be predictable with over 67% accuracy. Missing, however, is a crucial bit of evidence. If speakers are accustomed to begin with what is salient in perception at a given moment, they should be faster to initiate utterances that allow them to do this.

Data of this kind are reported in Flores d'Arcais (1987) from a similar sort of task. In these studies, simple animated figures (large and small squares, circles, and triangles) individually or together engaged in three kinds of actions, called *moving*, *bouncing*, or *vibrating*. In free descriptions of the actions, speakers showed a tendency to mention perceptually more prominent objects first, either a larger object or the first object to move in an event.[1] They did this on average 69% of the time over a range of conditions. But it did not make them faster to start speaking. Generally, speakers were actually slower to begin when they led with the more prominent object. Heightening the paradox, simple naming of the objects did yield faster initiation of the names for the more prominent figures.

So, while there is evidence that perceptual prominence *can* affect starting points, it is not obvious that speakers are naturally inclined to begin their utterances with perceptually salient information or that doing so facilitates production. The strength of the effect and its boundary conditions are far from certain, particularly in light of the possibility that prominent starting points impede utterance initiation. Contributing to the uncertainty in existing research is the absence of independent validation of perceptual salience or the locus of speakers' attention.

Conceptual Prominence   For understandable reasons, it is even harder to characterize conceptual than perceptual prominence. Levelt (1989, p. 267) aptly characterized the difficulty when he noted that it is tantamount to cataloguing the varieties of human interest. Compounding the difficulty, there is again an absence of convergence between perceptual and psycholinguistic research in establishing objective criteria for conceptually mediated prominence. All of this makes it correspondingly more difficult to specify what role conceptual prominence might play in establishing a starting point.

A broad array of research on starting points has relied on intuitive assessments of conceptual prominence, on normative ratings of factors presumed to be associated with prominence, or on operationalizations of linguistic factors hypothesized to influence word order (e.g., topicalization, referential status, and lexical repetition). Among the factors considered have been vividness or salience (James, Thompson, & Baldwin, 1973; Osgood & Bock, 1977), imageability or concreteness (Bock & Warren, 1985), prototypicality (Kelly, Bock, & Keil, 1986), affective valence or empathy (Cooper & Ross, 1975; Ertel, 1977; Kuno & Kaburaki, 1977), animacy (Clark & Begun, 1971; Dewart, 1979; Harris, 1978; McDonald, Bock, & Kelly, 1993; Prat-Sala & Branigan 2000), conversational topicality, referential status, or givenness (Carroll, 1958; Bock, 1977; Prat-Sala & Branigan 2000), implicit direction of attention (Anisfeld & Klenbort, 1973; Prentice, 1967; Tannenbaum & Williams, 1968; Tomlin, 1983; Turner & Rommetveit, 1967, 1968), and mental accessibility (Bock, 1986, 1987a, 1987b; Bock & Irwin, 1980; Chafe, 1974, 1994; Fenk Oczlon, 1989; Perfetti & Goldman, 1975; Prentice, 1966). The results of all of this work can be broadly summarized as demonstrating a strong tendency for conceptually prominent referents to take the lead in utterances. In fact, these tendencies are considerably stronger than those created by perceptual prominence (Levelt, 1989; Prat-Sala & Branigan, 2000).

The paradox of conceptual prominence as an explanation for starting points is that the factors reliably associated with starting points in discourse include some that are mutually contradictory and some that appear to be diametrically opposed to the kinds of factors associated with perceptual prominence (for discussion see Bock, 1982; Costermans & Hupet, 1977; Johnson-Laird, 1977). Discourse fronting typically involves repeated mention or familiarity (Birner, 1994), conditions that are seemingly opposed to what leads to attentional capture and perceptual prominence, which involve novelty, transience, and deviation from a local norm. If the prominence associated with starting points in discourse stems from frequent exposure and familiarity, while the prominence associated with starting points in the descriptions of scenes stems from novelty and change, there is little hope for a unified explanation of starting points in language production and little merit in a general notion of prominence.

So is prominence, either perceptual or conceptual, really necessary or sufficient to account for variations in starting points or variations in word order more generally? At present, it is impossible to say. There is a clear need to know whether and to what degree the factors associated with variations in perceptually or conceptually driven attending are demonstrably the same factors that induce variations in the starting points of utterances. Without such evidence, we remain in the circle begun with the assumption that important things go first, following around inexorably to the idea that if something goes first, it is important. Setting aside grammatical constraints of the sort that create language variation, it could turn out that there is no single factor characterizable as cognitive prominence or importance associated with individual referents, in or out of context, that reliably predicts starting-point or word-order alternations.

This would be bad news for elemental accounts of word order. But before abandoning the approach, there is a new tack to try. Suppose we could tell, with some degree of precision, what is perceptually prominent for a speaker at a given moment relative to the onset of an utterance. If we could do that, we could see whether prominence defined in this objective fashion can predict variations in word order. Here is where eye-movement methodology comes into the picture.

WHAT EYES SAY

We begin with the caveat that the linkage between the locus of eye fixation and the focus of visual attention is imperfect. It is nonetheless a good barometer of what is in the mind's eye and well suited to our purpose, which is to assess how well an object of initial fixation (and by inference, attention) corresponds to a speaker's starting point.

More explicitly, the hypothesis is that if the selection of a starting point for an utterance is sensitive to the focus of a speaker's attention, the speaker is likely to be looking at the corresponding referent if it is present in the visual field at the outset of sentence formulation. For simple technical reasons, this hypothesis until recently has not been readily amenable to empirical test. Though automated eye-tracking technology began to be widely used in cognitive research in the early 1970s, fueling the study of online reading comprehension, it involved eye tracking while the reader's head was stabilized. To achieve this, a bite bar is typically employed. The difficulty of talking with a sizeable hunk of dental compound in one's mouth is enough to make this situation uncomfortable for studying eye movements during speaking, and the further complication that speech in such circumstances is labored makes the temporal relationships between eye movements and speech uncertain at best. This changed dramatically with the development of head-mounted, eye-tracking technology, which allows the locations of the eyes to be determined with precision even when the head is not stabilized, by correcting for movements of the head. With simultaneous time-stamped recording of speech, the temporal relationship between eye movements and the contents of extemporaneously produced utterances can be accurately measured.

Because empirical work on eye tracking coupled to production is in its infancy, there are relatively few findings relevant to the starting point hypothesis. One comes from Griffin and Bock (2000). Using eye tracking during relatively unconstrained sentence production, Griffin and Bock assessed the timing of event apprehension (that is, how long it took for speakers to understand a pictured event that he or she was about to describe) and the timing of utterance onsets relative to successive fixations on the elements of events. Speakers described simple events such as the one depicted in Figure 8.1, and while they did so, their eye movements were monitored. A major finding was that speakers' eye movements went in turn to the elements of the pictured event, and each eye movement anticipated the onset of corresponding parts of the utterance by about 800 ms. As this implies, the eyes normally went first to the elements that began the utterances.

To determine whether this was because the eye was naturally drawn to whatever served as the sentence subject, the eye-fixation patterns from the production task were compared to those in a control condition. In the control task, participants simply viewed the pictures without describing them, and the sequence of fixations along with the durations of gazes to different event elements were analyzed. The findings did not bode well for a simple attentional account of starting points. The subjects of sentences (the first noun phrases) did not correspond to the elements that drew the most or the earliest fixations in the free-viewing situation, nor were they straightforwardly predictable from the conceptual features of individual entities. Because event comprehension occurred within the same time frame as the selection of a starting point for production, Griffin and Bock proposed that the subject was identified on the basis of causal and aspectual coding carried out during initial apprehension. This implies that when speakers produce fluent utterances to describe events, the eye is sent not to the most salient element in a scene, but to an element already established as a suitable starting point.

Findings from experiments by Bock, Irwin, Davidson, and Levelt (2003) paint a complementary picture for very different kinds of utterances. Speakers' eye movements were monitored as they told times from analog or digital clocks, producing either expressions that put the minute first (*ten past two*) or expressions that put the hour first (*two-ten*). As in Griffin and Bock's work, the speakers spontaneously made successive saccades to different parts of the visual array corresponding to different parts of their utterances. In time expressions, those different parts correspond to the hour and minute information. Almost always, the speakers began to move their eyes toward the information represented in the first part of the time expression within 400 ms of the onset of the clock display.

The speed of these looks does not mean that the eyes were drawn to prominent landmarks in the display. In some sense it reflects obedience to instructions: Half the time, speakers were instructed to use the expressions that put the minute first and the other half of the time to use expressions that put the hour first. What is remarkable is the alacrity with which these instructions were fulfilled. The fact that the eyes sought first the information that was needed first for the expressions to be produced, and did so within 400 ms or less from the onset of the clock displays, indicates that the scene was analyzed well enough to identify the location of the needed information *before* the eyes were directed there. This in turn implies that the eyes were sent to the information needed for a structure that was already in mind.

It could still be that in the absence of grammatical constraints or imposed utterance structures, the focus of a speaker's attention would tend to determine the starting point. In Griffin and Bock's production task, speakers were not constrained to produce particular kinds of structures, but the grammatical constraints of English were naturally operative: The utterances contained subjects, verbs, objects and so on, which, because of the demands of English, may have obscured any relationship between prominence and the sentence subject (the starting point in all of the sentences). Some results from Meyer, Sleiderink, and Levelt (1998) suggest that this may be the case. Speakers in these experiments named objects in simple phrasal frames that did not constrain the order (e.g., *the cat and the chair*). In these circumstances, speakers showed a very strong tendency to scan the pictures from left to right and to name the objects in the order in which they were viewed. On the assumption that the scanning pattern is a byproduct of reading habits, the naming pattern supports the hypothesis of starting point prominence.

Of course, because the structural frame was constant, these results are also compatible with the structural alternative. To distinguish the accounts, we need a situation in which different starting points involve different structural commitments, preferably without the demands imposed by grammatical relations (such as subjecthood) or other constraints on the structures speakers employ. In the next section we set out some findings from an exploratory study that satisfied these requirements.

From the Speaker's Eye to the Mind's Eye?

To examine the relationship between where the eye first alights and the kind of time expression produced, we conducted an experiment in which college-age American English speakers viewed analog clock displays for 3000 ms. They were given no explicit instructions about the kinds of expressions to use, and they produced whatever time expressions they pleased. Because of the strong preference among speakers in this age group for absolute expressions such as *ten-twenty* (Bock et al. 2003), we expected such forms to dominate. To increase the likelihood of observing relative expressions (e.g., *twenty past ten*) without coercion, half the speakers received examples of relative expressions in the experimental instructions and half received examples of absolute expressions. This instructional manipulation did increase the propensity to employ relative expressions (from 1.6% to 10.8%), though the difference was not significant.

All of the speakers produced time expressions for each of the 144 five-minute times on a 12-hour clock. The displays were schematic analog clock faces like the one in Figure 8.2, containing no numbers or minute marks. To evaluate performance, we carried out analyses similar to those reported in Bock et al. (2003). These included analyses of voice-onset latencies, of fixation locations, latencies, and durations, and of eye-voice spans for the first and second terms in the time expressions.

Figures 8.3 and 8.4 show the distributions of eye fixations associated with the production of absolute and relative expressions. Plotted are the proportions of fixations to the hour hand out of all fixations to the hour and minute hand, relative to display onset (Figure 8.3) and expression onset (Figure 8.4). Because there was a stronger tendency to fixate the hour than the minute hand overall, the proportions are generally higher than 0.5, but positive deflections indicate increased numbers of fixations to the hour, and negative deflections indicate increased numbers of fixations to the minute. Recall that the hour hand is associated with the starting point in absolute expressions (the hour term) and the minute hand with the starting point in relative expressions (the minute term). Because it takes roughly 200 ms for the initial saccade to be initiated and reach its target, the critical fixations for evaluating starting-point effects are those shown in Figure 8.3 at 200 and 300 ms. There is little evidence

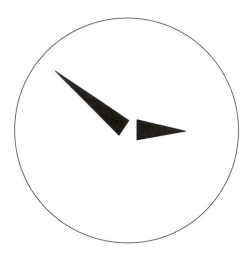

FIGURE 8.2. Sample analog clock face used in time-telling experiment.

of a difference in looking to the hour and minute as a function of upcoming expression type. Regardless of the eventual expression, initial fixations were predominantly to the hour hand.

To set this out in more detail, Table 8.1 gives the percentages of fixations
to the hour and minute at 100 ms intervals for the first 500 ms after display
onset. At 200 ms after display onset, fixations to the hour hand constituted
33% of all fixations and fixations to the minute hand constituted 22% of all fixations when absolute expressions ensued. When relative expressions ensued,
the corresponding percentages were exactly the same: 33% to the hour hand
and 22% to the minute hand. At 300 ms after display onset, 61% of all fixations
were on the hour and 21% on the minute when absolute expressions later occurred, compared to 58% on the hour and 22% on the minute when relative
expressions later occurred. Not until 400 ms was there some indication of ex-
pression-associated looking toward the minute, when the amount of looking to
the minute hand (as a proportion of fixations on the hour and minute hand
only) was larger for relative (0.20) than for absolute expressions (0.08).

A similar picture emerges from a different vantage point, the locations of
initial individual fixations on the clock. Table 8.2 shows, for the first three fixations after display onset, the percentages of fixations to the hour and minute as
a function of ordinal position. Of the first fixations that preceded absolute expressions, 50.5% were to the hour hand and 24.9% to the minute. Of the first
fixations that preceded relative expressions, the corresponding percentages
were 43.8% and 29.9%. Though the difference is slightly smaller for relative
than absolute expressions, there is nothing to suggest that the locus of the first
fixation determines or plays a dominant role in the selection of a starting point.

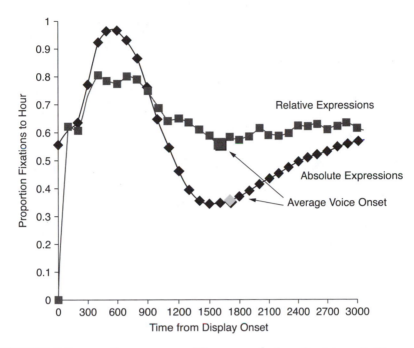

FIGURE 8.3. Overall proportions of fixations to the hour hand (out of all hour- and minute-hand fixations) associated with producing absolute and relative time expressions during successive 100 ms intervals after clock onset.

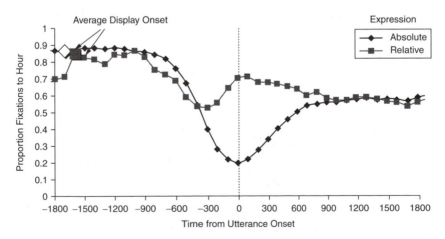

FIGURE 8.4. Overall proportions of fixations to the hour hand (out of all hour- and minute-hand fixations) associated with producing absolute and relative time expressions from the time of expression onset.

TABLE 8.1. Percentages (and Raw Numbers) of Fixations to the Hour and Minute Hands during the First 500 ms after Clock Display Onset prior to the Production of Absolute and Relative Expressions

Time past display onset	Eventual expression	Fixation location	
		Hour hand	Minute hand
100 ms	Absolute	1.5% (36)	1.0% (23)
	Relative	3.3% (5)	2.0% (3)
200 ms	Absolute	32.9% (725)	18.9% (417)
	Relative	33.3% (49)	21.8% (32)
300 ms	Absolute	61.3% (1389)	18.0% (407)
	Relative	51.81% (86)	21.6% (32)
400 ms	Absolute	83.7% (1926)	6.8% (156)
	Relative	73.5% (111)	17.9% (27)
500 ms	Absolute	90.8% (2171)	3.0% (71)
	Relative	73.95% (116)	20.4% (32)

Perhaps starting points are triggered by looks that immediately precede speech, rather than the looks associated with the initial uptake of information. We will call this an immediacy account. Figure 8.4 shows the fixation patterns relative to expression onset. There, differences can be seen in looks toward the hour and minute hands as a function of when speech began, but the differences for relative expressions are not what the immediacy hypothesis would predict. The average eye-voice span for time telling, the difference between the point of fixation on a time-relevant region, and the utterance of the corresponding time term, is 770 ms (Bock et al. 2003). In roughly the same time window in the present experiment, of the fixations that preceded absolute expressions at 800 ms prior to expression onset, 84% were directed to the hour hand; the corresponding percentage for relative expressions was 75%. At 700 ms prior to expression onset, the respective percentages of fixations to the

TABLE 8.2. Percentages of First, Second, and Third Fixations Directed to the Hour and Minute Hands prior to the Production of Absolute and Relative Expressions

Fixation #	Eventual expression	Fixation location	
		Hour	Minute
1	Absolute	50.5%	24.9%
	Relative	43.8%	29.9%
2	Absolute	85.2%	7.2%
	Relative	77.0%	20.1%
3	Absolute	68.3%	23.4%
	Relative	64.7%	33.1%

hour hand were 82% and 72%. This means, assuming the bare minimum of preparation time for speaking, that speakers who were about to produce relative expressions were looking at the same place as those who were about to produce absolute expressions. Evidently, relative expressions were triggered neither by the locus of the first fixation nor by the information fixated within the typical eye-voice span for the first time-term.

Maybe initial fixations are random, with decisive fixations coming at an indeterminate later time. Countering this conjecture, looks to the minute and hour hand diverged significantly from chance (taken as equal probabilities of fixation) by 200 ms after the onset of the display. Similarly, in Bock et al. (2003), speakers, instructed about the kind of expression to employ, fixated the hour and minute hands differentially in less than 400 ms. Most of the time, the very first or, at most, second fixation was on the information that initiated the utterance.

The trigger for putting minutes first is apparently some other kind of information. What was that information? A comparison of the actual clock times associated with absolute and relative expressions reveals a striking difference between them that suggests some possibilities. On average, excluding the whole hour, each of the 5-minute times would be expected to elicit 9% of all the relative times produced. In fact, just three times together elicited more than 60% of the relative times, and they were :45, :50, and :55. Several things distinguish these times from others. First, the minute numbers are high in magnitude, and there may be a preference to avoid them in favor of lower-magnitude numbers. Second, these minute number-names are long in comparison to their relative alternatives. Third, the part of the display that contains this information is the upper-left quadrant of the clock. Fourth, these are the times that, if absolute expressions were used, precede the change in the reference hour from the current hour to the next hour.

Although we cannot rule out any of these possibilities, our results make one of them more credible than the others. The magnitude hypothesis suffers from the problem that at <u>any</u> point past the half hour, the minute names in relative expressions are smaller than those in absolute expressions, but the effect doesn't emerge until :45. The length hypothesis does not work consistently: If the length of the first word-form is what matters, the emergence of the effect at :45 is problematic, because *quarter* is no longer than *forty*. If the lengths of the expressions as wholes were critical, even more problems arise for the length story: The number of syllables in *three forty-five* is the same as the number of syllables in *quarter to four*, and *three fifty* is the same as *ten to four*. If length is counted in words, the prediction is wrong for two of the three times.

The upper-left quadrant of the clock might be privileged in some way, such that information presented there receives more attention, independently of eye fixations, than other regions. By itself it is hard to see why this would elicit more relative expressions, but in combination with alternative locations of the hour hand, it makes sense that when the minute is on the left side of the display and the hour on the right side, a predisposition toward relative expressions would arise because of reading habits. A similar predisposition toward relatives might be present when the minute hand is above the hour hand, since there is a general bias toward top-before-bottom (Clark & Chase, 1974), and the upper portion of an analog clock face tends to be fixated more than the bottom (Bock et al. 2003). Together, these predispositions would favor the upper-left quadrant, and that would make sense on an attentional account of starting points: Time expressions begin where attention is most likely to fall first.

To evaluate this, we examined the proportions of relative expressions used when the minute and hour hands were in the same quadrants, when they were in opposite left-right quadrants, and when they were in opposite top-bottom quadrants. Table 8.3 shows these data. First, consider the patterns predicted by the attentional account (minute left, hour right, and minute top, hour bottom contrasted with their opposites, minute right, hour left, and minute bottom, hour top). The prediction would be that more relatives should occur when the minute hand is to the left and the hour to the right than the other way around, and when the minute hand is above and the hour below than the other way around. The data appear to support this hypothesis. Overall, when hand positions were congruent with the order of information in relative expressions, the proportion of relatives produced was 0.09. In comparison, when the hand positions were incongruent with the order of information in relative expressions, the proportion of relatives produced was 0.03.

Unfortunately for the attentional hypothesis, there is more to the story. When the hour and minute hands occupied the *same* quadrants of the clock, eliminating the left-right difference, the rate of producing relative expressions was almost identical to the rate when the minute hand alone occupied the quadrant. Inspection of individual times within the quadrants (in terms of whether the hour or minute hand was above, below, left, or right) revealed no

TABLE 8.3. Mean Proportions of Relative Expressions Produced when Hour and Minute Hands Occupied the Same or Different Analog Clock Regions

Minute-hand location	Hour-hand location	
	Left	Right
Left (7, 8, 9, 10, 11)	0.10	0.09
Right (1, 2, 3, 4, 5)	0.04	0.04
	Top	Bottom
Top (10, 11, 1, 2)	0.09	0.09
Bottom (4, 5, 7, 8)	0.03	0.01

effect whatsoever of these variations. In short, the location of the hour hand had virtually no impact on the frequency of relative expressions. Only the minute hand mattered, and only when it was in the upper-left quadrant.

So, what is special about the upper-left quadrant? The remaining hypothesis has to do with reference-point changes. For a speaker who relies on absolute expressions, as our speakers did, it is in the last 15 minutes of the hour that the reference hour turns over. For example, the time at 10:55, expressed absolutely, is *ten fifty-five*. Five minutes later, the first time-term becomes *eleven*. The reference-point hypothesis is that naming patterns in the region of a reference-point change suffer interference from the increased activation of the upcoming reference hour.

Why would this lead to a *switch* in time expressions, from absolute to relative? Because the names of relative times in the second half of an hour include the name of the upcoming hour, competition from the approaching change in the reference hour in the absolute system may serve to activate relative times. For instance, at 10:55, where we hypothesize that the upcoming transition to the eleven o'clock hour interferes with saying "ten fifty-five," the corresponding relative time is "five till eleven."

Other evidence for effects of reference points on time telling comes from variations in preferred time names (reported in Bock et al. 2003). When English speakers name times from digital clocks, where there is no spatial difference between times during different parts of the hour, the preference for absolute expressions is weaker at :55 than at any other time except :25 (where, interestingly, there is an imminent change in the reference hour in the *relative* system, suggesting that points of change in either system introduce variability). Even more telling are the variations that arise in Dutch. The favored Dutch time names are structured like English relative expressions, but the loci of reference-point changes in Dutch are different than in English. At twenty past the hour (:20), the reference point switches to the upcoming hour: The preferred expression at this point is "ten before half" of the upcoming hour. So, 4:20 is expressed as *ten before half five*. This structure is maintained through :40, with 4:40 being (for example) *ten after half five*. At :45, the reference point changes from the half-hour to the full hour, with the favored expression being analogous to the English *quarter till five*. Notice that Dutch reference-point changes occur in a completely different region of the analog clock than the English changes. But in Dutch, it is at these points that the most variations in expression preference are observed on analog clocks. The fact that it is not a spatial effect is again confirmed by the occurrence of a similar pattern for digital displays.

The only related phenomenon we are aware of occurs when people count. In backwards counting, Nairne and Healy (1983; see also Healy & Nairne, 1985) reported that people tend to skip whole-decade numbers, proceeding from ninety-one (for example) to eighty-nine, from sixty-one to fifty-nine, and so on. When the task was changed so that speakers named only the digits in the numbers (e.g., saying nine-one instead of ninety-one) while counting back-wards, the rate of these errors decreased, as would be expected if a structural frame is no longer involved. Although forward counting yielded no such effect for the adults tested by Nairne and Healy (1983), it may be present in counting by children (Miller, Smith, Zhu, & Zhang, 1995). Reference-point contributions to these phenomena could come from the change in frame at a decade boundary as well as earlier, from competition created by an imminent decade change (e.g., from ninety to eighty-nine in backward counting or from twenty-nine to thirty in forward counting) disrupting the production of the final number in the current decade.

Returning to time telling, what seem to be responsible for most of the variations in clock expressions are not changes in the prominence or accessibility of alternative starting points. Were this the case, we would expect to see changes between expression types with variations in the prominence of hour and minute information, since absolute and relative expressions are perfectly complementary in permitting hour and minute starting points. What seems to matter instead to variability in expression is competition from an alternative structural frame. This competition is ignited by reference-point changes (or imminent reference-point changes), suggesting that the reference points anchor the structural frames.

One objection to generalizing this account of our results to the production of other kinds of utterances is that time expressions are not *like* other kinds of utterances. They may seem more like names or idioms than productive expressions. While we acknowledge that time telling has a highly re-stricted vocabulary and calls on formulaic structures, it is in critical respects very much like other kinds of language production. Specifically, the expressions are structured, and there is variability in those structures that extends to permitting different starting points. The evidence suggests that the information in the structural frames is assembled compositionally, because there are discrete eye movements to corresponding parts of a visual display that antici-pate the production of corresponding elements of time expressions. And ob-jectively, the timing and trajectories of saccades and fixations are remarkably similar to what occurs when speakers formulate sentences they have never produced before (Griffin & Bock, 2000).

Don't Start What You Can't Finish   Returning to the elemental and structural stories about starting points, we see the evidence pointing toward a structural view. What cements a starting point is not the relative salience of el-ements in the perceptual or conceptual underpinnings of a message, but the identification of something that affords a continuation or completion; that is, a predication. Another way of putting this is that people begin with what it is they have something to say about, and they tend to avoid initiating utterances until they are fairly sure what the beginning of *that* something is. This implies that the rudiments of an utterance frame are present when an utterance is initiated. In short, speakers don't like to start what they can't finish. At least, they don't like to start what they can't continue. This in turn means that something other than the relative salience of potential starting points matters. Their relative predicability matters, too, and in the first instance may matter more.

We are hardly the first to have come to this conclusion. To name just a few others, Lindsley (1975) found that accounting for the timing of sentence initiations required a model that included not only preparation of the sentence subject, but the beginnings of preparation for the verb. Ferreira and Swets (2002) showed that speakers reporting the solutions to arithmetic problems were disinclined to begin producing a tens digit (for instance) before they knew what the subsequent digit would be. Like our time tellers, above and in Bock et al. (2003), the speakers in these experiments tended to start only when they knew how to go on.

DO THE EYES HAVE IT?

We hope we have shown how data from eye tracking can be brought to bear on a long-standing issue in the study of language production. In 1971, discussing some findings from an early examination of experimentally elicited sentences, Osgood wrote that "the entity which is the focus of the speaker's momentary interest or attention...is...likely to be represented in his first encoded noun phrase" (p. 520). Decades of work on production have been concerned with manipulating the focus of attention, using indirect means to do so. Eye tracking has made it possible to know with some certainty what the focus of the speaker's momentary interest or attention actually is at the outset of a production episode. We can now verify whether attentional manipulations work in the context of speaking and how they affect production.

We have argued that the effects on production are not what the traditional starting point hypothesis predicts. But we cannot claim to have settled the issue. Rather, we have tried to breathe new life into an account of starting points that is different from the time-worn approaches that have dominated research on this question without satisfactorily resolving it. Further efforts must go substantially beyond what we sketched above, where we only correlated the locations of initial eye fixations with the starting points of subsequent expressions. More powerful and decisive approaches are feasible, permitting the manipulation of where the eyes are or where they go at critical points in time. Naturally, it will be useful to revisit earlier attempts to draw attention to alternative elements of scenes, to see how effective such manipulations can be and what their impact is on subsequent speech.

Based on our results and others, we believe it will be useful to combine manipulations of perceptual and conceptual prominence with manipulations of the predicability or codability of alternative starting points. If structural accessibility is important to decisions about starting points, we would expect that, other things being equal, elements with more predicable linguistic realizations will be preferred to those with less predicable realizations. More broadly, the structural position that we have outlined says that the selection of a starting point goes hand in hand with a commitment to a structurally supported continuation. This need not mean that the structure is entirely prepared. It may, nonetheless, be latent in the selection of a verb or other continuation.

The coupling of eye tracking to this question also makes available new diagnostics for structural commitments. To take one example of how this works, we can look at more data from time telling that suggest the readying of a structure at utterance onset. Eye tracking gives a continuous readout of the temporal relationship between the eyes and the mouth: The strong tendency for the eyes to successively fixate the referents of phrases or words in an utterance means that the onset of looking at an object can be linked to the onset of a reference to it in speech. This creates a measure of the eye-voice span. Bock et al. (2003) used measures of eye-voice span to try to distinguish two kinds of incrementality that might characterize production processes as they are revealed in the behavior of the eyes. One is linear incrementality, which is roughly word-by-word (or phrase-by-phrase) incrementality, where the amount of time separating a fixation onset from a voice onset is proportional to the complexity of the upcoming increment of speech only. The other is hierarchical incrementality, which entails preparation beyond an initial increment of something about the structure as a whole.

In eye-voice spans, linear incrementality would be manifested in uniform effects of complexity within the production of an expression. For instance, when formulating a time expression for which minute and hour information are equally accessible, the eye-voice span for the minute should be the same as the eye-voice span for the hour. If the clock display complicates the extraction of minute information more than hour information, the eye-voice span for the minute might be longer than the eye-voice span for the hour, but under linear incrementality, the span should not change as a function of the location of the less-accessible information. In other words, the effects of complexity should be localized to the individual elements of an expression. Hierarchical incrementality implies that eye-voice spans at the outset of an expression may be longer than spans within an expression. For instance, structurally more complex expressions might have proportionally longer eye-voice spans only at the beginning of an utterance.

Bock et al.'s (2003) results were more consistent with hierarchical than linear incrementality. The hierarchical effects manifested themselves not as simple effects of utterance complexity, but as effects of the compatibility between an upcoming structure and the kind of clock being read. Eye-voice spans at the onset of absolute expressions were longer when time was being told from analog than from digital clocks, while eye-voice spans at the onset of relative expressions were longer when time was being told from digital than from analog clocks. This suggests an effect of perceptual and linguistic *compatibility*, with absolute expressions and digital displays or relative expressions and analog displays, being compatible when other combinations are not. The second terms in time expressions revealed no effect of compatibility on eye-voice spans, though the complexity of displays and of expressions made independent contributions. So, display complexity and expression complexity mattered throughout the production of utterances, but at the outset, what affected the timing between the eye and the voice was the relationship between perception and language.

CONCLUSION

With the refinement of means for tracking how one's understanding of another's spoken or written words emerges and changes from moment to moment, psycholinguistic approaches to comprehension have flourished during the last quarter century. Similar means have been beyond reach in the study of fluent language production. Unlike comprehension, the impetus for a production episode is hard to specify, and the observable parts of the episode are hard to measure with precision. What happens between start and finish, between the mind and the mouth, remains very much a mystery.

Eye tracking now promises to do for the study of language production what eye tracking has done for language comprehension. We may be able to follow the covert, mental run-up to an overt utterance, charting the details of formulation across ongoing time in terms of both difficulty and attentional focus. Though the enterprise is still in its infancy, its promise is evident in the work reviewed here and in other chapters in this volume.

We have tried to show how the methodology can be used to pursue a long-standing question about how utterances are initiated. We have raised the distinct possibility that the answers that emerge from this pursuit will contradict traditional wisdom. Speakers may not be naturally inclined to begin their utterances with whatever naturally draws or captures their attention. Instead, the behavior of the eyes suggests that the mechanisms of sentence production weigh the information provided by perception within a broader cognitive and communicative context in order to select a starting point. What makes a starting point is the mind, and not the eye. And it is the eye that tells us so.

NOTES

1. Unfortunately, the kinds of utterances that speakers produced are not explicitly related to the results, although it seems likely that only two alternatives were used

frequently: *The [noun1] and the [noun2] [verb]*, or *The [noun1] [verb] and the [noun2] [verb]*.

ACKNOWLEDGMENTS

Work on this chapter was supported in part by research and training grants from the National Science Foundation (BCS-0214270 and NSF BCS 01-32272) and the National Institute of Mental Health (R01-MH66089 and T32-MH18990). We thank Lisa Octigan for her assistance.

REFERENCES

Anisfeld, M., & Klenbort, I. (1973). On the functions of structural paraphrase: The view from the passive voice. *Psychological Bulletin, 79,* 117-126.

Bates, E., & Devescovi, A. (1989). Crosslinguistic studies of sentence production. In B. MacWhinney & E. Bates (Eds.), *The crosslinguistic study of sentence processing* (pp. 225-253). Cambridge: Cambridge University Press.

Berlyne, D. E. (1958). The influence of complexity and novelty in visual figures on orienting responses. *Journal of Experimental Psychology, 55,* 289-296.

Biederman, I., Mezzanotte, R. J., & Rabinowitz, J. C. (1982). Scene perception: Detecting and judging objects undergoing relational violations. *Cognitive Psychology, 14,* 143-177.

Birner, B. (1994). Information status and word order: An analysis of English inversion. *Language, 70,* 233-259.

Bloomfield, L. (1914). *An introduction to the study of language.* New York: Holt.

Blumenthal, A. L. (1970). *Language and psychology: Historical aspects of psycholinguisitics.* New York: Wiley.

Bock, J. K. (1982). Toward a cognitive psychology of syntax: Information processing contributions to sentence formulation. *Psychological Review, 89,* 1-47.

Bock, J. K. (1987). Coordinating words and syntax in speech plans. In A. Ellis (Ed.), *Progress in the psychology of language* (Vol. 3, pp. 337-390). London: Erlbaum.

Bock, J. K. (1990). Structure in language: Creating form in talk. *American Psychologist, 45,* 1221-1236.

Bock, J. K., & Irwin, D. E. (1980). Syntactic effects of information availability in sentence production. *Journal of Verbal Learning and Verbal Behavior, 19,* 467-484.

Bock, J. K., Irwin, D. E., Davidson, D. J., & Levelt, W. J. M. (2003). Minding the clock. *Journal of Memory and Language, 48,* 653-685.

Bock, J. K., Loebell, H., & Morey, R. (1992). From conceptual roles to structural relations: Bridging the syntactic cleft. *Psychological Review, 99,* 150-171.

Boucher, J., & Osgood, C. E. (1969). The Pollyanna hypothesis. *Journal of Verbal Learning and Verbal Behavior, 8,* 1-8.

Boyce, S. J., Pollatsek, A., & Rayner, K. (1989). Effect of background information on object identification. *Journal of Experimental Psychology: Human Perception and Performance, 15,* 556-566.

Buswell, G. T. (1935). *How people look at pictures: A study of the psychology of perception in art.* Chicago: University of Chicago Press.

Carroll, J. B. (1958). Process and content in psycholinguistics. In *Current trends in the description and analysis of behavior* (pp. 175-200). Pittsburgh: University of Pittsburgh Press.

Chafe, W. L. (1974). Language and consciousness. *Language, 50,* 111-133.

Chafe, W. L. (1994). *Discourse, consciousness, and time: The flow and displacement of con-*

scious experience in speaking and writing. Chicago: University of Chicago Press.

Chomsky, N. (1959). Review of Skinner's Verbal Behavior. *Language, 35,* 26-58.

Clark, H. H., & Begun, J. S. (1971). The semantics of sentence subjects. *Language and Speech, 14,* 34-46.

Cooper, W. E., & Ross, J. R. (1975). World order. In R. E. Grossman & L. J. San & T. J. Vance (Eds.), *Papers from the parasession on functionalism* (pp. 63-111). Chicago: Chicago Linguistic Society.

Costermans, J., & Hupet, M. (1977). The other side of Johnson-Laird's interpretation of the passive voice. *British Journal of Psychology, 68,* 107-111.

De Graef, P., Christiaens, D., & d'Ydewalle, G. (1990). Perceptual effects of scene context on object identification. *Psychological Research, 52,* 317-329.

Dewart, M. H. (1979). The role of animate and inanimate nouns in determining sentence voice. *British Journal of Psychology, 70,* 135-141.

Ertel, S. (1977). Where do the subjects of sentences come from? In S. Rosenberg (Ed.), *Sentence production: Developments in research and theory* (pp. 141-167). Hillsdale, NJ: Erlbaum.

Fenk-Oczlon, G. (1989). Word frequency and word order in freezes. *Linguistics, 27,* 517-556.

Ferreira, F. (1993). The creation of prosody during sentence production. *Psychological Review, 100,* 233-253.

Ferreira, F., & Swets, B. (2002). How incremental is language production? Evidence from the production of utterances requiring the computation of arithmetic sums. *Journal of Memory and Language, 46,* 57-84.

Flores d'Arcais, G. B. (1975). Some perceptual determinants of sentence construction. In G. B. Flores d'Arcais (Ed.), *Studies in perception: Festschrift for Fabio Metelli* (pp. 344-373). Milan, Italy: Martello-Giunti.

Folk, C. L., & Annett, S. (1994). Do locally defined feature discontinuities capture attention? *Perception & Psychophysics, 56,* 277-287.

Folk, C. L., & Remington, R. W. (1996). When knowledge does not help: Limitations on the flexibility of attentional control. In A. F. Kramer, M. Coles, & G. Logan (Eds.), *Converging operations in the study of visual selective attention* (pp. 271-296). Washington, DC: American Psychological Association.

Folk, C. L., Remington, R. W., & Johnston, J. C. (1992). Involuntary covert orienting is contingent on attentional control settings. *Journal of Experimental Psychology: Human Perception and Performance, 18,* 1030-1044.

Folk, C. L., Remington, R. W., & Johnston, J. C. (1993). Contingent attentional capture: A reply to Yantis. *Journal of Experimental Psychology: Human Perception and Performance, 19,* 682-685.

Forrest, L. B. (1996). Discourse goals and attentional processes in sentence production: The dynamic construal of events. In A. E. Goldberg (Ed.), *Conceptual structure, discourse and language* (pp. 149-161). Stanford, CA: CSLI Publications.

Frazier, L. (1989). Against lexical generation of syntax. In W. Marslen-Wilson (Ed.), *Lexical representation and process* (pp. 505-528). Cambridge, MA: MIT Press.

Garrett, M. F. (1975). The analysis of sentence production. In G. H. Bower (Ed.), *The psychology of learning and motivation* (Vol. 9, pp. 133-177). New York: Academic Press.

Garrett, M. F. (1988). Processes in language production. In F. J. Newmeyer (Ed.), *Linguistics: The Cambridge survey, III: Language: Psychological and biological aspects* (Vol. 3: Language: Psychological and biological aspects, pp. 69-96). Cambridge: Cambridge University Press.

Gernsbacher, M. A. (1990). *Language comprehension as structure building.* Hillsdale, NJ: Erlbaum.

Harris, M. (1978). Noun animacy and the passive voice: A developmental approach. *Quarterly Journal of Experimental Psychology, 30,* 495-501.

Henderson, J. M., Weeks, P. A., & Hollingworth, A. (1999). The effects of semantic consistency on eye movements during complex scene viewing. *Journal of Experimental Psychology: Human Perception and Performance, 25,* 210-228.

Hochberg, J., & Brooks, V. (1978). Film cutting and visual momentum. In J. W. Senders, D. F. Fisher, & R. A. Monty (Eds.), *Eye movements and the higher psychological functions* (pp. 293-313). Hillsdale, NJ: Erlbaum.

Hollingworth, A., & Henderson, J. M. (1998). Does consistent scene context facilitate object perception? *Journal of Experimental Psychology: General, 127*, 398-415.

Irwin, D. E., Colcombe, A. M., Kramer, A. F., & Hahn, S. (2000). Attentional and oculomotor capture by onset, luminance, and color singletons. *Vision Research, 40*, 1443-1458.

Itti, L., & Koch, C. (2000). A saliency-based search mechanism for overt and covert shifts of visual attention. *Vision Research, 40*, 1489-1506.

James, C. T., Thompson, J. G., & Baldwin, J. M. (1973). The reconstructive process in sentence memory. *Journal of Verbal Learning and Verbal Behavior, 12*, 51-63.

Jespersen, O. (1924). *The philosophy of grammar.* London: Allen and Unwin.

Johnson-Laird, P. N. (1977). The passive paradox: A reply to Costermans and Hupet. *British Journal of Psychology, 68*, 113-116.

Jonides, J. (1981). Voluntary vs. automatic control over the mind's eye's movement. In J. B. Long & A. D. Baddeley (Eds.), *Attention and performance IX* (pp. 187-203). Hillsdale, NJ: Erlbaum.

Kempen, G., & Hoenkamp, E. (1987). An incremental procedural grammar for sentence formulation. *Cognitive Science, 11*, 201-258.

Krieger, G., Rentschler, I., Hauske, G., Schill, K., & Zetzsche, C. (2000). Object and scene analysis by saccadic eye-movements: An investigation with higher-order statistics. *Spatial Vision, 13*, 201-214.

Kuno, S., & Kaburaki, E. (1977). Empathy and syntax. *Linguistic Inquiry, 8*, 627-672.

Lashley, K. S. (1951). The problem of serial order in behavior. In L. A. Jeffress (Ed.), *Cerebral mechanisms in behavior* (pp. 112-136). New York: John Wiley and Sons.

Levelt, W. J. M. (1989). *Speaking: From intention to articulation.* Cambridge, MA: MIT Press.

Levelt, W. J. M., & Maassen, B. (1981). Lexical search and order of mention in sentence production. In W. Klein & W. Levelt (Eds.), *Crossing the boundaries in linguistics* (pp. 221-252). Dordrecht: Reidel.

Lindsley, J. R. (1975). Producing simple utterances: How far ahead do we plan? *Cognitive Psychology, 7*, 1-19.

Loftus, G. R., & Mackworth, N. H. (1978). Cognitive determinants of fixation location during picture viewing. *Journal of Experimental Psychology: Human Perception and Performance, 4*, 565-572.

Lounsbury, F. G. (1965). Transitional probability, linguistic structure, and systems of habit-family hierarchies. In C. E. Osgood & T. A. Sebeok (Eds.), *Psycholinguistics: A survey of theory and research problems* (pp. 93-101). Bloomington: Indiana University Press.

MacDonald, M. C., Pearlmutter, N. J., & Seidenberg, M. S. (1994). The lexical nature of syntactic ambiguity resolution. *Psychological Review, 101*, 676-703.

Mackworth, N. H., & Morandi, A. J. (1967). The gaze selects informative details within pictures. *Perception & Psychophysics, 2*, 547-552.

MacWhinney, B. (1977). Starting points. *Language, 53*, 152-168.

MacWhinney, B., & Bates, E. (1978). Sentential devices for conveying givenness and newness: A cross-cultural developmental study. *Journal of Verbal Learning and Verbal Behavior, 17*, 539-558.

MacWhinney, B., & Bates, E. (Eds.). (1989). *The cross-linguistic study of sentence processing.* Cambridge: Cambridge University Press.

McDonald, J. L., Bock, J. K., & Kelly, M. H. (1993). Word and world order: Semantic, phonological, and metrical determinants of serial position. *Cognitive Psychology, 25*, 188-230.

Mowrer, O. H. (1954). The psychologist looks at language. *American Psychologist, 9*, 660-694.

Osgood, C. E. (1954). Effects of motivational states upon decoding and encoding. In C. E. Osgood & T. A. Sebeok (Eds.), *Psycholinguistics: A survey of theory and re-

search problems. Bloomington: Indiana University Press.

Osgood, C. E. (1957). A behavioristic analysis of perception and language as cognitive phenomena. In J. Bruner (Ed.), *Contemporary approaches to cognition.* Cambridge, MA: Harvard University Press.

Osgood, C. E. (1957). Motivational dynamics of language behavior. In M. R. Jones (Ed.), *Nebraska symposium on motivation.* Lincoln, Nebraska: University of Nebraska Press.

Osgood, C. E. (1963). On understanding and creating sentences. *American Psychologist, 18,* 735-751.

Osgood, C. E. (1971). Where do sentences come from? In D. D. Steinberg & L. A. Jakobovits (Eds.), *Semantics: An interdisciplinary reader in philosophy, linguistics, and psychology* (pp. 497-529). Cambridge, England: Cambridge University Press.

Osgood, C. E. (1980). *Lectures on language performance.* New York: Springer-Verlag.

Osgood, C. E., & Bock, J. K. (1977). Salience and sentencing: Some production principles. In S. Rosenberg (Ed.), *Sentence production: Developments in research and theory.* Hillsdale, NJ: Erlbaum.

Parkhurst, D., Law, K., & Niebur, E. (2002). Modeling the role of salience in the allocation of overt visual attention. *Vision Research, 42,* 107-123.

Paul, H. (1886/1970). The sentence as the expression of the combination of several ideas. In A. L. Blumenthal (Ed. and Trans.), *Language and psychology: Historical aspects of psycholinguistics* (pp. 34-37). New York: Wiley.

Perfetti, C. A., & Goldman, S. R. (1975). Discourse functions of thematization and topicalization. *Journal of Psycholinguistic Research, 4,* 257-271.

Prat-Sala, M., & Branigan, H. P. (2000). Discourse constraints on syntactic processing in language production: A cross-linguistic study in English and Spanish. *Journal of Memory and Language, 42,* 168-182.

Prentice, J. L. (1966). Response strength of single words as an influence in sentence behavior. *Journal of Verbal Learning and Verbal Behavior, 5,* 429-433.

Prentice, J. L. (1967). Effects of cuing actor versus cuing object on word order in sentence production. *Psychonomic Science, 8,* 163-164.

Rayner, K. (1998). Eye movements in reading and information processing: 20 years of research. *Psychological Bulletin, 124,* 372-422.

Remington, R. W., Johnston, J. C., & Yantis, S. (1992). Involuntary attentional capture by abrupt onsets. *Perception & Psychophysics, 51,* 279-290.

Skinner, B. F. (1957). *Verbal behavior.* New York, NY: McGraw-Hill.

Sridhar, S. N. (1988). *Cognition and sentence production: A cross-linguistic study.* New York: Springer.

Tanenhaus, M. K., & Trueswell, J. C. (1995). Sentence comprehension. In J. L. Miller & P. D. Eimas (Eds.), *Handbook of perception and cognition* (Vol. 11, pp. 217-262). San Diego: Academic Press.

Tannenbaum, P. H., & Williams, F. (1968). Generation of active and passive sentences as a function of subject or object focus. *Journal of Verbal Learning and Verbal Behavior, 7,* 246-250.

Theeuwes, J. (1994). Stimulus-driven capture and attentional set: Selective search for color and visual abrupt onsets. *Journal of Experimental Psychology: Human Perception and Performance, 20,* 799-806.

Theeuwes, J., Kramer, A. F., Hahn, S., & Irwin, D. E. (1998). Our eyes do not always go where we want them to go: Capture of the eyes by new objects. *Psychological Science, 9,* 379-385.

Tomlin, R. S. (1983). On the interaction of syntactic subject, thematic information and agent in English. *Journal of Pragmatics, 7,* 411-432.

Tomlin, R. (1995). Focal attention, voice, and word order: An experimental, cross-linguistic study. In M. Noonan & P. Downing (Eds.), *Word order in discourse* (pp. 521-558). Amsterdam: John Benjamins.

Tomlin, R. (1997). Mapping conceptual representations into linguistic representations: The role of attention in grammar. In J. Nuyts & E. Pederson (Eds.), *Language and conceptualization* (pp. 162-189). Cambridge: Cambridge University Press.

Treisman, A., & Gelade, G. (1980). A feature-integration theory of attention. *Cognitive Psychology, 12,* 97-136.

Turner, E. A., & Rommetveit, R. (1967). Experimental manipulation of the production of active and passive voice in children. *Language and Speech, 10,* 169-180.

Turner, E. A., & Rommetveit, R. (1968). Focus of attention in recall of active and passive sentences. *Journal of Verbal Learning and Verbal Behavior, 7,* 543-548.

van de Weijer, J. (1998). *Language input for word discovery.* Nijmegen, the Netherlands: MPI Series in Psycholinguistics.

Williams, L. G. (1967). The effects of target specification on objects fixated during visual search. *Acta Psychologica, 27,* 355-360.

Yarbus, A. L. (1967). *Eye movements and vision.* New York: Plenum.

9

Referential Domains in Spoken Language Comprehension: Using Eye Movements to Bridge the Product and Action Traditions

MICHAEL K. TANENHAUS
CRAIG G. CHAMBERS
JOY E. HANNA

INTRODUCTION

*M*ost psycholinguistic research on language comprehension falls into one of two traditions, each with its roots in seminal work from the 1960s (Clark, 1992; 1996) and each with its own characteristic theoretical concerns and dominant methodologies. The *language-as-product* tradition has its roots in George Miller's synthesis of the then emerging information processing paradigm and Chomsky's theory of transformational grammar (e.g., Miller, 1962; Miller & Chomsky, 1963). The product tradition emphasizes the individual cognitive processes by which listeners recover linguistic representation—the "products" of language comprehension. Psycholinguistic research within the product tradition typically examines moment-by-moment processes in real-time language processing, using fine-grained reaction time measures and carefully controlled stimuli.

The *language-as-action* tradition has its roots in work by the Oxford philosophers of language use, e.g., Austin, (1962), Grice (1957) and Searle (1969), and work on conversational analysis, e.g., Schegloff & Sachs (1973). The action tradition focuses on how people use language to perform acts in conversation, arguably the most basic form of language use. Psycholinguistic research within the action tradition focuses primarily on investigations of interactive conversation using natural tasks, typically in settings with real-world referents and well-defined behavioral goals.

It is tempting to view these traditions as complementary; research in the product tradition examines the early perceptual and cognitive processes that build linguistic representations, whereas research in the action tradition focuses on subsequent cognitive and social-cognitive processes that build upon these representations. Although there is some truth to this perspective, it masks some fundamental disagreements. This becomes apparent when we focus on *context*, a concept that has featured prominently in research in both traditions.

Context in the Product and Action Traditions

In the product tradition, context is typically viewed either as information that enhances or instantiates a context-independent core representation or as a *correlated constraint* in which information from higher-level representations can, in principle, inform linguistic processing at lower levels of representation. Specific debates about the role of context include whether, when and how: (a) lexical context affects sublexical processing, (b) syntactic and semantic context affect lexical processing, and (c) discourse and conversational context affect syntactic processing. Each of these questions involves debates about the architecture of the processing system and the flow of information between different types of representations—classic information-processing questions. Because linguistic processing occurs incrementally as a sentence is read or heard, answering these questions requires response measures that are closely time-locked to the unfolding utterance. These *online* tasks track changes in processing difficulty, e.g., monitoring fixations in reading (Rayner & Liversedge, this volume), or changes in representation, e.g., lexical priming, as linguistic input is encountered.

Consider, for example, the well-known cross-modal lexical priming paradigm. This paradigm builds upon the classic finding that response times to a target word are facilitated when the target is preceded by a semantically related prime word (Meyer & Schvaneveldt, 1971). A schematic of a widely used variant of this task, introduced by Swinney, Onifer, Prather & Hirshkowitz (1978), is illustrated in Figure 9.1.

FIGURE 9.1. Schematic of prototypical product experiment: Cross-modal lexical priming with lexical decision.

The participant, who is wearing headphones, listens to sentences that have been prerecorded by the experimenter. A sentence or short sequence of sentences is presented on each trial. At some point in the sentence, a target letter string appears on a computer monitor, allowing for experimenter control over the timing of the probe with respect to the input. The participant's task is to make a forced-choice decision indicating whether the letter string is a word. The pattern of decision latencies is used to assess comprehension processes. For example, when the target word follows *testified*, a verb whose subject, *doctor*, has been separated by a relative clause, lexical decisions to words that are associated to the subject are faster compared to lexical decisions to unrelated target words. Context is manipulated by varying the properties of the linguistic stimuli that precede the probe word.

In the action tradition, context includes the time, place, and participant's conversational goals, as well as the collaborative processes that are intrinsic to conversation. A central tenet is that utterances can only be understood relative to these factors. For example, Clark points out that in the utterance "Look at the stallion," the expression *the stallion* could refer to a horse in a field, a painting of a horse, or a test tube containing a blood sample taken from a stallion, depending upon the context of the utterance. Thus, researchers within the action focus primarily on interactive conversation using natural tasks, typically with real-world referents and well-defined behavioral goals.

Consider, for example, the referential communication task originally introduced by Krauss and Weinheimer (1966). A schematic of a well-studied variant of this task introduced by Clark and his colleagues (e.g., Clark & Wilkes-Gibbs, 1986) is illustrated in Figure 9.2.

Two naïve participants, a *matcher* and a *director,* are separated by a barrier. Each has the same set of shapes arranged in different positions on a numbered grid. The participants' goal is for the matcher to rearrange the shapes on his grid to match the arrangement on the director's grid. The resulting conversation can then be analyzed to provide insights into the principles that guide interactive conversation. While this paradigm abstracts away from certain aspects of typical conversation, such as a shared visual environment and face-to-face interaction, it preserves many central characteristics, including unscripted dialogue between participants who have clear behavioral goals.

With two such different views about so fundamental a notion as context, one might ask why, with the exception of an occasional shot fired across the bow (e.g., Clark & Carlson, 1981; Clark, 1997), the action and product traditions have not fully engaged one another. One reason is methodological. The traditional techniques in the psycholinguist's toolkit for studying real-time language processing required using either text or prerecorded audio stimuli in contextually limited environments. One cannot, for instance, use cross-modal

FIGURE 9.2. Schematic of prototypical action experiment: Referential communication task with Tangrams.

lexical priming to examine real-time language comprehension (or production) in a referential communication task.

Recently, the development of accurate, relatively inexpensive, head-mounted eye-tracking systems has made it possible to examine real-time spoken language processing in rich behavioral contexts. The use of eye movements in spoken language comprehension was pioneered by Cooper (1974), who demonstrated that the timing of participants' eye movements to pictures was related to relevant information in a spoken story. More recently, Tanenhaus, Spivey-Knowlton, Eberhard & Sedivy (1995) showed that when participants follow spoken instructions to manipulate objects in a task-relevant "visual world," fixations to task-relevant objects are closely time-locked to the unfolding utterance, providing insights into the resolution of referential and syntactic ambiguities. Subsequent studies have shown that this technique provides a continuous real-time measure of comprehension processes at a temporal grain fine enough to track even the earliest moments of speech perception and lexical access (e.g., McMurray, Tanenhaus & Aslin, 2002; Tanenhaus, Magnuson, Dahan & Chambers, 2000). Moreover, a clear quantitative linking hypothesis between underlying processes and fixations makes it possible to use eye movements to evaluate predictions made by mechanistic models (Allopenna, Magnuson & Tanenhaus, 1998, Dahan, Magnuson & Tanenhaus, 2001). Thus the eye-movement paradigm meets the strictest methodological criteria of researchers in the product tradition. At the same time, the language relates to salient real-world referents and is relevant to achieving behavioral goals. Moreover, one can naturally extend the paradigm to interactive conversation, using referential communication tasks. Thus, the eye-movement paradigm can be used with tasks that satisfy the methodological criteria of the action tradition.

Although eye-movement paradigms enable researchers to extend real-time measurement to more natural linguistic settings, including interactive conversation, it is prudent to ask whether the considerable effort that is required to do so is worthwhile. We believe the investment is likely to prove fruitful for at least two reasons. First, the use of eye-tracking paradigms with natural tasks will allow researchers from both traditions to investigate phenomena that would otherwise prove intractable. Second, and perhaps most importantly, this research is likely to deepen our understanding of language processing by opening up each tradition to empirical and theoretical challenges from the other tradition. For example, the product-based construct of priming provides an alternative mechanistic explanation for phenomena such as lexical and syntactic entrainment, i.e., the tendency for interlocutors to use the same words and syntactic structures, that does not require appeal to the action-based claim that such processes reflect active cooperation among speakers and addressees. Conversely, the action-based notion of context offers a challenge to the product-based assumption that there are core linguistic processes, e.g., word recognition and syntactic parsing, supported by quasi-independent processing modules that do not take into account context-specific information.

In the remainder of this chapter we focus on definite reference in order to examine how people update referential domains in real-time comprehension. We consider how actions, intentions, real-world knowledge, and mutual knowledge circumscribe referential domains and how these domains affect syntactic ambiguity resolution. Thus, we examine whether variables central to the action view of context influence the earliest moments of syntactic processing, which comprises the core of sentence processing, according to many within the product tradition. We first present a brief discussion of the notion of domains for definite reference and evidence that listeners dynamically update referential domains taking into account the real-world properties of objects and their affordances with respect to task-relevant actions. We then review results demonstrating that syntactic ambiguity resolution takes place with respect to these task-relevant referential domains, contrary to claims made by proponents of modularity. The next section presents evidence that addressees can use information about speaker perspective to guide even the earliest moments of reference resolution. We then present preliminary results from an ongoing investigation of real-time reference resolution and generation using a completely unscripted referential communication task, which further highlight the importance of action-based referential domains. We conclude with a brief discussion of implications and future directions.

REFERENTIAL DOMAINS AND DEFINITE REFERENCE

Many linguistic expressions can only be understood with respect to a circumscribed context or referential domain. Consider definite descriptions, such as "the new eyetracker," in a conversation overheard one morning in late May in East Lansing:

    A: What did you guys do after dinner?
    B: We stayed up until 2 AM drinking beer and debating whether the new
        eyetracker is better than the old one.

Felicitous use of a definite noun phrase requires reference to, or introduction of, a uniquely identifiable entity. For example, if there were two martini glasses in front of you at the table, your dinner partner could not felicitously ask you to "Pass the martini glass." Instead, your partner would have to use the indefinite version, "a martini glass." Yet, B's use of the definite noun phrase "the new eyetracker" is easily understood in the example discourse, despite the fact that the speaker and addressee were aware of many different eyetrackers. The definite expression is felicitous here because the satisfaction of uniqueness must be qualified by an all-important caveat, namely, *with respect to a relevant context*. A definite noun phrase can be used with multiple potential referents so long as the relevant domain defines a unique interpretation. For example, at a banquet one could ask the person sitting next to you to please pass the red wine even if there were six bottles of the same red wine on the table, but only one was clearly within reach of the addressee.

A considerable body of research demonstrates that listeners dynamically update referential domains based on expectations driven by linguistic information in the utterance (Altmann & Kamide, 1999; Chambers, Tanenhaus, Eberhard, Filip & Carlson, 2002; Eberhard, Spivey-Knowlton, Sedivy & Tanenhaus, 1995). The question we asked is whether referential domains take into account the affordances of potential referents with respect to the action evoked by the instruction. If so, this would provide strong evidence in support of the action-based claim that language processing takes place with respect to a particular behavioral context.

In Chambers et al. (2002, Experiment 2), participants were presented with six objects in a workspace, as is illustrated in 9.3A. On critical trials, the objects included a large and a small container, e.g., a large can and a small can. The critical variable manipulated in the workspace was whether the to-be-mentioned object, in 9.3, the cube, could fit into both of the containers, as was the case for the small version of the cube, or could only fit into the larger container, as was the case for the large version of the cube. Critical instructions for the display in Figure 9.3 are given in:

1. Pick up the cube. Now put it inside a/the can.

We will refer to the can containers as the *goal-objects* and the to-be-moved object as the *theme-object*. Thus the size of the theme-object determined whether one or two of the potential goal-objects were compatible referents. The instructions manipulated whether the goal was introduced with the definite article, *the*, which presupposes a unique referent, or the indefinite article, *a*, which implies that the addressee can choose from among more than one goal.

First, consider the predictions for the condition with the small cube. Here we would expect confusion when the definite article was used to introduce the goal because there is not a unique referent. In contrast, the indefinite article should be felicitous because there is more than one referent. This is precisely what we found. Eye-movement latencies to fixate the goal-object chosen by the participant were slower in the definite condition compared to the indefinite condition. This confirms expectations derived from the standard view of how definite and indefinite articles are interpreted. Now consider predictions for the condition with the large cube, the theme-object that would fit into only one of the goal-objects, i.e., the large can. If the referential domain consists of those objects in the visual world that meet the linguistic description in the utterance,

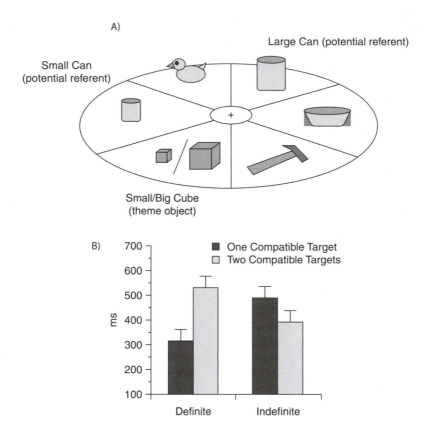

FIGURE 9.3. The top panel shows sample stimuli. The small cube will fit into both cans, but the large cube will fit into only the big can. The bottom panel shows the mean latency to launch an eye movement to the goal with definite and indefinite instructions and one and more than one compatible goal referents.

then the pattern of results should be similar to that for the small cube, resulting in a main effect of definiteness and no interaction with the compatibility. If, however, listeners dynamically update referential domains to include only those objects that afford the required action, that is, containers that the object in hand would fit into, then only the large cube would be in the relevant referential domain. Therefore, use of a definite description, e.g., the can should be felicitous, because there is only one can that the cube could be put into, whereas an indefinite description, e.g., a can, should be confusing. Thus, there should be an interaction between definiteness and compatibility.

As Figure 9.3B shows, this what we found. Eye-movement latencies to the referent for the definite referring expressions were faster when there was only one compatible referent compared to when there were two, whereas the opposite pattern occurred for the indefinite expressions. Moreover, latencies for the one-referent compatible condition were comparable to control trials in which there was only a single object that met the referential description in the instruction, e.g., trials with only a single large can. These results demonstrate that referential domains are dynamically updated to take into account the real-world properties of potential referents with respect to a particular action.

To further evaluate the claim that the participant's intended actions were constraining the referential domain, we conducted a second experiment in which we modified the second instruction to make it a question, as in this example:

2. Pick up the cube. Could you put it inside a/the can?

In order to prevent participants from interpreting the question as an indirect request, the participant first answered the question. On about half of the trials when the participant answered "yes," the experimenter then asked the participant to perform the action. Unlike a command, a question does not commit the speaker and the addressee to the assumption that the addressee can, and will, perform an action. Thus, the referential domain should now take into account all the potential referents that satisfy the linguistic description, not just those that would be compatible with possible action mentioned in the question. If referential domains take into account behavioral goals, then under these conditions, definite expressions should be infelicitous regardless of compatibility, whereas indefinite expressions should always be felicitous,. This is what we found. Time to answer the question was longer for questions with definite compared to indefinite referring expressions. Crucially, definiteness did not interact with compatibility (i.e., size of the theme-object). Moreover, compatibility had no effect on response times for questions with definite articles (for details, see Chambers, 2001).

These results demonstrate that referential domains are dynamically updated using information about available entities, properties of these entities, and their compatibility with the action evoked by an utterance. This notion of referential domain is, of course, compatible with the view of context endorsed by researchers in the action tradition. However, it is important to note that assignment of reference necessarily involves mapping linguistic utterances onto entities in the world, or a conceptual model thereof. A crucial question, then, is whether these contextually defined referential domains influence core processes in language comprehension that arguably operate without access to contextual information. In order to address this question, we examined whether action-based referential domains affect the earliest moments of syntactic ambiguity resolution.

REFERENTIAL DOMAINS AND SYNTACTIC AMBIGUITY RESOLUTION

As the utterances in (3) unfold over time, the italicized prepositional phrase, *on the towel,* is temporarily ambiguous because it could introduce the goal as in (3a) or modify the theme, as in (3b).

3. a. Put the apple *on the towel*, please.
    b. Put the apple *on the towel* into the box.

Temporary "attachment" ambiguities like these have long served as a primary empirical test-bed for evaluating models of syntactic processing (Tanenhaus & Trueswell, 1995). Crain and Steedman (1985) (also Altmann & Steedman, 1988) called attention to the fact that many classic structural ambiguities involve a choice between a syntactic structure in which the ambiguous phrase modifies a definite noun phrase and one in which it is a syntactic complement (argument) of a verb phrase. Under these conditions, the argument analysis is typically preferred. For instance, in example (3a), readers and listeners will initially misinterpret the prepositional phrase *on the towel* as the goal argument of *put* rather than as an adjunct modifying the noun phrase *the apple,* resulting in a garden-path.

Crain and Steedman (1985) noted that one use of modification is to differentiate an intended referent from other alternatives. For example, it would be odd for (3a) to be uttered in a context in which there was only one perceptually salient apple, such as the scene in Figure 9.4, Panel A, whereas it would be natural in contexts with more than one apple, as in the scene illustrated in Panel B. In this context, the modifying phrase *on the towel* provides information about which of the apples is intended. Crain & Steedman proposed that listeners might initially prefer the modification analysis to the argument analysis in situations that provided the appropriate referential context. Moreover, they suggested that referential fit to the context, rather than syntactic complexity, was the primary factor controlling syntactic preferences (cf. Altmann & Steedman, 1988).

Tanenhaus et al. (1995) and Spivey, Tanenhaus, Eberhard & Sedivy (2002) investigated the processing of temporarily ambiguous sentences such as (4a) and unambiguous control sentences, such as (4b), in contexts such as the ones illustrated in Figure 9.4.

The objects illustrated in the figures were placed on a table in front of the participant. Participants' eye movements were monitored as they performed the action in the spoken instruction:

4. a. Put the apple on the towel in the box.
    b. Put the apple that's on the towel in the box.

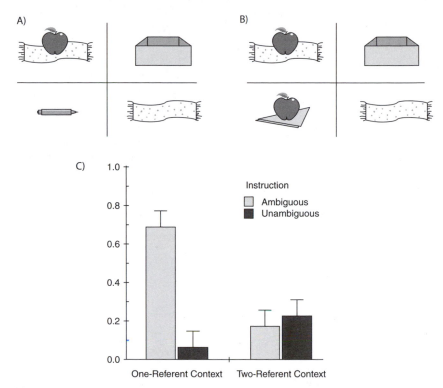

FIGURE 9.4. The top panel shows sample stimuli for one-referent (pencil) and two-referent (apple on napkin) conditions. The bottom panel shows the proportion of looks to the competitor goal (the towel) for instructions with locally ambiguous and unambiguous prepositional phrases in one-referent and two-referent contexts.

The results, which are presented in the bottom panel of Figure 9.4, provided clear evidence for immediate use of the visual context. In the one-referent context, participants frequently looked at the false (competitor) goal, indicating that they initially misinterpreted the prepositional phrase *on the towel* as introducing the goal. In contrast to the results for the one-referent context, looks to the competitor goal were dramatically reduced in the two-referent context. Crucially, participants were no more likely to look at the competitor goal with ambiguous instructions compared to the unambiguous baseline. Moreover, the timing of the fixations provided showed that the prepositional phrase was immediately interpreted as modifying the object noun phrase (for details see Spivey et al., 2002). Participants typically looked at one of the potential referents as they heard the beginning of the instruction, e.g., put the apple. On trials in which participants looked first at the incorrect Theme (e.g., the apple on the napkin), they immediately shifted to the correct Theme (the

apple on the towel) as they heard towel. The timing was identical for the ambiguous and unambiguous instructions. For similar results, see Trueswell et
al., (1999; Trueswell & Gleitman, this volume).

Clearly, then, referential context can modulate syntactic preferences from
the earliest moments of syntactic ambiguity resolution. We are now in a position to ask whether the relevant referential domain is defined by the salient
entities that meet the referential description provided by the utterance or
whether it is dynamically updated based on real-world constraints, including
action-based affordances of objects. In Chambers, Tanenhaus & Magnuson (in
press), we addressed this issue using temporarily ambiguous instructions, such
as "Pour the egg in the bowl over the flour," and unambiguous instructions,
such as "Pour the egg that's in the bowl over the flour," with displays such as
the one illustrated in Figure 9.5.

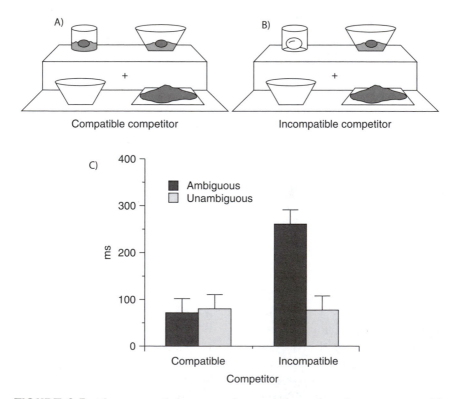

FIGURE 9.5. The top panel shows sample stimuli for trials with action-compatible
competitor (liquid egg in glass) and action-incompatible competitor (solid egg in glass).
The bottom panel shows the mean proportion of time spent looking at the competitor
goal (the empty bowl) for instructions with locally ambiguous and unambiguous prepositional phrases with action-compatible and action-incompatible competitors.

The display for the test trials included the goal (the flour) a competitor goal (the bowl), the referent (the egg in the bowl), and a competitor referent (the egg in the glass). The referent was always compatible with the action evoked by the instruction, e.g., the egg in the bowl was liquid and therefore could be poured. The critical manipulation was whether the affordances of the competitor referent were also compatible with the action evoked by the verb in the instruction. For example, one can pour a liquid egg, but not a solid egg. In the compatible competitor condition, the other potential referent, the egg in the glass, was also in liquid form. In the incompatible competitor condition, it was an egg in a shell. The crucial result was the time spent looking at the competitor goal, which is presented in Figure 9.5.

When both potential referents matched the verb (e.g., the condition with two liquid eggs, as in Panel A, there were few looks to the false goal (e.g., the bowl) and no differences between the ambiguous and unambiguous instructions. Thus, the prepositional phrase was correctly interpreted as a modifier, replicating the pattern observed by Spivey et al. (also see Tanenhaus et al., 1995; Trueswell et al., 1999; Trueswell & Gleitman, this volume). However, when the properties of only one of the potential referents matched the verb, (e.g., the condition where there was a liquid egg and a solid egg), we see the same data pattern as Spivey et al. (2002) found with one-referent contexts. Participants were more likely to look to the competitor goal (the bowl) with the ambiguous instruction than with the unambiguous instruction. Thus, listeners misinterpreted the ambiguous prepositional phrase as introducing a goal only when a single potential referent (the liquid egg) was compatible with a pouring action.

While these results are problematic for many classes of processing models, it can be argued that they do not provide definitive evidence that nonlinguistic constraints can affect syntactic processing. Note that, unlike the Chambers et al. (2002) study, which used the verb *put*, all of the relevant affordances were related to properties that can plausibly be attributed to the semantics of the verb. For example, *pour* requires its theme to have the appropriate liquidity for pouring. There is precedent going back at least to Chomsky (1965) for incorporating a subset of semantic features, so-called selectional restrictions, into linguistic lexical representations, as long as those features have syntactic or morphological reflexes in at least some languages. Thus it could be argued that only a restricted set of real-world properties influence syntactic processing, viz., those properties that are embedded within linguistic representations stored in the lexicon.

Chambers et al. (in press) addressed this issue in a second experiment. The critical instructions contained *put*, e.g., "Put the whistle (that's) on the folder in the box," a verb that obligatorily requires a goal argument. Figure 9.6 shows a corresponding display, containing two whistle referents, one of which is attached to a loop of string. Importantly, *put* does not constrain which whistle could be used in the action described by the instruction.

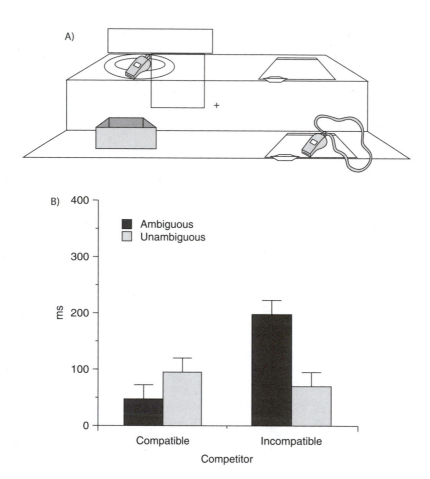

FIGURE 9.6. The top panel shows sample stimuli. Both whistles can be moved by hand, but only the whistle with the string attached can be picked up with a hook. The bottom panel shows the proportion of looks to the competitor goal when the presence of absence of an instrument makes the competitor action-compatible or action-incompatible.

The compatibility of the referential competitor was manipulated by varying whether or not participants were provided with an instrument. The experimenter handed the instrument to the participant without naming it. We also avoided semantic associations between the instrument name and the target referent name. For example, before participants were given the instruction described earlier, they might be given a small hook. Critically, this hook could be not be used to pick up the competitor whistle without a string. Thus, upon hearing "put the...," the competitor could be excluded from the referential domain based on the affordances of the object with respect to the intended action, i.e., using the hook to move an object. If so, participants should misinterpret on the folder as the goal only when ambiguous instructions are used *and* when an instrument is provided. If, however, the relevant referential domain is defined using only linguistic information, then a goal misanalysis should occur, regardless of whether an instrument is supplied beforehand.

Figure 9.6 shows the mean time spent fixating the false goal object within the 2500 ms after the first prepositional phrase. The false goal is most often fixated when ambiguous instructions are used, and the competitor cannot afford the evoked action. The remaining conditions all show fewer fixations to the false goal.

The experiments described in this section provide clear evidence that the syntactic role assigned to a temporarily ambiguous phrase varies according to the number of possible referents that can afford the action evoked by the unfolding instruction. The same results hold regardless of whether the constraints are introduced linguistically by the verb, or nonlinguistically by the presence of a task-relevant instrument. Thus the referential domain for initial syntactic decisions is determined by the listener's consideration of how to execute an action, rather than by information sources that can be isolated within the linguistic system. The results show that provisional syntactic structures are established as part of the process of relating a sentence to the context, taking into account communicative goals. This process requires the simultaneous use of multiple information sources—a property that is consistent with constraint-based theories as well as action-based approaches to language performance. Of critical importance is the *nature* of the information used in this process. Syntactically relevant referential context is established by evaluating the affordances of candidate referents against the action evoked by the unfolding sentence. This action itself can be partially determined by situation-specific factors such as the presence of a relevant instrument. The syntactic role assigned to an unfolding phrase, in turn, depends on whether these factors jointly determine a unique referent without additional information.

These results add to the growing body of literature indicating that multiple constraints can affect even the earliest moments of linguistic processing. Moreover, they present a strong challenge to the claim that the mechanisms underling linguistic processing include encapsulated processing modules. If modular systems are characterized by domain specificity and isolation from high-level expectations, including perceptual inference (Coltheart, 1999; Fodor, 1983), then the mechanisms underlying on line syntactic processing do not meet these criteria.

REFERENTIAL DOMAINS AND SPEAKER PERSPECTIVE

Thus far we have established that listeners dynamically update referential domains, taking into account real- world properties of potential referents, including their affordances with respect to intended actions evoked by the unfolding instruction. We now turn to the question of whether a listener's referential domain can also take into account the perspective of the speaker.

Clark and his colleagues have argued that language processing is a form of joint action (Clark, 1996). Interlocutors can cooperate and communicate successfully only if they monitor what is mutually known about a situation and use that knowledge effectively to create common ground (e.g., Clark, 1992; 1996; Clark & Brennan, 1989; Clark & Marshall, 1981; Clark & Schaefer, 1987; Clark & Wilkes-Gibbs, 1986). Common ground includes information established on the bases of community membership, physical co-presence, and linguistic co-presence. For example, conversational participants would be able to infer that they share various types of knowledge on the basis of both being in a particular city, by looking at a particular object at the same time, or by maintaining a record of what has been discussed. A logical consequence of the joint action perspective is that one of the primary roles of common ground is to act as the domain of interpretation for reference.

In real-time comprehension, however, addressees must rapidly access, construct, and coordinate representations from a variety of subsystems. What would constitute optimal use of common ground under these conditions? One possibility is that conversational partners continuously update their mental representations of common ground, such that a dynamically changing representation of common ground defines the domain within which utterances are typically processed. Updating common ground at this temporal grain would require participants to continuously monitor each other's utterances and actions in order to gather evidence about each other's beliefs. Alternatively, common ground might be interrogated at a coarser temporal grain. If so, many aspects of linguistic processing, including reference resolution, might take place without initial appeal to common ground. Thus, while common ground might control language performance at a macrolevel, the moment-by-moment processes necessary for production and comprehension could take place relatively egocentrically for speakers and listeners. Keysar and colleagues' monitoring and adjustment (Horton & Keysar, 1996) and perspective adjustment (Keysar, Barr, Balin, & Brauner, 2000) models adopt this approach.

In the perspective adjustment model (Keysar et al. 2000), the initial interpretation of utterances is egocentric. Common ground is used as a second-stage filter to rule out inappropriate interpretations. A number of theoretical arguments can be marshaled in support of the common ground as filter approach. Computing common ground by building, maintaining, and updating a model of a conversational partner's beliefs could be inefficient because it is extremely memory intensive. In addition, many conversational situations are constrained enough that an individual participant's perspective will provide a sufficient approximation of true common ground. Moreover, information about another's beliefs can be uncertain at best. Thus, adjustment from monitoring and explicit feedback might be the most efficient mechanism for correcting the occasional confusions or misunderstandings that arise from adopting an egocentric perspective.

Perhaps the strongest evidence that common ground might not initially restrict referential domains comes from a study by Keysar, Barr, Balin, and Brauner (2000; see also Keysar, Barr, & Horton, 1998). Keysar et al. (2000) monitored eye movements during a referential communication task. Participants were seated on opposite sides of a vertical grid of squares, some of which contained objects. A confederate speaker played the role of director and instructed the naïve participant, who wore a head-mounted eyetracker, to reorganize the objects in different locations in the grid. Most of the objects were in common ground on the basis of physical co-presence since they were visible from both sides of the display, but a few objects in the grid were hidden from the director's view, and thus were in the matcher's privileged ground. On critical trials, the director used a referring expression that referred to a target object in common ground, but that could also refer to a hidden object in privileged ground. For example, one display had three blocks in a vertical row, and the block at the very bottom was hidden. If the director said, "Put *the bottom block* below the apple," the italicized definite noun phrase referred to the middle block from the common ground perspective, but to the hidden object from the matcher's egocentric perspective. The results showed that matchers were not only just as likely to look at the hidden object as the target object, but, in fact, initially preferred to look at the hidden object and, on some trials, even picked it up and began to move it.

However, this result does not necessarily support the claim that addressees ignore the speaker's perspective. In the critical conditions, the hidden object was always a better perceptual match for the referring expression than the visible object. For example, when the director said, "Put the bottom block...," the hidden block was the one on the absolute bottom of the display. Similarly, when the director said, "Put the small candle...," the hidden candle was the smallest candle in the display, and the visible candles were medium- and large-sized.

Hanna, Tanenhaus, and Trueswell (2003, Experiment 1) eliminated the typicality confound in a referential communication task using an explicit grounding procedure with common ground established on the basis of linguistic co-presence. Participants wore a head-mounted eyetracker while they played the role of addressee in a referential communication task with a confederate speaker. For ease of exposition, we use "she" to refer to the addressee and "he" to refer to the confederate. The confederate, who was hidden behind a divider, instructed the naïve participant to manipulate colored shapes on a display board with the pretense of getting the participant's board to match the confederates. The confederate followed a script so that the form of the referring expressions could be controlled and linked to addressees eye movements and actions.

On critical trials, the confederate gave an instruction containing a definite noun phrase that referred to a particular shape as a target location (e.g., "Now put the blue triangle on *the red one*"). On these trials there were two identical shapes (among others) already in place on the board that could serve as the intended location, the target shape and the competitor shape (e.g., two triangles). The target shape was always in common ground because it had been referred to and placed on the board during the course of the matching task. We manipulated whether the competitor shape was also in common ground, or whether it was in the addressee's privileged ground. When a shape was in privileged ground, it was identified only to addressee, who placed this "secret shape" in a space on the display board before the matching task began. In addition to manipulating the ground of the competitor shape, the target and competitor shapes were either the same or a different color. A sample display is presented in Figure 9.7.

The competitor shape was a possible referent (e.g. for the red one) only when it was the same color as the target shape. Thus, the different color condition provided a baseline, and looks to the competitor should have been infrequent and should not have varied as a function of whether the competitor was in common or privileged ground. The critical question was whether a same color competitor would compete when it was in privileged ground as strongly as when it was in common ground. When the same color competitor was in common ground, addressees should have considered both the target and competitor shapes as possible referents, and in fact should have asked for clarifying information to determine which location was intended by the confederate. The crucial condition was when the same color competitor was in privileged ground. If the language processing system makes immediate use of common ground, addressees should quickly choose the target shape in common ground and there should be little if any interference from the secret shape. However, if common ground is used to filter initially egocentric interpretations, then addressees should initially consider the secret shape equally as often as the target shape in common ground.

Instructions for each trial were typed on index cards and placed in envelopes. The confederate's instructions contained the configuration of shapes for his board as well as the script he would follow for that trial; the addressee's instructions indicated the secret shape and where to put it on the display board. The addressee's envelope also contained seven shapes, five of which were needed for the trial. The confederate chose shapes for each trial from a box located on his side of the table.

The confederate's scripts for the critical trials consisted of the following series of instructions: (1) a question asking the addressee what shapes she had in her envelope; (2) a statement telling the addressee which shapes she needed for that trial; (3) three separate statements instructing the addressee to place a shape on the board in a particular location; (4) a critical instruction telling the

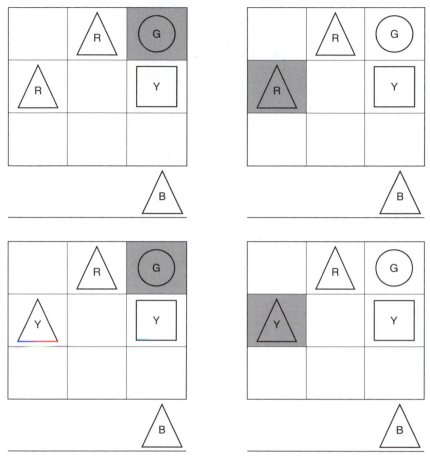

Now put the blue triangle on the red one.

FIGURE 9.7. Example displays and critical instruction for a single item rotated through the conditions in which the competitor was in common ground (left column) or privileged ground (right column), and when it was the same color (top row) or a different color (bottom row). All of the shapes on the board were known to both the confederate speaker and the participant addressee except for the secret shape, indicated here with a gray background, which was only known to the addressee. The target shape location in this display was the topmost red (R) triangle.

addressee to stack the final shape on one of the shapes that was already on the board; and (5) a statement that the confederate was finished or, 25% of the time, a question asking the addressee to describe where her shapes were to double-check that the boards matched. On trials where the target and competitor shapes were both in common ground and were the same color, the addressee typically asked which location was meant. The confederate then apologized for his mistake and told the addressee the specific location.

The results for the different color competitors were as predicted: few looks to the competitor and no effects of type of ground. Figure 9.8 presents the proportion of fixations on the shapes in the display for the same color competitors in the common and privileged ground conditions over the course of 2000 ms in 33 ms intervals, beginning with the point of disambiguation, which we defined as the onset of the disambiguating word. At the point of disambiguation, participants were most often fixating on the stacking shape, which was either in the resource area or, if they had picked it up already, in their hand. The average offset of the disambiguating region is indicated on each graph.

When there was a same color competitor in common ground (Figure 9.8a), participants initially looked roughly equally at any of the objects on the board, and within 600 ms after the onset of the disambiguating word, began looking primarily at either the target or the competitor shape. The critical question was whether a same-color competitor in privileged ground would compete to the same extent as a competitor in common ground. As Figure 9.8b shows, participants most often made initial looks to the target shape. Within 400 ms after the onset of the adjective, participants were fixating on the target more often than the privileged ground competitor. The proportion of fixations to the target then rose steadily and quickly. The proportion of fixations to the competitor began to rise about 400 ms after the onset of the adjective, and rose along with the proportion of looks to the target until about 800 ms after the onset of the adjective. Note, however, that the proportion of looks to the privileged ground competitor was always lower than the proportion of looks to the target.

The pattern and timing of results demonstrate that (1) addressees used common ground from the earliest moments of reference resolution, and (2) there was some degree of interference from a potential referent in privileged ground. Our evidence that common ground modulated the earliest moments of reference resolution is consistent with similar studies by Arnold, Trueswell, & Lawentmann (1999) and Nadig & Sedivy (2002). Arnold et al. (1999) conducted an experiment similar to ours, but with a simplified display that was designed for children. They found that attentive adults experienced competition from a common ground competitor, but not from a privileged ground competitor. Nadig and Sedivy (2002) used a display of four physically co-present objects, one of which was hidden from a confederate speaker. Children from 5 to 6 years of age experienced interference from a competitor in common ground, but no interference from a privileged ground competitor.

Although the research strategy of comparing the effects of information in common ground and privileged ground has been quite fruitful, this class of experimental design is subject to a potentially problematic ambiguity of interpre-

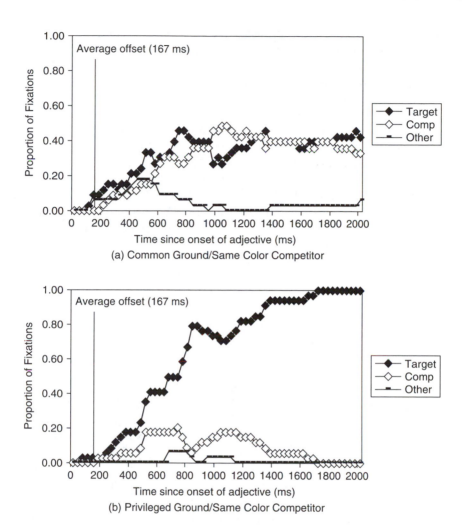

FIGURE 9.8. Proportion of fixations for each object type over time in the common ground with a same color competitor condition (upper graph) and the privileged ground with a same color competitor condition (lower graph).

tation. Privileged ground objects are, by necessity, not referred to by confederates. Therefore, it is unclear whether addressees' preference for referents in common ground arises because they are taking into account the perspective of the speaker, or whether they are performing a kind of probability matching, keeping track of the likelihood with which specific referents are mentioned. Therefore, Hanna et al. (2003) conducted a second experiment to determine the time course with which an addressee can utilize information taken from a speaker's perspective when (1) it conflicts with perceptually salient information in the addressee's privileged ground, and (2) conflicting perspectives are not confounded with likelihood or recentness of reference.

Hanna et al. manipulated the perspectives of the conversational participants in a referential communication task such that the domain of interpretation was different from each conversant's perspective; that is, from the speaker's point of view, only one subset of objects would make sense as the domain in which reference would be interpreted, while for the addressee, a different set of objects would potentially constitute the domain of interpretation. The participant addressee was again seated across a table from a confederate speaker who was completely hidden from view by a vertical divider. (In this case, the confederate speaker was female and will be referred to as *she*, and participant addressees will be referred to as *he*.) The experimenter placed four objects on a shelf on the addressee's side of the table and then named them in order from left to right to inform the confederate of their identity. The confederate repeated the object names in the same order to ground them and firmly establish her perspective and then instructed the addressee to pick one of them up and place it in one of two areas on the table surface.

The point in the spoken instructions where the referent of the noun phrase became unambiguous was manipulated with respect to the visual display. The point of disambiguation was varied by taking advantage of the different uniqueness conditions carried by definite and indefinite descriptions, and the contrastive property of scalar adjectives (Sedivy, Tanenhaus, Chambers, & Carlson, 1999). To give an example using a definite description, consider a display such as the top array of objects in Figure 9.9 in which there are two sets of two identical objects: two jars, one with olives and one without, and two martini glasses, one with olives and one without. As the instruction "Pick up the empty martini glass" unfolds, the addressee cannot identify the referent as the martini glass without olives until relatively late in the instruction. *The empty* could refer to either the empty jar or the empty martini glass in this display, and it is not until the addressee hears martini that the referent is disambiguated. Now consider the same instruction in combination with a display such as the middle array of objects in Figure 9.9 in which both jars and one martini glass are empty, but the other martini glass has olives in it. In this case, the intended referent could be disambiguated upon hearing the empty. The definite article *the* signals a uniquely identifiable referent, which eliminates the set of jars as potential referents and locates the referent within the set of martini glasses, and *empty* uniquely identifies the martini glass without olives. Indefinite instructions, such as "Pick up one of the empty martini glasses," were also combined with displays to produce late and early points of disambiguation, but we will not discuss the results with indefinites here (for details, see Hanna et al., 2003).

The point of disambiguation was either late or early as described above (e.g., martini versus the empty). We will consider the point of disambiguation

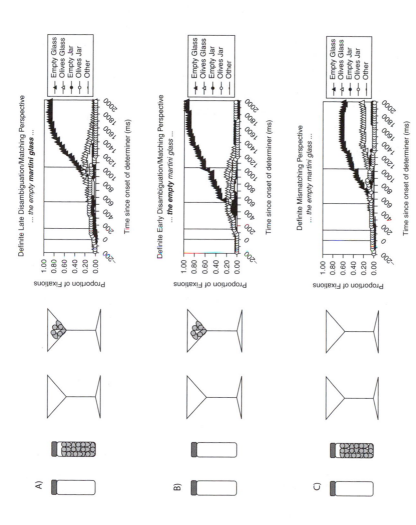

FIGURE 9.9. Left panels show sample displays for the late disambiguation/matching perspective, early disambiguation/matching perspective, and mismatching perspective conditions. Right panels show proportions of fixations on each object type over time. Points of disambiguation in the instructions are indicated in bold.

to be the onset of the disambiguating word. The perspectives of the participant addressee and the confederate speaker either matched or mismatched. In the matching perspective conditions, the experimenter described the objects to the confederate accurately. In the mismatching perspective conditions, the experimenter described the early disambiguation displays inaccurately (from the addressee's perspective) to the confederate. Mismatching perspectives for both the definite and indefinite instructions were achieved by describing the objects with the modification switched between the sets. For example, for the definite instruction "Pick up the empty martini glass," the objects were described as two empty jars, an empty martini glass, and a martini glass with olives in it, but the group really consisted of an empty jar, a jar with olives in it, and two empty martini glasses. See the bottom array of objects in Figure 9.9 for the mismatching perspective conditions.

With matching perspectives, we expected to see a clear point of disambiguation effect depending on the uniqueness properties of the objects in the display. In the late disambiguation conditions, addressees should identify the target relatively slowly. Early fixations should be equally distributed to both the target set of objects (e.g., the set of martini glasses) and the competitor set of objects (e.g., the set of jars). Looks to the target should not rise until after the onset of the object name. This condition is a baseline, since under all circumstances the latest point at which disambiguation can occur is at the object name; that is, there is always at least one object that matches the description of the intended referent, disregarding the definiteness of the referring expression. In the early disambiguation conditions, addressees should identify the target more quickly; fixations to the target set of objects should begin soon after the onset of the article and adjective, and there should be few looks to the competitor set of objects.

The crucial question was what would happen when there was a mismatch between the confederate's and the addressee's perspectives in the context of a display that would, under matching conditions, normally provide an early point of disambiguation. Taking the speaker's perspective in these conditions requires that the addressee remember what the confederate thinks the sets of objects are like while ignoring conflicting perceptual information. If use of common ground information is delayed, then addressees should initially interpret the referring expression from their own perceptual perspective, which conflicts with what the speaker believes. Thus, there should be early looks to the competitor objects (e.g., to the single empty jar in response to the empty), and a delay in the identification of the intended referent. However, if addressees are able to adopt the speaker's perspective, then reference resolution should still show an advantage compared to the late disambiguation conditions.

Figure 9.9 also presents the proportion of fixations in each condition over the course of 2000 ms in 33 ms intervals, beginning with the onset of the referring expression.

In the matching perspective conditions, looks to the target object begin to separate from looks to other potential referents earlier for the early disambiguation condition (Figure 9.9B) compared to the late disambiguation condition (Figure 9.9A). The results demonstrated that addressees assigned reference as soon as a potential referent was uniquely identifiable given the information provided by contrast and definiteness, replicating and extending the findings of Eberhard et al. (1995), Sedivy et al. (1999), and Chambers et al. (2002).

Critically, the same pattern held with mismatching perspectives. Although addressees had to remember that the speaker thought that the objects were different than they really were, they were still able to make rapid use of information provided by uniqueness and contrast. There was some cost associated with perspective taking, but as the comparison of Figure 9.9C and Figure 9.9A reveals, participants identified the referent faster in the mismatching condition than in the late matching condition.

In sum then, the results presented in this section confirm Keysar et al's (2000) conclusion that common ground does not completely circumscribe the referential domain for referring expressions. However, we found clear evidence that addressees can take into account information about common ground during the earliest moments of reference resolution. Note, however, that while our results demonstrate that addressees can use limited capacity cognitive resources to consciously track a speaker's knowledge and hold onto this information in memory, this may not be the natural way that addressees keep track of the speaker's perspective. Factors such as eye gaze, gesture, head position, and postural orientation are likely to provide cues that allow participants to track each other's perspectives, attentional states, and intentions, without requiring memory-intensive cognitive models of mutual belief. Just as basic low-level cognitive mechanisms such as priming may be at least partially responsible for many phenomena that support coordination (e.g., lexical entrainment), tracking the perspective of a conversational participant might be accomplished in part via basic low-level mechanisms that social primates use to monitor each other during interaction. Whether or not these mechanisms result in fully developed internal representations of the intentions and beliefs of a conversational partner is an important question; but this question is orthogonal to the more basic question of how conversational partners achieve the coordination necessary for successful real-time communication.

How can we reconcile the results reported here with some of the striking demonstrations of speaker and addressee egocentricity provided by Keysar and colleagues? We have proposed that common ground can be most fruitfully viewed as a probabilistic constraint within the framework of constraint-based processing models (e.g., MacDonald, 1994; Tanenhaus & Trueswell, 1995; Trueswell & Gleitman, this volume). In constraint-based models, different information sources or constraints each contribute probabilistic evidence for alternative interpretations during processing. The constraints are weighted according to their salience and reliability and are integrated with each other in parallel, causing the alternative interpretations to compete with each other (Spivey & Tanenhaus, 1998; McRae, Spivey-Knowlton, & Tanenhaus, 1998). Factors such as speaker perspective can be incorporated into constraint-based models through expectation-based constraints, such as the likelihood that a speaker will refer to a particular entity (cf. Arnold, 2001).

Thus far, constraint-based models have been applied primarily to situations where the strength of constraints, even contextual constraints such as the prior discourse, can be estimated from relatively static experience-based factors such as frequency and plausibility. In conversational interactions in which the participants have behavioral goals, however, the state of the context must be based upon the speakers' and addressees' intentions and actions. Under these circumstances, the strength and relevance of different constraints will have to be computed with respect to continuously updated contextual models because the relevancy of constraints changes moment by moment. Developing formal models of dynamically updated context will be a major challenge for constraint-based models of comprehension, as well as for other classes of models. We should note that this challenge is similar to that faced by models of perception and action as they seek to accommodate the increasing evidence that basic perceptual processes are strongly influenced by attention and intention, which are guided by behavioral goals.

REFERENTIAL DOMAINS IN NATURAL INTERACTIVE CONVERSATION

Thus far, we have provided empirical evidence that even the earliest moments of language comprehension are affected by factors that are central to the language-as-action view of context and are typically ignored in real-time language processing. We have not, however, established that one can actually conduct research that combines fully interactive conversation with rigorous examination of moment-by moment processing. It is important to do this for at least two reasons. First, there are likely to be differences in the behavior of participants who are participating in conversations with confederates using scripted responses compared to conversations with true interlocutors, who are generating their language on the fly. Second, there is a general methodological concern about results from experiments with scripted utterances that motivates the importance of developing complementary paradigms with nonscripted language. Despite the best efforts of experimenters to avoid creating predictable contingencies between the referential world and the form of the utterances, most controlled experiments are likely to draw attention to the feature of the language being studied. Sentences or utterances of a particular type are likely to be overrepresented in the stimulus set, and the participant's attention is likely to be drawn to small differences in structure or usage that are being investigated in the experiment. Thus, it would be desirable to replicate results from experiments with scripted utterances using more natural spontaneous utterances.

In a recent study (Brown-Schmidt, Campana, & Tanenhaus, in press), we used a modified version of a referential communication task to investigate comprehension of definite referring expressions, such as the red block. Pairs of participants, separated by a curtain, worked together to arrange blocks in matching configurations and confirm those configurations. The characteristics of the blocks afforded comparison with findings from scripted experiments investigating language-driven eye movements, specifically those demonstrating point of disambiguation effects during reference resolution. We investigated: (1) whether these effects could be observed in a more complex domain during unrestricted conversation, and (2) under what conditions the effects would be eliminated, indicating that factors outside of the speech itself might be operating to circumscribe the referential domain.

Figure 9.10 presents a schematic of the experimental setup. In order to encourage participants to divide up the workspace (e.g. the board) into smaller

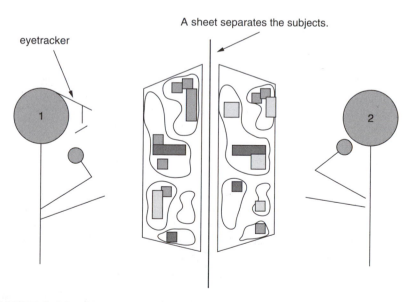

FIGURE 9.10. Schematic of the setup for the referential communication task. Solid regions represent blocks; striped regions represent stickers (which will eventually be replaced with blocks). The scene pictured is midway through the task, so some portions of the partners' boards match, while other regions are not completed yet.

referential domains, we divided participants' boards into five physically distinct subareas. Initially, subareas contained stickers representing blocks. The task was to replace each sticker with a matching block. While partners' boards were identical with respect to subareas, partners' stickers differed: where one partner had a sticker, the other had an empty spot. Pairs were instructed to tell each other where to put blocks so that in the end their boards would match. No other restrictions were placed on the interaction. The entire experiment lasted approximately 2.5 hrs. For each pair we recorded the eye movements of one partner and the speech of both partners.

The stickers (and corresponding blocks) were of two types. Most of the blocks were of assorted shapes (square or rectangle) and colors (red, blue, green, yellow, white, or black). The initial configuration of the stickers was such that the color, size, and orientation of the blocks would encourage the use of complex noun phrases and grounding constructions. Some of the stickers (and corresponding blocks) contained pictures which could be easily described by naming the picture (e.g. "the candle"). We selected pairs of pictures that referred to objects with initially acoustically overlapping names—cohort competitors such a clown and cloud. Half of the cohort competitor stickers were arranged such that both cohort competitor blocks would be placed in the same subarea of the board. The other half of the cohort competitor stickers were arranged such that the cohort competitor blocks would be placed in different subareas of the board. All of the cohort competitor pairs were separated by approximately 3.5 inches.

The conversations for each of the four pairs were transcribed, and eye movements associated with definite references to blocks were analyzed. The non-eye-tracked partners generated a total of 436 definite references to colored blocks. An analysis of these definite references demonstrated that just over half (55%) contained a linguistic point of disambiguation, while the remaining 45% were technically ambiguous with respect to the subarea that the referent was located in (e.g. "the red one" uttered in a context of multiple red blocks). Two researchers coded the noun phrases for their point of disambiguation (POD), defined as the onset of the word in the noun phrase uniquely identified a referent, given the visual context at the time. Average POD was 864ms following the onset of the noun phrase. Eye movements elicited by noun phrases with a unique linguistic point of disambiguation were analyzed separately from those that were never fully disambiguated linguistically. The eye-tracking analysis was restricted to cases where at least one competitor block was present. This left 74 linguistically disambiguated trials and 192 ambiguous trials.

Eye movements elicited by disambiguated noun phrases are pictured in Figure 9.11A. Before the POD, subjects showed a preference for looking at the target block. Within 200ms of the onset of the word in the utterance that uniquely specified the referent, looks to targets rose substantially. This point of

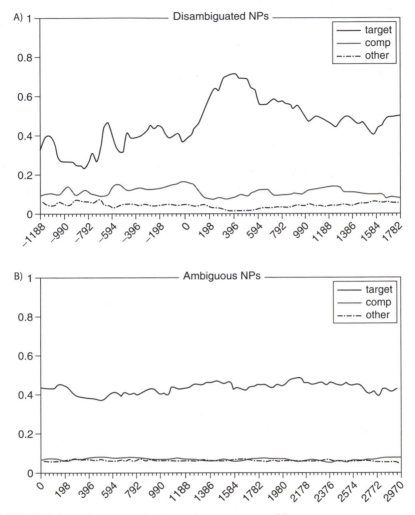

FIGURE 9.11. The top graph shows the proportion of fixations to targets, competitors, and other blocks by time (ms) for linguistically disambiguated definite noun phrases. The graph is centered by item with 0 ms = POD onset. The bottom graph shows the proportion of fixations for the linguistically ambiguous definite noun phrases.

disambiguation effect for looks to the target is similar to that seen by Eberhard, et al. (1995), demonstrating that we were successful in using a more natural task to investigate online language processing. The persistent target bias and lack of a significant increase in looks to competitors are likely due to additional pragmatic constraints that we will discuss shortly.

Most remarkably, while we found a clear point of disambiguation effects for disambiguated noun phrases, for ambiguous utterances (see Figure 9.11B), fixations were primarily restricted to the referent. Thus the speaker's under-specified referential expressions did not confuse listeners, indicating that ref-erential domains of the speaker and the listener were closely coordinated. These results suggest that (1) speakers systematically use less specific utter-ances when the referential domain has been otherwise constrained, (2) the at-tentional states of speakers and addresses become closely coordinated, and (3) utterances are interpreted with respect to referential domains circum-scribed by contextual constraints.

In order to identify what factors led speakers to choose underspecified re-ferring expressions, and enabled addresses to understand them, we performed a detailed analysis of all of the definite references, focusing on factors that seemed likely to be influencing the generation and comprehension of referen-tial expressions. Our general hypothesis was that speakers would choose to make a referential expression more specific when the intended referent and at least one competitor block were each salient in the relevant referential domain.

We focused on *recency, proximity* and *compatibility with task con-straints*. These factors are similar to those identified by Beun and Cremers (1998) using a "construction" task in which participants, separated by a screen, worked together in a mutually co-present visual space to build a structure out of blocks.

Recency

We assumed that recency would influence the saliency of a referent, with the most recently mentioned entities being more salient than other (nonfocused) entities. Thus, how recently the target block was last mentioned should predict the degree of specification, with references to the most recently mentioned block of a type, resulting in ambiguous referring expressions. For example, if the green block were uttered in the context of a set of 10 blocks, two of which were green, recency would predict that the referent should be the green block that was most recently mentioned.

Proximity

We examined the proximity of each block to the last mentioned block, because partners seemed to adopt a strategy of focusing their conversation on small re-gions within each sub-area. In the following segment of the discourse, we see an example where the referent of an otherwise ambiguous noun phrase is con-strained by proximity:

> Speaker 2. OK, so it's four down, you're gonna go over four, and then you're gonna put the piece right there.

Speaker 1. OK…how many spaces do you have between this green piece and *the one to the left of it, vertically up*?

The italicized referring expression is ambiguous, given the visual context; there are approximately three green blocks up and to the left of the previously focused block (the one referred to in the NP as this green piece). In this case, the listener does not have difficulty dealing with the ambiguity because he considers only the block closest to the last mentioned block.

Task Compatibility

Task compatibility refers to constraints on block placement due to the size and shape of the board, as well as the idiosyncratic systems that partners used to complete the task. In the following exchange, compatibility circumscribes the referential domain as the participants work to agree where the clown block should be placed:

Speaker 1. OK, you're gonna line it up…it's gonna go <pause> one row ABOVE the green one, directly next to it.
Speaker 2. Can't fit it.
Speaker 1. Cardboard?
Speaker 2. Can't, yup, cardboard…
Speaker 1. Well, take it two back.
Speaker 2. The only way I can do it is if I move, all right, should the green piece with the clown be directly lined up with *thuuh square*?

Again, the italicized referring expression is ambiguous given the visual context. While the general task is to make their boards match, the current sub-task is to place the clown piece (which they call the green piece with the clown). In order to complete this subtask, Speaker 2 asks whether the clown should be lined up with the target, *thuuh square*. The listener does not have difficulty dealing with this ambiguous reference because, although there are a number of blocks one could line up with the green piece with the clown, only one is task-relevant. Given the location of all the blocks in the relevant sub-area, the target block is the easiest block to line up with the clown. The competitor blocks are inaccessible because of the position of the other blocks or the design of the board.

For all ambiguous and disambiguated trials, each colored block in the relevant subarea was coded for recency (number of turns since last mention), proximity (ranked proximity to last mentioned item) and task constraints (whether or not the task predicted a reference to that block). Targets consistently showed an advantage for all three constraints, establishing their validity

Planned comparisons revealed that target blocks were more recently mentioned and more proximal than competitor blocks; additionally, target blocks best fit the task constraints. However, recency, proximity, and task compatibility of the target blocks did not predict speaker ambiguity. Instead, speaker ambiguity was determined by the proximity and task constraints associated with the *competitor* blocks. When a competitor block was proximate and fit the task constraints, speakers were more likely to linguistically disambiguate their referential expression. A logistic-regression model supported these observations: noun phrase ambiguity was significantly predicted by a model which included task and proximity effects, with no independent contribution of recency.

These results demonstrate that the relevant referential domain for the speakers, and addressees was restricted to a small task-relevant area of the board. Striking support for this conclusion comes from an analysis of trials in which there was a cohort competitor for the referent in the addressee's referential domain. When referential domains are unrestricted, listeners typically look at cohort competitors more often than distracters with unrelated names (Allopenna et al. 1998; Dahan et al., 2001). Moreover, fixations generated while the word is still ambiguous are equally likely to be to the cohort competitor as to the target. However, Brown-Schmidt et al. found that looks to cohort competitors were no more likely than looks to competitors with unrelated names. This is not simply a null effect. Because of the length of the experiment, participants occasionally needed to take a bathroom break. Following the break, the eyetracker had to be recalibrated. The experimenter did so by instructing the participant to look at some of the blocks. Under these conditions, the referential domain consists of the entire display because there is no constraining conversational or task-based goal. When the intended referent had a cohort competitor, the participant also frequently looked at the competitor, showing the classic cohort effect.

In sum, these results demonstrate that it is possible to study real-time language processing in a complex domain during unrestricted conversation. When a linguistic expression is temporarily ambiguous between two or more potential referents, reference resolution is closely time-locked to the word in the utterance that disambiguates the referent, replicating effects found in controlled experiments with less complex displays and prescripted utterances. Most importantly, our results provide a striking demonstration that participants in a task-based or "practical dialogues" (Allen et al. 2001), closely coordinate referential domains as the conversation develops. Speakers chose referential expressions with respect to a circumscribed, task-relevant, referential domain. Speakers were more likely to choose a specific referential expression when both the referent and a competitor were salient in the immediate task-relevant environment (saliency of competitors was predicted by task and proximity constraints). When only the referent was salient, speakers were less likely to add additional modification, generating utterances whose referents would be ambiguous if one took into account only the local visual context and the utterance. This, by itself, makes sense and is unremarkable, though the degree of ambiguity is perhaps surprising. What *is* remarkable, however, is that listeners were rarely even temporarily confused by underspecified referential expressions. This demonstrates that the participants in the conversation had developed closely matching referential domains, suggesting that referential domains become closely aligned as proposed by Pickering and Garrod (in press). Moreover, reference resolution appeared to be affected by collaborative constraints that developed during the conversation. Our participants spontaneously created collaborative terms for troublesome words (such as horizontal and vertical), and tuned their utterances, and comprehension systems for such details as the recency of mention of each particular kind of block, proximity of blocks to one another, and task constraints idiosyncratic to our block-game. These observations suggest that the attentional states of the interlocutors become closely tuned during the course of their interaction.

SUMMARY AND IMPLICATIONS

We began this chapter by noting that most research on language comprehension has been divided into two distinct traditions, language-as-product and language-as-action, each with its own conception of what comprise the fundamental problems in language processing and each with its own preferred methodologies. The product tradition emphasizes the cognitive processes by which listeners recover linguistic representations in real time, using response measures that are closely time-locked to the linguistic stimuli. The action tradition emphasizes the processes by which interlocutors cooperate to achieve joint goals, using natural tasks, typically with real-world referents and well-defined behavioral goals. We also argued that these traditions have conflicting views of what constitutes the context for comprehension. For the product tradition, context is one of many factors that might modulate core processes that are fundamentally context independent, whereas context is intrinsic to language processing in the action tradition. We then asked whether the notion of context espoused by the action tradition affects the earliest moments of real-time language processing, focusing on the referential domain for definite referring expressions. We showed that actions, intentions, real-world knowledge, and mutual knowledge circumscribe referential domains and that these context-specific domains affect core processes, such as syntactic ambiguity resolution.

In order to appreciate how this notion of context-specific referential domain alters the standard product-based view of real-time sentence processing, consider the utterance in "After John put the pencil below the big apple, he put the apple on top of the towel."

A traditional account goes something like this. When the listener encounters the scalar adjective *big*, interpretation is delayed because a scalar dimension can only be interpreted with respect to the noun it modifies; compare, for example, a *big* building and a *big* pencil. As apple is heard, lexical access activates the apple concept, a prototypical apple. The apple concept is then modified resulting in a representation of a *big apple*. When *apple* is encountered in the second clause, lexical access again results in activation of a prototypical apple concept. Because *apple* was introduced by a definite article, this representation would need to be compared with the memory representation of the *big apple* to decide whether the two corefer. (See, e.g., Tanenhaus, Carlson & Seidenberg, 1985, for an outline of such an approach.)

This account of moment-by-moment processing seems reasonable when we focus on the processing of just the linguistic forms. However, let's reconsider how the real time interpretation of (5) proceeds in the context illustrated in Figure 9.12, taking into account results we have reviewed. At *big*, the listener's attention will be drawn to the larger of the two apples, because a scalar adjective signals a contrast among two or more entities of the same semantic type. Thus *apple* will be immediately interpreted as the misshapen green apple, despite the fact that there is a more prototypical red apple in the scene. When the apple is encountered in the second clause, it will be immediately interpreted as the large green apple, despite the fact that there is also a co-present prototypical red apple in the scene. Moreover, *put* would be interpreted as a specific action, involving either John's hand or, if John were holding an instrument, an action using the instrument, and the affordances it introduced.

A common product-based view is to construe the goal of real-time sentence processing research as determining how listeners compute context-independent representations. The output of this "input" system will be a linguistic representation that can be computed quickly because the system is encapsulated. One of the appealing aspects of context-independent representations is

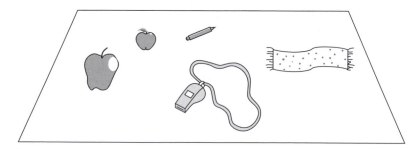

FIGURE 9.12. Hypothetical context for utterance, *After John put the pencil below the big apple, he put the apple on top of the towel*, to illustrate the implausibility of some standard assumptions of context-independent comprehension. Note that the small (red) apple is intended to be a more prototypical apple than the large (green) apple.

that they can be computed by fast, limited-domain, processing systems. More-over, such representations would be general enough to serve as the skeleton for more computationally complex context-specific representations. Now, however, we see that people can, and do, map linguistic input onto action-based representations from the earliest moments of processing. Moreover, we find increasing evidence throughout the brain and cognitive sciences that (a) behavioral context, including attention and intention affect even basic per-ceptual processes (e.g., Gandhi, Heeger, & Boyton, 1998; Colby & Goldberg, 1999) and (b) brain systems involved in perception and action are implicated in the earliest moments of language processing (e.g., Pulvermüller, Härle, & Hummel, 2001). Given these developments, focusing solely on context-independent, form-based processing is unlikely to prove fruitful (cf., Barsalou, 1999; Glenberg & Robertson, 2000; Spivey, Richardson & Fitneva, this vol-ume). Thus an important goal for future research will be integrating action-based notions of linguistic context with perceptual and action-based accounts of perception, language, and cognition in order to develop more realistic mod-els of real-time language processing.

This perspective appears to be increasingly shared by researchers in re-lated fields of study. For example, as work in theoretical linguistics continues to marshal evidence that even basic aspects of semantic interpretation involve pragmatic inference (e.g., Levinson, 2000), "embodied" approaches to dis-course understanding have concurrently demonstrated that semantic repre-sentations incorporate perceptual factors and knowledge of how referents are acted upon in specific situations (e.g., Barsalou, 1999; Glenberg & Robertson, 2000; also Altmann & Kamide, this volume; Spivey, et al. this volume). In addi-tion, there is now substantial evidence that social pragmatic cues such as joint attention and intentionality are critical in early language development (e.g., Bloom, 1997; Sabbagh & Baldwin, 2001), as well as evidence showing that nonlinguistic gestures contribute to the understanding of speech (e.g., Goldin-Meadow, 1999; McNeill, 2000). By moving towards a methodological and the-oretical union of the action and product traditions, work in language process-ing can more fruitfully identify points of contact with these areas of research.

NOTES

1. This conclusion depends on the assumption that behavioral data about syntactic preferences in parsing bear on questions about the architecture of the language pro-cessing system. Thus, just as the absence of context effects is claimed to be evidence for modularity, the presence of context effects provides evidence against modularity (Fodor, 1983, Frazier, 1999). Note, however, that there is an alternative view in which behavioral data reflect the output of rapid general-purpose cognitive deci-sions that act upon the output of a modular parallel parser. With apologies to

William James, we will refer to this as "turtles" modularity because it assumes that an unobservable process underlies a second observable process.

ACKNOWLEDGMENTS

This work was partially supported by NIH grants HD-27206 and NIDCD DC-005071 to MKT, NSERC 69-6157 to CGC, and NRSA MH1263901A1 to JEH. We thank John Henderson, Fernanda Ferreira, Zenzi Griffin, and Sarah Brown-Schmidt for helpful comments.

REFERENCES

Allen, J. F., Byron, D. K., Dzikovska, M., Ferguson, G., Galescu, L., & Stent, A. (2001). Towards conversational human-computer interaction. *AI Magazine, 22*, 27-35.

Allopenna, P. D, Magnuson, J. S., & Tanenhaus, M. K. (1998).Tracking the time course of spoken word recognition: Evidence for continuous mapping models. *Journal of Memory and Language,38*, 419-439.

Altmann, G. T. M., & Kamide, Y.(1999). Incremental interpretation at verbs: Restricting the domain of subsequent reference. *Cognition, 73*, 247-264.

Altmann, G. T. M., & Kamide, Y. (2004). Now you see it, now you don't: Mediating the mapping between language and the visual world. In J. M. Henderson & F. Ferreira (Eds.), *The interface of language, vision, and action: Eye movements and the visual world*. New York: Psychology Press.

Altmann, G. T. M., & Steedman, M. J. (1988). Interaction with context during human sentence processing. *Cognition, 30*, 191-238.

Arnold, J. E. (2001). The effect of thematic roles on pronoun use and frequency of reference continuation. *Discourse Processes, 31*, 137-162.

Arnold, J. E., Trueswell, J. C., & Lawentmann, S. M. (1999, November). Using common ground to resolve referential ambiguity. Paper presented at the 40th annual meeting of the Psychonomic Society. Los Angeles, CA.

Austin, J. L. (1962). *How to do things with words*. Oxford: Oxford University Press.

Barsalou, L. (1999). Language comprehension: Archival memory or preparation for situated action? *Discourse Processes, 28*, 61-80.

Beun, R.-J., & Cremers, A. H. M. (1998). Object reference in a shared domain of conversation. *Pragmatics & Cognition, 6*, 121-152.

Bloom, P. (1997). Intentionality and word learning. *Trends in Cognitive Sciences, 1*, 9-12.

Brown-Schmidt, S., Campana, E., & Tanenhaus, M. K. (in press). Real-time reference resolution in a referential communication task. In J. C. Trueswell & M. K. Tanenhaus (Eds.), *Processing world-situated language: Bridging the language-as-action and language-as-product traditions*. Cambridge, MA: MIT Press.

Chambers, C. G. (2001). The dynamic construction of referential domains. Doctoral dissertation, University of Rochester.

Chambers, C. G., Tanenhaus, M. K., & Magnuson, J. S. (in press). Action-based inference and syntactic ambiguity resolution. *Journal of Experimental Psychology: Learning, Memory & Cognition*.

Chambers, C. G., Tanenhaus, M. K., Eberhard, K. M., Filip, H., & Carlson, G. N. (2002). Circumscribing referential domains during real-time language comprehension. *Journal of Memory and Language, 47*, 30-49.

Chomsky, N. (1965). *Aspects of the theory of syntax*. Cambridge, MA: MIT Press.

Clark, H. H. (1992). *Arenas of language use.* Chicago: University of Chicago.

Clark, H. H. (1996). *Using language.* Cambridge: Cambridge University Press.

Clark, H. H. (1997). Dogmas of understanding. *Discourse Processes, 23,* 567-598.

Clark, H. H., & Brennan, S. E. (1989). Grounding in communication. In L. Resnick, J. Levine, & S. Teasley (Eds.), *Perspectives on socially shared cognition.* American Psychological Association: Washington, DC.

Clark, H. H., & Carlson, T. (1981). Context for comprehension. In J. Long & A. Baddeley (Eds.), *Attention and performance IX* (pp. 313-330). Hillsdale. N J : Erlbaum.

Clark, H. H., & Marshall, C. R. (1981). Definite reference and mutual knowledge. In A. H. Joshi, B. Webber, & I. A. Sag (Eds.), *Elements of discourse understanding* (pp. 10-63). Cambridge: Cambridge University Press.

Clark, H. H., & Wilkes-Gibbs (1986). Referring as a collaborative process. *Cognition, 22,* 1-39.

Colby, C. L., & Goldberg, M. E. (1999). Space and attention in parietal cortex. *Annual Review of Neuroscience, 22,* 97-136.

Coltheart, M. (1999). Modularity and cognition. *Trends in Cognitive Sciences, 3,* 115-120.

Cooper, R. M. (1974). The control of eye fixation by the meaning of spoken language: A new methodology for the real-time investigation of speech perception, memory, and language processing. *Cognitive Psychology, 6,* 84-107.

Crain, S., & Steedman, M. (1985). On not being led up the garden path: the use of context by the psychological parser. In D. Dowty, L. Karttunen, & A. Zwicky (Eds.), *Natural language parsing: Psychological, computational, and theoretical perspectives* (pp. 320-358). Cambridge: Cambridge University Press.

Dahan, D., Magnuson, J. S., & Tanenhaus, M. K. (2001). Time course of frequency effects in spoken word recognition: evidence from eye movements. *Cognitive Psychology, 42,* 317-367.

Eberhard, K. M., Spivey-Knowlton, M. J., Sedivy, J. C., & Tanenhaus, M. K. (l995). Eye-movements as a window into spoken language comprehension in natural contexts. *Journal of Psycholinguistic Research, 24,* 409-436.

Epstein, R. (1998). Reference and definite referring expressions. *Pragmatics & Cognition, 6,* 189-207.

Fodor, J. A. (1983). *Modularity of mind.* Cambridge, MA: Bradford Books.

Frazier, L. (1999). Modularity and language. In R. A. Wilson & F. C. Keil (Eds.), *MIT encyclopedia of cognitive science* (pp. 557-558). Cambridge, MA: MIT Press.

Gandhi, S. P., Heeger, M. J., & Boyton, G. M. (1998). Spatial attention affects brain activity in human primary visual cortex. *Proceedings of the National Academy of Science 96,* 3314-3319.

Glenberg, A. M., & Robertson, D. A. (2000). Symbol grounding and meaning: A comparison of high-dimensional and embodied theories of meaning. *Journal of Memory and Language, 43,* 379-401.

Goldin-Meadow, S. (1999). The role of gesture in communication and thinking. *Trends in Cognitive Sciences, 3,* 419-429.

Grice, H. P. (1957). Meaning. *Philosophical Review, 66,* 377-388.

Hanna, J. E., Tanenhaus, M. K., & Trueswell, J. C. (2003). The effects of common ground and perspective on domains of referential interpretation. *Journal of Memory and Language. 49,* 43-66.

Horton, W. S., & Keysar, B. (1995). When do speakers take into account common ground? *Cognition, 59,* 91-117.

Keysar, B., Barr, D. J., Balin, J. A., & Brauner, J. S. (2000). Taking perspective in conversation: The role of mutual knowledge in comprehension. *Psychological Science, 11,* 32-37.

Keysar, B., Barr, D. J., & Horton, W. S. (1998). The egocentric basis of language use: Insights from a processing approach. *Current Directions in Psychological Science, 7,* 46-50.

Krauss, R. M., & Weinheimer, S. (1966). Concurrent feedback, confirmation, and the encoding of referents in verbal communication. *Journal of Personality and Social Psychology, 4,* 343-346.

Levinson, S. C. (2000). *Presumptive meanings*. Cambridge, MA: MIT Press.

MacDonald, M. C. (1994). Probabilistic constraints and syntactic ambiguity resolution. *Language and Cognitive Processes, 9,* 157-201.

McMurray, B., Tanenhaus, M. K., & Aslin, R. N. (2002). Gradient effects of within-category phonetic variation on lexical access. *Cognition, 86,* B33-42.

McNeill, D. (Ed.) (2000). *Language and gesture*. Cambridge, UK: Cambridge University Press.

McRae, K., Spivey-Knowlton, M. J., & Tanenhaus, M. K. (1998). Modeling the influence of thematic fit (and other constraints) in online sentence comprehension. *Journal of Memory and Language, 38,* 283-312.

Meyer, D. E., & Schvaneveldt, R. W. (1971). Facilitation in recognizing pairs of words: Evidence of a dependence between retrieval operations. *Journal of Experimental Psychology, 90,* 227-234.

Miller, G. A. (1962). Some psychological studies of grammar. *American Psychologist, 17,* 748-762.

Miller, G. A., & Chomsky, N. (1963). Finitary models of language users. In R. D. Luce, R. R. Bush, & E. Galanter (Eds.), *Handbook of mathematical psychology*. New York: Wiley.

Nadig, A. S., & Sedivy, J. C. (2002). Evidence of perspective-taking constraints in children's on-line reference resolution. *Psychological Science, 13,* 329-336.

Pickering, M., & Garrod, S. A. (in press). Towards a mechanistic psycholinguistics of dialogue. *Brain and Behavioral Sciences.*

Pulvermüller, F., Härle, M., & Hummel, F. (2001). Walking or talking? Behavioral and neurophysiological correlates of action verb processing. *Brain and Language, 78,* 143-168.

Rayner, K. E., & Liversedge, S. P., (2004). Visual and linguistic processing during eye fixations in reading. In J. M. Henderson & F. Ferreira (Eds.), *The interface of language, vision, and action: Eye movements and the visual world*. New York: Psychology Press.

Sabbagh, M. A., & Baldwin, D. A. (2001). Learning words from knowledgeable versus ignorant speakers: Links between pre-schoolers' theory of mind and semantic development. *Child Development, 72,* 1054-1070.

Schegloff, E. A., & Sacks, H. (1973). Opening up closings. *Semiotica, 8,* 289-327.

Searle, J. R. (1969). *Speech acts. An essay in the philosophy of language*. Cambridge: Cambridge University Press.

Sedivy, J. C., Tanenhaus, M. K., Chambers, C. G., & Carlson, G. N. (1999). Achieving incremental processing through contextual representation: Evidence from the processing of adjectives. *Cognition, 71,* 109-147.

Spivey, M. J., Richardson, D. C., & Fitenva, S. A (2004). Thinking outside the brain: Spatial indices to visual and linguistic information. In J. Henderson & F. Ferreira (Eds.), *The interface of language, vision, and action: Eye movements and the visual world*. New York: Psychology Press.

Spivey, M. J., & Tanenhaus, M. K. (1998). Syntactic ambiguity resolution in discourse: Modeling the effects of referential context and lexical frequency. *Journal of Experimental Psychology: Learning, Memory and Cognition, 24,* 1521-1543.

Spivey, M. J., Tanenhaus, M. K., Eberhard, K. M., & Sedivy, J. C. (2002). Eye movements and spoken language comprehension: Effects of visual context on syntactic ambiguity resolution. *Cognitive Psychology, 45,* 447-481.

Swinney, D. A., Onifer, W., Prather, P., & Hirshkowitz, M. (1978). Semantic facilitation across sensory modalities in the processing of individual words and sentences. *Memory and Cognition, 7,* 165-195.

Tanenhaus, M. K., Carlson, G., & Seidenberg, M. S. (1985). Do listeners compute linguistic representations? In D. Dowty, L. Kartunnen, & A. Zwicky (Eds.), *Natural language parsing: psychological, computational, and theoretical perspectives* (pp. 359-408). Cambridge: Cambridge University Press.

Tanenhaus, M. K., Magnuson, J. S., Dahan, D., & Chambers, C. G. (2000). Eye movements and lexical access in spoken language comprehension: Evaluating a linking hypothesis between fixations and linguistic processing. *Journal of Psycholinguistic Research, 29,* 557-580.

Tanenhaus, M. K., Spivey-Knowlton, M. J., Eberhard, K. M., & Sedivy, J. C. (1995). Integration of visual and linguistic information during spoken language comprehension. *Science, 268,* 1632-1634.

Tanenhaus, M. K., & Trueswell, J. C. (1995). Sentence comprehension. In J. Miller & P. Eimas (Eds.), *Speech, language, and communication* (pp. 217-262). San Diego, CA: Academic Press.

Trueswell, J. C., & Gleitman, L. A., (2004). Children's eye movements during listening. Developmental evidence for a constraint-based theory of sentence processing. In J. M. Henderson & F. Ferreira (Eds.), *The interface of language, vision, and action: Eye movements and the visual world.* New York: Psychology Press.

Trueswell, J. C., Sekerina, I., Hill, N., & Logrip, M. (1999). The kindergarten-path effect: Studying on-line sentence processing in young children. *Cognition, 73,* 89-134.

10

Children's Eye Movements during Listening: Developmental Evidence for a Constraint-Based Theory of Sentence Processing

JOHN TRUESWELL
LILA GLEITMAN

Many comprehension studies of grammatical development have focused on the ultimate interpretation that children assign to sentences and phrases, yielding somewhat static snapshots of children's emerging grammatical knowledge. Studies of the dynamic processes underlying children's language comprehension have to date been rare, owing in part to the lack of online sentence processing techniques suitable for use with children. In this chapter, we describe recent work from our research group, which examines the moment-by-moment interpretation decisions of children (age 4 to 6 years) while they listen to spoken sentences. These real-time measures were obtained by recording the children's eye movements as they visually interrogated and manipulated objects in response to spoken instructions. The first of these studies established some striking developmental differences in processing ability, with the youngest children showing an inability to use relevant properties of the referential scene to resolve temporary grammatical ambiguities (Trueswell, Sekerina, Hill, & Logrip, 1999). This finding could be interpreted as support for an early encapsulated syntactic processor that has difficulty using non-syntactic information to revise parsing commit-

ments. However, we will review evidence from a series of follow-up experiments which suggest that this pattern arises from a developing interactive parsing system. Under this account, adult and child sentence comprehension is a "perceptual guessing game" in which multiple statistical cues are used to recover detailed linguistic structure. These cues, which include lexical-distribution evidence, verb semantic biases, and referential scene information, come "online" (become automated) at different points in the course of development. The developmental timing of these effects is related to their differential reliability and ease of detection in the input.

INTRODUCTION

This chapter describes much of what is currently known about how young children go about interpreting the sentences that they hear against their surrounding real-world environments. As we will describe further, we have the advantage of being able, by recording children's eye movements, to measure their moment-to-moment visual attention to objects in the world while they hear spoken sentences unfolding over time. This eye-gaze-during-listening paradigm was originally developed by Tanenhaus and colleagues to study adults' sentence comprehension abilities (e.g., Tanenhaus, Spivey-Knowlton, Eberhard, & Sedivy, 1995; Sedivy, Tanenhaus, Chambers, & Carlson, 1999; cf. Cooper, 1974). As discussed extensively in this volume, the basic idea behind this paradigm is that by measuring how visual-attentional states line up in time with the successive arrival of words and phrases, researchers can gain insight into the real-time processes by which listeners organize sentences structurally and semantically and how they map these representations onto the events and objects that they denote (Tanenhaus & Spivey-Knowlton, 1996). To accept this link between data and interpretation, one need only believe that, to a useful approximation, the mind is going where the eye is going.[1]

How the mechanics of "language processing," so studied and described, relate to more static descriptions of "language knowledge" or "knowledge of grammar" is a hotly debated topic. At one extreme, some investigators have held that these real-time processes (how the listener comes to understand particular instances of language use) impose only minimal constraints on the theory of mental grammar (a person's relatively stable knowledge of the design features of a language). At the opposite end of the theoretical continuum, other investigators hold that linguistic representations are highly constrained by the form of their use (linearly in time, word-by-word), such that, at the extreme, a single theory describes both "knowledge" and "use" of language.

Until quite recently, such questions concerning the architecture of language knowledge could not even be raised realistically for the case of young children. After all, most sentence-processing techniques relied on the experimental subject's ability to deal comfortably with written text, techniques that are transparently unsuitable for preschoolers and even novice readers in the early school years. Eye-movement techniques that link responses to *speech events* have the potential to revolutionize how we examine the child's emerging understanding of language. Accordingly, we and our colleagues have adapted this online experimental paradigm for use with children as young as 4 years of age.

In the present paper we will first briefly review the results and theoretical approaches that have emerged from the adult sentence-comprehension literature, based on such real-time measures as eye tracking. We will then describe the extension of such techniques and findings to children—to the question of how one learns to parse. In doing so, we review both the original study that introduced eye-tracking techniques and their rationale for this age range (Trueswell et al., 1999) and several later studies that have clarified and refined interpretation of the original findings. Our most general ambition is to understand how the processes of language use and language learning interact in the young child to yield the mature state that all normal language-using humans attain.

HOW ADULTS RECOVER GRAMMATICAL INFORMATION FROM AN UTTERANCE: THE CONSTRAINT-BASED LEXICALIST ACCOUNT

In order to understand the intended meaning of a sentence, a reader or listener must detect much or all of the sentence's grammatical structure. This is because the grammatical operations of a language convey complex combinatory and referential meaning that single words cannot. By finding clues in the sentence about the grammatical operations that gave rise to it, a reader or listener is in a position to recover the intended meaning of the sentence as a whole. Adults are known to be marvelously adept at this process. In fact, numerous studies show that adult listeners and readers are so skilled that they typically achieve sentence interpretations in real time, packaging words into phrases and making provisional commitments to interpretation as each word is perceived (e.g., Altmann & Steedman, 1988; Frazier & Rayner, 1982; Marslen-Wilson & Tyler, 1987; Trueswell, Tanenhaus, & Garnsey, 1994). In this straightforward sense, sentence understanding comes about through a process that is "immediate" and "incremental." Each word makes its contribution to the interpretation at the point of its occurrence in the flow of speech and influences the interim structure and interpretation of the sentence that is being built.

An important implication of this online nature of processing is that readers and listeners sometimes make interpretation errors that require revision when further words in the sentence are encountered. In this sense they are "led down the garden path" at a point of ambiguity and only later make their way back to the intended interpretation. This garden-path phenomenon is something of a gift from nature to the researcher interested in sentence processing. This is because it can be used as a means for examining which kinds of evidence (syntactic, semantic, discourse context) inform initial commitments to interpretations, thus providing insight into the internal organization of the comprehension system. Investigations of this kind comprise a broad experimental effort in which sources of evidence are parametrically manipulated and their effect on parsing preferences is measured. For example, consider the following sentence:

(1) Anne hit the thief with the stick.

There are two primary ways that we can interpret the prepositional phrase *with the stick:* either as the Instrument with which the action is performed, in which case it is structurally linked to the verb phrase (VP) (*to hit using a stick*—VP attachment[2]), or as a modifier of the direct object, in which case it is syntactically linked to that noun phrase (NP) (*the thief that has the stick*—NP attachment). It has been confirmed experimentally that readers and listeners have a tendency to commit to the so-called instrument interpretation when encountering the ambiguous preposition *with* in sentences like (1) (e.g., Rayner, Carlson, & Frazier, 1983; Taraban & McClelland, 1988). This finding is consistent with our intuition of a misinterpretation, or garden-path, when we encounter the final word in such sentences as:

(2) Anne hit the thief with the wart.

Many early studies of readers' eye-movement patterns for this and other ambiguities suggested that the comprehension device had general structural biases (e.g., for VP-attachment) that were initially uninfluenced by nonsyntactic facts such as plausibility (warts vs. sticks) or situation-specific discourse cues (e.g., Rayner et al. 1983; Ferreira & Clifton, 1986; Ferreira & Henderson, 1991). The findings supported modular theories of parsing, whose initial stage rapidly structured the input words (each represented by its lexical class label, e.g., noun, preposition) based solely on phrase structure rules of the language and resolved ambiguities using a syntactic simplicity metric —the Minimal Attachment Principle (Frazier, 1987, 1989; Frazier & Fodor, 1978).

However, during the past 20 years, an accumulating body of evidence on the pattern of garden paths supports a different characterization of the processing system, in which far more detailed and probabilistic linguistic properties of the input are tracked, detected, and used incrementally. First, it has been found that parsing commitments are often guided by the syntactic preferences of individual lexical items, such as whether a particular verb frequently denotes an instrument via a prepositional phrase (Taraban & McClelland, 1988; Trueswell & Kim, 1998; MacDonald, 1994; Trueswell, Tanenhaus, & Kello, 1993). To see this point, compare the likely interpretation of sentence (1) when the verb *noticed* is substituted for *hit*. Second, the semantic fit of preceding complements also rapidly constrains initial parsing commitments, especially when the information precedes the ambiguity (e.g., readers assume a main clause analysis of *The defendant examined...*, but a relative clause analysis for *The evidence examined...*, see Tabossi, Spivey-Knowlton, McRae, & Tanenhaus, 1994; Trueswell et al., 1994).

Third, constraints from the immediate referential context can influence the course of parsing decisions. For instance, in sentence (1), a two-thief context encourages an initial modifier interpretation of *with the stick* (e.g., Altmann & Steedman, 1988; Crain & Steedman, 1985; Trueswell & Tanenhaus, 1991). This is because listeners realize that NPs are most often modified so as to distinguish between referential alternatives made available by either the discourse or situational context. Uttering a plain vanilla *thief* is sufficient for identification when there's only a single criminal in sight; but if there are two or more, then the modified *thief with the wart* is needed to select the guilty party. Finally, the measured effectiveness of these probabilistic constraints on interpretation depends upon whether the verb makes available the appropriate syntactic alternatives (e.g., Britt, 1994; Garnsey, Pearlmutter, Myers, & Lotocky, 1997; Trueswell, 1996).

The theory that we would argue best captures the existing evidence is the constraint-based lexicalist theory (henceforth, CBL: see MacDonald, Pearlmutter, & Seidenberg, 1994; Trueswell & Tanenhaus, 1994). This theory assumes a constraint-satisfaction approach to ambiguity resolution (Marslen-Wilson & Tyler, 1987; McClelland, 1987), in which multiple sources of information are used to converge as rapidly as possible on a single interpretation. The central component of this theory is a grammatical processing system that is highly tuned to the structural preferences of individual lexical items; hence "lexicalist." The recognition of a word includes activation of rich argument structures that define the initial set of possible interpretations. For example, the preference for VP attachment in sentences 1 and 2 is explained as arising from a system that is sensitive to the grammatical preferences of the verb "hit," which include the use of the instrument role, typically headed by the preposition "with" (for related evidence, see Taraban & McClelland, 1988; Garnsey et al., 1997; MacDonald, 1994; Trueswell et al., 1994; Britt, 1994). It is significant that linguistic (Bresnan & Kaplan, 1982; Pollard & Sag, 1987) and computational linguistic (Joshi, Vijay-Shanker, & Weir, 1991; Steedman, 1995; Srinivas & Joshi, 1999) theorizing have also in the same period been converging toward a lexicalized picture of the organization of language (Kim, Srinivas, & Trueswell, 2002). Relatedly, recent theories of the acquisition of word meaning give independent support for a lexically organized grammar (Landau & Gleitman, 1985; Gleitman, 1990; Fisher, 1996; Gillette, Gleitman, Gleitman, & Lederer, 1999).

DEVELOPMENTAL PREDICTIONS FROM THE CONSTRAINT-BASED LEXICALIST THEORY

With the adult processing patterns and CBL account in mind, we sketch here a developmental version of the CBL theory of sentence processing.[3] First, this theory assumes that the computational procedures involved in sentence comprehension remain constant over development. This means that from a very early age, the learner's comprehension machinery can best be characterized as a perceptual guessing game in which multiple probabilistic cues are used to converge on the grammatical operations that gave rise to the utterance. The assumption that the analysis of the input is driven by statistical learning mechanisms has experimental support. Very young infants, when exposed to 2 to 3 minute sequences of artificially generated syllable sequences, begin to recover the phonological and grammatical tendencies of the language (e.g., Saffran, Newport, & Aslin, 1996; Marcus, 2000; see also Hudson & Newport, 2003). It seems plausible, therefore, especially in the light of adult processing findings above, that statistical tracking is accomplished at multiple levels of utterance representation, and this forms a deep continuity between learning and comprehension processes over the course of the language system's development.

Under this assumption, the CBL theory can be used to make developmental predictions about the development of sentence processing abilities, in particular about developmental differences in how children might resolve temporary syntactic ambiguity. Below, we sketch three such predictions, which will be examined in the child eye movement studies described in this chapter.

Prediction 1: Early Reliance on Lexical Information. Given the probabilistic nature of grammatical processing in CBL, the theory most naturally predicts that the degree of informativity of various sources of evidence (e.g., lexical, semantic, referential) should predict the order in which these cues "come on-line," i.e., become automatized for use in syntactic ambiguity resolution. Of the sources of evidence we have discussed, the CBL theory most naturally predicts a developmentally early reliance on lexical cues to structure. The reason for this is that lexical information (in the form of verb-argument information, for instance) highly determines the likelihood of local structure, a fact that has been noted time and again by linguists (e.g., Carlson & Tanenhaus, 1988; Jackendoff, 2002), psycholinguists (e.g., Fisher, Gleitman, & Gleitman, 1991) and computational linguists constructing lexically contingent parsing systems (e.g., Srinivas &

Joshi, 1999). Indeed, in the adult system we see evidence for a bias to rely on such information when resolving syntactic ambiguities, which is of course rapidly constrained by other evidence, such as plausibility and referential information (Britt, 1994; Garnsey et al., 1997). Thus, we should expect that the distribution of lexical items (and their meaning) should overly constrain children's parsing commitments to ambiguity, more so than they would for older children and adults, who have learned to recruit referential cues to structure. As experience builds knowledge of how contextual facts predict structure in the utterance, these sources of evidence should begin to exert effects on online parsing commitments.

Prediction 2: Interactive Processing When Cues Are Highly Constraining. Given our interactive processing account, it should in principle be possible to find children using multiple evidential cues, including nonlinguistic cues, to resolve ambiguity, provided that they highly constrain the possible structure of the utterance. That is, evidence for reliance on a particular cue to structure, such as lexicosyntactic information, should not be understood as an early ban on other sources of evidence for resolving ambiguity. Easy to track nonlinguistic cues that are highly constraining should be predicted to combine with lexical evidence, even in younger children.

Prediction 3: Comprehension-Specific Deficits. Our comprehension theory assumes that multiple sources of evidence automatically combine to influence a child's estimate of the intended meaning of a sentence. Thus, it makes the somewhat counterintuitive prediction that children who readily produce particular syntactic structures in appropriate referential contexts could very well show an inability to detect and understand these very same structures in a comprehension setting where evidential sources support an alternative analysis.

CHILDREN'S COMPREHENSION IN REAL TIME

The launch point of our research endeavor is a pair of eye movement studies that we conducted with 5-year-olds (N = 16) and 8-year-olds (N = 16), first reported in Trueswell et al. (1999). In this study, which was modeled after an adult sentence-parsing study by Spivey, Tanenhaus, and colleagues (Tanenhaus et al., 1995; Spivey, Tanenhaus, Eberhard, & Sedivy, 2002), children's eye movements were recorded as they acted upon spoken instructions to move objects in an array (see Figure 10.1). The participants in Trueswell et al. (1999) heard spoken instructions, which on critical trials contained a temporary prepositional phrase- (PP-) attachment ambiguity, as in

(3) Put the frog on the napkin in the box.

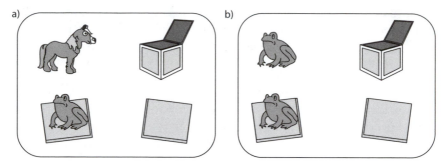

FIGURE 10.1. Illustrations of (a) 1-Referent scene and (b) 2-Referent scene. In both cases, children look to the empty napkin upon hearing "on the *napkin*", showing a strong VP-attachment bias. The initial commitment also influences the final interpretation: most children move a frog to the empty napkin, regardless of context. (Truswell et al., 1999)

Here the phrase *on the napkin*, when first encountered, could in principle link to the verb *put* as a goal, indicating where to put a frog, or link to the NP *the frog* as a modifier, specifying a property of a particular frog. The phrase though is disambiguated toward the modifier interpretation by the presence of a second goal phrase (*in the box*).

The striking finding was that 5-year olds showed a strong preference to interpret *on the napkin* as the goal of *put*, even when the referential scene supported a modifier interpretation (e.g., two frogs, one on a napkin, see Figure 10.1b). Upon hearing *on the napkin*, 5-year olds typically looked over to a potential goal in the scene, the empty napkin, regardless of whether there were two frogs present (supporting a modifier interpretation) or one frog present (supporting a goal interpretation). In fact, 5-year olds' preference for VP-attachment was so strong that they showed little sign of revising it: upon hearing *napkin,* children would look to the empty napkin as a potential goal and then frequently move a frog to that location. In two-referent cases, children were at chance even when selecting which frog to move, suggesting they never considered a modifier interpretation.

Importantly, this child parsing behavior was localized to the ambiguity and not to the complexity of the sentence. This is shown by the fact that 5-year-olds' eye movements and actions became adult-like when the temporary ambiguity was removed, as in the unambiguous modifier form:

(4) Put the frog that's on the napkin in the box.

The near-perfect performance on unambiguous forms rules out a more mundane explanation of our results, namely that long "complicated" sentences puzzle young children. Here, sentence 4, an even longer sentence with the same intended structure, doesn't flummox the child. Why? Because we have removed the temporary ambiguity.

In contrast to 5-year-olds, adults' responses to the temporarily ambiguous stimuli were found to depend on the referential scene provided. In particular, the mere presence of a two-referent scene eliminated measurable signs of syntactic misanalysis of the ambiguous phrase: there were few looks to the potential goal and few incorrect actions, as compared to one-referent scenes. This finding is consistent with the earlier work on adults with this ambiguity (Tanenhaus et al., 1995; Spivey et al., 2002).

Thus, as CBL theory predicts, younger children appear to be relying more heavily on local lexical cues than referential scene cues to resolve syntactic ambiguity. Specifically, younger children appear to be relying heavily on the grammatical preferences of the verb *put* which almost always denotes a goal, typically as a prepositional phrase.[4] The finding displays a striking paradox: Young children are often presumed to be very well tuned to the semantics and pragmatics of scenes and events in the extralinguistic world and far less attuned to the formal (presumably "boring") formal facts about words and sentences. Yet these initial findings have been that it is the adults who are more sensitive to the referential scene as a guide to parsing commitments, whereas the children seem—on the surface of the matter—to be little lexicalist grammarians, parsing the heard sentence in fine indifference to the reference world.

THE ROLE OF VERB BIAS IN CHILD- AND ADULT-PARSING PREFERENCES

Snedeker, Thorpe, & Trueswell (2001), and Snedeker & Trueswell (submitted) explored in detail the claim that children's parsing preferences are driven by their verb-specific syntactic and semantic knowledge. Such an account predicts that child-parsing preferences for ambiguous phrases should be heavily influenced by manipulations of the type of verb, pursuing the analysis that is consistent with the most likely argument structure for that verb. Recall that this is not a guaranteed outcome, for a general structural bias could also account for the original Trueswell et al (1999) child-parsing outcomes. Certain acquisition theories make this prediction, proposing that the child parser might avoid more complex syntactic structures in favor of simpler ones (e.g., Minimal Attachment Principle, Goodluck, & Tavakolian, 1982; Frazier & Fodor, 1978) or place a general ban on complex syntactic operations (e.g., the No-Adjoin Principle, Frank, 1998), predicting little or no influence of verb bias.

We were also interested in better understanding a paradox in the adult literature regarding verb-bias information. Whereas adult-reading studies indicated an important role for verb biases in the initial consideration of syntactic alternatives (Britt, 1994), studies of adult listeners in world-situated, eye-gaze studies suggest an almost exclusive role for referential cues in determining initial syntactic choices (Tanenhaus et al., 1995; Spivey et al., 2002). Almost all constraint-satisfaction views of parsing, including our own, would expect some difficulty with *put* instructions, like the ones used in those studies. If, in the adult system, both lexical and referential facts were weighed simultaneously (as supported by reading studies), why would referential cues completely eliminate adult difficulty with *put* instructions, which are heavily lexically biased toward the incorrect destination analysis?

To meet these two exploratory goals, Snedeker et al. (2001) followed the lead of the prior adult-reading studies that have, in a single experiment, fully crossed verb bias with manipulations of referential context (e.g., Britt, 1994), except that we performed these manipulations in the world-situated, eye-gaze task. Such manipulations should reveal the relative contributions of these several factors under all possible combinations, for both adults (N = 36) and 5-year olds (N = 36). Target constructions contained a PP-attachment ambiguity (e.g., "Feel the frog with the feather") in both two-referent and one-referent contexts (see Figure 10.2 below; clip-art images are provided for illustrative purposes only—real-world, beanie-baby objects were actually employed, as in our previous study). Linguistic materials were prenormed, and we compared three different types of verbs: those that typically take an instrument phrase (*hit*), those that rarely do so (*choose*), and equibiased verbs (*feel*). The semantic fit of the instrument noun was controlled across conditions via normative ratings: all nouns, e.g., *fan, feather,* and *stick,* were rated as being approximately equally good-or-poor instruments for their respective verbs.

The results were systematic and striking. Five-year olds' eye movements and actions showed a sole reliance on the verb preferences, almost perfectly

- Three levels of Verb Bias:
  Tickle the pig with the fan. (Instrument Bias)
  Feel the frog with the feather. (Equi Bias)
  Choose the cow with the stick. (Modifier Bias)
- Crossed with Referential Scene...

FIGURE 10.2. Manipulating both verb-bias and referential scene. From Snedeker, Thorpe, & Trueswell, 2001.

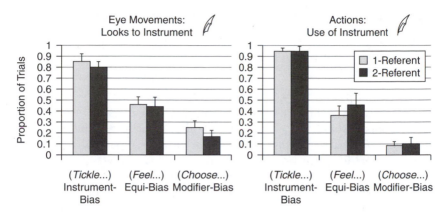

FIGURE 10.3. Five-year-olds (N = 36) show sensitivity to verb bias and not referential scene manipulation (Snedeker et al., 2001).

matching rates of instrument use to the semantic preferences of individual verbs. As shown in Figure 10.3, the proportion of looks to the potential instrument upon hearing "with the X" systematically decreased across instrument-biased, equibiased and modifier-biased conditions. Additionally, absolutely no sensitivity to the referential scene was observed, even for equibiased verbs. These means reflected a reliable effect of verb type, no effect of referential scene, and no interaction in subject and item ANOVAs. In contrast, adults' initial eye movements and actions showed simultaneous sensitivity to both verb-bias manipulations and referential context in the expected directions: Two-referent scenes and modifier-biased verbs both reduced looks to, and use of, a potential instrument (e.g., a large feather), resulting in reliable effects of both the verb type and referential factors.

These findings are in line with what is predicted by a CBL parsing system that gradually recruits reliable information over development. As the processing exposure with modifier expressions increases, children become increasingly sensitive to scene-contingent factors for their use.

It is important to note that although two-referent scenes greatly decreased instrument looks and instrument actions in adults, there were still effects of verb bias in two-referent scenes. That is, instrument-biased verbs resulted in adults considering the contextually *inappropriate* instrument interpretation significantly more often than in unambiguous forms. This stands in contrast with adults in our earlier *put...* study and the study of Tanenhaus, Spivey and colleagues, where the same two-referent scene removed all signs of the contextually inappropriate VP-attachment interpretation. As discussed in the paper, we suggest that the apparent ease that adults show in *put...* instructions comes from the immediately following disambiguating material (*in the box*), which is integrated into ongoing parallel estimates of parse likelihoods.

Lexical Modularity or Informativeness of the Scene?

Thus far, our experimental work has shown a near-exclusive role of lexical evidence for informing children's parsing decisions. In particular, the child parser does not appear to make consistent use of all potentially relevant cues in the scene to inform parsing decisions. Five-year olds relied on language-internal information such as the syntactic preferences of verbs and the linkages of these preferences to argument-structure interpretation. In contrast, 8-year-olds and adults were measurably influenced not only by these language-internal cues, but also by several other sources of information that were available in the utterance and the situation.

These results in hand, we can now reapproach our original questions: What accounts for the restrictions on early child processing? And what are the mechanisms (or expansions of the knowledge base) that allow these restrictions to be lifted? At least two viable and distinguishable developmental accounts exist.

The Modular/Single-Cue Hypothesis First, contra the account given thus far, it is possible that the observed child-adult differences regarding the child's reliance on lexical cues arise from changes or expansions in processing ability. For instance, a limited, single-cue, or encapsulated, parsing system might become more interactive as processing ability grows with age. Indeed, several current modular theories of parsing propose a special status for lexical cues to structure for architectural reasons, where the lexicon exclusively proposes syntactic and semantic structure (Boland & Cutler, 1996). Our observed 5-year-old preference to use lexical cues might very well reflect an encapsulated, lexicalist parsing system "in the raw," which, as it increases in processing power, becomes increasingly interactive. Similarly, it is possible that even when children control multiple cues, they may only be able to use one cue at a time for ambiguity resolution, perhaps due to an early inability to coordinate multiple cues.

Multiple Cue System from the Start In contrast, our own account assumes a probabilistic multiple cue comprehension system from the start, with the ordering of cue use over development reflecting changes in each cue's relative reliability. As various evidential databases are built and discovered to be informative, they come into use in the comprehension process.[5] Under this account, the child-parsing system shows an earlier reliance on lexical sources (above and beyond other relevant information sources such as referential sources) precisely because of the high degree of reliability of lexical sources for syntactic structuring. By age 5, the child has learned a great deal about the possible and probable syntactic/semantic environments in which particular verbs can appear—especially, for the common verbs we have tested thus far. Other sources, such as referential scene constraints on syntax, might simply take longer to acquire and use because they are less reliable over the input database as a whole and arguably more difficult to track in particular instances of use than lexicosyntactic contingencies. Thus, the child- parsing system can, in principle, use multiple evidential sources to guide a syntactic choice, but, in practice, the usefulness of particular sources of evidence is a matter of discovery and, hence, changes with experience.

Under this multiple-cue, informativity account, a crucial question becomes whether a child listener can deduce from scene information alone the need for referential specificity, that is, the need for a speaker to provide restrictive modification of a definite NP. In particular, can the child look out into the visual world and easily anticipate a speaker's need to utter *the little star* (and not *the star*), *the toy closest to you* (and not *the toy*), or *the frog on the napkin* (and not *the frog*)?

Our assumption thus far has been that a speaker's use of a bare definite NP (*the frog*) in the presence of multiple entities of that sort (multiple frogs) ought to be a near-perfect predictor of the need for further linguistically specification, i.e., a post-NP restrictive modifier (e.g., *the frog you caught yesterday*). But is this the case? A recent adult-to-adult referential communication study suggests that there would be only sporadic evidence for this scene-contingent inference (Brown-Schmidt, Campana, & Tanenhaus, 2002). It was observed that adults do not utter restrictive modifiers every time there is more than one potential referent. In particular, nearly half of all definite NPs uttered (48%) did not have a unique referent in the scene (e.g., "Okay, pick up the square" might be uttered in the presence of multiple squares.) However, conversants' eye movements, actions, and vocal responses all showed that they routinely achieved referential success under these conditions. Obviously, this success isn't evidence for psychic abilities on the part of the conversants. Rather, success occurred because the shape of the discourse and the goals of the task had narrowed the field of possible referents down to one (e.g., only one of the squares was currently a plausible referent). Definite NPs containing restrictive modifiers were uttered only when more than one potential referent was currently under discussion.

What this means is that the discourse and its goals relative to the scene, rather than the scene itself, ought to be a far better predictor of restrictive modifier use for the younger child. In prior referential scene-parsing studies (Trueswell et al., 1999; Spivey et al., 2002), adults and older children might have shown a proclivity to use scene evidence as *a proxy for the discourse*, when such a discourse is absent. Or perhaps humans develop an understanding of how scene cues partially predict structure gradually over developmental time, given the sporadic nature of the cue.

To this end, we have begun to ask whether potentially potent evidence from the discourse can influence 5-year-old parsing decisions (Hurewitz, Brown-Schmidt, Trueswell, & Gleitman, in progress). Here a preceding discourse, in the form two conversing puppets, establishes the referential goal to contrast multiple referents in the scene prior to hearing an ambiguous PP. If these discourse goals provide a strong constraint on the need for the otherwise ambiguous PP to be a modifier, we might expect even 5-year-olds to be sensitive to this fact, combining it with lexical cues to structure. If a single-cue, modular system is at work, we would expect to see continued use of only lexical cues to structure.

In the study, children (N = 24; Age = 4;0-5;6) were tested in a modified version of the Truth Verification task (Crain & Thornton, 1998). On each trial, the child heard a beanie-baby story acted out in the presence of a puppet ("Mr. Walrus," who is known to be not terribly bright). At the end of the story, a second puppet (the clever Ms. Rabbit, who had been hiding under the table listening to the story) appeared and asked Mr. Walrus questions about the story. The child's job was to evaluate and, if necessary, correct Mr. Walrus's answers to her questions.

On critical trials, each child was always presented with a two referent scene (as in Figure 10.4, two cats, one on a book, one on a fence, a toy barn, another fence, and a turtle; again, real-world objects, not clip-art images, were used). The story, prerecorded and acted out by the experimenter (E)

FIGURE 10.4. Illustration of stimulus scene from Hurewitz, Brown-Schmidt, Trueswell, & Gleitman (in progress).

deictically referred to each animal and established the pair of cats in distinct events; it is paraphrased below:

> "This cat [E grabs the cat on the book] and this turtle [E grabs turtle] decided to go for a walk, and met up on top of the barn [E moves animal to barn]. Suddenly, the turtle tickled the cat. 'Tickle, tickle tickle!' 'Hee! Hee! Hee!' [E performs appropriate actions with the animals.] And then they went home. [E returns each animal to original starting place.] And, this cat [E grabs cat on fence] saw all this and laughed and laughed as well."

With all the animals back in their original locations, Ms. Rabbit returned to ask Mr. Walrus a question. In all conditions, Walrus's answer contained an attachment ambiguity: "I know, the turtle tickled the cat on the fence." Here *on the fence* can indicate where the tickling happened (locative VP-attachment) or indicate a particular cat (locative NP-attachment). Mr. Walrus's utterance, however, was preceded by a question from Ms. Rabbit that either supported the need to contrast the cats (the contrastive question condition, "Which cat did the turtle tickle?") or did not support this goal (the noncontrastive question condition, "Can you tell me something about the story?"). In all cases, *both* interpretations of the ambiguity *are incorrect* because the story actually involved the cat on the book being tickled by the turtle, in a different location, i.e., when they both had been on the barn. Hence, however the child parsed the sentence, she still must correct Mr. Walrus. It is the child's *particular* correction of Mr. Walrus that can reveal the implicit parse choice ("No! It happened OVER HERE on the barn!" or "No! THIS CAT was tickled, the one on the book!").

The question-type factor (contrastive vs. noncontrastive) was crossed with a verb manipulation. Half the trials involved eventive verbs (such as *tickle*), which easily allow for locative (VP-attached) modifiers such as "on the barn." The other half involved stative verbs, where the story and the critical sentence involved, e.g., *liking* ("The turtle liked the cat on the fence."). These verbs do not usually permit locative modifiers; such modifiers would indicate a particular moment in time that the verb would have to denote going, against the lexical semantics of such verbs.

Given the importance of conversation cues in modifier use (see above), our multiple-cue account predicts that constraining discourse cues (here, question-type), as well as lexical cues (verb-type) should influence parsing preferences, even in 5-year-olds. That is, contrastive questions and stative verbs should both induce greater modifier interpretations and resulting corrections by the child. In contrast, a modular lexicalist account predicts children will continue to do what they have done in our previous studies: rely on lexical cues. That is, children should show only an effect of the type of verb, with increased modifier responses for stative verbs.

Figure 10.5 plots the rates of VP-attach interpretations exhibited by children in the four conditions. As one can see, the pattern of VP-attach corrections across conditions supports our interactive account. This resulted in reliable effects of question type and verb type (p's < .05). And, interestingly, adult controls exhibited an even stronger reliance on the discourse needs of the questions, with adults even coercing stative verbs into eventive readings. Taken together, these data suggest a general progression toward overcoming local lexical biases that are in conflict with strong discourse requirements.

The Production/Comprehension Dissociation

It should be emphasized that our account of the child parsing phenomenon is that it is the product of a system that automatically combines multiple evidential sources, all to serve the purpose of coming up with an estimate of the intended meaning of an utterance. If this is the case, we should expect to observe striking differences in children's use of structures in production and comprehension tasks under particular comprehension conditions. That is, children might correctly produce a particular structure in the right referential context, but then fail to understand this same structure during comprehension, when the evidential sources support an alternative analysis.

To test these claims, Hurewitz, Brown-Schmidt, Thorpe, Gleitman & Trueswell (2000) examined 5-year-olds' production and comprehension abilities in two-referent scenes, e.g., two frogs, as in Figure 10.6. Children heard a

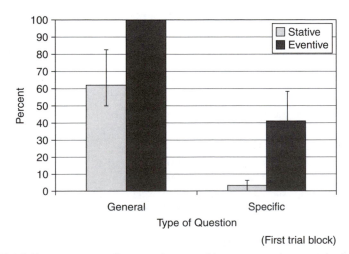

FIGURE 10.5. Proportion of locative (VP-attach) corrections (e.g., "No! It happened in the barn!" (N = 24, Age = 4;0 to 5;6).

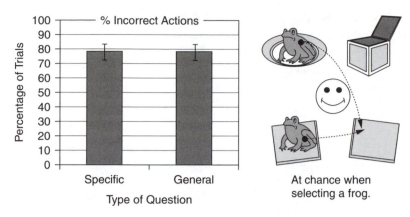

FIGURE 10.6. Children distinguish frogs in their own speech but then garden-path on "Put the frog on the napkin into the box" (Hurewitz et al., 2000).

story (acted out by the experimenter), which introduced salient differences between the two frogs (by having them doing different things). Afterwards, they were tested by asking them a specific question: "Which frog visited Mrs. Squid's house?" To answer this question required (a) understanding the story, (b) understanding that the question requires an answer that distinguishes the frogs via locative modification, as these frogs were otherwise identical, and (c) producing in the answer a restrictive modifier, namely, "The frog/one on the napkin." Immediately thereafter, the same child was asked to perform the *put...* task of Trueswell et al. (1999): "Very good. Touch the Smiley Face. Now put the frog on the napkin into the box." As a control, another group of children were asked a general question ("Can you tell me something about the story?") prior to doing the *put...* task.

Children's production performance on the specific question showed they were able to perform all of the relevant nonlinguistic and linguistic acrobatics to specify uniquely a referent through restrictive modification; 72% of all answers to the specific question were correct, providing answers like "The frog on the napkin." In striking contrast, these same children's response to the *put...* instruction showed the *same* misanalysis effects as those reported in Trueswell et al. (1999). They typically performed incorrect actions, all of which involved the incorrect destination (see Figure 10.6). And, children were at chance in selecting between the two frogs. That is, the very same child who had just correctly responded to the story-question by producing a PP-modified NP (*the frog on the napkin*) might now in response to "Put the frog on the napkin into the box," pick up the other frog, move it over to the empty napkin, and then put it into the box. The sheer differences in *complexity* between the two sentences cannot account for the findings as we know from earlier experimentation (the same children have no difficulty with unambiguous control sentences of equal complexity, e.g., "Put the frog that's on the napkin into the box").

A further experiment in this line (Hurewitz et al. 2000, Exp. 2) investigated the possibility that children just weren't inclined to notice napkins as salient components of scene description. Making the platforms on which frogs were ensconced more salient (frilly umbrellas and royal thrones) generally increased performance in production (87% restrictive modifiers in production), but still the striking asymmetry between production and comprehension was preserved (60% errors in comprehension). In addition, in this version of the experiment we eye-tracked the young subjects, with the online results replicating Trueswell et al. (1999).

So, in both of these experiments, we observe, like in the Rabbit-Walrus study of the previous section, children understanding how the discourse can specify the need for an NP restrictive modifier. In particular, in the case of the Rabbit-Walrus study, we see this discourse-syntax knowledge at work in comprehension: a contrastive question generates an increased chance of interpreting an ambiguous PP as an NP modifier, though this knowledge must battle against lexical evidence that may support an alternative interpretation (e.g., eventive verbs generated some question/discourse-inappropriate responses in children). The experiments in the present section demonstrate this discourse-syntactic knowledge in children's own productions. Contrastive questions generated a need for referential specificity in the form of a modifier ("The frog/one on the napkin."), which the children often uttered in response to this question type. However, when we then pull out a *put...* sentence from our lexical arsenal, we see that we can swamp the comprehension statistics in favor of VP-attachment interpretations, even in the same child who had just a moment ago demonstrated knowledge of the discourse-syntax facts in his or her own productions.

It should be noted, though, that the discourse conditions are indeed slightly different between our production and comprehension test conditions. The distinction between the frogs had just been made by the child in his or her utterance, and thus the discourse-goal of contrasting the frogs had been achieved by the time we tested for comprehension abilities in our *put...* instruction. We strongly suspect though that *put* was exerting detrimental effects, since unpublished work from our lab has examined *put...* sentences as part of an answer to a contrastive question (Rabbit: "Which frog should I move?" Walrus: "I know. Put the frog on the napkin into the box."). Here we still find strong VP-attachment preferences despite the immediately preceding contrastive question (Hurewitz, Gleitman & Trueswell, in progress). Thus, the data strongly support the automatic use of verb statistics in the young-child parsing system.

THE CONSTRAINT-BASED LEXICALIST LEARNER: A SUMMARY OF FINDINGS

We have presented the results of several experiments which, taken together, support the CBL approach to language comprehension by children during the period when they are constructing the automatic mechanisms for rapid and efficient language understanding, in the age range from 4 to 6 years. All these studies took advantage of the fact, well documented in the adult parsing literature, that the resolution of lexicosyntactic ambiguities can shed light on the internal workings of the comprehension system. An act of comprehension, followed along its course with real-time measures such as eye gaze, gives evidence about how features of the input (e.g., an ambiguous word; a complex visual scene; the preceding discourse) influence the construction of an interpretation and when in this process they are having their effects.

As we showed, children's comprehension is already highly nuanced and efficient early in life. Much like adults, children can make use of detailed statistical facts about verbs' individual complementation preferences and the details of the discourse and scene contingencies to converge on an interpretive choice under conditions of ambiguity. As the CBL theory predicts, then, the young learner—like the adult—appears to be a statistics-based incremental device, sensitive to varied cue types as it tries to recover the sense of what is meant by the sequence of words arriving at the ear. This incremental, multicue picture of the child parser contrasts with some interpretations of our initial studies (Trueswell et al, 1999), in which the child parser is perceived as "modular," at least in the sense of being subject to severe limitations on the types of evidence it will recruit at all. Although not fully resolved at this point, because of the early state of this research endeavor, our current evidence lends strong support for a multiple-cue interactive and probabilistic system at work at all ages.[6]

At the same time, these same studies reveal important differences between children and adults that are consistent with our account. As just stated, we do not think these differences are of kind (modular vs. interactive parsing architectures). Rather, the younger language user has yet to discover the full range of evidence pertaining to particular linguistic choices regarding the input. He or she needs to build up relevant linguistic databases, several of which vary cross-linguistically. Minimally, the learner must build up a library of English (or French, or Hindi, etc.) word forms and the sentential contexts (of other words and phrase types) in which each such word occurs, as well as a picture of the language-specific phrasal types and organization (e.g., that in English PP's serially follow their dominating head NP's).[7] This being so, and learning being what it is, it follows that *the more frequent and reliable in the input is an observable property of the system being learned, the sooner a learner will exploit this property in making parsing decisions.* Thus, a youngster may appear to be deaf to a particular cue, such as contextual scene information, not because his or her comprehension architecture is immune to such information, but because the relevant knowledge base for using such a cue type either doesn't exist (yet), isn't fully automatized, or hasn't been integrated with other cue types.

To take a specific example, earlier we predicted that younger children would be most efficient and adult-like in their use of lexical cues to structure, as indeed they are: As the experiment showed, they are highly sensitive to the frequency facts about complementation type for particular verbs as a clue to the status of a PP as a VP- versus NP- modifier (e.g., *hitting* is more likely than *choosing* to be followed by a VP-attached PP whose noun denotes an instrument).[8] In contrast, learners at early ages are sporadic and quite errorful in their use of a particular situational cue (one frog/two frog) compared to older children and adults. By hypothesis, this is because such cues are harder to come by, and less reliable, in the input. Indeed, the range of complement privileges for common verbs is just about fully attested within single, hour-long, mother-infant (age range approx. 15 months) conversations (Lederer, Gleitman, and Gleitman, 1995; Li, 1994; Geyer, 1997). Maternal usage "errors" in this regard (e.g., saying "Don't come your toys into the living room" or "Put your apple.") are rare to nonexistent. Thus, the information is both bountiful and reliable.

In sharp contrast, the correlation between seeing two entities (let us say, two frogs) and hearing a modified, definite NP referring to a member of the set rather than a bare NP is surprisingly weak ("the green frog," "the frog on the napkin" rather than just "the frog" or even "a frog"). The Brown-Schmidt et al. (2002) referential study of adults indicates that referential specificity is discourse defined, not just scene defined: A modified, definite NP description will happen largely on those occasions when (a) you see a pair of frogs, (b) the two frogs are the topic of conversation, (c) the conversation requires, for communication, that the two frogs be distinguished from each other, and (d) this distinction has not been established in sentences that preceded the one you are now hearing. Thus this information is less available and is less reliable. Accordingly, novices often fail to use scene cues to disambiguate sentences, but show reasonable (but not perfect) understanding when the discourse goals specify the need for modification. By hypothesis, then, the youngest learners come to use syntactic-distributional evidence before this particular contextual evidence because evidence concerning the former has been, in the child's experience, easier to come by. To the naked eye, these early tendencies to make systematic use of only a subset of the cues used by adult comprehenders might masquerade as a modular architecture. In this regard, it is very important to keep in mind that our participants' disinclination to rely on contextual cues is by no means across the board. If such a cue is rendered relevant by the discourse, our child subjects were able to use it.

In sum, the comprehension machinery appears to be incremental and interactive from the earliest developmental times that we can measure it, sensitive to a variety of cues to sentential meaning. But all the same we see a change in the reliance on (or weighting of) several cues depending on the amount and generality of information that the learner has accrued concerning each cue type.

CLOSING REMARKS: THE PLACE OF COMPREHENSION IN A THEORY OF LANGUAGE ACQUISITION

In closing, we want to take a little space here to ask how "learning to parse" fits in with other topics relevant to language learning.

Phrase Learning and Word Learning

We have focused in this paper on the question of how the child and adult listener goes about resolving the meaning of an ambiguous phrase. Several sources of evidence, including scene and distributional evidence, are brought to bear, and the reliance on these over development will differ either because of their informativeness for a particular item, or because the relevant evidence is not yet in place in the young child. In this regard, resolving the meaning of a PP for the child (and the adult) resembles the computational problem facing a language user when he or she is asked to discover the intended meaning of other abstract expressions, notably the computational problem facing a language user when he or she is asked to discover the intended meaning of a new word. Multiple sources of evidence—the observed scenes, the distribution of syntactic structures it can reside in, and its discourse setting—are in this case also potentially available. However, depending on the actual meaning of this word, only some of these sources are likely to be informative; for instance, it is easier to see that somebody is *jumping* than to see that he is *thinking*, and so the observed scene is more informative for the first of these words than it is for the second. Moreover, some potentially informative sources of evidence require time and experience to construct. For instance, the syntactic environment of *think* is highly predictive of aspects of its meaning: This word, like many verbs whose semantic content pertains to mental acts and states, occurs with tensed sentence complements (compare "John thinks that the ceiling is falling" with the nonoccurring "John jumps that the ceiling is falling,"; see Gleitman, 1990). Yet the youngest learners cannot exploit this evidentiary source because they have not yet acquired the requisite syntactic knowledge of the exposure language (Gleitman, 1990 and sources cited earlier in this chapter).

In the case of PPs occurring in an utterance, the child listener is also faced with the problem of discovering the conditions under which a linguistic expression has a particular abstract meaning, that is, when it denotes a contrastive property of an object relative to another object. It is not easy to look out into the world to see when such meanings arise (since relationships like these are typically in the eye of the beholder, who in this case is the speaker). In contrast, distributional facts in the sentence itself are there for the taking by the listener and constrain meaning in the relevant ways. Therefore, these ought to exert an early influence. Discourse evidence, which often points toward how the speaker perceives the world (such as communicative acts that align the speaker's and listener's discourse model of the world), ought to facilitate the discovery of the appropriate conditions for referential specificity. And, indeed, our Rabbit-Walrus study suggests that these discourse functions of aligning perceptions and goals exert their expected influence on this sort of meaning discovery.[9]

"Parsability" as a Factor in Linguistic and Psycholinguistic Theorizing? Parsibly!

We believe our work also has implications for psycholinguistic theorizing on grammatical formalisms that are designed for language use. As mentioned in the introduction, recent experimental work on adult sentence processing has had much to say about grammatical representation in the mind. In particular, the data have been most consistent with the notion that grammatical information is highly *lexicalized*, in the sense that a lexical event triggers the computation of detailed grammatical structures that can permit the local processing of what (on the surface) appears to be longer-distance grammatical and semantic relationships (e.g., Srinivas & Joshi, 1999; MacDonald et al. 1994; Trueswell & Tanenhaus, 1994; Kim et al. 2002). The fact that, as predicted, young children show an early greater reliance on lexical information of this sort lends support to the notion that grammars are organized along these lines and implicitly implemented as such in the comprehension system.

Indeed, we believe it is no accident that the grammatical formalisms most compatible with this psycholinguistic account have been independently developed within computational circles, especially among those interested in formalisms for natural language parsing. Here, many have noted the computational advantages of lexicalized/localized structure (CCG, Steedman, 2000; LTAG, Joshi et al., 1991; HPSG, Pollard & Sag, 1987; LFG, Bresnan & Kaplan, 1982) and the need for and success of statistical mechanisms in parsing (Srinivas & Joshi, 1999; Collins & Brooks, 1995; Marcus, 1995; Kim et al., 2002). This consistency of theory suggests that linguistic and psycholinguistic formalisms are causally related to an extent not appreciated a decade or two ago. A particular contribution from the psycholinguistic inquiries of the past two decades has been to add *incrementality* as a desideratum: Language design is what it is, in part, because the sentence has to be interpreted in real time. Syntactic and semantic formalisms, if they are to be psychologically plausible, need to allow for the incremental building of structure and the rapid computation of contextual dependencies reflected in the meaning of these structures (for some of the most elegant and linguistically sophisticated discussions of these matters, see Altmann & Steedman, 1988; Sedivy et al., 1999; Sedivy, 2002).

In the present paper, we have taken the position, in common with many prior researchers, that the problems of learning vocabulary and language-specific syntax also fit into the same broad picture; that is, that language design is also constrained by aspects of how it is learned (e.g., the introduction of "learnability constraints" such as those proposed by Wexler and Culicover, 1980; Wexler & Hamburger, 1973, Osherson & Weinstein, 1982; Pinker, 1984; but see also Seidenberg, 1997, and Elman, 1993, for related, but quite different, perspectives on how learning may constrain language design). Here again we have tried to show that, for psychological plausibility, the notion of incrementality enters into the account but in new ways. First, there is a natural ("intrinsic") ordering among features of the evolving language system. As one crucial instance, the child receives a database of reliable lexical evidence that can be deciphered, stored, and organized early on. The individual verbs have their discernable distributions (e.g., instruments for hitting acts) and are similarly selective in their syntactic structures. The lexically specific learned facts leave their footprints in the design of the mature system, which, as we have stated above, continues to operate from lexically derived information. Second, there are practical constraints on which evidence will come on line when, as the reliability of the evidence for constructing databases differs in the input. Overall, children's comprehension ability looks the way it does because they are building a linguistic ladder, so to speak, as they are climbing it.

NOTES

1. Such an assumption seems even less radical and more familiar when we reconsider the often unspoken assumptions behind such measures as reaction time, as assessed by the stroke of a finger on a key or lever. Nevertheless, we are not advocating that psycholinguistics or any other research field rely on a single experimental technique. The linking assumptions of this new measure certainly need to be more carefully stated and tested as we proceed with its development.
2. Throughout, we use the abbreviations NP (Noun Phrase), VP (Verb Phrase) and PP (Prepositional Phrase).
3. In certain ways, our developmental account (and the CBL account generally) is reminiscent of the Bates & MacWhinney's (1987) Competition Model. For instance, both theories assume constraint-satisfaction mechanisms for language discovery and

use, and therefore emphasize information reliability when accounting for developmental patterns. However, most of the similarities end there. One crucial difference is that the CBL account assumes a central role for detailed linguistic representations in language use along multiple, partially independent dimensions (phonology, syntax, semantics). Representational modularity in the presence of interactive processing, a key assumption of CBL, is crucial for accounting for a broader range of phenomena (Trueswell & Tanenhaus, 1994, see also Jackendoff, 2002).

4. Alternatively, this could be evidence that children are "mini-minimal-attachers," showing a general structural bias toward VP-attachment. This issue has been addressed below and reported in Snedeker, Thorpe, & Trueswell (2001).

5. This means that some inherent ordering to cue use is imposed even on a constraint-based system, since the building of certain linguistic representations (i.e., evidential sources), serve as prerequisites to building other, often higher level, linguistic representations (see Fisher & Gleitman, 2002).

6. We say this because, for instance, online measures need to be collected on our discourse-based (Rabbit-Walrus) effects, to assure us that children are not using discourse cues at a later stage of processing, such as during revision. A pattern of this sort would be consistent with a modular developmental account.

7. If the highly "incremental" approach to parsing is correct - i.e., if the listener makes use of information as soon as it becomes available - then parsing in different languages can look materially different. For instance, in English, certain information that can be gleaned from the subject NP usually becomes available first, temporally preceding information about the verb and about the verb's complement structure. In other languages, object NP's or main V's canonically capture first serial position. Depending on the scope and reliability of "first received" information, later-arriving information is often redundant. Parsing in one language might be more "verb-based" and in another more "noun-based" depending on just when, given serial ordering facts, each reaches the ear. Thus, a uniform system might be at work across languages but differ in how information is weighed and used (Kaiser & Trueswell, in progress). To the extent that this is so, it follows that the infant is building comprehension machinery that is specifically tailored to exploit surface properties of the exposure language.

8. In a reasonable world, understanding what these verbs mean equivalently predicts these complementation likelihoods. To that extent one might hold that the language learner never has to record the frequency with which each verb occurs with a VP-attached PP complement. This expectation is a consequence of the verb's logical structure (for a relevant linguistic discussion, see e.g., Baker, 2001; Jackendoff, 2002), a matter of knowing the semantics of the verb rather than a matter of knowing probabilistic facts about its distributional contexts (which latter could arise as an artifact of the meaning). However, these two approaches to how children come to acquire verb complement relations (via the semantics or via the observed distributions) are not as different as they may seem at first glance. They are different only insofar as the claim can be sustained that the verb meanings are acquired independently of and prior to acquiring knowledge of their distributional structure. And this does not seem to be the case. Current evidence is consistent with a word-learning process that uses situational and distributional evidence interactively to converge on the semantics of verbs—much like the interactive comprehension-learning machinery

that is the topic of the present paper; for many kinds of words, it just isn't possible to learn their meanings before and independently of acquiring information about their distributional structure (Gleitman, 1990; Gillette et al., 1999; Gleitman & Trueswell, forthcoming).

9. One might wonder whether verb learning is also influenced by how discourse and joint attention shape a listener's perception of the world. We have been asking this very question in ongoing research, where we find that the alignment of the speaker's and listener's perception of the scene does indeed partially influence a listener's guess of verb use (Nappa, Trueswell, & Gleitman, in progress).

REFERENCES

Altmann, G., & Steedman, M. (1988). Interaction with context during human sentence processing. *Cognition, 30,* 191-238.

Baker, M. C. (2001). *The atoms of language: The mind's hidden rules of grammar* Basic Books.

Bates, E., & MacWhinney, B. (1987). *Competition, variation, and language learning. In B. MacWhinney (Ed.),* Mechanisms of language acquisition. (pp. 157-193) Hillsdale, NJ.: Lawrence Erlbaum Associates.

Boland, J., & Cutler, A. (1996). Interaction with autonomy: Multiple output models and the inadequacy of the Great Divide. *Cognition, 58,* 309-320.

Bresnan, J., & Kaplan, R. (1982). Lexical functional grammar: A formal system of grammatical representation. In J. Bresnan (Ed.), *Mental representation of grammatical relations.* Cambridge, MA: MIT Press.

Britt, M. A. (1994). The interaction of referential ambiguity and argument structure in the parsing of prepositional phrases. *Journal of Memory and Language, 33,* 251-283.

Brown-Schmidt, S., Campana, E., & Tanenhaus, M. K. (2002). Reference resolution in the wild: On-line circumscription of referential domains in a natural, interactive problem-solving task. *Proceedings of the 24th annual conference of the Cognitive Science Society.* Hillsdale, NJ: Lawrence Erlbaum.

Carlson, G.N., & Tanenhaus, M. K. (1988). Thematic roles and language comprehension. In W. Wilkins (Ed.), *Syntax and Semantics, Vol. 21: Thematic Relations,* pp. 263-289. Academic Press.

Collins, M., & Brooks, J. (1995). Prepositional phrase attachment through a backed-off model. *Proceedings of the third workshop on very large corpora* .

Cooper, R.M. (1974). The control of eye fixation by the meaning of spoken language. *Cognitive Psychology, 6,* 84-107.

Crain, S., & Steedman, M. (1985). On not being led up the garden path: The use of context by the psychological parser. In D. Dowty, L. Karrattunen, & A. Zwicky (Eds.), *Natural language parsing: Psychological, computational, and theoretical perspectives.* Cambridge, MA: Cambridge University Press.

Crain, S., & Thornton, R. (1998). *Investigations in universal grammar: A guide to experiments on the acquisition of syntax and semantics.* Cambridge, MA: MIT Press.

Ferreira, F., & Clifton, C. Jr. (1986). The independence of syntactic processing. *Journal of Memory and Language, 25,* 348-368.

Ferreira, F. & Henderson, J.M. (1991). How is verb information used during syntactic parsing? In G. B. Simpson (Ed.), *Understanding word and sentence.* North Holland: Elsevier Science Publishers.

Fisher, C. (1996). Structural limits on verb mapping: The role of analogy in children's interpretations of sentences. *Cognitive Psychology, 31*(1), 41-81.

Fisher, C., Gleitman, H., & Gleitman, L. (1991). On the semantic content of subcategorization frames. *Cognitive Psychology, 23*(3), 331-392.

Fisher, C., & Gleitman, L. (2002). Breaking the Linguistic Code: Current Issues in

Early Language Learning. In C.R. Gallistel (Ed.) *Steven's handbook of experimental psychology: Vol. 2, Learning, motivation and emotion.* John Wiley & Sons: New York.

Frank, R. (1998). Structural complexity and the time course of grammatical development. *Cognition, 66,* 249-301.

Frazier, L. (1987). Sentence processing: A tutorial review. In M. Coltheart (Ed.), *Attention and performance XII: The psychology of reading.* Hillsdale, NJ: Erlbaum.

Frazier, L. (1989). Against lexical generation of syntax. In W. D. Marslen-Wilson (Ed.), *Lexical representation and process.* Cambridge, MA: MIT Press.

Frazier, L., & Fodor, J. D. (1978). The sausage machine: A new two-stage parsing model. *Cognition, 6,* 291-325.

Frazier, L., & Rayner, K. (1982). Making and correcting errors during sentence comprehension: Eye movements in the analysis of structurally ambiguous sentences. *Cognitive Psychology, 14,* 178-210.

Garnsey, S. M., Pearlmutter, N. J., Myers, E., & Lotocky, M. A. (1997). The contributions of verb bias and plausibility to the comprehension of temporarily ambiguous sentences. *Journal of Memory and Language, 37,* 58-93.

Gillette, J., Gleitman, L., Gleitman, H., & Lederer, A. (1999) Human simulations of vocabulary learning, *Cognition, 73,* 153-190.

Gleitman, L. (1990). The structural sources of verb learning. *Language Acquisition, 1,* 3-35.

Gleitman, L., & Gleitman, H. (1970) *Phrase and paraphrase.* New York: Norton.

Gleitman, L., & Gleitman, H. (1997) What is a language made out of? *Lingua 100,* 29-55.

Goodluck, H. & Tavakolian, S. (1982). Competence and processing in children's grammar of relative clauses. *Cognition, 11,* 1-27.

Geyer, H. (1997). Subcategorization as a predictor of verb meaning: Evidence from modern Hebrew. Unpublished manuscript, University of Pennsylvania.

Hudson, C. L., & Newport, E. L. (2003). Regularizing unpredictable variation in the transition from pidgin to creole: An experimental investigation of the role of adult learners in pidgin/creole development. Manuscript submitted for publication.

Hurewitz, F., Brown-Schmidt, S., Thorpe, K., Gleitman, L., & Trueswell, J. (2000) One frog, two frog, red frog, blue frog: Factors affecting children's syntactic choices in production and comprehension. *Journal of Psycholinguistic Research, 29,* 597-626.

Hurewitz, F., Brown-Schmidt, S., Trueswell, J., & Gleitman, L. (in progress). The contribution of conversation goals and verb-preferences to children's syntactic decisions.

Jackendoff, R. (2002). *Foundations of language.* Oxford: Oxford University Press.

Joshi, A., Vijay-Shanker, K. & Weir, D. (1991). The convergence of mildly context sensitive formalisms. In P. Sells, S. Shieber, & T. Wasow (Eds.), *The processing of linguistic structure,* 31-91. Cambridge, MA: MIT Press.

Kim, A., Srinivas, B., & Trueswell, J.C. (2002). The convergence of lexicalist perspectives in psycholinguistics and computational linguistics. In P. Merlo, & S. Stevenson (Eds.), *Sentence processing and the lexicon: Formal, computational and experimental perspectives.* Philadelphia: John Benjamins Publishing.

Landau, B., & Gleitman, L. (1985) *Language and experience.* Cambridge, MA: Harvard University Press.

Lederer, A., Gleitman, L., & Gleitman, H. (1995) Verbs of a feather flock together: Structural properties of maternal speech. In M. Tomasello, & E. Merriam (Eds.), *Beyond words for things: Acquisition of the verb lexicon.* New York: Academic Press.

Li, P. (1994). Maternal verb usage in Mandarin Chinese. Unpublished manuscript, University of Pennsylvania.

MacDonald, M. C. (1994). Probabilistic constraints and syntactic ambiguity resolution. *Language and cognitive processes, 9,* 157-201.

MacDonald, M. C., Pearlmutter, N. J., & Seidenberg, M. S. (1994). The lexical nature of syntactic ambiguity resolution. *Psychological Review, 101,* 676-703.

Marcus, G. F. (2000). Pabiku and Ga Ti Ga: Two mechanisms infants use to learn about the world. *Current Directions in Psychological Science, 9*(5), 145-147.

Marcus, M. (1995). New trends in natural language processing: Statistical natural language processing. *Proceedings of the National Academy of Science, 92*, 10052-10059.

Marslen-Wilson, W. D., & Tyler, L. K. (1987). Against modularity. In J. Garfield (Ed.), *Modularity in knowledge representations and natural language understanding*. Cambridge, MA: MIT Press.

McClelland, J. L. (1987). The case for interactionism in language processing. In M. Coltheart (Ed.), *Attention and performance XII*. London: Erlbaum.

Nappa, R., Trueswell, J., & Gleitman, L. (in progress) Referential cues to perspective verbs.

Osherson, D.N., & Weinstein, S. (1982). Criteria of language learning. *Information and Control 52*(2), 123-138.

Pinker, S. (1984) *Language learnability and language development*, Cambridge MA: Harvard Univ. Press.

Pollard, C., & Sag, I. (1987). *Information-based syntax and semantics*. CSLI Lecture Notes.

Rayner, K., Carlson, M., & Frazier, L. (1983). The interaction of syntax and semantics during sentence processing. *Journal of Verbal Learning and Verbal Behavior, 22*, 358-374.

Saffran, J., Newport, E., & Aslin, R. (1996). Word segmentation: The role of distributional cues. *Journal of Memory and Language, 35*, 606-621.

Sedivy, J. (2002). Invoking discourse-based contrast sets and resolving syntactic ambiguities. *Journal of Memory and Language*, 341-370.

Sedivy, J. Tanenhaus, M., Chambers, C., & Carlson, G. (1999). Achieving incremental semantic interpretation through contextual representation. *Cognition, 71*, 109-147.

Seidenberg, M .S. (1997). Language acquisition and use: learning and applying probabilistic constraints. *Science, 275*, 1599-1604.

Snedeker, J., & Gleitman, L. R. (in press). Why it is hard to label our concepts. In Hall, & Waxman (Eds.) *Weaving a lexicon*. Cambridge, MA: MIT Press.

Snedeker, J., Thorpe, K., & Trueswell, J. C. (2002). On choosing the parse with the scene: The role of visual context and verb bias in ambiguity resolution. *Proceedings of the 22nd annual conference of the Cognitive Science Society*, Edinburgh, Scotland.

Snedeker, J., & Trueswell, J. C. (submitted). The developing constraints on parsing decisions: The role of lexical-biases and referential scenes in child and adult sentence processing.

Spivey, M. J., Tanenhaus, M. K., Eberhard, K. M., & Sedivy, J. C. (2002). Eye movements and spoken language comprehension: Effects of visual context on syntactic ambiguity resolution. *Cognitive Psychology, 45*, 447-481.

Spivey-Knowlton, M., & Tanenhaus, M. K. (1994). Referential context and syntactic ambiguity resolution. In C. Clifton, Jr., & L. Frazier, et al. (Eds.) *Perspectives on sentence processing*. Hillsdale, NJ: Lawrence Erlbaum Associates.

Srinivas, B., & Joshi, A. K. (1999). Supertagging: An approach to almost parsing. *Computational Linguistics, 252*(2), 237-265.

Steedman, M. (1995). *Computational aspects of the theory of grammar*. Cambridge, MA: MIT Press.

Steedman, M. (2000). *The syntactic process*. Cambridge, MA: MIT Press/Bradford Books.

Tabossi, P., Spivey-Knowlton, M. J., McRae, K., & Tanenhaus, M. K. (1994). Semantic effects on syntactic ambiguity resolution: Evidence for a constraint-based resolution process. In C. Umilta, & M. Moscovitch (Eds.), *Attention and performance 15: Conscious and nonconscious information processing*. Cambridge, MA: MIT Press.

Tanenhaus, M. K., Spivey-Knowlton, M. J. (1996). Eye-tracking. *Language & Cognitive Processes, 11*(6), 583-588.

Tanenhaus, M. K., Spivey-Knowlton, M. J., Eberhard, K. M., & Sedivy, J. C. (1995). Integration of visual and linguistic information in spoken language comprehension. *Science, 268*, 1632-1634.

Taraban, R., & McClelland, J. (1988). Constituent attachment and thematic role assignment in sentence processing: Influences of content-based expectations. *Journal of Memory and Language, 27*, 1-36.

Trueswell, J. C. (1996). The role of lexical frequency in syntactic ambiguity resolution. *Journal of Memory and Language, 35*, 566-585.

Trueswell, J. C., & Kim, A. E. (1998). How to prune a garden-path by nipping it in the bud: Fast-priming of verb argument structures. *Journal of Memory and Language, 39*, 102-123.

Trueswell, J. C., Sekerina, I., Hill, N. M., & Logrip, M. L. (1999). The kindergarten-path effect: Studying on-line sentence processing in young children. *Cognition, 73*, 89-134.

Trueswell, J. C., & Tanenhaus, M. K. (1991). Tense, temporal context and syntactic ambiguity resolution. *Language and Cognitive Processes, 6*(4), 303-338.

Trueswell, J. C., & Tanenhaus, M. K. (1994). Toward a lexicalist framework for constraint-based syntactic ambiguity resolution. In C. Clifton, K. Rayner, & L. Frazier (Eds.), *Perspectives on sentence processing.* Hillsdale, NJ: Erlbaum.

Trueswell, J. C., Tanenhaus, M. K., & Garnsey, S. M. (1994). Semantic influences on parsing: Use of thematic role information in syntactic ambiguity resolution. *Journal of Memory and Language, 33*, 285-318.

Trueswell, J. C., Tanenhaus, M. K., & Kello, C. (1993). Verb-specific constraints in sentence processing: Separating effects of lexical preference from garden-paths. *Journal of Experimental Psychology: Learning, Memory and Cognition, 19*(3), 528-553.

Wexler, K., & Culicover, P. (1980). *Formal principles of language acquisition.* Cambridge, MA: MIT Press.

Wexler, K., & Hamburger, H. (1973). On the insufficiency of surface data for the learning of transformational languages. In K. J. J. Hintikka, J. M. E. Moravcsik, & P. Suppes, (Eds.), Approaches to natural language. *Proceedings of the 1970 Standard Workshop on Grammar and Semantics* (pp. 167-179). Dordrecht: Reidel.

11

Now You See It, Now You Don't: Mediating the Mapping between Language and the Visual World

GERRY T. M. ALTMANN
YUKI KAMIDE

The goal of much psycholinguistic research is to understand the processes by which linguistic input is mapped onto a hearer's mental representation of his or her world. Within the context of a sentence such as "The mouse chased the cat into the basket," we can ask questions such as "At what stage is the cat interpreted as the thing being chased?" "At what stage do we determine which cat?" and, more generally, "How, and when, do we map the components of a sentence onto components of the world?" Historically, there has been somewhat of a shift in respect of the answer to these questions. In the 1960s, "click-detection" studies suggested the possibility that interpretation may be bounded by clausal structure, with clause boundaries being the site of significant processing effort (see Fodor, Bever, & Garrett, 1974, for review); in the 1980s, researchers proposed that interpretation does not "lag" behind syntactic parsing, but takes place incrementally, as each word is encountered (Altmann & Steedman, 1988; Crain & Steedman, 1985; Tyler & Marslen-Wilson, 1977); and more recently, it has been demonstrated that interpretation can on occasion be driven by expectations made on the basis of linguistic input that precedes the actual linguistic items that confirm those expectations (Altmann, 1999; Altmann & Kamide, 1999; Tanenhaus, Carlson, & Trueswell, 1989). In this chapter, we review a number of these latter studies. Specifically, we explore the timing of interpretive processes in relation to the mapping of language onto a concurrent visual world.

We shall review first a series of studies that explore the mapping of sentences onto the visual world and that show that the processor is able to anticipate what is likely to be referred to next. We then review a series of studies that show how, in fact, the mapping is not onto the visual world but rather onto a mental world; this is shown by exploring patterns of eye movements when the visual world is absent at the time of the linguistic input , and, in other studies, when the visual world remains constant, but certain "facts" about that world are changed in the linguistic context that precedes the target sentence . Finally, we review a study that delves a little deeper into the relationship between linguistic structure and the structure of events that are portrayed in the visual world. This last study demonstrates additional complexities regarding the interpretation of the visual world. With reference to thematic interpretation (the interrelation of the entities referred to by that sentence in respect of their roles within the event described by that sentence), we shall conclude in the final section that the interpretation of a sentence situated in a visual world may be as much to do with non-linguistic, primarily visually driven, processes as with linguistic processes.

BACKGROUND: MAPPING SENTENCES ONTO THE VISUAL WORLD

The goal of much work within the "visual world paradigm" (monitoring eye movements around a visual scene in response to a concurrent linguistic input: Cooper, 1974; Tanenhaus, Spivey-Knowlton, Eberhard, & Sedivy, 1995) has been to investigate how (and when) the language that we hear makes contact with the world that we see. The evidence to date suggests that certain aspects of the language make contact with the visual world at the theoretically earliest opportunity. For example, Allopenna, Magnuson, and Tanenhaus (1998) asked subjects to "Pick up the candle. Now put it…" in the context of a visual scene containing, among other things, a candle and a piece of candy. They found that looks to both the candy and the candle increased as more of the word *candle* was heard, but that soon after its acoustic offset, looks to the candy decreased while looks to the candle continued to increase. This study demonstrated a standard "competitor" effect as predicted by the cohort model of auditory word recognition (e.g., Marslen-Wilson, 1987). Allopenna et al. also observed increased looks to a *rhyme* competitor (e.g., towards a *handle*) during *candle*, suggesting that lexical hypotheses may be activated according to the partial fit between the acoustic input and a corresponding lexical hypothesis (presumably, as a function of the goodness-of-fit of the lexical candidate given the acoustic input). Importantly, the study demonstrated these effects in real-time, as the acoustic signal unfolded. And given that it takes a certain amount of time to execute an eye movement once a signal to move the eyes has been given (estimated at around 200 ms.; e.g., Matin, Shao, & Boff, 1993; Saslow, 1967; and see Appendix I), the Allopenna et al. result demonstrated that the effects of acoustic mismatch manifested themselves in the eye-movement record at the theoretically earliest possible moment in time; thus, looks towards the candy began to decrease in comparison with looks towards the candle at the final segment of the input corresponding to *candle* (and looks towards the handle only began to increase a little later than, and not so sharply as, looks towards either the candle or the candy).

Allopenna et al.'s (1998) findings are significant for two reasons. The first, as just outlined, concerns the speed with which the acoustic input can be mapped onto the visual world, as evidenced by the eye-movement record. The second concerns the nature of competitor effects in lexical access and what they offer theories of sentence processing. The fact that during the earliest moments of *candy*, lexical hypotheses corresponding to both *candy* and *candle* are activated (cf. Marslen-Wilson, 1987; Zwitserlood, 1989) indicates that the processor in effect uses the currently available input (e.g., the input corresponding to the partial fragment *cand*) to anticipate possible ways in which the input might continue (with the rhyme findings indicating similar anticipation, albeit on the basis of a poorer fit between the acoustic input and the initial segment of the rhyming candidate). Presumably, it does this on the basis of lexical knowledge, itself derived on the basis of the processor's experience of how the acoustic input can unfold in different circumstances.

Thus, lexical knowledge constrains the range of continuations after the fragment *cand* to just those continuations corresponding to words compatible with *cand* as onset. But is such anticipation restricted only to lexical access? What might happen if, instead of "Pick up the candy," participants heard "Eat the candy"? On the basis of the processor's experience of how a *sentence* can unfold in different circumstances, lexical knowledge associated with *eat* might in principle constrain the range of continuations to just those continuations corresponding to things compatible with *eat* as the verb—namely to just edible things (these constraints are more often referred to as "selectional restrictions"). We might therefore expect looks to the candy (or any other edible thing) to start rising even before the word *candy* is heard. This would be similar to the situation in which looks to the candy start rising even before the final segment (/i/) is heard; the principle is the same, albeit applied across larger linguistic units.

With this last prospect in mind, Altmann and Kamide (1999) presented participants with an auditory sentence such as "The boy will eat the cake" and a concurrent scene portraying a boy, a cake, a toy train, a toy car, and a ball. The cake was the only object that satisfied the selectional restrictions of the verb (something edible). A second condition used sentences such as "The boy will move the cake" presented with the same scene. In this condition, the verb's selectional restrictions no longer exclusively selected for the cake: the other objects in the scene—the toy train, the toy car, and the ball—were all moveable and thus satisfied the selectional restrictions of the verb. The participants' task in this and all subsequent studies was simply to look at each scene and listen to each sentence (they were told that they would be asked questions about some of these pairings later, but they never were). We found that the probability of launching a saccadic eye movement to the cake was significantly higher in the *eat* condition than in the *move* condition and that this difference manifested itself even before the actual noun (*cake*) was encountered; the difference reached statistical significance before the onset of the expression *the cake* (note 1). These data were interpreted as suggesting that the processor, anticipating at the verb a forthcoming postverbal argument, immediately applies the semantic constraints afforded by the verb's selectional restrictions and immediately evaluates the result against, in this case, the visual context.

In a subsequent study (Experiment 2 in Kamide, Altmann, & Haywood, 2003), we explored whether this last effect was driven purely by the verb, or by the combination of the verb with its grammatical subject. The Altmann and Kamide (1999) result could be explained by assuming that the processor anticipated something that could plausibly be eaten, rather than something that could plausibly be eaten *given that the boy was to do the eating*. In the new study, we kept the verb the same but manipulated, across the conditions, the verb's grammatical subject—thus, for the verb *taste* (to pick one example), we contrasted "'The man will taste the beer" with "The child will taste the sweets" (sweets = candy). At the same time as they heard one or other of these sentences, participants saw a fairground scene portraying a young girl and a man, and among other things, a jar of sweets and a glass of beer. The stimuli were designed so that the man would more plausibly taste the beer than the sweets, while the opposite would be true for the child. In the event, we observed more anticipatory looks towards the beer at *taste* in "The man will taste the beer" than in "The girl will taste the sweets", and more looks towards the sweets at *taste* in "The girl will taste the sweets" than in "The man will taste the beer." To ensure that this result was not simply due to participants associating men with beer and children with sweets (irrespective of the verb), we had two other conditions also: "The man will ride the motorbike" and "The girl will ride the carousel" (the scenes contained these other objects also). The idea here was that if the anticipatory looks towards the beer or the sweets were independent of the verb, we would observe the same patterns in these latter conditions. But we did not; instead, there were more looks to the motorbike at *ride* after *the man* than after *the girl*, and conversely, for the carousel after *the girl*. The data thus showed that, in this experiment at least, it was the *combination* of the verb with its grammatical subject that drove the anticipatory process.

It is notable that these effects were observed at the verb, whose average duration was around 410 ms (range: 320-600 ms). Given that it takes around 150-200 ms to program and execute a saccadic eye movement (see Appendix I), it is all the more remarkable that we see evidence of the combination of the verb and its subject during the lifetime of the verb itself. Indeed, the effects appear to have occurred at the theoretically earliest possible moment—quite literally within moments of the lexical meaning of the verb being activated (and it is conceivable that these effects in fact occurred even before the point in the acoustic input at which each word became uniquely identifiable—information from the visual context could have constrained the interpretation of the unfolding auditory input). Further research, controlling for the time it takes to recognize each verb used in this study, would be required to establish the relationship between our combinatory effects and the dynamics of lexical access).

In each of these studies, anticipatory looks towards an object that would be referred to postverbally were found at the main verb. This may not be so surprising in light of the information conveyed by a verb. This includes its argument structure—a specification of what may come before and what may come after. However, anticipatory effects are not restricted to verbs; we have found similar anticipatory effects in Japanese (Experiment 3 in Kamide et al. 2003)—a language in which the main verb always comes at the end of the sentence. For example, the sentence corresponding to "The waitress will cheerfully bring the customer the hamburger" would be spoken as *"waitress*-nominative *customer*-dative *cheerfully hamburger*-accusative *bring"* (where *waitress*-nominative indicates that the Japanese word for *waitress* is followed by a nominatively case-marked particle). We presented Japanese participants with visual scenes portraying a waitress, a customer, a hamburger, and various other objects, and monitored their eye movements as they listened to this last sentence. We hypothesized that on hearing *customer*-dative, the processor would use the dative case-marking to interpret this expression as referring to a goal (the thematic role associated with a recipient in an act of transference initiated by the nominatively marked agent—the waitress). The processor could then anticipate a plausible theme object (that is, an object that could fill the theme role—the object being transferred). Thus, we predicted anticipatory eye movements towards the hamburger immediately after *customer*-dative (during *cheerfully*). We contrasted this last case with a condition with the sentence *"waitress*-nominative *customer*-accusative *cheerfully greet"* (the accusatively marked customer cannot be a goal, and thus no theme should be anticipated, and there should be no reason to look towards the hamburger). We found, as expected, more looks towards the hamburger in the first case (*customer*-dative) than in the second (*customer*-accusative).

Taken together, these data suggest that the processor can determine thematic fit between the language and the entities portrayed in the visual world (and, as we shall argue later, assign the appropriate thematic roles) in advance of linguistic material that will unambiguously signal which entity should receive which thematic role. Whether the processor does this by predicting (i.e., representing) future input and subsequent reference, or does this without making any assumptions at all regarding subsequent linguistic input, is something we shall leave until later discussion (informed, in part, by some of the studies that follow). In the meantime, we shall use the terms *prediction* and *anticipation* interchangeably and to refer, in the context of the present studies, to the process by which thematic dependencies can be established prior to the point at which those dependencies are unambiguously signaled within the linguistic input. Whether this process in fact involves the projection of structure (syntactic or otherwise) that is explicitly tagged as representing future input, or whether it does not, is less relevant to the present discussion than the fact that thematic dependencies *can* be computed in advance of their corresponding grammatical dependencies.

We turn now to the question to which the next two sections are devoted: To what extent do the anticipatory processes we have observed generalize from processing language in the context of the visual world to processing language in the context of a *mental* world? Does the processor, in the visual-world paradigm, map language onto the visual world (or its perceptual correlate) directly, or does it instead map language onto a mental representation of that world that has an existence that is, at least in part, independent of the perceptual correlates of the visual world?

MAPPING LANGUAGE ONTO THE MENTAL WORLD: THE BLANK-SCREEN PARADIGM

One of the defining features of language is that it enables objects to be referred to even though they are absent from the immediate context. It is this feature of language that requires the maintenance/recall of a mental correlate of whatever is being referred to. Thus, seeing a cake, which then disappears, leaves an episodic trace that can form the basis for subsequent reference. We can make use of this to explore whether the eye movements we have observed in our previous studies are contingent on the object to which those movements are directed being present in the visual context—if it is a mental representation of the objects, rather than the objects themselves, that drives those movements, we might see equivalent movements when the visual scene is *removed* before participants hear the description that, in previous studies, has mediated eye movements towards the different objects within the scene. Such a result would be consistent with recent findings that suggest that patterns of eye movements when recalling a stimulus, or information associated with a stimulus, reflect the spatial properties of the now-absent stimulus (e.g., Brandt &

Stark, 1997; Laeng & Teodorecu, 2002; Richardson & Spivey, 2000; Spivey & Geng, 2001; and see Spivey, Richardson, & Fitneva, this volume).

In a study based on the earlier Altmann & Kamide (1999) experiment (Altmann & Kamide, in press), we generated 20 visual scenes containing, to take one example, a man, a woman, a cake, and a newspaper. For each scene, two sentences were recorded; for this example, "The man will eat the cake" and "The woman will read the newspaper." The materials were designed so that there were always two animate and two inanimate objects, and each verb could apply to one of the inanimate objects (so there was only one edible object and one readable object in the scene just described). On each trial the visual scene was presented for five seconds. The screen then went blank, and after a 1 s delay, the auditory sentence was played. Participants were told that the sentence would describe something that might happen in the picture that had just been presented and that they would be asked some questions about the sentence and picture later in the experiment (in fact, this last phase never happened; this was simply a ruse to try and get participants to attend to both the picture and the subsequent sentence). We recorded participants' eye movements as they listened to the sentence (when the screen was blank).

We analyzed the data in a number of ways. First, and because we expected eye movements towards where the objects had been to be relatively scarce and somewhat inaccurate, we simply counted as a fixation any eye movements towards the quadrant where the corresponding object had been located (the scenes were constructed so that each object was in a separate quadrant). The graph in Figure 11.1 shows the percentage of trials with looks to each object synchronized against the speech input (see Appendix II for discussion of alternative ways of synchronizing and graphing such data). Thus, it shows that during, for example, *the man*, looks were directed to the quadrant that had contained the man on 16% of trials (in fact, this figure is the average of looks towards where the man had been during *the man* and looks towards where the woman had been during *the woman*, but for the sake of describing the data, we shall refer to the data in terms of the "man eating the cake" example). There are two aspects of these data that are noteworthy: First, as each object was referred to in the sentence, so the eyes were directed to where that object had been; there were more looks to where the man had been during *the man* than to where the woman had been (and conversely, for looks to the woman) and more looks to where the cake had been during *the cake* than towards where the newspaper had been. The fact that looks towards where the man had been increased during *will* is most likely a kind of "spillover," with looks during *will* still being in response to *the man*. Second, the increase in looks towards where the cake had been relative to looks towards where the newspaper had been became significant during the verb *eat*[2]. Thus, we observed in this study the same sensitivity to selectional restrictions as in previous studies, and with the same temporal

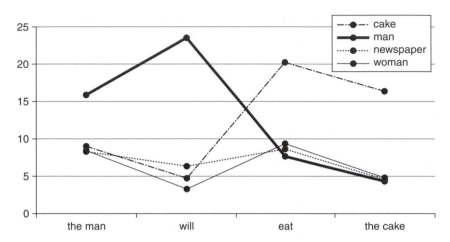

FIGURE 11.1. Percentage of trials with looks to each object (for the quadrant analysis). What is labeled as "looks to the cake" here is, in fact, the average of looks to the cake during *"the man"* and looks to the newspaper during *"the woman"* (in the condition *"the woman will read the newspaper"*). Similarly, what is labeled as "looks to the man" is, in fact, the average of looks to the man during *"the man"* and looks to the woman during *"the woman."*

dynamics, even though the visual scene was, in fact, absent during the auditory presentation of the target sentence.

Figure 11.2 shows the same data but now including as fixations only movements to the actual pixels which the object had previously occupied. Although broadly similar to the data graphed in Figure 11.1, there were statistically no more looks towards where the man had been during *the man* than towards where the woman had been—the difference became significant only during *will*. And overall, there were fewer trials with looks towards the "target" pixels. Nonetheless, the pattern of looks towards where the cake had been is essentially the same, with more looks towards this location than towards where the newspaper had been, both during the verb itself, and during *the cake*. Again, the fact that we observed the effect on the verb means that even here, when the image was *absent*, we observed the effects of verb semantics (selectional restrictions) at the theoretically earliest opportunity, within moments of lexical activation.

The data demonstrate that what we have termed *anticipatory eye movements*—language-mediated eye movements directed towards an object that is yet to be referred to in the linguistic input—are not simply an artifact that is contingent on the object being co-present with the linguistic stimulus. These movements are not driven by the visual world (in combination with the concurrent linguistic input) but are driven by the mental world—a world that encodes the spatial properties of the objects it contains.

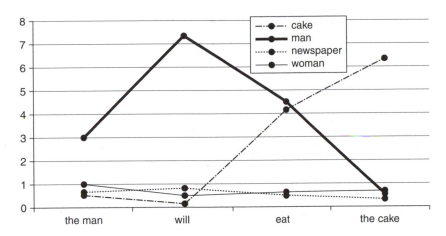

FIGURE 11.2. Percentage of trials with looks to each object, for the pixel analysis. The labeling convention used here is the same as that used in Figure 11.1.

Clearly, further research is required to explore further the mechanism underlying these data. For example, what would happen if participants saw a scene depicting a fireman and some objects, then a scene depicting a policeman and some other objects, and then one depicting a nurse? On hearing a sentence starting *The fireman…* would participants "retrieve" the mental representation corresponding to the first scene and thereafter behave in much the same way, and with the same temporal dynamics, as observed in the study just described? It is unlikely that our data are due to some form of visual iconic memory (the initial eye movements would "smear" the memory as the retinal input changed). Nonetheless, we do not know for how long such mental representations remain available, and to what extent (and to what level of detail) they can subsequently be retrieved. Studies of this kind are in the planning. For the present, it is enough to know that language-mediated eye movements toward a particular location are not contingent on the object that is about to be referred to actually being in that location. We explore this effect further in the next section.

MAPPING LANGUAGE ONTO THE MENTAL WORLD: DISCOURSE-MEDIATED EFFECTS

Why, in the previous study, did the eyes move to a particular location when there was nothing there? One possibility, proposed by Richardson and Spivey (2000), is based on the idea that very little information about one part of a visual scene is maintained internally when the eyes move to another part of the scene. They propose that the visual system instead uses the scene itself as a kind of external memory, using oculomotor coordinates (defined relative to the configuration of cues within the scene) as pointers towards this external memory (cf. Ballard, Hayhoe, Pook, & Rao 1997). The activation of these pointers causes the eyes to move to the corresponding coordinate from where information about the contents of that part of the scene can be retrieved. Interestingly, Richardson & Spivey (2000) demonstrated that these pointers are not necessarily determined by saccades to, and subsequent fixations on, absolute positions within the visual field, but can be determined relative to the configuration of the parafoveal information surrounding those positions (see Richardson & Spivey, 2000, Experiment 5). Thus, the encoding of these pointers need not require any eye movements per se. Our own effects, in the "blank-screen" experiment, can be explained in terms of a system that cues eye movements towards particular locations on the premise that further information about whatever is in that location might be retrieved once the eyes reach their destination. Hearing *the man* causes activation of the corresponding pointer, which, in turn, drives the eyes towards the corresponding location in order that further information might be gathered from the scene, despite the fact that the location will subsequently be found to be empty.

This last account, or at least one version of it, assumes that eye movements in the absence of a visual scene (i.e., the "blank-screen" case above) are due to the memory that something has been present at a particular location. In effect, the coordinate-as-pointer is the spatial component of the episodic trace of whatever had been there. But this assumes that the spatial representation that drove the eye movements in our blank-screen study relied on there actually having been something at a particular location (as defined relative to other cues within the scene) during a previous scan of the scene. But what would happen if the visual pointer corresponding to the *current* location of an object were at odds with the location of that object as encoded within some mental representation of that object? Which would win out?

To explore this question, we conducted a study in which participants would hear "The woman will pour the wine into the glass." — We knew from previous studies that during *the wine*, we would observe anticipatory looks to whatever the wine could be poured into (Experiment 1 in Kamide et al., 2003). But we were, in fact, interested in what would happen if participants heard "The woman will put the glass on the table. Then, she will pick up the wine, and pour it carefully into the glass." Critically, neither the glass nor the wine were on the table in the visual scene (in this example, they were on the floor). During *it carefully*, would eye movements be directed toward the actual glass (as depicted in the concurrent image) or towards the table—the putative location of the glass? (We included the adverb *carefully* in the critical region because of the short duration of *it*.)

We constructed 16 scenes, each of which was accompanied by one of two spoken stimuli. One of these corresponded to the example above, and the other corresponded to "The woman will wipe the table. Then, she will pick up the wine, and pour it carefully into the glass." This functioned as a control condition in which the glass was unmoved. In fact, we used the same acoustic token of "Then, she will pick up the wine, and pour it carefully into the glass" in both cases. There were two aspects to the data that warrant mention: first, there were fewer trials with looks towards the actual glass when the glass had "moved" (according to the context sentence) than when it had not (30% vs. 42%). Second, there were correspondingly more trials with looks towards the table when the glass had "moved" there than when it had not (18% vs. 4%). Thus, the "mental location" of the glass engendered a significant bias to look away from the actual glass and towards that location (the table).

On the one hand, these data seem to suggest that the mental location of the objects depicted in the visual scene can drive anticipatory eye movements. On the other hand, the data are also compatible with the view that the context sentence "The woman will put the glass on the table" sets up a simple association, through co-occurrence, between the glass and the table—on subsequently activating the representation of the glass (during *and pour it carefully*), the representation of the table is automatically activated because of this association and, hence, increased eye movements towards the table. If this is the correct explanation for the effect, it is certainly interesting that the system is so sensitive to even a single co-occurrence (with interesting consequences for how visual attention may be spuriously directed in real-world situations). We are currently exploring this possibility by using a control condition such as "The woman is too lazy to put the glass on the table. Instead, she will pick up the wine and pour it carefully into the glass." The point here is that the co-occurrence between the glass and the table is maintained, but the semantics indicates that the glass was unmoved. In the absence of the relevant data, however, we cannot rule out the possibility that co-occurrence information drives the effect in this case. But we do have alternative data that are suggestive of our original hypothesis. In another study, we presented participants with a scene depicting a woman, a bottle of water, a glass, and a mug. Concurrently, participants heard either "The woman will clean the glass. Then, she will pour the water into the glass" or "The woman will break the glass. Then, she will pour the water into the mug"(and again, the acoustic tokens corresponding to *she will pour the water into* were identical across conditions). We found significantly fewer anticipatory looks towards the glass during *the water* when the glass had been broken than when it had been cleaned (17% vs. 21%), and significantly more anticipatory looks towards the mug when the glass had been broken than when it had been cleaned (18% vs. 14%). Although these effects are small, they demonstrate a bias to look away from the object that is set up in the context as being an implausible location for the pouring (i.e., the glass when it has been broken), and to look towards the object that has become more plausible a location as a result (i.e., the mug when the glass has been broken). In this study there is no possibility that the data are confounded with co-occurrence phenomena.

The bias to look towards the mental location of the glass is entirely compatible with the spatial-pointer approach to visual encoding described earlier. Particularly so in the context of language comprehension as "simulation" (Barsalou, Simmons, Barbey, & Wilson, 2003). According to this view, a sentence such as "The woman will put the glass on the table" will engender a mental simulation of the described event, in which case the spatial pointer corresponding to the glass might be "adjusted" to reflect the new, simulated, position of the glass. An analysis of eye movements during the preamble "The woman will put the glass on the table" revealed that on only 30% of trials in which participants looked towards the mental location of the glass during the critical period ("'Then, she will pick up the wine and pour <u>it carefully</u> into the glass") had they previously moved their eyes, during the preamble, from the glass to the table. These data, although not conclusive, do suggest that *overt* perceptual simulation of the glass being moved to the table, in which the eyes "re-enact" the movement, is not a prerequisite for subsequent looks towards the mental location of the glass.

To summarize this section: The anticipatory eye movements that we have observed in previous studies (Altmann & Kamide, 1999; Kamide et al., 2003) do not appear to be contingent on a concurrent image; the locations to which eye movements are directed appear to be determined, at least in part, by the mental representation of the scene rather than by the scene itself. The spatial representations that drive the eye movements in these studies need not, therefore, rely on objects actually having occupied particular locations within the scene. In short, sentences are not mapped onto static representations of the concurrent visual input, but rather they are mapped onto interpreted, and dynamically changing, representations of that input.

MAPPING SENTENCE STRUCTURE ONTO EVENT STRUCTURE

Thus far, we have been concerned primarily with the interpretation of the linguistic input and the mapping of that input onto some representation of the visual scene. Knowledge of grammar enables this mapping. In fact, it enables the mapping between the form of a sentence and the structure of the *event* that sentence describes. We have so far ignored this aspect of language processing. Indeed, we have so far ignored this aspect of visual scene processing. Our studies have been quite artificial insofar as the sentences we have used are dynamically unfolding representations of events, while the scenes we have used are simply static representations of the objects that can take part in these events. They have no event structure per se, unlike the sentences onto which they are mapped. This has interesting consequences, which we explore in this final empirical section of the chapter—consequences for how the "mental locations" alluded to in the previous section can be determined, as well as for the nature of the processes that underpin the eye movement patterns we have observed across the range of studies reported here.

Events unfold in time, just as sentences do. They have a beginning and an end. Within a sentence, the combination of tense and aspect determine the beginning and end of the event that sentence describes. Real-world events are quite different from the static images we have employed in our previous studies: These images do not unfold in time (they could, and future research in our laboratory will employ moving images), nor do they indicate a beginning nor an end of any event. Indeed, they do not identify an event at all (although they could, and other studies, reviewed in Griffin, this volume, use static scenes that do identify specific events, such as "kicking"). Instead, they identify, at least as we have used them, *states*. That is, they identify the state of a part of the world before an event took place (such as before the man will eat the cake, or before the woman will pour the wine). But static images of these kinds need not identify just the *initial* state before an event will take place. They could, in principle, identify the *final* state after an event has taken place, or even a *substate* that is passed through as the event unfolds (a plate half-full of food could portray the state between the initial case when the plate is full and the final case when it is empty). Thus, the processor (not necessarily "the language processor") must determine which state is identified by the visual scene when mapping a sentence onto that scene (or vice versa). At what point does this happen? And on what basis?

In the Altmann and Kamide (1999) study, the sentence "The boy will eat the cake" was accompanied by a visual scene depicting a boy and a whole cake. The cake was uneaten, and the future tensed *will eat* indicated that the eating had yet to happen. Thus, the scene could be interpreted as representing the initial state before the event had taken place. If the sentence had been "The boy has eaten the cake," the past-tensed *has eaten* would have indicated that the eating had already happened (and concluded), and a scene that would be felicitous with such a sentence might include, for example, an empty plate on which the cake (or a piece of cake) could be inferred to have been located prior to the eating. In this case, the scene would be interpreted as representing the final state after the event had concluded. And in principle, the theoretically earliest moment at which it could be inferred that the scene portrays the initial state in the *will eat* case, or the final state in the *has eaten* case, is at the verb *eat* or *eaten*. But is this in fact when such inferences are made?

To explore this question, we conducted a study that manipulated the tense of the target sentence. Participants heard either "The man will drink the beer" or "The man has drunk the wine." Concurrently, participants saw a scene portraying a man, a full beer glass, an empty wineglass, and various other distractor objects. We reasoned that in the *will drink* condition, we would observe anticipatory eye movements during *drink* toward the beer. In the *has drunk* condition, we reasoned that we would observe eye movements towards the wineglass *if* the processor had (a) interpreted the scene on the basis of the tense marking as representing the final state of the drinking event and (b) assumed, on the basis of world-knowledge, that the most likely location of the object that was affected by the event (i.e., the thing that was drunk) was the wineglass.

We constructed 16 scenes similar to the one just described, and using the same "look and listen" paradigm as before recorded eye movements during the main verb (*drink* or *drunk*) in each sentence. We found that there was no difference in the number of anticipatory looks towards the beer as a function of the tense of the verb (33% and 32% in the future and past conditions respectively). Most likely, this is because the fragment *the man will drink* could continue *some beer* and the fragment *the man has drunk* could also continue *some beer*— in other words, the presence of the beer need not imply that no beer has been drunk (and although, in this example, the glass was full of beer, in the other examples used in this study, the target object corresponding to the beer was indeed compatible with both a future and past tense fragment). More interesting were the looks towards the wineglass. There were significantly more looks to this glass during *drunk* than during *drink* (30% vs. 22%). Of course, one might argue that this is simply because the *drunk* items might have been longer than the *drink* items—a difference of 54 ms, and perhaps the data are simply an artifact of the fact that the likelihood of directing a movement towards an item may be proportional to the amount of time in which to direct it. Two factors mitigate against this. First, there was no hint of an effect of verb on looks to the beer. Second, a post-hoc analysis revealed that there was in fact no correlation between the duration of the verb and the number of looks directed towards either the wineglass or the beer.

The data suggest that the system can very rapidly, at the earliest possible opportunity, use the tense marking associated with the verb to determine whether the visual scene is to be interpreted as indicating the initial or the final state associated with the event described by the sentence. Even more impressive is the fact that the system can equally rapidly determine (at least some of) the real-world contingencies associated with that event—namely, that the object affected by the event (and which underwent a change of state) was most likely associated with a particular location in the scene (the wineglass in the example given). Thus, during *has drunk*, the system may not know what it was that was drunk, but it has some idea (based presumably on probabilistic information derived from its experience of real-world contingencies) as to the likely location of whatever it was. Again, the spatial information that drives the eye movements need not be based on information contained within the scene, but can be based on information derived through knowledge that may be linguistic in origin (the discourse-mediated effects from the previous section) or nonlinguistic in origin (the "wine glass" effect just described).

We return to the significance of this result more fully in the theoretical section that follows.

INTERPRETING THE WORLD

What manner of process is responsible for the anticipatory eye movements we have observed in each of these studies? What kinds of representation drive the process? We shall start our exploration of these questions by considering first the anticipatory effects observed in the *will eat* and *will pour the wine* cases—namely, the cases where the language indicates an event that will occur at some time in the future.

One interpretation of our anticipatory effects is that the system uses information conveyed by the verb to project an upcoming noun-phrase constituent that is immediately interpreted with respect to both the selectional restrictions of the verb (and any real-world knowledge regarding the combination of that verb with its sentential subject) and the objects in the concurrent visual scene (or its mental equivalent). In effect, the system thus predicts which object in the concurrent scene will be referred to postverbally and, hence directs the eyes towards this object. In this case, the mental representation constructed at the verb includes a projection, forward in time, of the kind of constituent that will come next and of the semantic conditions that upcoming referring expression must meet. Another interpretation is based on a process that attempts to organize thematically the objects in the visual context, both with regard to each other and with regard to whatever representations are available (e.g., from the language) which may constrain their thematic interpretation. In effect, then, the processing system (linguistic and/or non-linguistic) assumes that some subset of the objects in the visual context will take part in the event being described linguistically and attempts to find roles for those objects as that description unfolds and as those roles become available. And when a role becomes available (e.g., at the verb) that can plausibly be assigned to a particular object, so attention is directed towards that object, and hence the "anticipatory" eye movements. This process need not entail any prediction of upcoming linguistic input—indeed, it makes no assumptions at all regarding subsequent linguistic input. At present, we do not have the data to decide between these two views.

We turn now to the *has drunk* condition described in the last section. How is that case to be explained? Looks towards the wineglass could not have been anticipatory in the sense of anticipating that the wineglass would be referred to next (it was not drinkable and thus violated the selectional restrictions of the verb—a condition that held across the different items in that study). The most parsimonious account of these data would be to assume that the same process underlies the *will eat* and *has drunk* cases. And again, there are two plausible interpretations of these data.

One version assumes, again, an account in which the language processor projects upcoming structure and immediately interprets it with reference to the concurrent visual scene. In this case, the processor anticipates that whatever will be referred to next has been drunk (to use that same example). At this point, knowledge of real-world contingencies identifies that the thing that has been drunk will be associated with some probability with the wineglass—the equivalent of a semantic priming effect, in essence (based on the real-world contingency between events of drinking and subsequently empty glasses). An alternative interpretation assumes the same process described earlier that attempts to organize thematically the objects in the visual scene with respect to each other and the available constraints that might limit the thematic interpretation of a particular object. In this case, the wineglass evokes the association with some probability that something may have been drunk from there. And as the language unfolds, a thematic role becomes available for something that must be drinkable and that must satisfy the semantic constraint of having been drunk. The processor then determines that the something associated with the wineglass can satisfy the role that has been made available for precisely such a thing.

What these last two interpretations have in common is that essentially the same process (augmented with a mechanism that can realize real world associative contingencies) can account for the future and past-tense conditions. The assumption that the scene represents the initial or final state in the event described by the language is implicit in the temporal constraints on the entities that are assumed to receive roles from the verb—they must either satisfy the condition of existing in the present, such that they can undergo a change in the future, or of existing in the past, such that they have already undergone the change effected by the event. While both alternatives have some a priori plausibility, we offer below yet another possibility, but one that we believe is even more plausible.

Dynamic Scene Perception

Whichever of the interpretations one subscribes to, language is seen as essentially driving inferences about the world in which the language is situated. These inferences may not be of the problem-solving variety, but may instead be the manifestation of low-level associative contingencies based on an experiential learning system. But whatever the nomenclature, language is interpreted, under this view, with reference to a static scene that is little more than the equivalent of a visually presented list of objects. The thematic interrelating of these objects is determined by the language. More plausible is the view that the representation of the scene is more than just an unstructured list of objects—indeed, no one would argue that this is all that such representations depict. In which case, what might the consequences be, for explaining the language-mediated eye movements that we have observed, of a richer interpretation of the visual scene?

One possibility is that the processing system can draw inferences about events that are likely to take place or to have taken place. The two panels in Figure 11.3 illustrate such inferences. In Panel A, the ball is on the desk, and that is all there is to it. In Panel B, it is on the edge of the desk and oriented in such a way as to suggest that it will fall off. Indeed, it is hard not to conclude that the ball will drop. Previous research (e.g., Freyd, 1987; Freyd, Pantzer, & Chenk, 1988) has found considerable evidence for the interpretation of static scenes in terms of an underlying temporal dynamics (and with reference to Figure 11.3B, there is a considerable literature on "representational momentum" — the implied motion of elements of a pattern; Freyd & Finke, 1984). The claim, then, is that the scene is interpreted with reference to the event structures that it supports (a claim that goes beyond the representational momentum findings based purely on motion events). But just how rich might this interpretation be? In the extreme, one might suppose that scene analysis involves the representation of "possible events" — a property of visual scenes that can be exemplified by the scenes used in the Kamide et al. (2003) study in which we contrasted "The man will ride the motorbike" with "The girl will ride the carousel" (see Figure 11.4). Real-world knowledge of children, of motorcyclists, and of the other objects in the scene, might define with some probability the likelihood that the man will drink/buy/look at the beer or ride/get on/lock up the motorbike, and with some lesser likelihood that he might ride/watch the carousel or eat/buy/steal the candy. Similarly for the girl. Within an interactive activation framework, there is no reason to suppose that the system *cannot* hold such representations in mind simultaneously (in much the same way as, during the process of lexical access, the system can hold in mind multiple representations of how the input perceived thus far might unfold). In this case, our explanation of the *will drink/has drunk* study in the last section changes from one where language drives inferences about the world in which the language is situated to one where language refers to inferences that have already been made in respect of how the world may change, or may have changed, on the basis of the objects and their configuration and real-world knowledge. For example, in the scene that accompanied the *will drink/has drunk* example (Figure 11.5), one might infer that the man will drink the beer, or that he

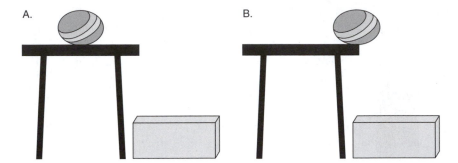

FIGURE 11.3.

poured the beer, or that he will give the beer to someone else, or that he will eat the cheese, and so on. One might also infer that the wineglass had had something in it that has been drunk, or that it will have something in it that will be drunk (some wine, or something yet to be brought into the scene). Less likely would be inferences such as that he will go shopping, is listening to the radio, is watching TV, or is about to brush his teeth. We return to discussion of the plausibility of such conjecture below. In the meantime, and on the assump-

FIGURE 11.4.

FIGURE 11.5.

tion that this conjecture is correct, we can explain the *has drunk* result by supposing that tense morphology restricts the set of inferences to a subset compatible with the corresponding event having taken place in the past, and a subset of this restricted set of possible events is further selected on the basis of verb semantics and real-world knowledge (so *has drunk* picks out a different subset of possible events than *has prepared*, for example).

Is it plausible to conjecture such a rich event-based interpretation of the visual scene? Given that most of our interactions with the outside world are not mediated by language, and that we can undeniably make inferences about what the state of that world will be or has been, we believe that it is entirely plausible. More contentious are the ideas that we maintain multiple interpretations of the visual world and that what we refer to here as *inference* may be based on low-level associative phenomena. Regarding the latter, the idea that the system is sensitive to probabilistic contingencies between objects is a natural one that is little different from the finding that the recognition of a word is sensitive to probabilistic contingencies between the object denoted by the word and other real-world objects. Seeing an empty wineglass may thus cause the activation of representations that reflect the contingencies between glasses and things having been drunk out of those glasses, or between wineglasses and things that could be poured into them prior to the drinking. We take the concept associated with an object to reflect, among other things (such as its physical form) the accumulated experience of the ways in which that object interacts with others in its real-world environment—an idea that is mirrored in the language literature as the view that the thematic roles that are associated with a verb reflect the accumulated experience of the entities that can play a role in the event to which a verb refers (McRae, Ferretti, & Amyote, 1997). In each case, the concept (whether associated with the object or with the verb-specific thematic role) is the accumulated experience of the interaction between one object and another. In this view, the *same* knowledge base underpins both the interpretation of the visual scene (in the absence of any language) and the interpretation of a sentence with reference to the verb's thematic roles and the entities filling those roles (in the absence of a concurrent visual scene).

To suggest that an empty glass activates representations reflecting not just the contingencies between glasses and things that may have been drunk (in the past) but also the contingencies between glasses and things that might be drunk (in the future) is no different than the proposal (or rather, the finding) that multiple representations become activated as a single word unfolds (e.g., Marslen-Wilson, 1987). And, if seeing two objects does not cause the activation of some representation of their plausible interaction, why does a parent so rapidly remove the piece of food from the hand of the infant who has picked that food up from the dirty sidewalk? Thus, we conjecture that, in certain circumstances at least, visual scenes are indeed interpreted with reference to plausible interactions that could take place, or may have taken place, between the objects within the scene. And hence, our further conjecture that in the experiments described above, language may, in effect, serve to pick out which of the several possible interactions is the right one to focus on.

The interpretations we have offered for our effects are not mutually exclusive; the effects we have observed may reflect the operations of all three kinds of process—the use of grammatical knowledge to predict upcoming linguistic material, the attempt to organize thematically the objects in the visual scene as new information about thematic roles becomes available through the language, and the use of probabilistic real world knowledge to interpret the scene in respect of the events which may have led to that state or which may ensue from that state (and the subsequent mapping of the language onto a subset of those events).

Mediating the Mapping between Language and the World

Thus far, we have focused on the knowledge that mediates the mapping between language and world and, thus, mediates the patterns of overt attention (as evidenced by the eye movements) we have observed in our studies. But what of the *representation* that mediates that mapping? Is it some kind of amodal representation onto which language and the visual world are each, separately, mapped? Or is it an intermodal representation that is not representationally distinct from the perception, or even sensation, of the world about us? If the latter, the representations that would be constructed in response to language input would simply be abstracted versions of the representations that would be constructed if the events described by the language were being played out, and observed by the hearer, in his or her immediate world (e.g., Altmann, 1997)—they would be abstract versions in the sense that mention of, for example, the dog in "Julie played with her dog" might not evoke the representation of a particular dog as might happen if Julie's dog were actually to be seen. Instead, it might evoke in a hearer who had never encountered that particular dog a representation that was abstracted across the hearer's experience of dogs. But except for this abstraction (and others corresponding to the act of play, and perhaps Julie herself), the mental representation would not be representationally distinct from that which would ensue if Julie were to be observed playing with her dog.

The idea that there is no representational distinction between the interpretation of language and the interpretation of the world about us is compatible with the approach to cognition termed *embodied cognition*. According to this view, cognition is rooted in the interactions between the cognitive agent and its environment and, hence, in perception and action (cognition is thus constrained by the sensory modalities through which we perceive and act on the world). The job of cognition is not to reconstruct, mentally, the external world, but rather, to enable interaction with that world. Cognition is therefore embodied in representations that are based on such interaction and is thus rooted in motoric and sensory representation (for recent reviews see Barsalou, 1999; Barsalou et al., 2003; Glenberg, 1997; Lakoff & Johnson, 1999; see also Spivey et al., this volume)[3]. However, the idea that the representations that result from language interpretation are in some sense equivalent to those that would result if the event being described by that language were being observed directly is not as straightforward as it may at first glance appear. There must be some distinction between the mental representation of the world (constructed through prior linguistic or visual input) and the real time perception of that world—if only because (a) the sensory component is lacking when we refer to an event that is not taking place before us, and (b) the temporal properties of the events that we can observe in the real world cannot be directly "mirrored" in the mental version of those events. An event that we observe to take place over a period of some minutes is not encoded in a form that itself takes a period of some minutes to unfold. And, of course, the temporal properties of events dynamically change as time passes: an event that was observed two days ago was not perceived, at the time of that event's unfolding, as taking place in the past, and its temporal encoding now (two days after) is different from the encoding it will have two months hence. To put it simply, the temporal properties of the perceived event and the corresponding temporal encoding within the mental representation of that event cannot be fully iso-morphic (but see, for example, Zwaan, 1996, and van der Meer, Beyer, Heinze, & Badel, 2002, for data suggesting some, perhaps limited, isomorphism). Thus, the distinction between the memory of an event and the perception of that event (in real time) does have implications for a representational distinc-tion between the two, at least with regard to the representation of the tempo-ral properties of that event and the sensory components that accompany real time perception.

While more general discussion of sensory encoding and temporal repre-sentation is beyond the remit of this chapter, their consideration does directly affect the interpretation of one of the studies described earlier: specifically, the study in which participants heard "The woman will put the glass on the table. Then, she will pick up the wine, and pour it carefully into the glass." If the rep-resentation that results from hearing "The woman will put the glass on the table" is in some sense equivalent to the representation that would result were one actually to see the glass moved to the table, how is one to explain the fact that participants do not perceive the visual world to change? The answer, of course, is that the sensory component that would accompany such direct per-ception is lacking (which may help explain, of course, how it is that we do not confuse memories of the world with the actual world). Future research, apply-ing the blank screen paradigm (see previous discussion) to this last study, will determine the extent to which looks to the glass, even when it had been "moved," were in part due to its sensory co-presence. But there is another dif-ference also, concerning the encoding of the temporal properties of the event that puts the glass on the table; it occurs at a different time (in the future) to that at which the glass is on the floor (in the present). It is because of this dif-ferent temporal index (cf. Zwaan, Langston, & Graesser, 1995) that both states—the glass on the floor and the glass on the table—can be represented simultaneously and this, presumably, is how each can influence the eye move-ment record.

One final issue, before concluding, concerns the mechanism that under-pins the eye movements we have observed across our studies. Much of the previous discussion has been concerned with why participants in the blank-screen study moved their eyes to where objects had previously been, or why, in the discourse-mediated case of the glass being moved to a new location, they moved their eyes towards this new location. This discussion did not, however, explain why the eyes moved *when* they moved. However, we would argue that the immediacy of those eye movements, and indeed, their automaticity (if one believes that they were indeed automatic—something that is yet to be estab-lished) is a consequence of the embodiment of cognition, and the idea that the representation of the world is embodied in the same neural substrate that sup-ports interaction with that world (cf. Glenberg, 1997). If this is in fact the case, then the representation of an object includes a component corresponding to the (episodic) experience of that object. That experience necessarily reflects the object's *location*, which will be encoded in the same substrate whose activation supported the experience of the object—in effect, when attending to an object in the visual scene, the neural substrate implicated in orienting towards it will encode its location. Thus, the representation of an object is the embodiment of the different aspects of its experience, and the (re)activation of that representation causes the reenactment of the experiential state(s) associated with the perception of that object (Barsalou et al., 2003). This reenactment—the reactivation of the embodied experience—entails the reactivation of the neural substrate implicated in orienting towards (or attending to) the object. Thus, and in the absence of any competing attentional demands, the eyes will move toward that object's location. This is a further reason (further to the "external memory" or visuospatial pointer account of vision) why, even though sentences are mapped onto internal representations of the concurrent visual input (see previous discussion), the eyes still move towards objects in the concurrent scene.

According to proponents of embodied cognition, the same representational medium encodes the interpretation of both visual and linguistic input, namely, that medium which supports *interaction* with the external world. However, there may be representational differences in the encodings that relate to the *content* of the representations (due to abstraction and the presence or absence of concurrent sensory input). Our data do not address directly the nature of the embodiment, or even whether the representation may instead be amodal (and as such, divorced from the perception that gave rise to that representation). What we do believe, however, is that our data have an experiential basis—our experience of how the world unfolds, whether in respect to objects or words, determines how we perceive that unfolding. And as it unfolds, so we anticipate the consequences of that unfolding. Future research will elucidate further the degree to which the interpretation of language, when situated in the visual world, is mediated by the interpretation of that world.

CONCLUSION

The interpretation we have arrived at of our data is that, in certain circumstances at least, the interpretation of language is predicated on an understanding of the world which that language can describe. The *will drink/has drunk* case (see previous discussion) can be interpreted in precisely this way, such that language is used to refer to inferences already made on the basis of the visual input and real-world knowledge about the contingencies between different objects in particular configurations. This would help explain the extraordinary rapidity with which language makes contact with the visual world—at the theoretically earliest opportunity, and with what seems to be as much information as is theoretically possible. And although there will be situations when, in the absence of a concurrent visual world, language *is* used to drive such inferences, ontologically, it makes sense that language use is predicated on understanding the world. What is the use of saying "Watch out for that lion over there," if the hearer could not deduce imminent danger simply by observing that lion directly?

Our anticipatory eye-movement data reflect only an initial foray into the relationship between the processes that underpin visual scene interpretation and those that underpin language interpretation when situated in the visual world. We believe that to fully explore the dynamics of such language understanding will require an understanding of the dynamics of real world interpretation.

APPENDIX I

Saccadic Launch Latencies and the Visual World Paradigm

Any muscular response takes time. How much time is an important issue in experimental psychology if one wishes to link response times to cognitive operations. Eye movements are no exception. The issue is simple: between presenting a visual stimulus and observing a saccadic eye movement towards that stimulus, the cognitive system must encode and process the stimulus (for instance, to determine whether an eye movement should be directed towards it), program the spatial coordinates to which the eyes should be launched, and then initiate the motor command that drives the musculature of the eye. It follows that if the eye movements are indicative of some particular cognitive process, the timing of those movements will be offset relative to the timing of that process. For example, in our own studies described in this chapter and elsewhere, we have observed eye movements towards particular objects in the visual scene that can only be explained through the combination, for example, of real-world knowledge with morphosyntactic information conveyed by the linguistic input. But what we want to know is *when* that combination took place. We thus need to know the extent of the delay between that combination and the ensuing eye movements—a delay caused, presumably, by the time it takes to program the eye movement and initiate the appropriate motor response.

Many researchers assume that it takes around 200 ms to program and launch a saccadic eye movement. This assumption is based on a body of research that stretches back as far as the 1930s (Travis, 1936) if not before. Much of the work required participants to fixate on successively appearing crosses on a computer screen (e.g., Rayner, Slowiaczek, Clifton, & Bertera, 1983) or successively lit bulbs (e.g., Saslow, 1967). Saccadic latencies of around 200-220 ms were observed in these studies, with the Saslow study suggesting that there was a reduction in the latency when it was known in advance of the stimulus appearing where it would appear. These studies measured the time from stimulus onset to saccadic initiation. Matin, Shao, and Boff (1993) attempted to measure the 'saccadic overhead'—roughly, the time to plan and launch a saccade minus the time to process the visual information. They estimated around 100 ms. However, they employed a particularly complex procedure that involved subtracting between conditions in which judgments about stimuli either did or did not require saccadic eye movements in order to view the stimuli. In addition, they did not monitor eye movements as such, but rather, based their estimates on participants' button presses.

There is a further limitation to the generalizability of these earlier results: these studies used the visual stimulus itself as a trigger for the saccadic eye movement—the target and trigger were the same. Zambarbieri, Schmid, Magenes, & Prablanc (1982) used auditory stimuli as both trigger and target (the auditory signal was generated at a particular spatial location that constituted that target of the eye movement) and found significantly longer latencies to auditory stimuli (380 ms). However, it is again unclear whether these data generalize to the visual world paradigm. In the visual world paradigm, the auditory input is the trigger for an eye movement towards a visual target, and thus the sequence of cognitive events between the trigger and the initiation of the movement towards the target is somewhat different. It was with these considerations in mind that we carried out the following study to establish whether the saccadic latencies we might observe with the stimuli we use would be comparable with the latencies used in the earlier studies.

There were three auditory conditions, each accompanying a visual scene of the type used in our previous studies. In one condition (the "tone" condition) participants heard "boy [silence] cake [silence] [tone] [silence] [tone]." They were instructed not to move their eyes when they heard the first two words, but that at the first tone, they should move their eyes as quickly as possible to the first-mentioned object (the boy) and stay there, and at the second tone they should move their eyes as quickly as possible to the second-mentioned object (the cake). In the "word" condition, participants heard "boy [silence] cake [silence] boy [silence] cake." This condition was included simply to see whether the acoustic complexity of a real word, as opposed to a tone, might play any part in the latencies (the participants' task was the same as in the first condition, in that they knew in advance which objects they would have to fixate on the first tokens of *boy* and *cake*, and the signal to move their eyes was the second token of each word). In the "recognition" condition, participants heard "boy [silence] boy [silence] cake." In this case, the first token of *boy* was a pre-cue to the subsequent token of *boy*, at which they had to move their eyes to the boy. But there was no pre-cue for the cake, and thus the first that participants knew of where their eyes should move next was when they heard *cake*. In each case, we were interested in the latency between the cue to move the eyes to the cake (or the equivalent object across different trials) and the onset of the corresponding saccadic movement.

Stimuli   Thirty of the visual stimuli used in the Altmann and Kamide (1999) study were used (stimuli that had constituted filler items in that study were included in the present study). Three auditory speech files were created for each visual stimulus that corresponded to the conditions described above. Each tone in the tone condition lasted 200 ms. Each period of silence lasted 2000 ms. The mean duration of the target corresponding to *cake* in the recognition condition ("boy [silence] boy [silence] cake") was 421 ms. The delay between the two trigger cues (the second token of each of *boy* and *cake*) varied at random across stimuli, in 100 ms increments, between 1600 and 2100 ms. This was to ensure that participants could not anticipate when the final cue would arrive. Each participant saw each visual stimulus only once, but was exposed to all three conditions in a Latin Square design. The different conditions were blocked, with order of blocks determined by Latin Square, and each block consisting of 10 trials. There were six practice trials.

Participants   Twenty-seven participants took part in this study, drawn from the University of York student community.

Procedure   Participants wore an SMI EyeLink head-mounted eyetracker, sampling at 250Hz from the right eye. Viewing was binocular. Visual stimuli were presented at a resolution of 640 x 480 on a 17" monitor. Participants were seated approximately 24" from the monitor. Auditory stimuli were played through two external loudspeakers situated on either side of the monitor. The onset of the auditory stimuli was 1000 ms after the onset of the visual stimulus (which remained on-screen for 2000 ms beyond the end of the auditory stimulus). Participants were informed of the aims of the experiment (to see how fast they could move their eyes). The entire experiment took approximately 25 minutes.

Results and Discussion   The onsets of the saccadic movements to the target object (the cake in the example above) were calculated relative to the onset of the preceding cue. Latencies in excess of 2000 ms were excluded from the following analyses (amounting to less than 0.25% of trials). The mean latencies to onset are given in Table 11.1. Overall, there was a significant difference across the conditions ($F1(2,52) = 96.0$, $p < .0001$; $F2(2,58) = 125.2$, $p < 0.0001$). There was a significant difference between the recognition condition and both the word and tone conditions (all $p < .0001$), but no difference between the word and tone conditions ($F1(1,52) = 1.9$, $p = .17$; $F2(1,58) = 2.9$, $p = .09$). There were a number of trials in which participants' first saccade was to an incorrect object. The percentages of trials in which participants made

TABLE 11.1. Percentage Trials with Errors, and Saccadic Latencies (in ms) to the Intended Target on All Trials and (in parentheses) on Error-Free Trials

	Condition		
	Tone	Word	Recognition
Errors	4	6	25
Mean	254	295	560
	(246)	(281)	(525)
Median	181	217	525
	(180)	(213)	(484)
Mode	132	207	466
	(132)	(207)	(460)

such errors were low in the tone and word conditions (4% and 6%, respectively), but relatively high in the recognition condition (25%). Nonetheless, the same statistical patterns were observed when comparing mean latencies when these trials were excluded from the analysis (with significant differences between the recognition and both the word and tone conditions—all $p < .0001$, but no difference between the word and tone conditions—both $p > .1$).

The relatively long latencies (given the 200 ms from the previous literature) are due to the skewed nature of the distributions. Figure 11.6 shows (for trials without errors) the number of saccades in each 10 ms bin relative to cue onset, and Table 11.1 shows, in addition to the mean latencies, the median and modal latencies. One can see from Figure 11.6 that there is indeed no difference between the distributions of latencies in the tone and word conditions, but that the distribution in the recognition condition is both shifted and broader (and less skewed). The data show that even in the tone and word conditions there is substantial variation in individual latencies to launch saccadic eye movements to the target. Although the mean latency in the tone condition (for error-free trials) was 246 ms, it is evident that the majority of saccades were launched less than 200 ms after cue onset (the median latency was 180 ms). In the recognition condition, in which participants did not know in advance of the cue where they would be required to look, the mean and median latencies were, respectively, 525 ms and 484 ms. The difference between the two conditions reflects the fact that in the tone condition, participants neither have to recognize the cue nor determine from the cue which is the intended target to which they should move their eyes. In the recognition condition, participants had to recognize the cue word in order to identify the intended target and, hence, the increased latencies.

Why were there so many errors in the recognition condition? On 25% of trials, participants looked first to an object that was not the target. Post-hoc analysis of the visual scenes and their corresponding target words indicated that these errors were not due to cohort competitor effects (cf. Allopenna et

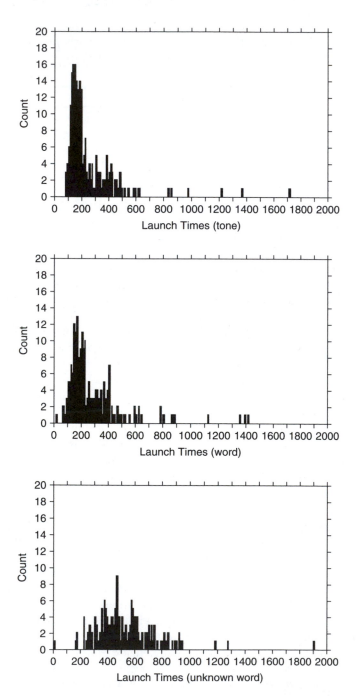

FIGURE 11.6. Histograms showing distribution of saccadic latencies (ms) in each of the three conditions described in Appendix I.

al., 1998). However, there *was* a factor that predicted the majority of errors: whether or not a distractor object lay between the launch position and the target object. There were almost twice as many errors to scenes with an intervening object (63% of errors) than to scenes where there was no such object (37% of errors), and the majority of errors constituted looks to these intervening objects (of the 30 scenes, 14 were in the "nothing in the way" category, and 16 were in the "something in the way" category). While this may seem, at first glance, a compelling account of the *kinds* of errors that were made, it cannot account for why such errors occurred predominantly in the recognition condition—the scenes and corresponding launch/target positions were identical across conditions, and thus any purely *visual* factors were constant across the conditions. One possibility is that in the recognition condition, participants were more likely to attempt to guess which target would be referred to (no such guesswork was required in the tone and word conditions because they knew in advance what the target object would be). In such a case, saccades launched towards incorrect targets might be expected to have shorter latencies than saccades to correct targets, simply because the chances of having recognized the word, and having avoided a saccade towards an incorrect target, are greater the more that has been heard of the unfolding target word. In fact, the launch time in the recognition condition on those trials when the eyes moved first to an incorrect target was ca. 340 ms (median: 337 ms; average: 338 ms), compared with a median launch time on error-free trials of ca. 480 ms. On the assumption that the median latency of 180 ms in the tone condition reflects the minimum planning/execution time of a saccade (see below), these erroneous launches appear to have been planned within the first 160-200 ms of the target word. We conclude that the task demands ("move your eyes as quickly as possible") may indeed have been responsible for the relatively high error rate in the recognition condition.

Conclusions and Implications

So what should we conclude about the time it takes to program and launch a saccade? Sixty percent of saccades in the tone condition were launched within 200 ms of cue onset, and the median latency (180 ms) is, therefore, a cautious estimate of how long it takes to program and launch a saccade when the target is known. This accords well with the previous literature. But what the previous literature fails to mention is the large, and skewed, range of latencies that can be observed in such studies. All we can conclude, in the face of this large distribution of latencies, is that on the majority of occasions when the eyes know where to move in advance of having to move, it takes around 180 ms after the decision, or signal, to move the eyes to initiate the saccade. But what should we conclude about the time it takes when the eyes do *not* know where to move? For example, in the original Altmann & Kamide (1999) case, information on the verb *eat* (in "the boy will eat the cake") apparently determined which was the appropriate target to move towards (i.e., towards the one edible object in the scene). The verb must have been recognized, and information regarding its likely object accessed, before the eyes could have been programmed to move. Even on the implausible assumption that hearing *eat* was in some sense equivalent to hearing *cake*, our data from the recognition condition suggest that it can take around 460 ms (the modal latency) from the onset of the word to launch a saccadic movement towards the corresponding object. That said, a considerable number of saccades (31%) were launched before word offset (with the word having a mean duration of 421 ms), and it is these early saccades (they are not "express saccades," which typically have a modal latency of around 100 ms; e.g., Fischer & Weber, 1993) that enable us to see the differential effects of our experimental manipulations (e.g., *eat* vs. *move*) during the acoustic lifetime of the target word.

How, then, are to interpret saccadic latencies in the visual world paradigm? If we see a difference in the eye-movement record emerging at some particular time, when should we assume that the programming of the eye movements that led to that difference first occurred? The data we have presented here suggest that 180 ms is a safe minimum— thus, if we were to observe a difference in the eye-movement record emerging, say, 180 ms after the offset of a particular word, it would be safe to conclude that the cognitive processes that led to that difference took place during the life time of that word. Similarly, if we were to observe a difference that emerged by that word's offset, it would be safe to conclude that the critical processing had taken place at least 180 ms before word offset.

Finally, and taken together with the results reported earlier in this chapter (e.g., eye movements reflecting combinatory processes at the verb), these data show, if nothing else, that saccadic eye movements are as closely time-locked as possible to the cognitive processes that spawn those movements. It is unclear how the eye movements could be more closely synchronized with those processes.

APPENDIX II

Plotting the Data

There are several different ways of plotting eye-movement data, and the choice of which to use depends in part on the hypothesis that underpins the linkage between the behavioral measure and the cognitive processes which that measure is intended to reveal. The four different plots in Figure 11.7 reflect four of the many different plots that are possible for the data described in this chapter and originally shown in Figure 11.1. This appendix describes the differences between these alternative plots and their implications for statistical analysis of the data. It is intended as a somewhat extended footnote to the plots employed in this chapter. Although the study described above involved monitoring eye movements in response to "the man will eat the cake," when the screen was blank, we shall for ease of exposition refer to "eye movements toward the cake" or "fixations on the cake" as simply shorthand for the more unwieldy "eye movements toward where the cake had been" and "fixations on where the cake had been."

The Synchronization Problem   Figure 11.1 (Panel A in Figure 11.7) plotted the proportion of trials in which a saccadic eye movement was directed towards each of the quadrants in the blank-screen study. For the purposes of this discussion, it does not matter whether movements were directed towards a particular quadrant, or a particular group of pixels (consequently, we shall on occasion refer to quadrants, and on occasion refer to e.g., "the man"). More specifically, the graph plotted the proportion of trials in which a movement was directed towards each of the quadrants during each word or phrase. Thus, the number of trials on which a movement occurred between the onset of the verb (*eat*) and the onset of the following word (*the*) is plotted against, on the x-axis, *eat*. Importantly, the plot takes into account the duration of the verb (or the region defined as verb onset to determiner onset) on a trial-by-trial basis. If, on one trial, the duration was 450 ms, only movements initiated within that 450 ms were recorded. If, on another trial, the duration was 550 ms, only movements initiated within that 550 ms were recorded. To understand the importance of this, we must consider the graph shown in Panel B of Figure 11.7. This plots the proportion of trials in which a saccadic movement was directed towards each of the quadrants during each 200-ms bin following sentence onset[4]. Thus, in the time window spanning 1000 to 1200 ms after sentence onset (labeled as 1100 on the x-axis), looks were directed towards the quadrant containing the appropriate subject (the man in this case) on 5% of trials. But what is the relevance of this particular time window? If we are interested in what happens, say, during the verb in "The man will eat the cake," would it not be useful to see on this graph where *eat* is located on the timeline represented on the x-axis?

Figure 11.8 is an enlarged version of Panel B of Figure 11.7, and on this plot, the mean onset of the verb and the mean onset of the following word *the* are marked (the region between the two corresponds to the critical region plotted as *eat* in Figure 11.1). Thus, mean onset occurred around 1180 ms after sentence onset, and mean offset of this region occurred around 2000 ms after sentence onset (the actual offset of the verb was on average 1620 ms after sentence onset—the 380ms until the onset of *the* was a postverbal pause. See Footnote 2.). According to the mean verb onset marked on the graph, it looks as if, by verb onset, looks towards the man had dropped to roughly the same

378

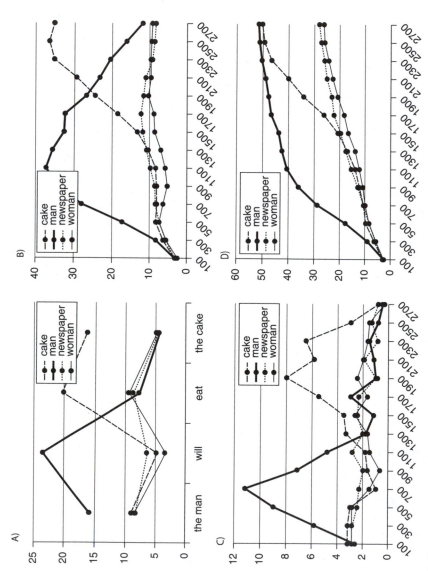

FIGURE 11.7. Four ways of plotting the same data. A - percentage trials with eye movements towards each target during each word as calculated on a trial-by-trial basis; B - percentage trials with eye movements towards each target calculated for each 200 ms bin since sentence onset; C - percentage trials with fixations on each target calculated for each 200 ms bin since sentence onset; D - cumulative percentage trials with eye movements towards each target calculated for each 200 ms bin since sentence onset.

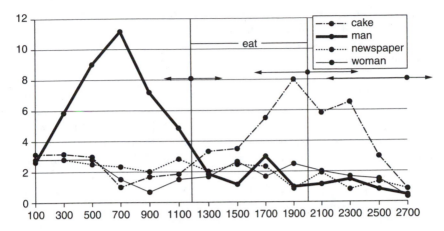

FIGURE 11.8. Percentage trials with looks to each quadrant. This figure corresponds to the same data as plotted in Figure 11.1. Here, the data are plotted in 200ms bins ("100" indicates saccades launched between 0 and 200 ms). The two vertical lines indicate verb onset and offset. The arrows indicate the range of individual (trial-by-trial) onsets and offsets relative to sentence onset (the origin of the x-axis). The right-most set of arrows indicate the range of individual sentence offsets relative to sentence onset.

(2%) as the looks towards the other quadrants (corresponding to the woman and the newspaper). Thus, those 5% of trials on which a look was directed towards the man most likely reflected looks before verb onset. However, Figure 11.8 also marks the *range* of verb onsets (as well as the range of determiner onsets and sentence offsets). For example, the verb's onset on one particular trial occurred 990 ms after sentence onset, while the verb's onset on another trial occurred 1400 ms after sentence onset. In which case, those 5% of trials between 1000 and 1200 ms after sentence onset, with looks to the man, may have reflected looks during the verb after all. The problem here is how to plot the data against time when, across different trials, critical points within the linguistic input occurred at different times. The data have to be synchronized to some point, and whether it is sentence onset, or the onset (or offset) of some specific word, there will always be a problem in interpreting the graph when a later point in the linguistic input is shown, but the time between the zero-point and this later point varies on a trial-by-trial basis. The plot shown in Figure 11.7 Panel A (Figure 11.1) is one way around this synchronization problem when it comes to plotting the data. One drawback with such plots, however, is that if the regions are too long, they may permit multiple fixations, in which case a single trial may "count" toward two different data points on the graph, and this can potentially lead to the sum of the percentages adding up to more than 100. Nonetheless, if one is interested in looks to a *specific* object, it may not matter that a particular trial counted for more than one data point if one simply wishes to know on what percentage of trials an eye movement was directed towards that object. However, such plots are limited in respect of their temporal resolution, as they do not say anything about how the pattern of eye movements or fixations unfolds as the word itself unfolds, and if one's main interest *is* in how the pattern of eye movements unfolds in time, as in the case, for example of the Allopenna et al. (1998) study mentioned in the introduction to the chapter, there is little alternative but to plot the data against a time axis. Crucially, however, the origin of the x-axis need not be at zero. If the intention is to show what happens by, for example, the offset of a particular word, there is no reason why the data cannot be synchronized to that offset, with data points to the right (positive) reflecting looks after word offset, and looks to the left (negative) reflecting looks before word offset.

Finally, synchronizing the data on a trial-by-trial basis to the region of theoretical interest is particularly important if one wants to establish that it was that particular region which gave rise to whatever cognitive representations drove the eye movements. If one did not synchronies on a trial-by-trial basis, but for example took the average duration of that region across all trials, and scored eye movements on each trial that fell within a region whose span was constant across trials and based on that average, the resulting data would reflect the fact that on some trials the scoring region would be too short (in which case relevant linguistic material may not have influenced those eye movements) and others too long (in which case linguistic material from outside that region may have influenced those eye movements).

Saccades or Fixations? All the data discussed thus far has been described in terms of saccadic eye movements. That is, at each moment of interest (be it a 200 ms bin, or a word), we have recorded the number of eye *movements* towards a particular region. But an alternative would be not to record movements, but fixations. That is, we could record on the graph at each moment in time the probability (or percentage of trials) of the eyes *fixating* a particular region. These data are shown in Panel C of Figure 11.7. The corresponding graph, showing saccades instead of fixations, is in Panel B, and the two graphs are evidently quite different. The reason, of course, is that the probability at each moment in time of fixating a particular region does not take into account when that fixation started.

Determining which measure to plot depends in part on the nature of the hypothesis that is being tested. For example, in our own work, we are interested in the manner in which language mediates overt visual attention to the objects in a scene. In particular, we are interested in how language can cause the system to *shift* its attention onto a new object. It is for this reason that we favor a measure which directly reflects such shifts — namely the *movement* of the eyes, rather than their fixation. However, in other work, the distinction is less important. For example, in the reaching task employed in the Allopenna et al. (1998) study, participants' eyes tend to fixate on the object as they reach for it. And given the interest in that study on when those fixations began, the distinction between plotting saccades or fixations becomes less relevant (and, of course, a rise in the probability of fixating a particular object may often be accompanied by a rise in the probability of launching a saccade towards that object). Another factor exemplified by that study was that the researchers were primarily interested in fixations on a single object—what mattered more was when those fixations started rather than when they ended or to which other objects attention was subsequently directed.

The fact that a rise in fixation probability may be accompanied by a rise in the probability of launching a saccade (immediately beforehand) means that there will be many situations in which it does not in fact matter whether fixation probabilities or saccadic launches are plotted. Where it does matter is when the probability of launching a saccade towards a particular region remains constant over some period of time; if the eyes stay in that region once they get there (for example, in a reaching task), the probability of fixation will rise (as more eyes land there over time) while the probability of launching a saccade might remain constant. Of course, in this scenario, the probability of launching a saccade towards a particular region must eventually fall when each participant has directed their eyes at that region and no more saccadic movements into that region are possible. And when the probability of launching a saccade does fall, the probability of fixating that region could remain the same (as in the scenario just described, in which case the probability of launching a saccadic movement towards the region will tend towards zero, but the probability of fixating that region will tend towards one), or it could fall also. In each case, the two measures provide different perspectives on exactly the same process—one either monitors when, and where, the eyes are still, or one monitors when, and to where, the eyes are moving.

An example of the dissociation between saccadic launch probabilities and fixation probabilities can be seen in Panel B of Figure 11.7. By around 1300 ms after sentence onset, the probability of launching a saccade towards the man has fallen to around the same level as the probability of launching a saccade towards the other objects. Not so in Panel C, which shows that the probability of fixating the man remains elevated until almost the end of the sentence. The distinction between the two panels shows that there is a dissociation in the data between the saccadic and fixation probabilities. Panel B shows that there were few saccadic movements towards the man after verb onset (assuming this was around 1200 ms after sentence onset), and that after this point there were more saccadic movements towards the cake. Panel C, however, suggests that the likelihood of fixating on the man does not change so dramatically—if the eyes had been fixating the man, they continue to do so even during and beyond the verb, with only a gradual decline. Indeed, examining only those trials in which looks to the cake had been preceded by looks to the man revealed that looks to the cake diverged from looks to the newspaper (the inappropriate object) around 400 ms later than they did on those trials in which looks to the cake had *not* been preceded by looks to the man.

This last observation must be treated with caution because we are dealing here with just one set of data from the (unusual) case in which the screen was in fact blank at the time of the eye movements. In other studies, one can find greater correspondence between falls in saccadic eye movements and falls in fixation probability. The fact that there *can* be a dissociation between the two does suggest, however, that useful information can be gleaned from both measures (as in the case of the observations surrounding the contingent analyses just mentioned).

Finally, several studies have plotted neither saccadic launches nor fixation probabilities. For example, Griffin (2001) reported gaze durations (the time spent fixating an object), and that study is a clear example of how different behavioral measures can be 'linked' with different aspects of the cognitive processes that underpin the behavior. Eye movements reflect not simply when an object in the scene is looked at, but for how long. No single plot can capture both these components of the eye movement pattern, and yet both are informative. One simplistic view of these two components would be that the saccadic movement plots reflect processes that shift attention around the visual scene, while the durational data reflect the processing load associated with whatever processes are required to interpret that object (or plan some consequent action on that object). The two are not independent: the "decision" to stop fixating and "move on" may be as much to do with the processing of whatever has been fixated as with the processes that cause attention to be redirected elsewhere.

Linking the Data Plots to the Statistics How should one best analyze, statistically, the data presented in graphs such as those shown in Figure 11.7? The answer is relatively simple. Consider, for example, Figure 11.8. If we wanted to know whether there were more looks during the verb towards the cake than towards the newspaper, we should simply calculate the area under the curve corresponding to looks towards the cake and compare this to the area under the curve corresponding to looks towards the newspaper. The area under the curve is simply the sum of the looks at each bin within the critical region (technically, this sum is only an approximation to the area under the curves as plotted; however, given that the individual data points that form the curve are based on quantized time steps, the sum of the looks is an accurate reflection of the actual data). In Panel D of Figure 11.7, we have plotted the cumulative sum of the looks (or the "cumulative probability" if the y-axis is scaled between one and zero). Where each curve crosses the y-axis at sentence offset corresponds to the area under each curve of Panel B (in fact, this is not quite true—the curves would need to be synchronized relative to sentence offset, not relative to sentence onset as shown in Figure 11.7). Often, researchers calculate not the sum of the individual data points, which corresponds to the area under the curve, but their mean, which corresponds to the mean amplitude of the curve. This is common, for example, in the analysis of ERP data, which also requires analyses equivalent to the area under a curve, but which tend to be reported in terms of amplitude. It is of course unlikely that one would want to analyze the data in this way (whether in terms of area or amplitude) for a region that spanned the entire sentence, but the same principle holds true for smaller regions of the sentence, even down to individual words or less.

One advantage of plotting saccadic movements rather than fixation probabilities is that the total number of saccadic movements within a temporal region is just that: the total number of individual eye movements. Each such event occurs, in effect, at only one moment in time. But the situation is somewhat different when plotting fixation probabilities. Fixations span multiple moments in time, and summing the proportion of trials in which a region was being fixated has the disadvantage that a fixation that contributes to that sum at one time point may be the same fixation that contributes to that sum at another time point. Consequently, it is more usual (cf. Griffin, 2001) to plot fixation durations and to analyze the proportion of time within some temporal region fixating a particular object.

To conclude: Eye movements are closely time-locked to the cognitive processes that conspire to drive those movements. It is that close time-locking that means that their interpretation is itself dependent on accurate synchronization in these studies between the timing of the movements and the timing of critical input in the auditory signal that underlies the linguistic mediation of those movements. Different studies will inevitably focus on different aspects of the eye-movement record, but this diversity may result, ultimately, in a better understanding of the linkage between the different components of the eye-movement record and their underlying cognitive processes.

NOTES

1. Throughout this chapter, data will be described as "significant" only if the statistical analyses achieved significance at $p < 0.05$ on both by-subjects *and* by-items analyses. In all the studies except the blank-screen study, there were 16 subjects per group (and as many groups as experimental conditions, employing a standard Latin Square design). The blank-screen study employed 15 subjects per group.

2. The region described as *eat* in Figure 11.1 in fact extended from the onset of the verb to the onset of the following word (*eat*). When the region was calculated as

between verb onset and verb offset, the same statistical patterns were found (by subjects and by items), with more looks to either the quadrant or the pixels that had contained the appropriate object (the cake) than to the quadrant or pixels that had contained the inappropriate object (the newspaper).

3. A very readable review, "Embodied Cognition" by Daniel Richardson (2000), can be downloaded from http://node15.psych.cornell.edu/home/docs/EC_B3_final_colour.pdf

4. The 200 ms figure is essentially arbitrary. The data could be plotted at the maximum resolution permitted by the eyetracker (in our case, 4 ms bins), but as the temporal resolution increases, so the curves become more jagged and less easily interpretable (simply because there may be one or more movements in one bin, but none in the following bin, something that increases in likelihood as the bin size is reduced). Note that this is a problem mainly for plots of saccadic movements; plots that show probability of fixation at each moment in time do not become jagged in this way, simply because fixations extend in time across many time samples, whereas saccade onsets register at a single sample only.

ACKNOWLEDGMENTS

The work reported here was made possible through funding from the Medical Research Council (G9628472N and G0000224), the Economic and Social Research Council (R000222798), and the Royal Society. The authors would like to thank the following: Ruth Ancliff and Andrew Thomas for their help in setting up and running the blank-screen experiment, Michael Spivey for neither setting up nor running the blank-screen experiment, Charlie Southgate for setting up and running the study on saccadic launch latencies described in Appendix I, Falk Huettig for discussion of alternative ways of plotting the data, Silvia Gennari for discussion of event structures and their temporal properties, Mike Tanenhaus for discussions that led to useful clarification of the theoretical components of this chapter, and Michael Spivey (again) for his comments on an earlier version of this chapter. Finally, thanks are due to the members of the original workshop on which this volume is based—their insightful presentations and subsequent discussions helped shape this chapter.

REFERENCES

Allopenna, P. D., Magnuson, J. S., & Tanenhaus, M. K. (1998). Tracking the time course of spoken word recognition using eye movements: Evidence for continuous mapping models. *Journal of Memory and Language, 38*(4), 419-439.

Altmann, G. T. M. (1997). *The ascent of Babel: An exploration of language, mind, and understanding.* Oxford: Oxford University Press.

Altmann, G. T. M. (1999). Thematic role assignment in context. *Journal of Memory and Language, 41*, 124-145.

Altmann, G. T. M., & Kamide, Y. (1999). Incremental interpretation at verbs: Restricting the domain of subsequent reference. *Cognition*, 73(3), 247-264.

Altmann, G. T. M. (in press). Language-mediated eye movements in the absence of a visual world: The "blank screen paradigm." *Cognition*.

Altmann, G. T. M., & Steedman, M. J. (1988). Interaction with context during human sentence processing. *Cognition*, 30(3), 191-238.

Ballard, D. H., Hayhoe, M. M., Pook, P. K., & Rao, R. P. N. (1997). Deictic codes for the embodiment of cognition. *Behavioral and Brain Sciences*, 20(4), 723-767.

Barsalou, L. W. (1999). Perceptual symbol systems. *Behavioral and Brain Sciences*, 22(4), 577-660.

Barsalou, L. W., Simmons, W. K., Barbey, A. K., & Wilson, C. D. (2003). Grounding conceptual knowledge in modality-specific systems. *Trends in Cognitive Sciences*, 7(2), 84-91.

Brandt, S. A., & Stark, L. W. (1997). Spontaneous eye movements during visual imagery reflect the content of the visual scene. *Journal of Cognitive Neuroscience*, 9, 27-38.

Cooper, R. M. (1974). The control of eye fixation by the meaning of spoken language: A new methodology for the real-time investigation of speech perception, memory, and language processing. *Cognitive Psychology*, 6(1), 84-107.

Crain, S., & Steedman, M. J. (1985). On not being led up the garden path: the use of context by the psychological parser. In D. Dowty, L. Karttunen & A. Zwicky (Eds.), *Natural Language Parsing: Psychological, Computational, and Theoretical perspectives* (pp. 320-358). Cambridge: Cambridge University Press.

Fischer, B. & Weber, H. (1993). Express saccades and visual attention. *Behavioral and Brain Sciences*, 16, 553-61.

Fodor, J. A., Bever, T. G., & Garrett, M. F. (1974). *The psychology of language: An introduction to psycholinguistics and generative grammar*. New York: McGraw-Hill.

Freyd, J. L. (1987). Dynamic mental representations. *Psychological Review*, 94(4), 427-438.

Freyd, J. L., & Finke, R. A. (1984). Representational momentum. *Journal of Experimental Psychology: Learning, Memory and Cognition*, 10(1), 126-132.

Freyd, J. L., Pantzer, T. M., & Chenk, J. L. (1988). Representing statics as forces in equilibrium. *Journal of Experimental Psychology: General*, 117(4), 395-407.

Glenberg, A. M. (1997). What memory is for. *Behavioral and Brain Sciences*, 20, 1-19.

Griffin, Z. M. (2001). Gaze durations during speech reflect word selection and phonological encoding. *Cognition*, 82, B1-B14.

Kamide, Y., Altmann, G. T. M., & Haywood, S. L. (2003). The time-course of prediction in incremental sentence processing: Evidence from anticipatory eye movements. *Journal of Memory and Language*, 49(1), 133-156.

Laeng, B., & Teodorecu, D. (2002). Eye scanpaths during visual imagery reenact those of perception of the same visual scene. *Cognitive Science*, 26, 207-231.

Lakoff, G., & Johnson, M. (1999). *Philosophy in the flesh: The embodied mind and its challenge to western thought*. New York: Basic Books.

Marslen-Wilson, W. D. (1987). Functional parallelism in spoken word recognition. *Cognition*, 25, 71-102.

Matin, E., Shao, K., & Boff, K. (1993). Saccadic overhead: information processing time with and without saccades. *Perception and Psychophysics*, 53, 372-380.

McRae, K., Ferretti, T. R., & Amyote, L. (1997). Thematic roles as verb-specific concepts. *Language and Cognitive Processes*, 12(2/3), 137-176.

Rayner, K., Slowiaczek, M.L., Clifton, C., & Bertera, J.H. (1983). Latency of sequential eye movements: implications for reading. *Journal of Experimental Psychology: Human Perception and Performance*, 9, 912-922.

Richardson, D. C., & Spivey, M.J. (2000). Representation, space and Hollywood squares: looking at things that aren't there anymore. *Cognition*, 76, 269-295.

Saslow, M. G. (1967). Latency for saccadic eye movement. *Journal of the Optical Society of America*, 57, 1030-1033.

Spivey, M.J., & Geng, J. J. (2001). Oculomotor mechanisms activated by imagery and memory: eye movements to absent objects. *Psychological Research*, 65, 235-241.

Tanenhaus, M. K., Carlson, G., & Trueswell, J. C. (1989). The role of thematic structures in interpretation and parsing. *Language and Cognitive Processes*, 4(3/4), SI 211-234.

Tanenhaus, M. K., Spivey-Knowlton, M. J., Eberhard, K. M., & Sedivy, J. C. (1995). Integration of Visual and Linguistic Information in Spoken Language Comprehension. *Science*, 268, 1632-1634.

Travis, R. C. (1936). The latency and velocity of the eye in saccadic movements. *Psychological Monographs*, 47, 242-249.

Tyler, L. K., & Marslen-Wilson, W. D. (1977). The on-line effects of semantic context on syntactic processing. *Journal of Verbal Learning and Verbal Behavior*, 16, 683-692.

Van der Meer, E., Beyer, R., Heinze, B., & Badel, I. (2002). Temporal order relations in language comprehension. *Journal of Experimental Psychology: Learning, Memory and Cognition*, 28(4), 770-779.

Zambarbieri, D., Schmid, R., Magenes, G., & Prablanc, C. (1982). Saccadic responses evoked by presentation of visual and auditory targets. *Experimental Brain Research*, 47, 417-427.

Zwaan, R.A. (1996). Processing narrative time shifts. *Journal of Experimental Psychology: Learning, Memory and Cognition*, 22(5), 1196-1207.

Zwaan, R.A., Langston, M.C., & Graesser, A.C. (1995). The construction of situation models in narrative comprehension— An event-indexing model. *Psychological Science*, 6(5), 292-297.

Zwitserlood, P. (1989). The locus of the effects of sentential-semantic context in spoken-word processing. *Cognition*, 32, 25-64.

Index

A

Absent objects, pointers to, 170
Absolute expressions, 263
Abstract letter codes, 70
Abstract word representation, 215
Accurate instruction, 228
Acoustic signal, 349
Action experiment, prototypical, 282
Active externalism, 163
Active vision, 17
Adjective-final utterances, 203
Ambiguity resolution, 60
Ambiguous phrases, 93
American Sign Language, 176, 178
Anticipatory eye movements, 354, 370
Antisaccade(s)
    paradigm, 116
    voluntary, 117
Arrays, semantic interpretation, 9
Attended processing, 117
Attention
    capturing of, 253, 256
    covert, 135, 139
        role of, 154
        stimulus factors and, 256
    display change and, 164
    dividing, 109
    effects of on memory, 113
    factors, eye movement direction and, 109
    -getting cues, 166
    overt, 136, 256
    pre-motor theory of visual, 155
    -requiring expectation, 124
    salience in, 255
    shifts, saccade-induced, 113
    speaker's momentary, 271
    two-process theory of, 124
    voluntary, 114
Auditory conditions, 371
Auditory information, recalled, 224
Auditory speech files, creation of, 372
Auditory word recognition, cohort model of, 348
Average saccade length, 62

B

Backwards counting, 269
Beat gestures, 178
Bias
    mental location, 358
    target, 307
Binocular coordination of eyes, 73
Blank-screen study, 356, 377
Block(s)
    competitor, 310
    pattern copying task, 169
Boundary paradigm, 65, 67, 68

C

Cambridge Research Systems shutter goggles, 74
Candid Camera, 165
Center of gravity
    averaging, 141
    effect, 71, 143
Central-biased representations, 6
Change blindness
    demonstrations, 136
    dramatic effects observed in, 165
    real-world scenario, 165
    studies, 69
Change-detection task, 109
Children's eye movements during listening, 319–346
    children's comprehension in real time, 325–327
    constraint-based lexicalist learner, 337–339
    developmental predictions from constraint-based lexicalist theory, 324–325
    how adults recover grammatical information from utterance, 321–324

place of comprehension in theory of language acquisition, 339–341
parsability as factor in linguistic and psycholinguistic theorizing, 340–341
phrase learning and word learning, 339–340
role of verb bias in child- and adult-parsing preferences, 327–336
lexical modularity or informativeness of scene, 330–334
production/comprehension dissociation, 334–336
Click-detection studies, 347
Clock expressions, variations in, 270
Cloze task, modified, 82
Codability, definition of, 194
Cognition, embedded, 367
Cognitive processing, fixation location and fixation duration as indices of, 105–133
cognitive processing during saccadic eye movements, 119–126
implications, 126
stimulus recognition and stimulus identification during saccades, 122–126
visuospatial processing confined to eye fixations, 119–122
eye position and cognitive control, 115–118
eye position, eye movements, and locus of visual attention, 110–115
fixation location and functional field of view, 106–110
Cognitive resources, limited capacity, 303
Color
competitor, 296, 298
report, 114
Common ground
competitor in, 297
establishment of, 295
fixations for object types in, 299
mental representations of, 294
Communication
hypothesis, 221
real-time, coordination necessary for, 303
Competitor
blocks, 310
effect, prediction of, 348
objects, 302

Comprehension
real-time, 294
research, eye tracking in, 214
Computer vision, 164
Conceptual metaphor, 183–184
Conceptual prominence, 259
Consistency effect, 12
Consistent objects, 32
Constant blocks, 202
Construction task, 308
Content-addressable memory, 162
Context-dependent memory, 173
Contextual constraint, 214
Conversation
interactive, 283
listeners, face-to-face, 213
natural interactive, referential domains in, 304
pointers in, 176
Coordinate-as-pointer, 356
Correlated constraint, 280
Cortical magnification, 20
Counting
backwards, 269
skills, 237
Covert attention, 135, 139
role of, 154
stimulus factors and, 256
Crossed fixation disparity, frequency of, 77
Cross-modal lexical priming paradigm, 280
Cumulative probability, 382

D

Data plots, linking of to statistics, 382
Deictic codes, 233
Deictic gestures, 177
Deictic pointer, 168, 173
Diagnostic object, 15
Digital video clips, 178
Disambiguation, 298, 302
Disappearing text, 79
Discourse
processing, 60
understanding, embodied approaches to, 313
Discrimination accuracy, 111
Display change, 66, 164
Distractor(s), 137
characters, 111
item location, 144

potentially interfering, 146
status, eye scanpath and, 148
Dual Purkinje Image eyetrackers, 75
Dual-task paradigm, 222
Dynamic scene perception, 362

E

Effort hypothesis, 222
Elemental explanation, varieties of, 253
Embedded cognition, 367
Episodic scene knowledge, 26
ERP signature, *see* Event-related potential
signature
Erroneous prosaccades, 116, 118
Ersatz scene, 7
Event(s)
description, eye movements during, 204
inferences about, 363
possible, 363
-related potential (ERP) signature, 14
structure, mapping of sentence structure
onto, 358
temporal properties of, 368
Experiential knowledge, 30
Express saccades, 80, 376
Externalism, 183
External memory, 356, 369
Extrafoveal objects, processing of, 200
Eye(s)
behavior, 273
binocular coordination of, 73
contingent display change techniques, 66
contingent probe paradigm, 88
gaze, speaker's, 206
-mind assumption, 106
monitoring, 192
position, cognitive control and, 115
Eye fixations in reading, visual and linguistic
processing during, 59–104
binocular coordination of eyes, 73–77
center of gravity and landing position effects, 71–72
express saccades, 80
gap effect, 78–80
implications of visual processing research
for language processing research,
89–95
inhibition of saccade return, 77–78
integration of information across saccades, 68–70

lexical and phonological ambiguity, 82–84
linguistic processing in reading, 80–81
on-line inferences, 88–89
perceptual span, 64–67
preview effects, 67–68
pronoun resolution, 86–88
range effects, 72–73
saccade programming, 70–71
sentence and clause wrap-up, 86
sentence parsing, 84–86
word frequency, 81
word predictability, 82
EyeLink head-mounted eyetracker, 372
Eye movement(s), *see also* Language production, reasons for eye movements related to
anticipatory, 354
basic facts, 19
behavior, experimental manipulation and,
92
conditions, 224
control, model of, 61
data
anticipatory, 370
types of research groups developed
using, 60
ways of plotting, 376
decision, 91
direction, attentional factors tied to, 109
experiential knowledge used to guide, 30
language-driven, 205
language-mediated, 354
latencies to referent, 286
noun phrases and, 192
object semantics and, 33
paradigms, 282
pattern, during face recognition, 40
recorded, 45
re-enactment of, 358
relationship between visual attention
and, 21
scan, covert scanning and, 138
scene description and, 204
speech-related, 215, 233
use of to study cognitive processing, 105
Eye scanning and visual search, 135–159
eyes directed to target during visual
search, 141–149
fixation of active visual search, 138–141
fovea and periphery, 136–138
preplanning in saccadic system, 153–156

saccade selection accuracy, 152–153
saccade targeting accuracy, 150–152
Eye-tracking, *see also* Sentence generation,
    use of eye tracking in studies of
  experiments, 89
  hardware, off-the-shelf, 90
  language production and, 271
  methodology, 83
  research, volume of data generated, 90
  studies, gender information and, 87
  system(s), 21
    high-accuracy, 191
    lead-mounted, 283
  technology, 261
Eye-voice span(s), 192, 199, 217, 263
  linear incrementality in, 272
  measurement of, 272
  time telling, 266
E-Z Reader model, 61

F

Face recognition, eye-movement pattern
    generated during, 40
Facial expressions, 167
False goal, fixation to, 293
Fingers of instantiation, 233
First fixation duration, 37, 61, 81
First-pass gaze duration, 37, 39
Fixation(s), 19
  box, 123
  clusters, 41
  density, semantic influences on, 36
  disparity, 75
    average, 74
    changed, 76
    frequency of crossed, 77
    magnitude of, 76
  duration(s), 126
    computing, 41
    data, 110
  location, 106, 127
  look-ahead, 28
  mean proportion of, 75
  multiple, 379
  number of, 380
  placement, 2–4, 21, 22
    control of, 25
    stimulus-driven control of, 25
    task influence on, 28
  positions, predicting individual, 26

probabilities, saccadic launch probabili-
    ties and, 381
processing of information during, 110
random initial, 267
sites, top-down factors modulating, 26
spatially contiguous, 62
temporally contiguous, 62
time, 36
  contextual constraint and, 82
  semantic factors and, 38
  visual factors and, 37
uncrossed, 76
Fixed-viewers, 232
Flicker paradigm, 46
fMRI study, 7
Focus particles, 88, 89
Forward return saccades, 78
Fovea, processing of information at, 110
Foveal vision, 106
Framework problem, 250
Free-scanning situation, 144
Free-viewers, 232
Functional field of view, 4, 43
  fixation location and, 106
  overestimate of, 46
  size of, 108
Fuzzy set theory, 179

G

Gabor patches, 142
Gap effect, 78, 80
Garden Path theory, 85
Gaze(s)
  center of, 110
  control, 31
  counting-like, 237
  duration, 37, 61, 81, 106, 194, 218
  fixation count, 35
  name-related, 216, 222, 238
  parallels between speech and, 214
  social-communicative functions of, 221
  speech-related, 236
  unnecessary appearance of, 233
Gazing, motivation for, 226
Gender information, 87
Gestures
  beat, 178
  deictic, 177
  function of in language production, 236
  hotly debated functions for, 236

iconic representational, 177
ideational, 237
interactive, 177
metaphoric representational, 177
sequencing words aided by, 237
speech-related, 236
Global effect, 71, 149
Goal
-objects, 285
reference to, 351
Go-past reading time, 93
Grammar, transformational, 279

H

Hand gestures, 167, 268
Hollywood Squares, 171, 172
Homophone target words, 84
Human interlocutors, 226
Human scale, 5
Hybrid images, 16
Hypothesis(es)
communication, 221
effort, 222
interference-avoidance, 225
memory-support, 223
production-support, 227
sequencing, 233
space-Y, 236
starting point, 249, 250, 271
why-not, 230

I

Iconic representational gestures, 177
Ideational gestures, 237
Identification accuracy, 125
Image(s)
-based saliency, 25
content, 42
differences between previously learned
and currently visible, 44
hybrid, 16
memory for, 40
properties, 22
static, real-world events and, 359
viewing time per, 42
Inaccurate-naming study, 228, 229
Indefinite instructions, 300, 302
Information, encoding of during recognition,
45
Inhibition of return, 77

Inner speech, 197
Instructional manipulation, 263
Instructions
ambiguous, 290
indefinite, 300, 302
series of, 296
Interactive conversation, 283
Interactive gestures, 177
Interference-avoidance hypothesis, 225
Internal information, externalizing of, 167
Internalism, 162, 163
Internet, navigation of, 183
Interobject saccades, 4
Interpretable arrays, 9
Intersaccadic interval, saccade destination
and, 154
Involuntary saccades, 118

J

Joint action, 294

K

Knowledge
episodic scene, 26
experiential, 30
grammatical, 366
lexical, 349
long-term episodic scene, 26
scene schema, 27
short-term episodic scene, 26
task, 27

L

Landing positions, 71, 73, 92
Language(s)
-as-action tradition, 280
comprehension, visual displays and, 19
-driven eye movements, 305
interactions not mediated by, 365
interpretation, 34
mediating mapping between world and,
366
processing
brain systems implicated in, 313
group, measuring of eye movements
in, 61
online, 307
real-time, 279–280, 311
research, 89
upcoming structure projected by, 362

salience in, 255
signed, 177
spoken, 177
variation problem, 251
Language production, reasons for eye movements related to, 213–247
articulating object names, 217–219
beyond name-related gazes in speaking,
239–240
communication hypothesis, 221–222
effort hypothesis, 222–223
hypotheses so far, 232–233
identifying objects, 219–220
interference-avoidance hypothesis,
225–227
memory-support hypotheses, 223–225
monitoring speech, 221
name-related gazes, 238–239
planning messages, 220
production-support hypothesis, 227–230
sequencing hypothesis, 233–235
space-Y hypothesis, 236–237
summary of hypotheses, 238
when speakers gaze, 215–217
why-not hypothesis, 230–232
Latencies, reversed length for, 197
Lateral masking, 136
Lemma, 215, 216
Length hypothesis, 267
Letter
identification, 107
report, 114
-string, 125
Levels problem, 250
Lexical accessibility, 199, 251
Lexical ambiguity, 82, 83
Lexical decision, 86
Lexical hypotheses, activation of, 349
Lexical knowledge, 349
Lexical priming, 280
Lexical processing, 126
Line drawing(s)
identification of, 43
manipulation of target objects in, 31
stimuli, 39
Linguistic compatibility, 273
Listening, *see* Children's eye movements
during listening
Logistic-regression model, 310
Long-term episodic scene knowledge, 26
Look-ahead fixations, 28

Low-pass filtered scenes, 23

M

Mapping, mediation of between language
and visual world, 347–386
background, 348–352
blank-screen paradigm, 352–355
discourse-mediated effects, 355–358
interpretation of world, 361–369
dynamic scene perception, 361–366
mediating mapping between language and world, 366–369
mapping sentence structure onto event
structure, 358–361
plotting of data, 376–383
saccadic launch latencies and visual
world paradigm, 370–375
Memory
access of information from, 162
accuracy, 171, 173
content-addressable, 162
context-dependent, 173
effects of attention on, 113
experiment, 224
external, 356, 369
items retained in, 113
list, key words, 87
short-term, 177
smeared, 355
strength, 225
-support hypotheses, 223
task, 195
test, 45
visual working, 178
Mental contents, fuzzy set of, 179, 180
Mental imagery experiment, 224
Mental location, bias toward, 358
Mental rotation, 119, 120
Mental scanning, covert, 138
Mental world
mapping language onto, 352, 355
processing language in, 352
Message(s), 215
planning of, 220
representations, 215
words expressing content of, 234
Metaphoric representational gestures, 177
Mind-as-just brain assumption, 163
Mirror-image reversals, 178
Model(s)

auditory word recognition, 348
constraint-based, 304
eye movement, 94
logistic-regression, 310
object naming, 193
saliency map, 25
serial spotlight, 141
stimulus salience, 256
visual saliency, 24
WEAVER++, 196
zoom lens, 141
Moment-by-moment processing, 80, 294, 312
Monosyllabic targets, 196
Motion parallax, 2
Moving-mask experiments, 65
Moving-window paradigm, 64, 108
Mudsplashes, 165
Multiple-object naming task, 193, 200, 205

N

Name-related gazes, 216, 230, 8
Natural interactive conversation, referential domains in, 304
Naturalistic conversation, 178
Natural scenes
    hierarchical structure of, 5
    properties of, 2
Natural-task studies, 4
Natural visuomotor processing, 169
New eyetracker, 284
No-saccade control trials, 120
Noun phrases, eye movements during production of, 192, 197
Number of regressions, 62

O

Object(s)
    absent, 170
    anticipatory looks toward, 351
    changed, 47
    color, 203
    competitor, 302
    concept associated with, 366
    consistent, 32
    deletions, detection of, 45
    detection paradigm, 12
    effects of name length on viewing times for, 195
    files, 233
    fixating on multiple, 239
    goal-, 285
    identification, 219
    initial fixation, 260
    location, experience reflecting, 369
    meaning, 30, 35
    memory representation of, 205
    mental location of, 357
    name(s)
        articulating, 217
        generation of in inner speech, 197
        models, 193
        onset of, 302
    pointers to, 169
    probability of fixating, 19
    recognition
        effect of saccades on, 125
        language production and, 220
    referent, 201, 206, 216
    repeated, 201
    semantics, functional field of view for, 44
    speaker gaze at, 214
    target, 33
    thematic interrelating of, 363
    theme-, 285
    trials with looks to each, 353, 354
    viewing times for, 194, 195
Objecthood, infant's concept of, 175
Oculomotor behavior, lower-level aspects of, 93
Oculomotor capture, 116, 118
Oculomotor tasks, 64
Off-the-shelf eye-tracking software, 90
Online auditory sentence comprehension, 105
On-line inferences, 88
Online language processing, 307
Online tasks, changes tracked by, 280
Ordering variations, 253
Overt attention, 136, 256

P

Parahippocampal place area (PPA), 6–7
Partial-report cue, 112
Passivization, 254
Patient detection task, 204
Pattern
    completion process, 174
    information, visual uptake of, 19–20
Perception, salience in, 255

Perceptual-motor routines, 178
Perceptual prominence, 257
Perceptual simulation, 167
Perceptual span, 64, 107
Peripheral objects, meaning of, 23
Peripheral preview, 154
Peripheral target stimulus, 108
Phonological ambiguity, 82
Phonological encoding, 70, 215
Photographs, categorized, 13
Physical constraint, violation of, 6
Picture
    perception, perceptual cues in, 255
    processing, 225
POD, *see* Point of disambiguation
Point of disambiguation (POD), 306
Pointer(s)
    coordinate-as-, 356
    deictic, 168, 173
    infancy, 176
    reading, 176
    visuospatial, 369
Pop-out search, 138
Positional markers, 233
Possible events, representation of, 363
PPA, *see* Parahippocampal place area
Predictability effect, 82
Prediction, 352
Preferred viewing location, 71
Pre-motor theory of visual attention, 155
Prepositional phrase, misinterpretation of
    ambiguous, 291
Preview
    advantage, 155
    effects, 67
Prime-mismatch trials, 122
Prime stimulus, 122
Priming, product-based construct of, 283
Probability of region entry, 35
Processing
    -cost effect, 72
    disruption to, 91, 92
    resources, 255
Product-based assumption, 283
Production
    eye tracking and, 262
    moment-by-moment processes necessary
        for, 294
    studies of eye tracking during, 250
    -support hypothesis, 227
    task, 261

Pronoun
    cataphoric, 88
    resolution, 86, 87
Proportionality, 8
Prototypical action experiment, 282
Prototypical product experiment, schematic
    of, 281
Proximity, 308
Psycholinguists, scene perception for, 1–58
    eye movement basic facts, 19–48
        fixation location, 21–36
        fixation time, 36–40
        functional field of view in scene per-
            ception, 43–48
        systematic scan patterns, 40–42
    eye movements in scene perception,
        17–19
    general issues in scene perception, 2–17
        definition of scene, 5–8
        displays used in psycholinguistic stud-
            ies, 8–11
        quick recognition of scenes, 15–17
        scene recognition speed, 12–15
Psychology
    behaviorist accounts of language in, 252
    internalism in, 163
Putting first things first, 249–278
    eyes have it, 271–273
    salience in perception, attention, and lan-
        guage, 255–260
        perceptual and attentional promi-
            nence, 255–256
        salience and linguistic starting points,
            256–260
    starting point hypothesis, 250–252
    starting point tradition, 252–255
    what eyes say, 260–271

R

Range effects, 72
Rapid categorization effect, 14
Rapid serial visual presentation (RSVP), 13
Reaction time (RT), 121, 122
Readiness for pronunciation, 195
Reading, *see also* Eye fixations in reading, vi-
    sual and linguistic processing dur-
    ing
    habits, 267
    linguistic processing in, 80
    pointers in, 176

process, disruption to, 92
self-paced, 84, 88
theory of, 106
time measures, 62, 63
Real-time behavioral index, 18
Real-time communication, coordination necessary for, 303
Real-time language processing, 279–280, 311
Real-world events, static images and, 359
Real-world referents, 281
Real-world scenes, substitute for, 2
Recency, 308
Recognition
    condition, 375
    tests, 108
Reference-point changes
    Dutch, 269
    structural frames and, 270
Referent(s)
    eye movement latencies to, 286
    object, 201, 206, 216
    potential, 291
    real-world, 281
    saliency of, 308
    unambiguous, 300
Referential communication task, 295, 300
Referential domains, 284, 288, 293
Refixation effect, 72
Regressive return saccades, 78
Remote distractor effect, 151
Repeated object, 201
Representational momentum, 363
Retinotopic maps, 141
Return saccades, 77
Rhyme findings, 349
Rings task, 145
RSVP, *see* Rapid serial visual presentation
RT, *see* Reaction time
Rye movements, studies of, 4

S

Saccade(s), 19, 110
    amplitudes, 42
    average amplitude of, 4
    destination, determination of, 151
    direction, 112
    distance, reaction time as function of, 120
    durations, 126
    express, 80, 376
-induced attention shifts, 113
integration of information across, 68
involuntary, 117, 118
landing point, 149
latency, 123
launch point, 149
length, average, 62
lexical processing during, 125
multistepping, 147
parallel programming of, 71
programming, 70, 121, 125
reflexive, 116
return, 77, 78
scene change during, 165
selection accuracy, 152, 156
target
    attentional phenomenon associated with, 155
    box, 124, 125
    location, 111, 115
    task, 143
targeting
    accuracy, 150, 156
    distractors influencing, 147
Saccadic destination, preprogrammed, 153
Saccadic eye movement, probability of launching, 350
Saccadic latencies, 373, 374
Saccadic launch latencies, 370
Saccadic movements, advantage of plotting, 383
Saccadic targeting, accuracy of, 149
Salience
    map, 24, 141, 151
    referent, 308
    starting points, 256
Same/different response, 123
Scanning process, efficient, 145
Scanpath, 40, 145, 146
Scan pattern, 10, 40
Scene
    assumption about, 362
    change detection in, 38
    characteristics missing in, 7
    components, 8
    construction, 360
    definition of, 5
    degraded, 44
    depiction(s)
        examples of, 3
        purpose of using, 2

studies, 4
description(s)
    advanced preparation of, 218
    eye movements during, 204
elements, gross overall spatial layout of, 15
empty regions of, 22
ersatz, 7
experiments, input to visual system in, 7
gist, 12, 13, 17
identification, initial stages of, 16
information, visual memory for, 49
low-pass filtered, 23
natural, properties of, 2
parsing of into multiple regions, 41
perception(s)
    dynamic, 362
    eye movements in, 4, 17
    fixation placement in, 21
    functional field of view in, 43
    role of PPA in, 7
processing systems, visual information available to, 20
recognition, quick, 15
region, fixation time, 36
schema knowledge, 27
semantic anomaly manipulation in, 32
sketch, 9, 15
static, 359
true, 7
viewing
    gaze durations during, 39
    systematic scan patterns and, 40
Search
    accuracy, 140
    difficulty, increasing, 144
    displays, 143
    selection accuracy, 152–153
    situation, center-of-gravity effects in, 142
Second-pass gaze duration, 37
Self-paced reading, 84, 88
Semantic anomaly
    detection of, 44
    manipulation, 31, 32
Semantic codes, 69
Sensory encoding, 368
Sentence
    -level planning processes, 191
    manipulated tense of, 360
    onset, 379
    parsing, 84

planning, time required for components of, 192
processing, core of, 284
production, 105, 273
structure, mapping of onto event structure, 358
wrap-up effects, 86
Sentence generation, use of eye tracking in studies of, 191–211
    complex noun phrases, 197–200
    processing of extrafoveal objects, 200–201
    repeated reference, 201–203
    scene and event description, 204–205
    simple noun phrases, 192–197
Sequencing hypothesis, 233
Serial search, 138
Serial spotlight model, 141
Short-term episodic scene knowledge, 26
Short-term memory, 177
Signed languages, 177
Signing space, 176, 178
Single fixation duration, 61, 81
SOA, *see* Stimulus onset asynchrony
Space-Y hypothesis, 236
Span of effective stimulus, 107
Spatial cue, activation of, 235
Spatial envelope, 17
Spatial index, 161, 168, 175
Spatial licensing, 6
Spatial scale, 41
Spatial selectivity, 155
Spatiotopic fusion hypothesis, 163–164
Speaker
    confederate, 295
    gaze, 214, 215, 237
    perspective, referential domains and, 293
Speaking, preparation time for, 267
Speech
    -to-gaze alignment, 198
    inner, 197
    monitoring of, 221
    onset latencies, 195
    parallels between gaze and, 214
    planning
        coordination of speech output and, 192
        theory of, 206
    -related gazes, 236
    spontaneous, 218
    time-stamped recording of, 261

Spillover, 62, 81, 353
Spoken language comprehension, referential domains in, 279–317
  context in product and action traditions, 280–284
  definite reference, 284–287
  implications, 311–313
  natural interactive conversation, 304–311
    proximity, 308–309
    recency, 308
    task compatibility, 309–311
  speaker perspective, 293–304
  syntactic ambiguity resolution, 288–293
Spontaneous speech, 218
Starting point(s)
  effect, manipulations required to elicit, 258
  hypothesis, 249, 250, 271
  selection of, 262
  structural view, 270
  tradition, 252
  triggering of, 266
Static-scene viewing, 128
Stereo-depth, conjunctions involving, 137
Stimulus
  auditory, 372
  onset asynchrony (SOA), 122, 123
  pictorial face, 140
  preview of, 67
  prime, 122
  processing, saccades interfering with, 125
  recognition, 122
  salience, biologically motivated computational model of, 256
  type, 125
Structural frames, information assembled in, 270
Synchronization problem, 377
Syntactic ambiguity, 214, 287, 288, 290
Syntactic parsing, 60
Syntactic word representation, 194

T

Tachistoscope, 64
Target(s)
  bias, persistent, 307
  block, preference for looking at, 306
  box, 120
  -distractor similarity, 108
  incorrect, 375

latency of eye movements to, 140
letter discrimination, antisaccades and, 118
monosyllabic, 196
object(s)
  saccadic movements to, 372
  search for, 33
pop-out, 137
selection, 155
sentence, manipulated tense of, 360
word(s), 67
  duration of fixation after leaving, 62
  homophone, 84
Task(s)
  block pattern copying, 169
  change-detection, 109
  cloze, 82
  compatibility, 309
  constraints, 308, 311
  construction, 308
  demand, 258
  eye-scanning patterns in, 144
  forced-choice, 107
  gazes in description, 239
  knowledge, 27
  memory, 195
  multiple-object naming, 193, 200, 205
  oculomotor, 64
  online, changes tracked by, 280
  patient detection, 204
  production, 261
  referential communication, 295, 300
  -relevant instrument, 293
  Rings, 145
  saccade-to-target, 143
  use of spatial indices in, 182
  viewing, 42
Temporally contiguous fixations, 62
Text
  disappearing, 79
  linguistic characteristics of, 94
Thematic Apperception Test, 11, 22
Theme-object, 285
Thinking outside brain, 161–189
  broader mindset, 182–183
  Hollywood Squares, 171–173
  internalism and externalism, 162–163
  internalism in psychology, 163–165
  look of mind, 178–182
  on context-dependent memory, 173–175
  pointers to absent objects, 170–171

pointers in conversation and gesture, 177–178
pointers in infancy, 175–176
pointers to objects, 169–170
pointers in reading and conversation, 176–177
pointers in space, 167–169
ramifications, 183–184
thinking outside brain, 165–167
Thought experiments, Twin Earth, 162
Time telling
average eye-voice span for, 266
experiment, 263, 264
Tip-of-the tongue (TOT) states, 182, 191
Tone
acoustic complexity of, 371
condition, cue recognition and, 373
Total fixation time, 36, 61
Total prime effect, 124
TOT states, *see* Tip-of-the tongue states
TRACE model, 16
Transformational grammar, theory of, 279
Transsaccadic change detection paradigm, 38
True scene, 7
Tumor-and-lasers problem, 166
Twin Earth thought experiments, 162
Two-process theory of attention, 124

U

Ultrarapid categorization, 14
Unambiguous referent, 300
Unattended processing, 117
Uniform resource locator (URL), 183
URL, *see* Uniform resource locator
Useful field of view, 107, 108, 127
Utterance(s), 249
adjective-final, 203
fluent, 262
initiated, 273
objects included in, 219
scripted, 304
selection of starting point for, 262
serial spell-out of, 254

V

Viewing
condition, 232
task, 42
Virtual post-it notes, 173
Vision

computer, 164
foveal, 106
research, accumulating evidence in, 161
Visual activity, common, 135
Visual acuity, 106
Visual attention, 110
covert, 110, 112
cues for guidance of, 110
pre-motor theory of, 155
relationship between eye movements and, 21
Visual cognition
literature, 9
research, 8
theory of, 18
Visual cues, 47
Visual displays
relationship of to scene, 8, 9
types of, 11
Visual field, size of functional, 109
Visual imagery, 178
Visual information, dynamic representation of, 150
Visual orthographic codes, 70
Visual periphery, 21, 33
Visual processing research, 89
Visual properties, memories of, 171
Visual psychophysics, 164
Visual saliency
computational models of, 24
image-generated, 30
Visual scenes, 363
Visual search, *see* Eye scanning and visual search
Visual stimuli, constrained, 60
Visual world
paradigm, 19, 29, 213, 348
importance of functional field of view in, 48
saccadic latencies in, 370, 376
task-relevant, 283
Visuomotor processing, 169
Visuospatial pointer, 369
Visuospatial processing, 119
Visuospatial sketchpad, 168
Vivid imagery, eye movements and, 168
Voice-onset latencies, 263
Voluntary attention, 114

W

WEAVER++ model, 196
When decision, 150
Why-not hypothesis, 230
Wine glass effect, 356, 360, 361
Word(s)
    acoustic form of, 19
    disambiguating, 84
    disruption at particular, 85
    erroneous, 228
    frequency, 81, 214
    integrity, 67
    launch site, 72
    length information, 68
    lexically ambiguous, 83
    memory list of key, 87
    number of fixations on, 91
    order
        alternations, 260
        elemental accounts of, 260

    phonological similarity between, 214
    predictability, 82
    preparation, processes of, 215
    recognition, processes involved in, 124
    selection, 215
    sequencing, 237
    span, 47
    substitution errors, self-corrected, 227
    target, 62, 67, 84, 281
Working memory system, 171
World
    interaction with external, 369
    interpretation of, 361
    mediating mapping between language
        and, 366

Z

Zoom lens model, 141